PLATO'S CARIBBEAN ATLANTIS

A SCIENTIFIC EXPLANATION OF PLATO'S ATLANTIS STORY

DR. P.P. FLAMBAS

ISBN: 978-1-923078-69-7

Published by Vivid Publishing
A division of Fontaine Publishing Group
P.O. Box 948, Fremantle
Western Australia 6959
www.vividpublishing.com.au

A catalogue record for this book is available from the National Library of Australia

Contents

Preface

What is Atlantis? For most people who have heard the name, it is just a vague notion about a mythical land that existed somewhere long ago but then sank beneath the sea. Some people may have seen speculative stories on Atlantis in movies, television programmes, magazines, or the internet. They also may have seen claims about someone's latest discovery of the location of Atlantis.

Regrettably, very few people who think they know something about Atlantis have read the Ancient Greek philosopher Plato's written accounts. Over two thousand years ago, Plato wrote of a powerful prehistoric civilisation that existed more than eleven thousand years before the present. Plato describes an advanced culture on what he calls an 'Atlantic island' outside the Mediterranean Sea in the Atlantic Ocean.

Why would anyone in the 21st century be interested in a story written over two thousand years ago about a long-lost civilisation? Even though ancient cultures preserved and retold many myths of lost lands worldwide, why does Plato's story of Atlantis intrigue people up to the present day? Possibly, the main reason people want to believe in something like Atlantis is to satisfy an inner need to know about our ancient ancestors' capabilities and achievements. We want to imagine an advanced civilisation in the very distant past, but somehow it became lost to us.

This book analyses Plato's writings on Atlantis and attempts to give a plausible scientific explanation for all of his descriptions. If Plato's Atlantis story is true, the people of Atlantis created the Earth's first civilisation on their Atlantic Island, thousands of years before any known civilisation.

From an early age, I have been fascinated by ancient history and the achievements of past human civilisations. As I have Greek heritage, my initial interest was in the history of Ancient Greece and its many myths and legends. As a child in the early 1960s, I was inspired by Hollywood epics such as *Ben Hur* and *Spartacus*, numerous Italian sword and sandal films set in Ancient Greece and Rome, and even the 1961 movie Atlantis the Lost Continent. I first read Homer's *Odyssey* and *Iliad* at the age of thirteen. I later read various histories by ancient writers such as Herodotus and Livy and modern historians who wrote about ancient civilisations. I learned of the archaeological discoveries at sites such as Troy in Asia Minor and the Minoan palaces of Crete, and also discoveries from the ancient civilisations of Mesopotamia, Egypt, India and China.

More recently, I began to wonder about the prehistory of our *Homo sapiens* species and its much more ancient predecessors. Archaeological discoveries about our origins have pushed back when we evolved into a separate species to well before two hundred thousand years ago. These discoveries started me thinking of the possibility that our human species had the intellectual potential to develop civilisations many thousands of years before those we now know.

In the last few years, the topical issue of global warming and a rising sea level made me wonder whether past climate changes would have affected prehistoric cultures. When I looked at current knowledge regarding the Earth's past climate, I learned that we now live in a warm period of a continuing Ice Age that began two and a half million years ago. During that unimaginably long time, there were many huge cyclical changes in global sea levels when enormous amounts of water lost from the oceans were deposited as thick sheets of glacial ice on land.

One important fact I came across was that the worldwide sea level had risen by one hundred and twenty metres in the past twenty thousand years. If any prehistoric civilisations once existed, much of their material remains would probably now lie well underwater. Despite knowing little about the subject then, I began to think of the legend of Atlantis and how its prehistoric civilisation sank beneath the sea. I then read translations of Plato's two written works on Atlantis, the *Timaeus* and *Critias*. If the Atlantis story were true, I realised it would force a revolutionary change in thinking about human prehistory and civilisations.

I began looking at a world map for a location that matched Plato's geographical descriptions of the Atlantic Island in his writings. The Caribbean region was the only location that exactly matched Plato's descriptions. Yet, my main problem was that the area I thought could once have been the Atlantic Island was much too far underwater to be covered just by the sea level rise.

There had to be a geological cause for how a large landmass like Plato's Atlantic Island could sink not merely hundreds but thousands of metres below the sea. It seemed possible that massive changes in the thickness of glacial ice sheets might have caused major geological changes on the Earth's surface. After learning about the nature of the Earth's geological structure, I developed an original Hydraulic Hypothesis that could explain many past rapid and large vertical movements of the Earth's surface. When applied to the Caribbean region, it became the Caribbean Hypothesis, which could describe the existence and destruction of Plato's Atlantic Island.

Existing scientific knowledge from various disciplines explains the geography and cultures Plato describes in his *Timaeus* and *Critias* writings. Key subject areas include Classical Literature, Ancient History, Archaeology, Human Prehistory, Palaeontology, Geology and Climate Science. I attempt to provide a single accepted scientific opinion in each area of expertise. Still, when experts dispute the science, there may be two or more conflicting views on a particular topic.

Although there is some discussion of myths from ancient civilisations that may be relevant to parts of the Atlantis story, I have avoided extreme and unsubstantiated opinions and interpretations of them. Too often in the past, many fantastic theories have tainted and trivialised serious discussions of Atlantis. Therefore, I have rejected any paranormal, occult, or extraterrestrial explanations for Atlantis or any speculation about lost super-advanced Atlantean technologies.

I was born in Sydney, Australia, in 1953 and attended the University of NSW medical school, graduating as a doctor in 1978. After practising medicine as a country GP for some years, I became interested in the commercialisation of new technologies and wanted a change of career. Returning to Sydney, I became the Managing Editor of a long-established medical journal. Realising that I needed more business knowledge to achieve his goals in technology transfer, I left medical publishing. I then began a full-time two-year Master of Business Administration (MBA) course at the University of NSW, graduating in 1992. Since then, I have worked as a hospital administrator, management consultant and equities analyst. Due to family commitments, I returned to full-time medical practice as a skin cancer surgeon for eighteen years and am now retired. I researched and wrote about Plato's Atlantis story for eight years in my spare time.

To adequately explain all of Plato's numerous descriptions, I used my scientific foundations as a doctor, my MBA analytical training and its application as a management consultant and equities analyst. Hundreds of technical papers were researched for the facts supporting my ideas and conclusions. All that information is publicly available on the internet; the only way I could have realistically found it all was by searching the internet. In the past, only large institutional libraries provided relevant technical information; physically finding all of it would have been a complicated process that might have taken a lifetime or more of study.

Amongst the many resources, *Wikipedia* was especially useful as an initial search for general information on a topic. The *Google Scholar* website was essential for specialised papers on narrow technical subjects, particularly Geology. *Google Earth* helped me visualise and represent Caribbean and Mediterranean geography, the main regions in the Atlantis story. I have tried acknowledging the sources for the many illustrations used to describe the story. Unfortunately, some have eluded me, so my apologies to anyone who recognises one of their original works but is uncredited.

One problem in writing for the general reader is limiting the volume of technical information. Too much information will overwhelm readers, mainly if it is in an academic field about which they know very little or nothing at all. On the other hand, too little technical information will not convince readers of the truth of the Atlantis story. This abridged edition of *Plato's Caribbean Atlantis* reduces much of the geological data that explains the creation and destruction of the Atlantic Island. Instead, that information has been put aside in case any geologists become interested in the book's technical contents.

Over the eight years or more it has taken to research and write about the Atlantis story, I have tried to be my greatest critic. I would have discarded the whole project if scientific information contradicted my explanations. That did not happen, so I carried on to my conclusions. Because some of those conclusions are very controversial, I expect and look forward to academics and scientific experts scrutinising and criticising those ideas.

Since Plato wrote about Atlantis, he has been accused of fabricating all of it rather than writing the truth. Ultimately, my purpose is to stimulate serious discussion about Atlantis. The aim is to present enough circumstantial evidence for people to consider that the Atlantis story could be a true account rather than something he made up. If the scientific community considers the possible existence of Plato's Atlantic Island and its remarkable civilisation, they might begin searching for some physical evidence of it.

Though there are several English translations of Plato's original works on Atlantis, only two are used here: Thomas Taylor, who published the *Timaeus* in 1793 and *Critias* in 1804, and Benjamin Jowett, who published both translations in 1871. If any Classics scholars are interested, they can still study the original Greek texts to find additional or different meanings to these English translations.

I deconstructed Plato's *Timaeus* and *Critias* dialogues to analyse them and placed only relevant quotes in this book's many sections. If you only read Plato's scattered quotes, the Atlantis story will appear fragmented and lack continuity. Before going further, I strongly advise you to read the translations of the *Timaeus* and *Critias* included in Appendix 1. Then, after reading the entire Atlantis story, you will better understand the scope and relevance of Plato's descriptions. Reading Plato's actual works will also do away with the many false or outlandish ideas proposed for Atlantis since Plato's time.

There are rational explanations for the many features in Plato's Atlantis story

Introduction

Plato wrote his Atlantis story in two documents called the *Timaeus* and *Critias*. These writings date from around 360 BCE and are the only known works that describe the Atlantean civilisation.

Anyone interested in Ancient History probably wonders what people like us created many thousands of years before any written records – in what we call prehistory. Plato's Atlantis story provides graphic descriptions of an advanced but long-lost civilisation that rose and fell in the distant past. The thousands of books and articles on Atlantis attempt to describe it and its locations, but none so far satisfy all of Plato's details. Nevertheless, there are rational explanations for the many features in Plato's *Timaeus* and *Critias*; this book will describe all of them.

Chapter 1 considers how the Atlantis story was transmitted through time and how Plato received it and must have believed it. Plato based his Atlantis story on the writings of the Athenian statesman Solon. Solon was a well-known historical figure in Athens in the 6th century BCE, almost two centuries before Plato lived, wrote, and taught philosophy in Athens. In the early 6th century BCE, Solon travelled to the city of Sais in the Nile Delta in Egypt. While there, Solon met with Egyptian temple priests who possessed ancient historical records concerning Atlantis. The Egyptian priests showed Solon those records and recounted the story of Atlantis. They told Solon about events nine thousand years before his time, or over eleven thousand years ago. In the early 4th century BCE, Plato accessed a document written by Solon about what he had seen and heard in Egypt concerning the Atlantis story. Plato then used Solon's document to write about Atlantis in the *Timaeus* and *Critias*.

Plato describes the Atlanteans as an aggressive imperial military power which originated on what he calls the 'Atlantic island', located outside the Mediterranean in the Atlantic Ocean. The Atlanteans conquered and enslaved Western Mediterranean cultures and then attempted to expand their empire by conquering the remaining free cultures in the Eastern Mediterranean. They were defeated in a war against the free Mediterranean people and eventually were driven entirely from the Mediterranean region. Sometime after the war in the Mediterranean, the Atlanteans' homeland on the Atlantic Island sank into the sea during devastating earthquakes and floods. Plato also describes a prehistoric society in Athens that fought against the Atlanteans but was destroyed by natural disasters.

In both the *Timaeus* and *Critias*, Plato repeatedly describes his Atlantis story as fact, not fiction. Yet, almost from when Plato wrote about Atlantis in the 4th century BCE, many philosophers and scholars have argued that he created the Atlantis story as a fiction or a 'noble lie'. They claim Plato fashioned a fictitious Atlantis and prehistoric Athens as a metaphor and moral message for discussing ideal societies. But in his many philosophical writings, Plato never wrote anything we would call a fiction genre. He believed the purpose of all philosophy was the search for truth, and his writings are devoted to seeking the truth of how the world works. The extraordinary degree of detail that Plato uses, particularly for the geography of the Atlantic Island and prehistoric Athens, is much more than he would have needed for a philosophical metaphor.

Plato wrote the *Timaeus* and *Critias* as a successful philosopher in the latter stage of his fifty-year professional life. Philosophers in the Greek world had studied his written works for decades while he was still alive and would do so for centuries after his death. Why would Plato open himself to criticism and ridicule from those philosophers and others if he had fabricated the Atlantis story and did not believe it was fact?

Chapter 2 analyses Plato's precise geographical descriptions of the 'Atlantic island'. It had to be located in the Caribbean region because no other location satisfies all of his exact details. The Atlantic Island would have been a vast landmass that once lay above sea level, but according to Plato, it eventually 'sank' beneath the sea. It is proposed that most of the Atlantic Island did sink below sea level and now lies on the floor of the eastern Caribbean Sea. Many of the geographical features such as mountain ranges that Plato describes, are now underwater.

The main academic objection to Plato's descriptions of Atlantean civilisation is that it existed several thousand years before any recognised civilisation developed anywhere on Earth; therefore, it is impossible. Current academic belief claims that the highest level of human culture at any time before 12,000 years ago was small groups of primitive hunter-gatherers. Those people are assumed to have lived just before or at the very start of the Neolithic Period – defined as the time when farming began and the first settled communities formed.

To consider whether the Atlantis story is true, we need to understand two crucial factors about the existence of prehistoric humans on Earth. One is that modern human intellectual and physical capabilities have existed for much longer than was once thought. The other is that over the relatively recent past, the Earth's climate and geography have been much more unstable than previously thought.

Recent scientific opinion is that *Homo sapiens* fully evolved in Africa at least 200,000 years ago. They are our ancestors and we must appreciate that they were virtually identical to us in body and mind as anatomically modern humans. Given the right environmental conditions, one can argue that extremely ancient but modern humans like us were mentally and physically capable of creating advanced civilisations many thousands of years ago. Therefore, we could develop the features of Atlantean civilisation much earlier than the beginning of the known Neolithic Period 12,000 years ago. Chapter 3 discusses human evolution and intellectual abilities.

The Egyptian priests explain that human cultures rise during periods of climate stability and then suffer major 'destructions of mankind' mainly due to 'the agencies of fire and water'. The destructions the Egyptians describe could be due to the effect of past major climate changes, discussed in Chapter 10.

Plato's Atlantean civilisation developed after the Last Glacial Maximum (LGM) around 20,000 years ago. At the LGM, vast glacial ice sheets were at their greatest extent, with ice thousands of metres thick covering much of North America, Eurasia, and all of Antarctica. After the LGM, the Earth warmed and much of the glacial ice rapidly melted. That melting caused the worldwide sea level to rise by around 120 metres before it stabilised to its present level from 8,000–6,000 years ago. Such an extreme sea level increase flooded millions of square kilometres of previously dry land all over the Earth.

The period of the first known ancient civilisations coincides with a stabilising global sea level 8,000–6,000 years ago. Nevertheless, it is possible that any number of prehistoric civilisations, including that of the Atlanteans, may have existed before 8,000 years ago. The increase in sea level and the long-term effects of erosion could have concealed or destroyed any physical evidence of them.

Flood myths exist in many ancient cultures worldwide. In virtually all of these myths, most of humankind is destroyed, with any survivors having to restart their culture. What is now generally accepted as the beginning of human civilisations in Mesopotamia, Asia, the Mediterranean, and the Americas may be a recovery from a Dark Age of planet-wide cultural destruction on the Antediluvian or Pre-Flood Earth. Advanced civilisations eventually emerged in all those regions and developed many of the same technological features of the Atlantean culture. Chapter 6 describes those ancient technologies and how the Atlanteans might have developed similar technologies thousands of years before those we know.

Much of the Caribbean Sea floor is now up to three thousand metres below sea level, so the Atlantic Island would have had to sink rapidly by hundreds or thousands of metres sometime after 11,000 years ago. The only way it could sink so far is through a series of major subsidences of parts of the Caribbean Tectonic Plate on which the Caribbean Sea rests. Tectonic plates are the many large segments of the Earth's solid outer shell.

No currently accepted geological mechanism can explain the rapid subsidence of any tectonic plate, including the Caribbean Plate. However, a novel geological hypothesis is proposed in Chapter 11 that could explain the emergence and submergence of the Atlantic Island. This Hydraulic Hypothesis is a radical departure from conventional thinking about the vertical movements of the Earth's tectonic plates.

It is often mistakenly believed that the LGM marked the end of the Ice Age. Yet, we still live in an Ice Age that began about 2.5 million years ago – the Quaternary Ice Age. The LGM of 20,000 years ago merely marks the most recent peak of glaciation. Still, many regular climate cycles of alternating warm and cold periods have occurred during the last 2.5 million years. Numerous times in the distant past, the Earth's climate cooled, kilometres-thick glacial ice sheets increased and the sea level fell. Then, the Earth warmed, the ice sheets melted and the sea level rose. These climate cycles will likely continue for millions of years as there is little likelihood that the Quaternary Ice Age has ended.

The basic concept of the Hydraulic Hypothesis argues that hydraulic pressure transfers from one tectonic plate to another through a fluid layer below the solid tectonic plates. During the Quaternary Ice Age, the weight of massive volumes of glacial ice on the tectonic plates of North America, Eurasia and Antarctica forced those plates down. That downward movement caused pressure to transmit through the fluid layer to distant tectonic plates not covered by ice, which forced those plates up. The opposite movement occurred when glacial ice melted: the ice-covered plates moved up, and the distant plates were pulled down.

The Caribbean Plate can be thought of as one of the distant plates affected by changes in underlying hydraulic pressure. The Caribbean Hypothesis is discussed in Chapter 12. It describes extremely long geological processes affecting the Caribbean Plate, including the emergence and later subsidence of the Atlantic Island. Millions of years of accepted geological evidence confirm many large vertical movements of parts of the Caribbean Plate. Those vertical plate movements seem to match changes in glacial ice thickness.

An often overlooked feature of Plato's Atlantis writings is the role of the prehistoric city of Athens at the time of the Atlanteans. Plato describes its geography, culture, and the natural disasters that occurred there. He also describes a war between the Atlanteans and the Athenians, which unfortunately lacks specifics but may relate to some ancient Greek myths. Chapters 8 and 9 cover these topics.

Several times, Plato writes that the Atlantis story is true and not a myth. The Atlanteans' civilisation was a culture where human intellectual and technological potential thrived long before the conventional view of history considers it possible. If the Caribbean region were the centre of an advanced Atlantean civilisation, then the first human civilisation developed in the New World of the Americas, not the Old World. Discovering the truth of the Atlantis story could help answer several questions about humanity – for how long have we behaved the way we do, what are we capable of achieving in the future, and what could prevent us from realising that potential?

This book's primary purpose is to vindicate Plato. It analyses Plato's writings as if they represent actual places and events the very early Egyptians recorded and Plato found in Solon's translation. There is currently no physical proof of the Atlanteans or their empire. Still, if there is enough convincing circumstantial evidence, it could inspire exploration in the most likely places where someone may find traces of Atlantean civilisation.

If you have not already done so, please read the Jowett translations of the *Timaeus* and *Critias* in Appendix 1. Only when you have read Plato's entire Atlantis story, rather than merely the scattered fragments in the body of this book, will you appreciate the scope and significance of Plato's writings.

BP (Before the Present) describes prehistoric periods – before any known written records. Once historical records exist, BCE (Before the Common Era) is used for what was once called Before Christ and CE (Common Era) for what was once called AD or Anno Domini. Geological events over much longer periods are represented by the term mya for millions of years ago and kya for thousands of years ago.

Plato states that the Atlantis story was knowledge about real places and events

CHAPTER 1

The Atlantis Story

In Athens around 360 BCE, the Ancient Greek philosopher Plato wrote two works or dialogues about Atlantis, the *Timaeus* and *Critias*, the only existing written records describing Atlantis and its civilisation. These dialogues tell of the journey to Egypt by the historical Athenian statesman Solon (638–558 BCE) in around 570 BCE. While Solon is in Egypt, some senior Egyptian temple priests tell him about the very ancient empire of Atlantis and its war against the nations of the Eastern Mediterranean. The Egyptian priests tell Solon that the war occurred 9,000 years before his time, around 9600 BCE or 11,600 BP.

The date of 11,600 BP often appears as a reference point, but it only estimates the time of the war against the Atlanteans. The many other events in the Atlantis story could have happened hundreds or possibly thousands of years on either side of 11,600 BP.

Plato was about seventy years old when he wrote them and eighty-two to eighty-four by the time he died in 347 or 348 BCE. He is known to have written thirty-six dialogues during his long and productive life as a philosopher, with the *Timaeus* and *Critias* considered part of his late dialogues written toward the end of his life. The *Timaeus* is thought to be the first of a possible trilogy of dialogues, followed by the *Critias* and finally, the *Hermocrates* (which is unknown and was possibly never written). The *Critias* appears incomplete and stops mid-sentence; it is uncertain whether it was unfinished or the remainder has been lost.

The *Timaeus* and *Critias* are in the form of conversations between several characters: the Athenian philosopher Socrates, Hermocrates, Timaeus and Critias. The Critias character responds to a previous talk by Socrates about ideal societies. Critias agrees to tell Socrates something 'not a fiction but a true story'. Critias claims that his true story originated from a visit by Solon to Egypt. While Solon was in the great Egyptian city of Sais in the Nile Delta, he spoke with senior priests at the Temple of the Egyptian goddess Neith. To further confirm such a conversation did occur, the Greek historian Plutarch (ca. 46–120 CE) wrote that Solon travelled to Egypt and met with 'Psenophis of Heliopolis, and Sonchis of Sais, the most learned of all the priests'.

The Egyptian temple priests at Sais tell Solon they possess a story about prehistoric Athens and Atlantis, a story the Egyptians had recorded from ancient times. The priests explain that 9,000 years before their time, Athens had engaged in a war in the Mediterranean against the vast Atlantean Empire, which had its centre on an enormous 'Atlantic island'. The Athenians eventually triumphed in the conflict and drove the Atlanteans from the Mediterranean. Sometime later, natural catastrophes destroyed the Atlantic Island and much of prehistoric Athens.

Solon wrote down the Egyptians' Atlantis story and returned to Greece. He then passed the written story on to Dropides, the great-grandfather of the Critias character in Plato's dialogues. The Critias character received the written story from his grandfather (also named Critias), who was the son of Dropides.

The Timeline of the Atlantis Story

- Indigenous people, or 'Earth-born men', inhabit a large island in the Atlantic Ocean long before 11,600 BP.
- Poseidon arrives on the 'Atlantic island'. With the indigenous woman Cleito, he creates the dynasty of Ten Kings of Atlantis who will rule various territories on the Atlantic Island.
- The Atlanteans build their Royal City on the Atlantic Island.
- The Atlanteans develop into a great power over many generations of the Ten Kings of Atlantis.
- The Atlantean Empire eventually controls parts of the continent adjacent to the Atlantic Island, various islands in the Atlantic Ocean, and lands in the Western Mediterranean.
- Athens is founded, possibly before 11,600 BP.
- A war is fought between the Atlanteans and the cultures of the Eastern Mediterranean around 9,000 years before Solon goes to Egypt, i.e. about 11,600 BP.
- Athens is victorious against the Atlanteans in the Mediterranean War. The Atlanteans are eventually driven out of the Mediterranean, freeing those they had enslaved in the western Mediterranean.
- The Egyptian city of Sais in the Nile Delta is founded one thousand years after the founding of Athens, possibly before 10,600 BP.
- Natural catastrophes occur sometime after the Mediterranean War of 11,600 BP. They cause the Atlantic Island to sink beneath the sea, and in a 'day and a night' they destroy Athens' Acropolis.
- Solon travels to Egypt in around 570 BCE and discusses the Egyptians' 'sacred registers' about Atlantis with senior priests at the Temple of Neith in the city of Sais.
- After several years of travels, Solon returns to Greece with a written Greek translation of the Atlantis story.
- A friend and relative of Solon named Dropides receives Solon's original written translation of the Atlantis story.
- Critias I, the son of Dropides, receives the Atlantis story from Dropides.
- Critias II, the character in Plato's dialogues, is the grandson of Critias I. Critias II receives the Atlantis story from Critias I and possesses Solon's original written translation.
- Socrates dies in 399 BCE, aged about 70.
- Plato visits Egypt soon after Socrates' death.
- Plato founds his philosophical school called the Academy in Athens in 387 BCE.
- Plato probably writes the *Timaeus* and *Critias* around 360 BCE, aged about 70.
- Plato dies in 348 or 347 BCE, aged over 80.
- The *Timaeus* and *Critias* are copied and studied by philosophers for several years while Plato is still alive and for hundreds of years later at the Academy and elsewhere in the classical world.
- In the late 4th century BCE, the Greek philosopher Crantor writes a commentary of Plato's *Timaeus* dialogue where he mentions visible temple hieroglyphs at Sais that describe the Atlantis story.
- Proclus is a 5th-century CE neo-Platonist philosopher who reports on Crantor's commentary of the *Timaeus*. Proclus states that the Egyptian hieroglyphs about Atlantis at Sais are still visible in his time in the 5th century CE, almost one thousand years after Solon's visit.

The Transmission of the Atlantis Story

Almost from when Plato first wrote about Atlantis in the 4th century BCE, he was accused of making up the entire story to prove a philosophical point. Though there was discussion throughout Antiquity about the possible existence of Plato's Atlantis, it was usually rejected and occasionally parodied by later classical authors. Many centuries later, modern scholars have argued that Plato's story is an allegory or metaphor inspired by Mediterranean Bronze Age events such as the volcanic eruption on Santorini or the Trojan War. Other scholars suggest later events familiar to Plato, such as the destruction of the city of Helike by an earthquake in 373 BCE or the failed Athenian invasion of Sicily in 415–413 BCE.

Contrary to all those opinions, Plato clearly states in his Atlantis dialogues that the Egyptians' Atlantis story was knowledge about real places and events in the very distant past. Yet, he stresses that the Greeks of his time had forgotten all that ancient knowledge.

How were the facts of the Atlantis story accurately recorded and passed on for eleven thousand years from the supposed existence of an Atlantean civilisation up to the present day? Over many thousands of years, the specifics of the Atlantis story had to be transmitted in three separate phases. Each phase had to correctly describe those details so they would reach our time unchanged.

Firstly, the Atlantis story begins when the Egyptians write about the story's ancient locations and events. They maintain their records for thousands of years before Solon visits Egypt. Secondly, Solon goes to Egypt in around 570 BCE and translates the Atlantis story from the Egyptian records into Greek. More than two hundred years later, Plato uses Solon's translation to write his two Atlantis dialogues: the

Timaeus and *Critias*. Thirdly, Plato's Atlantis dialogues are copied, translated, and studied for hundreds of years by Greeks, Romans, Byzantines and Arabs. Copies of the Atlantis dialogues in Plato's original Ancient Greek language eventually reach scholars in Western Europe hundreds of years later, and they are still available.

The Egyptian 'Sacred Registers'

Plato states that Solon spoke at the Temple of Neith in Sais with Egyptian priests who kept 'sacred registers' containing the Atlantis story.

One of the temple priests tells Solon: 'whatever happened either in your country (Greece) or in ours (Egypt), or in any other region of which we are informed – if there were any actions noble or great or in any other way remarkable, they have all been written down by us of old, and are preserved in our temples'…'As touching your (Athenian) citizens of nine thousand years ago, I will briefly inform you of their laws and of their most famous action; the exact particulars of the whole we will hereafter go through at our leisure in the sacred registers themselves.'

Thousands of years before Solon's time, the Egyptians must have developed a writing system to record the Atlantis story in their sacred registers. The Egyptians preserved those records until Solon saw them in the 6th century BCE.

Human prehistory usually refers to the time between the evolution of the first modern humans like us and the invention of writing systems that recorded history. Current thinking is that writing systems were first developed in the Old World in the Early Bronze Age. From around the 4th millennium BCE, Sumerian cuneiform script and Egyptian hieroglyphs are considered the earliest known complete writing systems. They apparently developed from even earlier symbol systems from 3400–3200 BCE, with the first known coherent texts dating from around 2600 BCE.

Even so, our modern human species, *Homo sapiens*, has physically recorded information for much longer than those accepted first writing systems. Also, there is recent evidence that human species, very much older than *Homo sapiens,* deliberately made recordings. The earliest known ancient art is a set of zigzags carved on a mussel shell found in Trinil, Indonesia. It dates to some 540,000 years ago and is thought to be the work of *Homo erectus*: a species of human that predates our species by at least one million years. A set of 65,000-year-old ochre sketches in the Cueva de los Aviones in south-eastern Spain were possibly crafted by Neanderthals, who predate our species by about half a million years.

Archaeological evidence of art or recording by our species, *Homo sapiens*, seems to have emerged in the Middle Palaeolithic (100,000–50,000 BP). Stones engraved with grid or cross-hatch patterns were discovered in Blombos Cave in South Africa and dated to 70,000 BP. In Europe, markings created by *Homo sapiens* around 30,000 BP were found in one hundred and forty-six different prehistoric European caves. The twenty-six specific signs consist of dots, lines and other geometric symbols. They might be a graphic code used by our species shortly after arriving in Europe from Africa around 40,000 BP. Otherwise, we *Homo* sapiens may have used these symbols in Africa before migrating to Europe.

The symbols found on Neolithic artefacts of the Vinča Culture of South-Eastern Europe date from the 6th–5th millennia BCE and are the oldest excavated example of proto-writing. They are a thousand years older than a proto-Sumerian pictographic script, usually considered the earliest known writing.

Current thinking is that Egyptian hieroglyphs emerged sometime after 4000 BCE. Simplified glyph forms then developed into demotic (popular) script

Inscribed object from the Karanovo Culture
Source: Wikimedia Commons

and a cursive hieroglyphic script called hieratic used for religious documents. Papyrus was manufactured and used as a writing material in Egypt since at least the 4th millennium BCE and was exported later and used throughout the Mediterranean region.

Papyrus is a paper-like material produced from the pith of the papyrus plant, Cyperus papyrus, a

Papyrus of Hunefer, 1275 *BCE*
Source: Wikimedia Commons – British Museum

type of wetland sedge. As well as for writing, the Ancient Egyptians used the papyrus plant for boats, mattresses, mats, rope, sandals and baskets. In ancient times, the papyrus plant was abundant in the Nile Delta in Egypt and the coastal regions of Ethiopia, along the Niger River, near the Tiberiade Lake in Palestine, and along the Euphrates River near Babylon.

The word papyrus is also used for documents written on papyrus sheets, often rolled into scrolls. Although papyrus was relatively cheap and easy to produce, it was fragile and easily damaged by moisture or excessive dryness. Papyrus is stable in a dry climate like Egypt, but moulds can destroy it quickly in humid conditions. As a more durable alternative to papyrus, Egyptians wrote documents on leather since at least the Fourth Dynasty (ca. 2550–2450 BCE), and the Greek historian Herodotus mentions that writing on skins was common in his time in the 5th century BCE.

The Seated Scribe – Painted Limestone
Statue ca. 2620–2500 *BCE*
Source: Wikimedia Commons – Louvre Museum, Paris

Scribes, or sesh, recorded much of what we know about Ancient Egypt. As well as being educated in writing, they supervised the construction of monumental buildings, documented administrative and economic activities and recorded stories from Egypt's lower classes or foreign lands. Scribes' sons were schooled in the scribal tradition, and when they entered the civil service, they inherited their fathers' positions.

A writing system possibly existed in Egypt 11,600 years ago, but no evidence would remain if written on papyrus or other perishable material. Scribes may have used some form of writing in Egypt before 4000 BCE to record important events such as the Atlantis story. If a writing system had existed at the time of the Atlantis story around 11,600 BP, it was five thousand years older than any presently known in Egypt. Over time, it may have evolved into the later Egyptian scripts.

Hieroglyphs on a temple wall - Medinet Habu

As the papyrus plant was native to Egypt, it possibly was manufactured as a writing material for thousands of years before the earliest known papyrus specimens. Egyptian priests or scribes would have copied the contents of the original Atlantis story onto a fresh papyrus when the previous version deteriorated. Scribes would have continued copying and transmitting the Atlantis story over thousands of years until Solon saw the physical sacred registers at Sais. It is also possible that important documents, such as the sacred registers at Egyptian temples, were written on leather or skins that were more durable than papyrus. Even so, they would have been copied if they had deteriorated after hundreds or thousands of years.

Other than writings about the Atlantis story on perishable material, there were inscriptions about the Atlantis story on columns at the Temple of Neith in Sais. It seems later travellers could still see those inscriptions many hundreds of years after Solon visited the Temple.

Solon

Solon (ca. 638–558 BCE) was an Athenian statesman, lawmaker and poet. Ancient authors such as Herodotus and Plutarch wrote about his life. Solon is best known for making laws against the political, economic and moral decline in archaic Athens. After instituting those laws, Solon left Athens and travelled for ten years to prevent the Athenians from making him repeal any of his laws.

After Solon left Athens, he first went to Egypt. Herodotus wrote that Solon visited the city of Sais and spoke there with the Pharaoh Amasis II, who assumed the Egyptian throne in 570 BCE. According to the Greek historian Plutarch (46–120 CE), Solon also discussed philosophy with two senior Egyptian priests: Psenophis of Heliopolis and Sonchis of Sais.

After leaving Egypt, Solon sailed to Cyprus and oversaw the construction of a new capital city for a local king, who named the city Soloi. Solon then went to Sardis, the capital of Lydia in Anatolia where, according to Herodotus and Plutarch, he met with the Lydian King Croesus. Solon then returned to Athens and became an opponent of the Athenian tyrant Pisistratus.

In Plato's *Timaeus* and *Critias*, Solon visits the Temple of Neith at Sais, where the priests tell him the Atlantis story and show him the sacred registers that record it. It seems unlikely that Plato would use Solon's respected name to legitimise an entirely fictional story about Atlantis. The documented life of the historical Solon fits Plato's account of his travels to Egypt, particularly his discussions with priests at Sais. So, one could assume that Solon discussed the sacred registers of the Atlantis story with Egyptian priests and then translated and wrote the story in Greek. Plato then based the *Timaeus* and *Critias* on Solon's actual written translation of the Atlantis story.

Solon
Source: Wikimedia Commons – National Museum, Naples

Herodotus
Source: Wikimedia Commons – Metropolitan Museum of Art

Herodotus

Herodotus was an Ancient Greek writer born around 484 BCE in the city of Halikarnassos in Asia Minor. He is called the Father of History because he was the first known historian to collect his materials systematically, test their accuracy, and arrange them in a well-constructed narrative.

Herodotus was a traveller and historian who documented his travels in the *Histories* around 430–425 BCE, the only work he is known to have produced. The *Histories* is a record of the ancient traditions, politics, geography and conflicts of the various cultures known in his time around the Mediterranean and western Asia.

Herodotus travelled to Egypt around 450 BCE, mainly in the Nile Delta but perhaps reaching as far south as Aswan along the Nile. Several of Herodotus' entries about Egypt in the *Histories* relate to Plato's Atlantis dialogues, written around one hundred years after Herodotus.

The Greeks in Egypt

Solon was not an unknown solitary Greek traveller when he went to Egypt around 570 BCE. The Egyptians must have considered Solon a very important guest if he had been allowed an audience with Pharaoh Amasis II and had a discussion with the most senior Egyptian temple priests. As it is unlikely that Solon understood Egyptian, he probably would have had interpreters for those meetings and to translate Egyptian documents into Greek.

The history of the Greeks in Egypt dates back over four thousand years. From at least the 3rd millennium BCE, the Minoans of Crete were long-distance, open-sea sailors known to have exported fine fabrics to Egypt. Regular Minoan trade routes extended from Crete and mainland Greece to Egypt, the Levant and Asia Minor.

The city of Avaris was located in the north-eastern Nile Delta and was once the capital of Egypt. It was occupied from 1783 to 1550 BCE and was a well-developed trading centre with a busy harbour. One temple excavated in Avaris has Minoan-like wall paintings with images of bull-leaping, bull-grappling, gryphons and hunts similar to those found in Minoan Crete at the Palace of Knossos.

When the Minoan civilisation declined, the later Mycenaean Greeks' trade routes extended west toward southern Italy and beyond, to the regions around the Aegean, and as far east as Cyprus and Asia Minor. The major Mycenaean export was pottery, and from 1400–1100 BCE it is often found in New Kingdom archaeological sites in Egypt. Other widely traded goods were silver, lead, copper and bronze. The Mycenaeans imported gold, ivory, lapis lazuli, amber, tin, copper and other metals from Egypt, Syria, the Near East and Europe. At Tell el-Amarna, the capital of Pharaoh Akhenaten, who ruled until 1334 BCE, a painted battle scene on a papyrus found there depicts Libyans fighting the Pharaoh's army, whose warriors include Mycenaean foot-soldiers.

After the collapse of Mycenaean Greek civilisation and the following Greek Dark Ages that lasted from 1100 to 750 BCE, the first report of Greeks in Egypt is in the 7th century BCE. Herodotus writes in the *Histories* about Ionian and Carian pirates from Asia Minor, forced by a storm to land on or near the Nile Delta, near Sais. At that time, the Pharaoh Psammetichus I (ca. 664–610 BCE) was overthrown, so he sought advice from the Oracle of Wadjet in the city of Buto. The oracle told him to seek the aid of brazen men who would come from the sea. When Psammetichus saw the bronze armour of the shipwrecked pirates, he enlisted them in his campaign to return to power. Following his military success, Psammetichus gave the Greek mercenaries two parcels of land or camps on either side of the Pelusian branch of the Nile.

In 570 BCE, the Egyptian Pharaoh Apries led a Greek mercenary army of 30,000 Carians and Ionians against a rebellious former general named Amasis. Apries was defeated in battle, with Amasis then becoming Pharaoh and reigning from 570–526 BCE. Amasis closed the Greek camps on the Pelusian branch of the Nile and sent the Greek soldiers to the city of Memphis, where they were 'to guard him against the native Egyptians'. This Pharaoh Amasis met with Solon in the capital city of Sais in Egypt.

Herodotus wrote: 'Amasis was partial to the Greeks, and among other favours which he granted them, gave to such as liked to settle in Egypt the city of Naucratis for their residence.' Naucratis was the first permanent Greek trading colony in Egypt, located 72 kilometres from the Mediterranean on

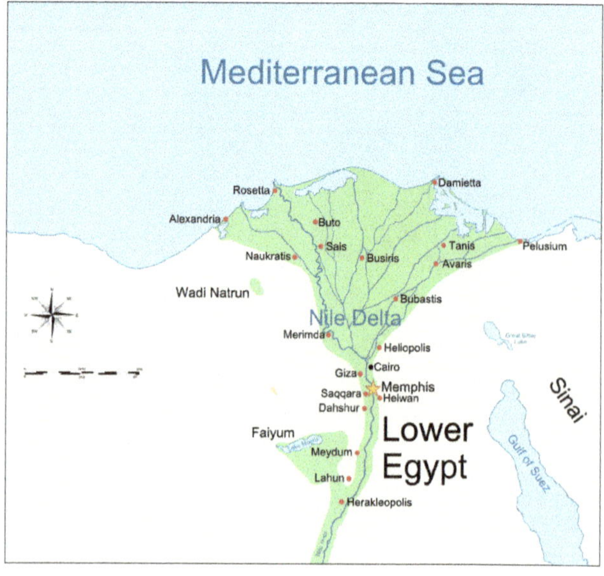

Ancient Cities of Lower Egypt
Source: Wikimedia Commons – Jeff Dahl

the Canopic branch of the Nile. Pharaoh Amasis gave the city to the Greeks in the years immediately after his victory in 570 BCE. He then converted Naucratis into a major emporion (trading post) shared by several Greek city-states.

The Egyptians supplied the Greeks mostly with grain, linen, and papyrus, whereas the Greeks mainly traded silver, timber, olive oil, and wine. Naucratis and the associated Greek forts in the Nile Delta also became a source of the Pharaohs' mercenaries, supplying superior Greek armour and tactics, and expertise in naval warfare.

Sais and the Nile Delta

In the *Timaeus* dialogue, Plato describes Solon's journey to Egypt and his discussions with priests at the Temple of Neith in the Nile Delta.

Plato – 'In the Egyptian Delta, at the head of which the river Nile divides, there is a certain district which is called the district of Sais, and the great city of the district is also called Sais, and is the city from which King (Pharaoh) Amasis came. The citizens have a deity for their foundress; she is called in the Egyptian tongue Neith, and is asserted by them to be the same whom the Hellenes (Greeks) call Athena; they are great lovers of the Athenians, and say that they are in some way related to them'…'To this city came Solon, and was received there with great honour; he asked the priests who were most skilful in such matters, about antiquity, and made the discovery that neither he nor any other Hellene knew anything worth mentioning about the times of old.'

The Nile Delta forms in northern Egypt (usually called Lower Egypt), where the Nile River branches and enters the Mediterranean Sea. It is one of the world's largest river deltas, 160 kilometres from north to south, with 240 kilometres of Mediterranean coastline. For most of the past 100,000 years, global sea levels were much lower due to increased glaciation, so there was little or no Nile Delta – the Nile emptied directly into the Mediterranean.

Nile River and Delta
Source: Google Earth

The known human occupation of the Nile Valley and Delta dates back to at least 7,000 BP. One reason farming settlements began in the Nile Delta may be due to sea level rise. After the peak of glaciation at 20,000 BP, when glacial ice melted the sea level rose 120 metres or more until it stabilised to its present level around 6,000 BP. As the sea level rose, it reduced the gradient of the Nile's course and formed a system of meandering Nile branches, which allowed silt from the river to accumulate and create a broad delta plain. The resultant fertile soil and abundant water of the Nile Delta allowed agriculture to evolve and farming communities to develop.

Records from ancient times, such as those of Pliny the Elder (23–79 CE), show that the Nile Delta once had seven branches. Due to accumulated silt, there are now only two main branches: the Damietta to the east and the Rosetta to the west.

The Atlantis story states that early Egyptian cultures fought during the Mediterranean War of 11,600 BP. They probably inhabited the Mediterranean coastal plain of Egypt and the early Nile Delta as it formed. As the sea level was much lower in 11,600 BP, a now-submerged coastal plain would have extended many kilometres from Egypt's present shoreline. One hundred and twenty metres of sea level rise and accumulated silt between 20,000–6,000 BP would have covered any evidence of prehistoric culture or civilisation on Egypt's coastal plain and early Nile Delta. Notably, there was a sixty metre sea level increase from the time of the Mediterranean War in 11,600 BP until the sea level stabilised at around 6,000 BP.

Sais was a city in the western Nile Delta on the Canopic branch of the Nile. Its Ancient Egyptian

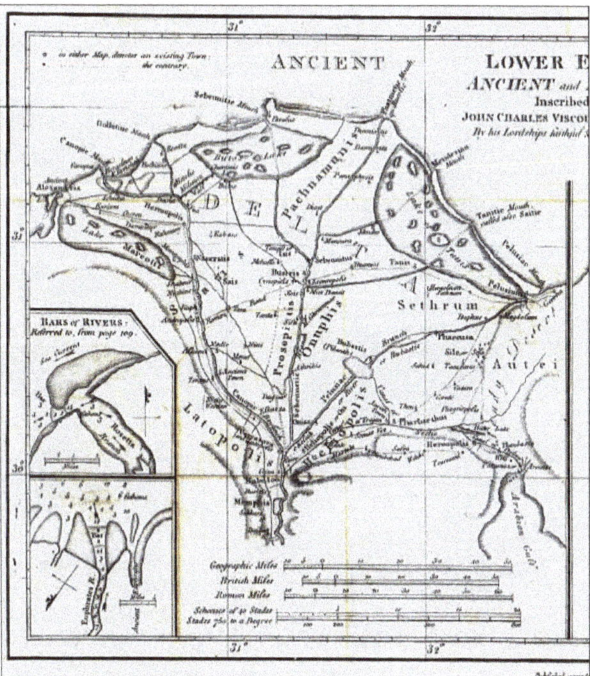

The Nile Delta at the time of Herodotus
Source: Wikimedia Commons – James Rennell (1800)

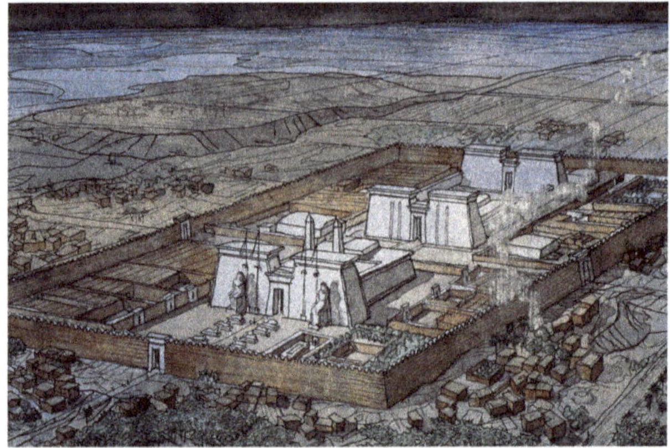

Temple of Neith Reconstruction.
Source: Jean-Claude Golvin

name was Zau, and it was already an important cult centre at the beginning of Egyptian history, around 3100 BCE. The city's patron goddess was Neith, whose cult was practised at least as early as the 1st Dynasty, ca. 3100–3050 BCE. Ancient Greek writers such as Herodotus, Plato and Diodorus Siculus identified Neith with the Greek goddess Athena, implying an extremely ancient link between Sais and Athens. The Egyptian priests at Sais tell Solon – 'She (Neith/Athena) founded your city (Athens) a thousand years before ours (Sais), receiving from the Earth and (the god) Hephaestus the seed of your race, and afterwards she founded ours, of which the constitution is recorded in our sacred registers to be eight thousand years old'.

Sais was Egypt's capital city during the 24th Dynasty (ca. 732–720 BCE) and the later Saite 26th Dynasty (664–525 BCE). The Saite Kings of the 6th and 5th centuries BCE restored temple buildings and made Sais one of the greatest cities in the known world. By the time of Solon, the Temple of Neith may have been as large as the vast Temple of Karnak in Luxor. Though an original ancient cult Temple of Neith may have existed at Sais for thousands of years before the Saite Kings, the buildings Solon saw after 570 BCE would have been much more recent. Herodotus travelled to Egypt probably sometime after 454 BCE. While in Sais, he saw large obelisks, a sacred lake and a massive granite naos (shrine) of Pharaoh Ahmose II at the Temple of Neith.

By the 14th century CE, the Temple of Neith was largely destroyed. There are no surviving traces of the great city of Sais that date before the Late New Kingdom (ca. 1100 BCE). The buildings of the modern town of Sa el-Hagar have spread over much of the archaeological site. Practically nothing remains at the city's site today because local farmers removed most of its massive mudbrick enclosure walls to use as fertiliser, and the town mound is destroyed.

Map of Sais Ruins
Source: Wikimedia Commons
- Jean-François Champollion, 1828

Socrates and Plato's Dialogues

In the *Timaeus* and *Critias*, Plato writes the Atlantis story through conversations or dialogues between various characters. Plato makes the Greek philosopher Socrates the central character who presides over the dialogues and questions the other characters to seek the truth in their discussions. The historical Socrates was Plato's mentor and intellectual hero. In both dialogues, the Socrates character never seems to doubt the truth of the Atlantis story. One can assume that if the Socrates character in the *Timaeus* and *Critias* appears to believe the Atlantis story without question, their author Plato also believed it.

Socrates was born in Athens around 469 BCE and is considered one of the founders of Western philosophy. He was the son of a stonemason and was trained and worked as a stonemason. Socrates also fought as a hoplite (frontline soldier) for Athens in several battles during the Peloponnesian War between Athens and Sparta.

Even though Socrates did not write any works himself, he is known through the accounts of later classical writers, especially of his students Plato and Xenophon, and from the plays of his contemporary, Aristophanes. In 399 BCE, at the age of about 70, Socrates was tried and convicted on two charges: impiety and corrupting Athenian youth. He was sentenced to death and was executed by having to drink a hemlock-based poison.

Socratic dialogue is a genre of prose writing developed in Greece at the beginning of the 4th century BCE. It is found mainly in the dialogues of Plato and the Socratic works of Xenophon and several other Greek authors. In a Socratic dialogue, several characters discuss moral and philosophical problems. Socrates is often the principal character of the dialogues, and he employs the Socratic Method as he questions the other characters of the dialogue. The Socratic Method is a form of inquiry and debate between individuals with opposing viewpoints. Questions are asked and answered to stimulate critical thinking. An initial hypothesis is proposed, and better hypotheses are found by identifying and eliminating prior hypotheses that lead to contradictions.

Plato (428/427 BCE–348/347 BCE) was a philosopher and mathematician. He was a student of Socrates and the writer of many philosophical dialogues. Plato was born in Athens and belonged to an aristocratic and influential Athenian family. He was named Aristocles at birth but is known by the nickname Plato, which his wrestling coach gave him because of his broad shoulders – platon means broad in Greek.

As an Athenian aristocrat, Plato would have studied grammar, music and gymnastics as a youth. He also attended courses in philosophy before he met Socrates. Plato, along with his teacher Socrates and his student Aristotle, laid the foundations of Western philosophy and science.

Unlike Socrates, Plato was both a writer and a teacher. For around fifty years, Plato wrote numerous Socratic dialogues with Socrates as the principal speaker. Plato never placed himself into any of the dialogues except in one called the Apology of Socrates, where Plato makes it clear that he was a devoted young follower of Socrates. In that dialogue, Socrates mentions Plato as one of those Athenian youths close enough to him to have been corrupted, as Socrates' accusers alleged at the trial before his execution.

Soon after Socrates was convicted and put to death in 399 BCE, Plato left Athens at the age of about twenty-eight. He travelled for around twelve years to study with the philosophers of his day. Plato stayed first in the Greek city of Megara but then went on to several other places, likely including Cyrene in North Africa, Italy, Sicily and Egypt.

Thirty-six dialogues and thirteen letters attributed to Plato have survived. The dialogues' exact ordering is unknown, although they can be roughly assigned to three periods: early, middle and late.

Plato began writing his early dialogues after the death of Socrates in 399 BCE; these are considered to be Plato's memorials to Socrates' life and teaching. Plato's middle to later works developed his own philosophy, where the main character speaks for Plato. The middle period includes his most famous work, the *Republic*. Modern scholars agree that the

Socrates
Source: Wikimedia Commons – Louvre Museum

Plato
Source: Wikimedia Commons – Capitoline Museum

Assumed Chronology of Plato's Dialogues	
Early - All written after the death of Socrates, but before Plato's first trip to Sicily in 387 BCE	*Apology, Charmides, Crito, Euthydemus, Euthyphro, Gorgias, Hippias Major, Hippias Minor, Ion, Laches, Lysis, Protagoras, Republic* Book I
Early-Transitional - Either at the end of the early group or the beginning of the middle group ca. 387-380 BCE:	*Cratylus, Menexenus, Meno*
Middle - ca. 380-360 BCE	*Phaedo, Republic* Books II-X, *Symposium*
Late-Transitional - Either at the end of the middle group or the beginning of the late group ca. 360-355 BCE:	*Parmenides, Theaetetus, Phaedrus*
Late - ca. 355-347 BCE; possibly in chronological order	*Sophist, Statesman, Philebus, Timaeus, Critias, Laws*

Source: Internet Encyclopedia of Philosophy

Timaeus and *Critias* containing the Atlantis story are among Plato's late dialogues.

Plato wrote extensively during his twelve years of travels before he returned to Athens. In around 387 BCE, at around the age of forty, he founded a philosophical school known as the Academy. It was located outside the city walls of ancient Athens and contained a sacred grove of olive trees dedicated since at least the Bronze Age to the goddess Athena. The archaic name for the site was Hekademia, which by classical times evolved into Akademia, linking it to a legendary Athenian hero called Akademos. The philosopher Aristotle studied at the Academy for twenty years (367–347 BCE) before founding his own school in Athens: the Lyceum.

In Plato's time, the Academy had no particular doctrine to teach. Plato and his other associates posed problems for students to study and solve using the Socratic Method. Plato was also one of Ancient Greece's most important patrons of mathematics, and he stressed mathematics as a way of understanding more about reality. In particular, Plato was convinced that geometry was the key to unlocking the secrets of the Universe. The sign above the Academy entrance read, 'Let no one ignorant of geometry enter here.'

For three hundred years, the Academy continued as a sceptical school until it was destroyed by the Roman general Sulla during a siege and sack of Athens in 86 BCE. Even though philosophers continued to teach Plato's philosophy in Athens during the Roman era, it was not until 410 CE that an Academy was re-established in Athens as a centre for Neo-Platonism. The Christian Byzantine emperor Justinian closed that school in 529 CE, and its remaining members went to Mesopotamia under the protection of the Sassanid King Khosrau I in his capital at Ctesiphon. They carried with them scrolls of literature, philosophy and science.

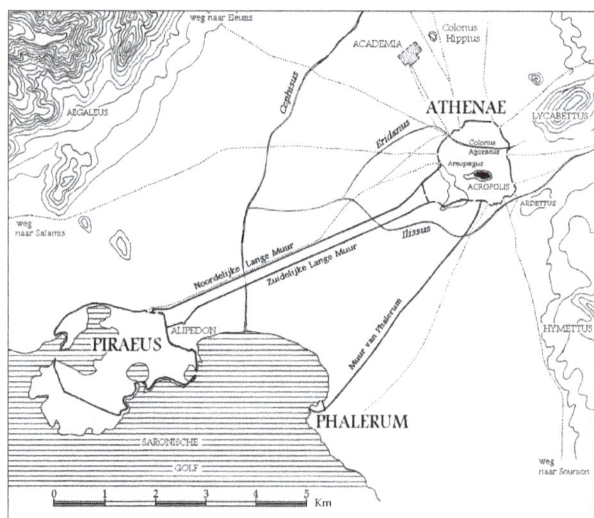

Ancient Athens with the Academy to the North-West
Source: Wikimedia Commons – Napoleon Vier

Archaeological Site of Plato's Academy
Source: Wikimedia Commons – Tomisti

Solon's Translation of the Atlantis Story

The Critias II character of Plato's dialogues states that while Solon was in Egypt, he wrote or received a Greek translation of the Egyptians' sacred registers about the Atlantis story. Critias II's family then kept Solon's original document for several generations. Critias II states: 'My great-grandfather, Dropides, had the original writing, which is still in my possession, and was carefully studied by me when I was a child'.

Plato: 'Then listen, Socrates, to a tale which, though strange, is certainly true, having been attested by Solon, who was the wisest of the seven sages (6th century BCE wise men of Greece). He was a relative and a dear friend of my great-grandfather, Dropides, as he himself says in many passages of his poems; and he told the story to Critias (Critias I), my grandfather, who remembered and repeated it to us'...'great and marvellous actions of the Athenian city, which have passed into oblivion through lapse of time and the destruction of mankind'...'which Critias declared, on the authority of Solon, to be not a mere legend, but an actual fact'...'if Solon had only, like other poets, made poetry the business of his life, and had completed the tale which he brought with him from Egypt'...'About the greatest action which the Athenians ever did, and which ought to have been the most famous, but, through the lapse of time and the destruction of the actors, it has not come down to us'.

Solon must have met with Pharaoh Amasis in the Egyptians' capital city of Sais shortly after Amasis' military victory in 570 BCE. Solon would have been around seventy years old and only recently departed Athens to begin his ten years of travels away from Greece. Regular trading contact between Greeks and Egyptians existed for over two thousand years before Solon arrived in Egypt. Many Greeks involved in trade and warfare would have lived permanently in Egypt. As a result, some Greeks and Egyptians must have learnt to speak and write each others' language and would have acted as interpreters. Assuming Solon used those interpreters, they would have been able to accurately translate the Atlantis story from the Egyptians' sacred registers into writings that he eventually took back to Greece.

Plato was a relative of the historical Critias II and a distant relative of Solon. Critias II speaks of Solon's 'original writing, which is still in my possession'. Because Plato quotes so much information about the Atlantis story in his dialogues, he likely saw and used Solon's original document or an exact copy. Though separated by almost three hundred years, the Greek language in Solon's writings would have been essentially the same as in Plato's time. Greek script underwent substantial changes over hundreds of years before Solon and Plato, but it was relatively standardised by their time.

At the time of Solon and Plato, the primary writing material in the Mediterranean world was papyrus imported from Egypt. Solon's original Greek translation of the Egyptians' Atlantis story was probably written on a papyrus scroll in the contemporary Greek alphabet. In damp European conditions like in Greece, papyrus lasted only decades, so a 200-year-old papyrus was considered extraordinary. If Plato used Solon's document over two hundred years later, it either was the original safeguarded from mould, or it may have been a copy or one of several later copies of Solon's original text. Otherwise, Solon's original account or a later copy may have been written on more durable leather or skins, which could have survived intact until Plato's time.

The Truth of the Atlantis Story

If Plato had manufactured the Atlantis story as an allegory of ideal societies, he likely would have used the Socratic Method to question the facts in the *Timaeus* and *Critias*. By introducing doubt and discussion, Plato would have created a more persuasive argument about societies than by merely stating facts. Instead, Plato has Socrates and Critias II repeatedly declare that Solon's Atlantis story is true. None of the characters in the dialogues questions any of the story's many exact details. For Plato, the Atlantis story is 'not a mere legend, but an actual fact'.

Plato had been the head or Scholarch of his Academy for forty years before he died around 347 BCE. The *Timaeus* and *Critias* were probably written around 360 BCE, about thirteen years before Plato died. Their contents, including the Atlantis story, would have been presented, discussed and critiqued by philosophers at the Academy for thirteen years while Plato was still alive. After Plato's death, the dialogues were studied for another three hundred years while the Academy functioned in Athens and then for centuries afterwards.

Plato's intellectual hero Socrates favoured truth as the highest value and argued that it could be discovered in discussion through reason and logic. In the *Timaeus* and *Critias*, the character of Socrates does not question any of the facts stated in the Atlantis story. All of the dialogues' characters emphasise clearly that truth and accuracy are essential when revealing the Atlantis story. There is no contrary opinion or scepticism from any of the characters in the dialogues.

From the *Timaeus* – Critias II: 'Then listen, Socrates, to a tale which, though strange, is certainly true, having been attested by Solon, who was the wisest of the seven sages.'

From the *Timaeus* (Taylor) – Socrates: 'You speak well. But what is this ancient achievement which was not only actually related by Solon, but was once really accomplished by this city (Athens).'

From the *Timaeus* (Taylor) – Critias II: 'what that event was which Solon asserted as a fact'.

From the *Critias* – Timaeus: 'grant that my words may endure in so far as they have been spoken truly and acceptably to him (God); but if unintentionally I have said anything wrong, I pray that he will impose upon me a just retribution, and the just retribution of him who errs is that he should be set right.'

From the *Critias* – Critias II: 'I would specially invoke Mnemosyne (the Ancient Greeks' goddess of memory); for all the important part of my discourse is dependent on her favour, and if I can recollect and recite enough of what was said by the priests and brought hither by Solon.'

In addition to Plato's statements about the truth of the Atlantis story in the *Timaeus* and *Critias*, some of Plato's quotes on philosophy, truth and reality show how unlikely it would be for him to completely invent a story and then pass it off as a true account:

'And isn't it a bad thing to be deceived about the truth, and a good thing to know what the truth is? For I assume that by knowing the truth you mean knowing things as they really are.'

'The philosopher is in love with truth, that is, not with the changing world of sensation, which is the object of opinion, but with the unchanging reality which is the object of knowledge.'

'He (the philosopher) will never willingly tolerate an untruth, but will hate it as much as he loves truth.'

'Is there anything more closely connected with wisdom than truth?'

'What is at issue is the conversion of the mind from the twilight of error to the truth, that climb up into the real world which we shall call true philosophy.'

'The object of knowledge is what exists, and its function is to know about reality.'

'One trait in the philosopher's character we can assume is his love of the knowledge that reveals eternal reality, the realm unaffected by change and decay. He is in love with the whole of that reality, and will not willingly be deprived even of the most insignificant fragment of it.'

The Other Characters of the *Timaeus* and *Critias*

Plato and some other Greek authors who wrote Socratic dialogues were students of Socrates. Even though they knew Socrates well, did they recall historical discussions with him in their dialogues? Or did they merely use Socrates' philosophical methods to present their arguments, mimicking how he would have spoken and behaved?

It is unknown whether the historical Socrates had actual discussions with any individuals named in the many Socratic dialogues written after his death. It is also unknown whether Plato or any other authors of Socratic dialogues were present at discussions Socrates might have had with those named individuals.

Two of the three characters of the *Timaeus* and *Critias* were known historical figures. They may have met with Socrates and discussed the Atlantis story before his death in 399 BCE, and Plato may have been present at those discussions. Nevertheless, it seems Plato did possess Solon's document of the Atlantis story when he wrote the *Timaeus* and *Critias* decades after the death of Socrates.

In the *Timaeus* and *Critias*, the Critias II character tells the story of Atlantis. From the first Ancient Greek commentaries on the dialogues up to the early 20th century CE, scholars identified Plato's Critias II character with the Athenian oligarch Critias (460–403 BCE). That historical Critias was a first cousin of Plato's mother, Perictione. Nevertheless, since the 20th century CE, the identity of the Critias character has been disputed as either the oligarch Critias (Critias II) or the grandfather of the oligarch (Critias I). Still, that academic dispute makes little difference to the contents of the Atlantis story.

Timaeus may or may not have been a historical figure, and little is known about the history of his supposed home city of Locri in Italy. Hermocrates (ca. 5th century BCE–407 BCE) was a Syracusan politician and general mentioned by the historian Thucydides (ca.460–400 BCE), among others. As the Hermocrates is a dialogue that possibly followed the *Critias* but may never have been written or has been lost, Hermocrates' contribution to the dialogues is unknown.

What Dialogue Came Before the *Timaeus*?

Plato sets the *Timaeus* dialogue on the day after a discussion of ideal societies. Another of Plato's dialogues must have contained that previous day's discussion and should have the same characters as the *Timaeus*. Those characters are Socrates, Timaeus, Critias, Hermocrates, and one other unnamed person.

Plato – from the first lines of the *Timaeus*:

Socrates: 'One, two, three; but where, my dear Timaeus, is the fourth of those who were yesterday my guests and are to be my entertainers today?'

Timaeus: 'He has been taken ill, Socrates; for he would not willingly have been absent from this gathering.'

Socrates: 'Then, if he is not coming, you (Timaeus) and the two others (Critias and Hermocrates) must supply his place.'

Classics scholars have long assumed that when Plato writes of the discussions of 'yesterday', he means the contents of the *Republic*, which is considered his most famous dialogue. Although the *Republic* does contain a discussion of ideal societies, it was probably written twenty to thirty years before the *Timaeus* or *Critias* with an entirely different cast of characters. Also, Plato wrote at least five dialogues between the *Republic* and the *Timaeus*, with no other known existing dialogue having the same characters as the *Timaeus* and *Critias*. One explanation for the Atlantis dialogues' different characters could be that Plato wrote a now-lost first dialogue that came before the *Timaeus* and *Critias* – not the *Republic* as is commonly alleged.

No one mentions the 'fourth' missing person's name from the discussion of 'yesterday', neither in the *Timaeus* nor in what remains of the *Critias*. A preceding first dialogue may have been named for this fourth missing person, and it could have repeated some of the themes about ideal societies written in the *Republic* many years earlier. There is also no known dialogue named Hermocrates, which may have once existed as an additional dialogue but is now lost. The Hermocrates may have been the first dialogue, and the fourth missing person may have been a character named in it. Whatever the case, Plato may originally have written at least three and possibly four related dialogues rather than only the two we now have.

Following a brief introduction to the Atlantis story, the *Timaeus* dialogue contains an account of the formation of the Universe and the nature of matter. Philosophers studied this technical part of the *Timaeus* for centuries, greatly influencing scientific thinking from late Antiquity to the European Renaissance of the 15th century CE. Why did Plato only briefly introduce the Atlantis story in the *Timaeus*? He could have entirely ignored it there and completely explained it in the following *Critias* dialogue. A possible explanation is that Plato may have wanted to introduce and link the Atlantis story to the hard facts in the remainder of the *Timaeus*. That connection would make it more credible for those studying it later at the Academy and elsewhere.

Writing with stylus and folding wax tablet, 500 BCE
Source: Wikimedia Commons – Museum Berlin

An overarching answer to the above possibilities is that although Plato wrote a story in the *Timaeus* and *Critias* that he believed to be true, it was of a remote past entirely unknown to his fellow Greeks. No Ancient Greek myths and legends mention Atlantis or a war between Athens and the Atlanteans, so the Atlantis story would probably have seemed unbelievable to the Greeks of Plato's time. Plato knew his Atlantis dialogues would be scrutinised and criticised by his followers and competitors, above all at his own Academy. The Atlantis dialogues must have been discussed at the Academy in Athens for at least ten years while Plato was alive and head of the school there. Plato might only have felt confident enough to write or release the Atlantis story after he had been a prominent philosopher in Athens for several decades.

Although it seems Plato based his complex Atlantis story on the actual writings of Solon, it is unclear how long he possessed them before he wrote the *Timaeus* and *Critias*. Regardless of whether Plato received them early or late in his career, Solon's writings may have given him a few possible features of an idealised Athenian society. Still, precise geographical details, such as the prehistoric Athenian Acropolis, seem unnecessary. Also, the many elaborate descriptions Plato gives about the Atlantic Island and Atlantean civilisation seem irrelevant to a debate on an idealised Athenian society. The Atlanteans were unlike any foreign civilisation known to the Greeks of Plato's time and are not described in Greek myths.

The Incomplete *Critias*

The *Critias* dialogue stops abruptly in mid-sentence. Modern scholars have long argued that Plato never completed the *Critias* because he stopped writing it or died before finishing it. Despite that common opinion, after Plato wrote the *Timaeus* and *Critias* and possibly one or two related dialogues, he wrote a separate dialogue called the Laws, his last known but unfinished work. Consequently, as the *Critias* was not Plato's final work, he could not have died while writing it. Also, what remains of the Atlantis story in the *Critias* does not seem to be a first draft that Plato abruptly abandoned before he finished it. Instead, the *Critias* reads like a well-constructed work that Plato completed after writing earlier drafts.

Ancient Greek writers used wax tablets as a reusable and portable writing surface since at least the 8th century BCE and probably for centuries before. The tablet was made of wood covered with a layer of wax, often linked loosely to a cover tablet. Writers used a pointed stylus to write on the wax surface and could erase it using a small spatula on the opposite end of the stylus tip. Writers used the wax tablet to make easy corrections on document drafts. Once a final document was prepared to be read by others, it was copied in ink onto the more permanent medium of papyrus or possibly skin. The entire wax tablet could then be erased for reuse by warming it to around 50°C and smoothing the softened wax surface.

Plato probably lived and worked in Athens for at least ten more years after he wrote about Atlantis. Sometime after writing the *Critias*, Plato wrote the *Laws* in twelve books written on wax tablets; however, it was unfinished and not copied to papyrus by the time Plato died. Philip of Opus was a disciple of Plato and a member of the Academy; he was responsible for transcribing the *Laws* to papyrus and then added a thirteenth and final book of his own.

The fact that Plato wrote the whole twelve books of the *Laws* on wax tablets and not on papyrus means that he would initially write and correct the drafts of an entire set of dialogues on several wax tablets. When Plato completed the dialogues' final draft, scribes would have copied them to a more permanent medium, such as papyrus, before Plato released them to the public. What remains of the *Critias* was written on papyrus, which means it must have been a complete final draft on wax before being transcribed to papyrus and circulated. Therefore, Plato did not abandon the Atlantis story in the *Critias* in mid-sentence as has usually been assumed.

The *Critias* dialogue was likely complete and significantly longer than what we now have. Plato specifically states that Solon's original Atlantis document 'was of great length'. Ancient Greek writers from the time of Homer in the 8th century BCE wrote lengthy works. For example, Homer's Iliad contains over one hundred and forty thousand words. In contrast, the *Timaeus* and what remains of the *Critias* dialogue have fewer than ten thousand words that describe the Atlantis story.

In the *Timaeus* dialogue, the Egyptian priest tells Solon: 'As touching your (prehistoric Athenian) citizens of nine thousand years ago, I will briefly inform you of their laws and of their most famous action; the exact particulars of the whole we will hereafter go through at our leisure in the sacred registers themselves.' The Athenians' 'most famous action' was their role in the Mediterranean War between the Atlanteans and the free people of the Eastern Mediterranean, so the Egyptians had 'exact particulars' of the Mediterranean War. Plato possessed Solon's record and would have included them in the *Critias* dialogue, where he states, 'this war I am going to describe'.

As for what a complete *Critias* may have contained, Plato declares: 'the history (of the Mediterranean War) will unfold the various nations of barbarians and families of Hellenes (Greeks) which then (9,000 years before) existed, as they successively appear on the scene' and 'you must not be surprised at often hearing me mention Grecian names of barbarous men.'

In the Atlantis story, the words barbarian and barbaric describe any non-Greek cultures. The Ancient Greeks used the word barbaros (barbarian in English) to describe a person speaking a non-Greek language, which sounded like bar-bar to a Greek's ears. It became a common term for all foreigners regardless of their level of sophistication, including the highly civilised societies of the Egyptians, Persians and Medes.

Plato states that the Atlantis story will describe 'the various nations of barbarians and families of Hellenes...as they successively appear on the scene.' That statement means Solon's original account and the complete *Critias* dialogue described the war between the Atlanteans and the Mediterraneans. Contrary to Plato's statement, the incomplete *Critias* does not name any Barbarians, Atlanteans or the 'families of Hellenes' involved in the war. There is no 'history' or narrative of the war in which they 'successively appear on the scene'. Even though Plato names a few legendary Athenian folk heroes who he claims participated in the war, their deeds are not discussed.

Rather than Plato leaving the *Critias* unfinished, a more likely explanation for its abrupt ending is that it was once complete and the remainder was lost, as have thousands of other Ancient Greek literary works. That loss may also include the Hermocrates dialogue, which possibly was the first or final part of a trilogy or yet another dialogue that would have created four related dialogues.

A lost work is a document or literary work with no known surviving copies. It may be lost either through the destruction of the original manuscript or all later copies of the work. Many hundreds of Ancient Greek writings are known to be lost because they were discussed or referenced in later classical works or compilations. Many thousands more must have been lost, but we know nothing of their existence.

A small selection of prominent Greek writers whose works are known to be lost gives some idea of how many more must be lost and forgotten:

- Lost plays of Aeschylus – believed to have written some ninety plays, of which six plays survive
- Lost plays of Aristophanes – wrote forty plays, eleven of which survive

- Lost plays of Sophocles – of one hundred and twenty-three plays, seven survive with only fragments of others
- Lost plays of Euripides – believed to have written over ninety plays, but only eighteen survive
- Lost works of Aristotle – it is thought that about one-third of his original works survive
- Lost works of Democritus – wrote extensively on natural philosophy and ethics, but little remains
- Lost works of Proclus – many of his commentaries on Plato's writings are lost

Crantor, Proclus and the Atlantis Hieroglyphs

Crantor was an Ancient Greek philosopher, born in Cilicia in Asia Minor around the middle of the 4th century BCE and died in 276/5 BCE. Crantor moved to Athens to study philosophy at the Academy after Plato's death and became a pupil of Xenocrates, the Academy's Scholarch at that time. Crantor was the first of Plato's followers to write commentaries on Plato's written dialogues, but only fragments remain. Whereas some ancient writers viewed the Atlantis story as fiction, others believed it was real. Crantor was one writer who thought the story was historical fact. He wrote a commentary on Plato's *Timaeus* dialogue, unfortunately now lost. Whether Crantor also wrote a commentary on the *Critias* is not known.

Proclus Lycaeus (412–487 CE) was a Neoplatonist philosopher of the 5th century CE who also wrote commentaries on Plato's dialogues. His commentary on the *Timaeus* is his most famous writing, especially influential on Western medieval philosophy and Islamic thought. Plato's *Timaeus* dialogue and Proclus' commentary on it were studied widely in the Middle Ages and Renaissance, notably by astronomers such as Copernicus and Keppler.

A passage from Proclus' 5th century CE commentary on the *Timaeus* claims that either Crantor or Plato visited Egypt, had conversations with temple priests, and saw the hieroglyphs at the Temple of Neith that confirmed the Atlantis story.

Proclus writes: 'As for the whole of this account of the Atlanteans, some say that it is unadorned history, such as Crantor, the first commentator on Plato. Crantor also says that Plato's contemporaries used to criticise him jokingly for not being the inventor of his *Republic* (dialogue) but for copying the institutions of the Egyptians. Plato took these critics seriously enough to assign to the Egyptians this story about the Athenians and Atlanteans, so as to make them say that the Athenians really once lived according to that system. He (Crantor or Plato) adds that this is testified by the prophets (priests) of the Egyptians, who assert that these particulars (of the Atlantis story) are written on pillars (of the Temple of Neith in Sais) which are still preserved.'

Proclus writes of 'pillars which are still preserved' in his time in the 5th century CE. That statement means the Atlantis story hieroglyphs were still visible at Sais almost one thousand years after Solon's visit there. Plato did travel to Egypt in his thirties after the death of Socrates in 399 BCE. His journey possibly was after an actual discussion of the Atlantis story between Socrates and Critias II, something that Plato may have witnessed. Another possibility is that Plato had a copy of Solon's account of the Atlantis story before he went to Egypt. Either way, if Plato already knew about Atlantis before going to Egypt, he may have looked for more evidence on the columns at the Temple of Neith.

Since Crantor was a student at the Academy in the 4th century BCE, he would have been familiar with Plato's *Timaeus* and *Critias*. As the *Critias* possibly was available as a complete work in Crantor's time, he may have travelled to Egypt or enquired from someone in Egypt about the temple inscriptions of the Atlantis story. Much later, in the 5th century CE, Proclus wrote that he knew the Atlantis story was still carved on pillars at the Temple of Neith at Sais.

Whether it was Plato, Crantor, an agent of Crantor, an acquaintance of Proclus or Proclus himself centuries later, someone besides Solon saw the Egyptian hieroglyphs about Atlantis. Those temple inscriptions likely were the same Solon would have seen in the 6th century BCE.

The Preservation of Ancient Greek Literature

Pre-Classical and Classical Greek literature starts with Homer's *Iliad* and *Odyssey* in the 8th century BCE and extends to the rise of Alexander the Great in the 4th century BCE. Fictional literature was written in verse; scientific literature was in prose. For thousands of years before the invention of the printing press in the 15th century CE, books were hand-written and relatively rare items. Scribes had to copy manuscripts that were stored and read in private and public libraries.

Plato's original Greek texts of the *Timaeus* and *Critias* were copied and preserved in an unbroken line exactly as Plato wrote them in the 4th century BCE. In addition to the texts in Ancient Greek, the dialogues were translated over many centuries into Latin, Arabic, English and other languages. Some of these translations may have changed the meaning of the original Ancient Greek. But Plato's entire *Timaeus* still survives unaltered, as does the incomplete *Critias* up to where it cuts off in mid-sentence.

The great libraries of the ancient world housed imperial archives, sacred writings, literature, and chronicles. They contained tens of thousands of

The Great Library of Alexandria
Source: Wikimedia Commons –
O. Von Corven, 19th Century CE

Scholars at an Abbasid Library, 13th century CE
Source: Wikimedia Commons –
Bibliotheque Nationale de France

works of fictional and scientific literature. Some of those ancient libraries may have included additional works about Atlantis by Plato or other ancient writers. If those unknown works once did exist, they are lost and forgotten after centuries of neglect and destruction.

The Royal Library of Alexandria in Egypt was founded in the late 3rd century BCE. It was part of a larger research institution for classical scholars called the Musaeum, which functioned for almost nine hundred years. The Royal Library was said to have housed an estimated 400,000 manuscripts and was considered the leading intellectual centre of the Hellenistic world. There were several partial or complete destructions of the Library over several centuries. These include a fire set by Julius Caesar in 48 BCE, an attack by the Roman Emperor Aurelian in the 270s CE, the decree of Coptic Pope Theophilus in 391 CE, and the Muslim conquest of Egypt in 642 CE.

The Library of Pergamum (197-159 BCE) in Asia Minor was the second-greatest Hellenistic library after Alexandria, collecting over 200,000 manuscripts. There is a legend that Mark Antony gave Cleopatra a wedding present of all the volumes stored at Pergamum for the Library in Alexandria.

The Library of Celsus at Ephesus (135 CE) in Asia Minor housed 12,000 manuscripts. It was a tomb and a shrine for Gaius Julius Celsus Polemaeanus, after whom it was named. A fire destroyed the library and all of its books when an earthquake struck the city in 262 CE.

The Imperial Library of Constantinople (330 CE) was the last of the great libraries of the ancient world. It stored some documents saved from the Library of Alexandria. Byzantine Emperor Constantius II established the library and had the rolls of papyrus copied onto parchment or vellum to be better preserved. Over the centuries, several fires destroyed much of the collection. A fire in 473 CE destroyed around 120,000 manuscripts, and in 1204 CE, the Normans of the Fourth Crusade totally destroyed the library.

Knowledge of the Ancient Greek language declined with the fall of Rome and the Western Roman Empire in the 5th century CE. Numerous surviving Greek texts remained untranslated, while any older texts written on papyrus deteriorated after a few decades and were lost unless copied onto longer-lasting parchment. Unfortunately, in the Eastern Roman Empire centred in Constantinople, the Greek-speaking Byzantines were more interested in Christian writings than Classical Greek works. Byzantine scribes often recycled old parchment books by scraping off Greek philosophical texts to create religious books.

In Western Europe, there was a lack of interest in Greek ideas, so only a few Irish monasteries kept or copied Greek works. The Irish monks learnt from Greek and Latin missionaries, who probably brought Greek texts from the East. Nevertheless, Arabic translators introduced much more Greek philosophy and science to the West than the Irish. The Arab military conquests began in the 7th century CE, with Islamic expansion continuing for centuries. After the Arabs invaded the southern portions of the Byzantine Empire, they were exposed to Ancient Greek writings and ideas. Arabic translations and commentaries on Greek ideas spread throughout their conquered territories, initially via Arab North Africa and then into Spain and Sicily, which became essential centres for the further transmission of Greek ideas.

The translation of ancient texts by Islamic Culture was one of the greatest transmissions of ideas in history and took place in two main stages. The first stage was in the 8th and 9th centuries CE when Greek works were translated into Arabic during Abbasid rule in Baghdad, in present-day Iraq. The second stage was in the 12th and 13th centuries CE, known as 'the great age of translation'. It occurred after Europeans conquered Islamic territories in Spain and Sicily, which allowed Western scholars from all over Europe to travel there and study Arabic learning and culture.

During the decline of the Byzantine Empire after 1200 CE, Byzantine and other scholars migrated from Sicily and Byzantium to Western Europe. Migration increased after the fall of Constantinople to the Ottoman Turks in 1453 CE and continued up to the 16th century CE. The migrants taught the Ancient Greek language to Western Europeans in universities or privately. The further spread of knowledge of Greek texts revived Greek and Roman studies in the West and inspired the humanism and science of the Renaissance in Europe.

Despite those hundreds of years when Ancient Greek texts were translated into different languages, Plato's writings in original Greek were lost to Western civilisation until the 15th century CE. Then, George Gemistus Plethon (ca. 1355–1452/1454 CE) took them from Constantinople to the West. Plethon was a Greek Neo-Platonist scholar and one of the chief pioneers of the revival of Greek learning in Western Europe. During the 1438–1439 CE Council of Florence, Plethon met and influenced Cosimo de Medici to found a new Platonic Academy in Florence, where all of Plato's surviving works were translated into Latin. The original Greek works Plethon took with him likely included Plato's entire *Timaeus* and the incomplete *Critias*.

The Clarke Plato is the oldest surviving manuscript in the original Greek for about half of Plato's dialogues. It was written in Constantinople in 895 CE and was acquired by Oxford University in 1809 CE.

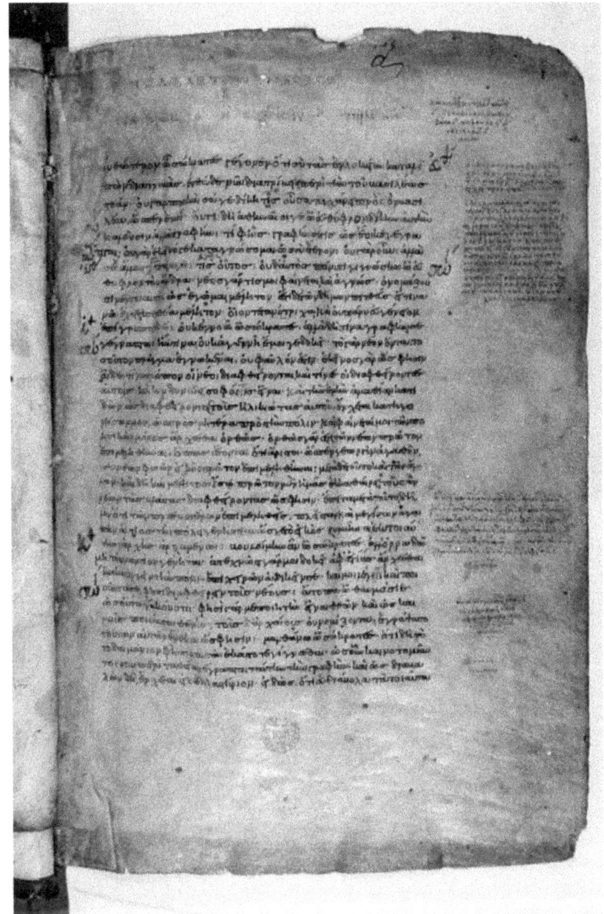

The Clarke Plato, 895 CE
Source: Wikimedia Commons – Bodleian Library

The Atlantic Island must be located in the Atlantic Ocean and be 'larger than Libya and Asia put together'

CHAPTER 2

Plato's Atlantic Island

Ever since Plato wrote the Atlantis story over two thousand years ago, many different sites were claimed to be his 'Atlantic island'. Several of these locations include the continents of North and South America; the Mediterranean islands of Sardinia, Santorini and Cyprus; the Black Sea; North-West Africa; southern Spain; the Bahamas, the Canary and Azores Islands in the North Atlantic; the Mid-Atlantic Ridge; Greenland; the submerged landmass of Sundaland in South-East Asia; and even the continent of Antarctica.

None of these or the many other claimed sites can satisfy all of the geographical features of Plato's 'Atlantic island', an enormous island that he insists was once a real place and not a myth. At the very least, any site claimed for the Atlantic Island must have two specific features – it must be located somewhere in the Atlantic Ocean and be 'larger than Libya and Asia put together'.

The Time of the Atlantean Empire and Prehistoric Athens

Modern scholars have long debated the units of time Plato uses in his Atlantis story. Some scholars have suggested that the Egyptians, Solon or Plato confused solar years with lunar months. They then argue that the 9,000-year time frame for the Atlantis story is merely 9,000 months, which would only be 750 years before Solon's time of around 600 BCE. This claim places Atlantis' destruction around 1400 BCE, toward the end of the Mediterranean Bronze Age. That would then roughly coincide with the volcanic destruction of the Aegean island of Thera (Santorini) and the decline of the Minoan civilisation on Crete, which many academics claim is the basis of Plato's Atlantis story.

It is highly improbable that the Ancient Egyptians confused months with years for any past events they recorded in their 'sacred registers'. By Solon's time in the 6th century BCE, the Egyptians had a highly literate and numerate civilisation since at least 3000 BCE, with written records dating back to the beginning of their civilisation.

Before Solon visited Egypt, the Egyptians had used two different calendars for thousands of years. Both of those commonly used Egyptian calendars had years the same length as the one we use now – a solar year of approximately 365 days, representing the Earth's complete orbit around the Sun. For at least hundreds of years before Solon and Plato's time, the Ancient Greeks had also used a solar year of twelve lunar months, similar to the Egyptians. So, it is unlikely that the Egyptians, Solon or Plato would have confused months with years. The length of Plato's 'year' in the Atlantis story can be assumed to be about the same as one of our solar years of about 365 days, not just one lunar month of four weeks.

Another argument against Plato's timescale is that the Egyptians, Solon or Plato himself confused the figure of 9,000 with 900. As well as a written script, the Ancient Egyptians used a system of numerals based on a scale of ten, as we do now. They must have used these symbols regularly to describe and calculate numbers in the hundreds of thousands and millions. It is doubtful that the Egyptians who

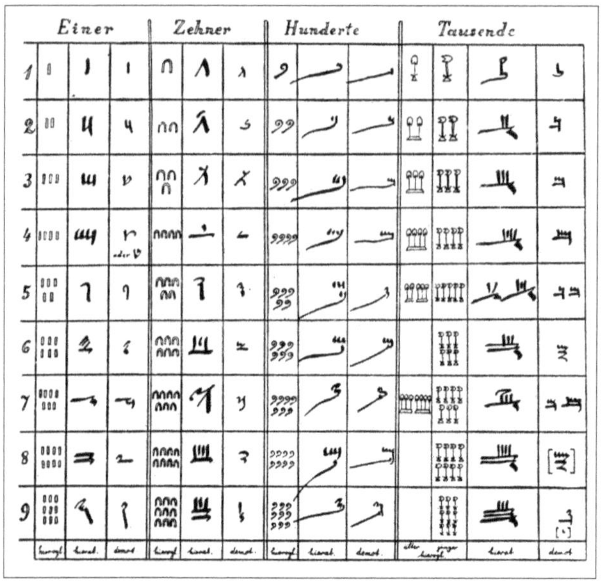

Egyptian Numerical Hieroglyphs
Source: Wikimedia Commons

recorded the Atlantis story confused their numbers and turned 9,000 years into 900 years.

From Minoan and Mycenaean times, the Greeks also used a numeral system with a scale of ten. By Solon and Plato's time, it was based on the Greek alphabet, which the Romans later modified into their Roman numerals. Again, like the Egyptians, the Greeks were accustomed to using large numbers accurately, so Solon and Plato would not have confused thousands with hundreds. As well as being a philosopher, Plato was an accomplished mathematician, so he was very unlikely to make the simple numerical mistake of confusing 9,000 with 900 years.

The Egyptian priests who spoke with Solon around 570 BCE told him about the founding of Athens and Sais: 'the goddess (Athena/Neith) who is the common patron and parent and educator of both our cities. She founded your city (Athens) a thousand years before ours (Sais), receiving from the Earth and Hephaestus the seed of your race, and afterwards she founded ours, of which the constitution is recorded in our sacred registers to be eight thousand years old.' If Sais was founded 8,000 years before Solon, that is around 10,600 BP. Therefore, Athens was founded 9,000 years before Solon or around 11,600 BP.

The Egyptians also told Solon the recorded time from the Mediterranean War against the Atlanteans up to his time: 'nine thousand was the sum of years which had elapsed since the war which was said to have taken place between those who dwelt outside the Pillars of Heracles and all who dwelt within them.' If the Mediterranean War occurred nine thousand years before Solon's time, it was around 11,600 BP, which is about the same time as the founding of Athens but a thousand years before the founding of Sais.

Plato claims that by the time of the Mediterranean War in around 11,600 BP, the Atlanteans had already constructed a vast Royal City on the Atlantic Island and possessed an extensive maritime empire that reached into the Mediterranean: 'these (the first Kings of Atlantis) and their descendants for many generations were the inhabitants and rulers of divers islands in the open sea; and also, as has been already said, they held sway in our (Egypt's) direction over the country within the Pillars (inside the Mediterranean) as far as Egypt and Tyrrhenia.' It must have taken hundreds if not thousands of years and 'many generations' before 11,600 BP for the Atlanteans to develop their advanced civilisation.

At some unspecified time after 11,600 BP, Plato states that the Mediterranean War ended. Then, catastrophic natural disasters of floods and earthquakes destroyed the Atlantic Island and much, if not all, of prehistoric Athens. It is improbable that these two geographically separate destructions happened simultaneously. Either event could have been anything from a few years to thousands of years after the Mediterranean War. Therefore, it is possible that the Atlantic Island and Atlantean Empire, as well as the prehistoric city of Athens, persisted long after 11,600 BP.

The Ancient Greeks' Worldview

The Greeks of Solon's time in the 6th century BCE had a minimal understanding of the shape and size of the Earth or the location and extent of the continents and oceans. There was little concept of the actual size of the continents of Europe, Asia or Africa (called Libya by the Greeks) or the extent of the Atlantic, Indian or Pacific Oceans. The continents of the Americas, Australia and Antarctica were entirely unknown to the Ancient Greeks.

By Plato's time in the 4th century BCE, most Greeks thought the Earth was a flat disc. Some early philosophers, such as Pythagoras (ca. 570–495 BCE), theorised that the Earth was a sphere, as did Plato. Later, around 240 BCE, the Greek astronomer Eratosthenes (276–194 BCE) believed the Earth was a sphere and calculated its circumference. Depending on the distance measure Eratosthenes used, his estimate was within a 2% to 20% margin of the Earth's actual circumference.

The Greek philosopher Anaximander (ca. 610–546 BCE) created one of the first known maps of the world at a time when the Greeks thought the Earth was a flat disc. Anaximander's map showed the extent of the Earth as imagined by the Greeks of Solon's time around 600 BCE. The map was circular and showed the known lands of the world arranged around the Mediterranean Sea. The Greek name for the Mediterranean was *Mesogeios*, meaning middle land or middle earth. The landmasses of Europe,

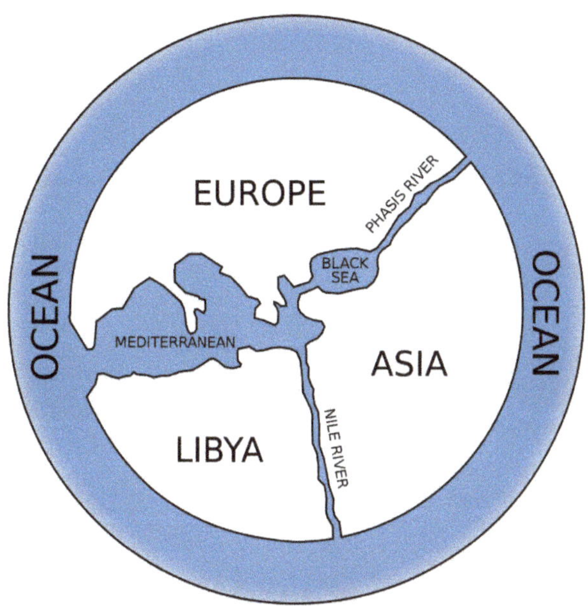

Reconstruction of Anaximander's map
Source: Wikimedia Commons – Bibi Saint-Pol

Reconstruction of Hecataeus' map
Source: Wikimedia Commons – Bibi Saint-Pol

Asia and Libya were of equal size on the map, and a single Ocean encircled them all.

Hecataeus of Miletus (ca. 550–476 BCE) is the first known Greek historian. He described the countries and inhabitants of the known world accompanied by a map based on Anaximander's map of the Earth. Hecataeus corrected and enlarged Anaximander's map, though he still depicted the Earth as a flat disc.

When Plato wrote the *Timaeus* and *Critias* in the 4th century BCE, the Greeks knew nothing about the extent of the Atlantic Ocean or the continents of the Americas to the west. This limited worldview was accepted as fact during Solon and Plato's lives and did not change for centuries until the European discovery of the Americas. Maps of the late 15th century CE clearly show that Europeans only knew of the American continents, what they called the New World, after Columbus' first voyage there in 1492 CE.

Plato – '(the Atlantic Island) was the way to other islands, and from these you may pass to the whole of the opposite continent which surrounded the true ocean.'

Neither Anaximander's nor Hecataeus' map includes any continent other than Europe, Libya and

Martellus world map (1489)
Source: Wikimedia Commons – Yale Library Archives

Cantino world map (1502)
Source: Wikimedia Commons – Biblioteca Estense Universitaria, Modena, Italy

Asia. Still, Plato is very specific in describing another continent outside the Mediterranean, beyond the encircling single Ocean and further than the Atlantic Island. Given the Greeks' limited concept of the Earth in Plato's time, it is extraordinary that he describes anything like the Atlantic Island or 'other islands' and another continent to the west of the Mediterranean. How and why would Plato fabricate their existence? Is it not more likely that Plato used some very ancient but forgotten knowledge for his geographical descriptions in the *Timaeus* and *Critias*?

Ancient Measurements of Length and Distance

The *Timaeus* and *Critias* contain precise measurements the Egyptians gave Solon, particularly the foot and the stadion (whose plural is stadia). In antiquity, various cultures used different measures for the foot and stadion. Still, one can assume that the Egyptian priests used their measures when they described the Atlantis story to Solon.

The first known standardised foot measure was from the ancient civilisation of Sumer around 2575 BCE, but several others have been used since then:

- Greek/English 1 foot (305mm) – one of the variations of Greek measures, called Olympian or Geographic
- Common Greek 1.028 ft (314mm) – widely used throughout Europe, surviving in England until the 14th century CE
- Royal Egyptian 1.142857 ft (349mm)
- Common Egyptian 0.979592 ft (299mm) – six-sevenths of the Royal Egyptian foot

For convenience, any measurements Plato gives in feet are converted to metres, with three feet to one metre. It is assumed that the Egyptian priests used the Royal Egyptian Foot in their sacred registers. At just less than 350 millimetres, three Royal Egyptian Feet are roughly equivalent to one metre. If the priests used the Common Egyptian Foot of 299mm, three feet would be even closer to one metre.

As well as the foot, the Ancient Greeks had a larger unit of length called the stadion. According to Herodotus, one stadion equalled 600 feet. As there were several different lengths of feet depending on the country of origin, each would produce a different length of stadion.

The Egyptian priests probably gave Solon their stadion measurements. Therefore, the Egyptian stadion length of 209 metres will be used for distance calculations.

Stadion Name	Length in Metres	Description
Olympic	176 m	600 × 294 mm
Attic/Italic	185 m	600 × 308 mm
Babylonian/ Persian	196 m	600 × 327 mm
Phoenician/ Egyptian	209 m	600 × 349 mm

Source: Wikipedia

The Location of the Atlantic Island

Plato repeatedly locates the Atlantic Island in the Atlantic Ocean. The oldest known mention of Atlantic is around 450 BCE in Herodotus' *Histories*, where he mentions *Atlantis thalassa* or Sea of Atlas. Although many location theories for the Atlantic Island place it within the Mediterranean, Plato clearly distinguishes between the Mediterranean Sea, the Atlantic Ocean, and the lands on either side of the Atlantic.

Plato – 'He (Poseidon) named them all (his sons); the eldest, who was the first king, he named Atlas, and after him the whole island and the ocean were called Atlantic.'

Plato – 'for this sea (the Mediterranean) which is within the Straits of Heracles is only a harbour, having a narrow entrance, but that other is a real sea (the Atlantic Ocean), and the surrounding land (Europe, Africa and the Americas) may be most truly called a boundless continent.'

The Mediterranean Sea
The Strait of Gibraltar on the Bottom Left
Source: Wikimedia Commons – NASA

The Strait of Gibraltar looking towards the Mediterranean – Rock of Gibraltar on the Left
Source: Wikimedia Commons – NASA

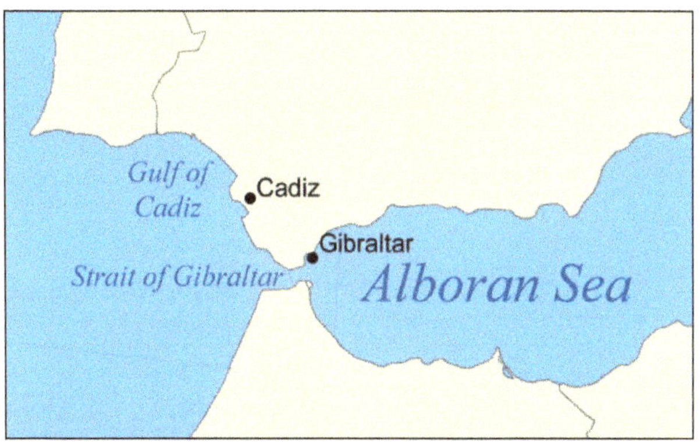

Location of Cadiz
Source: Wikimedia Commons – Adapted from Norman Einstein

Plato's statement that the 'real sea' of the Atlantic Ocean has 'surrounding land' that forms 'a boundless continent' contradicts the Ancient Greeks' worldview. To the Greeks of Solon and Plato's time, only one Ocean encircled the known continents of Europe, Libya and Asia, so no other lands lay beyond Ocean. Plato also clearly states that the Atlantic Island was outside 'the Straits of Heracles'. In Antiquity, the Pillars of Heracles were the headlands on either side of the Strait of Gibraltar. To the north, the European Pillar is the Rock of Gibraltar, but the southern location of the North African Pillar is disputed; it is either Monte Hacho or Jebel Musa.

The Pillars of Atlas is a more ancient name for the Strait, as used in the Greek myth of Perseus and by Homer in the *Odyssey*. Euripides (ca. 480–406 BCE) wrote in his play *Hippolytus*: 'Of those mortals who look upon the light of the sun and who live between the very edges of the east, the Black Sea and the farthest ends of the west, the great Pillars of Atlas.' By Euripides' time, the Greeks were aware of the western end of the Mediterranean as they had been sailing beyond it for centuries.

The following passage from Plato further describes the Atlantic Island's location outside the Mediterranean: 'To his (Atlas') twin brother, who was born after him, and obtained as his lot the extremity of the (Atlantic) island towards the Pillars of Heracles, facing the country which is now called the region of Gades in that part of the world, he gave the name which in the Hellenic language is Eumelus, in the language of the country which is named after him, Gadeirus.'

The location of 'Gades' or 'Gadeirus' is present-day Cadiz, a port city on the Atlantic coast of south-western Spain. If one end of the Atlantic Island faced Cadiz and the Strait of Gibraltar, it further confirms that the Atlantic Island was in the Atlantic Ocean, not inside the Mediterranean or any other sea or ocean.

Cadiz is the most ancient city continuously inhabited in Western Europe. The Phoenicians founded the city, initially known as Gadir but later known by the Greek name Gadeira, which became Gades in Latin and finally Cadiz. Traditionally, the city's founding date is 1104 BCE, but no archaeological finds are dated earlier than the 9th century BCE.

The Phoenicians used the city to trade with a more ancient city-state called Tartessos, believed to be somewhere near the mouth of the Guadalquivir River, thirty kilometres north-west of modern Cadiz. By around 600 BCE, the Greeks had founded important trading colonies just inside the Mediterranean, in what is now southern France and Spain. By then, Cadiz had been established for centuries, so the Greeks of Solon and Plato's time would have known it was outside the Mediterranean.

The Size of the Atlantic Island

In each of his Atlantis dialogues, Plato describes the size of the Atlantic Island. From the *Timaeus*: 'the (Atlantic) island was larger than Libya and Asia put together.' From the *Critias*: 'was an island greater in extent than Libya and Asia.'

What we now call Libya and Asia are very different from when Solon visited Egypt in the early 6th century BCE. When the Egyptian priests at Sais spoke with Solon, they likely compared the size of the Atlantic Island with those geographical regions of 'Libya and Asia' well-known to the Egyptians and Greeks in Solon's time. However, the original Egyptian sacred registers were likely written thousands of years before Solon and may not have used the same geographical descriptions. Those very ancient records might have described the Atlantic Island's size in units of measure or compared it to the landmasses the prehistoric Egyptians knew well in their time.

The exact boundaries of Ancient Libya are unknown, but it lay west of Ancient Egypt, and the Egyptians called it IMNT. Libyan tribes frequently fought against the Egyptians, with the major tribes being the Tjehenu, the Tamahu, the Libu (or Ribu), and the Meshwesh. The oldest known written references to the Libyans or Libu date to Ramesses

Ancient Libya – Locations of the Libyan Tribes
Source: The Eastern Libyans – Oric Bates, 1914

called all the native Berbers of North Africa Libyans, and their lands were called Libya. Berber territory extended along the Mediterranean from the western borders of Ancient Egypt to the Atlantic in modern Morocco.

When Solon visited Egypt in the early 6th century BCE, the Egyptians would likely have described Libya in its older context: the territory immediately to the west of Egypt. It was a region occupied for thousands of years by the Libyan tribes the Egyptians knew well and fought regularly. By Solon's time, the Greeks had only recently colonised the city of Cyrene. Like the Egyptians, the Greeks probably used a narrower definition of Libya's size rather than all of North Africa. That older definition of Libya would include the regions later called Cyrenaica and Marmarica, whose combined dimensions are roughly 700km east-west by 400km north-south. Those dimensions would then give Plato's 'Libya' a total area of about 280,000km^2.

II and his successor Merneptah, who were Egyptian rulers during the 13th century BCE.

In Greek and Roman mythology, Libya is the daughter of Epaphus (a mythical king of Egypt), and she personified the land of the ancient Libyans. By Roman times, the Latin name Libya referred to the region west of the Nile Valley, generally corresponding to modern Northwest Africa and extending to the Atlantic. Still, a more ancient and narrower definition of Libya could also mean the country immediately west of Egypt, comprising what was later called Cyrenaica (Libya Superior) and Marmarica (Libya Inferior).

Before the rise of the Romans, the Greeks colonised Libya in 630 BCE and founded the city of Cyrene. Within 200 years, they established four more cities in the region that became known as Cyrenaica. Together with Cyrene, the combined cities were called the Pentapolis or Five Cities. Eventually, over several hundred years of colonisation, the Greeks

In Greek mythology, Asia is the name of a Titan goddess who once lived in the land of Lydia in Anatolia. In Greek, *Anatolia* meant east or sunrise, but it was also called Asia Minor from the Greek term *Mikra Asia*, meaning Small Asia. These two Greek names defined the westernmost extension of the continent of Asia, in what is now most of the Republic of Turkey.

The earliest known place name for Asia is the Hittite word *Assuwa*: a region in central-western Anatolia. The name may be connected to the Mycenaean Greek *a-si-wi-ja*, found in inscriptions in Greece at Pylos. The early Greeks considered the extent of Asia to be central-western Anatolia. Later, the region became a province of the Roman Empire and was also called Asia.

The Hittites were a Bronze Age people who established a kingdom centred at Hattusa in

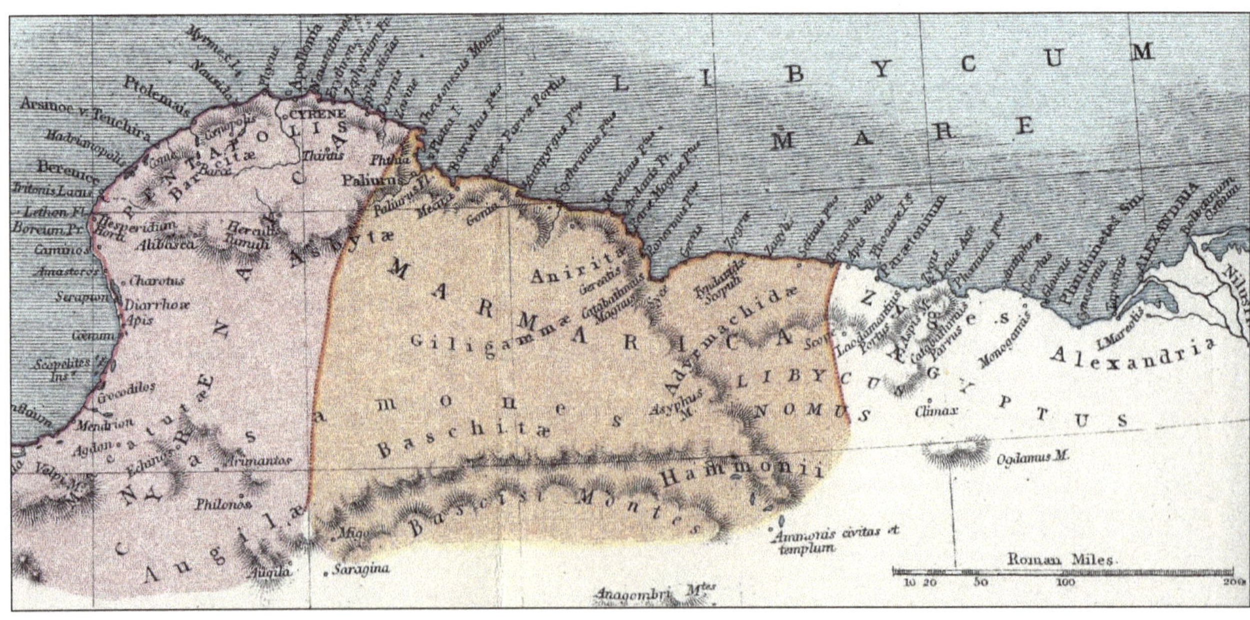

Map of Cyrenaica and Marmarica in the Roman era
Source: Wikimedia Commons – Samuel Butler, J.M. Dent, E.P. Dutton, 1907

'Libya' in the time of Solon – Nile Delta to the Right
Source: Google Earth

The Hittite Kingdom at the height of its power ca. 1300 BCE (red), bordering on the Egyptian Empire (green)
Source: Wikimedia Commons – D. Bachmann

north-central Anatolia in the 18th century BCE. The Hittite Empire reached its height in the 14th century BCE; by 1300 BCE, the Hittites bordered the Egyptian sphere of influence. The rivalry led to the Battle of Kadesh between the Egyptians and Hittites in 1274 BCE.

From at least the time of their conflict with the Hittites in the 13th century BCE, the Egyptians would have considered Asia as the land the Greeks later called Anatolia or Asia Minor. That narrow definition of Asia was probably the same as in Solon's time when the Egyptian priest described the size of the Atlantic Island. The dimensions of Asia Minor are roughly 900km east-west by 650km north-south, which gives Plato's 'Asia' a total area of about 585,000km^2.

Plato twice describes the Atlantic Island as 'larger than Libya and Asia put together'. Using the approximate size of those regions known by the Ancient Egyptians and Greeks in Solon's time, if 'Libya' is 280,000km^2 and 'Asia' is 585,000km^2, the combined area is 865,000km^2. If the Atlantic Island was larger than Libya and Asia put together, it may have been around 1,000,000km^2 in size.

An Atlantic Island of one million square kilometres is hundreds of times greater than any island known to the Egyptians or Greeks of Solon and Plato's time. All of the Mediterranean islands are very much smaller: Sicily is the largest at 25,711km^2;

Asia Minor
Source: Wikimedia Commons – Samuel Butler, 1907 CE

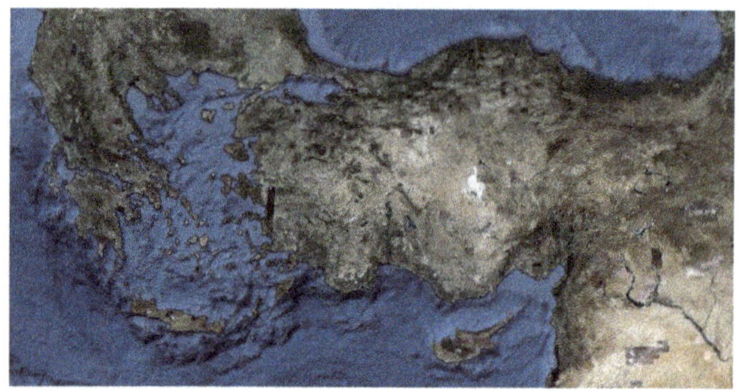

Greece and Asia Minor
Source: Google Earth

Sardinia is 20,090km^2; Cyprus is 9,251km^2; Corsica is 8,680km^2, and Crete is 8,336km^2.

An Atlantic Island in the Caribbean

Plato – 'This power (the Atlantean Empire) came forth out of the Atlantic Ocean'...'and there was an island situated in front of the straits which are by you called the Pillars of Heracles'...'(the Atlantic Island) was the way to other islands, and from these you may pass to the whole of the opposite continent which surrounded the true ocean.'

Plato's use of the term 'in front of the straits' is often interpreted to mean the Atlantic Island was close to the Mediterranean's entrance at the Strait of Gibraltar. A more likely meaning is that the Atlantic Island was opposite the Strait of Gibraltar and was not far to the south or north of the Strait. Being opposite the Strait means the Atlantic Island would also 'face' Cadiz, as Plato describes it. These two descriptions eliminate locations in the Atlantic Ocean off the coast of West or Southern Africa, or off-shore from Western Europe, Britain and Scandinavia.

There are claims that various islands or island groups in the North Atlantic are possible locations of the Atlantic Island, including the Canary, Madeira and Cape Verde Islands. There is no geological evidence of past catastrophic subsidence of any of these islands, nor has the ocean bottom surrounding them ever been dry land in the past. Also, all of these islands are far too small and nothing like Plato's geographical descriptions of the enormous Atlantic Island.

Some claim the Azores island chain is a remnant of the sunken Atlantic Island. The Azores are small, steep-sided volcanic seamounts. They emerged from the Azores Platform, a 5.8 million km^2 region located on the Mid-Atlantic Ridge at a depth of 2,000 metres. The Azores islands began to emerge around 8 million years ago, with the last island emerging approximately 270,000 years ago. Drilling cores taken from the Azores Platform show it has been an undersea plateau for millions of years. Regardless of its vast size, the Azores Platform has never been above sea level, so it could never have formed Plato's Atlantic Island.

The North Atlantic and Surrounding Landmasses
Source: Google Earth

Others claim that several other North Atlantic regions were the Atlantic Island's location. These areas were once dry land but were submerged by rising sea levels after the Last Glacial Maximum 20,000 years ago. One example is the now-submerged land bridge known as Doggerland, which connected England and Denmark until about 8,000 years ago. Other claimed candidates are various submerged coastal regions of Britain, Ireland, Denmark, Finland and Sweden. All of these areas are too far north to be opposite the Strait of Gibraltar and far too small and very unlike Plato's descriptions of the Atlantic Island.

No known recently submerged landmasses in the Atlantic Ocean can compare with Plato's Atlantic Island of approximately one million square kilometres. Also, the Atlantic Island had to be 'situated in front of the straits' or opposite Gibraltar. It was the way to the Americas, the only 'opposite continent' to Europe and Africa. Also, beyond the

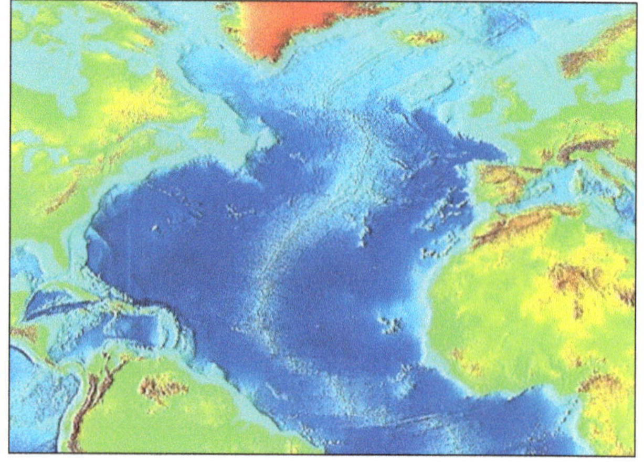

The Mid-Atlantic Ridge – North Atlantic Portion
Source: Wikimedia Commons – adapted from NOAA

The Caribbean Region
Source: Wikimedia Commons – CIA

Atlantic Island were 'other islands' from where a ship could reach the opposite continent of the Americas.

All of Plato's highly specific geographical descriptions make the Caribbean region the most likely location for a now-submerged Atlantic Island. The following section briefly describes the Caribbean's geography, geology, and the mechanism of the Atlantic Island's creation and destruction.

If a large part of the Caribbean Sea floor were once above sea level, an Atlantic Island of about one million km^2 would easily fit within the Caribbean Sea. The Caribbean Sea has an area of 2.75 million km^2, with an average depth of 2,400 metres. It sits on the Caribbean Plate, a tectonic plate roughly 3.2 million km^2 in area that extends from the Lesser Antilles in the east to the Pacific margin of Central America in the west, from the Greater Antilles in the north to the northern margin of South America in the south. The Caribbean Plate borders the North American, South American, Nazca and Cocos Plates.

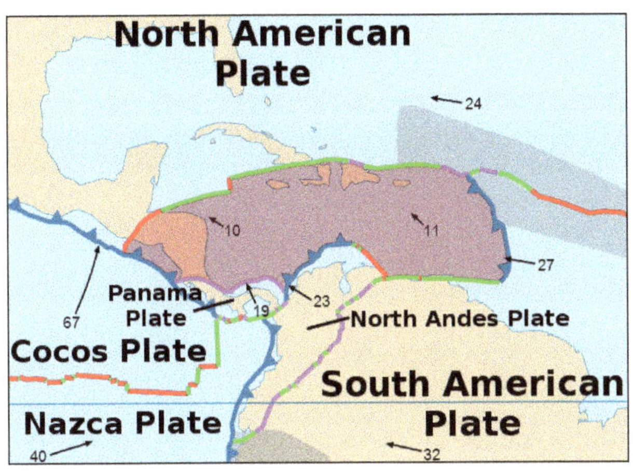

The Caribbean Plate (Red)
Source: Wikimedia Commons

Underwater ridges and mountain ranges divide the Caribbean Sea floor into five basins. From east to west, those five basins are the Grenada, Venezuelan, Colombian, Cayman and Yucatan Basins. The Aves Ridge and Beata Ridge subdivide the eastern part of the Caribbean Plate into the Grenada Basin, Venezuelan Basin and Colombian Basin.

This book's Caribbean Hypothesis argues that sometime in the extremely distant past, the Atlantic Island formed out of the combined landmasses of the Greater Antilles islands of Hispaniola and Puerto Rico in the north, the Venezuelan Basin in the centre, the Aves Ridge to the east, and the Beata Ridge to the west.

An Atlantic Island of that size and shape has an east-west length averaging about 1,300km and the north-south length averaging about 800km, giving a total area of 1,040,000km^2. This landmass fits Plato's explanation of the Atlantic Island being

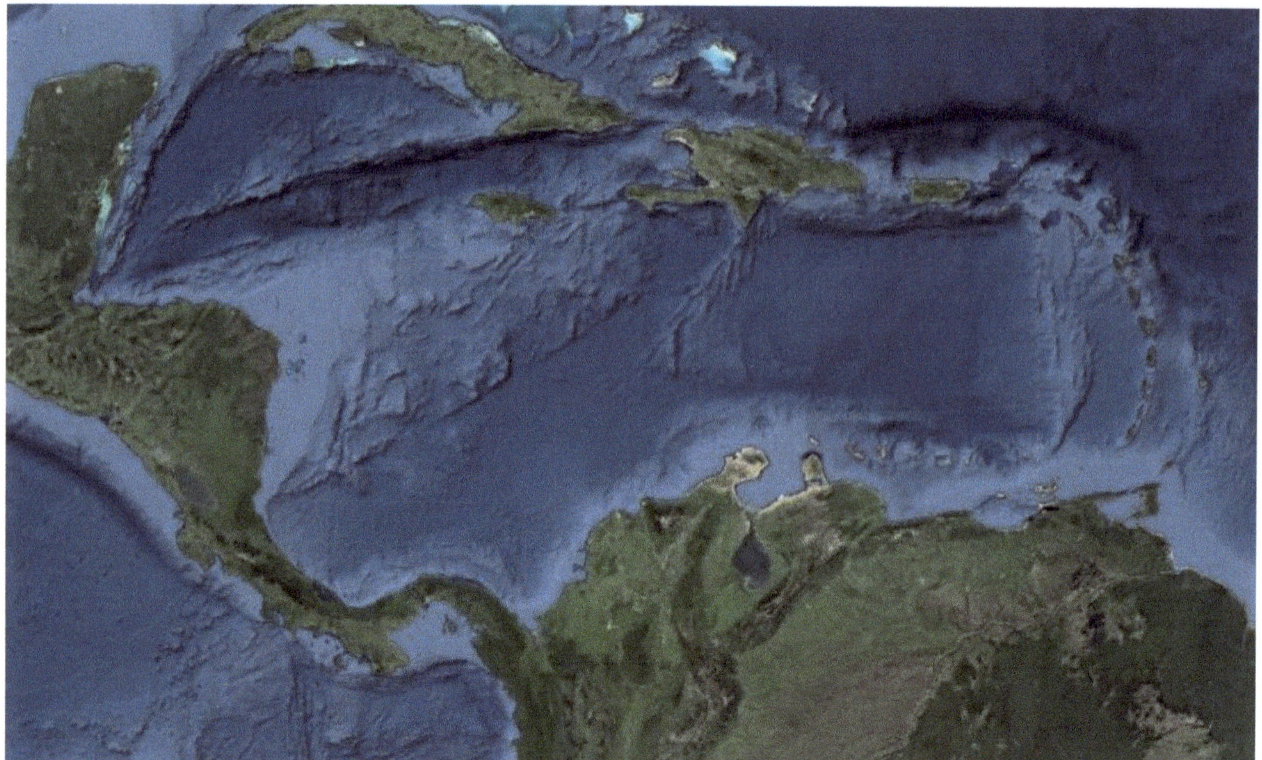

The Caribbean Region
Source: Google Earth

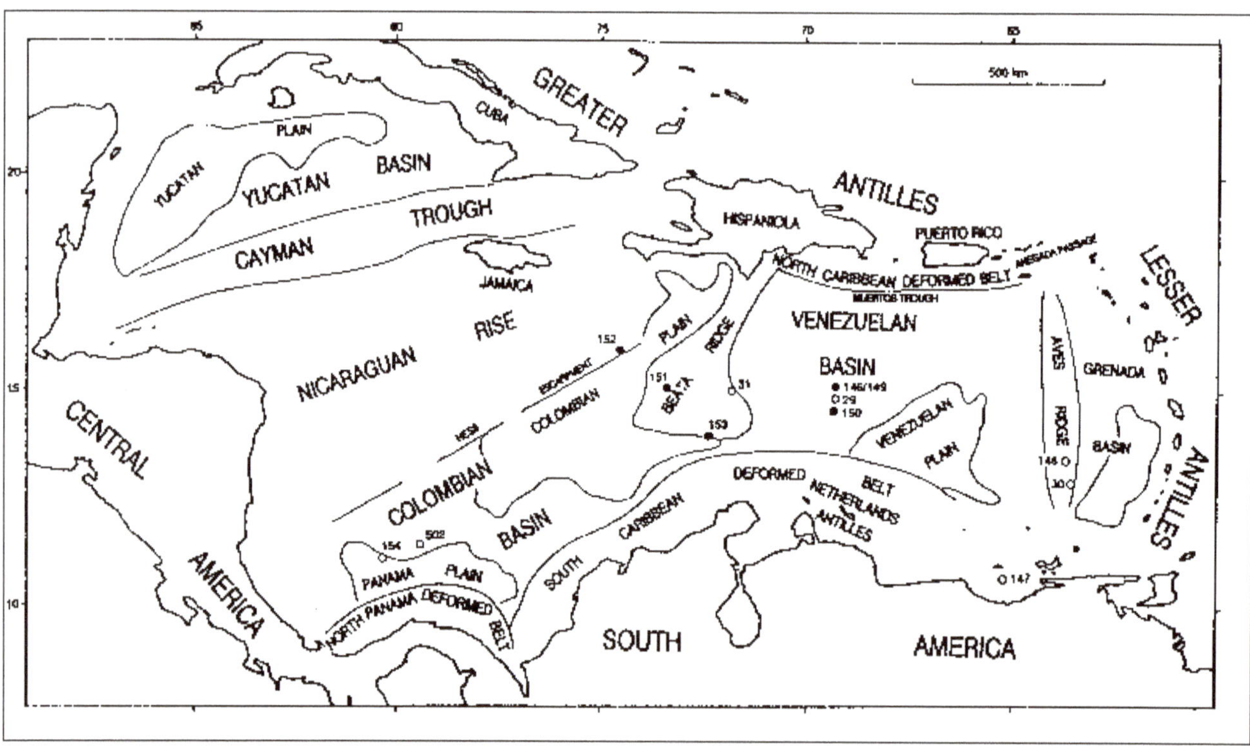

Map of the Caribbean showing major named features
Source: Case, J.E., MacDonald, W.D. & Fox, P.J. 1990. Caribbean crustal provinces; seismic and gravity evidence: in Dengo, G. & Case, I.E. (eds), The Geology of North America, Volume H, The Caribbean Region, 15–36. Geological Society of America

larger than Libya and Asia put together – an area estimated earlier at over 865,000km^2.

Until now, there is no accepted geological explanation for how a vast landmass of one million square kilometres was above sea level before 11,600 years ago but is now hundreds to thousands of metres below sea level. However, a novel geological mechanism could explain how a large part of the Caribbean Plate sank in a relatively short time of a few thousand years. The Hydraulic Hypothesis connects past great vertical movements of the Caribbean Plate with changes in the size of the massive ice sheets at the Earth's polar regions. It

The Caribbean – North America at the top; Mesoamerica and South America on the left; the Greater and Lesser Antilles on the right
Source: NASA

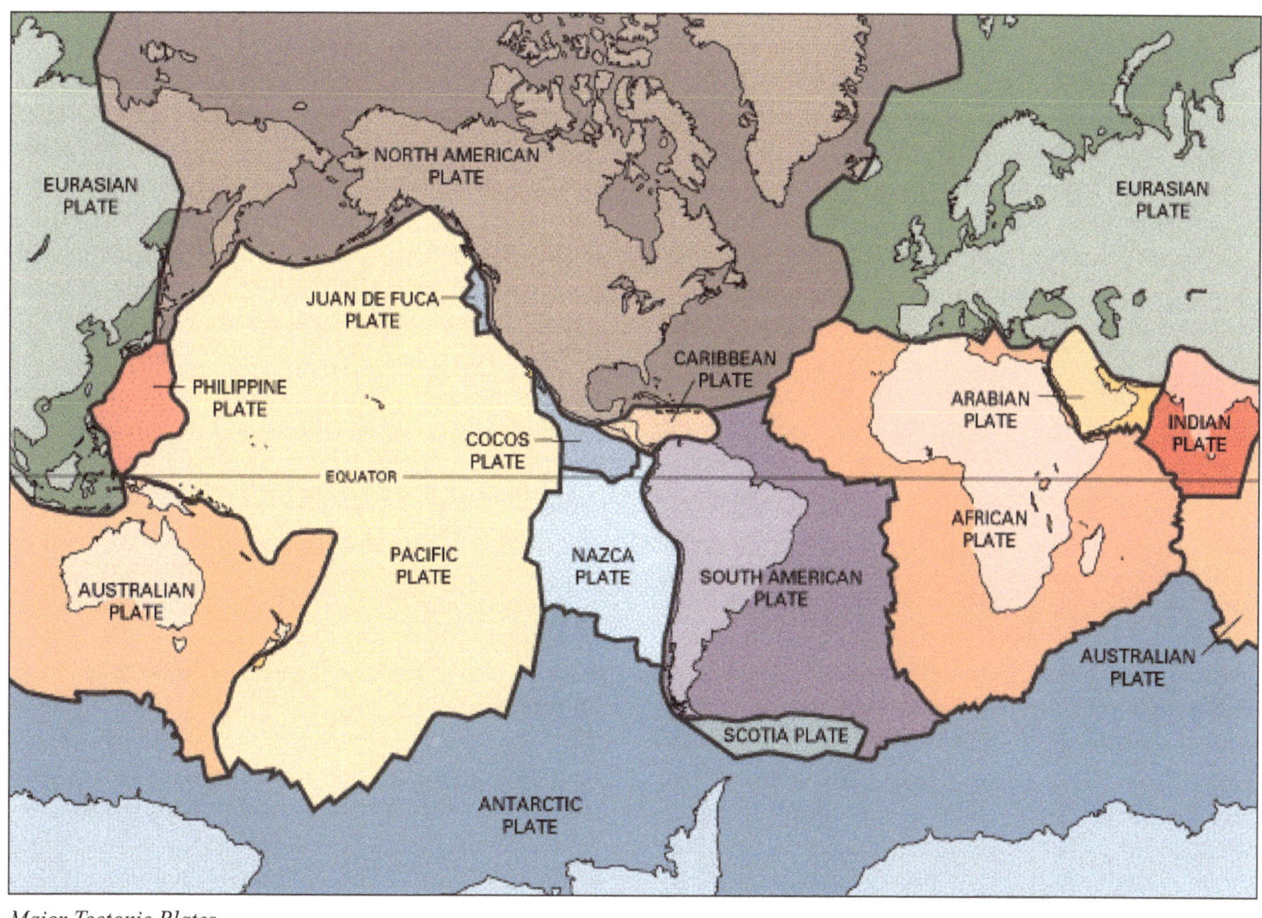

Major Tectonic Plates
Source: Wikimedia Commons – USGS

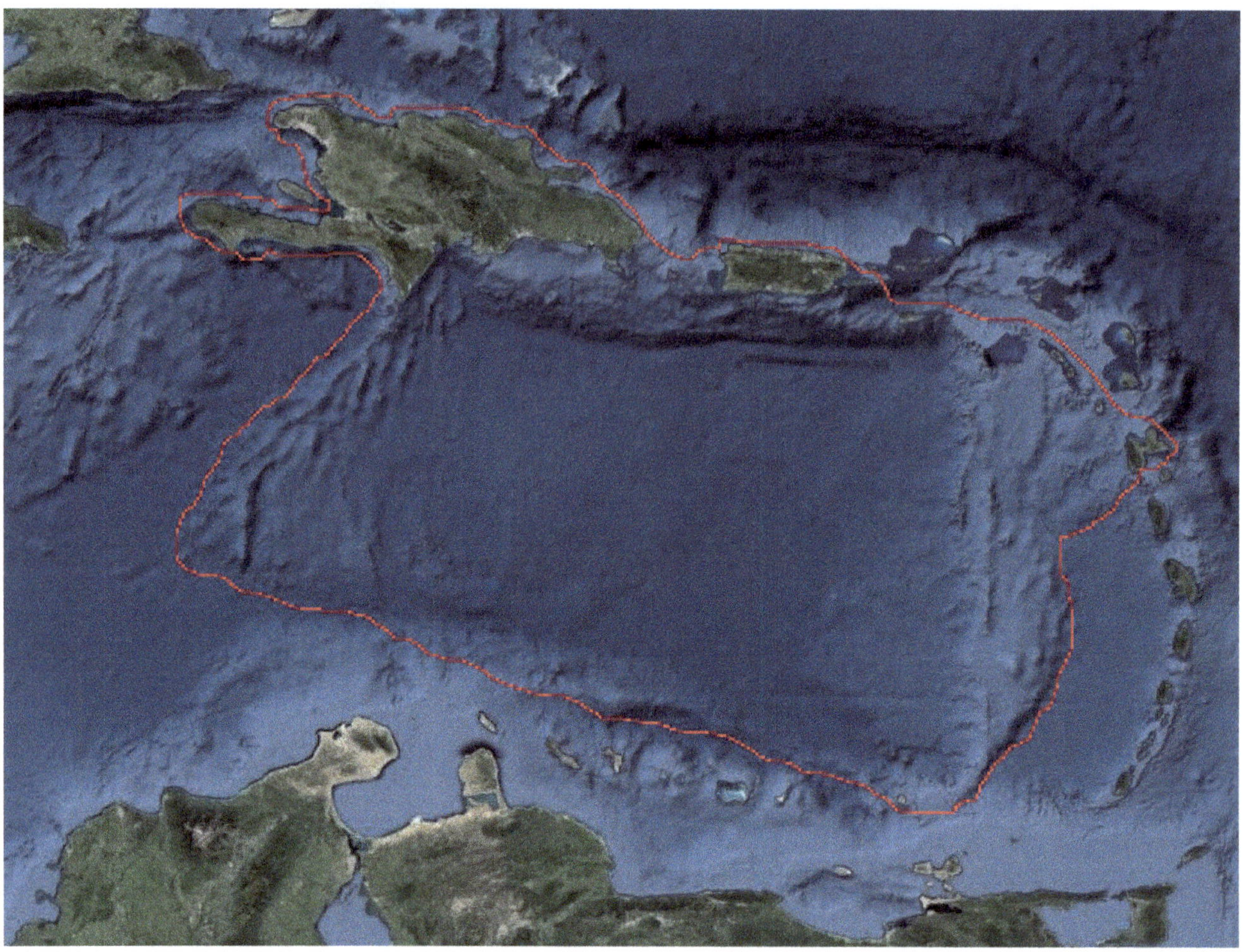

Possible Rough Outline of the Atlantic Island
Source: Modified from Google Earth

may explain both the creation and destruction of the Atlantic Island.

We live in an Ice Age called the Quaternary Ice Age that began about 2.5 million years ago. For much of that time, glacial ice sheets thousands of metres thick covered much of North America, Eurasia, and all of Antarctica. The glacial ice sheets were at their greatest extent at the Last Glacial Maximum (LGM) about 20,000 years ago. After the LGM, the Earth warmed and much of the glacial ice melted rapidly.

The LGM is the most recent peak of glaciation, but there have been many prior climate cycles during the Quaternary Ice Age. Numerous times in the distant past, the Earth's climate cooled, and the glacial ice sheets increased; the Earth then warmed, and the ice sheets decreased. These climate cycles will likely continue for millions of years as it is unlikely the Quaternary Ice Age has ended.

The Hydraulic Hypothesis describes a natural hydraulic system located inside the liquid Asthenosphere layer. This hydraulic system transmits pressure changes beneath any of the Earth's tectonic plates to the other tectonic plates. Put as simply as possible, if some tectonic plates are pushed down because of an increase in ice thickness covering them, other remote plates not covered by ice will go up. The opposite movement occurs when the ice thickness decreases over ice-covered plates, and the remote plates go down. The Hydraulic Hypothesis is further explained in chapter 11

Over the past 2.5 million years, huge volumes of glacial ice have covered the landmasses of Antarctica, North America and Eurasia. The Hydraulic Hypothesis argues that the weight of accumulated ice pushed down those tectonic plates located below the ice. The Earth's hydraulic system transmitted this downward pressure and caused the uplift of some remote tectonic plates not covered by ice.

The Caribbean Hypothesis argues that the Caribbean Plate is one of the remote tectonic plates not covered by ice and was affected by changes in hydraulic pressure below it. As glacial ice increased over the polar tectonic plates, hydraulic pressure increased below the Caribbean Plate, pushing it upwards to form the complete Atlantic Island.

There is some geological evidence of past uplift and emergence above sea level of previously submerged components of the Caribbean Plate. The Caribbean Hypothesis claims that those emergent parts were the Venezuelan Basin and the adjoining Aves and Beata Ridges. These structures rose above sea level and joined onto Hispaniola and Puerto Rico islands, which had already been above sea level for millions of years. Once all the landmasses combined, they formed Plato's Atlantic Island of over one million square kilometres. The Caribbean Hypothesis is explained at length in Chapter 12.

Some parts of the Atlantic Island 'sank' sometime after 11,600 years ago because of a large, rapid fall in underlying hydraulic pressure. After the Last Glacial Maximum 20,000 years ago, a massive amount of glacial ice that had covered the continents of Antarctica, North America and Eurasia melted rapidly over just a few thousand years. This rapid melting caused a relatively sudden fall in hydraulic pressure beneath the Caribbean Plate. That pressure drop caused the Venezuelan Basin, Beata, and Aves Ridges to separate from the remainder of the Caribbean Plate and submerge. Virtually all that remained of the great Atlantic Island were the Hispaniola and Puerto Rico islands, which stayed above sea level.

The Caribbean Islands – Remnants of the Atlantic Island

Plato – '(the Atlantic Island) was the way to other islands, and from these you may pass to the whole of the opposite continent (North and South America) which surrounded the true ocean (the Atlantic).'

The Caribbean region has over 7,000 islands, islets, reefs and cays. These Caribbean islands mainly form island arcs called the Antilles along the eastern and northern edges of the Caribbean Sea. The Greater Antilles are to the north, and the Lesser Antilles are to the south and east.

When the entire Atlantic Island was above sea level, the other islands on the way to the 'opposite continent' of North America would have been Cuba, Jamaica, the Swan and Cayman Islands, and the Bahamas. The islands on the way to the 'opposite continent' of South America would have been Trinidad and Tobago, the Leeward Antilles islands of Aruba, Curacao and Bonaire, and several smaller islands off the Central American and Venezuelan coasts.

A clue to what remained of the Atlantic Island after it sank below the sea comes from the following passage in Proclus' 4th century CE commentary on Plato's *Timaeus* dialogue. It is the only surviving work other than Plato's that gives a possible location for the Atlantic Island.

Proclus – 'That an (Atlantic) island of such nature and size once existed (as Plato describes in the *Timaeus*) is evident from what is said by certain authors who investigated the things around the outer sea (the Atlantic Ocean). For according to them, there were seven islands in that sea in their time, sacred to Persephone, and also three others of enormous size, one of which was sacred to Pluto, another to Ammon, and another one between them to Poseidon, the extent of which was a thousand stadia (210km); and the inhabitants of it – they add – preserved the remembrance from their ancestors of the immeasurably large island of Atlantis which had really existed there and which for many ages had reigned over all islands in the Atlantic sea and which itself had likewise been sacred to Poseidon. Now, these things Marcellus has written in his *Aethiopica*.' The author Marcellus has never been identified, and his *Aethiopica* is a lost work.

The Caribbean Islands
Source: Wikimedia Commons – Karl Musser

From L to R – Cuba, Jamaica and Hispaniola
Source: Google Earth

The unknown author Marcellus describes a group of three islands 'of enormous size' in the 'outer sea', but there are no such large islands in the Atlantic Ocean. The only location that fits Proclus' description is the Caribbean Sea, where the three large islands could be Cuba, Jamaica and Hispaniola (Haiti/Dominican Republic) in the Greater Antilles. In that case, Cuba and Hispaniola would be Marcellus' islands sacred to the gods Pluto and Ammon. Cuba is 1,100km long, and Hispaniola is 650km long. The middle island between them sacred to Poseidon would then be Jamaica, which is around 230km long and almost identical in length to the one thousand stadia (210km) Marcellus describes.

Compared to these three islands of the Greater Antilles, the largest Mediterranean islands any Ancient Egyptian, Greek or Roman writers would have known were Sicily, Sardinia, Crete and Cyprus, all less than 300km long. To any ancient Mediterranean writers, islands such as Cuba and Hispaniola over 600km long would have been considered 'enormous'. Even Jamaica at 230km long is larger than all Mediterranean islands except Sicily and Sardinia.

Puerto Rico and the Lesser Antilles
Source: Google Earth

Marcellus also describes seven islands sacred to the goddess Persephone, but unlike the three 'enormous' islands, he does not mention their size. If these seven smaller islands were in the Caribbean, they could be Puerto Rico and several larger islands of the Lesser Antilles island arc.

It is unknown who Marcellus was or when he wrote about the remnants of the Atlantic Island in his *Aethiopica*. Still, it must be before Proclus wrote about Marcellus in the 4th century CE. Another unknown factor is who were the 'authors who investigated the things around the outer sea'? Those authors must have spoken with Caribbean islanders who 'preserved the remembrance' of their Atlantean ancestors. There are only two possible locations for those discussions. The first is the Caribbean, which means someone from the Old World travelled to and from the Caribbean before the 4th century CE – more than a thousand years before Columbus. The second location is the Old World, meaning Caribbean people travelled there before the 4th century CE – a much less likely scenario.

The ancient travellers to the Caribbean may have been Phoenician sailors. For several centuries after 1200 BCE, the Phoenicians were the foremost naval and trading power of the Mediterranean and had ships capable of long-distance ocean travel. Depending on the route taken, the sailing distance from Gibraltar to the Caribbean and back is 13,000–14,000km. According to Herodotus, Pharaoh Necho II of Egypt sent a Phoenician expeditionary fleet down the Red Sea in around

Carthaginian-held territory in the early 3rd century BCE
Source: Wikimedia Commons

600 BCE. After three years of sailing during that single voyage, the Phoenician fleet circumnavigated Africa and returned to Egypt through the Pillars of Heracles. The total distance sailed would have been around 26,000km.

The Phoenicians established the city of Carthage in North Africa in about 800 BCE. From there, the Carthaginians developed an extensive empire over the next few hundred years. In the 5th century BCE, the Carthaginians dispatched an expeditionary fleet led by Hanno the Navigator. The fleet comprised sixty ships with 30,000 aboard, and its mission was to explore and colonise the north-western coast of Africa.

Leaving Gades (Cadiz) in Spain, Hanno founded or repopulated seven colonies along the African coast of what is now Morocco. He then explored the Atlantic coast of Africa as far as the Gulf of Guinea before returning. The total distance the Carthaginians sailed was around 14,000km.

Carthage eventually became the dominant naval power in the Western Mediterranean. By 300 BCE, it had a navy of over 300 warships and a large merchant fleet for trade. In what later became known as the Punic Wars from 264–146 BCE, Carthage engaged in a series of three large-scale wars with Rome for control of the western Mediterranean. Following Carthage's defeat in the Third Punic War, the Romans destroyed the city in 146 BCE.

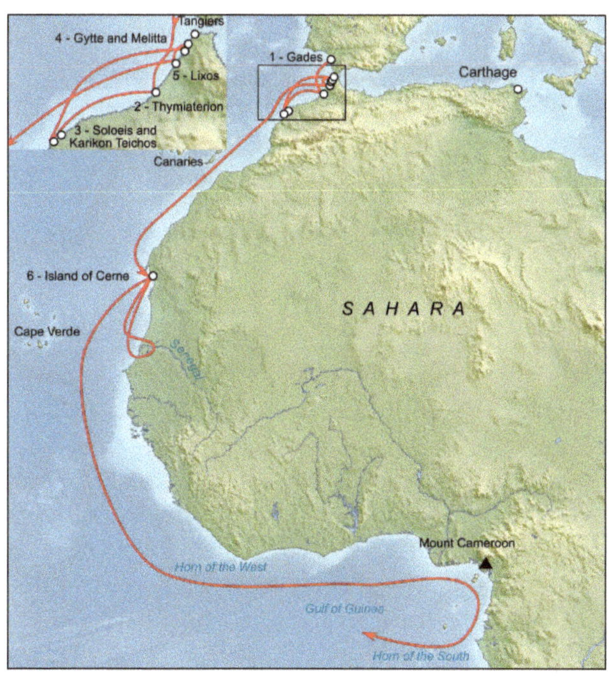

Hanno's voyage
Source: Wikimedia Commons – Bourrichon

There is no surviving continuous Carthaginian literary or historical narrative because the Romans destroyed virtually all of its culture and records. As a result, much of what we know about Carthaginian civilisation is based on Greek and Roman historical records.

In the 4th century CE, Proclus quotes Marcellus and his now-lost *Aethiopica*. Whoever Marcellus was, he may have had access to an original Carthaginian account or a Greek or Roman translation of a Carthaginian voyage to the Americas. It was a voyage that would have preceded the destruction of Carthage in 146 BCE. The *Aethiopica* may have included discussions between the Carthaginian sailors and the natives of the Caribbean islands who recounted their stories of the vanished 'immeasurably large island of Atlantis'.

The Venezuelan Basin is the Plain of Atlantis

In the Caribbean region, the submerged Venezuelan Basin closely matches the size, shape, and geographical features of Plato's description of the vast Plain of Atlantis.

Plato – 'Looking towards the sea, but in the centre of the whole (Atlantic) island, there was a plain which is said to have been the fairest of all plains and very fertile'…'it was smooth and even, and of an oblong shape, extending in one direction three thousand stadia (627km) but across the centre inland it was two thousand stadia (418km).'

Like the Plain of Atlantis, the submerged Venezuelan Basin is rectangular ('oblong'), flat and featureless ('smooth and even'). Plato also gives quite precise dimensions in stadia for the size of the Plain – 3,000 by 2,000 stadia. If the assumed length of a stadion is 209 metres, then Plato's dimensions for the Plain of Atlantis are about 630km by 420km, which gives it a land area of just over 260,000km^2.

The submerged Venezuelan Basin's dimensions are around 700km west to east from the foot of the Beata Ridge to the foot of the Aves Ridge. It is around 400km north to south from Hispaniola and Puerto Rico to the Southern Caribbean Deformed Belt. These dimensions closely match those Plato gives for the Plain of Atlantis: approximately 630km by 420km. The total area of the submerged Venezuelan Basin is around 280,000km^2, which is extremely close to Plato's 260,000km^2 for the Plain of Atlantis. For comparison, the Venezuelan Basin is

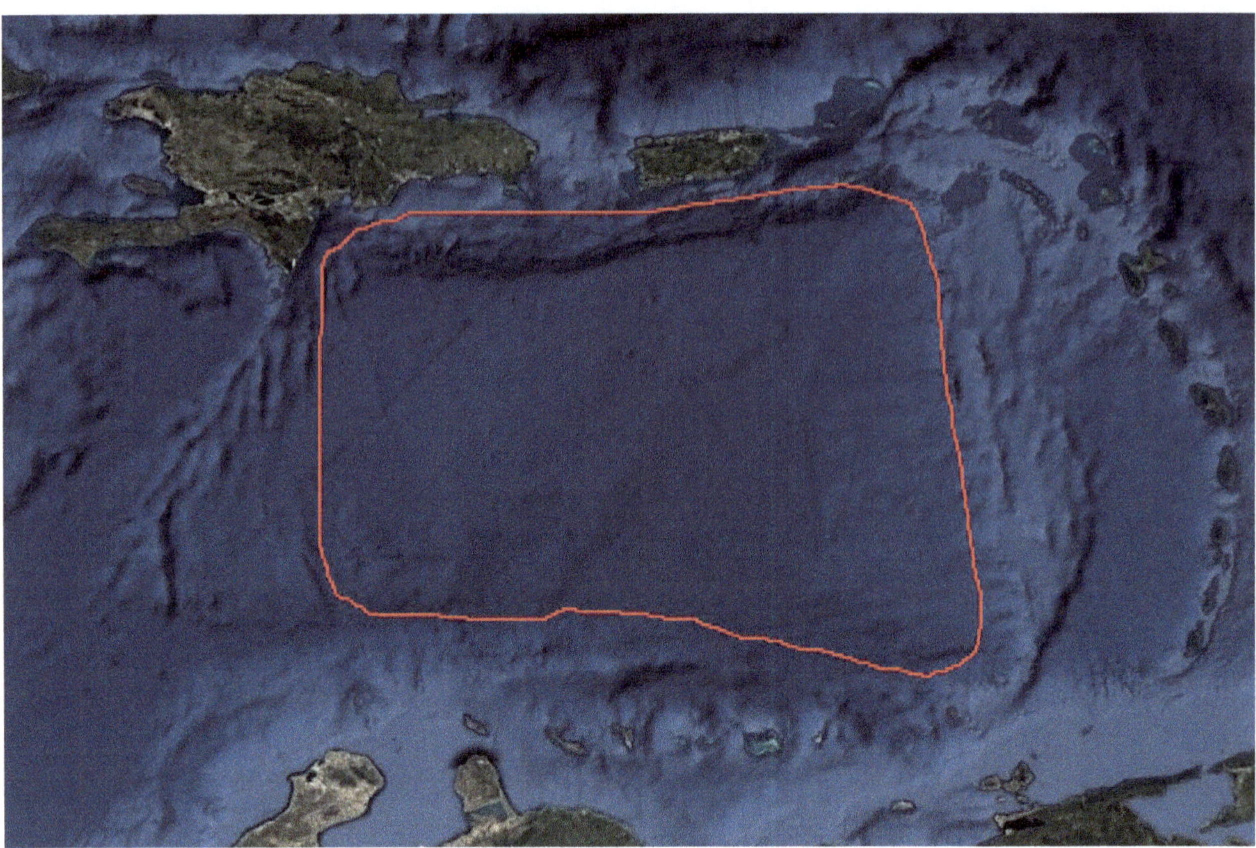

The Venezuelan Basin
Source: Modified from Google Earth

roughly the same size as Arizona in the USA or all of mainland Italy and twice the size of Java.

It must be emphasised again that Plato was a mathematician who believed in the precision of numbers and geometry, so he would not have randomly chosen the measurements in his Atlantis dialogues.

The Mountains of the Atlantic Island

Plato – 'The surrounding mountains (around the Plain of Atlantis) were celebrated for their number and size and beauty, far beyond any which still exist, having in them also many wealthy villages of country folk, and rivers, and lakes, and meadows supplying food enough for every animal, wild or tame, and much wood of various sorts, abundant for each and every kind of work.'

The Ancient Egyptians and Greeks who retell the Atlantis story claim they do not know of any mountain ranges that can compare with the 'number and size and beauty' of those surrounding the Plain of Atlantis.

The Ancient Egyptians would have been familiar with several mountain ranges within Egypt. The High Mountain Region is part of the Sinai Peninsula in Southern Egypt; the Halayeb Triangle is on the Red Sea's African coast, and the Eastern Desert mountain range is in the Sahara Desert. Each of these mountain ranges is 200–300 kilometres long. The highest mountain peak in Egypt is Mount Catherine in the Sinai at 2,642 metres, but several others are over 2,000 metres. The Ancient Egyptians may have also known the Atlas Mountains in North-West Africa, even though they are over 1,500 kilometres west of Egypt. The Atlas Mountains extend around 2,500 kilometres through present-day Morocco, Algeria and Tunisia. Their highest peak is Toubkal in South-Western Morocco, with an elevation of 4,167 metres.

As for any mountains the Ancient Greeks would have known: although Greece is mainly mountainous, its mountains do not form long ranges and are not exceptionally high. The Pindus Mountain Range is the longest in Greece at 160 kilometres and is an extension of the Dinaric Alps to the north, which gives a total length of 230 kilometres. Mount Olympus is the highest mountain in Greece and has fifty-two peaks; its highest peak is 2,917 metres.

The only other large mountain ranges the Greeks of Solon and Plato's time possibly knew may have been the European Alps in northern Italy, the Caucasus to the east, and perhaps the Atlas Mountains in North-West Africa. The European Alps are 1,200 kilometres long, and the Greater Caucasus is 1,200 kilometres long. Mont Blanc is the highest mountain in the European Alps at 4,810 metres; the highest peak in the Caucasus is Mount Elbrus at 5,642 metres.

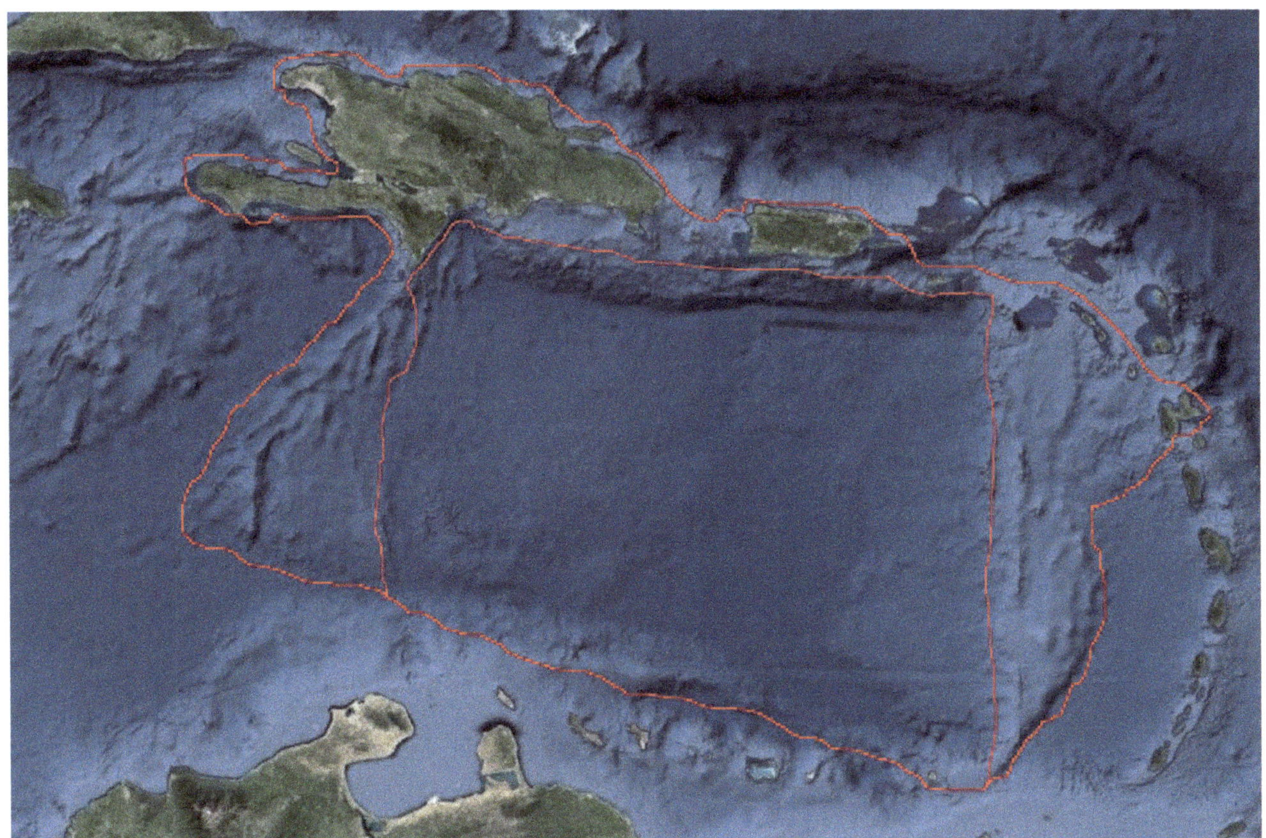

Hispaniola and Puerto Rico (Top); Beata Ridge (L); Aves Ridge (R)
Source: Modified from Google Earth

The Atlantic Island's Western and Eastern Mountains

The Caribbean Hypothesis claims that the Beata and Aves Ridges and the Venezuelan Basin were uplifted in the distant past and eventually emerged above sea level. These geological structures joined with the already emergent islands of Hispaniola and Puerto Rico to form the complete Atlantic Island.

When they were above sea level, the Beata and Aves Ridges bordered the emergent Venezuelan Basin to the west and east, extending over the entire north-south length of the Plain of Atlantis. Suppose the Plain of Atlantis once was the emergent Venezuelan Basin and had 'surrounding mountains', as Plato describes. In that case, the Beata Ridge could be called the Western Mountains and the Aves Ridge the Eastern Mountains.

The Beata Ridge is on the western border of the submerged Venezuelan Basin. It extends south-west from Cape Beata in Hispaniola and ends at the South Caribbean Deformed Belt. The Beata Ridge is over 400 kilometres long and has an elevation of 2,000–3,000 metres above the submerged Venezuelan Basin. It has a series of north-south trending subsidiary ridges that become less pronounced towards the south.

The Western Mountains formed by an emergent Beata Ridge would have risen 2,000–3,000 metres above the Plain of Atlantis with a central spine 400km long. Many subsidiary ridges at their eastern border descended onto the Plain of Atlantis. The Western Mountains would have had a total area of over 50,000 square kilometres. The Western Ghats in India typify a mountain range rising from a plain.

Western Ghats, India
Source: Wikimedia Commons – Magnetic Manifestations

To the east of the submerged Venezuelan Basin, the Aves Ridge is a broad plateau that extends 600 kilometres from north to south. The plateau is 50–150 kilometres wide with a steep 600km-long and 2,000–3,000-metre-high escarpment that borders the Venezuelan Basin.

The Eastern Mountains of an emergent Aves Ridge would have formed a 600km-long plateau 2,000 metres above the Plain of Atlantis, with an area of over 60,000 square kilometres. At the mountains' western boundary with the Plain of Atlantis is a steep escarpment over 600km long, rising 2,000 metres directly from the Plain. The

Kakadu Escarpment, Northern Australia
Source: Wikimedia Commons – Tourism NT

Kakadu Escarpment in Australia is one example of an escarpment rising from a plain.

The Atlantic Island's Northern Mountains

When the Venezuelan Basin emerged and formed the Plain of Atlantis, its northern margin would likely have been at about the same level as the southern coastal regions of Hispaniola and Puerto Rico. The combined mountain ranges of Hispaniola and Puerto Rico would have formed the Plain's 'surrounding mountains' to the north – the Atlantic Island's Northern Mountains.

The island of Hispaniola has five major mountain ranges that run east-west across the island. The Central Range, or Cordillera Central, has the highest peak in the Greater Antilles at 3,087 metres above sea level. Hispaniola's neighbouring island of Puerto Rico is mostly mountainous, with flatter coastal areas to the north and south. Puerto Rico's main mountain range's highest elevation is 1,339 metres.

Hispaniola (L) and Puerto Rico (R)
Source: Google Earth

If the mountains of Hispaniola and Puerto Rico combined to form the Northern Mountains of the Atlantic Island, they would have been a mountain range 1,000 kilometres long, with several peaks from 1,000 to 3,000 metres high.

The 'surrounding mountains' of the Plain of Atlantis

If the Atlantic Island's mountains were combined, there would have been an almost continuous 2,000-kilometre-long mountain range to the west, north and east of the Plain of Atlantis. Compared to the mountain ranges of the Atlantic Island, the South American Andes is the Earth's longest mountain chain at 7,000 kilometres; the Rocky Mountains in the USA are 4,800 kilometres and the Himalayas are 2,500 kilometres long.

The Atlantic Island's mountain range of 2,000 kilometres was probably much more extensive than any mountains known to the Ancient Egyptians and Greeks of Solon and Plato's time. To those ancient people, the mountains would have been in 'number and size and beauty, far beyond any which still exist'.

When seen from the Plain of Atlantis, the surrounding mountains with heights over 2,000 metres rose directly up from the Plain. They continued for hundreds of kilometres until well out of sight and would have impressed any observer from any time, including the prehistoric Egyptians who first recorded the Atlantis story.

If these vast mountains were covered with fertile soil and had a combined area well over 120,000km^2, they would have contained 'rivers, and lakes, and meadows supplying food enough for every animal, wild or tame, and much wood of various sorts, abundant for each and every kind of work.'

The Fully Emergent Atlantic Island

Once the Beata and Aves Ridges and the Venezuelan Basin rose above sea level and combined with the landmasses of Hispaniola and Puerto Rico, the total land area of the fully emergent Atlantic Island was around 1,040,000km^2.

Compared to the complete Atlantic Island, France is 550,000km^2, Texas is 700,000km^2, and Thailand is 500,000km^2. If an intact Atlantic Island still existed, it would now be the second-largest island on Earth. Presently, Greenland is the largest with an area of over 2.1 million km^2; New Guinea is the second largest with an area of 786,000km^2.

The Atlantic Island
Source: Modified from Google Earth

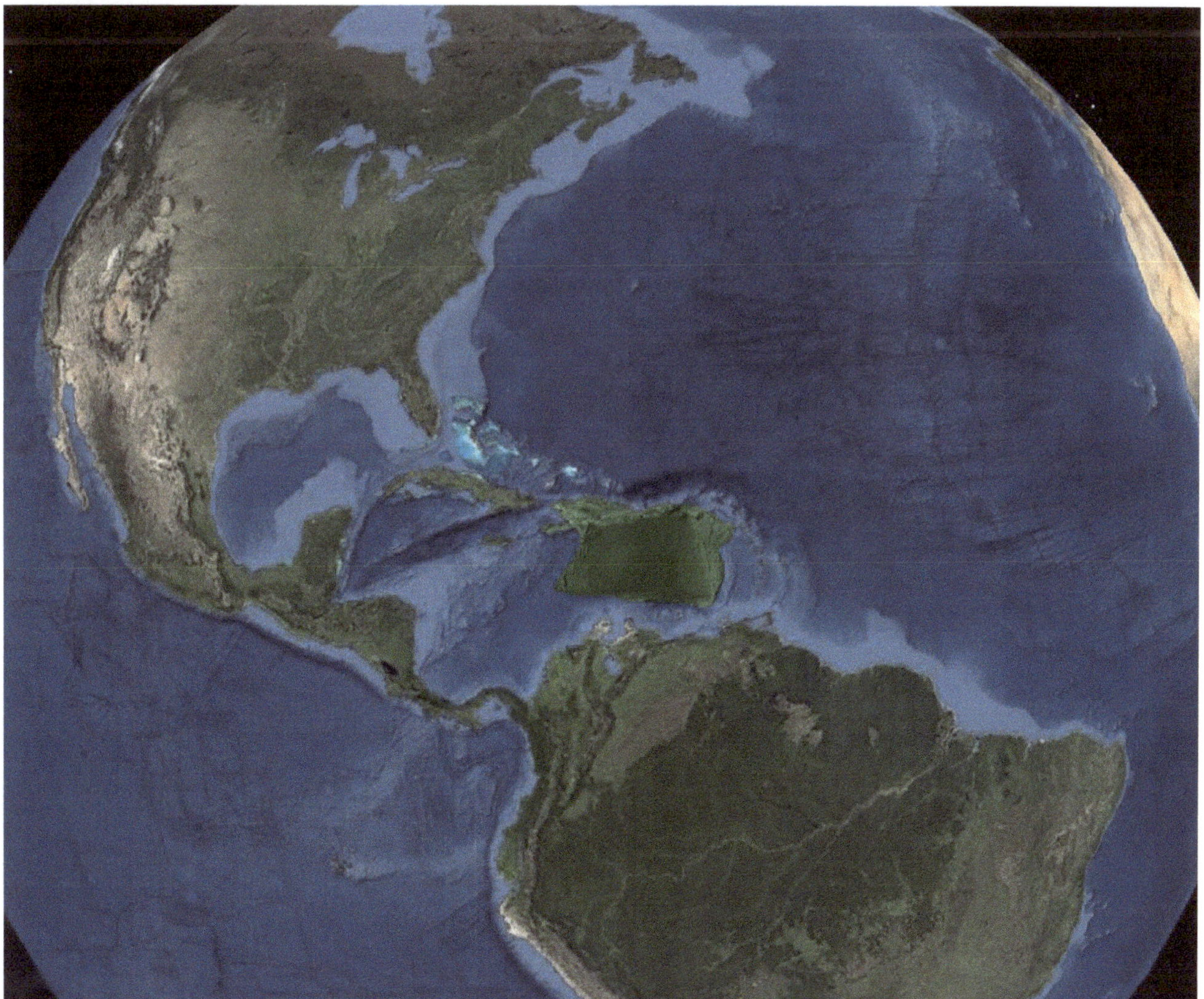

The Location of the Atlantic Island
Source: Modified from Google Earth

The Biology of the Atlantic Island

Plato states the Atlantic Island was exceptionally fertile. It had varied forests, abundant plants and wild animals, and the Atlanteans farmed plentiful crops and domestic animals. An Atlantic Island in the Caribbean would have contained native plants and animals similar to those now existing in the Caribbean, Central America, and the northern part of South America. Plato also describes some animals on the Atlantic Island that once lived in the prehistoric Americas but later became extinct.

Plants

Plato – 'whatever fragrant things there now are in the Earth, whether roots, or herbage, or woods, or essences which distil from fruit and flower, grew and thrived in that land (the Atlantic Island)'...'The surrounding mountains...having in them...rivers, and lakes, and meadows supplying food enough for every animal, wild or tame, and much wood of various sorts, abundant for each and every kind of work.'

The plant life on a large, fertile Atlantic Island would likely have included the present Caribbean and Central American plant species. With an estimated 13,000 native plant species in the region, the Caribbean Islands are considered a biodiversity hotspot. Forests dominated the pre-Columbian Caribbean and included timber species such as Caribbean mahogany, walnut, West Indian ebony and poui. As well as having tropical species, the existing forests in Southern Mexico and Central America contain many species typical of temperate North America, including oaks, pines, fir and cypress.

Animals

Plato's *Critias* dialogue mentions several species of large animals that lived on the Atlantic Island over 11,600 years ago.

Plato – 'there were a great number of elephants in the (Atlantic) island'...'there were separate baths for...horses and cattle'...'There were bulls who had the range of the temple of Poseidon'...'(there were) other animals of the yoke'.

The co-existence of elephants, horses and cattle on the Atlantic Island eliminates virtually all of its previously suggested locations. Yet, when Europeans first arrived in the Americas in the 15th century CE, they found no elephants, horses or domesticated cattle. The only large domesticated animals were the llama and alpaca in the Andes region of South America. But it will surprise many people that elephants, horses, and several species of cattle were plentiful in the Americas until they became extinct well after 11,600 years ago. Also, there were now-extinct species of larger animals that the Atlanteans could have domesticated to become Plato's 'other animals of the yoke'.

Plato describes several animal species on the Atlantic Island that we know did once coexist in the prehistoric Americas. Significantly, Plato sets his Atlantis story around 11,600 BP before they all became extinct. For instance, if Plato had fabricated the Atlantis story and dated it to around 7,000 BP or later, it would have been well after all those animal species became extinct.

Debate continues over when and how the ancestors of the larger animals now living there colonised the Caribbean's Greater and Lesser Antilles Islands. The prevailing model is that they came mainly from South America and dispersed over open seas. That can happen when smaller animals are trapped on rafts of floating vegetation washed down rivers and out to sea, eventually landing on a remote location and colonising it.

An alternative model is for travel and colonisation from the Americas over land bridges and between stepping-stone islands that may have existed millions of years ago. If such connections had once existed and remained there for many thousands or millions of years, they would have allowed larger animals from the Americas to colonise the Antilles Islands.

When the Atlantic Island fully emerged, the Beata and Aves Ridges and the Venezuelan Basin connected with the long-emergent islands of Hispaniola and Puerto Rico, which large animals might have previously colonised. That new land connection would have allowed large animal species already on Hispaniola and Puerto Rico to migrate south to the rest of the Atlantic Island. Another possibility is that large animals migrated along land bridges between

Megafauna of Mexico ca. 10,000 BP
Source: Wikimedia Commons – Sergio de la Rosa

the Americas and the Atlantic Island after the island partially or fully emerged.

Horses

Plato states that the Atlanteans used domesticated horses for racing and warfare on the Atlantic Island around 11,600 BP. In that case, the Atlanteans domesticated the horse several thousand years earlier than the Ancient Egyptians, Greeks, or other Old World civilisations.

Over tens of millions of years, the continent of North America was the first region on Earth where most horse species evolved. By 55mya, the first dog-sized members of the horse family lived in the forests that covered North America; by 10mya, up to a dozen different species of horses lived in North America. These relatives of the modern horse varied greatly in shape and size; some lived in the forest, others in open grassland.

The genus *Equus* includes all living modern horses, asses and zebras. *Equus* first evolved in North America between eight and five million years ago and then quickly spread westward over a land bridge into Asia and the rest of the Old World. Over millions of years, there were additional westward migrations to Asia, return migrations to North America and several extinctions of *Equus* species in North America. Though several horse species similar to the modern horse existed throughout the Americas until around 10,000 BP, they suddenly became extinct. The *Equus* species then survived only in Eurasia and Africa, where they became the ancestors of the Earth's seven living species of horses.

In the Old World, horses appeared in Palaeolithic cave art as early as 30,000 BP, when they were probably hunted for meat. The earliest archaeological evidence for horse domestication is in the Ukraine and Kazakhstan, dating to approximately 5,500–6,000 BP. By 5,000 BP, horses were completely domesticated and were used throughout Europe by 4,000 BP.

Horses were not native to Egypt and were introduced there during the Second Intermediate Period of 1700–1550 BCE. They were animals of the military elite and the ruling class and usually were used to pull chariots. In Greece, the Minoan civilisation used horses and chariots by at least the 2nd millennium BCE. According to Homer, the later Mycenaeans employed them in the Trojan War in the 12th century BCE.

Because horses became extinct in the Americas thousands of years before the Spaniards arrived in the 15th century CE, they and later European colonists imported their horses to the Americas. As a result, all domesticated and wild horses now in the Americas are descendants of those Old World horses.

Wild horses possibly lived on the Atlantic Island long before 11,600 BP. If there had been one or more land connections between the Americas and the components of the Atlantic Island, several ancient horse species could have migrated over them. Also, horses can swim in herds for many kilometres and may have swum between stepping-stone islands to the Antilles. Another less likely possibility is that the Atlanteans introduced domesticated horses from the Americas to the Atlantic Island.

Elephants

Plato – 'there were a great number of elephants in the (Atlantic) island.'

Not only did 'a great number of elephants' live on the Atlantic Island around 11,600 BP, but a few different elephant species could have lived there simultaneously. Several elephant species co-existed in the Americas before 11,600 BP, but all became extinct over the following few thousand years. All of those extinct elephant species were at least as large as modern elephants.

As well as walking to the Antilles or Atlantic Island directly from the Americas over land bridges,

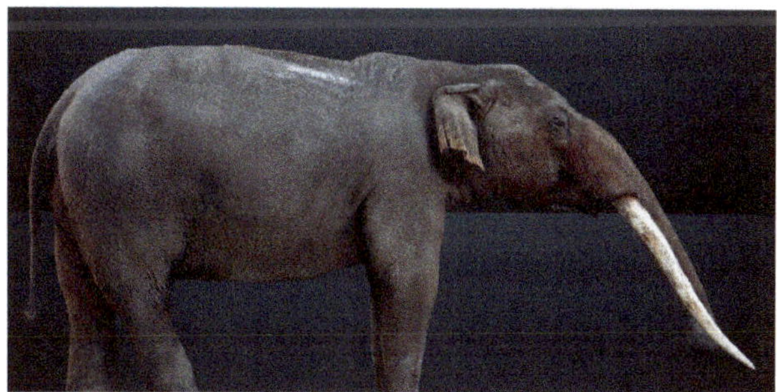

Cuvieronius
Source: Wikimedia Commons – Sergio de la Rosa

Stegomastodon
Source: Wikimedia Commons – Sergio de la Rosa

American Mastodon
Source: Wikimedia Commons – Sergio de la Rosa

Columbian Mammoth
Source: Wikimedia Commons – Sergio de la Rosa

elephants are known to be long-distance swimmers and may have swum there via stepping-stone islands. Elephants have been observed to swim for forty-eight hours in herd formation across African lakes and, in one reported case, a distance of nearly fifty kilometres at sea.

The Gomphotheres were a diverse family of extinct elephant-like animals that included the species Cuvieronius and Stegomastodon. They were widespread in North America between 12–1.6mya, but beginning at around 5mya, modern elephants gradually replaced them. Still, Gomphotheres survived in Mexico and Central America until at least 11,600 BP.

Cuvieronius initially evolved in North America around 10mya. It stood 2.7 metres tall and looked like a modern elephant except for its spiral-shaped tusks. Cuvieronius colonised South America around 3mya, living as far south as Chile. The last two South American species did not become extinct until as recently as 9,100 BP.

Stegomastodon lived in both North and South America. They evolved initially in North America and migrated to South America around 3mya. Standing 2.8 metres tall, they weighed about 6 tonnes and looked like a robust version of the modern elephant. Stegomastodon remains have been dated as recently as 6,060 BP in Colombia, South America.

The American mastodon (Mammut americanum) lived from around 3.7mya until it became extinct around 12,000 BP. It resembled a woolly mammoth, with a thick coat of shaggy hair and with tusks occasionally over five metres long. It could grow to over three metres tall and weigh over 10 tonnes. Mastodon fossils have been found in a range from present-day Alaska and New England to Florida, southern California and Honduras. Until recently, it was thought mastodons were confined to North America, but in 2011 a mastodon skull was found in Santiago, Chile.

The first mammoths entered North America from Asia via a land bridge 1.5–1.8mya. The mammoths are closely related to living elephants, especially the Asiatic elephant (Elephas maximus). By 12,000 BP, three species of mammoths lived on the mainland of the United States: the Columbian Mammoth, Jefferson's Mammoth and the Woolly Mammoth.

Most species of mammoth were about as large as a modern Asian elephant and weighed 6–8 tonnes. However, the Columbian Mammoth was the largest mammoth species and one of the largest elephants to have ever lived. It was four metres tall and weighed up to 10 tonnes, with two-metre-long spiralled tusks and short grey hair similar to a modern elephant. The Columbian Mammoth inhabited North America and has been found as far south as Nicaragua and Honduras. It was one of the last members of the American megafauna to go extinct. Several specimens were dated to 9,000 BP or less, with one near Nashville, Tennessee, dated around 7,800 BP.

Cattle

Plato – 'There were bulls who had the range of the temple of Poseidon.'

There were several species of bovine (cattle-like) animals in the prehistoric Americas by 11,600 BP, but there is no archaeological evidence that they were ever domesticated. Bovine species that once coexisted in the Americas were the Steppe Bison, the Ancient Bison and *Bison occidentalis*. If any of these bison species reached the Atlantic Island via land bridges or stepping-stone islands, the Atlanteans might have domesticated them over hundreds or thousands of years.

The aurochs and their domesticated descendants are the only type of 'cattle' the Ancient Egyptians and Greeks would have known in Solon and Plato's time. The aurochs are an extinct type of large wild cattle that once inhabited Europe, Asia and North Africa. It is estimated to have weighed up to 1,500 kg and is the ancestor of all modern domesticated cattle. Wild aurochs survived in Europe until the last recorded individual died in Poland in 1627 CE. There is no evidence that aurochs ever existed in the Americas.

After 10,000 BP, humans in the Old World domesticated aurochs at least twice. One domestication was an Indian subspecies that led

Aurochs
Source: Wikimedia Commons – Jaap Rouwenhorst

Steppe Bison (Bison priscus)
Source: University of Maryland

Bison latifrons

Ancient bison (Bison antiquus)

to zebu cattle; the other was a Eurasian subspecies leading to taurine cattle. In Asia, other large but unrelated species of wild bovines, such as the water buffalo, gaur and banteng, had been domesticated over thousands of years.

The Steppe Bison, or Steppe Wisent, lived on grasslands throughout Europe and Central Asia after around 2.5mya. It is believed to have evolved in South Asia and appeared at roughly the same time and region as the aurochs. The Steppe Bison entered Alaska via a land bridge from Asia around 300,000 BP. It was over two metres tall and could weigh 900 kg. The tips of its horns were over one metre apart, with the horns themselves more than half a metre long.

The Steppe Bison became extinct around 11,600 BP. It was replaced in Europe by the modern wisent (European Bison) and in America by a sequence of species that ended in the American Bison. In North America, the Steppe Bison was replaced by the long-horned bison, *Bison latifrons*, and somewhat later by the Ancient Bison or Antique Bison (*Bison antiquus*).

Bison latifrons appears to have died out by around 20,000 BP, but the Ancient Bison became increasingly abundant in parts of North America from 18,000 BP until around 10,000 BP. Its range extended from southern Canada into Mexico and from coast to coast. The Ancient Bison was 15–25% larger than the modern American Bison. It was up to 2.27 metres tall, 4.6 metres long, and weighed over 1,500 kg.

The Ancient Bison evolved into the *Bison occidentalis*, then into the yet smaller two subspecies of the modern American Bison (the Plains Bison and the Wood Bison) sometime between 10,000–5,000 BP. Therefore, it is unlikely that the American Bison was present on the Atlantic Island.

Other Animals of the Yoke

Plato's term 'other animals of the yoke' implies that the Atlanteans domesticated some large working animals besides horses and cattle. The camelids are another group of big animals that may have been

American Bison
Source: Wikimedia Commons – Jack Dykinga

Camelops hesternus
Source: Wikimedia Commons – Sergio de la Rosa

Guanaco
Source: Wikimedia Commons

Alpaca
Source: Wikimedia Commons

Llama
Source: Wikimedia Commons

Vicuna
Source: Wikimedia Commons

present on the Atlantic Island. Camelids are members of the biological family *Camelidae*, which includes the modern species of Dromedary and Bactrian camels, llamas, alpacas, vicunas and guanacos. As with other large animals such as horses and elephants, camelids may have migrated to the emergent Atlantic Island via land bridges or stepping-stone islands. Eventually, the Atlanteans may have domesticated them.

Camelids first evolved in North America around 45mya. They were confined to the North American continent until 2–3mya when some crossed via a land bridge into Asia. The camelids in North America diversified into a much wider variety than modern species. Several original North American camelid species remained common until around 10,000 BP but then became extinct.

One North American genus, *Titanotylopus*, stood 3.5 metres at the shoulder, compared with the approximately two metres of the largest modern camelids. Other extinct camelids included small, gazelle-like animals and some tall, giraffe-like camelids. *Camelops hesternus* is an extinct genus of camels from western North America, where it disappeared around 10,000 BP. It was slightly taller than modern Bactrian camels and would have been a useful size if it had been domesticated.

Guanacos, llamas, vicunas and alpacas are the only surviving American camelid species. Guanacos and vicunas are wild species, with llamas domesticated from guanacos and alpacas from vicunas. Excavations at Telarmachay Rock shelter north-east of Lima, Peru, showed that from 9,000 BP, the cave's occupants initially hunted guanaco and vicuna. Domesticated alpacas and llamas were present by 6,000–5,500 BP, with a herding economy based on llama and alpaca established by 5,500 BP.

Early Humans in the Americas

Plato – 'In this mountain (on the Atlantic Island) there dwelt one of the Earth born primaeval men

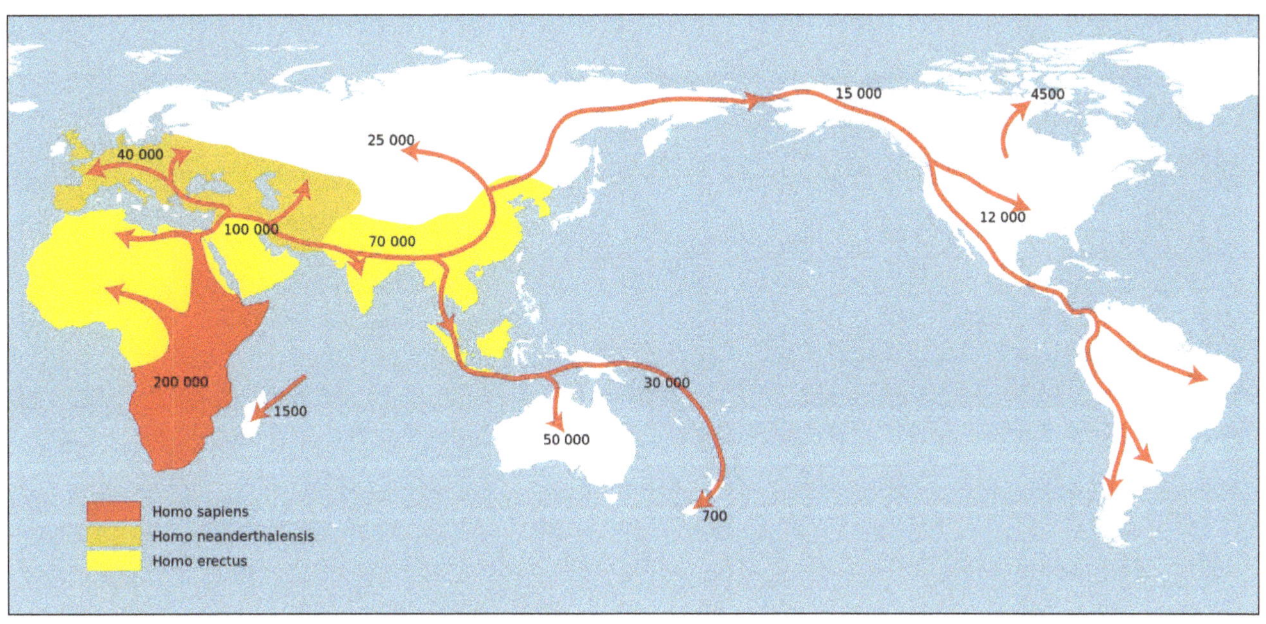

Possible 'Out of Africa' Migration Routes for Homo Species
Source: Wikimedia Commons – NordNordWest

of that country, whose name was Evenor, and he had a wife named Leucippe, and they had an only daughter who was called Cleito.'

Plato states that aboriginal inhabitants or 'primaeval men' lived on the Atlantic Island before Poseidon arrived there and before the Atlantean civilisation began. By the time of the Mediterranean War of 11,600 BP, Plato describes an Atlantic Island with a large human population, most likely of many millions. For a population of that size, humans must have reached the Atlantic Island and successfully multiplied on it for thousands of years before 11,600 BP.

The important point is that the original people on the Atlantic Island and any later arrivals were of our human species, *Homo sapiens*. The dominant view on the origin of *Homo sapiens* is the Out of Africa hypothesis. It claims that anatomically modern humans like us arose as a distinct human species solely within Africa sometime before 200,000 BP. We *Homo sapiens* then began to migrate out of Africa around 100,000 BP, replacing existing populations of more ancient human species, such as *Homo erectus* in Asia and *Homo neanderthalensis* in Europe. Over many thousands of years, *Homo sapiens* eventually migrated eastward to Australia, the Pacific, and the Americas.

The first humans on an Atlantic Island in the Caribbean most likely arrived there by sea from the Americas. The conventional theory of initial human migration into the Americas is that early *Homo sapiens* migrants from Asia moved into the Bering Land Bridge or Beringia between eastern Siberia and present-day Alaska. It is thought that this migration eastward occurred between 40,000 and 16,500 BP when sea levels were much lower during the most recent glacial period of the current Quaternary Ice Age.

When sea levels were at their lowest, the Beringia land bridge was roughly 1,600km wide from north to south and had diverse plant and animal habitats. Even though the human migrants colonised

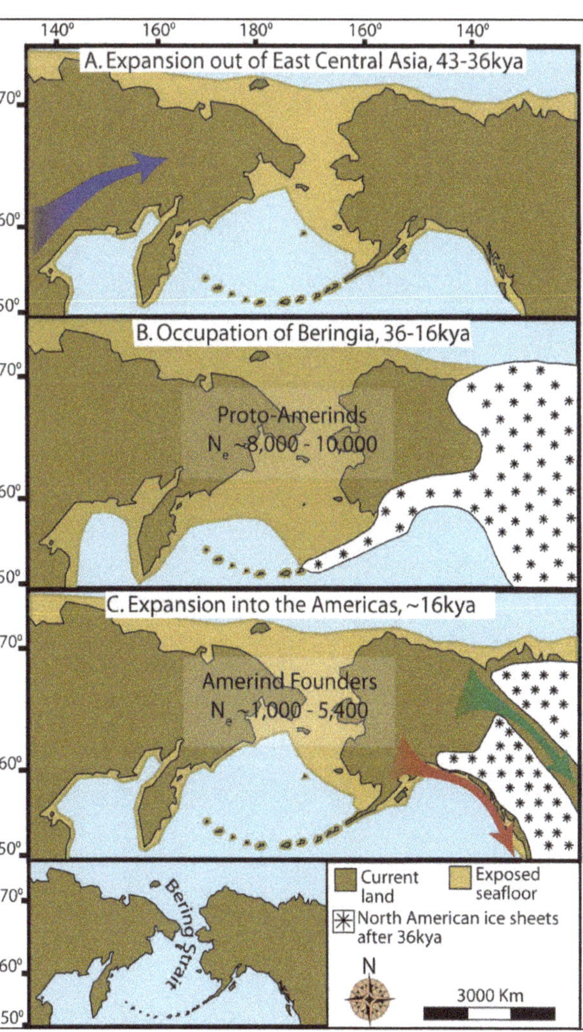

Early Human Migrations via Beringia
Source: Wikimedia Commons – Kitchen A, Miyamoto MM, Mulligan CJ (2008) A Three-Stage Colonization Model for the Peopling of the Americas

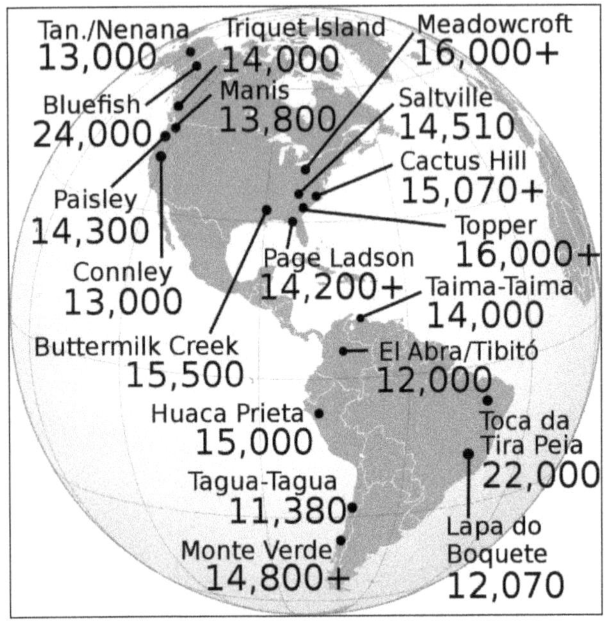

Pre-Clovis Sites in the Americas
Source: Wikimedia Commons – Pratyeka

Beringia for thousands of years, the North American Laurentide and Cordilleran ice sheets seem to have blocked them from travelling overland into the Americas. Supposedly, ice-free corridors formed between the Laurentide and Cordilleran ice sheets, allowing the people from Beringia to follow herds of now-extinct megafauna into North America and then travel onward to South America. Rising sea levels completely inundated Beringia by 10,000 BP, so no further overland migration from Asia could have occurred after that.

Recent investigations suggest that the presumed ice-free corridor between the ice sheets into North America was blocked between 30,000 until at least 14,000 BP and possibly until 11,500 BP. Any blockage would have prevented people from migrating into the Americas by that central overland route. One suggested alternative migration route is that either on foot or using boats, people travelled down the Pacific North-West coast to South America as far as Chile. Several other alternative routes of human migration into the Americas before 14,000 BP have been proposed, and they all depend on travel by sea.

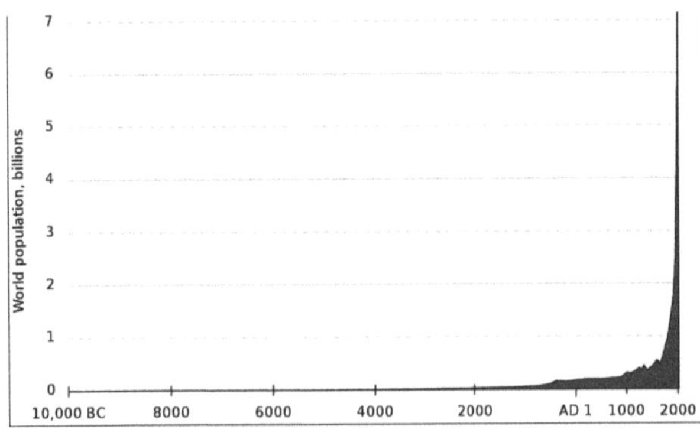

Estimates of the world population from 10,000 BP to 2000 CE
Source: Wikimedia Commons – El T

For many decades during the 20th century, the prevailing theory was that the original human inhabitants of the Americas were the hunter-gatherer Clovis people. They were named Clovis after the site in New Mexico where their artefacts were first found. The Clovis Culture is thought to have appeared at approximately 13,500 BP. It is characterised by the manufacture of fluted stone projectile points called Clovis points and by distinctive bone and ivory tools.

Clovis Culture artefacts have been found throughout most of the United States and as far south as Panama. Nevertheless, recent archaeological evidence indicates that modern humans lived in the Americas many thousands of years before the Clovis people appeared around 13,500 BP. The standard theory of Clovis First has been challenged in recent decades by the discovery of several pre-Clovis sites, including Monte Verde in Chile, Cactus Hill in the USA, and Pedra Furada in Brazil.

Monte Verde is an archaeological site in Southern Chile. Radiocarbon dating of 14,800 BP and possibly 33,000 BP makes Monte Verde the oldest known site of human habitation in the Americas. Coastal migration down along the western coast of the Americas is a widely accepted model for the occupation of Monte Verde.

Cactus Hill is an archaeological site in south-eastern Virginia, USA, with multiple levels of early occupation. Stone tools associated with the Clovis Culture are dated to 10,920 BP, but a lower level has artefacts with ages ranging from 15,000–17,000 BP, with charcoal from a hearth on this level dated to 15,070 BP.

Pedra Furada is a collection of over 800 archaeological sites and rock paintings in North-Eastern Brazil. Some well-excavated archaeological levels have dates between 32,000 BP and 17,000 BP. Other excavations have found artefacts dated 48,000–32,000 BP, with some possible dates to 60,000 BP. The Toca da Tira Peia rock shelter, close to Pedra Furada, has yielded 113 knapped stone artefacts from four well-preserved layers dated from 22,000–4,000 BP. The oldest confirmed dates are 10,000 years earlier than Clovis.

If a Bronze Age level of civilisation developed on the Atlantic Island and peaked at around 11,600 BP, it is unlikely that the Clovis people created it. If they were the first humans to arrive in the Americas around 13,500 BP, two thousand years would probably not have been enough time to develop into the Atlantean civilisation that Plato describes. A more extended pre-Clovis occupation of the Americas and the Atlantic Island by five, ten or fifteen thousand years or more may have been enough time for the Atlanteans to develop from hunter-gatherers to an advanced Bronze Age civilisation with a large population.

The Earth's human population subsisted on hunting and foraging for tens of thousands of years until the beginning of known agriculture around 13,000 BP. Because of this subsistence lifestyle, the total global population of *Homo sapiens* is thought to have remained stable at around three million people. After the invention of agriculture and secure food sources, the population growth rate increased but has remained steady at about 2% per year.

The population figures for the Americas before the first voyage of Columbus in 1492 CE rely on archaeological evidence and the written records of European settlers. Most scholars writing at the end of the 19th century CE estimated the pre-Columbian population of the Americas was about 10 million. By the end of the 20th century CE, the consensus was about 50 million, with some arguing for 100 million or more. In comparison, the population estimate for 15th-century CE Europe (excluding Russia) is around 70 million.

If the Americas of the 15th century CE had an estimated human population of 50–100 million, it confirms how America's natural environment and resources could support a large agriculture-based population. If a fertile one million square kilometre Atlantic Island had been settled and farmed intensively for thousands of years before 11,600 BP, it could have produced and supported a human population of many millions.

Our prehistoric ancestors were the same as us for at least 30,000 years and probably for well over 100,000 years

CHAPTER 3

Human Evolution and Intellectual Potential

Regardless of how many thousands of years ago; how many times; or from where humans entered the Americas and colonised the Atlantic Island, they were all the same as our species of modern humans: *Homo sapiens*.

Did the Atlanteans have the physical and intellectual capacity to create the technology of a Bronze Age sea-going civilisation and empire before 11,600 BP? Until recent decades, it was commonly believed that modern human intelligence was a relatively new development, occurring only in the last ten or twenty thousand years of our species' evolution. The assumption was that before then, we could only live as primitive hunter-gatherers with insufficient mental ability to create any civilisation.

Recent archaeological discoveries have shown that our prehistoric ancestors were physically and intellectually the same as us for at least 30,000 years and probably for well over 100,000 years. It now appears that our very ancient ancestors had the same physical and intellectual capacity as everyone now living on Earth. Modern humans like us would have travelled to and colonised the Atlantic Island and would later develop a civilisation there.

Conventional thinking is that from the time we *Homo sapiens* evolved in Africa before 200,000 BP, we lived for tens of thousands of years as simple hunter-gatherers in all parts of the Earth we colonised. Then, from around 12,000 BP, more advanced cultures evolved independently in several regions, such as China, India, Mesopotamia, the Mediterranean, and the Americas. Small hunter-gatherer groups developed into settled farming cultures in each of these regions and then progressed over thousands of years into Bronze Age or Iron Age civilisations. This accepted progression assumes that no cultures besides hunter-gatherer groups existed before 12,000 BP, with no previous eras of more advanced societies anywhere on Earth.

It can be argued that we *Homo sapiens* have had the physical and intellectual potential to create a civilisation, even to our present level of social and technological development, since at least 30,000 years ago and possibly before leaving Africa 100,000 or more years ago. The most basic environmental conditions humans need to create a civilisation are fertile land and a mild and stable climate. These two factors must last long enough for people to develop agriculture and establish permanent settlements. Once societies achieve that level of culture, they require mineral resources to exploit and develop more advanced metal technologies.

All of the necessary environmental conditions to create a civilisation have been present for tens of thousands of years in various regions on Earth occupied by groups of modern humans like us. Then, it is possible that something like the past 12,000-year cycle of technological development, with people like us progressing from hunter-gatherers to advanced civilisations, could have occurred several times somewhere on Earth over the past 100,000 years or more.

Once humans arrived and established themselves on the Atlantic Island, a cultural and technological sequence may have begun with agriculture and permanent settlements long before 11,600 BP. If the

Australopithecus
Source: Wikimedia Commons

Atlantic Island had a climatically stable and resource-rich environment, its people could have developed their Bronze Age civilisation thousands of years before known civilisations anywhere else on Earth.

In the relatively recent past, numerous civilisations and empires worldwide flourished for a relatively brief time of one or two thousand years and often much less. These advanced civilisations collapsed from various causes, with any survivors regressing to a more primitive way of life. The collapse of Atlantean civilisation sometime after 11,600 BP may have had the same result. There could have been an initial regression of culture, with civilisation redeveloping gradually in the Americas thousands of years later.

Human Evolution

Human evolution describes the evolutionary history of primates, particularly the genus Homo (including our species *Homo sapiens*) as a distinct species of hominins or Great Apes. Primate evolution likely began sometime between 85 and 55mya. The family Hominidae (Great Apes) diverged from the Hylobatidae family (Gibbons) 15–20mya. Then, Chimpanzees diverged from that lineage 5–6mya. That split eventually led to the genus Homo, from which our *Homo sapiens* species later developed.

It is now thought that early human Homo species evolved in Africa from the last common ancestor of the Hominini and the species Australopithecines 2.3–2.4mya. After the Australopithecines, two critical physical characteristics developed in all Homo species: an upright stance (bipedalism) and an opposable thumb. These features allowed our ancestors to walk and run long distances for hunting and to grasp objects to create and use tools.

Several migrations of early human species out of Africa began 1.8mya when the species *Homo erectus* first migrated to Eurasia. This migration was followed by *Homo antecessor* into Europe around

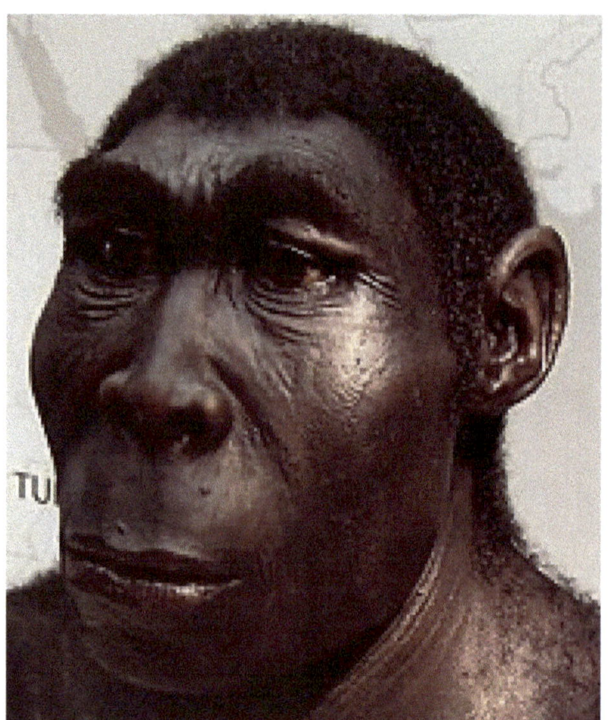

H. erectus
Source: Wikimedia Commons

H. heidelbergensis
Source: Wikimedia Commons

800,000 BP, then by *Homo heidelbergensis* around 600,000 BP. *Homo heidelbergensis* is the most likely ancestor of our species of Modern Humans (*Homo sapiens*), who evolved in Africa and the Neanderthals (*Homo neanderthalensis*), who evolved in Europe.

The Out of Africa hypothesis argues that *Homo sapiens* evolved only in Africa from the species *Homo heidelbergensis*, which created an archaic form of *Homo sapiens* between 400,000–250,000 BP. Anatomically modern humans like us then evolved from archaic *Homo sapiens* by at least 200,000 BP. Those modern *Homo sapiens* migrated out of Africa sometime after 100,000 BP and replaced existing populations of *Homo erectus* in Asia and Neanderthals in Europe. Genetic evidence shows that when modern humans left Africa, they met and interbred with at least two other hominin species: the Neanderthals and Denisovans.

An alternative but less accepted multiregional hypothesis argues that *Homo sapiens* evolved from geographically separate and more ancient Homo populations, which interbred inside and outside Africa. This more gradual evolution would have occurred during the almost two million years after *Homo erectus* and other later Homo species left Africa.

Human Intelligence and Behavioural Modernity

Entirely modern human behaviour was well-established for tens of thousands of years before the existence of the Atlanteans, Greeks, Egyptians and 'barbarians' of the Atlantis story. Over those tens of thousands of years, all people on Earth had the same range of mental and physical abilities as we now have. Our prehistoric ancestors had to survive in many environments, from forests to deserts to snow-covered regions, living in kin groups and societies of varying sizes.

Our ancestors had the same range of positive and negative emotions and motivations as we do: from love and joy to hate and fear. In essence, they probably also had the same personality types and mental disorders as we now have. That means if you or I were born into a group of our species, say 100,000 years ago, we would fit in physically and intellectually with the others in that group. We would look like them and be able to participate in the same physical activities as them. We would communicate in the group's language, coordinate essential activities, raise families and care for the less able to ensure the group's survival.

The evolution of human intelligence is closely linked to the development of the human brain, which tripled in size over nearly seven million years. Most of this rapid brain growth was in the past two million years. By 2.4mya, *Homo habilis* had appeared in East Africa and is considered the first human species and the first known to make stone tools. The use of tools gave an evolutionary advantage and required a larger and more sophisticated brain to coordinate fine hand movements. Opinions vary on when early humans developed language, but some primitive language may have been present as early as *Homo habilis* (2.4mya), *Homo erectus* (1.8mya), or *Homo heidelbergensis* (0.6mya).

Behavioural modernity describes a set of traits that separates modern humans and our recent Homo ancestors from other now-extinct hominins and any of the living primates. It is when we *Homo sapiens* began to demonstrate symbolic thought and cultural creativity. Modern human behaviour is a combination of cultural universals shared by all groups of people: language, religion, art, music, myth, cooking, games, and jokes. Physical evidence of behavioural modernity includes finely-made tools, fishing, long-distance exchange or barter among groups, use of pigments such as ochre and jewellery for decoration or self-ornamentation, figurative art such as cave paintings, petroglyphs and figurines, and ritual burial.

When our species *Homo sapiens* first appeared in Africa before 200,000 years ago, it is not clear whether we had developed language, music, religion, or any other modern behaviour by that time. Nevertheless, there is some physical evidence of early modern behaviour, with a 90,000-year-old ritual burial including grave goods at Qafzeh in the Levant and the use of pigment at several sites in Africa from before 100,000 BP. Increasing sophistication in tool-making and other behaviour appears from 80,000 BP, and archaeological evidence of fully modern behaviour such as figurative art, music, self-ornamentation and trade appears well before 30,000 BP.

Name	**Brain Size (cm³)**
Homo habilis	550–687
Homo ergaster	700–900
Homo erectus	600–1250
Homo heidelbergensis	1100–1400
Homo neanderthalensis	1200–1750
Homo sapiens	1400

Brain Sizes of Hominids
Source: Wikipedia

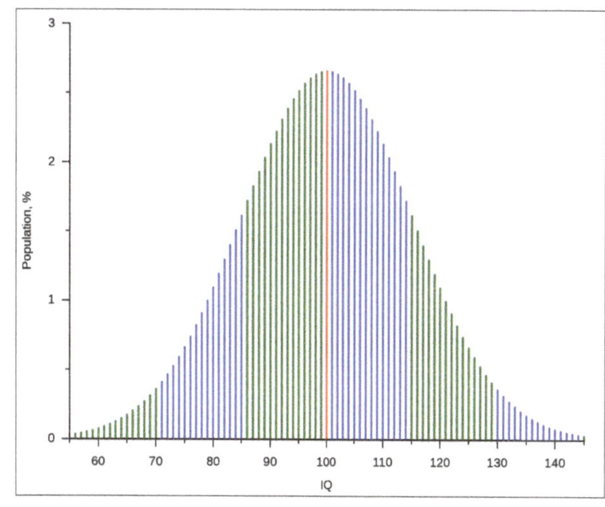

The Bell Curve for IQ
Source – Wikimedia Commons – Alessio Damato, Mikhail Ryazanov

An Intelligence Quotient (IQ) is a score derived from standardised tests designed to assess human intelligence. Modern IQ tests are designed to give an average score of 100 within a particular age group; approximately 95% of that age group scores between 70 and 130. The IQs of a large population match a normal distribution, or Bell Curve.

If human intelligence has not significantly changed for at least 30,000 years, then the range of individual intelligence would also not have changed dramatically over that time. If it were possible to perform an IQ test on a large group of our ancestors 30,000 years ago, the IQ Bell Curve would be about the same as now. It would also be the same for the Atlanteans and all the other modern humans of the Atlantis story.

Periods of Human Prehistory

Human prehistory is all of the time the genus Homo has existed as a separate species. Prehistorians have divided human prehistory into three consecutive periods. Each period is named for its primary tool-making technology – the Stone Age, Bronze Age, and Iron Age. Not all cultures have gone through these stages of development, so societies with different development levels have often co-existed in the same geographical region.

The Stone Age is subdivided into the Palaeolithic, Mesolithic, and Neolithic. Palaeolithic means Old Stone Age. It began with the first use of stone tools when very early humans before *Homo sapiens* lived as nomadic hunter-gatherers. The earliest known stone tools are dated to around 3.3mya. The Palaeolithic is further divided into the Lower (3.3mya–300kya), Middle (300–45kya), and Upper Palaeolithic (40–10kya). The Lower Palaeolithic was before the evolution of our species, *Homo sapiens*; it began with *Homo habilis* and other related early Homo species.

We *Homo sapiens* originated at least 200,000 BP during the Middle Palaeolithic. Features of the Middle Palaeolithic include the systematic burial of the dead, music, early art, and increasingly sophisticated multi-part tools. The Upper Palaeolithic from 40–10kya has the earliest known evidence of organised *Homo sapiens* settlements in the form of campsites and the first evidence of fishing. There was a marked increase in the diversity of artefacts such as cave paintings, petroglyphs, carvings, and engravings on bone or ivory. It was also when our earlier Homo relatives, such as Neanderthals and Denisovans, became extinct.

The Mesolithic or Middle Stone Age is a period between the Palaeolithic and the Neolithic, characterised by small composite flint tools. The Mesolithic has starting and ending dates that vary by geographical region. Depending on local circumstances, it may be as short as a thousand years or as long as 15,000 years.

The Neolithic or New Stone Age began with farming, which produced the Neolithic Revolution and the development of early villages, agriculture, animal domestication, and the earliest recorded incidents of warfare. The Neolithic began 12,000 BP in some parts of the Middle East and later in other regions of the Earth, ending between 6500–4000 BP. In the Americas, a similar set of events had occurred by around 6,500 BP but possibly began as early as 13,000–12,000 BP.

The Chalcolithic or Copper Age was a transitional period when early copper metallurgy appeared alongside the widespread use of stone tools. The Bronze Age began when copper and tin ores were smelted and combined to make bronze. The place and time of the introduction and development of bronze technology varied:

- In the Near East, it began with the rise of Sumer in the 4th millennium BCE.
- On the Indian subcontinent, it began ca. 3300 BCE.
- In Ancient Egypt, it began in the Protodynastic period ca. 3150 BCE.
- The Aegean Bronze Age began ca. 3200 BCE.
- The Mesopotamian Bronze Age began ca. 2900 BCE.
- The Atlantic Bronze Age was a cultural complex from 1300–700 BCE that included different cultures in Portugal, Andalusia, Galicia, and the British Isles.
- In the Americas, there is evidence of the smelting of copper sulphide in the Altiplano region of Southern Peru, Bolivia and Chile ca. 1000–200 BCE.

The Iron Age began when iron was smelted and used. Iron production is more complicated than tin and copper smelting because iron requires hot-working and can be melted only in specially designed furnaces. Iron production was thought to have begun in Anatolia around 1200 BCE, but new dates from India suggest that iron was being worked there as early as 1800 BCE, and some African sites have dates as early as 1500 BCE. By the Middle Bronze Age (ca. 2100–1550 BCE), increasing numbers of smelted iron objects appeared in the Middle East, South-East Asia, and South Asia. Ironworking arrived in Europe in the late 11th century BCE.

Notably, there is no evidence of iron production in the Ancient Americas. Although Plato mentions several metals used by the Atlanteans, there is no mention of iron in the Atlantis story. That omission occurs despite Greece and Egypt being well into their Iron Age by Solon and Plato's time. As Plato did not include the use of iron by the Atlanteans or any other cultures of 11,600 BP, it again indicates that Plato did not invent the Atlantis story.

All present human cultures consist of people with fully developed intelligence and modern behaviour. The main difference between existing cultures is their level of technological development. In various parts of the world, some cultures remained at a Palaeolithic or Neolithic level until recently and into the present. They survived successfully in their environments for thousands of years without further developing their technology. Recent Palaeolithic cultures include the Australian aborigines and the San peoples of Southern Africa. A few uncontacted Palaeolithic and simple Neolithic societies continue to exist in remote parts of the Amazon, Papua New Guinea, and elsewhere.

The term civilisation refers to a society with a sophisticated use of technology and the division of labour. Civilisation is often measured by progress in agriculture, long-distance trade, occupational specialisation, a governing class, and urbanism. Also, a civilisation usually has several secondary elements, such as a developed transportation system, writing, standardised measurement, currency, contractual and legal systems, original art and architecture, mathematics, scientific knowledge, metallurgy, political structures, and an understanding of astronomy.

If all of the above criteria are applied to Plato's descriptions of Atlantean culture, it had the characteristics of an advanced Bronze Age civilisation. If there was such an Atlantean civilisation over 11,600 years ago, it existed more than six thousand years before any currently known ancient Bronze Age civilisation. At the same time as the Atlanteans' Bronze Age civilisation, the prehistoric Athenians were at a Neolithic level. The Athenians had domesticated crops and animals, but Plato does not describe them using metals. Likewise, the Greeks elsewhere and 'barbarians' such as the Egyptians and other Mediterranean cultures of 11,600 BP were probably either at a Mesolithic or Neolithic level.

Genius, Invention and Cultural Evolution

If the people of the Atlantis story 11,600 years ago had the same level of intelligence as we now have, some geniuses would have lived amongst them. A genius can be defined as someone who displays exceptional intellectual ability, creativity or originality associated with achieving an unprecedented leap of insight.

No universally accepted IQ level defines genius or what percentage of the human population are geniuses. For instance, one in one hundred has an IQ over 135, but only one in one thousand has an IQ over 145. One current view of genius is that a minimum IQ of around 125 is necessary but only when combined with other influences on the individual development of genius. External social factors provide the opportunity for talent development, while internal factors are the personality characteristics of drive and persistence.

If human intelligence has remained virtually unchanged for at least the past 30,000 years, hundreds of thousands of potential geniuses must have existed over that time in all cultures worldwide. Those gifted individuals, singly or in collaboration with other like-minded people, produced leaps in cultural and technological development that were not achievable for most of the population.

Over thousands of years, diverse societies developed from hunter-gatherers into Neolithic cultures and then into Bronze Age and Iron Age civilisations. The rise of many great civilisations over the past six or seven thousand years can be viewed as an accumulation of the technical advances of inventions. Inventions can be new ideas or technologies that often are conceived by geniuses. Once someone creates an invention, the general population employs it and further refines it to advance their society. Then, another invention comes along that again changes the usual way society functions. For example, the Industrial Revolution introduced mechanisation to the world in the last three hundred years. The ongoing sequence of inventions that followed, stepwise from the steam engine to the internet, radically changed the way of life in most of Earth's societies.

A potential genius cannot flourish if isolated from a supporting culture. Recognised geniuses, such as Archimedes, da Vinci, Newton, Edison and Einstein in the sciences, or even musical geniuses like Bach, Mozart and Beethoven, could not have achieved much success without a supportive physical and social environment. All those individuals built on the work of previous geniuses their culture had nurtured. If any of them had been born into a hunter-gatherer social group or a subsistence farming society, they probably would have achieved little, if anything, revolutionary in their lifetimes.

On the Atlantic Island, if a stable physical and social environment existed for thousands of years before 11,600 BP, it would have supported any geniuses who lived there. Over time, a succession of gifted individuals and groups created inventions that allowed the Atlanteans to develop at least a Bronze Age civilisation thousands of years before any now known.

Indigenous American civilisations developed many of the same features as Atlantean civilisation

CHAPTER 4

The Ancient Americas

If a maritime-based Atlantean Empire had spread out from the Atlantic Island before 11,600 BP, it initially would have occupied the coastal regions of the Americas near the Caribbean Sea. Those regions would likely have included the Lesser and Greater Antilles, Mesoamerica and the eastern coast of North America around the Gulf of Mexico, and the northern coast of South America from Colombia to Brazil. The Atlantean Empire may also have extended down the Pacific coast of South America into Ecuador, Peru and Bolivia.

If the Atlantic Island subsided sometime after 11,600 BP and its Bronze Age civilisation and empire were destroyed, any survivors in the Americas may have regressed to a more primitive level of culture. Also, there would have been Palaeolithic hunter-gatherer groups or Neolithic farming communities in the Americas that co-existed with the more technologically advanced Atlanteans. These more primitive cultures could have remained intact on the fringes of the ruined Atlantean Empire. Over the next several thousand years, advanced civilisations slowly arose in the Americas. They most likely developed there independently, but they may have also used some prior technical knowledge that survived the destruction of the Atlantean civilisation.

Long before Christopher Columbus arrived in the Americas in 1492 CE, various indigenous American civilisations developed many of the same features Plato describes for Atlantean civilisation. Over thousands of years, those American civilisations built great cities and empires; they waged wars with huge armies and traded long-distance over land and sea. From around 5,000 BP, a continuous line of indigenous civilisations culminated in the Aztec Empire in Mesoamerica and the Inca Empire in north-eastern South America. During the 16th century CE, within one hundred years of first arriving in America from Europe, the Spanish conquerors and colonists systematically destroyed almost all features of those great civilisations.

Following the peak of the most recent cold period, around 20,000 BP, glacial ice melted and the worldwide sea level rose more than 120 metres until it stabilised to its present level around 6,000 BP. In particular, the sea level rose 60 metres after 11,600 BP when the Atlantean Empire was probably at its greatest extent. Any cultural evidence of Atlantean civilisation, such as coastal towns and cities from before the civilisation's destruction, would now be under many metres of water. Any Atlantean towns or cities that did remain above the present sea level would likely be destroyed or buried by thousands of years of natural processes.

In 1958, Gordon Willey and Philip Phillips first described the conventional view of a sequence of cultural stages in the Americas:

- The Lithic stage before 10,000 BP is the earliest period of human occupation in the Americas and began with the first appearance of flaked stone tools. Hunter-gatherers lived in small, mobile groups that survived on hunting, fishing and plant gathering.
- The Archaic stage or Meso-Indian Period from around 10,000–4,000 BP is characterised by subsistence economies supplemented by gathering

nuts, seeds and shellfish. The Archaic stage ended with the beginning of farming settlements, but this date varies across the Americas.

- The Formative Stage or Neo-Indian Period between 4,000 BP and 500 CE is when societies used pottery and weaving and produced food. There were permanent towns and villages as well as the first ceremonial centres.
- The Classic Stage from 500–1200 CE is when cultures had specialised crafts and the beginnings of metallurgy. Social organisation involved urbanism and large ceremonial centres.
- The Post-Classic Stage is applied to North American and Mesoamerican societies between 1200 CE and European contact. Cultures of the Post-Classic Stage had developed metallurgy, and their social organisation involved complex urbanism and militarism.

Willey and Phillips developed their classification system in the 1950s when Clovis First was the dominant theory on the peopling of the Americas. As a result, for most of the 20th century, it was commonly assumed that no one occupied the Americas before 13,000 BP. Yet, the human occupation of the Americas appears to have begun thousands of years before 13,000 BP. Also, there is increasing archaeological evidence of sophisticated Neolithic cultures emerging in the Americas before 5,000 BP. It is also possible that some civilisations in the Americas emerged far earlier than 5,000 BP. Any signs of them could be covered by the rising sea level from 20,000 to 6,000 BP, or they could remain buried and undiscovered on land.

Thousands of years before the Spanish arrived, typically called pre-Columbian times, sophisticated indigenous American civilisations arose in eastern North America, Mesoamerica, and north-western South America. All these regions are relatively close to the Caribbean location of the Atlantic Island and would likely have been part of any prehistoric Atlantean Empire.

Several known New World civilisations had societies and technologies equivalent to the pre-mechanised civilisations of the Old World. The following sections give a brief overview of the most prominent pre-Columbian cultures and civilisations in various regions of the Americas. The issue is not whether Atlantean civilisation directly influenced the ancient civilisations of the pre-Columbian Americas, as there probably was a gap of thousands of years between the demise of the Atlantean Empire and the rise of those later civilisations. The critical point is that indigenous American civilisations could create similar social and technical achievements to those of the Atlanteans.

Eastern North America

An array of ancient cultures of North America are collectively called the Mound Builders, which flourished from before 5,500 BP to the 16th century CE. They lived in the regions of the Great Lakes, the Ohio River Valley, and the Mississippi River Valley and its tributary waters. For over 5,000 years, these cultures constructed assorted styles of earthen mounds for religious, ceremonial, burial and elite residential purposes.

The Old Copper Complex was a culture in present-day Michigan and Wisconsin in the northern United States. They used native copper for tools, weapons and other implements. Native copper is a relatively pure form of copper that occurs as a natural ore and does not require smelting. The primary copper sources were deposits of up to 99% pure copper found along 200 kilometres of the Keweenaw Peninsula on the southern shores of Lake Superior.

Copper mining began around 7,000 BP and possibly as early as 8,000 BP. Over 15,000 Old Copper artefacts have been discovered so far. They cover various implement types such as axes, adzes, knives, perforators, fishhooks and harpoons, and projectile points. These objects were traded in a network from the Rocky Mountains to the Gulf Coast. But by 3,500 BP, much less copper was mined, and artefacts began to change from tools to personal or symbolic ornaments.

Old Copper Complex artefacts
Source: copperculture.homestead.com – collection of David Johnson

Poverty Point
Source: Wikimedia Commons – Herb Roe

Cahokia Reconstruction
Source: Wikimedia Commons – Heironymous Rowe

Poverty Point in Louisiana was constructed by a culture that inhabited the lower Mississippi Valley and surrounding Gulf Coast from 4,200–2,700 BP. Over 100 sites of this culture have been identified from that time, with Poverty Point being North America's largest known settlement. It had six concentric earthworks forming ridges with a total embankment length of 12 kilometres. Archaeologists believe that 500 to 1,000 inhabitants lived in homes on these ridges.

Many tools and other objects found at the site were made from raw materials such as slate, copper, galena, jasper, quartz, and soapstone. These materials came from as far as 1,000 kilometres away, which indicates an extensive long-distance trading network in the present eastern USA.

From approximately 800–1600 CE, the Mississippian Culture was a later mound-building culture of the Midwestern, Eastern, and South-Eastern USA. Cahokia was the largest and most influential urban settlement of the Mississippian Culture. It covered 15km^2 and included 120 earthen mounds in various sizes, shapes and functions. The town population is estimated at 10,000–40,000, with more people in farming villages that supplied the urban centre. When Cahokia peaked from 1050–1200 CE, it was larger than many European cities, including London.

The Caribbean

Based on Proclus' commentary on Plato's *Timaeus*, it is assumed that some of the Greater and Lesser Antilles Islands are the remnants of the sunken Atlantic Island. Most, if not all, the Antilles would once have been part of the Atlantean Empire until the destruction of the Atlantic Island. Still, no human cultural artefacts dating before 8,000 BP in the Greater or Lesser Antilles have been identified.

The first known hunter-gatherer cultures are believed to have begun on the Greater and Lesser Antilles around 8,000 BP. If the Atlantean civilisation once occupied the Antilles Islands, there should be evidence of human occupation dating before 8,000 BP. Those occupation sites may now be underwater or are undiscovered if they are on land. Another possibility is that before 8,000 BP, any Atlantean inhabitants on the Antilles died out or were significantly depleted after the Atlantic Island's destruction. In that case, some descendants of the Atlantean Empire's survivors on the American mainland migrated from the Americas to the Antilles after 8,000 BP. They repopulated the islands, bringing their culture and stories of the sunken Atlantic Island.

The first known occupation in the Antilles was the Banwari Culture from Trinidad, around 7,900 BP. From then to 1,200 BP, several waves of immigrants from the Americas travelled by sea to the Greater and Lesser Antilles. Because of these many different migrations, at least eight separate ethnic groups were present in the Caribbean during European contact in the late 15th century CE. All these groups travelled from areas that once would have been part of the Atlantean Empire. Any or all of these cultures may have had myths and religions that included memories of the sunken Atlantic Island.

Mesoamerica

Mesoamerica describes the region of present-day Southern Mexico, Guatemala, Belize, El Salvador, western Honduras, and the Pacific lowlands of Nicaragua and north-western Costa Rica. If the Atlantic Island were adjacent to Mesoamerica, Atlantean civilisation would probably have been well-established there by 11,600 BP. Any remnants of Atlantean civilisation following the destruction of the Atlantic Island may have survived in Mesoamerica, with civilisation redeveloping there over thousands of years.

Mesoamerica
Source: Wikimedia Commons

Known complex cultures began to form in Mesoamerica after 5,000 BP. Some matured into advanced civilisations such as the Olmec, Maya, Teotihuacan, Zapotec, Mixtec, Huastec, Purepecha,

Toltec and Mexica (Aztec). These indigenous Mesoamerican civilisations flourished for 4,500 years before the appearance of Europeans.

Mesoamerican civilisations did not use metals until just before the Spaniards arrived in the late 15th century CE. By definition, they were Neolithic civilisations, but they were much more technologically advanced and socially sophisticated than small Neolithic farming communities.

The Olmec

The Olmec Culture flourished from as early as 1500 BCE to 400 BCE, and they are often considered the mother culture of pre-Columbian Mexico. The Olmec appear to have originated in the early farming cultures of Tabasco, which began between 7,100 BP and 6,600 BP. What these people called themselves is unknown; the name Olmec comes from the later Nahuatl language of the Aztecs. Olmec means rubber people because they were associated with the use of rubber. Olmec Culture was unknown until the mid-19th century CE when Olmec artefacts were recognised as belonging to a unique artistic tradition. The first scientific excavations of Olmec sites were in the 1930s and '40s.

What is now called the Olmec Heartland contains the major Olmec sites of La Venta, San Lorenzo Tenochtitlan, Laguna de los Cerros, and Tres Zapotes. Although Pre-Olmec cultures had occupied the area since 2500 BCE, by 1600–1500 BCE Olmec Culture had emerged and was centred on the San Lorenzo Tenochtitlan site.

San Lorenzo Tenochtitlan was the major centre of Olmec Culture from 1200 BCE to 900 BCE, when it was the largest city in Mesoamerica. It seems to have mainly been a ceremonial site without city walls and was at the centre of a widespread agricultural population. The urban centre covered 55 hectares and may have housed 5,500, while the entire area including the hinterlands may have reached 13,000.

Laguna de los Cerros was settled around 1400 BCE; by 1200 BCE, it was a regional centre covering 150 hectares. By 1000 BCE, it had nearly doubled in size, with forty-seven smaller sites within a 5km radius. The central city consists of long, parallel mounds alongside rectangular plazas and conical mounds at the ends of the plaza. Laguna de los Cerros was occupied for over 2,000 years, from Olmec times until the Classic era (300–950 CE).

La Venta was a civic and ceremonial centre, with most of the population at outlying sites. Occupation dates to 1200 BCE, but it peaked after 900 BCE following the decline of San Lorenzo Tenochtitlan. A sacred area, the Great Pyramid, and a large plaza to the south dominate La Venta. The Great Pyramid is one of Mesoamerica's earliest known pyramid structures; it is 33m high and contains an estimated 100,000m^3 of earth fill. After 500 years of dominance, La Venta was virtually abandoned by 400 BCE.

Fish Vessel
Source: Wikimedia Commons

'The Wrestler' Statuette
Source: Wikimedia Commons

The Olmec Heartland
Source: Wikimedia Commons

Jade Face Mask
Source: Wikimedia Commons

'Hollow Baby' Figurine
Source: Wikimedia Commons

Tres Zapotes was founded sometime before 1000 BCE and emerged as a regional centre early in the Middle Formative period around 900–800 BCE, roughly coinciding with the decline of San Lorenzo Tenochtitlan. Tres Zapotes appears abandoned by 900 CE, though a later, smaller occupation existed.

The Olmec Culture created sophisticated art in many media, such as jade, clay, basalt and greenstone. They had no metals and made cutting tools such as axes, hammers, drills, saws and other simple tools from hard stone such as chert and obsidian (volcanic glass).

Olmec Colossal Head – La Venta 1947 CE

The most well-known examples of Olmec art are the colossal heads carved from basalt, with seventeen discovered in four sites within the Olmec Heartland. The sculptures vary in height from 1.47 to 3.4 metres and weigh between six and fifty tonnes. Most colossal heads are dated to the Early Preclassic period (1500–1000 BCE), with some to the Middle Preclassic (1000–400 BCE) period.

The colossal heads were usually sculpted from spherical basalt boulders sourced from Veracruz's Sierra de los Tuxtlas Mountains and transported over 150 kilometres. It has been estimated that 1,500 people took three to four months to move a colossal head.

All colossal heads represent mature men with fleshy cheeks, flat noses, and slightly crossed eyes. It is generally accepted that these heads are portraits of Olmec rulers, perhaps dressed as ballplayers of the Mesoamerican Ball Game. Rubber ball games were played for thousands of years throughout the Americas, and several rubber balls were discovered at the Olmec site of El Manati near San Lorenzo, confirming that the Olmec played the game. A later section in Chapter 6 will describe the Mesoamerican Ball Game.

The Maya

The Yucatan Peninsula was the centre of the Maya civilisation; the earliest known Maya sites date to around 2600 BCE. Nevertheless, there may have been even earlier Maya cultures as the Maya calendar is based on the Mesoamerican Long Count Calendar, which commences on a date equivalent to 11th August 3114 BCE. Although writing and the calendar did not originate with the Maya, their civilisation fully developed them.

The Maya can be classified as a Neolithic civilisation because they had just begun experimenting with metals by the Spanish conquest. They used obsidian for cutting tools and weapons. Various outside influences are found in Maya art and architecture

The Maya Region – Map showing the extent of the Maya civilization (red) compared to all other Mesoamerican cultures (black). Source: Wikimedia Commons – adapted from K. Musser

because of cultural interaction throughout the Mesoamerican region. Maya influence can be detected from Honduras, Guatemala, and Northern El Salvador to Central Mexico, more than 1,000km from the Maya area.

Many Maya cities were established during the Pre-Classic period (ca. 2000 BCE to 250 CE), although they reached their highest state of development during the Classic period (ca. 250–900 CE). Some cities continued throughout the Post-Classic period, from 900 CE until the arrival of the Spanish. The

Reconstruction of El Mirador
Source: T.W. Rutledge, National Geographic

Palenque – Palace and Aqueduct
Source: Wikimedia Commons – Rickraider

Extent of the Zapotec Civilisation
Source: Wikimedia Commons

Classic Maya occupied small hierarchical states with a hereditary ruler. These small kingdoms usually consisted of a capital city and several smaller towns. However, greater kingdoms controlled larger territories and extended patronage over smaller states. The Maya employed warfare in each development period to obtain sacrificial victims, settle competitive rivalries, acquire critical resources and gain control of trade routes.

The Maya transported various trade goods, including cacao, salt, seashells, jade and obsidian, along the Yucatan Peninsula. That trade linked dynastic Maya leaders from separate distant cities, and they also had long-distance trade with other Mesoamerican cultures. Maya settlement of offshore islands from the Late Preclassic through to the Post-Classic periods required waterborne travel and maritime skills, as did trade with more distant non-Mesoamerican groups in the Caribbean.

There were two collapses of the Maya civilisation – one at the end of the Pre-Classic Period and a better-known one at the end of the Classic Period. The Pre-Classic Maya Collapse was the systematic decline and abandonment of several major Pre-Classic cities, such as El Mirador, around 100 CE.

El Mirador was a large Maya city in Guatemala that flourished from the 6th century BCE. El Mirador peaked from the 3rd century BCE to the 1st century CE, having an area of 16km^2 and a population of more than 100,000. The site contains the three huge pyramid complexes of El Tigre, La Danta and Los Monos. The La Danta pyramid is 70 metres tall and has a total volume of 2.8 million cubic metres, making it one of the most massive pyramids on Earth. El Mirador and the other Maya centres of the Mirador Basin were abandoned by 150 CE, as were nearly all other major sites during the Pre-Classic collapse. The cause of the Pre-Classic Collapse is unknown.

The later Classic Maya Collapse refers to the decline of the Maya Classic Period (300–900 CE) and the abandonment of cities in the southern Maya lowlands between the 8th and 9th centuries CE. Palenque, Copan, Tikal, Calakmul and many other Maya centres declined and were abandoned shortly afterwards.

The Classic Maya Collapse did not end Maya civilisation because some Maya cities continued to prosper in the northern Yucatan. The state of Chichen Itza built an empire that united much of the Maya region, and centres such as Mayapan and Uxmal flourished, as did the Highland states of the K'iche and Kaqchikel. Maya civilisation continued until the arrival of the Spanish in the first half of the 16th century CE.

The Zapotec

The Zapotec civilization flourished in the Valley of Oaxaca in southern Mexico. Their culture goes back at least 3,500 years, with the earliest Zapotec city of San Jose el Mogote founded around 1600–1400 BCE. It was abandoned about 500 BCE when the Zapotec founded their capital, Monte Alban, one of the first major cities in Mesoamerica. It was the socio-political and economic centre of the Zapotec state for a thousand years after 500 BCE. The population rose to 25,000 from 400–700 CE when the city reigned over more than one thousand settlements spread across the Oaxaca Valley.

The Zapotec state began an expansion from 400 BCE–200 CE. It seized control over the provinces

Monte Alban pyramid complex
Source: Wikimedia Commons – DavidConFran

outside the valley of Oaxaca and had trade and cultural links with the Olmec, Teotihuacan and Maya civilisations. The Zapotec developed a calendar and a system of writing that had a separate glyph to represent each syllable of the language. This writing system possibly was the predecessor of those used by the Maya, Mixtec and Aztec civilisations.

Monte Alban lost its political dominance by the end of the Late Classic (ca. 500–750 CE) and was later abandoned. The cause of the Zapotec civilisation collapse at Monte Alban is not known. Even though there is no trace of violent destruction, the collapse happened at the same time as the end of the Teotihuacan civilisation, with an increased conflict between states.

Teotihuacan

Teotihuacan is a vast archaeological site in the Basin of Mexico, 40km north-east of modern-day Mexico City. In Mexico, a power vacuum after the decline of Olmec civilisation led to the rise of the city of Teotihuacan. The early history of Teotihuacan and the origin of its founders are unknown, as is the city's original name, which appears in Maya hieroglyphic texts as *puh* or Place of Reeds. The name Teotihuacan was given by the Nahuatl-speaking Aztecs several centuries after the city's fall.

First settled in 300 BCE, Teotihuacan appears well established by 100 BCE, with construction continuing until 250 CE. It remained occupied for over one thousand years until sometime between the 7th and 8th centuries CE when Teotihuacan was destroyed either by invaders or by an internal uprising against the ruling class.

At its peak, Teotihuacan was the largest city in the pre-Columbian Americas. Covering over 30km^2 and with more than 200,000 inhabitants, it was one of the largest cities in the world at the time, with multi-floor apartment compounds to accommodate its large population. Archaeological evidence suggests that Teotihuacan was a multi-ethnic city, with distinct quarters occupied by Otomi, Zapotec, Mixtec, Maya and Nahua peoples.

Because the land was swampy in the Basin of Mexico, the farmers of Teotihuacan constructed raised artificial islands or floating gardens called chinampas to grow their crops. Chinampas measured roughly 30 by 3 metres, with canals between them that allowed canoes to transport food to the city. The chinampas had exceptionally high crop yields with up to seven crops a year and were commonly used throughout Ancient Mexico and Central America.

The Ciudadela is a square public enclosure located at the geographical centre of Teotihuacan. It measures around 400 metres on each side and is bordered by four large platforms surmounted by

The Ciudadela and the Avenue of the Dead with the Pyramid of the Sun on the Left
Source: Wikimedia Commons

Pyramid of the Sun
Source: Wikimedia Commons – Mario Roberto Durán Ortiz

pyramids. The central plaza had a capacity of about 100,000, and one of its principal functions may have been ritual performance.

Teotihuacan contains some of the largest pyramidal structures built in the pre-Columbian Americas. The Pyramid of the Sun is roughly 65 metres high and 215 metres wide. It was built around 100 CE by labourers who transported three million tonnes of brick, rubble and stone without using the wheel, metal tools or draught animals.

Population decline began in Teotihuacan in the 6th century CE and continued for the next one or two centuries until the city was destroyed and abandoned. No single cause appears for its decline, but it was likely a combination of prolonged drought, internal unrest and interstate conflict with surrounding cultures.

Cholula

The Cholula archaeological zone is 6km west of the city of Puebla, Mexico. While the occupation of the area began around 2,000 BCE, Cholula eventually grew into a regional centre between 600 and 700 CE. It became an important trade centre between the cultures of the Gulf Coast, the Valley of Mexico, and the Pacific Coast. Though Cholula developed at the same time as Teotihuacan, it seems to have avoided Teotihuacan's violent destruction. When the Spanish under Hernan Cortez conquered Cholula in 1519, it was the second-largest city in central Mexico. The Aztec capital Tenochtitlan had a population of 200,000, whereas Cholula had 100,000.

The Cholula temple-pyramid complex was built in four stages from the 3rd century BCE to the 9th century CE and was dedicated to the deity Quetzalcoatl. The central ceremonial precinct included several pyramids and a central plaza. The most massive structure in the complex is the Great Pyramid of Cholula. Its base is 450 by 450 metres with a height of 66 metres, making it the biggest pyramid and the largest monument ever constructed anywhere on Earth. The Cholula Pyramid's total volume is estimated to be over 4.45 million cubic metres, much larger than the 2.5 million cubic metres of the Great Pyramid of Giza in Egypt.

When it was intact, the Great Pyramid of Cholula would have resembled the Pyramid of the Sun at Teotihuacan. Still, it was far bigger, and archaeologists have estimated eight kilometres of tunnels inside the pyramid. The Great Pyramid was abandoned in the 8th century CE. Its external structure deteriorated afterwards to the point where the Spaniards built a Catholic church at the top of it in 1594 CE, without realising it was a pyramid and not a natural hill.

The Great Pyramid of Cholula
Source: Wikimedia Commons

The Toltec

The Toltec are thought to have originated from the Tolteca-Chichimeca people. They migrated during the 9th century CE from the deserts of north-west Mexico to Culhuacan, in the Valley of Mexico. Toltec Culture dominated a state centred in the Toltec capital Tula (Tollan). The Toltecs conquered the city of Teotihuacan around 900 CE, and the Toltec Empire then reigned over central Mexico from the 10th to 12th centuries CE. The later Aztec Culture considered the Toltecs their intellectual and cultural predecessors, describing Toltec Culture as the epitome of civilisation.

The Toltec capital at Tula grew to an area of 14km^2, with a population of around 60,000 in the city and 25,000 more in the surrounding area. The city's centre was laid out in a grid pattern similar to the Maya city of Chichen Itza. This city layout and other architectural similarities suggest a close cultural link between the Toltec and Maya civilisations.

Tula

The archaeological site includes two large pyramids, a collonaded walkway, a large palace building, and two ball-courts. There was dense urban housing outside the central area, with groups of up to five flat-roofed residences centred on a courtyard and surrounded by a wall. During the mid-12th century CE, Tula shows signs of violent destruction and many architectural columns and statues were burnt and purposely buried. Later, the Aztec systematically looted the site.

The Aztec

Aztec refers to the Mexica people, whose principal city was Tenochtitlan. They called themselves Mexica Tenochca or Colhua-Mexica. Sometimes Aztec also includes Tenochtitlan's two allied city-states, Texcoco and Tlacopan. Together with the Mexica, they formed the Aztec Triple Alliance, which controlled the Aztec Empire.

The Basin of Mexico
Source: Wikimedia Commons Christine Niederberger Betton

Initially, the Mexica was a semi-nomadic tribe that migrated from northern Mexico and arrived at the city of Chapultepec in the Valley of Mexico around 1248 CE. Several established city-states were already in the Valley, the two most powerful being Culhuacan to the south and Azcapotzalco to the west. After the ruler of Azcapotzalco expelled the Mexica from Chapultepec, the Culhuacan ruler permitted the Mexica to settle the unoccupied lands of Tizapan in 1299 CE.

In 1325 CE, the Mexica migrated to a small swampy island in Lake Texcoco, where they founded the town of Tenochtitlan – now the location of Mexico City. For the next 50 years, the Mexica were a tributary of the city-state of Azcapotzalco, which had become a regional power. In 1427 CE, the Mexica allied with Texcoco's exiled ruler and the city-state of Tlacopan. This coalition of three

Tenochtitlan Reconstruction
Source: Wikimedia Commons – Diego Rivera

Northern South America
Source: Ian Macky

city-states was the foundation of the Aztec Triple Alliance, which defeated the dominant city-state of Azcapotzalco in 1428 CE.

The Valley of Mexico was the centre of Aztec civilisation, and the city of Tenochtitlan became the capital of the Aztec Triple Alliance. The Mexica built Tenochtitlan on raised islets in Lake Texcoco. By the time of the Spanish conquest in the early 1500s CE, it was one of the largest cities in the world. The most common estimates put Tenochtitlan's population at over 200,000; compared to Europe at that time, only Paris, Venice and Constantinople were larger.

The Aztec Triple Alliance created a tributary empire that dominated the Valley of Mexico and conquered other city-states throughout Mesoamerica. Tenochtitlan was the dominant partner despite the empire being an alliance of three cities. Over the next 100 years, from 1428 CE, the Aztec Empire extended its power from the Gulf of Mexico to the Pacific. Most areas within the empire were organised as small city-states ruled by a local king from a dynasty. The Aztec did not interfere in local affairs as long as the city-states made tribute payments.

In 1521 CE, after eighteen months of sporadic fighting in Mexico, the Spaniard Hernan Cortes and his soldiers conquered Tenochtitlan, defeating the Aztec Triple Alliance led by Hueyi Tlatoani Moctezuma II. Cortes was assisted in battle by many Nahuatl-speaking indigenous allies the Aztec Empire had subjugated. The Spanish then systematically destroyed and levelled the city of Tenochtitlan.

South America

The north-west corner of South America appears to have the earliest known areas of human culture and civilisation in all of the Americas. Many sophisticated civilisations developed in this region, beginning before 5,500 BP and continuing until the Spanish Conquests of the 16th century CE.

This region is adjacent to Mesoamerica and may have been part of an Atlantean Empire that extended into South America, particularly along the Pacific Coast. As with Mesoamerica and North America, remnants of Atlantean civilisation may have survived there only to regress to a more primitive lifestyle of hunter-gatherers or Neolithic farmers before redeveloping civilisation. As elsewhere, any physical evidence of Atlantean civilisation dating from before 11,600 and up to 6,000 BP may be underwater or buried.

Colombia

Columbia's present territory linked the populations of Mesoamerica, the Caribbean, the Andes,

Tairona Gold Pendant
Source: Wikimedia Commons

and the Amazon. Excavations in the Altiplano Cundiboyacense highlands in northern Colombia show evidence of human activity since the beginning of the Holocene Epoch. El Abra is dated to 13,000 BP and is one of the most ancient archaeological sites in the Americas. At least from that time, Colombia was inhabited by indigenous people, including the Muisca and Tairona.

The Muisca migrated to the Altiplano Cundiboyacense around 7,500 BP and transitioned from hunters to farmers. They were organised into a loose union of sovereign states, with each tribe ruled by a chief. The Muisca had permanent housing and farmed maize, potato, quinoa and cotton; and traded worked gold, emeralds, blankets, ceramic handicrafts, coca and salt with neighbouring nations.

The Tairona inhabited northern Colombia in the isolated Andes mountain range of the Sierra Nevada de Santa Marta and farmed yucca and maize from around 3,200 BP. They built terraced stone platforms, house foundations, stairs, sewers, tombs and bridges; and made highly developed pottery.

Tairona civilisation had distinctive goldwork, the earliest known from the Neguanje Period (about 300–800 CE). Gold artefacts comprised pendants, lip-plugs, nose ornaments, necklaces and earrings.

Venezuela

Human habitation of Venezuela commenced by at least 15,000 BP. Hunting artefacts dating from 15,000–9,000 BP were found at a series of sites known as El Jobo in north-western Venezuela. Excavation at Taima-Taima recovered artefacts and the butchered remains of a juvenile mastodon dated to 13,000 BP.

During the Meso-Indian period from 9,000 BP to 1000 CE, megafauna hunters and gatherers started using other food sources and established the first tribal structures. The most advanced culture was the Timoto-Cuicas, who inhabited the Andean region of western Venezuela. They had pre-planned permanent villages surrounded by irrigated, terraced fields and regional crops, including maize, potatoes and ullucos (a root and leaf vegetable). Their houses were made primarily of stone and wood with thatched roofs. The Timoto-Cuicas produced works of art, particularly anthropomorphic ceramics, but no major monuments. They spun vegetable fibres to weave into textiles and mats for housing.

Ecuador

The Las Vegas Culture is the first known culture in Ecuador, occupying the Santa Elena Peninsula on the coast of Ecuador between 11,600–8,000 BP. Although initially hunter-gathers and fishers, by around 8,000 BP, the Las Vegas Culture was among the first known to begin farming in the Americas.

The Valdivia Culture emerged from the Las Vegas Culture and thrived from 5,500–3,800 BP. The Valdivians were sedentary people who lived primarily by farming and fishing. They cultivated maize, kidney beans, squash, cassava, hot peppers and cotton plants used to make clothing and were among the first Americans known to use pottery. The Valdivians sailed balsa rafts and established a trade network with tribes in the Andes and the Amazon. The Machallia Culture that followed the Valdivians was a farming culture along the coast of Ecuador from 4,000 to 3,000 BP. From 2,900 to 2,300 BP, the Chorrera Culture occupied Ecuador's Andes and coastal regions.

From 2,500 BP onwards, various clans joined into large tribes, with some tribes allying to form powerful confederations such as the Confederation of Quito. Each culture developed distinctive architecture, pottery, and religious interests but was consolidated under a confederation called the Shyris. The Shyris organised trading and bartering between the different regions, with political and military power held by a hereditary ruler. The Incan conquest of the tribes of Ecuador began in 1463 CE under the leadership of the ninth Inca, Pachacuti Inca Yupanqui.

Peru

It is thought that hunter-gatherers initially inhabited Peru sometime between 20,000–12,000 BP. These people created sophisticated stone arrow points and fine blades and made cave paintings of animals, hunting scenes and dances.

Some of the oldest identifiable cultures in Peru appeared around 8,000 BP in the coastal provinces of Chilca and Paracas and the highlands province of Callejon de Huaylas. Over the next three thousand

Ancient Sites of Peru

years, these cultures began cultivating plants such as maize and cotton. They also domesticated animals, including alpaca and llama, and developed domestic crafts such as basketry, pottery and the spinning and knitting of cotton and wool.

By 5,000 BP, a succession of more sophisticated cultures began to appear in Peru. They eventually developed into advanced civilisations with a Bronze Age level of technology equivalent to the ancient civilisations of the Old World.

The Sechin Alto Complex

Sechin Bajo is a stone plaza amid a group of ruins called the Sechin Alto Complex, located in the Andes foothills 330 kilometres north-west of Lima, Peru.

Sechin Bajo Sunken Plaza

The plaza is one of the oldest surviving buildings discovered in the Americas. It is 14 metres across and was built of rocks and adobe bricks between 5,500–5,000 BP.

The Sechin Alto Complex covers over 10km^2 and comprises the sites of Sechin Alto, Taukachi-Konkan and Sechin Bajo. Successive cultures lived in the area and constructed adjacent buildings on the site. The final and largest structure was Sechin Alto, which had several courtyards and patios, curved corners and niched walls. Because of the similarity in mound forms and site layout, they may have formed part of a single, large, continuous settlement.

The Norte Chico Civilisation

The Norte Chico Valley is roughly 240km south of the Sechin Alto Complex, in what is now called the Norte Chico region of north-central coastal Peru. Known archaeological sites cover 1,800km^2 and are concentrated in three principal valleys that share a coastal plain.

The Norte Chico civilisation – also known as Caral or Caral-Supe civilisation – flourished between 5,000–3,800 BP and is the oldest known civilisation in the Americas. Complex society in Norte Chico arose a thousand years after Sumer in Mesopotamia, was contemporary with the Egyptian pyramids, and pre-dated the Olmec in Mesoamerica by nearly two thousand years. The Norte Chico civilisation built monumental architecture, including large earthwork platform mounds and sunken circular plazas, but it completely lacked ceramics and had almost no art.

During the 5th millennium BP, Norte Chico may have been the Earth's most densely populated area. It included 30 major population centres with

Norte Chico Civilisation Sites
Source: Proyecto Arqueologico Norte Chico

View of the Caral Amphitheatre and City
Source: Wikimedia Commons

individual sites from 10–100 hectares. Each site had between one and seven large platform mounds and rectangular, terraced pyramids ranging in size from 3,000 to over 100,000 cubic metres. There is no evidence of warfare, and none of the settlements appear to have defensive structures. The major inland centres of Norte Chico possibly were in the middle of a regional trade network that traded as far as the Amazon. Only two confirmed coastal sites exist, but cotton fishing nets and domesticated plants have been found all along the Peruvian coast.

Caral (or Caral-Supe) was one of the larger settlements in the Supe Valley, inhabited between 4,600 and 4,000 BP with a population of approximately 3,000. However, 19 other pyramid complexes are scattered across the 80km^2 of the Supe Valley, with a possible total population of 20,000 people. Caral's central zone contains monumental architecture and covers an area of 65 hectares. There are six platform mounds, many smaller mounds, two sunken circular plazas and a variety of residential architecture.

The Piramide Mayor is the largest of Caral's platform mounds; it measures 160 by 150 metres at the base and is 18 metres high. In another of Caral's pyramids, there were 32 flutes made of condor and pelican bones and 37 cornets made of deer and llama bones.

Kotosh

Kotosh is an archaeological site on the eastern side of the Andes in Peru's central highlands. The Kotosh site gave its name to the Kotosh Religious Tradition, a term used for the ritual buildings constructed in the Andes between 5,000 and 3,800 BP. The first of these temples discovered was at Kotosh, with further examples found later at several other sites.

An image of crossed arms is a characteristic of Kotosh temple iconography. Kotosh also contains artefacts of later origin, mostly belonging to Chavin Culture. Kotosh people cultivated crops, used marine resources, and built permanent settlements with multi-storeyed ceremonial buildings.

Chavin Culture

The earliest Chavin archaeological finds are from 4,000 BP in the northern Andean highlands of Peru. Chavin civilisation flourished for 700 years, from 2,900–2,200 BP, when they extended their influence to other civilisations along the coast.

Caral Pyramids
Source: Wikimedia Commons – KyleThayer

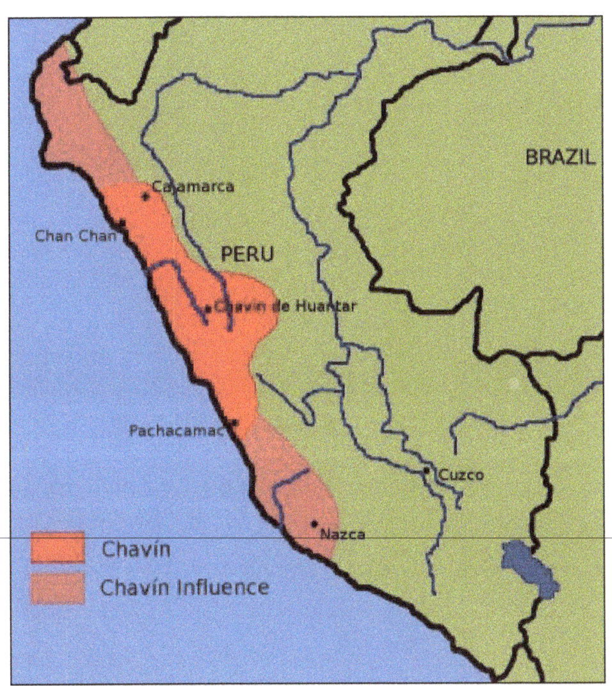

Chavin Culture
Source: Wikimedia Commons – Zenyu

The Chavin domesticated llamas and alpacas for use as pack animals, for fibre to weave, and for meat. They developed irrigation systems for farming and cultivated several crops, including potatoes, quinoa and maize. The Chavin had advanced skills and knowledge of metallurgy, such as soldering, anodising, and metal plating.

The greatest example of Chavin architecture is the massive Chavin de Huantar temple in the Andean highlands north of Lima at an elevation of 3,180 metres. Initial occupation at Chavin de Huantar was carbon-dated to at least 5,000 BP. Ceremonial centre activity occurred primarily toward the end of the 4th millennium BP and through the middle of the 3rd millennium BP, but most major construction ended by 2,750 BP.

The Chavin built a drainage system with several canals under the temple to avoid flooding during the highland rainy season. Chavin art on the temple's walls includes carvings, sculptures and pottery. Rather than local plants and animals, Chavin artists depicted exotic creatures such as jaguars and eagles found in more remote regions.

Chavin metalwork

The Moche

The Moche civilisation followed the Chavin and flourished in northern Peru from 100–800 CE, co-existing with the Ica-Nazca Culture to the south. The capital was called Moche and is near present-day Moche and Trujillo. Other major Moche sites are Sipan, Loma Negra, Dos Cabezas, Pacatnamu, the El Brujo complex, Mocollope, Cerro Mayal, Galindo, Huanchaco, and Panamarka.

The capital city of Moche once covered 300 hectares and contained urban housing, plazas, storehouses and workshop buildings. It also had monumental buildings, including two massive adobe brick pyramid-like mounds called *huacas*.

Built around 450 CE, the Huaca del Sol was the largest pre-Columbian structure in Peru at 50 metres high and 340 by 160 metres at the base. It was constructed with over 140 million mud-bricks and was brightly coloured in red, white, yellow and black. A smaller structure known as the Huaca de la Luna was built 500 metres away around the same time.

Moche society was based on agriculture, with a network of irrigation canals to divert river water to

The Main Temple of Chavin de Huantar
Source: Wikimedia Commons – Martin St-Amant

Huaca del Sol
Source: Wikimedia Commons – Martin St-Amant

From L to R: Alpaca Wool Tapestry; Moche Ceramic; Moche Earrings
Source: Wikimedia Commons

supply their crops. The Moche wove fine textiles, mainly using wool from vicuna and alpaca, and they are known for their elaborately painted ceramics and goldwork.

The Moche state preceded both the Wari Empire and Tiwanaku. Moche civilisation declined after the 5th century CE, probably due to a combination of factors such as an extended period of drought, Wari Empire expansion, and internal conflict with evidence of fire damage to many buildings.

Wari (Huari) and Tiwanaku

The Wari Empire emerged around 600 CE and lasted for 500 years until around 1100 CE. It co-existed with the Tiwanaku Culture and covered much of the highlands and coast of modern Peru. The capital city was called Wari, located 11km north-east of the modern city of Ayacucho, Peru. It covered some 16km^2 and was highly organised, with residential, administrative and religious areas.

The Wari people built an extensive network of roadways linking provincial cities. Each city had major religious complexes with plazas surrounded by residential blocks in walled compounds separated by streets. The Wari grew corn and potatoes and raised llama and alpaca. They traded figurines, ceramic vessels, textiles and metal objects through a trading network extending across the Andes. Centuries of prolonged drought caused the Wari Culture to deteriorate around 800 CE, and the Wari state structure collapsed. The city of Wari was largely depopulated by 1000 CE, with no further major construction.

Tiwanaku is an archaeological site in western Bolivia, located at an elevation of over 3,800 metres near the south–eastern shore of Lake Titicaca, 72km west of La Paz. While the area around Tiwanaku may have been inhabited as early as 1500 BCE, Tiwanaku became a religious centre of pilgrimage between 300 BCE and 300 CE.

Tiwanaku's power expanded significantly around 400 CE when it became the ritual and administrative capital of a large state for five hundred years. At its maximum extent, the city of Tiwanaku covered approximately 6.5km^2 with an estimated 15,000–30,000 inhabitants. Tiwanaku's culture and way of life spread to other cultures in Peru, Bolivia and Chile, becoming one of the most important predecessors of the Inca Empire.

The Tiwanaku people developed a farming technique known as flooded-raised field agriculture called *suka kollus*, where shallow canals filled with water separated artificially raised planting mounds. Suka kollus agriculture yielded an average of 21 tonnes of potatoes per hectare compared to more

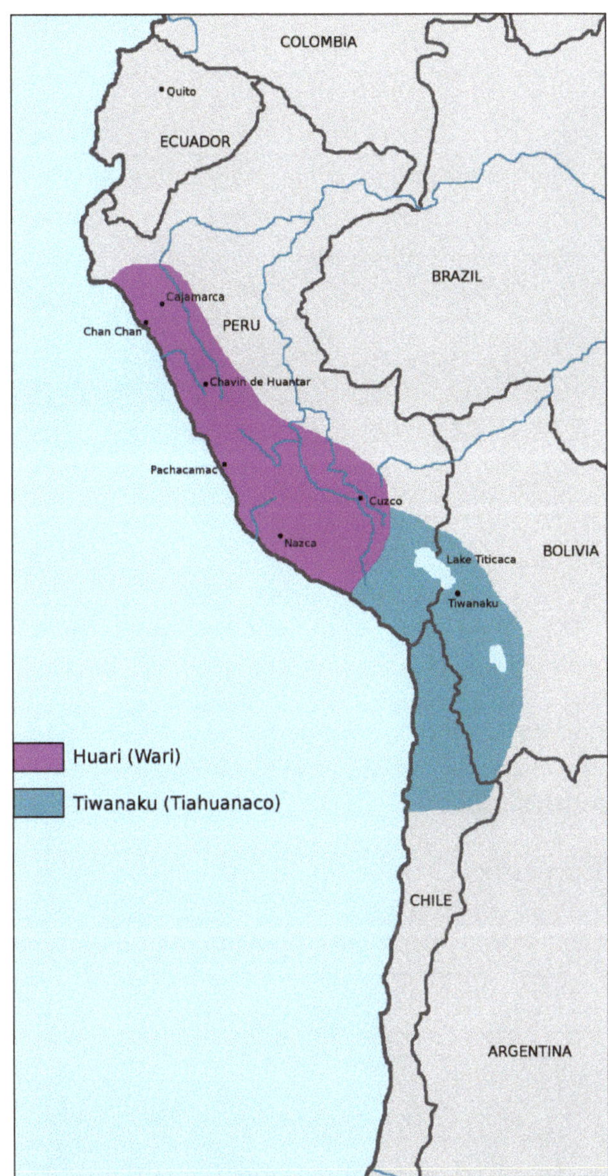

The Tiwanaku and Wari Areas of influence
Source: Wikimedia Commons – Zenyu~commonswiki

The Kalasasaya – Tiwanaku
Source: Wikimedia Commons – Pavel Spindler

Masonry Blocks – Tiwanaku
Source: Wikimedia Commons – Janikorpi

Gate of the Sun – as discovered and a reconstruction

recent traditional agriculture, producing only 2.4 tonnes per hectare. Satellite imaging shows that the extent of fossilised suka kollus across the three primary valleys of Tiwanaku could have fed a population of anywhere between 250,000 and 1.5 million people, which is a much larger population than present estimates for the city alone.

There are several monumental buildings in the city of Tiwanaku. The Kalasasaya dates back to at least 200 BCE. It is a low platform-mound of 120 by 130 metres and contains a large courtyard surrounded by high stone walls. Like several other platform mounds within Tiwanaku, it has a sunken central court reached by a monumental staircase through an opening in its eastern wall.

The Pumapunku is part of a large temple complex or monument group. It is a terraced earthen mound 167 metres long and 117 metres wide, faced with megalithic blocks. The Akapana is a cross-shaped pyramidal structure 257 metres long, 197 metres wide at its maximum and 16.5 metres tall, with a sunken court at its centre. The Pumapunku complex and its surrounding temples were probably spiritual and ritual centres for the people of Tiwanaku.

Tiwanaku had irrigation systems, hydraulic mechanisms and waterproof sewage lines. Tiwanaku metallurgy was advanced and included gold, silver,

Kuelap Stone Walls
Source: Wikimedia Commons – Martin St-Amant

copper and bronze alloys of copper-arsenic-nickel, copper-tin and copper-arsenic.

Tiwanaku stone architecture mainly used rectangular blocks that could be interchanged. Much of the masonry consists of accurately cut blocks that may have been prefabricated and mass-produced. It was a technology far more advanced than that of the Inca hundreds of years later.

The red sandstone used at Tiwanaku came from a quarry 10km away, with the largest stones weighing 131 tonnes. Green andesite stones used for elaborate carvings and monoliths came from 90 kilometres away, across Lake Titicaca. One hypothesis is that these andesite stones, some weighing over 40 tonnes, were transported on reed boats and then dragged another 10 kilometres to the city.

The Gate of the Sun is a megalithic solid stone arch or gateway that weighs an estimated ten tonnes. The lintel is carved with forty-eight squares containing a winged effigy, which surround a central figure that may represent a Sun God.

At around 950 CE, rainfall dropped drastically in the Titicaca Basin, resulting in fewer crops and causing the Tiwanaku elites to lose power. The entire region was depopulated around 1000 CE, and the land remained uninhabited for years.

Chachapoya Culture

The Chachapoyas, also called the Warriors of the Clouds, were a culture of Andean people living at 2,000–3,000 metres altitude in the cloud forests on the eastern flank of the Andes in the Amazonas Region of present-day Peru. The Chachapoyas civilisation developed around 750–800 CE, covering an estimated 65,000km^2.

The Chachapoya were tall, fair-skinned people who lived primarily on ridges and mountaintops in circular stone houses. Their major urban centres, such as Kuelap and Gran Pajaten, may have developed as defences against the Wari civilisation of the coast and highlands. The great fortress of Kuelap contained more than four hundred interior buildings and had massive exterior stone walls reaching up to twenty metres in height.

The Inca conquered the Chachapoyas in the second half of the 15th century CE. To pacify the Chachapoyas, the Inca installed garrisons in the region and arranged the transfer of groups of villagers under the system of *mitmac* or forced resettlement.

Chimor

Chimor was the political grouping of the Chimu Culture, which ruled the northern coast of Peru

Chan Chan – Aerial View, 1931

Ciudadela Wall Reconstruction
Source: Wikimedia Commons – Marrovi

from around 850 to 1470 CE. It was the largest kingdom in Peru then, covering 1,000 kilometres of Peru's coastline. The greatest surviving ruin of Chimu civilisation is the imperial capital city of Chan Chan, located four kilometres north-west of modern Trujillo city. Built of adobe and covering 20km^2, it was the largest pre-Columbian city in South America, with an estimated population of 40,000–60,000.

The dense 6km^2 urban centre of Chan Chan contained nine walled citadels known as Ciudadelas that housed ceremonial rooms, burial chambers, temples, reservoirs and residences. Each Ciudadela was surrounded by large adobe walls four metres thick at the base and up to nine metres tall. Around these nine major complexes were thirty-two semi-monumental compounds and four production sectors for weaving, wood, and metalworking.

The Chimu created a vast network of canals to divert water from the Moche River for farming. Extensive agricultural areas and a remnant irrigation system have been found further to the city's north, east and west.

The Inca

The Inca people were an unimportant pastoral tribe in the Cuzco region around the 12th century CE. In the early 13th century CE, under the leadership of Manco Capac, they formed the small city-state Kingdom of Cuzco. The Inca began a military expansion in 1438 CE. Within one hundred years, they controlled much of the Andes region of modern Peru and Ecuador.

Under their leader, Pachacuti Inca Yupanqui (1438–71), the Inca conquered territory south to the Titicaca Basin and north to present-day Quito. In 1462 CE, an Inca army of 250,000 narrowly defeated the Caras people and their allies around Quito in the battles of Tiocajas and Tixan. In 1470 CE, Tupac Inca Yupanqui (1471–93) conquered Chimor, the largest remaining rival to the Inca; the Inca Empire then reached its southernmost extent in central Chile. Huayna Capac (1493–1525) pushed the empire's northern boundary to the Ancasmayo River.

The Inca Empire was the largest in pre-Columbian America. The city of Cuzco in modern-day Peru was the empire's administrative, political and military centre. At its height, the Inca Empire included what is now Peru, Bolivia, most of Ecuador and a large part of Chile. Population estimates of the Inca Empire range from as few as four million to more than thirty-seven million people. The Inca Empire was a federalist system with a central government; its leader, the Sapa Inca, was its head. The territory was divided into four quarters, with the four corners meeting at the centre – the imperial city of Cuzco.

Spanish conquistadors led by Francisco Pizarro and his brothers explored south from what is now Panama, reaching Inca territory by 1526 CE. A few years later, the Inca were involved in a civil war that weakened the Inca Empire. Pizarro captured the Sapa Inca Atahualpa in the 1532 CE Battle of Cajamarca and executed him shortly afterwards. The numerous kingdoms and tribes that had been conquered or persuaded to join the Inca Empire then joined the Spanish to overthrow the Inca. In 1572 CE, the Spanish conquered the last Inca stronghold of Vilcabamba; the last Inca ruler, Tupac Amaru, was captured and executed.

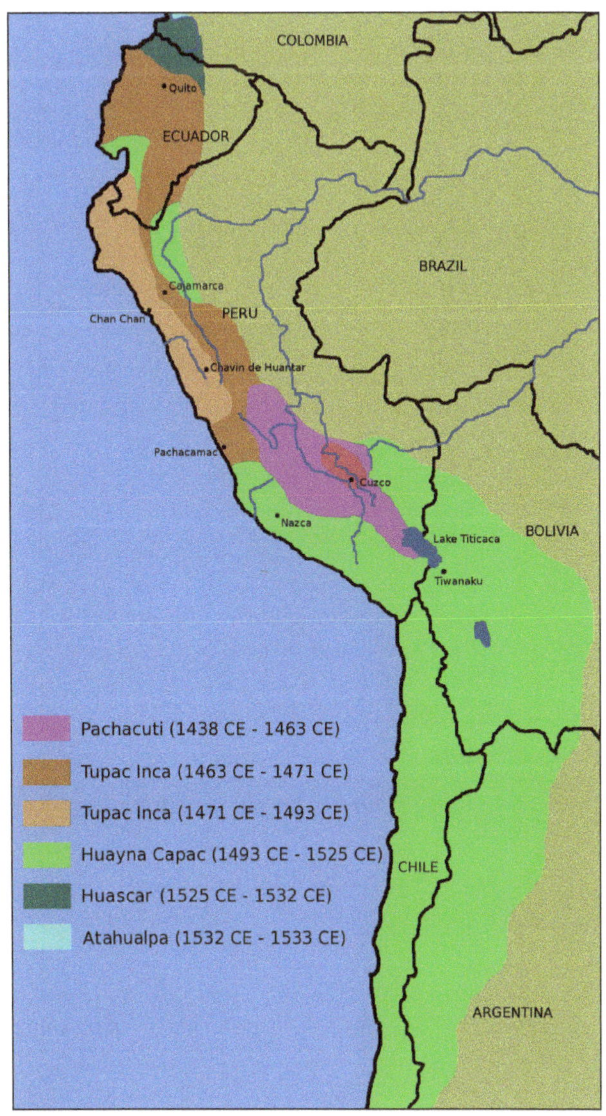

*Inca expansion (*1438–1533 *CE)*
Source: Wikimedia Commons – Zenyu

The Atlanteans had 'many temples built and dedicated to many gods'

CHAPTER 5

Gods and 'foreigners'

In his Atlantis dialogues, Plato uses Greek names for any mentioned Greeks or Greek gods and Greek translations for the names of 'foreigners' and their gods. Plato states he does this because the early Egyptians who wrote the 'sacred registers' translated any foreign names into Egyptian equivalents. Then, when Solon received the Atlantis story, he translated the Egyptian names into Greek equivalents, which Plato then used in his *Timaeus* and *Critias*.

Plato – 'you must not be surprised if you should perhaps hear Hellenic names given to foreigners. I will tell you the reason of this: Solon, who was intending to use the tale (the Atlantis story) for his poem, enquired into the meaning of the names, and found that the early Egyptians in writing them down had translated them (from the Atlantean or any other foreign language) into their own language (Egyptian), and he (Solon) recovered the meaning of the several names and when copying them out again translated them into your (Greek) language.'

Plato only mentions four gods in his Atlantis dialogues: Poseidon, Athena, Hephaestus and Zeus. The Greeks had worshipped these gods and numerous others for centuries before Plato wrote the *Timaeus* and *Critias*. Herodotus writes in his *Histories* that many Greek gods were based on the Ancient Egyptians' gods. In contrast, the remainder were the gods of the Pelasgians, who later Greeks considered to be the prehistoric aboriginal occupants of Greece. One specific exception was Poseidon, who began as a god of the Libyans.

In Proclus' 4th century CE commentary on the *Timaeus*, Marcellus describes several islands that remained after the Atlantic Island sank. Marcellus states that two large remnant islands were sacred to Ammon (Amun) and Pluto, also known as Hades. A smaller island between them was sacred to Poseidon, whose Roman equivalent is Neptune. Seven smaller islands were sacred to Persephone, the Greek goddess the Romans called Proserpina.

Suppose ancient Old World travellers, possibly Carthaginians, did sail to regions around the Caribbean and talked with the native people about their local gods. In that case, the travellers may have transferred the characteristics of the Caribbean natives' gods to their gods. Later, Old World writers may have transferred the travellers' gods' attributes into their existing Egyptian, Greek or Roman gods.

Plato states that the Atlanteans had 'many temples built and dedicated to many gods'. After the destruction of Atlantean civilisation, there may have been continued worship of Atlantean gods in any remnants of the Atlantean Empire. Those gods may have had equivalents in the later mythologies of Mesoamerica and northern South America and possibly within the Mediterranean.

In the Americas, there were over two hundred and fifty deities in the pantheon of the Maya alone. However, the mass burning of Maya books by Bishop Diego de Landa in 1562 CE destroyed much information about Maya culture and gods. Similar destructions of other polytheistic native religions by the Christian Spanish occurred throughout Mesoamerica, the Caribbean and South America, so little is known about those indigenous gods.

Poseidon and the Origin of Atlantean Civilisation

Plato states that Poseidon was one of several gods who each went to a different part of the Earth to settle. This statement might describe the dispersal of several colonising groups from a single original mother culture. Much later, the local populations of the various settled lands may have transformed individual leaders of the colonising groups into gods in their origin myths.

Plato – 'of the allotments of the gods, that they distributed the whole Earth into portions differing in extent, and made for themselves temples and instituted sacrifices. And Poseidon, receiving for his lot the island of Atlantis, begat children by a mortal woman, and settled them in a part of the island'... 'there dwelt one of the Earth born primaeval men of that country (the Atlantic Island), whose name was Evenor, and he had a wife named Leucippe, and they had an only daughter who was called Cleito. The maiden had already reached womanhood, when her father and mother died; Poseidon fell in love with her and had intercourse with her.'

Plato describes indigenous people living on the Atlantic Island before Poseidon arrived there. Yet, there is no indication from where Poseidon came, whether he was alone or in a group, or how he or they travelled to the Atlantic Island. Possibly, Poseidon was a foreign cultural leader who went there with a group of followers who then colonised the Atlantic Island and intermarried with the indigenous people. Later generations on the Atlantic Island may have made Poseidon the creator-god of their civilisation.

Poseidon's Origin

Plato states that Poseidon was the first god of the Atlanteans. Long before 11,600 BP, Poseidon supposedly arrived on the already inhabited Atlantic Island and initiated civilisation there.

Herodotus writes that the Libyans worshipped Poseidon in their remote past, and the Greeks learnt of Poseidon from the Libyans. If the Atlantean Empire of 11,600 BP did extend over North Africa to the borders of Egypt, it would have included the lands of the prehistoric Libyan tribes. The Libyans may have mythologised their contacts with the Atlanteans, including worshipping the Atlanteans' god Poseidon in his various aspects and attributes.

The Libyan myths of Poseidon may have been passed on later to the Greeks, but exactly how and when the Greeks came to worship Poseidon is unknown. However, Mycenaean Linear B tablets show that Poseidon was already worshipped in Bronze Age Greece during the 2nd millennium BCE.

After the Bronze Age ended in Greece, by the 1st millennium BCE, Poseidon was integrated into the twelve Olympian gods. They were called Olympians because they lived in palaces on Mount Olympus in Central Greece. The Olympians are usually considered to be Zeus, Hera, Poseidon, Demeter, Athena, Apollo, Artemis, Ares, Aphrodite, Hephaestus, Hermes and either Hestia or Dionysus. Though the Greeks also believed in many other gods, by the time of Homer, Solon and Plato, the Olympian gods were the principal deities of the Greek pantheon.

Poseidon is called the God of the Sea in Greek mythology. He is also the Earth-Shaker because he caused earthquakes and is the Tamer of Horses. Poseidon was a major civic god of several Ancient Greek cities or polis. In Athens, he was second only to Athena in importance; in Corinth and several cities of *Magna Graecia* (Greek colonies in Southern Italy and Sicily), he was the city's chief god.

Poseidon is usually depicted as an older male with curly hair and a beard. He was the sea's ruler, with all other marine divinities subject to him. Poseidon created new islands and calmed the seas in his benign role, but he could also gather clouds and call forth storms. One of the primary symbols of Poseidon is the trident: a three-pronged spear he could use to shatter rocks and create thunderstorms, tsunamis and earthquakes.

Poseidon – Roman mosaic from the 3rd century CE, Tunisia

Homer wrote that Poseidon's palace was under the sea near Aegae, a town on the island of Euboea, to the north of Attica. Poseidon kept horses there with brazen hooves and golden manes. With these horses, he rode in a chariot over the waves of the sea, which became smooth as he approached. The sea's creatures recognised him and played around his chariot.

Poseidon was also regarded as the creator of the horse. In some myths, Poseidon is their father; he either spilled his seed upon a rock or mated with a creature that gave birth to the first horse. He taught men the art of managing horses by the bridle and was the originator and protector of horse races. He was often represented on horseback or riding in a chariot drawn by two or four horses, and he has the epithets Poseidon hippios (horse) or hippios anax.

All of Poseidon's attributes can be associated with the Atlantis story. The Atlanteans were an imperial maritime power with a large navy, so Poseidon's depiction of holding a trident in a chariot on the sea may be a later mythologising of Atlantean naval power. Poseidon's epithet as the Earth Shaker may be a myth representing the massive earthquakes and deluges that destroyed Poseidon's Atlantic Island. The Atlanteans were a horse culture that raced horses and had a large military force with horse-drawn chariots. The Ancient Greeks' connection of horses with Poseidon may represent how the Atlanteans introduced domestication of horses to the Greeks or possibly how the Atlanteans used horses and chariots in their battles against the Greeks. Besides Plato's Atlantis story, Proclus' commentary on the Timaeus mentions that Poseidon was worshipped on one of the remnant Caribbean islands, probably Jamaica, thousands of years after 11,600 BP.

Chaac Incense Burner, Maya
Source: Wikimedia Commons – Leonard G.

Chaac and Tlaloc

In Ancient Mesoamerica, there were several gods with similar attributes to Poseidon. He may have been worshipped there long after the collapse of Atlantean civilisation, with his appearance modified over thousands of years.

Chaac is the name of the Maya rain deity who strikes the clouds and produces thunder and rain with his lightning axe. He is usually depicted with a human body covered with reptilian or amphibian scales. Chaac has a non-human head with two curling fangs, a long turned-up nose with tears streaming from his large eyes, and hair made up of a tangle of knots.

Chaac corresponds to the Aztec god Tlaloc, their god of rain, fertility and water. Many Mesoamerican goggle-eyed rain gods are now generically referred to as Tlaloc, although called by different or unknown names. Tlaloc was worshipped in Mesoamerica well before the Aztec and was a prominent god in Teotihuacan at least 800 years before the Aztec settled near there in the 13th century CE.

Tlaloc was a benevolent god who gave life and sustenance, but he was also feared for his ability to send hail, thunder and lightning and for being lord of the primal element of water. In depictions of both Chaac and Tlaloc, he appears to have an elephant-like trunk and tusks. As all species of elephants apparently became extinct in the Americas around 10,000 BP, a god with elephant-like features must have been worshipped in Mesoamerica for millennia, possibly before the extinction of elephant species.

In several Aztec codices, Tlaloc ruled the fourth layer of the Upper World or heavens called Tlalocan (place of Tlaloc), also recognised in wall paintings of the much earlier Teotihuacan Culture. Tlalocan is described as a place of eternal Springtime and a paradise of green plants. It was the destination in the afterlife for those who died violently from water-

Tlaloc in the Aztec Codex Borgia
Source: Wikimedia Commons

associated phenomena, such as lightning, drowning and water-borne diseases. Given its various features, Tlalocan may have been a mythologised Atlantic Island.

Viracocha

In the prehistoric religions of the Andes, Viracocha was a god with similar attributes to Poseidon. His full name and some spelling alternatives are Apu Qun Tiqsi Wiraqutra and Con-Tici (also spelt Kon-Tiki) Viracocha. Viracocha is the great creator god in pre-Inca and Inca mythology; he created the universe, sun, moon, stars, time, and civilisation. Viracocha was worshipped as the god of the sun and storms and is closely associated with the sea. He was depicted wearing the sun for a crown, with thunderbolts in his hands and tears descending from his eyes as rain.

Viracocha made humankind by breathing into stones, but his first creations were brainless giants that displeased him, so he destroyed them with a flood and made new, better human creations from smaller stones. He wandered the Earth disguised as a beggar, teaching humanity the basics of civilisation and working numerous miracles. The Spanish chronicler Pedro Sarmiento de Gamboa noted that the Inca described Viracocha as 'a man of medium height, white-skinned and dressed in a white robe like an alb secured round the waist, and that he carried a staff and a book in his hands'.

In Inca legend, the original name of Viracocha was Kon-Tiki or Illa-Tiki, which means Sun-Tiki or Fire-Tiki. Kon-Tiki was a high priest and sun-king of legendary white men who left enormous ruins on the shores of Lake Titicaca, now thought to be the city of Tiwanaku. A chief named Cari came from the Coquimbo Valley and attacked the bearded white men. They had a battle on an island in Lake Titicaca. Most of the fair race was massacred, though Kon-Tiki and his closest companions managed to escape and later arrived on the Pacific coast. The legend ends with Kon-Tiki and his companions disappearing westward, out to sea.

Viracocha – Gateway of the Sun, Tiwanaku
Source: Wikimedia Commons

The Foundation of Athens and Sais

Plato emphasises that the citizens of Sais in Egypt worshipped Neith and identified her with the Greek goddess Athena, as did other Ancient Greek writers such as Herodotus and Diodorus Siculus.

The priest at Sais tells Solon – 'the goddess (Athena/Neith) who is the common patron and parent and educator of both our cities (Athens and Sais). She founded your city (Athens) a thousand years before ours, receiving from the Earth and Hephaestus the seed of your race, and afterwards she founded ours (Sais), of which the constitution is recorded in our sacred registers to be eight thousand years old.'

In the Atlantis story, Athena/Neith founded Athens nine thousand years before Solon's time or 11,600 BP. Plato states that Athena founded Athens after the Earth (the goddess Gaia) and the god Hephaestus provided 'the seed of your race (of Athenians)'. This statement may mean that colonisers who were identified with Athena/Neith and Hephaestus arrived in the region of Athens from a distant place and united with the pre-existing native population to create the city.

Athena/Neith then founded the Egyptian city of Sais one thousand years later, or around 10,600 BP, without the apparent help of Hephaestus or any other gods. That may mean colonisers from the established city of Athens travelled to Egypt and founded Sais one thousand years after the founding of Athens.

Athena

Athena was the patron goddess of the city of Athens. She appears at Mycenaean Knossos in Crete in the 2nd millennium BCE, before any known mention of the god Zeus. Later, Athena was remade in the Olympian pantheon as the favourite daughter of Zeus, born fully grown and fully armed, springing from Zeus' forehead.

Some Ancient Greeks identified Athena's birthplace as being in Libya. In the myth of the birth of the Libyan Athena, Triton (a Libyan sea-god sometimes identified with Poseidon) and Tritonis (the goddess of the Libyan salt lake Tritonis) were the parents of two daughters – the Libyan Athena and Pallas. The first daughter, Athena, accidentally killed the second daughter, Pallas, in a mock battle. This story was re-enacted in an annual festival by the ancient Makhlyes and Ausean Libyan tribes.

Athena was the goddess of wisdom, civilisation, warfare, strength, strategy, female arts, crafts, justice,

Athena Promachos on the Acropolis
Source: Wikimedia Commons – G.P. Stevens

and skill for the Ancient Greeks. As the goddess of handicrafts, she created the potter's wheel, vase, spinning and weaving, horse bridle, chariot and ship. Athena was the patron of architects and sculptors, and she invented numbers and mathematics. She gave farmers the rake, plough and yoke and taught them how to use oxen to cultivate their fields. She had the epithet *Athena Hippeia* or *Athena Hippia* as the inventor of the chariot and was worshipped under this title in Athens, Tegea and Olympia.

Reproduction of the Athena Parthenos statue in Nashville, Tennessee, USA
Source: Wikimedia Commons – Dean Dixon; Sculpture by Alan LeQuire

In Plato's time, there were two main statues of Athena on the Athenian Acropolis. One stood in the open and was called *Athena Promachos*. Made of bronze and nine metres tall, it depicted Athena standing with her shield resting upright against her leg and a spear in her right hand. The other statue of Athena was inside the Parthenon temple: *Athena Parthenos*. It was twelve metres tall and made of wood covered in 100 kilograms of gold, except for skin made of elephant ivory.

Athena's prehistoric connection with Bronze Age Knossos confirms a much older origin for her than most of the other Olympian gods. As with Poseidon, Athena's association with Libya may point to her origin in that distant part of the Atlantean Empire.

Neith

In Egyptian mythology, Neith (also known as Nit, Net, and Neit) was a very early goddess in the Egyptian pantheon. She was a great mother-goddess and creator. Nu or Nun is the deification of the primordial watery abyss, and in some creation stories, Neith brings forth the original mound of land from the waters of Nun. The earliest known references to Neith are from the First Dynasty, before 3000 BCE. She was the patron goddess of the Red Crown of Lower Egypt and the patron deity of the city of Sais, the centre of her cult, where a great yearly festival called the Feast of Lamps was held in her honour.

Neith's symbol was two crossed arrows over a shield on top of her head. She was a goddess of hunting and war, known by the epithet Mistress of the Bow, Ruler of Arrows. As a goddess of war, she made the weapons of warriors and guarded their bodies when they died. Neith's symbol and part of her hieroglyph also resembled a weaver's loom, and

Neith
Source: Wikimedia Commons – Jeff Dahl

in later Egyptian myths, she also became the goddess of weaving.

Hephaestus

Hephaestus was the Greek god of blacksmiths, craftsmen, artisans, sculptors, metals, metallurgy, fire, and volcanoes. He was depicted as misshapen, with crippled feet. Hephaestus is probably associated with the 2nd millennium BCE Mycenaean Greek inscription *A-pa-i-ti-jo*, found at Knossos. His name in Greek has a root found in place-names of pre-Greek Pelasgian origin.

Even though Hephaestus was not one of the twelve Olympian gods, he did have his own palace on Mount Olympus. It contained his workshop with twenty bellows that worked at his bidding, where he crafted much of the equipment of the gods and heroes. Hephaestus also built metal automatons to work for him, including tripods that walked to and from Mount Olympus. In some myths, Hephaestus built himself a wheeled chair or horse-less chariot to move around on, and in Homer's *Iliad*, he built some bronze human-like machines to transport himself.

Hephaestus, Thetis and the Armour of Achilles
Source: Wikimedia Commons – Museum of Antiques, Berlin

Ptah

The Greeks identified Hephaestus with the Egyptian god Ptah. Ptah was originally the local deity of Memphis, the capital of Egypt from the 1st Dynasty onward, after which his cult spread across Egypt. Ptah was the primal creator, the first of all the gods, the creator of the world and everything in it. He was represented as a man in mummy form, wearing a skullcap and a short, straight, false beard.

In the Egyptian Book of the Dead, Ptah was a master architect and was responsible for building the framework of the universe. He created the immense metal plate that was the floor of heaven and the roof of the sky, as well as the supports that held it up. He was the patron of architects, artists and sculptors and built boats for the souls of the dead to use in the afterlife.

The Gods of the Remnant Islands

From Proclus' commentary on the *Timaeus* dialogue: 'there were seven islands in that sea in their time, sacred to Persephone, and also three others of enormous size, one of which was sacred to Pluto, another to Ammon, and another one between them to Poseidon' 'and the inhabitants of it – they add – preserved the remembrance from their ancestors of the immeasurably large island of Atlantis' 'which itself had likewise been sacred to Poseidon.'

Amun (Ammon)

According to Proclus, the ancient Old World travellers who went to the remnant islands of the Atlantic Island identified one of the three large

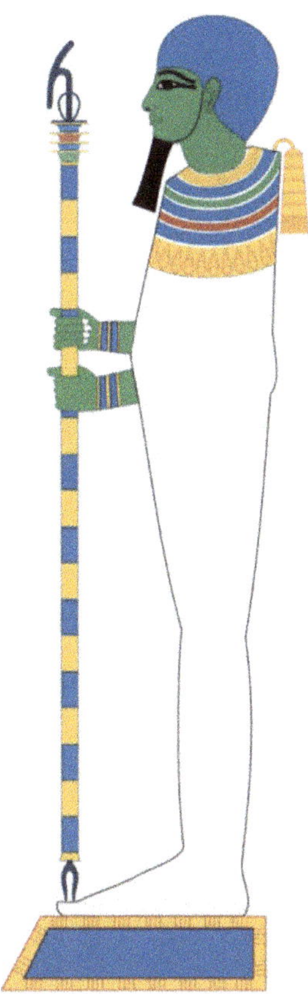

Ptah
Source: Wikimedia Commons – Jeff Dahl

islands as sacred to Amun. Amun was a primordial Egyptian god who was self-created, without a mother and father. His name means the hidden one, and he was initially a god of wind and ruler of the air.

During the 11th Dynasty (2133–2000 BCE), Amun became the Sun God of Thebes and was worshipped there as Amun-Re. Later, he became the supreme god of all Egypt and king of the gods. His position as King of Gods developed to the point of virtual monotheism, where the other gods became manifestations of him.

The natives in the Americas may have told Proclus' Old World travellers about their own Sky God or Sun God worshipped on one of the Caribbean islands. Because Amun was the Egyptian sky or sun god with similar attributes, the travellers may have called the natives' god Amun. Either that or the travellers might have used the name of their own sun god, which was translated later into the Egyptians' sun god, Amun. The Carthaginians' chief god and sun god was Baal Hammon (Baal Amon).

Hades (Pluto)

One of the three large remnant islands of the Atlantic Island was sacred to the god Pluto, also known as Hades. In Ancient Greek religion and myth, Hades was the name of the ruler of the underworld and the name of the underworld itself. The natives would have used the name and attributes of their god of the underworld when describing the main god of the island. The Phoenicians' god of the underworld and death was Melqart, the chief deity of Tyre and its two colonies: Carthage and Gadir (Cadiz).

Amun
Source: Wikimedia Commons – Jeff Dahl

The god Hades received the rule of the underworld in the three-way division of the world with his two brothers, Zeus and Poseidon. In older Greek myths, the realm of Hades is the misty and gloomy abode of the dead, also called Erebus, where all mortals go. Several sections of the realm of Hades included Elysium, the Asphodel Meadows, and Tartarus.

The Greek name Plouton gradually replaced the name of the god Hades. Plouton was frequently merged with the name of the Greek god of wealth, Plutus or Ploutos because mineral wealth was found underground. Pluto is the Latinised name of Plouton, which the Romans used for the ruler of the underworld.

Persephone

In Proclus' commentary on the *Timaeus*, Marcellus claims that some of the remnant islands of the Atlantic Island, possibly some of the Lesser Antilles islands in the Caribbean, were 'the seven islands sacred to Persephone' – a very ancient Greek goddess of vegetation, especially grain.

Though the origins of the Persephone cult are uncertain, it was based on cults of agricultural communities. Second millennium BCE tablets from Mycenaean-era Pylos record sacrificial goods destined for the Two Queens and Poseidon and to the Two Queens and the King. The Two Queens may be Demeter and Persephone, goddesses not associated with Poseidon in the later Classical period.

Persephone and her mother Demeter were vegetation goddesses and the central figures of the Eleusinian mysteries, which predated the Olympian pantheon. In later Olympian Greek mythology, Persephone was the daughter of Zeus and Demeter. Persephone became queen of the underworld after being abducted by the god Hades. She had to stay in the underworld during the winter months each year; she then returned above for the remainder of the year. Persephone's abduction to the underworld represents vegetation, which rises in Spring but then withdraws into the Earth after the harvest in Winter.

The natives on the remnant islands must have worshipped a vegetation goddess, so the Old World travellers equated the natives' goddess with Persephone. The Carthaginians adopted the Greek cults of Persephone and Demeter in 396 BCE due to a plague seen as divine retribution for the Carthaginian desecration of these goddesses' shrines at Syracuse.

Hades with Cerberus
Source: Wikimedia Commons – Heraklion Archaeological Museum

Zeus

Plato – 'Zeus, the god of gods, who rules according to law, and is able to see into such things, perceiving that an honourable race (the Atlanteans) was in a woeful plight, and wanting to inflict punishment on them, that they may be chastened and improve, collected all the gods into their most holy habitation, which, being placed in the centre of the world, beholds all created things. And when he had called them together, he spake as follows'...(the rest of the *Critias* dialogue has been lost).

At the end of the incomplete *Critias* dialogue, Zeus is about to pronounce the Atlanteans' fate. Other than at the beginning of the Atlantis story, where Poseidon, Athena and Hephaestus are mentioned briefly as creators of culture, there is no further involvement of any Greek gods in human affairs. In the *Timaeus* and *Critias*, none of the works or behaviours of the Atlanteans, Athenians, or Egyptians contain any divine actions, interventions, or pronouncements. In his many other dialogues, Plato does not describe individual Olympian gods interfering in the activities of people.

As Zeus was not mentioned previously in either the Timaeus or Critias, it seems strange that he would enter the Atlantis story in such an important role that decides the fate of the Atlanteans. Unfortunately, as the remainder of the Critias is lost, we do not know Zeus' proclamation or whether the gods played any further role in the Atlantis story. Also, a later writer possibly added Zeus' part after the remainder of Plato's Critias was lost, giving a final moral meaning to the Atlantis story. But there is no pronouncement by Zeus, so even a possible later addition may have been lost.

As the leader of the Olympian gods, Zeus only dates from the Late Greek Bronze Age, many thousands of years after the action of the Atlantis story in 11,600 BP. Before the Greeks began to worship the Olympian gods, the prehistoric Aegean, Anatolian, and ancient Near Eastern cultures worshipped a Mother Goddess or Great Goddess in the forms of Cybele, Gaia and Rhea. In later Classical Greece, Olympian goddesses, including Hera and Demeter, had mother-goddess attributes.

In Greek mythology, when Zeus, Poseidon and Hades drew lots to see who would become the supreme ruler of the gods, Zeus won and reigned as the leader of the Olympian gods. He became the presiding ruler of Heaven and Earth, the god of all aerial phenomena, the personification of the laws of nature, the lord of state life, and the father of gods and men. His weapon was the thunderbolt, which he hurled at those who displeased him.

Unlike Athena and Hephaestus, Zeus has no direct Egyptian equivalent. Nevertheless, during the height of Amun's cult, the Egyptians considered Amun their supreme god. So when Greeks travelled to Egypt, they thought Amun was the Egyptian pantheon's ruler. Being similar to Zeus as the leader of the Greek pantheon, the Greeks identified Amun and Zeus as the same deity. Likewise, Amun's consort Mut became associated by the Greeks with Zeus' consort, Hera. Therefore, a possible explanation for mentioning Zeus in the Atlantis story is that Solon translated the Egyptian god Amun into the interchangeable Greek deity of Zeus. Still, that does not explain why Zeus/Amun had any role in the Atlantis story.

'foreigners'

In the 'sacred registers' that Solon viewed at Sais, the very early Egyptians had translated the literal meaning of the names of 'foreigners' into equivalent Egyptian names. Solon translated the Egyptian names into comparable Greek names, and Plato then used those Greek names in his Atlantis dialogues.

The most likely foreigners in the Atlantis story would be any Atlanteans or non-Greek allies of the Athenians engaged in the Mediterranean War. But in what survives of the Atlantis story, the only foreigners' names are of a few Atlanteans from the origin story of Atlantis. There are no names of any Atlanteans or non-Greek military allies participating in the Mediterranean War. Their feats were most likely in the lost part of the *Critias* dialogue, which would have described the War's participants and events.

Statue of Zeus at Olympia
Source: Wikimedia Commons

Plato – '(on the Atlantic Island) there dwelt one of the Earth born primaeval men of that country, whose name was Evenor, and he had a wife named Leucippe, and they had an only daughter who was called Cleito' 'He (Poseidon) also begat and brought up five pairs of twin male children'…'And he named them all; the eldest, who was the first king, he named Atlas, and after him the whole island and the ocean were called Atlantic. To his (Atlas') twin brother' 'he gave the name which in the Hellenic language is Eumelus, in the language of the country which is named after him, Gadeirus'…'Of the second pair of twins he called one Ampheres, and the other Evaemon'…'To the elder of the third pair of twins he gave the name Mneseus, and Autochthon to the one who followed him'…'Of the fourth pair of twins, he called the elder Elasippus, and the younger Mestor'…And of the fifth pair he gave to the elder the name of Azaes, and to the younger that of Diaprepes.'

Atlas is the only Atlantean name from the Atlantis story mentioned anywhere in Greek mythology. Atlas was the primordial Titan who supported the heavens; his name's origin is uncertain but probably pre-Greek. Despite being associated with various locations, Atlas became commonly identified with the Atlas Mountains in North-West Africa. As stated by Plato, North-West Africa was a part of the Atlantean Empire, so any later ancient people living there might have mythologised and linked that region with the Atlantean name Atlas.

The translation sequence of the Atlanteans' names would have been Atlantean to Egyptian to Greek. None of the Greek names represents any significant known character in Greek mythology or history. Therefore, it seems extremely unlikely that Plato randomly chose them for the Atlantis story.

The following are approximate English meanings of the Greek names for the Atlanteans:

- Evenor – the joy of men or perhaps abounding in men
- Leucippe – white horse – a woman's name
- Cleito – famous – a woman's name
- Eumelus – good-song
- Ampheres – fitted on both sides
- Evaemon – good-blood
- Mneseus – something to do with memory – perhaps memorable
- Elasippus – horse-driving or horse-riding
- Mestor – advisor
- Azaes – something to do with heat/dry
- Diaprepes – distinguished

Ancient Old and New World cultures had technologies and social structures identical or similar to those of the Atlanteans

CHAPTER 6

Atlantean Civilistaion and Ancient Technologies

Atlantean technology of 11,600 BP is consistent with at least a Bronze Age level of civilisation. If true, the Atlanteans developed those technologies thousands of years before archaeological evidence for them anywhere else on Earth. A key argument against Atlantean culture insists such a sophisticated civilisation could not have existed around 11,600 BP. Despite that assumption, the Atlanteans were all *Homo sapiens* like us, whether they were the original inhabitants of the Atlantic Island or later migrants to the island. As discussed in Chapter 3, those ancient people had the same intellectual and physical capabilities as everyone living now and had the same potential to develop a civilisation.

In both the Old and New Worlds, within a few thousand years and with the right physical environment, known civilisations developed from hunter-gatherers to Neolithic farming cultures and then into much more advanced civilisations. The Atlanteans' ancestors possibly created a Neolithic culture well before 11,600 BP, and they might have done so before or after they arrived on the Atlantic Island. It would then have taken many hundreds or possibly thousands of years for the Atlanteans to progress from a Neolithic to a Bronze Age civilisation by 11,600 BP.

Ancient cultures in the Old and New Worlds had technologies and social structures identical or similar to those of the Atlanteans. Notably, the ancient civilisations of the Americas seem to have created most of the features of Atlantean civilisation without any obvious Old World influences. The following sections give some examples of pre-mechanised technology equivalent to Atlantean technology. Those technologies reveal the mostly forgotten achievements of past Neolithic, Bronze, and Iron Age societies. There is no logical reason to reject the Atlantean people's capacity to create similar technologies or any other features of the Atlantean Empire that Plato describes.

The Royal City of Atlantis

The Atlanteans' Royal City is much larger than any of the world's cities of Plato's time or until the beginning of the 20th century CE. Plato describes the Royal City precisely. He includes information on its location, exact measurements of its size and design, descriptions of its buildings, and the functions of different parts of the city. It is doubtful whether Plato needed such elaborations to prove a philosophical point about the Atlanteans.

The Location of the Atlanteans' Royal City

Plato – 'Near the plain (of the Atlantic Island – the Venezuelan Basin) again, and also in the centre of the (Atlantic) island at a distance of about fifty stadia (from the nearest coast), there was a mountain not very high on any side (at the centre of the Royal City)'...' This part of the island looked towards the south, and was sheltered from the north.'

Plato – 'The whole country (of the Atlantic Island) was said by him (Solon) to be very lofty and precipitous on the side of the sea, but the country immediately about and surrounding the (Royal) city was a level plain, itself surrounded by mountains which descended towards the sea.'

The central point of the Atlanteans' Royal City was a small mountain or hill located 'fifty stadia' or 10.5 kilometres from the nearest coast. But, the Royal City was in the 'centre of the island'. If the island's geographical centre were in the middle of the Plain of Atlantis (the Venezuelan Basin), it would be hundreds of kilometres from any coastline, not just 10.5km inland. By 'centre of the island', Plato must mean the Royal City was near the 'centre' of one of the island's coastlines. Because the area around the City 'looked towards the south', that coastline must be on the Atlantic Island's south side.

Plato describes high cliffs, 'very lofty and precipitous', along the coast at the Royal City's location. If the southern edge of the now-submerged Venezuelan Basin were once tilted upward and raised above sea level, the Atlantic Island's southern coastline would have been a sea cliff hundreds of kilometres long. Despite this, the centre of the Royal City was only a few kilometres from the coast, and ships could sail into the City from the sea. Therefore, some section of the southern coastline was at or near sea level and close to the City.

Though the Royal City was 'Near the plain', it was not actually on the vast Plain of the Atlantic Island. The Royal City was on 'a level plain, itself surrounded by mountains which descended towards the sea'. This description implies it was on a separate, smaller plain alongside the much larger Plain of Atlantis and was 'sheltered from the north' by mountains.

Molokai Sea Cliffs
Source: Wikimedia Commons – Jay

To the west of the Plain of Atlantis, the southern end of the Western Mountains (the emergent Beata Ridge) has high parallel ridges coming off the central mountain range. Some of those secondary ridges may have held a small plain between them that contained the Royal City and sheltered it from the north wind.

Putting all of Plato's geographical descriptions together, the most likely location of the Atlantean Royal City is somewhere along the western part of the Atlantic Island's southern coast. This location would place it in the 'centre of the island' and 'Near the plain' of Atlantis. It is also where the Western Mountains' secondary ridges would have 'descended towards the sea' to create a small plain around the Royal City.

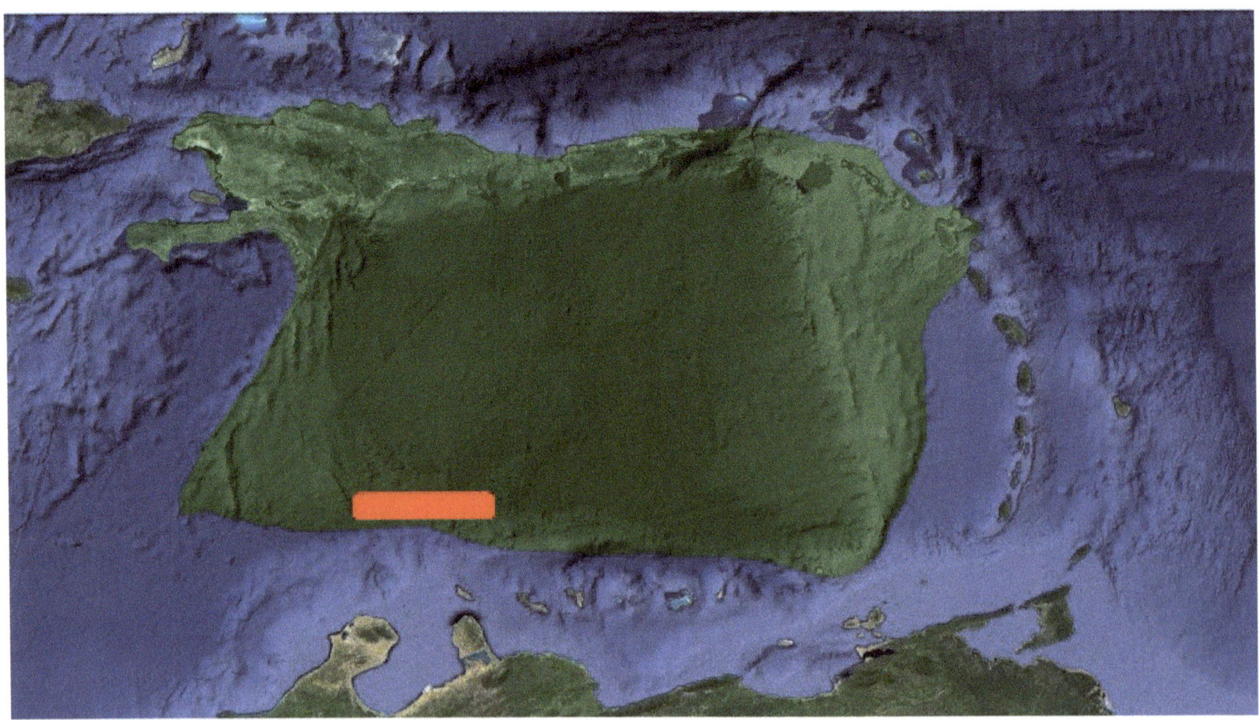

Possible Locations of the Royal City
Source: Modified from Google Earth

The Circular Zones of Sea and Land

The central part of the Royal City was on a small hill surrounded by several concentric rings of sea and land. The hill was highest in the centre and sloped evenly down to the surrounding land – 'a mountain not very high on any side'.

Plato – 'Poseidon...breaking the ground, inclosed the (Royal City's central) hill'…'all round, making alternate zones of sea and land larger and smaller, encircling one another; there were two of land and three of water'…'as if made by a turner's wheel, (they) were in all parts equidistant from the middle of the (central) island.'

A natural formation called a dome could have been the initial geological structure of those concentric rings of land and water. A dome forms an elliptical or circular outcropping on the Earth's surface. It consists of folded rock layers that are concave downward and dip outward from a central point.

A dome is formed by an uplift of less dense material from below (diapirism), usually partially molten rock, pushing up the overlying rock. If the top of a dome is eroded flat, it looks like a bulls-eye from above. The youngest rock layers are on the outside, with each ring being older toward the centre. The Richat Structure in Mauritania is an example of a dome.

Millions of years ago, there was volcanic activity on the floor of the Venezuelan Basin, possibly creating a dome there. The dome surface eventually eroded once the Venezuelan Basin rose above sea level. The small hill formed the centre, with the concave rings of the dome filling naturally with water to form the three zones of water, while the higher rings formed the two zones of land.

If the Atlanteans eventually mythologised Poseidon as a powerful god and Earth Shaker, they may have believed he created the initial geological formation of the concentric rings of the Royal City.

Dome Structure

Richat Structure, Oudane, Mauritania
Source: Wikimedia Commons – NASA/GSFC/MITI/ERSDAC/JAROS

The Circular Zones and the 'Canal to the Sea'

The Atlanteans dug a canal from the sea to the outermost zone of water around the centre of the Royal City. The canal allowed ships to sail directly into the Royal City, and the outermost water zone became a harbour. Plato gives precise dimensions for the canal and each circular land and water zone and describes how the Atlanteans used each land zone.

Plato – 'beginning from the sea they (the Atlanteans) bored a canal of three hundred feet (100 metres) in width and one hundred feet (30 metres) in depth and fifty stadia (10.5 kilometres) in length, which they carried through to the outermost (water) zone, making a passage from the sea up to this, which

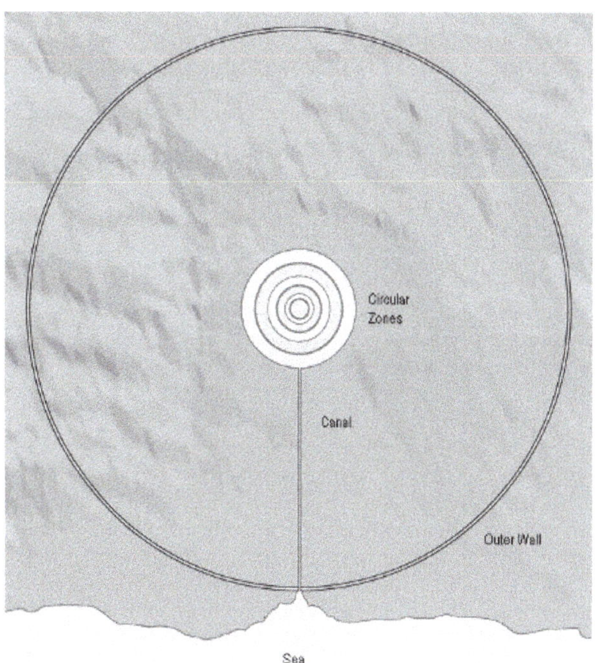

Outline of the Royal City

became a harbour, and leaving an opening sufficient to enable the largest vessels to find ingress'...'as they quarried, they at the same time hollowed out double docks, having roofs formed out of the native rock'... 'The docks were full of triremes and naval stores, and all things were quite ready for use.'

Plato – 'the largest of the (circular water) zones into which a passage was cut from the sea was three stadia (630 metres) in breadth, and the zone of land which came next of equal breadth (630 metres); but the next two zones, the one of water, the other of land, were two stadia (420 metres), and the (water) one which surrounded the central island was a stadium (209 metres) only in width.'

Using Plato's dimensions for the Central Island and the Outer Zones, the land areas are:

- Central Island – 0.78km2 or 78 hectares
- First zone of land – 2.42km2 or 242 hectares
- Second zone of land – 7.33km2 or 733 hectares

Whether the zones were initially the natural ring formations of a geological dome or not, the Atlanteans would have further excavated them to the dimensions Plato describes. They also excavated a 10.5-kilometre-long canal that connected the water zones to the sea.

Plato – 'In the next place (the first land zone out from the central island), they had fountains, one of cold and another of hot water.' A fountain of hot water could only have had two sources: a natural hot spring or artificially heated water. As there is evidence of past volcanic activity in the Venezuelan Basin, there may have been hot springs when the floor of the Basin was above sea level.

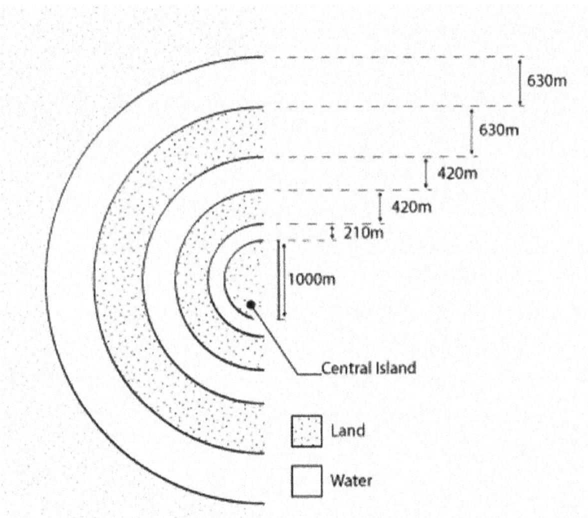

The Dimensions of the Circular Zones of Land and Water

Plato – 'Of the water which ran off (from the fountains in the first land zone) they carried some to the grove of Poseidon, where were growing all manner of trees of wonderful height and beauty, owing to the excellence of the soil, while the remainder was conveyed by aqueducts along the bridges to the outer circles; and there were many temples built and dedicated to many gods.'

Plato – 'They constructed buildings about them and planted suitable trees, also they made cisterns, some open to the heavens, others roofed over, to be used in winter as warm baths; there were the kings' baths, and the baths of private persons, which were kept apart; and there were separate baths for women, and for horses and cattle'...'also gardens and places of exercise, some for men, and others for horses in both of the two islands formed by the zones; and in

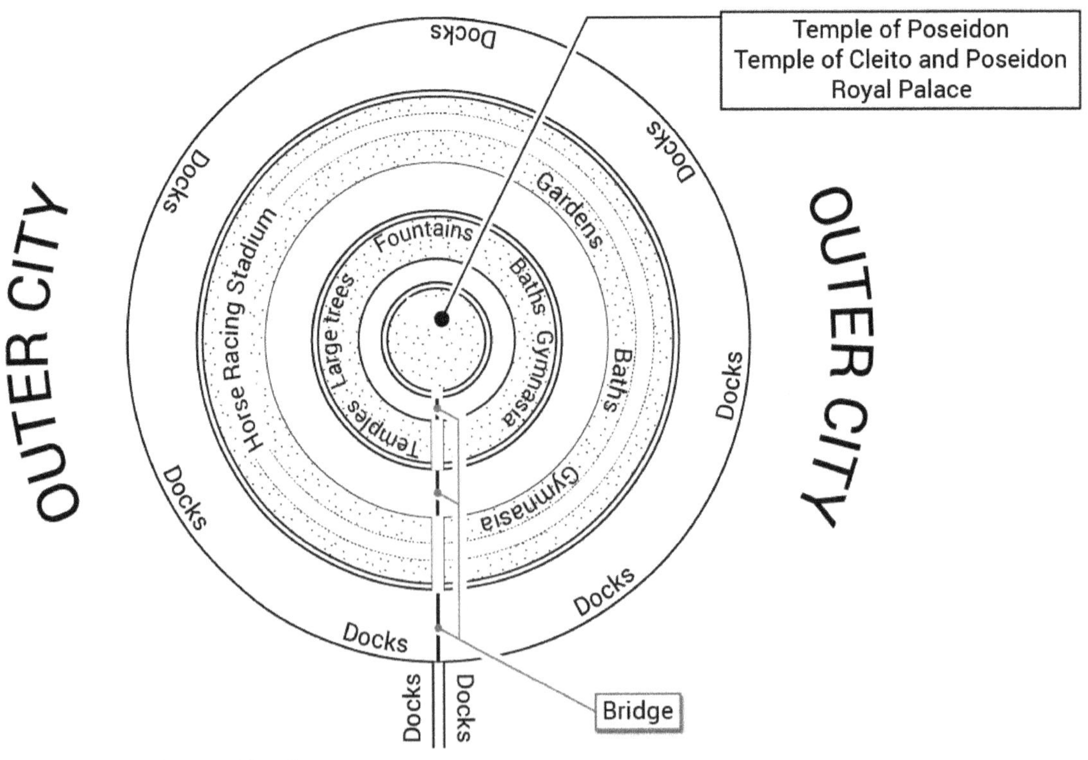

The Central Island and Zones of Sea and Land

The Royal City of the Atlantic Island

the centre of the larger of the two (the second land zone out from the Central Island) there was set apart a race-course of a stadium (209 metres) in width, and in length allowed to extend all round the island, for horses to race in.'

Plato – 'Also there were guardhouses at intervals for the guards, the more trusted of whom were appointed to keep watch in the lesser zone (first land zone out from the Central Island), which was nearer the (Central) Acropolis while the most trusted of all had houses given them within the citadel (on the Central Island), near the persons of the kings.'

The Central Island

Plato – 'The (Central) island in which the (Royal) palace was situated had a diameter of five stadia (one kilometre)'…'they bridged over the zones of sea which surrounded the ancient metropolis (on the Central Island), making a road to and from the royal palace'…'All this including the zones and the bridge, which was the sixth part of a stadium (35 metres) in width, they surrounded by a stone wall on every side, placing towers and gates on the bridges where the sea passed in.'

Plato – 'The palaces in the interior of the citadel were constructed on this wise: in the centre was a holy temple dedicated to Cleito and Poseidon, which remained inaccessible, and was surrounded by an enclosure of gold; this was the spot where the family of the ten princes (the children of Poseidon and Cleito) first saw the light, and thither the people annually brought the fruits of the Earth in their season from all the ten portions (kingdoms), to be an offering to each of the ten'…'at the very beginning they built the (Royal) palace in the habitation of the god (Poseidon) and of their ancestors (on the Central Island), which they continued to ornament in successive generations, every king surpassing the one who went before him to the utmost of his power, until they made the building a marvel to behold for size and for beauty.'

The Temple of Poseidon

Plato – 'Here (on the Central Island) was Poseidon's own temple (separate to the Temple of Cleito and Poseidon) which was a stadium in length (209 metres) and half a stadium in width (105 metres) and of a proportionate height, having a strange barbaric appearance. All the outside of the temple, with the exception of the pinnacles, they covered with silver, and the pinnacles with gold. In the interior of the temple the roof was of ivory, curiously wrought everywhere with gold and silver and orichalcum; and all the other parts, the walls and pillars and floor, they coated with orichalcum.' Orichalcum is a metal mentioned in several ancient writings and is thought to be either a gold-copper, copper-tin or copper-zinc alloy or a metal no longer known.

At 209 metres long by 105 metres wide, Plato's dimensions for the Temple of Poseidon are much greater than any known temple of the Ancient Egyptians or Greeks. However, several Old and New World buildings indicate how pre-mechanised civilisations could create very large stone structures.

Hypostyle Hall, Karnak
Source: Wikimedia Commons – Nadine Lee

Reconstruction of the Temple of Artemis, Ephesus

Temple of the Warriors, Chichen Itza
Source: Wikimedia Commons – Andre Moller

Governor's Palac, Uxmal
Source: Wikimedia Commons – Wolfgang Sauber

The Hypostyle Hall at the Karnak Temple Complex in Egypt is one-quarter the size of the Atlanteans' Temple of Poseidon. Built around the 19th Egyptian Dynasty (ca. 1290–1224 BCE), it measures 103 metres long and 52 metres wide, with an area of 5,000m². It has 134 massive columns, each with a diameter of over three metres. One hundred and twenty-two of these columns are 10 metres tall, while the other 12 are 21 metres tall. They are arranged in 16 rows and once supported a ceiling 24 metres high.

The Greek Temple of Artemis at Ephesus, constructed around 323 BCE, was considered one of the Seven Wonders of the Ancient World. It was 137 metres long by 69 metres wide and 18 metres high, with more than 127 columns.

In Mesoamerica, the Maya constructed columned buildings of a scale similar to those in the Old World. The Temple of the Warriors at Chichen Itza was built on a three-tiered, stepped pyramid with four recessed terraces and a single stairway on the west, facing the Great Plaza. Its base is approximately 40 metres square. To the west and the south are two colonnades known as the Court of the Thousand Columns; the portion facing the plaza is 182 metres by 23 metres.

The Governor's Palace at the Maya site of Uxmal sits on a triple terrace 15 metres high and covers two hectares. The palace itself is 100 metres long, 12 metres wide, 8 metres high, and contains twenty-four chambers. Elaborate mosaics decorate its four facades with 20,000 specially cut and fitted stone elements.

Most Mesoamerican civilisations built large pyramid structures with a temple on the summit. Successive rulers often added to these pyramids, which grew layer upon layer until they reached a massive size. The Atlanteans' Temple of Poseidon may have resembled a pyramidal structure rather than a columned temple.

In South America, at the remote Inca fortress of Incallajta, the Kallanka is a rectangular building of

Pyramid of the Magician, Uxmal
Source: Wikimedia Commons – Sybz

Inca Walls in Cuzco

78 by 26 metres, covered by a gable roof supported by columns. It is the largest known roofed building in the Inca Empire and was used for ceremonies and mass meetings. Larger Inca buildings may have once existed but have not survived.

Apart from its enormous size, Plato describes Poseidon's temple as having a 'strange barbaric appearance' with 'curiously wrought' decoration, so it must have looked quite different to any Egyptian, Greek or Mesopotamian temples known in Solon or Plato's time.

The monumental buildings of Mesoamerica and South America, built in the Americas thousands of years after the fall of Atlantean civilisation, may indicate the possible architectural style of Atlantis. In particular, the temple decorations of Mesoamerican civilisations were unlike anything found in the Old World, so they would appear 'strange' and 'curiously wrought' compared to those known to the Ancient Egyptians and Greeks.

The Statue of Poseidon

Plato – 'In the temple (of Poseidon) they placed statues of gold: there was the god himself standing in a chariot, the charioteer of six winged horses, and of such a size that he touched the roof of the building with his head; around him there were a hundred Nereids riding on dolphins.' In Greek myths, the

Mesoamerican Ornamentation

Nereids were fifty Nymphs or goddesses of the sea who were the patrons of sailors and fishermen, coming to their aid if in distress. Together with the Tritones (fish-tailed mermaid-like sea creatures), they formed the retinue of Poseidon.

Monumental statues were common in the ancient cultures of Mesoamerica and the Andes. A colossal basalt statue carved around the 5th century CE was discovered in the town of Coatlinchan, Mexico. It is thought to represent the god Tlaloc and weighs an estimated 168 tonnes, making it the largest existing ancient monolith in the Americas.

The Atlanteans' statue of Poseidon had him riding in a chariot pulled by 'six winged horses'. A possible explanation for several winged horses on Poseidon's statue is that the winged horse initially may have been a mythological creation of the Atlantean horse-raising culture many thousands of years before the Greeks adopted Pegasus into their myths.

Colossal Tlaloc Statue

Pegasus on Attic red-figure jug, 480–460 BCE
Source: Wikimedia – Bibi Saint-Pol

In Greek art, there are many representations of Poseidon driving a chariot pulled by horses but never winged horses. The divine white stallion Pegasus is the only winged horse mentioned in Greek mythology before Plato's time, and there are no winged horses in Egyptian mythology. There is never more than one winged horse in Greek art, and Pegasus never pulled a chariot. Unlike the Atlanteans' Poseidon statue, there are no Greek myths or images of several winged horses pulling a chariot, so it is doubtful that Plato fabricated such an image.

The Greek poet Hesiod (ca. 700 BCE) gave a folk origin of the name Pegasus, derived from *pēgē*, meaning spring or well. The cult of Pegasus may have begun in Egypt, as the oldest shrine of Osiris at Abydos (ca. 2000 BCE) centred on a sacred spring called Pega. In Greek mythology, Pegasus had a direct connection with Poseidon. Pegasus' father was Poseidon, while his mother was the snake-haired Gorgon called Medusa. Pegasus and his brother Chrysaor were born together at precisely the same time the hero Perseus decapitated their mother, Medusa.

Pegasus and Chrysaor were born in a distant place at the edge of Earth. It was beyond the Pillars of Atlas at the springs of Oceanus, which the Greeks thought was the single ocean encircling the inhabited Earth. Chrysaor was often depicted as a young man and is said to have been the king of Iberia (Andorra, Gibraltar, Spain, and Portugal). In the Atlantis story, the region of Iberia would once have been part of the Atlantean Empire.

Gold and Silver Statues and Temple Decorations

Plato – 'also in the interior of the temple (of Poseidon), other images which had been dedicated by private persons'...'around the temple on the outside were placed statues of gold of all the descendants of the ten kings and of their wives, and there were many other great offerings of kings and of private persons, coming both from the city itself and from the foreign cities over which they held sway'...'All the outside of the temple, with the exception of the pinnacles, they covered with silver, and the pinnacles with gold. In the interior of the temple the roof was of ivory, curiously wrought everywhere with gold and silver.'

Gold was the first metal to be manipulated by ancient South Americans. Andean cultures began smelting gold and other nonferrous ores in the Early Horizon period (1000–400 BCE). Silver first appeared in the late 1st millennium BCE in small personal adornments. It was less valuable than gold as tribute, so it was less used.

The Inca equated gold with the sun god Inti. Some Inca buildings in the capital of Cuzco were

Reconstruction of the Altar to Zeus in the Pergamonmuseum, Berlin
Source: Wikimedia Commons - Lestat (Jan Mehlich)

covered in gold, and most buildings contained numerous gold and silver sculptures. In the Temple of the Sun in Cuzco, there was a garden filled with life-sized plants, animals, men and women made of gold. The Inca Emperor Atahualpa had a portable throne of solid gold that reportedly weighed 83 kilograms. When the Spanish captured Atahualpa in 1532 CE, he agreed to fill a large room half-full with gold and twice-full with silver in return for his freedom. There were over 5,000 kilograms of gold and twice that much silver when melted down, but the Spanish executed him regardless.

Gold metalwork occurred relatively late in Mesoamerica, with distinctive objects appearing in west Mexico from around 800 CE. Artisans focused on making jewellery, display items, sheet metal breastplates, crowns, and objects that could produce sound.

(Maya) Stela E, Quiriguá, Guatemala
Source: Alfred Maudsley

Altars

Plato – '(in the Temple of Poseidon) there was an altar too, which in size and workmanship corresponded to this magnificence (of the statue and Temple of Poseidon).'

An altar is any structure upon which offerings such as sacrifices are made for religious purposes. In Mesoamerica, altars at the top of the great pyramid temples were used for human and animal sacrifice to appease the gods. Sacrificial altars were also a part of religious ceremonies in the ancient cultures of South America.

In Egypt, an offering hall in a temple included one or more altars where sacrifices were made to the gods. Ancient Greek ceremonies and rituals were usually performed at altars and were devoted to one or a few gods. Votive offerings such as food, drinks and precious objects would be left at the altar, where there would be a statue of the particular deity.

The Greeks would also perform animal sacrifices, with most of the flesh eaten and the offal burnt as an offering to the gods. During special religious ceremonies, a *hecatomb* was a sacrifice to the gods of one hundred cattle, but in practice, as few as twelve cattle could make up a hecatomb.

Pillars and Stelae

Plato – 'the commands of Poseidon which the law had handed down. These were inscribed by the first kings (of Atlantis) on a pillar of orichalcum, which was situated in the middle of the (central) island, at the temple of Poseidon.'

In Mesoamerica, the tradition of raising stelae (upright stone slabs or columns) had its earliest known origin among the Olmec, and hundreds of stelae are found in the Maya region. These stelae range in height from one to ten metres and are often made of limestone, with one or more faces sculpted with figures and hieroglyphic text.

In Peru, in the temple at Chavin de Huantar, the Lanzon is a 4.53-metre-tall carved granite shaft erected in about 500 BCE. It is carved with

The Lanzon

an image of a fanged deity, the main cult image of the Chavin people. Also at Chavin de Huantar, the 2.52-metre-tall Tello Obelisk features images of plants and animals, including caymans, birds, crops and human figures.

Sacred Animals and Animal Sacrifice

Plato – 'There were bulls who had the range of the temple of Poseidon'…'the bull which they (the Kings of Atlantis) caught they led up to the pillar (of orichalcum in the Temple of Poseidon) and cut its throat over the top of it so that the blood fell upon the sacred inscription.'

The Olmec, Maya and Aztec revered the jaguar as a symbol of fertility and warrior spirit. The tribes of Peru worshipped great snakes in pre-Inca times, while feline figures and eagles were significant religious motifs in Chavin art.

Although the Olmec possibly originated the practice of animal sacrifice in Mesoamerica, it may have existed before them. It is unclear whether the Olmec practised human sacrifice, but it was common in all later Mesoamerican cultures. The Maya had many festivals and rituals on fixed days of the year, many of which involved animal sacrifices and bloodletting. White-tailed deer were the most common sacrificial and festive food animal. Other sacrificial animals were dogs, various birds, and a

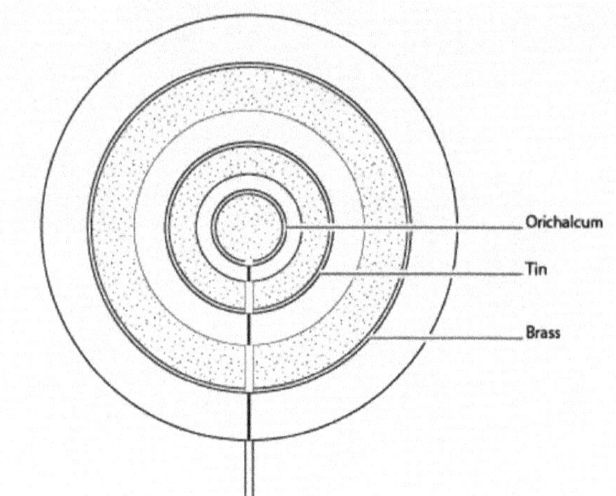

The Inner Walls of the Royal City

wide range of more exotic creatures, from jaguars to alligators.

In South America, the Inca and earlier Andean indigenous cultures practised animal and human sacrifice. Guinea pigs, alpacas, llamas, prepared food, coca leaves, and chicha (an alcoholic maize beverage) were used in Inca sacrifices.

The Inner Walls of the Royal City

Plato – 'the entire circuit of the wall, which went round the outermost zone (second land zone out from the Central Island), they (the Atlanteans) covered with a coating of brass, and the circuit of the next wall (first land zone out from the Central Island) they coated with tin, and the third, which encompassed the citadel (Central Island) flashed with the red light of orichalcum.'

The approximate length of the circuit for each wall around the outer side of the land zones is:

- Central Island – 3 kilometres
- First zone of land – 7 kilometres
- Second zone of land – 13 kilometres

It is assumed that the walls were built of stone or brick and then covered with metal sheets. To estimate the quantity of metal required to cover the walls, if each wall was ten metres high and the metal sheet five millimetres thick, then:

- Central Island – 150 cubic metres of orichalcum
- First zone of land – 350 cubic metres of tin
- Second zone of land – 650 cubic metres of brass

The Outer Wall and the Royal City's Population

Plato – 'Leaving the (Royal) palace and passing out across the three (zones of land) you came to a wall which began at the sea and went all round (the Royal City): this was everywhere distant fifty stadia (10.5 kilometres) from the largest zone (of water) or harbour, and enclosed the whole (Royal City), the

The Entire Atlantean Royal City

ends meeting at the mouth of the channel which led to the sea'…'The entire area (from the inner walls to the outer wall) was densely crowded with habitations; and the canal (to the sea) and the largest of the harbours were full of vessels and merchants coming from all parts.'

Plato describes a circular Outer Wall surrounding the entire Royal City. The radius from the middle of the central island to the Outer Wall is 13 kilometres, so the Outer Wall's circumference is around 80 kilometres, enclosing an area of 530km². After subtracting the areas of the circular zones and any internal canals, the part of the Royal City that was 'densely crowded with habitations' was around 500km². In comparison, the total area of New York City is 1,200km², Greater London is 1,600km², and Tokyo is 2,100km².

Archaeologists use various estimates of population density for ancient cities and towns, ranging from 100 people per hectare to over 400 per hectare. If the outer part of the Royal City had an area of 500km² (50,000 hectares) 'densely crowded with habitations', a conservative population density of 100 people per hectare would give the Royal City a population of around five million.

Ancient Cities

If the Atlanteans developed large cities by 11,600 BP, they did so several thousand years before anywhere else known on Earth. The conventional view is that cities first formed after the Neolithic Revolution when hunter-gatherer groups abandoned nomadic lifestyles to begin farming. Agriculture increased food output per unit of land and allowed enough surplus food to support trade and a relatively large settled population.

Although there are no exact criteria to define a city, there are some general conditions:

- Increased size and density of the population more than that of small settlements
- An organised system of government
- Differentiation of the population where not all residents grow their own food, leading to specialised occupations
- Trade and import of raw materials
- Payment of taxes to a deity or king
- Those not producing their own food are supported by the resources controlled by the king or priesthood

- Monumental public buildings
- A system of writing or recording information
- Systems of practical science
- Development of symbolic art

Over thousands of years, early cities developed in several regions of the ancient world. In the Old World in the 4th millennium BCE, the Sumerians in Mesopotamia had the earliest known cities, such as Eridu, Uruk and Urin. Each of these cities had populations in the tens of thousands. In the north-west Indian subcontinent, Mohenjo-Daro was one of several cities of the Indus Valley Civilisation and had a population of 50,000 or more from 2600 BCE.

In the 7th century BCE, Babylon was the first city known to have had a population of over 200,000. Ancient Rome had a population of one million by the end of the 1st century BCE, making it the largest city in the world at the time. In Egypt, Alexandria's population was also close to Rome's in the 1st century BCE, while in China, Changan's (Xi'an) population was 420,000. In the 1st century CE, the population of Antioch in Asia Minor was 150,000 and Anuradhapura in Sri Lanka was 130,000.

In Mesoamerica, large cities developed in several cultural regions, including the Preclassic Maya, the Zapotec of Oaxaca, and Teotihuacan in central Mexico. The Olmec city of San Lorenzo was the largest in Mesoamerica from roughly 1200 BCE to 900 BCE, with a population of up to 13,000. The Maya settlement of El Mirador flourished from the 6th century BCE and reached its height from the 3rd century BCE to the 1st century CE, with a peak population of more than 100,000. In the first half of the 1st millennium CE, Teotihuacan was the largest city in the pre-Columbian Americas, covering over 30km^2 and may have had more than 200,000 inhabitants. In the early 1500s CE, the Aztec capital of Tenochtitlan was one of the largest cities in the world, with the most common estimates of the population being over 200,000.

In the Andes, the first urban centres developed from 3000 BCE in the Norte Chico, Chavin and Moche civilisations, followed by major cities in the Huari, Tiwanaku, Chimu and Inca civilisations. Before the Spanish arrived, the population of the Inca capital Cusco is estimated at 126,000 for the urban zone plus 100,000 for the rural district, giving a total population of around 225,000.

Defensive Walls

Based on Plato's description, the Atlantean Royal City's circular Outer Wall was 80 kilometres long. Still, he does not specify whether the Outer Wall was for the City's defence, though that seems likely because the Atlanteans were a warlike society.

For thousands of years, defensive walls were necessary around ancient cities in the Old World. The town of Jericho in the Middle East was 2.5 hectares in size and had a wall surrounding it as early as the 10th millennium BP, making it the oldest known defensive wall. Uruk in ancient Sumer in Mesopotamia is one of the world's oldest known walled cities. At its height around 2900 BCE, Uruk probably had a population of 50,000–80,000 living within 6km^2 of walled area, making it the largest city in the world at that time. Some settlements in the Indus Valley Civilisation (3300–1900 BCE) were fortified, and large rammed-earth walls were being built in Ancient China since at least the Liangzhu Culture (ca. 3400–2250 BCE).

Besides long defensive walls being built around cities, they enclosed regions or marked territorial boundaries. The Great Wall of Gorgan is a series of ancient defensive fortifications near Gorgan in the Golestan Province of North-Eastern Iran. Probably built during the Parthian Empire (247 BCE–224 CE), it was restored during the Sassanid era (3rd to 7th century CE). It is 195km long, with over 30 fortresses spaced at 10 to 50 kilometres intervals.

The Great Wall of China is a series of fortifications comprising several walls, some built as early as the 7th century BCE. The walls were joined and extended until the 17th century CE and are collectively known as the Great Wall. When all branches are added together, the total length is 21,196km.

In Mesoamerica, many Maya cities had defensive walls, usually made of stone supported by wooden posts. In South America, the Huari site

Sacsayhuaman
Source: Wikimedia Commons

of Cotocotuyoc in Peru has an extensive perimeter wall, suggesting that the site functioned as a fortress. Near Cuzco, the Inca site of Sacsayhuaman is a 15th-century CE complex of tiered defensive walls built with stones weighing up to 300 tonnes.

Circular Walled Cities

The Atlantean Royal City had several concentric circular walls, starting with the wall around the Central Island and ending with the 80-kilometre-long wall around the periphery of the City. Some known ancient cities had a radial structure where main roads converged on a central point. The circular configuration was often due to several growth phases, with widening concentric town walls and citadels for each phase.

Mari was an ancient Sumerian and Amorite city on the Euphrates and was surrounded by two circular walls. It was probably inhabited since the 5th millennium BCE, with a series of superimposed palaces built over a thousand years from 2900 BCE until 1759 BCE when the Babylonian king Hammurabi sacked it.

Ecbatana, founded in 715 BCE in what is now Iran, was the capital of the Medes and later became the summer residence of the Achaemenid Persians. Herodotus described the city as being ringed with seven concentric walls: 'The circuit of the outer wall is very nearly the same with that of Athens. On this wall, the battlements are white, of the next black, of the third scarlet, of the fourth blue, the fifth orange; all these colours with paint. The last two have their battlements coated respectively with silver and gold.' The king and his court lived in the centre; lesser officials stayed in the outer rings in order of rank; commoners lived outside.

The 3rd century BCE Parthian city of Hatra in ancient Persia was surrounded by two circular walls and had a large temple complex in the centre. Another Parthian city, Darabjerd in southern Iran, had two rock formations within its circular wall; one was a castle, the other a temple.

Buildings of White, Black, and Red Stone

Plato – 'they (the Atlanteans) went on constructing their temples and palaces and harbours and docks'...'The stone which was used in the work they quarried from underneath the centre island, and from underneath the zones, on the outer as well as the inner side'...'One kind was white, another black, and a third red'...'Some of their buildings were simple, but in others they put together different stones, varying the colour.'

Limestone is the most likely type of rock the Atlanteans quarried and cut into blocks and slabs for

Red, white and black limestone

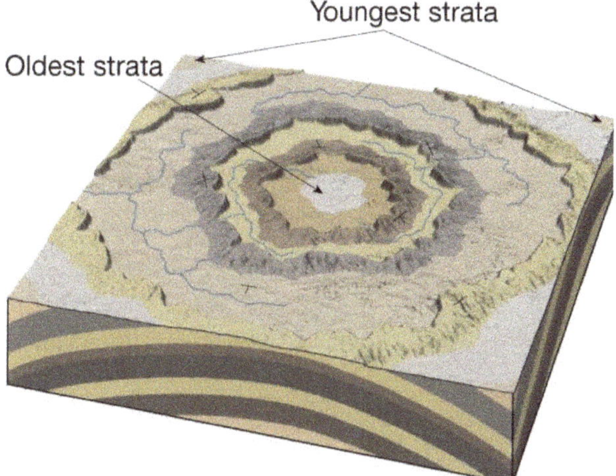

Dome Structure

construction. Limestone mainly comprises calcium carbonate ($CaCO_3$), with most limestones forming in shallow, calm, warm marine waters. Small marine organisms are the main source of the calcium carbonate. When these animals die, their shell and skeletal debris accumulate as sediment that can form limestone.

Impurities such as clay, sand, organic remains, iron oxide and other materials produce different colours in limestone. Those colours include white, black, and red – like the coloured stone the Atlanteans used to construct their buildings.

Before it emerged as the Plain of Atlantis, the Venezuelan Basin formed the bottom of a shallow sea for millions of years. That is the typical environment to create limestone, and different coloured layers would have formed there. A particular colour would depend on when the limestone layer formed and what impurities were present.

The Atlanteans quarried their building stone from the Central Island and the Circular Zones at the centre of the Royal City. If a dome structure lay under the centre of the Royal City, it may have contained several layers of limestone of different ages and colours. When the Venezuelan Basin was above sea level, the dome was eroded and formed a typical bullseye structure. The dome's various layers could have included white, black and red limestone. These different coloured limestones would have been close enough to the surface for the Atlanteans to quarry and shape building blocks for construction.

Reconstruction of Trajan's Bridge – E. Duperrex, 1907
Source: Wikimedia Commons

Bridges and Aqueducts

As stated by Plato, the Atlanteans built a set of bridges and aqueducts that went from the Central Island of the Royal City over the circular sea and land zones to the outer part of the City. The combined length of the bridges would have been 2,300 metres.

Plato – 'the bridge, which was the sixth part of a stadium (35 metres) in width'…'they (the Atlanteans) divided at the bridges the (circular) zones of land which parted the zones of sea, leaving room for a single trireme to pass out of one zone into another, and they covered over the channels so as to leave a way underneath for the ships; for the banks were raised considerably above the water.'

Compared to the Atlanteans' bridge, the Roman-era Trajan's Bridge (105 CE) across the Danube River was over 1,100 metres long, 15 metres wide and 19 metres high. Each arch spanned 38 metres and was set on masonry pillars made of bricks, mortar and cement.

In Mesoamerica, Maya engineers constructed numerous bridges using timber beams, with spans of up to 20 metres. Short-span bridges crossed streams, canals and moats in cities. A recently discovered three-span Maya suspension bridge was constructed in the late 7th century CE in the city of Yaxchilan. The Yaxchilan bridge reached 113 metres across a river, from the city's grand plaza to the northern shore.

Yaxchilan Bridge
Source: James O'Kon/David Morgan

The Yaxchilan bridge comprised a wooden deck suspended from rope cables stretched between cast-in-place concrete and stone towers topped by a Maya arch. The centre span was 63 metres long and rose 22 metres above the river. The bridge is considered to have had the longest single span in the ancient world until Italian engineers constructed a longer span in 1377 CE.

The Aztec capital of Tenochtitlan was situated on an island on the western side of the shallow Lake Texcoco. Three major causeways ran from the mainland into the city and were spanned by drawbridges that could be raised for defence.

Plato – 'while the remainder (of the water from the fountains in the first land zone) was conveyed by aqueducts along the bridges to the outer circles (of land zones).'

Despite being associated with the Romans in the Old World, aqueducts were devised much earlier in the Indian subcontinent, the Near East, and Greece. The Indian subcontinent has some of the earliest known aqueducts; those near the Tungabhadra River supplied irrigation water and were once 24 kilometres long. In the 7th century BCE, the Assyrians built an 80-km-long limestone aqueduct to carry water to their capital city of Nineveh. The aqueduct included a 10-metre-high section that crossed a valley 300 metres wide.

In Mesoamerica, at the 2nd millennium BCE Olmec site of San Lorenzo, joined sections of U-shaped carved stones covered with capstones formed elaborate drainage systems and hydraulic works. Aqueducts channelled water into sacred and decorative pools and created streams running throughout the complex for drinking and bathing. The Aztec capital Tenochtitlan was watered by two double-aqueducts, each more than four kilometres long and made of terracotta. They supplied the city of 200,000 with fresh water from springs on a mountain kilometres to the west of the city.

In South America, at an elevation of approximately 3,500 metres, Cumbe Mayo is the site of an eight-kilometres-long aqueduct constructed by an

Tambomachay
Source: Wikimedia Commons – Diego Delso

advanced pre-Inca culture around 1500 BCE. Near the Peruvian town of Nazca, an extensive connected system of underground aqueducts called *Puquios* was built by the Nazca Culture ca. 540–552 CE, and some are still used to draw water from underground aquifers.

Tambomachay is an Inca archaeological site near Cuzco that has a series of aqueducts, canals and waterfalls running through the terraced rocks, with warm water channelled from nearby thermal springs.

The Plain, the Ditch and the Canals

Plato – 'It (the Plain of Atlantis) was for the most part rectangular and oblong, and where falling out of the straight line followed the circular ditch'…'it (the Ditch) was fashioned by nature and by the labours of many generations of kings through long ages'… 'the depth, and width, and length of this ditch were incredible'…'it was carried round the whole of the plain, and was ten thousand stadia (2,090 kilometres) in length'…'It was excavated to the depth of a hundred feet (33 metres), and its breadth was a stadium (209 metres) everywhere'…'It received the streams which came down from the mountains, and winding round the plain and meeting at the (Royal) city, was there let off into the sea.'

Plato states that the water-filled Ditch around the Plain of Atlantis was roughly 2,100 kilometres long and extended 'round the whole of the plain'. The now-submerged Venezuelan Basin has a perimeter 2,200 kilometres long, virtually identical to the Ditch's length. That nearness in length again indicates Plato based the Atlantis story on exact measurements recorded by the Egyptians and given to Solon.

The Ditch was 'fashioned by nature' and the 'labours of many generations' of Atlanteans. These statements mean that a natural watercourse was initially around the edges of the Plain of Atlantis. This watercourse may have run along the base of the surrounding mountains to the north, east and west of the Plain, then along the elevated southern coastline until its arms met and emptied into the sea where the Atlanteans later built the Royal City. Subsequent excavations by the Atlanteans possibly deepened and widened the Ditch to Plato's dimensions.

Plato – 'Further inland, likewise, straight canals of a hundred feet (33 metres) in width were cut from it (the Ditch) through the plain, and again let off into the ditch leading to the sea'…'these canals were at intervals of a hundred stadia (21 kilometres), and by them they (the Atlanteans) brought down the wood from the mountains to the city, and conveyed the fruits of the Earth in ships, cutting transverse passages from one canal into another, and to the (Royal) city.'

The Atlanteans used the many large canals on the Plain of Atlantis for irrigation and transport. From Plato's estimations, they were more extensive

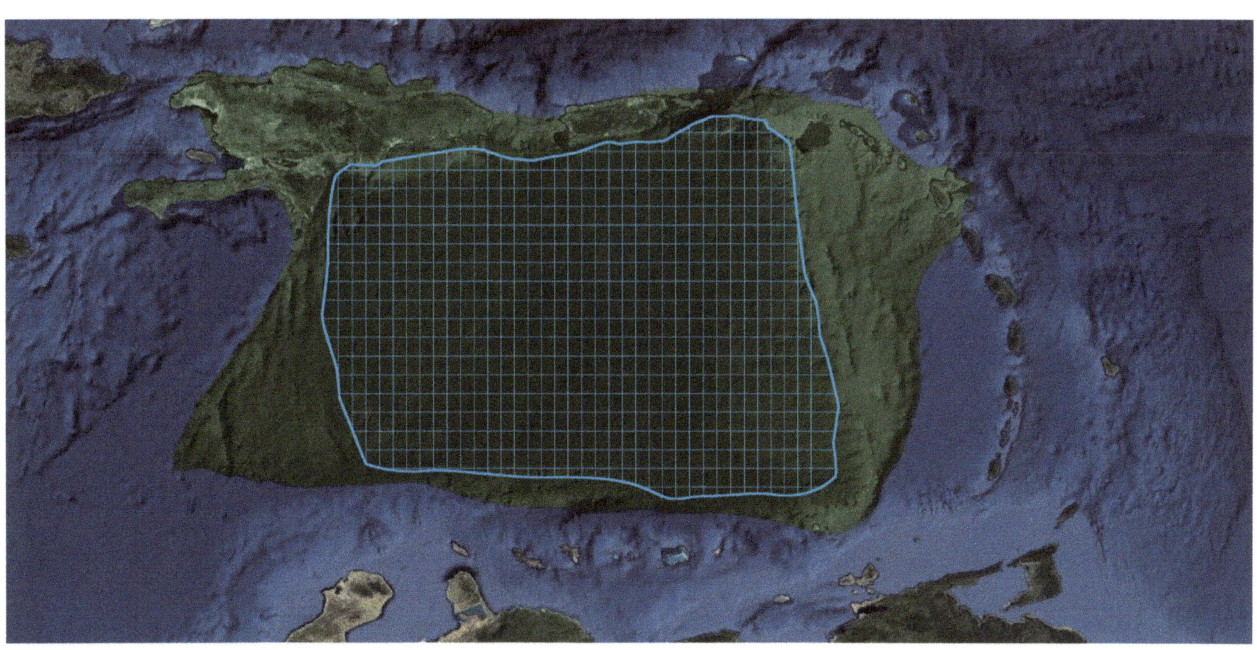

The Ditch and Canals on the Plain of Atlantis
Source: Modified from Google Earth

than any Old World canals the Ancient Greeks and Egyptians knew. Plato describes the canals as 'cutting transverse passages from one canal into another', which likely means they formed a grid pattern, possibly running north-south and east-west.

The submerged Venezuelan Basin is approximately 700 kilometres long by 400 kilometres wide, with a total area of 280,000 square kilometres. If the canals were spaced 21 kilometres apart and formed a grid pattern on the Plain of Atlantis, there would have been 35 canals running east-west and 20 north-south. The canals divided the Plain into 700 squares of land, with each square being 400km^2 in area. The combined length of the canals would have been 28,000 kilometres.

In the Old World, there is evidence of irrigated crops in Mesopotamia and Egypt as far back as the 8th millennium BP. The oldest known Old World canals are irrigation canals built in Mesopotamia around 6,000 BP, now in modern-day Iraq and Syria. The Indus Valley Civilisation in India also had sophisticated irrigation and storage systems, including reservoirs built at Girnar in about 5,000 BP.

In Egypt, transport canals date back at least to the time of Pepi I Meryre (reigned 2332–2283 BCE), who ordered one built to bypass the cataract on the Nile near Aswan. The Ancient Suez Canal (Canal of the Pharaohs) between the Nile Delta and the Red Sea may have been first excavated around the 13th century BCE, or it possibly was commenced earlier, in the 18th century BCE. Over more than 1,500 years, the canal was abandoned, silted up, re-dug and reopened several times. As early as the 3rd century BCE, Greek engineers were the first to use canal locks to regulate the water flow in the Ancient Suez Canal.

Canal of the Pharaohs
Source: Wikimedia Commons – Annie Brocolie

In Ancient China, large canals were used for river transport during the Warring States Period (481–221 BCE). Irrigation infrastructure called the Dujiangyan was built in 256 BCE by the State of Qin. It is still used to irrigate an area of over 5,300km^2. The Dujiangyan, along with the Zhengguo and the Lingqu Canal, are known as the three great hydraulic engineering projects of the Qin Dynasty. The longest canal was the Grand Canal of China; at 1,794 kilometres, it remains the longest canal in the world.

Many ancient civilisations in the Americas developed water technologies. In Florida in North America, the oldest known canals were dug around 1700 BP and averaged six metres wide, one metre deep, and up to twelve kilometres long. They allowed native peoples to move from the interior of Florida to the Gulf of Mexico and the Atlantic coast. Some of the canals had lock systems that allowed canoes to travel uphill. In what is now Arizona, the Hohokam people began to build a complex system of irrigation canals before 300 CE along the Salt and Gila River Valleys. For five hundred years, the Hohokam constructed more than 240 kilometres of canals, with the longest being 23 kilometres.

In Mesoamerica, the Olmec's first established city of San Lorenzo (1200–900 BCE) has evidence of intensive agriculture, with the draining and filling of swamps and the creation of canal systems. Maya raised-field cultivation was used from at least 1000 BCE in seasonally flooded lowlands where soils were often highly fertile but poorly drained. The Maya constructed raised dirt platforms and complex canal systems for drainage, with most of the large canals associated with grids of smaller canals. Some larger canals were probably used for transportation as they connected archaeological sites to rivers or the coast.

Inca Terraces
Source: Wikimedia Commons – AlexSP

Six major canals ran through the Aztec capital of Tenochtitlan, and smaller canals crisscrossed the entire city for water travel. The Aztec farmed irrigated artificial island plots called chinampas in the shallow lakes that surrounded the city. Crops were transported to market along the canals and lakes surrounding the chinampas to feed the city's population of 200,000.

In the Zana Valley of the Andes Mountains in Peru, there are the remains of three irrigation canals dated from the 6th millennium BP, the 5th millennium BP and the 9th century CE. These canals are the earliest record of irrigation in the Americas, but traces of a canal possibly dating from the 7th millennium BP were found below the 6th millennium BP canal. The Moche, who lived on the northern coast of what is now Peru from 200 BCE to 600 CE, built extensive irrigation ditches and flumes. Because the terrain where they lived was hilly, they built stone causeways or aqueducts to span the valleys.

All over the Peruvian Andes, Inca-built irrigation canals once distributed water to elaborate terrace systems. To build the terraces, the Inca piled large stones on a clay soil base with gravel laid above and finished off with a metre of topsoil. Water percolated slowly through each terrace to the one below, with the clay retaining moisture.

Atlantean Agriculture

Plato – 'whatever fragrant things there now are in the Earth, whether roots, or herbage, or woods, or essences which distil from fruit and flower, grew and thrived in that land (the Atlantic Island)'...'twice in the year they (the Atlanteans) gathered the fruits of the Earth, in winter having the benefit of the rains of heaven, and in summer the water which the land supplied by introducing streams from the canals.'

Plato claims the Atlantic Island had a great variety of natural vegetation, fertile soil, abundant rain, and irrigation water for domesticated food crops. He also states that the Plain of Atlantis was 'the fairest of all plains and very fertile' and was crisscrossed by irrigation canals.

If the submerged Venezuelan Basin is the Plain of Atlantis, it has a total area of 280,000 square kilometres or 28 million hectares. The carrying capacity of agricultural land is the number of people an area can support with food and will vary depending on soil type, water supply, and farming methods used. A conservative carrying capacity is 0.5 hectares of productive land per person, so the fertile Plain of Atlantis alone could have supported over 50 million people. Also, substantial lands elsewhere on the Atlantic Island, such as on Hispaniola, Puerto Rico, and the Beata and Aves Ridges, would have supported domesticated crops and animals.

The Climate of the Atlantic Island

Plato describes a well-established Bronze Age civilisation on the Atlantic Island by 11,600 BP, so agriculture probably would have begun thousands of years before. Over those thousands of years, the local climate in the Caribbean region had to be optimal for crop growth throughout the year. Plato states there were two distinct growing seasons on the Atlantic Island, with rain falling in winter and irrigation water used during a dry summer.

The Late Quaternary (the past 1.0–0.5 million years) climate of north-eastern South America has been studied by analysing river, coastal plain, and shallow marine systems. That climate information would be a close match for an Atlantic Island located in the nearby Caribbean. The region's climate was unstable for the period 60,000–30,000 BP. Then, from 24,000–18,000 BP, it was much drier than at present. It became warmer and wetter from 18,000–10,000 BP; from 9,500–8,500 BP, it was hot and wet. Therefore, the climate on the Atlantic Island from at least 18,000 BP would have been very suitable for agriculture and the development of Atlantean civilisation.

Agriculture in the Ancient Americas

If the Bronze Age Atlantean civilisation collapsed sometime after 11,600 BP, any surviving population probably reverted to a simpler Neolithic or hunter-gatherer state. As a result, some or all of Atlanteans' domesticated crops may have regressed into their wild types over time. As civilisation returned to the region over possibly hundreds or thousands of years, Neolithic tribes may again have cultivated and bred the wild varieties into domesticated food crops.

Known agriculture in the Americas dates to the Archaic period from 10,000–4,000 BP when hunter-gatherers began cultivating wild plants. Squash (Cucurbita) was grown in Mexico at around 10,000 BP. Maize-like plants derived from the wild teosinte plant date to 9,000 BP; beans were domesticated around the same time. From then on, squash, maize and beans formed the 'Three Sisters' nutritional foundation of native populations in North and Central America. When combined with peppers, these crops provided a balanced diet for much of the continent.

Around 4,500 BP, the inhabitants of what is now the eastern United States domesticated squash, sunflower, sumpweed, and goosefoot. When maize was introduced from Mexico after 1,800 BP, the population slowly changed from growing indigenous plants to a maize-based agricultural economy. Maize spread through much of the Americas, and the region developed a trade network based on

Timeline of American Crop Cultivation		
Date	**Crops**	**Location**
10,000 BP	Squash, Chilli Peppers, Avocados, Amaranth	Mexico
10,000 BP	Potatoes, Manioc, Sweet Potato	South America
9,000 BP	Maize	Central America
7,000 BP	Cotton	Mexico
6,000 BP	Common Bean	Central America
6,000 BP	Peanuts	South America
4,000 BP	Sunflowers, Beans	Mexico, Peru
3,500 BP	Cocoa	Mexico
3,500 BP	Sweet potato	South America

Timeline of American Crop Cultivation
Source: Wikipedia

Ancient American Crops	
Cereals	Maize (corn), maygrass, and little barley
Pseudocereals	Amaranth, quinoa, erect knotweed, sumpweed, and sunflowers
Pulses	Common beans, tepary beans, scarlet runner beans, lima beans, and pinto beans
Fibre	Cotton, yucca, and agave
Roots and Tubers	Jicama, manioc (cassava), potatoes, sweet potatoes, oca, mashua, ulloco, arrowroot, yacon, and leren
Fruits	Tomatoes, chilli peppers, avocados, cranberries, blueberries, huckleberries, cherimoyas, papayas, pawpaws, passionfruits, pineapples and strawberries
Melons	Pumpkins, zucchini, marrow, acorn squash, butternut squash
Nuts	Peanuts, black walnuts, shagbark hickory, pecans and hickory nuts
Peppers	Capsicum, bell peppers, jalapeños, paprika and chilli peppers

Ancient American Crops
Source: Wikipedia

varieties of maize crops. After that, the cultivation of domesticated indigenous plants declined and was eventually abandoned, with the domesticated plants reverting to their wild forms.

In South America, potatoes, sweet potatoes and manioc were domesticated from 10,000 BP; potatoes were eventually developed into hundreds of varieties. Other ancient food crops were quinoa, maize, lima beans, common beans, peanuts, oca and squashes.

Ancient Old World Agriculture

Old World agriculture is thought to have developed around 11,500 BP in the Near East, where the ancestral plants of wheat, barley and peas were first cultivated. There is evidence of the cultivation of figs in the Jordan Valley as long ago as 11,300 BP and cereal production in Syria from approximately 9,000 BP. During the same period, farmers in China began to cultivate rice and millet. Fibre crops were domesticated as early as food crops; hemp was domesticated in China, cotton in Africa, and flax in the Near East.

The use of soil improvers, including manure, fish, compost and ashes, developed independently in several areas, including Mesopotamia, the Nile Valley, and Eastern Asia. One example in the Americas is the creation of terra preta in the Amazon, where a mixture of charcoal, bone, broken pottery, compost and manure was added to low-fertility Amazonian soil.

Ancient Greece

At the time of Solon and Plato, cereals formed the staple diet of Ancient Greece, the two main grains being wheat and barley. Wheat grains were softened by soaking and then either reduced into a gruel or ground into flour and formed into loaves or flatbreads and baked. Cereals were often served accompanied by *opson* or relish, which was anything that accompanied bread, including vegetables such as cabbage, onions, lentils, sweet peas, chickpeas, broad beans and garden peas. These vegetables were eaten as a soup, boiled or mashed and seasoned with olive oil, vinegar, herbs, or a fish sauce.

Ancient Egypt

The staple foods of the Egyptians were beer and bread, with the bread usually made from emmer wheat. There was little meat, game or fish in the Egyptian diet, and the principal protein sources were pulses and legumes such as peas, beans, lentils and chickpeas. Vegetables were eaten as a complement to beer and bread. The most common vegetables were long-shooted green scallions and garlic, but there was also lettuce, celery, certain types of cucumber, and some Old World gourds and melons. Lily and similar flowering aquatic plants and tubers of sedges including papyrus were eaten raw, boiled, roasted or ground into flour. Tiger nut (Cyperus esculentus) was used to make a dessert from the dried and ground tubers mixed with honey.

Atlantean Food

Plato – 'also the fruit which admits of cultivation, both the dry sort, which is given us for nourishment and any other which we use for food – we call them all by the common name pulse.'

In the Atlantean diet, Plato does not mention any familiar vegetables or fruits of the Old World. Nor does he mention barley and wheat, the most common cereals the Ancient Egyptians and Greeks ate. If Plato had fabricated the Atlantis story, he would likely have referred to those typical food crops known to the Greeks of his time.

Cereals

The 'dry sort' of nourishment Plato describes may mean some grinding or processing of dried grain, which is then made into food. For thousands of years in the Ancient Americas, maize, maygrass, and little barley were cereals ground, baked and eaten, but they were unknown in the Old World. The Olmec and Maya cultivated maize in numerous varieties throughout Mesoamerica, and it was usually dried and stored for later use.

Pulses

In the Ancient Americas, widely used domesticated pulses included common beans, tepary beans, scarlet runner beans and lima beans. Wild potato species occur throughout the Americas, from the United States to southern Chile. Since the potato was unknown in the Old World, the Ancient Egyptians may have considered it a 'pulse' as it is not a 'dry sort' of nourishment.

Fruit

Plato – 'and the fruits having a hard rind, affording drinks and meats and ointments and are fruits which spoil with keeping, and the pleasant kinds of dessert, with which we (Greeks) console ourselves after dinner.'

In Ancient Greece, fresh or dried fruits and nuts were often eaten as desserts, especially figs, raisins and pomegranates. Dried figs were also eaten as an appetizer or when drinking wine and were often accompanied by grilled chestnuts, chickpeas and beechnuts. In Ancient Egypt, the most common fruits were dates, figs, grapes and raisins, certain species of mimusops, nabk berries, and dom palm nuts that were eaten raw or made into juice.

Some Native Fruits of the Americas		
Acai	Guarana	Papaya
Avocado	Guava	Peumo
Barberry	Keule	Pineapple
Cainito	Lardizabala	Sapote
Capuli cherry	Mamey	Sea grape
Cherimoya	Maqui	Strawberry
Coconut	Mora Común	Soursop
Feijoa	Mortiño	Sugar-apple
Giant Colombian blackberry	Naranjilla	Ugni

Some Native Fruits of the Americas
Source: Wikipedia

Many fruits native to the Americas, particularly Mesoamerica and South America, might also have been present on the Atlantic Island. Fruits of American origin would have been entirely unknown in the Old World. Plato does not describe any particular fruit eaten by the Atlanteans or mention them eating any Old World fruits. But he does describe the fruits of the Atlantic Island as 'fruits having a hard rind', as do many of the native fruits of the Americas. Most American fruits are also 'fruits which spoil with keeping' and must be eaten fresh, unlike Old World figs, grapes and dates that can be dried, stored, and consumed much later.

Wine

Plato – 'they (the Atlantean Kings) filled a bowl of wine.'

To the Ancient Greeks and Egyptians, 'wine' meant an alcoholic drink they prepared from domesticated grapes and made into red and white wines. Wine is known to have been consumed in the Eastern Mediterranean region from at least 5,000 BP. Wine-making in Egypt goes back to the 3rd millennium BCE and the earliest evidence of Greek wine dates from the 4th millennium BCE. The earliest known form of grape-based fermented drink, possibly mixed with rice and other species, was found in northern China in 9,000-year-old pottery jars. The earliest known grape wine was discovered in the north-western Zagros Mountains of Kurdistan, dated ca. 7,400 BP.

Though several native grape species did exist in the prehistoric Americas and probably were eaten, there is no known history of wine production there. Nevertheless, several Ancient American civilisations developed and regularly used alcoholic drinks:

- Pulque or octli is fermented maguey (agave) juice, a traditional native beverage of Mesoamerica.
- Balche is a honey wine brewed by the Maya and associated with the Maya deity Acan.
- Tepache is a mildly alcoholic beverage indigenous to Mexico, made from fermented pineapple.
- Tejuino is a maize-based beverage made from fermented masa dough.
- Chicha is a variety of traditional fermented beverages from the Andes region of South America, made from maize, manioc root (also called yuca or cassava) or fruits. The Inca used chicha for ritual purposes and consumed it in large quantities during religious festivals.
- Cauim is a traditional alcoholic beverage of Brazil and is similar to chicha.
- Tiswin is a mild, fermented, ceremonial beverage usually brewed from maize and produced by various cultures living in the south-western United States and northern Mexico. The Tohono O'odham of south-eastern Arizona brewed tiswin using the sap of the saguaro cactus.

'Chestnuts and the like'

Plato – 'good store of chestnuts and the like'.

The only Atlantean food crop Plato mentions is 'chestnuts', also commonly eaten in Ancient Greece. There are four main chestnut species: European, Chinese, Japanese and several subspecies of American chestnuts.

Prehistoric Americans ate the American chestnut species long before Europeans introduced their foreign stock to the Americas. By adding 'and the like', Plato implies the Atlanteans had other nut-like crops besides chestnuts. Several common indigenous American nut crops included peanuts, black walnuts, shagbark hickory, pecans and hickory nuts.

Domesticated Animals

The inhabitants of the Fertile Crescent of Western Asia were the first known to have domesticated animals in the Old World. Between 13,000 and 10,000 BP, they domesticated the ancestors of modern cattle, sheep, goats and pigs.

When Plato describes the Atlantic Island, the only animal species he names are horses, cattle and elephants. He does not refer to any commonly domesticated Old World animals, such as sheep, goats or pigs, that would have been familiar to the Ancient Egyptians and Greeks. These Old World species did not exist in the Americas before European colonisation, so if Plato had included them, it would have indicated that he fabricated the Atlantis story.

Working Animals

Plato – 'horses and other animals of the yoke'.

A yoke is a wooden beam between domesticated animals to pull together on a load when working in pairs, such as when ploughing a field or pulling a cart or wagon. Plato states that the Atlanteans yoked horses and 'other animals'. Although Plato does not say what species those other animals were, the Atlanteans would have used them to plough fields or pull a vehicle. As the Atlanteans had wheeled chariots pulled by horses, they likely had larger wheeled vehicles used to haul loads.

In the Old World, yoked working animals included oxen, horses, mules, donkeys, water buffalo, and camels. Some of these species were also used as pack animals, with goods placed directly on their backs. Apart from horses, Plato does not mention any of the usual domesticated species yoked in the Old World. Still, several large animal species existed in the Americas of 11,600 BP but are now extinct. The Atlanteans could have domesticated several elephant species, bison and camelids if they were present on the Atlantic Island.

Working Asian Elephants

War Elephants

Elephants

Plato – 'there were a great number of elephants in the (Atlantic) island.'

Plato does not mention whether the Atlanteans domesticated elephants on the Atlantic Island, but it is possible. Several elephant species existing in the prehistoric Americas were similar to the Asian Elephant, which had been domesticated in the Old World for thousands of years. Asian Elephants have been used as working animals since at least the Indus Valley Civilisation of 5,000 BP and can be trained to respond to over thirty commands.

The Atlanteans may have trained elephants for war. One of the earliest references to war elephants is in the Indian epic *Mahabharata*, written in the 4th century BCE but describing events between the 11th and 8th centuries BCE. Later Indian kingdoms made great use of war elephants: the Nanda army (5th to 4th centuries BCE) had 3,000, while the Mauryan army (4th to 2nd centuries BCE) may have had 9,000.

In the 3rd century BCE, the Ptolemies and the Carthaginians used African elephants for war, as did the Numidians and the Kushites. The animal they used was the North African Forest Elephant, which was smaller than the Asian Elephant. Although the African Savanna Elephant is much larger than either the African Forest Elephant or the Asian Elephant, it was difficult to tame and little used.

Bullock Train

Cattle

Plato – 'abundance of food for cattle'...'separate baths for women, and for horses and cattle'.

Plato describes domesticated 'cattle' on the Atlantic Island, which may have been used for haulage similarly to oxen or bullocks. The Atlanteans may have domesticated any or all of the several bison species that still existed in the Americas before 11,600 BP, such as the Steppe Bison, *Bison latifrons* and *Bison antiquus*.

Camelids

Camelops is a genus of camels of North America that became extinct about 10,000 BP. It was around two metres tall at the shoulder, making it slightly taller than modern Bactrian camels. *Camelops* may have been present on the Atlantic Island and domesticated by the Atlanteans before 11,600 BP.

The two surviving species of camel in the Old World are the Dromedary, a one-humped camel from the Middle East, and the Bactrian or two-humped camel from Central Asia. Dromedaries may have been first domesticated in Arabia at around 5,000 BP, whereas the Bactrian was domesticated in Central Asia at about 4,500 BP. Both of these domesticated camels provided milk, meat, and hair for textiles or goods. They were used as working animals for human transport and bearing or pulling loads.

Camel Cart

Harnessed Llamas

Camels are not native to Africa and were probably unknown to those prehistoric Egyptians who initially recorded the Atlantis story many thousands of years ago. Domesticated Dromedaries were probably first introduced into Africa from Arabia and have been in Egypt since the beginning of the 2nd millennium BCE. However, the invading Persians introduced camels into Egypt in much larger numbers in the 5th century BCE.

Even though the Egyptians and Greeks of Plato's time would have been well aware of Old World domesticated camels, Plato does not mention them being 'animals of the yoke' for the Atlanteans.

Llamas have been domesticated and herded in Peru since at least 5,500 BP. In the Inca Empire, llamas were the only beasts of burden and used as pack animals, but many earlier Andean civilisations had long traditions of llama herding. Several llamas can be harnessed together and trained to pull a cart. Similar camelid species may have been domesticated by the Atlanteans and used for haulage.

Atlantean Government and Laws

Plato – 'He (Poseidon) also begat and brought up five pairs of twin male children; and dividing the island of Atlantis into ten portions, he gave to the first-born of the eldest pair (Atlas) his mother's (Cleito's) dwelling and the surrounding allotment (the Royal City and the plain around it), which was the largest and best, and made him king over the rest; the others he made princes, and gave them rule over many men, and a large territory.'

Plato – 'Atlas had a numerous and honourable family, and they retained the kingdom (whose capital was the Royal City), the eldest son handing it on to his eldest for many generations'...'Each of the ten kings (of Atlantis) in his own division and in his own city had the absolute control of the citizens'... 'the order of precedence among them and their mutual relations were regulated by the commands of Poseidon which the law had handed down. These were inscribed by the first kings on a pillar of orichalcum, which was situated in the middle of the (Central) island, at the temple of Poseidon.'

Plato – 'the kings were gathered together every fifth and every sixth year alternately'...'they consulted about their common interests, and enquired if any one had transgressed in anything and passed judgment and before they passed judgment they gave their pledges to one another on this wise: They were not to take up arms against one another, and they were all to come to the rescue if any one in any of their cities attempted to overthrow the royal house'...'they were to deliberate in common about war and other matters, giving the supremacy to the descendants of Atlas.'

Though it is improbable that five sets of male twins could be born naturally to one couple, it is not impossible. The largest officially recorded number of children born to one mother is sixty-nine: a peasant woman in 18th century Russia had twenty-seven confinements, resulting in sixteen pairs of twins, seven sets of triplets, and four sets of quadruplets.

A more likely explanation for Poseidon and Cleito's ten male children might be that prominent male members of Poseidon's colonising group, or their male offspring, received titles and territories to govern. Then, that original division created the ruling dynasties of the ten kingdoms of Atlantis.

Neither the Ancient Egyptians, Greeks, nor any other Old World culture had a system of government like the Atlanteans, making it unlikely that Plato invented the Atlantis story to demonstrate any specific political philosophy. The Atlanteans had a confederation of the Atlantic Island's ten kingdoms, with inherited kingship in each of them. Each kingdom had a principal city, but the king of the Royal City had supreme rule over the other nine kings.

As the Atlanteans conquered surrounding territories, the ten Kings of Atlantis gained control over them and created an Atlantean Empire. Written laws regulated the ten kingdoms and the relationship of the kings with each other. All ten kings gathered at set intervals to perform a sacrificial bonding ritual, discuss common interests and resolve potential conflicts.

Plato – 'There were bulls who had the range of the temple of Poseidon; and the ten Kings, being left alone in the temple, after they had offered prayers to the god that they may capture the victim which was acceptable to him, hunted the bulls, without weapons but with staves and nooses; and the bull which they caught they led up to the pillar (of orichalcum) and cut its throat over the top of it so that the blood fell upon the sacred inscription.'

Plato – 'Now on the pillar, besides the laws, there was inscribed an oath invoking mighty curses on the disobedient. When therefore, after slaying the bull in the accustomed manner, they (the ten kings) had burnt its limbs, they filled a bowl of wine and cast in a clot of blood for each of them; the rest of the victim they put in the fire, after having purified the column all round. Then they drew from the bowl in golden cups and pouring a libation on the fire, they swore that they would judge according to the laws on the pillar, and would punish him who in any point had already transgressed them'...'when darkness came on, and the fire about the sacrifice was cool, all of them put on most beautiful azure robes, and, sitting on the ground, at night, over the embers of the sacrifices by which they had sworn, and extinguishing all the fire about the temple, they received and gave judgment, if any of them had an accusation to bring against any one; and when they had given judgment, at daybreak they wrote down their sentences on a golden tablet, and dedicated it together with their robes to be a memorial.'

The Atlantean ritual of bull sacrifice was repeated every five and six years by the many generations of the ten Kings of Atlantis who had ruled before 11,600 BP. Several ancient Old World cultures sacrificed bulls, including the Greeks of Plato's time. Yet, the rituals of the Kings of Atlantis have no equivalent in the cultures of the Ancient Egyptians, Greeks, or any other known ancient Old World culture. As Plato did not describe an existing ritual he may have known, particularly those of the Egyptians and Greeks, it seems unlikely that he made up the Atlanteans' ritual bull sacrifice.

At any one time, several 'bulls had the range of the temple of Poseidon' on the Central Island of the Royal City. As the now-extinct bison species such as the Steppe Bison, *Bison latifrons* and *Bison antiquus* were probably still living in the Americas by 11,600 BP, any of these species may have been present on the Atlantic Island.

If bison bulls were at the Temple of Poseidon, they might have been bred to be tame enough to wander about the Temple and its grounds without disturbing worshippers. Still, all of these bison species were huge animals. They were over two metres tall at the shoulder, weighed up to 1,500 kilograms, and probably were dangerous to catch and subdue with 'staves and nooses'. To capture one of them would have been a test of an individual Atlantean King's mental and physical abilities and the ten men's ability to cooperate in a dangerous task.

In Ancient Egypt, sacred bulls were worshipped but never sacrificed. Apis was the most popular of the three great bull cults, with the others being the Mnevis and Buchis bulls. The Apis bull was the most important of all the sacred animals in Egypt and embodied the god Ptah and later Osiris. The god's priests identified a long series of ritually perfect Apis bulls and once selected, the Apis bull was housed in a temple for its lifetime. When it died of natural causes, it was embalmed and encased in a giant stone sarcophagus. A new Apis bull was then found and worshipped over its lifetime.

Bull-Leaping Fresco from Knossos
Source: Wikimedia Commons – ChrisO

The bull was a central theme of the Bronze Age Minoan civilisation on Crete, with bull heads and horns used as symbols in the Knossos palace. Some modern scholars equate the Minoan sport of bull-leaping with the Atlantean Kings' hunt of bulls, but the Minoans did not use 'staves and nooses' to capture them. Instead, it appears that Minoan male and female athletes performed gymnastic feats with the bulls, with no evidence that the Minoans sacrificed bulls in their rituals. Later Greeks did sacrifice many bulls at religious festivals, but those rites were nothing like the Atlantean Kings' ritual sacrifice.

Atlantean Writing

Plato describes a literate Atlantean culture with an established writing system from the time of the early Kings of Atlantis, 'many generations' before 11,600 BP.

Plato – 'the commands of Poseidon which the law had handed down…were inscribed…on a pillar of orichalcum…besides the laws, there was inscribed an oath'…'they (the ten Kings) wrote down their sentences on a golden tablet'.

There were highly literate civilisations in the Ancient Americas for thousands of years before the Spanish arrived. There might also be undiscovered writing systems in the Americas from the more distant past. As with the Egyptians and other ancient cultures, evidence of very early writing may be lost if written on perishable materials that decayed over thousands of years. Some American cultures may have also become illiterate following a societal collapse, only to reinvent the art of writing after a long lapse.

Mesoamerica

Mesoamerica is one of only five world regions where writing was developed independently. The region produced several indigenous writing systems in the form of glyphs from at least the 1st millennium BCE onwards. The Cascajal Block is the earliest-known example in the Americas of an extensive text thought

A Drawing of the Cascajal Block
Source: Wikimedia Commons – Michael Everson

Some Mesoamerican Glyphs

1 2 3 4 5 6 7 8 9 10 11 12 13 14 15 16 17 18 19

Mesoamerican Number System

to be writing. This tablet of Olmec hieroglyphs has been dated to approximately 900 BCE and contains sixty-two signs.

Five or six different ancient scripts have been documented in Mesoamerica, but it is unknown which was the earliest and from which the others developed. Maya script, also known as Maya glyphs or Maya hieroglyphs, is the only Mesoamerican writing system to be substantially deciphered. The earliest inscriptions found that are identifiably Maya date to the 3rd century BCE.

As well as being highly literate, the ancient Mesoamerican civilisations were highly numerate. A feature of all Mesoamerican writing systems is a number system of bar-and-dot notation – where a dot represents a value of one, and a bar represents five. Numbers less than twenty were written in bar-and-dot notation, but different systems used different methods for quantities larger than twenty. For example, the Aztec used symbols such as a flag representing 20, a feather representing 400, and an incense bag representing 8,000.

Maya codices are folded books written in Maya hieroglyphic script on bark cloth made from the inner bark of particular trees, mainly the wild fig tree or *amate* (*Ficus glabrata*). It is unknown where or when papermaking began in Mesoamerica, but 9th-century BCE stone images depict items thought to be paper. During the Aztec Empire, amate paper was widely produced and used for communication, records, and rituals. Over forty villages manufactured paper as tribute in territory controlled by the Aztec, with around 480,000 sheets made annually.

Books and writing were common in Mesoamerica when the Spanish arrived. The codices and other texts were written by scribes who usually were members of the priesthood. Scribes wrote on a variety of media depending on the purpose. Stone was carved for public or monumental purposes; clay objects were inscribed to claim ownership; human and animal bones were carved to record lineages and identities; amate and deerskin were painted to record history.

South America

Quechuan is a South American language family spoken primarily in the Andes and derived from a common ancestral language long before the Inca. There is no known written representation of Quechua in any of the pre-Inca civilisations of the region. Instead of writing, the Inca used assemblages of knotted strings called Quipu to

Quipu
Source: Wikimedia Commons – Larco Museum, Lima

Chasqui Carrying a Quipu
Source: Wikimedia Commons

record information, but its exact meaning is no longer known.

The Quipu record-keeping system is probably much older than the Inca civilisation. Among the artefacts found at the prehistoric site of Caral is a knotted textile piece thought to be a Quipu, which would predate the Inca Quipu by well over two thousand years.

The Inca used Quipu to collect data and keep records, monitor tax obligations, properly collect census records and calendrical information, and for military organization. Once thought to be used only as mnemonic devices or to record numerical data, Quipu are now believed to record history and literature.

The Chasquis were highly trained runners who delivered messages and other objects throughout a road system of 40,000 kilometres in the vast Inca Empire. Each Chasqui carried a Pututu (a trumpet made of a conch shell), a Quipu containing information, and a Quepi on his back to hold objects for delivery.

The Azure Robes of the Atlantean Kings

Plato (Jowett) – 'all of them (the ten Kings of Atlantis) put on most beautiful azure robes'.

Plato (Taylor) – 'all of them, invested with a most beautiful azure garment'.

The Atlanteans must have used weaving and dyeing processes well before 11,600 BP. Taylor calls the Kings' outer clothing a garment, whereas Jowett describes them as robes: a long, loose-fitting outer garment, usually with sleeves. But both translations describe the Kings' clothing as azure, a variation of blue described as the colour of the sky on a clear summer's day.

Weaving

In the Old World, there are indications that weaving and dyeing were already known in the Palaeolithic era. At Dzudzuana Cave in Georgia, 30,000-year-old spun plant fibres were found that had been dyed pink, black and turquoise blue. Woven textiles are well known by the Neolithic era, with one fragment found at Fayum in Egypt at a site dated to 7,000 BP.

Weaving techniques were widespread and advanced in the ancient cultures of the Americas. The ancient Maya wove two natural types of cotton, one white and the other light brown, which were often dyed. Maya weavers used three different natural dyes. Indigo was used for shades of blue. Cochineal is an insect that makes red when crushed and dried. A coastal mollusc was used to whiten cloth by extracting fluid from its glands. Besides cotton, fibres from an agave plant called Maguey were used as a cordage material for nets, hammocks and bags.

In Peru, textiles found in burial sites date to 7,800 BP. Weavings show a great variety of techniques, including tapestry, embroidery, and pile weaves. Cotton was grown along coastal areas and was the predominant fibre used there. In mountainous regions, the Peruvians raised llama and alpaca for their wool for weaving.

Textile weaving, using cotton dyed with pigments, was an important craft among tribes of the American south-west, including the Pueblo peoples, the Zuni, and Ute tribes. In Amazonia in South America, various tribes used Aguaje palm-bast and the frond spears of the Chambira palm to weave fabric and for cordage, hammocks, mosquito netting and tents.

Old World Blue Dyes and Pigments

In the Old World, the earliest known blue dyes came from plants, such as woad in Europe and indigo in Asia and Africa. Blue pigments for paints were made from minerals, usually either lapis lazuli or azurite.

The Ancient Egyptians used blue dye, probably made from the woad plant (*Isatis tinctoria*) to colour cloth used to wrap mummies, but they do not appear to have used blue for the clothes of the living. The Egyptians made a blue pigment known as Egyptian Blue for their paintings by grinding silica, lime, copper and alkali together and heating it to 800–900°C.

The Minoans also used Egyptian Blue in the wall paintings of Knossos in Crete around 2100 BCE. The later Greeks imported indigo dye (*Indigofera tinctoria*) from India and called it *indikon*. Like the Egyptians, the Greeks do not appear to have used blue dye for their clothing. The Romans also imported indigo dye, but blue was the colour of working-class clothing, whereas nobles and the wealthy wore white, black, red, or violet.

Maya Blue

Maya Blue is an azure colour used by the Maya and other Mesoamerican cultures on textiles, ceramics, sculptures, and murals. It is a synthetic pigment produced by mixing Anil (indigo) leaves and a mineral called Palygorskite with smaller amounts of other mineral additives. *Indigofera suffruticosa*, commonly known as Anil, is a type of indigo plant native to the subtropical and tropical Americas. Palygorskite is a form of clay soil common to the south-eastern United States.

Azurite is another source of blue pigment used in the Americas in ancient times. It is a soft, deep blue copper mineral produced by the weathering of copper ore deposits. The Maya, Aztec and Inca all believed in the spiritual properties of azurite.

'Maya Blue' in Maya Mural Background

Azure was not a commonly used colour for fabrics in the Old World, but it was widely used in the form of Maya Blue in the Ancient Americas for thousands of years. The formulation of Maya Blue required the Anil plant and Palygorskite, while Azurite was another source of blue pigment. All of these ingredients would probably have been available to the Atlanteans on the Atlantic Island or nearby Americas.

The fact that Plato specifies 'azure' as the colour of the Atlantean Kings' robes, rather than just calling them blue, does set them apart from any coloured garments worn by the Ancient Egyptians or Greeks. Plato describes something unlikely in his time; another example that he did not invent the Atlantean Kings' 'most beautiful azure robes'.

Atlantean Mining and Metallurgy

Plato states that the Atlanteans mined, smelted and used a large amount and variety of metals and alloys, giving them the technology of a Bronze Age civilisation at the least.

Plato – 'they (the Atlanteans) dug out of the Earth whatever was to be found there, solid as well as fusile (formed by casting or melting), and that which is now only a name and was then something more than a name, orichalcum, was dug out of the Earth in many parts of the (Atlantic) island, being more precious in those days than anything except gold.'

Plato – 'All the outside of the temple (of Poseidon), with the exception of the pinnacles, they covered with silver, and the pinnacles with gold'... 'In the interior of the temple the roof was of ivory, curiously wrought everywhere with gold and silver and orichalcum; and all the other parts, the walls and pillars and floor, they coated with orichalcum'...'In the temple they placed statues of gold'...'around the temple on the outside were placed statues of gold'.

Plato – 'The entire circuit of the wall (in the Royal City), which went round the outermost (circular) zone, they covered with a coating of brass, and the circuit of the next wall they coated with tin, and the third, which encompassed the citadel, flashed with the red light of orichalcum.'

The Atlanteans had to extract and process large quantities of minerals to produce workable pure metals such as gold, silver, copper, tin, and zinc. They then had to combine some of those metals to make alloys of copper such as bronze, brass and 'orichalcum'. Bronze is an alloy of copper and tin, whereas brass is copper and zinc. Though orichalcum's exact nature is uncertain, it was probably an alloy of copper and gold.

All of the metals Plato mentions in the Atlantis story exist as ore deposits in the Americas. The ancient civilisations of South America and Mesoamerica mined, smelted and used these metals in pure form or combined them into alloys. The Atlantic Island was on the Caribbean Tectonic Plate, created by volcanic activity many millions of years ago. Volcanoes directly or indirectly produce copper, zinc, lead, gold, silver, and tin deposits. Therefore, all the metals that Plato states the Atlanteans used would likely have been present as ore deposits on the Atlantic Island itself and surrounding lands in the Americas that were part of the Atlantean Empire.

The Caribbean, Central America and northern South America have rich mineral deposits, particularly copper, tin, iron, silver, and gold. The Greater Antilles Islands in the Caribbean have some of the world's largest deposits of bauxite and nickel. Gold, silver, copper, zinc, manganese, cobalt, and chromium are also present.

Ancient Metallurgy

Native metal is mined almost pure and then shaped using heat and cold-hammering techniques without smelting or chemically altering the metal. In contrast, smelting uses heat and a chemical reducing agent to break down the ore and remove unwanted elements as gases or slag, leaving only the pure metal base. The reducing agent is commonly a carbon source, such as coke or charcoal.

In the Old World, the earliest known evidence for using native copper dates to the late 11th millennium BP at the site of Çayönü in Asia Minor. Very early cultures in the Americas used native metal, with copper finds dated to approximately 7,000 BP from the Old Copper Complex in present-day Michigan and Wisconsin in the United States.

The earliest evidence of Old World copper smelting is by the Vinča Culture in Serbia, from 7,500 BP. The Bronze Age began in the Old World around 5,500 BP when copper and tin were combined to make bronze alloy. Iron appears to have been invented by the Hittites of Asia Minor around 3,500 BP, which began the Iron Age in the Old World. However, iron does not appear to have ever been used in the New World of the Americas.

South American metalworking seems to have first developed in the Andean regions of present-day

Chimu Gold and Turquoise Vase

Peru and Bolivia, with the earliest known gold-work from around 4,000 BP and copper-work around 3,400 BP. In Northern Peru, the Moche civilisation (100–800 CE) had sophisticated metallurgy based on copper. Moche smiths worked primarily with sheet metal hammered into three-dimensional shapes and used solder to join metals. They also created bronze as well as gold-copper and silver-copper alloys. The Moche used lost-wax casting but not as frequently as in other parts of the Andes. Moche metal objects had ritual uses, such as headdresses, masks and jewellery, but also as weapons and tools.

In Mesoamerica, metallurgy occurred late in the region's history. Before then, the complex civilisations such as the Olmec, Maya, Zapotec and Teotihuacan had no metals. By definition, they were Neolithic cultures, though in a very advanced form. Metallurgical techniques developed in two main stages in Mexico and likely diffused northward from Central or South America along maritime trade routes. The earliest phase began around 600 CE and produced small copper-based objects, far fewer gold or silver objects, and some alloys. The second expansion phase was not until 1200 CE when alloying copper with tin and arsenic produced a wide range of silver and gold-coloured bronze objects.

Gold

Plato – 'In the temple (of Poseidon) they placed statues of gold'…'around the temple on the outside were placed statues of gold.'

The earliest gold artefacts found so far in the Americas are from the Andean region, dating to 4,000 BP. Gold in the Ancient Americas was used for personal ornaments but was also valued for its religious symbolism. For the Inca and other Andean cultures of South America, gold was the 'Sweat of the Sun', the most sacred of their gods.

From Mexico to Chile, most pre-Columbian gold-mining was along streams using wooden pans and digging sticks. Few gold mines went underground, except in north-western Colombia, where miners dug pits and shafts.

Metalsmiths used gold and gold alloys to make cast and hammered objects, cut, engraved, and beaten into thin sheets. The artisans of ancient South American cultures, such as the Nazca and Paracas, used sheet gold for wristbands and head-dress plumes.

Silver

Plato – 'All the outside of the temple (of Poseidon) with the exception of the pinnacles, they covered with silver.'

Silver-working requires greater technical skill than gold, as it must be smelted and refined before being formed into objects. Despite massive silver deposits in the mountains of Mexico and Honduras, it was only in the Andes region of South America that silver mining and metallurgy were developed in pre-Columbian times. Silver first appeared there as small personal adornments in the late 1st millennium BCE.

When the Lords of the Chimu Kingdom ruled over the northern part of the Peruvian coast from the 12th to 15th century CE, silver was used for objects of all kinds, ranging from jewellery to discs and vessels and to sheath large wooden-framed works. Following the arrival of the Spanish, the silver mines of South America produced as much as 100,000 metric tonnes of refined silver from 1500–1800 CE.

Chimu Silver Beakers

Copper

Over several thousand years, the Old Copper Complex located in present-day Michigan and Wisconsin in the United States used native copper to produce tens and possibly hundreds of thousands of tools, weapons and other implements. Carbon-14 testing of organic materials found with some artefacts shows that they were manufactured before 6,000 BP.

The primary copper sources were natural ore deposits along 200 kilometres of the southern shores of Lake Superior, where there are thousands of copper pits from 3–10 metres deep, some with connecting tunnels. Though the exact amount of native copper ore extracted during the prehistoric period is unknown, estimates range from 250,000–750,000 tonnes.

The next known location for copper mining was in the western coastal areas of South America and some parts of Central America, where it was often mixed with gold. The Atacama Desert's highlands have the oldest mining evidence from the Formative Period (1800 BCE–200 CE). Despite evidence for the smelting of copper sulphide in the Altiplano region around 900 BCE–200 CE, fully developed smelting only appears with the Moche Culture of the northern coast from 200 BCE–600 CE.

Copper-working developed later in Mesoamerican civilisations because of the lack of surface copper and little contact with the copper cultures to the north or south. One area in Mesoamerica that did develop copper-work was West Mexico in 800 CE. Copper was also found and worked in Colombia and Costa Rica, but deposits were much scarcer.

Tin

Plato – 'the circuit of the next wall they coated with tin'.

Tin deposits exist in South America, with significant deposits in northern Bolivia and minor deposits in southern Peru, Colombia, Brazil, and north-western Argentina. In North America, the only known exploitable source of tin during ancient times was in Zacatecas province in north-central Mexico.

Alloys

Ancient American artefacts composed of pure silver or gold are rare, but alloys of copper with gold or silver are much more common. Metalsmiths used the depletion gilding technique to produce a layer of nearly pure gold on an object made of a gold alloy by removing the other metals from its surface. When alloys of gold, silver, platinum and copper were rubbed with a plant juice containing oxalic or citric acid and then heated, the copper was removed, giving the object a golden appearance. Also, ammonium carbonate soaked in urine may have been used instead of plant juice for the same effect.

The Chavin, Moche, Nazca, Chancay and Inca people used two depletion gilding techniques. The first produced a reddish bronze-coloured copper-gold alloy that contained different amounts of gold and silver. The second technique made a pale green-white silver-gold-copper alloy with a high proportion of silver.

Brass

Plato – 'The entire circuit of the wall, which went round the outermost zone, they covered with a coating of brass.'

Brass is an alloy of copper and zinc. The earliest manufactured brasses may have been natural alloys made by smelting zinc-rich copper ores, as zinc commonly occurs with copper, lead, and silver ores. Copper-zinc alloys are known in China from as early as the 7th millennium BP. In West Asia and the Eastern Mediterranean, copper-zinc alloys have been found from 5th millennium BP sites.

Peru's pre-Columbian zinc production dates from the same period as its silver, gold and copper mining in the 1st millennium BCE. Zinc is now mined from many deposits across Latin America.

Bronze

Bronze is an alloy of copper and other metals, usually tin and sometimes arsenic, and it is a much harder metal than pure copper. Though Plato does not specifically mention bronze, the Atlanteans used its component metals of copper and tin and probably combined them into a bronze alloy.

In the Old World, bronze was initially made by combining copper and arsenic to form arsenical bronze. Arsenic is rarely found as a pure metal but is often a component in sulphur-containing minerals. Later, tin was used instead of arsenic and became the principal non-copper ingredient of bronze by the late 3rd millennium BCE. Tin bronze was superior to arsenical bronze because the alloying process could be more easily controlled, and the resulting alloy was stronger and easier to cast. Also, unlike arsenic, tin is not toxic to humans.

In the Old World, the earliest known arsenical bronze artefacts have been found on the Iranian Plateau from the 7th millennium BP. The earliest tin-alloy bronze in the Old World dates to 6,500 BP from a Vinča Culture site in Plocnik, Serbia.

Arsenical bronze was the earliest copper alloy in the Americas in north-west Argentina and southern Peru. Arsenical bronze was used by 400 CE for tools such as axes, chisels and wedges, and finer domestic items such as awls, needles, bracelets, and tweezers.

Arsenical bronze was the primary alloy in Ecuador and North and Central Peru because of the rich arsenic-bearing ores there.

The Moche civilisation discovered and developed bronze smelting in South America, with tin deposits exploited as early as 1000 CE. There was no arsenical bronze in the South and Central Andes, southern Peru, and Bolivia, as there was abundant tin ore called Cassiterite. Bronze technology was developed further by the Inca, who considered bronze the imperial alloy and used it widely for useful objects and sculptures. Tin deposits in north-central Mexico supplied West Mexican cultures with enough tin for their bronze production.

Orichalcum

Plato – 'that which is now only a name and was then something more than a name, orichalcum, was dug out of the Earth in many parts of the (Atlantic) island, being more precious in those days than anything except gold'...'the walls and pillars and floor (of the Temple of Poseidon), they coated with orichalcum'...'and the third (wall), which encompassed the citadel, flashed with the red light of orichalcum.'

The name orichalcum derives from the Greek *oreikhalkos* (from *oros*, mountain and *chalkos*, copper or bronze) – meaning mountain copper or mountain metal. The Romans later transliterated orichalcum as aurichalcum, meaning golden copper. Aurichalcum then became the Romans' standard term for brass: the gold-coloured alloy of copper and zinc.

Tairona Tumbaga Object

Tumbaga is the name the Spanish gave to an alloy of gold and copper widely used in pre-Columbian Mesoamerica and South America. Tumbaga fits the description of orichalcum because it has a 'red light' – it has a warmer hue than gold but is not as reddish as pure copper.

Tumbaga can be cast, drawn, hammered, gilded, soldered, welded, plated, hardened, annealed, polished, engraved, embossed, and inlaid. Depletion gilding of tumbaga leaves a layer of nearly pure gold on top of the harder and more durable copper-gold alloy below.

In ancient times, the Roman author Pliny the Elder (23–79 CE) described how orichalcum had come from ore deposits in Cyprus, but they had been exhausted by the 1st century CE. A similar ore containing gold and copper that could be smelted into Plato's 'orichalcum' may have existed on the Atlantic Island. If that combined gold-copper ore was rarer than gold ore alone, it might have been considered 'more precious in those days than anything except gold'. Then again, the most likely source of the Atlanteans' orichalcum was the smelting of separate ores of copper and gold, then combining the metals to produce an alloy like tumbaga.

Athletics, Horse and Chariot Racing

The Atlanteans had specific areas for men and horses to exercise in the Royal City, with a track for horse races.

Plato – '(there were) also gardens and places of exercise, some for men, and others for horses in both of the two islands (in the Royal City) formed by the (land) zones; and in the centre of the larger of the two (land zones) there was set apart a race-course of a stadium (209 metres) in width, and in length allowed to extend all round the island, for horses to race in.'

Athletics

Plato's description of 'places of exercise...for men' may mean the Atlanteans had athletic contests or games, but he does not describe any particular athletic activities.

Over several thousand years in Mesoamerica, there is no evidence of any organised sport played apart from the Mesoamerican ballgame and its variations, which will be described later in this chapter. In South America, Spanish chroniclers of the Inca Empire mentioned physical activities such as the Warachicuy, Inti Raymi, the practice of ball games, and the participation of the trained runners called Chasquis. The Warachicuy was an initiation ceremony in which young men got their first Wara (breechcloth) by passing different athletic tests and sham battles. The Inti Raymi was a religious ceremony in honour of the sun god Inti that lasted nine days and was filled with dances and processions.

In the Old World, athletic contests in running, walking, jumping and throwing are among the oldest sports. Athletics events were depicted in Ancient Egyptian tombs in Saqqara, with illustrations of running and high-jumping appearing in tombs from as early as 2250 BCE. Cretan stone vases, frescos and seal-stones show that the Minoans practised several sports in the 2nd millennium BCE, such as boxing, wrestling, bull-leaping, and acrobatics. For the later Mycenaeans in Greece, the main sports were wrestling and boxing, with athletic games organised during religious ceremonies. The Tailteann Games were an ancient Celtic festival founded in Ireland around 1800 BCE; the thirty-day meeting included running and stone-throwing among its sporting events.

In Ancient Greece, the earliest and only event at the first Olympic Games, held at Olympia in the Peloponnese in 776 BCE, was a stadium-length running event known as the stadion. Athletic events at later Olympic Games expanded to include shot-put and discus, long jump, boxing, wrestling, a pentathlon, and a form of no-holds-barred fighting called *pankration*. Similar regular athletics competitions also took place at other Panhellenic Games, such as those held at Delphi and Corinth, and there were many lesser local games in other Greek cities.

Several competitive forms of exercise were practised by the Greeks of Solon and Plato's time. Still, Plato does not describe the Atlanteans as having any of these, only that there were 'places of exercise…for men'. A lack of detail for any Atlantean exercise again indicates that Plato did not invent the Atlantis story.

Equestrian Sports

Plato – 'a race-course of a stadium (209 metres) in width, and in length allowed to extend all round the island (the second land zone from the central island), for horses to race in'.

Because the various horse species became extinct in the Americas after 10,000 BP, indigenous cultures and civilisations did not use horses until Europeans reintroduced them after the 15th century CE.

In the Old World, horses were used for racing in Babylon, Syria, Egypt, and Ancient Greece. In the 2nd millennium BCE, the Mycenaeans' use of the horse and chariot in Greece brought chariot races into their culture. Equestrian sports were introduced to the Olympic Games in 680 BCE. Both chariot and mounted horse racing were regular events in the Ancient Greek Olympics by 648 BCE.

The hippodrome was a Greek stadium used for both horse and chariot racing. The hippodrome used during the Olympic Games was 320 metres wide and 780 metres long, divided into two parallel tracks by a stone or wooden barrier to form the circuit.

Horse Riders – Greek Vase ca 500–480 BCE
Source: Wikimedia Commons – Walters Art Museum

Chariot Race – Attic black-figure hydria ca 510 BCE
Source: Wikimedia Commonsm Metropolitan Museum of Art

Racing with a rider on horseback was six laps of the hippodrome for a total distance of 6,500 metres. However, chariot racing was the most prestigious equestrian event in the Olympic Games and the various other Panhellenic Games in Greece. There were two-horse and four-horse chariot races over different distances. In each race, as many as twenty chariots would compete for up to twelve laps of the hippodrome, a total length of 13,000 metres. There were also separate races for chariots drawn by foals and carts drawn by a team of two mules.

Chariot racing remained among the most popular Ancient Greek and later Roman and Byzantine sports. It continued until the 13th century CE at the Hippodrome of Constantinople, where the stands could hold 100,000 people.

While Plato mentions that the Atlanteans raced horses, he does not explicitly mention chariot racing. As chariots were a significant component of the Atlanteans' military, it seems likely that they would have raced chariots as well as horses with a rider.

Using Plato's dimensions, if the Atlanteans used the Royal City's second land zone for horse-racing,

Reconstruction Circus Maximus, Rome
Source: Wikimedia Commons – Pascal Radigue

Ballcourt at Monte Alban
Source: Wikimedia Commons – Andrew McMillan

the racing track would have been a circuit of 10,000 metres. The hippodromes of the Ancient Greeks of Solon and Plato's time had nothing in common with the Atlanteans' horse-racing track, neither in its shape, length, or width. This contrast is yet another example that Plato did not base Atlantean culture on Greek culture.

Rubber Ball Games

Plato (Taylor) – 'there were trees, whose fruits are used for the sake of sport and pleasure, and which it is difficult to conceal'.

Plato (Jowett) – 'and the fruits…which furnish pleasure and amusement'.

The rubber tree is the only tree likely to produce any 'fruit' that the Atlanteans could use for 'sport and pleasure' or 'pleasure and amusement'. That 'fruit' would be in the form of a rubber ball, and the Atlanteans possibly played various games that used rubber balls.

Rubber was made from the latex of the Mexican rubber tree, *Castilla elastica*. The latex was mixed with the juice of *Ipomoea alba* (a species of morning glory) to make rubber. Archaeological evidence indicates that rubber was already used in Mesoamerica by the Early Formative Period, around 2000 BCE. By the time of the Spanish Conquest, more than three thousand years later, rubber was being exported from the tropical zones to sites all over Mesoamerica. Since the rubber tree is indigenous to the tropical areas of southern Mexico, Mesoamerica and northern South America, it would likely have grown on the nearby Atlantic Island.

What the ancient Olmec people of Mesoamerica called themselves is unknown. Thousands of years later, the Aztec referred to the people who then inhabited that region as the Olmeca or rubber people because the area was strongly identified with latex. A dozen rubber balls found in the Olmec heartland at the El Manati sacrificial bog were dated to roughly 1600 BCE. Rubber balls like these were used in the Mesoamerican ballgame or *Tlatchtli* in the Nahuatl language. It is not known precisely when or where the game originated, but the Olmec must have played it well before 1600 BCE. The oldest ballcourt discovered dates to approximately 1400 BCE at Paso de la Amadain, in the coastal lowlands along the Pacific Ocean.

The Mesoamerican ballgame had ritual aspects, with major formal ballgames held as ceremonial events and often featuring human sacrifice. The ritual ballgame was played within a large masonry structure. Over 1,300 ballcourts have been identified throughout Mesoamerica, as far south as Nicaragua and possibly as far north as Arizona, USA. In the Caribbean, the Tainos played a rubber ballgame known as *batey* in rectangular ballcourts.

Despite a considerable variation in ballcourt size, its overall form changed little over 2,700 years. All ballcourts have a long, narrow playing alley flanked by horizontal and sloping walls, or more rarely, vertical walls. The Maya playing field of the Great Ballcourt at Chichen Itza measures 96.5 metres long by 30 metres wide. In contrast, the Ceremonial Court at Tikal is only 16 metres by 5 metres.

The hip-ball version is usually considered the main Mesoamerican ballgame and was the primary or possibly only version played in the masonry ballcourts. Games were played between two teams, who hit the ball back and forth using only the hips until one team failed to return it or the ball left the court. The hip-game player's outfit consisted of a loincloth and sometimes leather hip guards. Further protection often was a thick girdle, most likely made of wicker or wood covered with fabric or leather. Kneepads, helmets and elaborate headdresses are common in ballplayer images but were probably used only in ritual games.

Apart from ritual games, the sport was played casually for recreation by men, children and possibly women. There were games where the ball was

Great Ballcourt at Chichen Itza
Source: Wikimedia Commons – Luis Fernandez Garcia

Ritual Ball Players

struck by racquets, bats, batons, hand-stones and the forearm. A mural at Teotihuacan shows a game that resembles field hockey. The various types of games each had their specific ball size, specialised gear, playing field and rules. The ball consisted of rubber strips wound around a solid rubber core. For the ritual ballgame, the ball was roughly 20 centimetres in diameter and weighed 3–4 kilograms.

The Ancient Egyptians and Greeks were unaware of the rubber tree or its products, so the idea of the Atlanteans playing with a bouncing rubber ball would have been strange to them. The rubber ball and the various forms of the Mesoamerican ballgame would have been unknown to Egyptians and Greeks. This strangeness may explain Plato's comments about a fruit used for 'sport and pleasure' 'which it is difficult to conceal'. In other words, an activity not known or understood in the Old World and is difficult to describe.

Ancient Ships and Sea Travel

Plato – 'the largest of the harbours (of the Royal City) were full of vessels and merchants coming from all parts, who, from their numbers, kept up a multitudinous sound of human voices, and din and clatter of all sorts night and day'...'because of the greatness of their (Atlantean) empire many things were brought to them from foreign countries.'

Plato states that the extensive Atlantean Empire of 11,600 BP possessed many warships and merchant vessels. The Atlanteans had to build ships to sail safely in open seas, initially from the Atlantic Island to the Americas and eventually to the rest of the expanding Atlantean Empire in Africa, Europe, and then into the Mediterranean. As the Atlanteans had at least a Bronze Age level of technology, it would have allowed them to build those seaworthy ships.

Over the past tens and hundreds of thousands of years, our species *Homo sapiens*, and even our *Homo erectus* ancestors before us, built vessels that could transport people safely over many kilometres of water. The first humans to colonise the Atlantic Island in the Caribbean most likely travelled there by sea from the Americas thousands of years before 11,600 BP. They needed to travel over water for tens to hundreds of kilometres, either directly from a nearby point in northern South America or by island–hopping from south–eastern North America. Those first settlers only required a Palaeolithic or Neolithic level of technology to build vessels that could travel relatively short distances.

By the time the Atlanteans could sail to the Mediterranean before 11,600 BP, their ships had

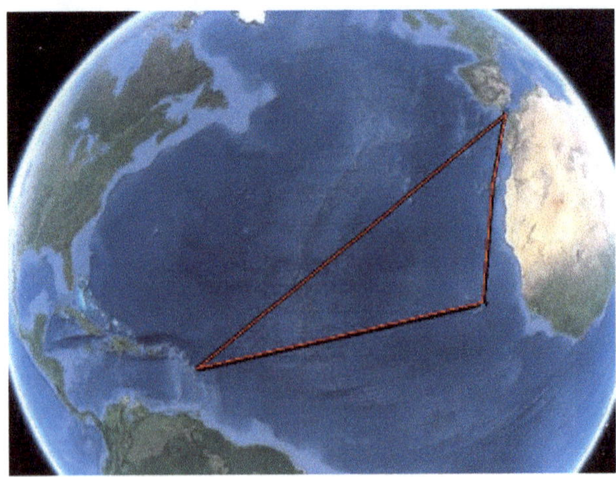

The Caribbean to Mediterranean Sea Routes
Source: Modified from Google Earth

to be seaworthy for open–ocean travel; they had to reach remote destinations and safely return to the Atlantic Island. To initially expand their empire into the Americas, the Atlanteans only had to sail distances of hundreds of kilometres, but it was much further to the Mediterranean.

The direct sailing distance across the North Atlantic from the Caribbean to the Mediterranean is around 6,000 kilometres. Indirectly, it is 4,000km east to the Cape Verde Islands off the coast of Africa, another 1,500km north to the Canary Islands, and then 1,300km further north to Gibraltar for a total distance of over 7,000km.

Since at least the Bronze Age and possibly the Neolithic, ancient Old World cultures have had shipbuilding technology for open–ocean sailing. In a few thousand years or less, ancient cultures in various parts of the Old World invented and built seaworthy ships for war and trade.

From the 9th century CE, the Vikings sailed small wooden boats of 25–30 metres across the Atlantic between Northern Europe and North America. Within a few hundred years, the Spanish and Portuguese routinely sailed in small wooden ships from Europe to trade with their colonies in the Americas.

Thousands of years before the Vikings crossed the Atlantic, the ancient shipbuilders and sailors of the Old World had the technical expertise to build and sail ships that were at least the equivalent of Viking, Spanish and Portuguese ships. If the Atlanteans had used those same ancient shipbuilding methods, they could have constructed reliable vessels for long-distance open-sea travel. They then could regularly sail to and from the Mediterranean and other parts of the Atlantean Empire.

Palaeolithic and Neolithic Sea Travel

Our early human ancestors, *Homo erectus*, invented rafts or other watercraft to travel over large bodies of water. By 800,000 BP, *Homo erectus* established a substantial population on the Indonesian island of Flores. But before they could get there, they had to settle the two major islands of Lombok and Sumbawa, which lie between Bali and Flores. Thirty-five kilometres of open water separates Lombok and Sumbawa, so the only way *Homo erectus* could travel between them was by sea.

Stone tools of Lower Palaeolithic type from 700,000–130,000 BP were found on the Greek island of Crete. The Mediterranean Sea has isolated Crete for at least five million years, so human ancestors such as *Homo erectus* must have arrived there by sea. The journey from Africa to Crete would have involved an open-sea crossing of 300 kilometres, while it is 100 kilometres to the nearest Greek mainland.

The oldest recognised marine crossing made by our species, *Homo sapiens*, was from Indonesia to Australia around 60,000 BP. In Japan, *Homo sapiens* from around 30,000 BP brought obsidian to the main island of Honshu from the small island of Kozushima, some 50 kilometres away, requiring regular sea crossings in both directions.

Evidence shows that *Homo sapiens* occupied northern Australia from at least 55,000 BP. The settlement of the Australia-New Guinea area (joined during lower sea levels as the continent of Sahul) could only have been by sea travel.

Oceania is a region centred on the islands of the South Pacific – divided ethnologically into the subregions of Melanesia, Micronesia and Polynesia. All of these island groups were settled by sea travel. In Melanesia, occupation dates are New Ireland at around 33,000 BP, the northern end of the Solomons chain by 29,000 BP, and New Britain by 11,400 BP. All of those island groups had to be reached by sea travel.

Between 5,000 and 3,000 BP, a new group travelled by sea through the islands of South-East

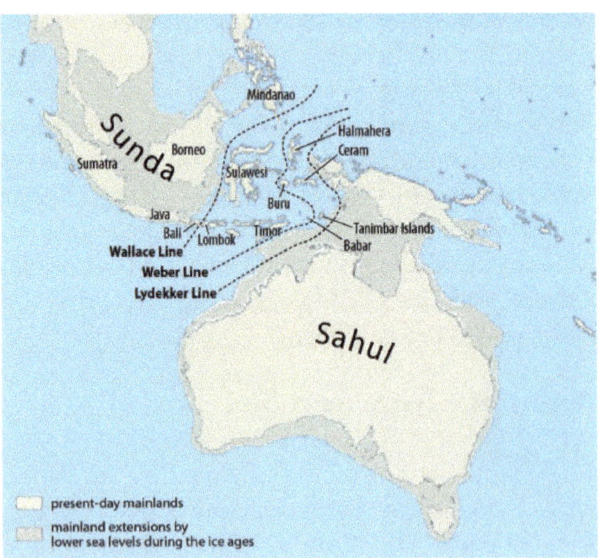

Sunda and Sahul
Source: Wikimedia Commons – Maximillian Dorrbecker

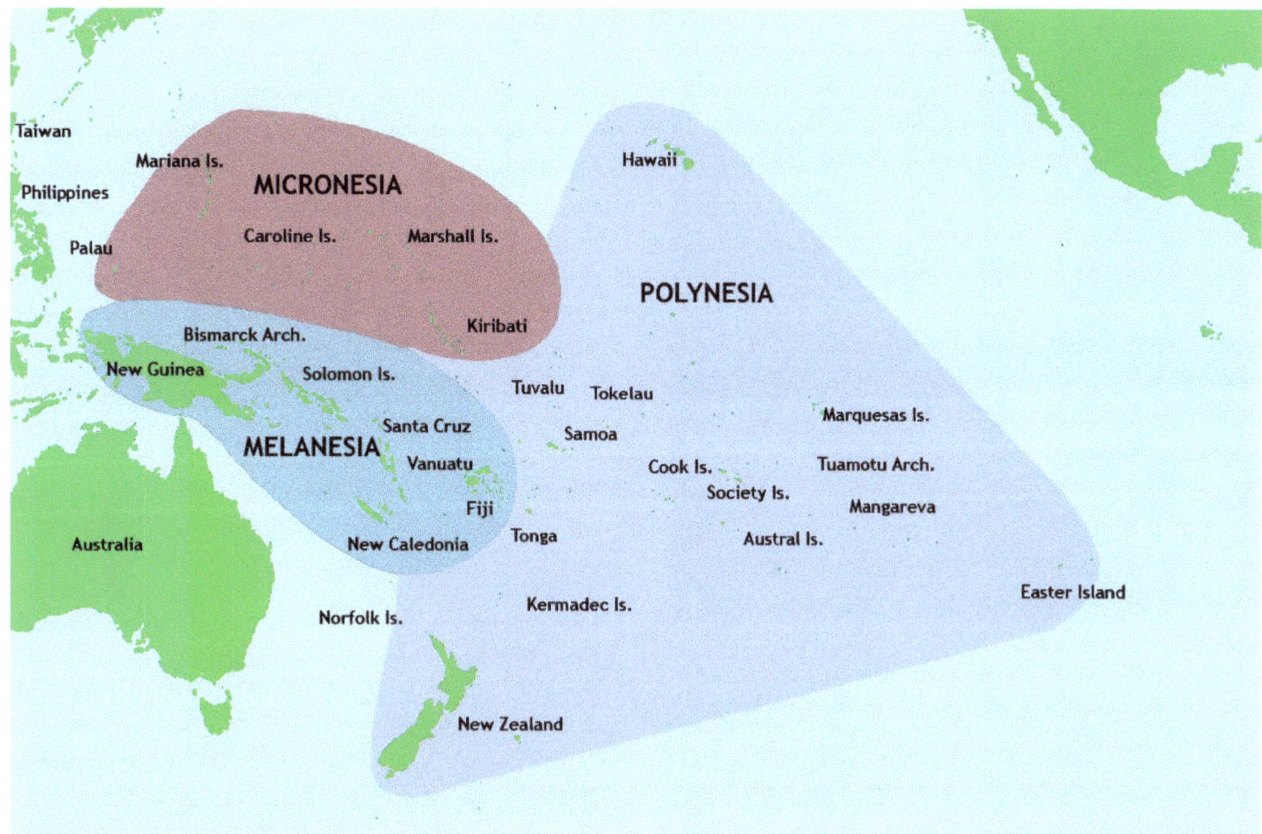

Ethno-cultural Divisions of Oceania
Source: Wikimedia Commons – Kahuroa

Asia. They started migrating from the island of Taiwan, where they were thought to have arrived from mainland South China around 8,000 BP. They then spread to the edges of western Micronesia and on into Melanesia.

In the mid-4th millennium BP, the Lapita Culture appeared suddenly in the Bismarck Archipelago in north-west Melanesia. Within three or four centuries, from 3,300–2,900 BP, the Lapita Culture spread 6,000 kilometres further east from the Bismarck Archipelago until it reached as far as Tonga and Samoa, where it developed into a distinctive Polynesian Culture. The Polynesians then spread out from the Samoan Islands as far as Easter Island and New Zealand.

Polynesian Voyaging Canoe
Source: Herb Kawainui Kane

Entire villages of people settled the new islands by sailing on large double-hulled voyaging canoes in Polynesia or canoes with an outrigger on one side in Micronesia. The Polynesians and their predecessors constructed their ships without using metals, building them from island materials such as plaited leaf sails, island woods, and organic webbing. The size of vessels for deep-sea voyaging was 15–23 metres, with a platform between the hulls. The canoes were planked vessels with broad planks fastened to each other, to ribs, and the keel, stitched or lashed together with coconut fibre.

In the Eastern Mediterranean during the Mesolithic and early Neolithic, obsidian was mined and exported from the island of Melos, with the first known obsidians from Melos appearing in Franchthi Cave in the Peloponnese around 13,000 BP. The inhabitants of Greece had to travel between the Greek mainland and the island of Melos for sea journeys of over 100 kilometres each way. Obsidian tools originating from Melos have been found in Crete, Cyprus and Egypt and must have reached there by sea.

The earliest representation of a ship under sail appears on a painted disc found in present-day Kuwait, dating between 7,000 and 7,500 BP. The earliest historical records of seafaring ships in Egypt are Neolithic petroglyphs (rock art) in Egypt's eastern desert. Dated to the Naqada period of Egyptian history from around 6,500–5,000 BP, they include the earliest known petroglyphs of sails.

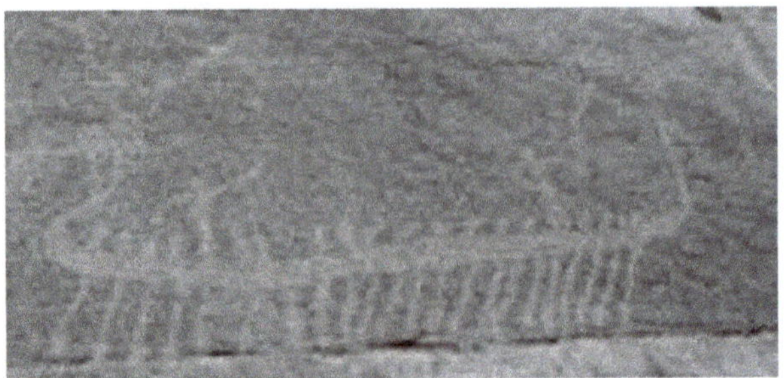

Naqada Boat Petroglyphs

Naqada petroglyphs of larger oared vessels appear to be simple images of a more advanced technology than the artists' culture. They show large ships with over twenty oarsmen per side, but they would likely have been assembled from planks for ships of that size. The petroglyph motifs suggest that distant cultures visited the Nile Valley for trade or that the Nile Valley Culture was sending regular expeditions to other cultures.

Bronze and Iron Age Ships

Some of the oldest wooden Egyptian ships yet discovered were excavated in Abydos and were ritually buried in boat graves shortly after 3000 BCE. This group of fourteen ships averaged twenty-five metres long and three metres wide. The Ancient Egyptians constructed their ships from sawn wooden planks and used mortise and tenon joints that were sewn together, and then reeds or grass were stuffed between the planks to seal the seams. They also fastened together planks of wood with wooden dowels and used pitch to caulk the seams.

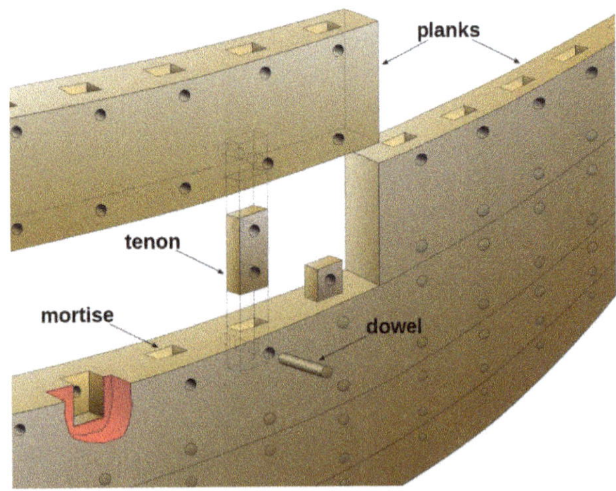

The mortise and tenon joint method of hull construction
Source: Wikimedia Commons – Eric Gaba

In the 15th century BCE, the Egyptian Queen Hatshepsut built a Red Sea fleet to trade between Egypt and as far south as the land of Punt, probably in the Horn of Africa. During Hatshepsut's reign, ships regularly crossed the Red Sea to obtain bitumen, copper, carved amulets, naphtha and other goods transported overland from civilisations in the east.

The Bronze Age Minoan civilisation (ca. 3100–1050 BCE) was based on the Aegean island of Crete. By 2000 BCE, it had evolved into a naval power controlling much of the Eastern Mediterranean. Minoan objects discovered outside Crete indicate two-way commerce with Egypt, Asia Minor, Cyprus, Canaan and the Levant, and Western Italy, where the Minoans obtained tin and copper to make bronze. Depictions of ships on Minoan seals and frescoes show vessels about 20 metres long with square sails and generally with 15 oars on each side.

Following the decline of the Minoan civilisation, Penteconters emerged during the Greek Mycenaean period (ca. 1600–1100 BCE). Penteconters were long-range ships capable of transporting freight or troops and were used for sea trade, piracy and warfare. They were 28 to 33 metres long and approximately four metres wide, with a midship mast and a square sail. They had fifty oarsmen in two rows of twenty-five on each side of the ship, with a top speed of 9 knots (18km/h). The Mycenaeans also used the

Egyptian Ship Model

Minoan Ship Model

triaconter, a shorter version of the penteconter with thirty oars.

The Mycenaeans used their ships for trade with Palestine, Egypt, and the centres of the Western Mediterranean in South Italy, Sicily and Sardinia. Evidence of Mycenaean trading posts has been identified in Italy, Spain, and Cornwall in England, where Mycenaean traders probably obtained tin to make bronze. The penteconter remained in use for over one thousand years until the Hellenistic period (ca. 330–320 BCE), when other designs such as the lembos, the hemiolia and the liburnian replaced it.

After 1200 BCE, from their base in several cities in the Levant, the Phoenicians became the Eastern Mediterranean's dominant naval and trading power. Initially, they traded mainly with the Greeks and provided timber, slaves, glass and powdered Tyrian purple (a violet-purple dye used by the Greek elite to colour garments).

The Phoenicians and Greeks gradually mastered navigation at sea, exploring and colonising the Mediterranean via ship. Herodotus described the Phoenicians making the first circumnavigation of Africa around 600 BCE, sailing clockwise from the Red Sea, around Africa and back into the Mediterranean.

Around 325 BCE, the Greek geographer and explorer Pytheas of Massalia (the Greek colony now called Marseilles in France) made a voyage of exploration to north-west Europe. Pytheas circumnavigated and visited much of Great Britain, and he is the first known person to describe the Midnight Sun, polar ice, and Germanic and possibly Finnic tribes.

Penteconter

A Junk from the 13th century CE, Song Dynasty
Source: Wikimedia Commons

While the Chinese used sails on ships from around 3,000 BCE, archives from the late Spring and Autumn Period (722 BC–481 BCE) describe various warship types. Large barge-like ships called castle ships had layered decks and cabins with ramparts, acting as floating fortresses. There were four other known ship types in that period, including a ramming vessel.

The Chinese developed a ship known as the Junk during the Han Dynasty (202 BCE–220 CE). During the Qin Dynasty (221–207 BCE), the Chinese sailed south into the South China Sea during their invasion of Annam, modern Vietnam. The 3rd century CE book *Strange Things of the South* by Wan Chen describes Junks capable of carrying 700 people with 260 tonnes of cargo. A 260 CE book by Kang Tai also describes ships with seven masts travelling as far as Syria.

The first explicit mention of a navy in India occurs in the mythological epic *Mahabharata*, written around 400 BCE but with its origins from the 8th and 9th centuries BCE. Historically, the first attempt to organise a navy in India was described by the Greek author Megasthenes (ca. 350–290 BCE) and is credited to Chandragupta Maurya (reign 322–298 BCE). The navy of the Mauryan Empire continued until emperor Ashoka (reign 273–232 BCE), who used it to send diplomatic missions to Greece, Syria, Egypt, Cyrene, Macedonia and Epirus.

Merchant Ships

Around 12,000 BP, fishing and sailing communities settled in coastal areas in South Asia – present-day India and Pakistan. These communities often combined fishing with trading ventures, with increasing maritime voyages from the region around the Indus River by 5,000 BP.

The Ancient Sumerians of Mesopotamia used square-rigged sailing boats around the same time as the Egyptians, in the 4th millennium BCE. They established sea trading routes as far as the Indus Valley Civilisation in north-west India. Mesopotamian inscriptions indicate that Indian traders from the Indus Valley shipped copper, hardwoods, ivory, pearls, carnelian and gold to Mesopotamia during the reign of Sargon of Akkad (ca. 2300 BCE).

Ancient Egyptian and Syrian communities had regular maritime trade links well before the formation of the Egyptian state around 3050 BCE. Some excavated artefacts in Egypt contain Mesopotamian motifs, suggesting travel by sea to and from the Persian Gulf and Euphrates River.

Egyptian Merchant Ship

Around 2500 BCE, the Egyptian Pharaoh Sneferu used a fleet of 40 ships to import cedar logs from Lebanon. By around 1500 BCE, the Egyptians built merchant ships displacing 60–80 tonnes, but they also had much larger vessels that transported building materials such as massive obelisks and stone blocks for pyramids.

Minoan traders from Crete were active in the Eastern Mediterranean by the 2nd millennium BCE. A Minoan shipwreck discovered off the north-eastern coast of Crete was between 10–16 metres long and had 209 ceramic containers that would have transported liquids such as wine and olive oil.

The Uluburun Shipwreck is a Late Bronze Age shipwreck discovered off south-western Turkey and dated to the late 14th century BCE. The ship was 15–16 metres long and constructed with mortise-and-tenon joints similar to those of later Graeco-Roman ships. The ship's cargo mainly consisted of trade items from nine or ten cultures ranging from Northern Europe to Africa, from as far west as Sicily to as far east as Mesopotamia.

The earliest evidence of Phoenician merchant ships comes from an Egyptian tomb relief of around 1400 BCE, which shows Phoenician ships unloading in an Egyptian port. The Phoenicians developed the round boat to carry trade items. It was a broad-beamed ship powered by sails rather than oars and had a much larger cargo space than narrow war galleys.

The Greeks built short, wide merchant ships similar to the Phoenicians. Their small ships sailed among the islands of the Aegean Sea and had shallow draughts to moor in the shallow waters of local ports. Larger ships for more distant voyages had 200–300 tonnes displacement. The Greeks regularly imported goods from the Black Sea coasts, Egypt and Sicily; and exported wine, oil, honey and craft items. Most of the products were carried in a ceramic container called an amphora with an average capacity of 20 litres. Fragments have been found of a sunken Greek merchant vessel 26 metres long and 12 metres wide, with 10,000 amphorae on board.

The Greeks carried out a large part of the sea trade of the later Roman Empire. Roman seagoing commercial ships made no significant advances over Greek ships of the previous centuries. They were round-hulled, with the majority having a capacity of over 100 tonnes, while the largest ships could carry 500 tonnes. The cost of sea transportation was 60 times lower than for land, so bulky, low-valued commodities such as grain and construction materials were traded only by sea.

The Byzantines' first merchant ships were comparatively small and round-hulled with one, two or three masts, each with a triangular (lateen) sail. Later, in the 14th and 15th centuries CE, Mediterranean merchant galleys traded high-value goods and carried passengers between the Mediterranean, the Black Sea, and the Atlantic coast of Europe. Merchant ship sizes ranged from the Venetian galera of 100–300 tonnes to the Genoese carrack of the 15th century CE of over 1,000 tonnes.

Medieval Western Europe

The ships of Medieval Europe were powered by sail, oar, or both. Shipbuilding in Southern Europe was influenced by Greek or Roman vessels, whereas in Northern Europe, it was influenced more by Viking vessels.

From the late 8th to the mid-11th century CE, Viking sailors from Scandinavia raided, traded, explored and settled areas of Europe, Asia and the North Atlantic islands. Vikings sailed from their homelands to the Faroe Islands, Iceland, Greenland, Newfoundland, the Mediterranean, the Black Sea, and Africa.

The Viking longship was built for warfare and exploration. It appeared in its complete form between the 9th and 13th centuries CE, but its design had evolved over thousands of years. Nordic shipbuilding developed the clinker technique, different from the Mediterranean mortise and tenon planking (Carvel) method. Though there were several types of Viking ships, they were all clinker-built, with overlapping planks riveted together.

Viking longships had a long, narrow hull and shallow draught for landings and troop deployment in shallow water. The Vikings used oars to complement the square sail set on a single mainmast. Longships ranged in size from the 20-metre-long Karvi with 13 rowing benches to the Busse with an estimated 34 rowing positions to large Dragon-ships carrying 100 warriors. The average speed of Viking ships varied depending on the ship type but was 5-10 knots. The maximum speed of a longship under favourable wind conditions was around 15 knots.

The Knarr was a dedicated Viking merchant sailing vessel designed to carry bulk cargo. It was

16 metres long, had a beam of 4-5 metres, a broad hull, deep draught and a few oars to manoeuvre in harbours. The Knarr had a crew of 20–30, could carry 120 tonnes of cargo and could sail 120 kilometres in one day. These merchant ships routinely crossed the North Atlantic, carrying livestock and stores to Viking colonies in Greenland.

Carvel planking gradually emerged in the medieval period and developed from the Ancient Mediterranean mortise and tenon method. Carvel was a skeleton-first hull-building technique, with hull planks fastened edge-to-edge over a timber frame. The planks formed a smooth surface in contrast to the overlapping clinker method the Vikings used.

By 1450 CE, the Portuguese developed the Caravel ship type based on African fishing boats. They were 15–25 metres long, with one to three masts and triangular lateen sails allowing windward sailing (beating). The Portuguese used Caravels to explore the West African coast and sail into the Atlantic Ocean.

Longer ocean voyages led to larger ships that were stable in heavy seas, with enough space to carry more provisions. The Carrack was a three or four-masted sailing ship developed in the 15th century CE for use in the Atlantic Ocean and could carry colonists, arms, tools and provisions. Carracks grew from 20 metres and 200 tonnes capacity to 45 metres and 500 tonnes capacity. The Carrack was usually square-rigged on the fore-mast and main-mast and lateen-rigged on the mizzen-mast.

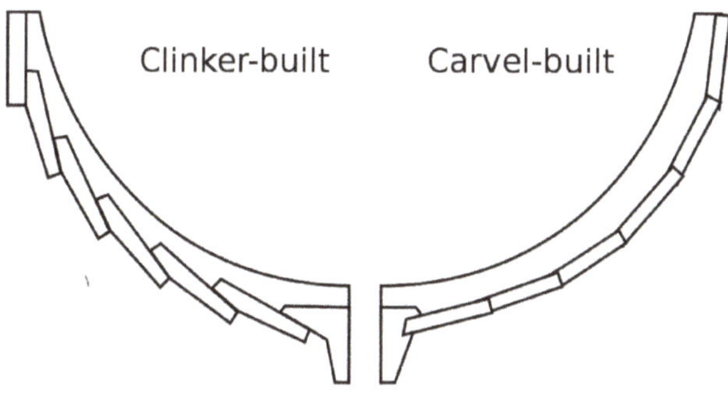

Clinker and Carvel Planking
Source: Wikimedia Commons – Willhig

Viking ship Sebbe Als of Augustenborg, Denmark under sail
Source: Wikimedia Commons

Lateen-rigged Caravel

Carrack

Carracks were used first by the Portuguese and later by the Spanish to explore the world's oceans. Portuguese sailors began exploring the coast of Africa and the Atlantic archipelagos in 1418–19 CE. In 1488 CE, Bartolomeu Dias rounded the southern tip of Africa, and Vasco da Gama reached India in 1498 CE.

With three small Spanish ships in 1492 CE, Christopher Columbus embarked on his first expedition across the Atlantic Ocean to the Americas while trying to find a shorter route to India. The Carrack Santa Maria was Columbus' flagship and the largest of his ships at 20 metres and 100–150 tonnes capacity. The Pinta and Nina were smaller Caravels of around 15–18 metres and 50–75 tonnes capacity.

In 1519 CE, Ferdinand Magellan left Seville in Spain in five ships with a crew of 270. The fleet comprised four Carracks and one Caravel. Magellan wanted to find a commercial western route to Asia around the southern tip of South

America. Losses occurred due to mutiny, desertion, storms, and battles against the indigenous peoples they encountered, which included the killing of Magellan in the Philippines. Only one ship and eighteen of the original crew sailed back to Spain in 1522 CE. They became the first people known to have circumnavigated the Earth.

Trade and Shipping in the Ancient Americas

Long-distance trade was a feature of Atlantean civilisation as 'many things were brought to them from foreign countries'. From the time of the earliest known civilisations in the Americas, long-distance trade over land and water was essential for their development.

Old Copper Culture

From at least 6,000 BP, the Old Copper Culture of the Great Lakes region of North America produced and traded tens of thousands of copper ingots, worked tools, and weapons. Old Copper Culture artefacts have been found in Canada from Alberta in the west to Quebec in the east, in the United States as far west as North Dakota, east as Delaware, and south as Kentucky.

Olmec

While the Olmec were not the first culture in Mesoamerica to organise long-distance exchanges of goods, the Olmec period after 1200 BCE saw a significant expansion in trade routes along rivers and overland. Like other Mesoamerican cultures, the Olmec used bitumen as an adhesive and decorative material. Another important use of bitumen was waterproofing for the planked boats that supported the vast Olmec trade network.

The Olmec were skilled artisans who traded their pottery, celts, statues and figurines in exchange for stone such as basalt, obsidian, serpentine and jadeite; commodities such as salt, and animal products such as pelts, bright feathers, and seashells. The wide distribution of Olmec artefacts and Olmecoid images throughout Mesoamerica and hundreds of kilometres into Mexico indicates extensive long-distance trade networks.

Maya and the Yokot'an

The first clear evidence of Maya sea trade is in the Maya Late Preclassic (400 BCE–100 CE), while trade between the coast and inland developed in the Classic period (250–900 CE). The coastal Maya called themselves the Yokot'anob or the Yokot'an but are now more commonly called the Chontal Maya. Their homeland was in the Mexican State of Tabasco. The Yokot'an claimed to be direct descendants of the Olmec, but the true Maya considered them illiterate barbarians.

Yokot'an Ship

The Yokot'an were proficient seafarers and dominated the coastal trade between the Mexican Highland civilisations and the Maya. They eventually became the principal merchants for all of Mesoamerica.

The Yokot'an built boats the same size and construction as the Viking longboat. Constructed from wooden planks, they were usually 20 metres long, used rudders for steering, and were propelled by oarsmen and one or more sails. These ocean-going ships regularly navigated the Gulf of Mexico and the Caribbean Sea.

After the Maya cities began collapsing in the 8th century CE, Yokot'an boats travelled longer distances in search of new trading markets. These later expeditions traded Gulf Coast and Caribbean Basin commodities with the Totonac and Toltec cities of Mexico's interior.

Caribbean

Canoes in the Caribbean were usually constructed from a single log with no sail. Small fishing canoes could hold one or a few individuals, whereas larger canoes could carry a few dozen people for inter-island travel and longer passages.

There are reports by Spanish chroniclers of much larger canoes, including ones that could hold between 50–60 people and even an apparent sighting of one near Jamaica that held over 100 people. These larger vessels were possibly built from wooden planks rather than hollow logs.

Ecuador and Peru

The balsa sailing raft was an Ecuadorian invention, used for trade at least since Valdivian times (5,000–3,800 BP). From 400 BCE to the 16th century CE, regular sea travel occurred between Ecuador and West Mexico, a distance of more than 3,000 kilometres. Ecuadorian merchants also used paddled or sailed canoes during this period.

In 1526 CE, when Spaniard Francisco Pizarro was on his second voyage of discovery down the Pacific coast of South America, his expedition found Peruvian merchant sailors on balsa rafts out at sea. The Spaniards reported that the rafts had masts and yards of very fine wood, with cotton sails the same shape as on the Spanish ships. They had stronger hemp rigging than the Spaniards' rope and used mooring stones for anchors.

Later Spanish records show these craft regularly sailed from Ecuador to Lima in the south and Panama in the north for over 1,100km. Balsa rafts had a length of 25–30 metres, a width of 8–10 metres, a freight capacity of 20–25 tonnes, and speeds of four to five knots. They were navigated by raising and lowering centreboards inserted in the gaps between the logs in different parts of the raft so that it could perform all the manoeuvres of a European sailing vessel.

Ancient Navigation

As well as having seaworthy ships, the Atlanteans needed navigational skills to sail throughout the Atlantean Empire. They would have sailed routinely in the Caribbean and coastal Americas, made frequent crossings of the Atlantic Ocean, and sailed within the Mediterranean. The Atlanteans could have made these voyages using observational techniques and some relatively simple instruments similar to those invented and used by early Old World navigators.

The Polynesians sailed across thousands of kilometres of the Pacific Ocean for thousands of years. They had to find their way between small inhabited islands in that vast ocean. Polynesians navigated by relying on their senses and knowledge passed by oral tradition from navigator to apprentice, often in the form of song. To locate directions, navigators memorised where particular stars would rise and set on the horizon, the weather during different seasons, the direction, size and speed of ocean waves, the colours of the sea and sky, and the angles to approach harbours.

The Marshallese islanders used stick-charts to navigate the Pacific Ocean. Stick-charts were usually made from the midribs of coconut fronds, tied together to form an open framework. The charts represented major ocean swell patterns and the ways the islands disrupted those patterns. They were studied and memorised before a voyage but were not used during the trip.

Ancient Mediterranean sailors used several navigation techniques, including staying in sight of land and understanding the prevailing winds. The Minoans used celestial navigation, where sailors located particular stars to orient the ship's direction. One navigational tool the Greeks, Phoenicians and Carthaginians used was a sounding weight. It was bell-shaped, made from stone or lead with tallow inside and attached to a long rope. When out to sea, sailors lowered the sounding weight to measure how deep the waters were, and the tallow would pick up a sample of the sea bottom. They could then estimate how far they were from land.

The Phoenicians, Greeks and Romans used the *periplus*: a manuscript document for a voyage that listed ports and coastal landmarks in order and the approximate distances between them. From the 6th century BCE, the Greeks used nautical charts and textual descriptions of sailing directions, while maps date back to the 2nd century BCE. Navigational maps called portolan charts began to appear in Italy at the end of the 13th century CE and later in Spain and Portugal.

In the 10th century CE, Vikings navigated using a circular wooden board notched at the edge with lines scored into it. It allowed ships to be steered

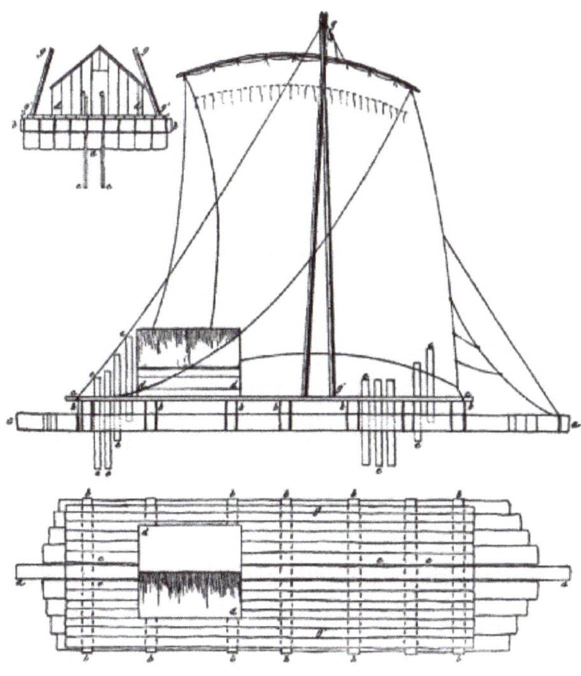

Balsa Raft
Source: F.E. Paris, 1841

Micronesian stick-chart
Source: Wikimedia Commons – Cullen328

Viking Sun-compass – speculative replica
Source: Wikimedia Commons – Praenomen3

accurately along an east-west line as the north and south position could be deduced from the Sun's shadow on the board. Vikings also used a polarising sunstone to navigate by locating the Sun even in an entirely overcast sky.

Islamic geographers and navigators developed a simple instrument called a kamal in the 9th century CE. They used it for celestial navigation and measuring the altitudes and latitudes of the stars. The kamal was a rectangular piece of either bone or wood called a transom, with a string with nine consecutive knots attached to it. The knotted string was held in one's teeth to standardise the arm's length distance at which the transom was held. Before leaving home, the navigator tied a knot in the line so that, when held in his teeth, he could sight the North Star Polaris just over the top of the transom and the horizon just below. To go home, he would sail north or south until Polaris lined up with the transom the way it did at home, then sail along that line of latitude.

The Arabs later introduced two other navigational instruments to Europe that were more advanced than the kamal: the quadrant and the astrolabe. When these instruments were combined with accurate maps, sailors could sail more confidently across open-ocean rather than skirt along the coast.

The quadrant was more accurate in measuring latitude than the kamal. It was shaped like a quarter-circle and was divided into ninety-degree intervals. The quadrant was held vertically in line-of-sight of the star selected as a reference point. A navigator would then mark the latitudes of his ports on the instrument, similar to tying a knot in the string of a kamal.

Kamal

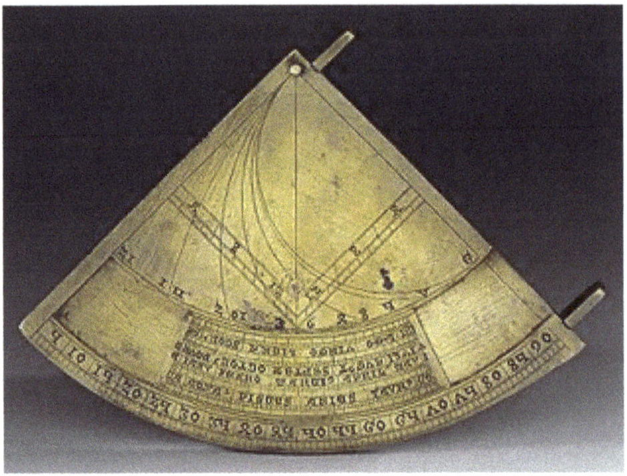

Quadrant – late 14th century–early 15th century
Source: Wikimedia Commons

The astrolabe is an instrument that measures the altitude of stars and planets above the horizon. An early astrolabe was invented in the Hellenistic world in 150 BCE and is often attributed to Hipparchus, a Greek astronomer, geographer and mathematician. Astrolabes were further developed in the medieval Islamic world. They could determine latitude on land but were awkward for use on the heaving deck of a ship. Sometime in the 13th century CE, Portuguese navigators developed the mariner's astrolabe to solve this problem. Navigators could determine a ship's latitude by measuring the Sun's altitude or declination at noon or the meridian altitude of a star of known declination. In the early 15th century CE, the Portuguese computed tables of the sun's declination and improved the mariner's astrolabe to determine latitude better.

The magnetic compass was developed in China sometime between 1040 and 1117 CE. The true mariner's compass, which used a pivoting needle in a dry box, was invented in Europe before 1300 CE.

Logs are nautical instruments designed to measure the speed of a ship through water. The Portuguese developed the chip log at the end of the 15th century CE. It consisted of a weighted wooden board attached to a line (the log-line) with knots tied at uniform spacings. A sailor would drop the board

Mariner's Astrolabe
Source: Wikimedia Commons – Museu da Marinha, Portugal

Chinese Mariner's Compass
Source: Wikimedia Commons – Victoria C

Chip Log

Marine Chronometer 1763 CE
Source: Wikimedia Commons – PHGCOM

over the ship's stern and count the number of knots that passed through his hands in a fixed time, usually measured with a sandglass. This measurement would then give the ship's speed in knots.

If the Atlanteans of 11,600 BP had a Bronze Age level of technology and had been sailing for hundreds of years or more, they could have invented and used all the navigation methods described so far. That basic level of navigation technology allowed European sailors to circumnavigate the Earth in the early 16th century CE. It allowed the European empires to colonise and trade with most of the world before the 17th century CE. The Atlanteans could have used the same technology to sail along the coastal Americas, cross the Atlantic and sail on into the Mediterranean.

Until the mid-1750s CE, accurate navigation at sea and out of sight of land was impossible because it was difficult to calculate longitude – the east-west position of a ship. Longitude is measured by imaginary lines known as meridians that run around the Earth vertically and meet at the North and South Poles.

Latitude, the north-south position, was calculated by observing with a quadrant or astrolabe. However, longitude requires accurate time-keeping, which came with the invention of the marine chronometer in 1761 CE. It accurately measures and keeps the time of a known fixed location. For example, if it is set for Greenwich in England, it gives Greenwich Mean Time (GMT). Longitude measures a location east or west of the meridian at Greenwich. At noon on a ship, a ship's navigator can use the time difference from GMT to determine the ship's longitude.

In the early 15th century CE, coiled steel springs powered portable timekeeping devices, including the marine chronometer. The Atlanteans could have developed chronometers if they had manufactured their essential parts of coiled springs and small gears.

During the 3rd century BCE, Greek engineer Ctesibius of Alexandria developed a process for making springy bronze by increasing the proportion of tin in the copper alloy, casting the part, and hardening it with hammer blows. That technique could have made coiled springs without steel, which the Atlanteans seem not to have possessed.

The Ancient Greeks had used small bronze gears in complex configurations from at least the 2nd century BCE. The Antikythera Mechanism is an ancient analogue computer that predicts astronomical positions and eclipses. It was recovered in 1901 CE from a shipwreck off the Greek island of Antikythera, located between the southern tip of the Peloponnese and Crete. The computer's construction dates to the 2nd century BCE and has been attributed to the Greeks.

The complex mechanism was housed in a wooden box and comprised 30 bronze gears, though it may have had more that are now lost. The Antikythera

Found Remains of Antikythera Mechanism
Source: Antikythera Mechanism Research Project

Computer Model of Antikythera Device
Source: University College London

device's complexity and workmanship did not appear again until the 14th century CE when mechanical astronomical clocks were built in Western Europe.

Atlantic Winds and Ocean Currents

Regardless of the Atlanteans' shipbuilding, sailing, and navigational skills at the height of their empire around 11,600 BP, they could not have sailed regularly from the Caribbean to the Mediterranean and back again without favourable ocean currents and winds.

The North Atlantic Gyre is a circular system of ocean currents that rotates clockwise from near the Equator almost to Iceland and from the east coast of North America to the west coasts of Europe and Africa. It assists east-to-west sailing in the south and west-to-east sailing in the north.

The Trade Winds are the prevailing pattern of surface winds found in the tropics and are named so because they trade, or tread, in one uniform track. They blow to around 30° latitude on either side of the Equator at around 20 kilometres per hour. In the Northern Hemisphere, they blow from the north-east and are known as the Northeast Trade Winds, which assist sailing from east-to-west. The Westerlies blow in the north of the North Atlantic and assist sailing from west-to-east.

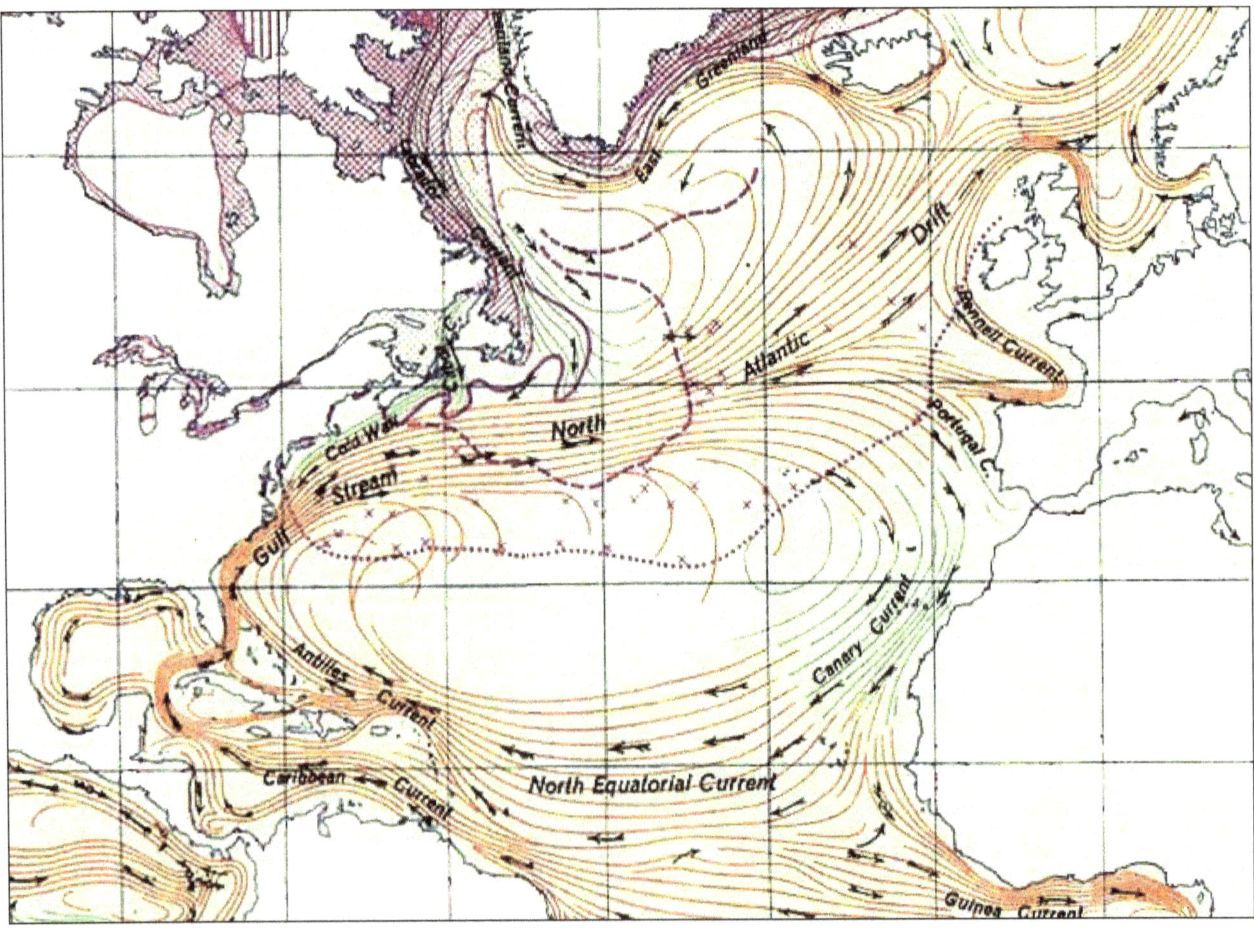

North Atlantic Gyre
Source: Wikimedia Commons – J. Rockley – modified from US Army Map

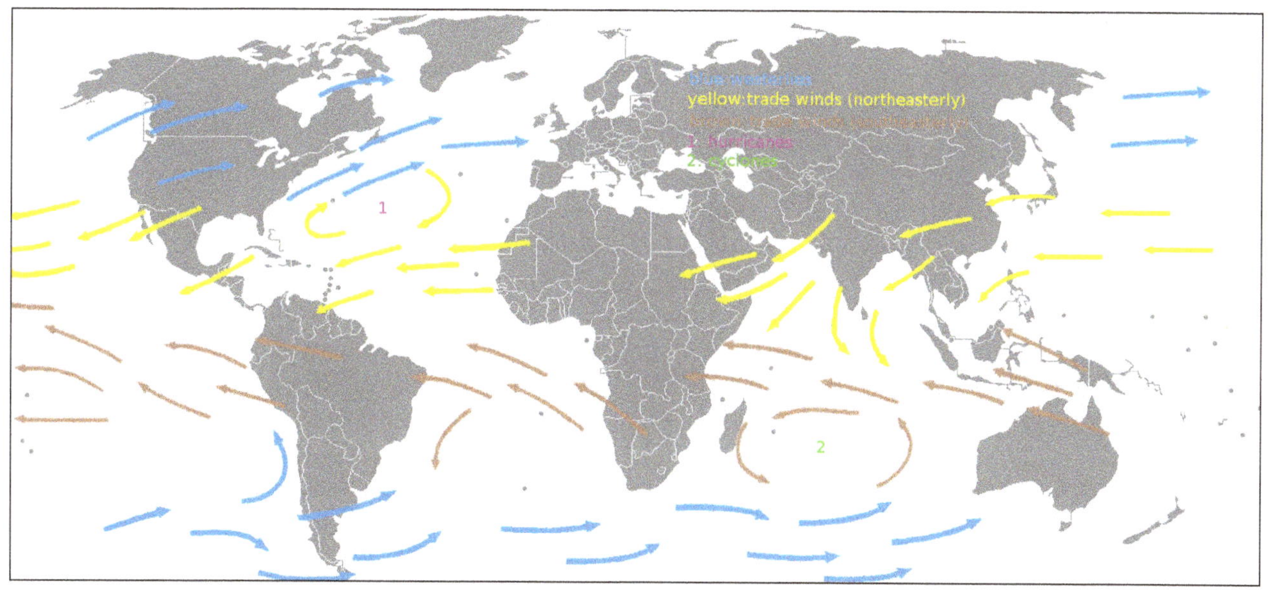

Trade Winds – westerlies (blue) and trade winds (yellow and brown)
Source: Wikimedia Commons – KVDP

The initial five-week voyage of Christopher Columbus from Spain to the Caribbean in 1492 CE and his three subsequent voyages all took the Northeast Trades outbound from east-to-west and the Westerlies back to Europe from west-to-east.

The prevailing Atlantic winds and ocean currents enabled European empires to expand into the Americas and establish regular trade routes across the Atlantic Ocean. From the 16th to the 18th century CE, Spanish ship convoys (the Spanish Treasure Fleet) numbering 30–90 vessels escorted by warships transported European goods to the Spanish colonies in the Americas and transported colonial products, especially gold and silver, back to Spain.

The Royal City's Military

The Atlantean Royal City's military was supplied and organised by dividing the great Plain of Atlantis into 60,000 small 'lots'. Each lot contributed a fixed quota of conscripted men and materials, including horses. Using calculations based on Plato's narrative,

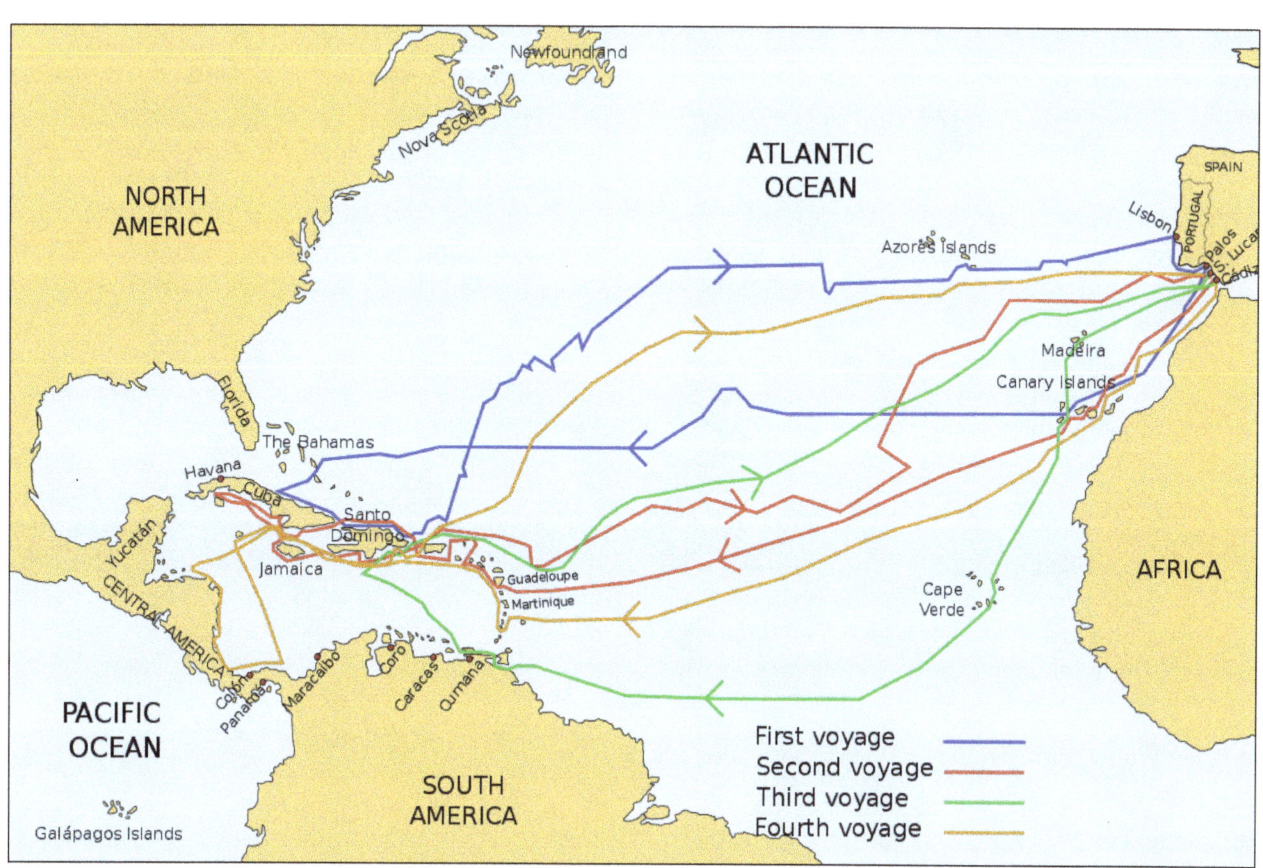

The Routes of the Four Voyages of Christopher Columbus
Source: Wikimedia Commons – Phirosiberia

the Royal City's military was huge, with over one million trained fighting men.

There is no mention of the military being sourced directly from the Royal City itself. Still, the Royal City's population may have been distributed among the lots, as was the rest of the Atlantic Island's population. Each lot had to provide troops already trained in specialised forms of combat, and an individual leader from the same lot controlled the supply and training of those troops.

Plato (Jowett) – 'As to the population, each of the lots in the plain (of the Atlantic Island) had to find a leader for the men who were fit for military service, and the size of a lot was a square of ten stadia each way (2km a side, or 4km^2), and the total number of all the lots was sixty thousand. And of the inhabitants of the mountains and of the rest of the country there was also a vast multitude, which was distributed among the lots and had leaders assigned to them according to their districts and villages.'

Plato (Jowett) – 'The leader (of each lot) was required to furnish for the war the sixth portion of a war-chariot, so as to make up a total of ten thousand chariots; also two horses and riders for them (mounted cavalry), and a pair of chariot-horses without a seat, accompanied by a horseman who could fight on foot carrying a small shield, and having a charioteer who stood behind the man-at-arms to guide the two horses'...'also, he (the leader) was bound to furnish two heavy-armed soldiers, two slingers, three stone-shooters and three javelin-men, who were light-armed, and four sailors to make up the complement of twelve hundred ships.'...'Such was the military order of the Royal City – the order of the other nine governments varied, and it would be wearisome to recount their several differences.'

There are a few differences between Jowett's and Taylor's translations of the Royal City's military. Taylor specifies that each of the 60,000 lots supplied 'two horses and two charioteers'...'two horses yoked by the side of each other, but without a seat, together with a man who may descend armed with a small shield, and who after the charioteer may govern the two horses'...'two heavy-armed soldiers'...'two slingers'...'three light-armed soldiers'...'three hurlers of stones'...'three ejaculators (javelin men)'...'four sailors'.

Taylor's translation differs from Jowett's because each lot supplied not one but two charioteers plus an armed man to fight from the chariot, two additional yoked horses, and three light-armed soldiers, as well as the two heavy-armed soldiers. Jowett mentions 'two horses and riders for them', implying mounted cavalry, but Taylor does not mention them at all. Instead, Taylor only mentions chariots, for which there are additional horses.

In both translations, there are far too many horses and charioteers for 10,000 war chariots. Regardless of whether each of the 60,000 lots provided two or four chariot-horses or one or two charioteers, 10,000 chariots would not require 120,000–240,000 chariot-horses and 60,000–120,000 charioteers.

If Jowett's translation is the more accurate and there was an Atlantean cavalry, then 'two horses and riders for them' from each lot would add up to 120,000 mounted men. Another possibility is that any additional horses and the men to handle them were used as the baggage train for the army, which may have used horse-drawn wagons or carts or horses carrying packs.

As a compromise for the differences in the two translations, the estimated size of the Atlantean Royal City's military is based on the following assumptions:

- 10,000 chariots – each with two horses, one charioteer, and one armed man
- a cavalry of 120,000 horses and riders
- 100,000 additional supply horses with men to handle them
- 1,200 ships
- Also, each of the 60,000 lots supplied:
    - one 'leader'
    - three 'light-armed soldiers'
    - two 'heavy-armed soldiers'
    - two 'slingers'
    - three 'stone-shooters' or 'hurlers of stones'
    - three 'javelin-men' or 'ejaculators'
    - four 'sailors'

Ancient military forces are commonly considered one-sixth the size of a city's population during peace and one-fifth the population size during crises and war. Using these ratios, if the Atlantean Royal City's military had over one million men, then the estimated combined population of the Royal City itself, plus that of the Plain and the Mountains, was between five and six million.

There also were the Atlantean Empire's 'other nine governments' on the Atlantic Island, which Plato states incorporated parts of the Empire beyond the Atlantic Island. They contributed more fighting men, horses, chariots, ships and other materials to the combined military of the Atlantean Empire. Therefore, the entire Atlantic Island population likely was several million more than five to six million, with many more in the remainder of the Atlantean Empire.

If the Atlanteans dug canals crisscrossing the Plain of Atlantis at 21-km intervals, they divided the Plain into large squares, each with an area of 400km^2. If every small 'lot' were a 'square of ten stadia each way' or 4km^2, there would have been 100 lots on each 400km^2 large square of land. Therefore, there

The Royal City's Military Manpower	
Lot Leaders	60,000
Charioteer + Armed Man	20,000
Cavalry	120,000
Light-Armed Soldiers	180,000
Heavy-Armed Soldiers	120,000
Slingers	120,000
Stone-Shooters	180,000
Javelin-Men	180,000
Supply Men	100,000
Sailors	240,000
Total Manpower	1,320,000

The Royal City's Military Materiel	
Chariots	10,000
Chariot-Horses	20,000
Ridden Horses	120,000
Supply Horses	100,000
Ships	1,200

must have been 600 large squares on the Plain of Atlantis for those sixty thousand smaller lots.

Plato's figure of 60,000 smaller lots located on 600 large squares on the Plain of Atlantis is relatively close to the earlier calculation of 700 large squares on the submerged Venezuelan Basin if divided by canals at 21-km intervals. This consistency of numbers further supports the argument that an emergent Venezuelan Basin was Plato's prehistoric Plain of Atlantis.

Ancient Armies

If several million people lived on the Atlantic Island, an organised and effective Atlantean military of over one million men would have been possible. For thousands of years, many ancient cultures in both the Old and New World equipped and organised large armies of tens and hundreds of thousands of men for war.

The Old World

Egypt had organised military units as early as the Old Kingdom (2686–2160 BCE), with a military hierarchy appearing in the Middle Kingdom (2055–1650 BCE). By the New Kingdom (1550–1069 BCE), the Egyptian military consisted of three major branches: infantry, chariotry and navy. Based on Herodotus, the Egyptian warrior class was divided into the Hermotubies and Kalasiries, who came from different districts of Egypt. The Hermotubies numbered 160,000, and the Kalasiries 250,000.

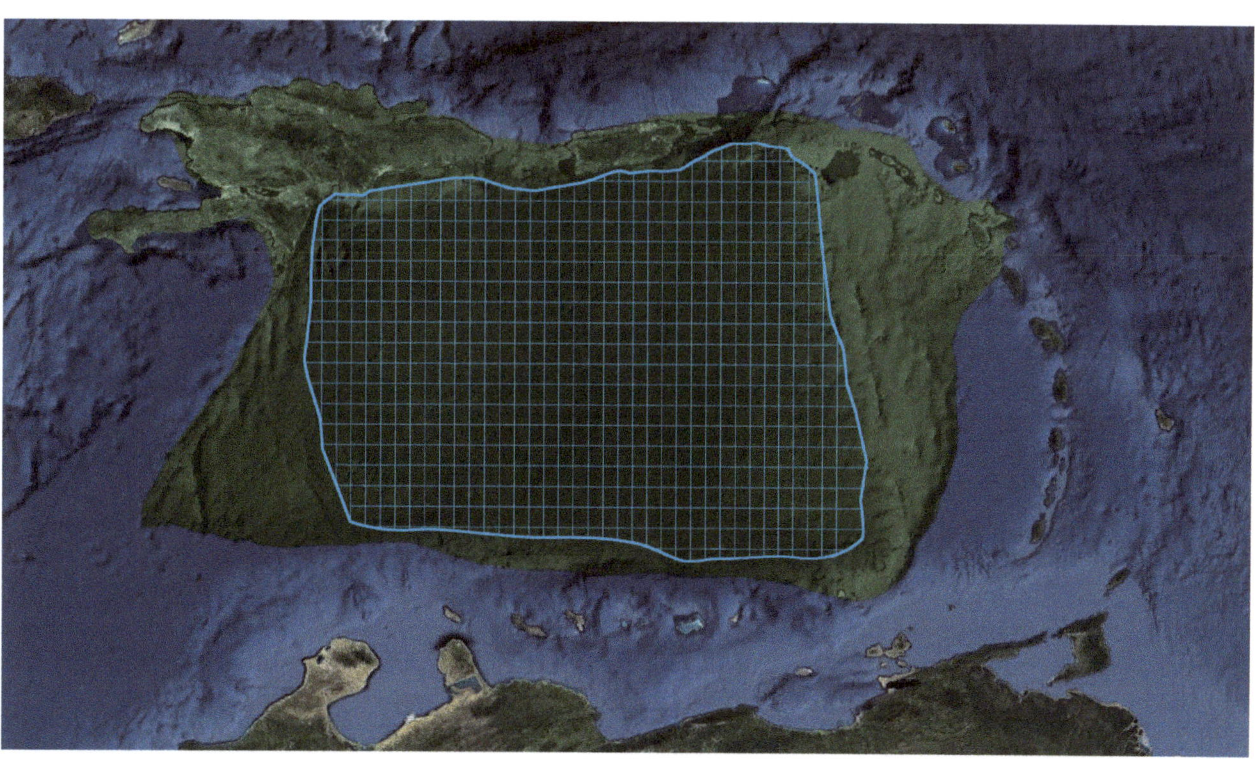

The Ditch and Canals on the Plain of Atlantis
Source: Modified from Google Earth

The Achaemenid Empire (559–330 BCE) of Persia had a national army of roughly 120,000–150,000 soldiers, plus tens of thousands of troops from their allies. Herodotus claimed that in 480 BCE, the Empire's invading army led by the Persian King Xerxes crossed into Greece from Asia Minor and numbered nearly two million men, with a cavalry of 80,000. In 331 BCE, at the Battle of Gaugamela, a Persian army of over 250,000 soldiers and 42,000 cavalry was defeated by around 47,000 Macedonian infantry and 8,000 cavalry led by Alexander the Great.

At its territorial height in 76–138 CE, the Roman Empire may have contained between 45–120 million people. Historian Edward Gibbon estimated that the size of the Roman army 'most probably formed a standing force of 375,000' at the Empire's territorial peak; other estimates are for up to 700,000, including auxiliaries.

The Vedas and other associated texts dating to the Vedic period (1100–500 BCE) contain the earliest written references to armies in India. The 4th century BCE Nanda Empire had an army of 80,000 cavalry, 200,000 infantry, 8,000 armed chariots, and 6,000 war elephants. At its height, the Indian Maurya Empire (332–185 BCE) had an army of 600,000 infantry, 30,000 cavalry, and 9,000 war elephants.

The recorded military history of China commences around 2200 BCE. The Ancient Chinese were involved in frequent wars of unification, expansion, and defence of their territories. Before 500 BCE, Chinese field armies numbered in the tens of thousands, but by 300 BCE, armies regularly included up to 200,000 infantry accompanied by cavalry.

The Americas

Most, if not all, of the early civilisations of the Americas engaged in large-scale warfare between cities, states, and empires. Little is known about the organisation of those early armies and conflicts. When the Spanish arrived and attempted to conquer the native armies of the Americas, they encountered large, organised resistance forces.

In Mesoamerica, the Maya regularly employed warfare to obtain slaves and sacrificial victims, settle competitive rivalries, acquire resources, and gain control of trade routes. They did not maintain standing armies but assembled militias of men and boys equipped from centralised arsenals in public buildings.

Aztec armed forces consisted of a large number of commoners with only basic military training who served part-time under the leadership of professional officers. A smaller number of elite warriors, who usually belonged to the nobility, were organised into several warrior societies. The size of the Aztec army varied from smaller units of a few thousand warriors to large armies with tens to hundreds of thousands of warriors. In the war against the state of Coixtlahuaca, the Aztec army numbered 200,000 warriors and 100,000 porters, while some other Aztec armies had up to 700,000 men.

In South America, the Inca Army was a multi-ethnic army that defended the Inca Empire, expanded its borders, and put down rebellions. It was also used for internal political purposes such as executions or coups. All the Inca Empire's citizens had to perform either military or community service, with one in every fifty men over twenty-five conscripted for military service. Conscripted commoners served mandatory military service called *mita*. Once he completed the mita, each commoner would return to his community.

Inca battalions contained a permanent staff of generals and officers. An individual battalion consisted of a single ethnic group directed by a warlord of the same ethnicity. The Inca could field armies of 100,000 at a time, with the largest units in the Inca army composed of 10,000 men under the command of a Major General. At the height of the empire under the reigns of Tupac Yupanqui and Huayna Capac, the Inca army grew to approximately 200,000 men.

Soldiers, Weapons and Armour in the Ancient Americas

Apart from horses, for thousands of years, the organised land armies of the Ancient Americas used all of the specialised roles and weapons that Plato describes for the Atlantean military.

Slings

There were 120,000 'slingers' in the Royal City's military.

The sling used for hunting and warfare was probably invented during the Upper Palaeolithic (50,000–10,000 BP) and was used worldwide except in Australia, where spear-throwing predominated.

The sling was known throughout the Americas and was employed by the Maya, Aztec and Inca armies. The Aztec used a sling made from maguey fibre, firing oval-shaped rocks or hand-moulded clay balls filled with obsidian flakes or pebbles. These projectiles could be thrown over 200 metres, further than arrows could be shot. In the ancient Andean civilisations, such as the Inca Empire, slings were made from llama wool. During the Inca resistance against the Spanish, one conquistador was quoted as saying that an Inca sling could 'break a sword in two pieces' and 'kill a horse'.

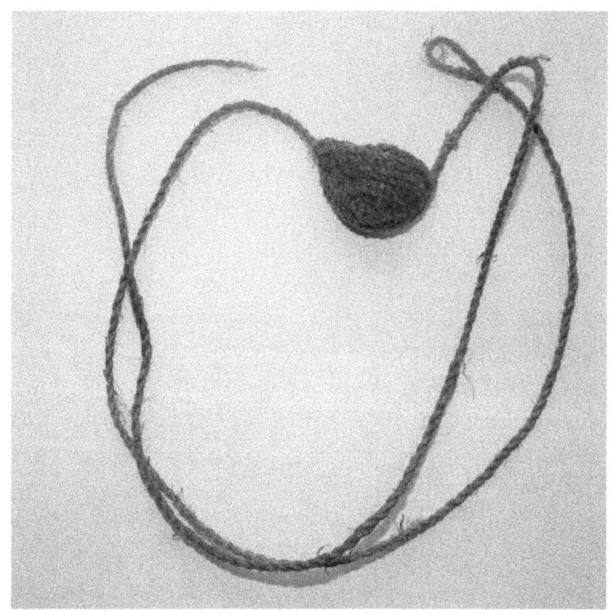

Braided sling weapon, Gambia
Source: Wikimedia Commons – Peter van der Sluijs

Bolas

There were 180,000 'stone shooters' in the Royal City's military.

Even though Plato distinguishes between 'slingers' and 'stone shooters', this weapon seems to have no Old World equivalent. Perhaps the Atlantean military used the bolas, a thrown weapon peculiar to the Americas.

Bolas (from Spanish bola or ball), also known as boleadoras or Inca ayllo, are made of weights on the ends of interconnected cords. Bolas are swung around the head and thrown at enemies or animals to entangle and immobilise them. Most bolas have two or three balls, but some may have up to eight or nine. The bola perdida (lost ball) is a single, large stone with a short rope tied to it, swung like a sling and then thrown to land a blow rather than entangle.

Bolas
Source: Wikimedia Commons

Bolas have been found in several excavations of prehistoric settlements in Patagonia in South America that date from around 7,000 BP. However, bolas were unknown in Europe until the Spanish conquest of South America, where the Inca army used them in battle.

Javelins

There were 180,000 'javelin men' in the Royal City's military.

Homo heidelbergensis used wooden spears for hunting around 500,000 years ago. Seven spears between 1.83 and 2.25 metres long were found in Schoningen, Germany. They date from 400,000 BP and are thought to have been made by *Homo heidelbergensis*. Neanderthals constructed stone spearheads glued with tar to the spear shaft as early as 300,000 BP.

From 200,000 BP onwards, our species *Homo sapiens*, began to make spearheads from stone blades with flaked edges. They were fixed to the spear shaft by gum, resin, or bindings made of animal sinew, leather strips, or vegetable matter. *Homo sapiens* designed different types of spears, depending on whether they were thrown or held in the hands for thrusting.

The javelin or dart is a light spear designed for throwing and resembles a large arrow or thin spear, typically from 1.2 to 2.7 metres long. Projectile points used for throwing-spears and darts are known from the Middle Palaeolithic, with a collection of stone blades found at a cave site at Pinnacle Point, South Africa, dated to around 70,000 BP.

An atlatl or spear-thrower is a wooden tool that increases the javelin's range by using leverage to increase the dart's speed. It can throw a dart well over 100 metres but is most accurate at distances of 20 metres or less. *Homo sapiens* have used the atlatl throwing-stick since at least the Upper Palaeolithic, around 30,000 BP.

It is thought that Palaeoindians introduced the atlatl into the Americas before 13,000 BP. Javelins were used extensively in ancient Mesoamerican warfare, usually with the atlatl. Murals at Teotihuacan show warriors using the atlatl hundreds of years before the Aztec. While it is characteristic of the Mesoamerican cultures of central Mexico, the Inca army also had spear throwers, used mainly by its jungle troops.

Aztec Warrior with Dart and Atlatl

Light and Heavy Armed Soldiers

Plato does not specify the types of arms carried by the 180,000 'light-armed' and 120,000 'heavy-armed soldiers' of the Royal City's military. In addition to specialised troops such as slingers, bolas and javelin throwers, the armies of the Ancient Americas did contain large numbers of warriors who used an array of weapons.

The Olmec were the first known group in Mesoamerica with specialised weapons and personnel for war. Murals, bas-relief carvings and ceramics depict armed warriors. The Olmec sent troops from their main population centres to support their distant trading operations. Olmec warrior societies provided weapons and combat training to a military elite. They used shock weapons for close combat, such as thrusting spears with obsidian points and clubs and maces. Hand-thrown javelins and atlatl-propelled darts were available but not much used in combat, and the Olmec do not appear to have used shields or armour.

In the Maya Classic Period (250–900 CE), shock weapons included stone clubs with leather strings or wooden handles, short stabbing spears, and wooden axes edged with flint or obsidian blades. Projectile weapons included blowguns, javelins and throwing sticks, and slings. Although bows and arrows were used, spears were much more common. Weapons were made mainly by shaping chert or obsidian into projectile points and attaching them to atlatl darts, spears and arrows. Maya soldiers typically carried long, flexible shields of leather or smaller, rigid round shields. Armour consisted of cotton vests stuffed with rock salt.

The weapons of Aztec warriors were derived from the various cultures that preceded the Aztec civilisation in southern Mexico and Mesoamerica. The Aztec used javelins, darts, and slings for projectile weapons and had bows 1.5 metres long with arrows pointed with flint, bone or obsidian. The Macuahuitl was a wooden sword with sharp obsidian blades embedded in its sides. It was the standard armament of the Aztec elite warrior societies and was reputedly capable of decapitating a horse. It came in one-handed and two-handed varieties: the one-handed version was ten centimetres wide and one metre long, while the two-handed version was slightly wider and as tall as a person. As they had no point for stabbing, they were used with a chopping action.

The Tepoztopilli was a standard Aztec front-lines weapon, comprising a pole-arm around 1.5 metres long with a broad wooden head edged with obsidian blades cemented in place with bitumen or plant resin. The Quauhololli was a mace-like weapon with a wooden handle topped with a copper, rock, or wooden ball. The Tripatlzachital was a copper club used only by the Aztec. The Huitzauhqui was a wooden club resembling a baseball bat and often studded with flint or obsidian on its sides. The Tepoztli was a small axe with either a stone or copper head. The Tecpatl was a twenty-centimetre-long dagger with a double-sided blade made out of flint or obsidian. Spaniard Bernal Diaz refers to a long scythe-like weapon so large that several warriors had to operate it. It was embedded with obsidian blades for up to three metres and was used to slice through enemy ranks.

Tlahuiztli were the decorated suits of prestigious Aztec warriors and members of warrior societies. They identified warriors for their battle achievements, rank, alliance, and social status. Chimalli were shields made with different materials such as wood (cuauhchimalli) or maize cane (otlachimalli), and there were ornamental shields decorated with motifs made in featherwork (mahuizzoh chimalli). Pamitl were identifying emblems that officers and famous warriors wore on their backs.

Ichcahuipilli was quilted cotton armour soaked in a saltwater brine and then dried so that the salt would crystallise inside it. It was three or four centimetres thick and resistant to obsidian swords and atlatl darts. Helmets were carved from hardwood in various shapes, including jaguars, eagles, and a demon of the air known as a tzitzimitl.

As with the Aztec in Mesoamerica, Inca weapons in South America were derived from earlier Andean cultures. Inca soldiers carried several types of simple weapons according to the ethnic group to which they belonged. Macana were wooden shafts topped

Maya Battle Scene

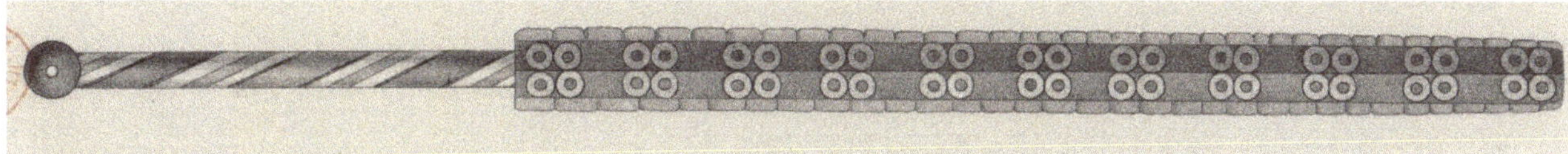

Macuahuitl
Source: Wikimedia Commons

Tlahuiztli of Eagle and Jaguar Knights
Source: Florentine Codex

Aztec Warriors with Pamitl Emblems
Source: Wikimedia Commons – Foundation for the Advancement of Mesoamerican Studies

Royal Standard of Ur, ca 2500 *BCE*
Source: Wikimedia Commons – British Museum

with a heavy, star-shaped object and were the most common Inca weapons. Projectile weapons were slings and two-stone or three-stone bolas. Estolica were similar to the Aztec atlatl and were used with javelins primarily by the jungle troops, as were bows and arrows. Some jungle tribes used two-metre-long arrows capable of going through several enemies simultaneously. Axes were made of stone or copper; wooden clubs, some with spikes, were used mainly by southern nations.

Cuzco elite troops and generals carried spears, considered symbols of power. Shields for higher-ranking soldiers were made of wood covered in leather and could be round, square or rectangular. Helmets were mostly wooden, but some were reinforced with copper for generals and high-ranking officers. Body armour used by officers and noblemen consisted of thick padded cotton tunics with wooden plates to protect the back. The highest-ranking officers wore metal armour.

The Absence of Archers

When Plato describes the Atlantean and prehistoric Athenian militaries, he does not mention bows and arrows. That is a significant omission because archers were used for millennia in most Old World armies before Solon and Plato's time, including the armies of the Ancient Egyptians and Greeks. As archers were essential components of Greek military forces by Plato's time, if he had invented the Atlantis story, he probably would have mentioned them as part of the Atlantean or prehistoric Athenian military rather than omit them.

The oldest known evidence of arrows comes from the South African site of Sibudu Cave, where the remains of bone and stone arrowheads were dated to 70,000–60,000 BP. The earliest definite remains of a bow and arrow from Europe are possible fragments from Germany found at Mannheim-Vogelstang dated 17,500–18,000 BP. The bow and arrow eventually replaced the spear-thrower as the primary technique to fire sharp projectiles on all continents except Australia.

Bows and arrows were used in Egypt long before 3000 BCE. By the time of the earliest Pharaohs, archery was widespread for hunting and warfare, with the bow and arrow the most common Egyptian weapon. In Bronze Age Greece, the Minoans practised archery before the 2nd millennium BCE, and archers were a significant component of later Mycenaean military forces in the first millennium BCE.

Several major wars occurred in Greece roughly halfway between the lives of Solon and Plato. In the series of wars known as the Graeco-Persian Wars (499–449 BCE), the Persians used massed archers against the Greeks. Later, during the thirty-year-long Peloponnesian War between Sparta and Athens (431–404 BCE), archers comprised roughly ten percent of an Ancient Greek city's military force.

Archery seems to have arrived in the Americas via Alaska by 8,000 BP, spreading south into the temperate zones as early as 4,000 BP and then into South America. Before that, the javelin and atlatl were the primary projectile weapons in the Americas. If the Atlanteans established their military structure thousands of years before archery arrived in the Americas, it might explain why the Egyptians speaking to Solon omitted archers from the Atlanteans' military. Again, if Plato invented the Atlantis story, he could have included archers in either or both the Atlantean and Athenian military.

War Chariots

Plato states that the Atlantean Royal City's military had 'a total of ten thousand chariots'. Horses existed in the Americas before 10,000 BP, so they would have been available to the Atlanteans to pull their chariots. Because horses became extinct after around 10,000 BP, no wheeled vehicles appear to be used in the Americas until Europeans introduced them after the 15th century CE.

The first archaeological evidence of horses used in warfare in the Old World dates to 6,000–5,000 BP, and the practice was widespread by the end of the Bronze Age. Near-simultaneously in the northern Caucasus of Central Europe and Mesopotamia, archaeological evidence of wheeled vehicles appears from the mid-6th millennium BP. The earliest depiction of vehicles used in warfare is from 2500 BCE on the Royal Standard of Ur from southern Mesopotamia. Before horses were introduced in around 2000 BCE, oxen or tamed asses pulled double-axled wagons or carts with solid wooden wheels.

The invention of the spoked wheel allowed the construction of the light, horse-drawn war chariots used in ancient warfare during the Bronze and Iron Ages. The earliest known spoked-wheel chariots date to 2000 BCE, and their usage peaked around 1300 BCE. The original horse chariot was two or four-wheeled and drawn by two or more horses hitched side by side. The car comprised a floor with a waist-high semicircular guard in front.

The chariot and the horse itself were introduced to Egypt by the Hyksos invaders from Western Asia in the 16th century BCE. In 1274 BCE, in what is now Syria, the Battle of Kadesh was fought between the forces of the Egyptian Empire under Ramesses II and the Hittite Empire under Muwatalli II. It is the earliest recorded battle in history, with an account of tactics and formations. It was probably the largest known chariot battle ever fought, involving 5,000–6,000 chariots.

In Greece, the earliest records of chariots are in the arsenal inventories of Mycenaean palaces found in Linear B tablets from the 15th–14th centuries BCE. Chariots feature in the *Iliad* and *Odyssey*, Homer's epic poems about the Trojan War, probably set around 1200 BCE. Although chariots ceased to have military importance by the 4th century BCE, the vehicle continued to be used for travel, processions, games and races. Chariot races continued to be popular in Constantinople until the 13th century CE.

In India, there is evidence of wheeled vehicles in the Indus Valley Civilization (2600–1900 BCE) but not of chariots. However, chariots do figure prominently in the *Rig Veda*, an ancient Indian collection of Vedic Sanskrit hymns, indicating their presence in India in the 2nd millennium BCE. The Ancient Chinese used the chariot as an attack and pursuit vehicle on open fields and plains from around 1200 BCE.

Cavalry

Plato (Jowett) – 'two horses and riders for them'.

As previously stated, Jowett's translation could mean the Atlanteans had a horse-mounted cavalry of 120,000 men. As horses became extinct in the Americas after 10,000 BP, there was no cavalry in any American culture until the arrival of European horses.

In the Old World before the Iron Age, light chariots performed the role of cavalry on the battlefield. Cavalry techniques began with the horse-mounted nomads of the Central Asian and Iranian steppe and with pastoralist tribes such as the Persian Parthians and Sarmatians. Assyrian cavalrymen in the early 1st millennium BCE had no spurs, saddles, saddlecloths or stirrups, but they did use swords, shields and bows. The cavalry acted in pairs, with the reins of the mounted archer controlled by his neighbour's hand. Later Assyrian cavalry used saddlecloths as primitive saddles, allowing each archer to control their own horse.

The Ancient Egyptians seldom used cavalry in warfare, preferring light chariots. Cavalry played a relatively minor role during the many wars between Greek city-states from the 9th–4th centuries BCE, with conflicts mainly decided by a phalanx of massed armoured infantry. This period coincides with the time of Solon and Plato, so the Atlantean Royal City's assumed cavalry of 120,000 would have been well out of proportion for any militaries of their day in Egypt, Greece, or anywhere else in the Mediterranean.

For the Ancient Greeks, massed cavalry was first used effectively in Greece and beyond by the Macedonian Kingdom, notably by Alexander the Great after 334 BCE. That was a time well after Plato wrote of Atlantis. Even by Alexander's time, his cavalry during his invasion of the Persian Empire numbered fewer than 8,000, not in the tens of thousands like the Atlanteans'. However, one of the armies Alexander faced in northern India had 38,000 infantry, 30,000 cavalry and 30 war elephants. Allegedly, another Indian army that Alexander

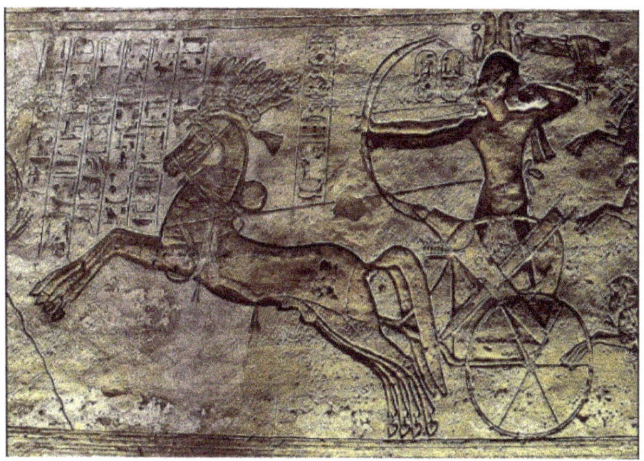

Egyptian Chariot

Assyrian Cavalry
Source: Wikimedia Commons – Iglonghurst

decided not to meet had 200,000 infantry, 80,000 cavalry, 8,000 chariots, and 6,000 war elephants.

In China, by the 3rd century BCE, infantry-based armies of 100,000–200,000 troops were complemented by several hundred thousand mounted cavalry. Mounted archers were a major part of the armies of the Mongol Empire. At the 13th century CE Battle of Liegnitz, a Mongol army with 20,000 horse-archers defeated a force of 30,000 European armoured troops.

The 'trireme'

Plato – 'The docks (in the Royal City) were full of triremes and naval stores, and all things were quite ready for use'…'room for a single trireme to pass out of one zone into another'.

The trireme was a warship that derived its name from its three banks of oars on each side. It was the commonest Mediterranean warship in Solon and Plato's time and would have been familiar to the Egyptian priests at Sais. That may be why the Egyptians described the Atlanteans' military vessels as 'triremes' and not another type of ship. Otherwise, the Atlanteans did develop ships with multiple levels of rowers by 11,600 BP.

The early trireme developed from the traditional penteconter and the bireme – a warship with two banks of oars, probably of Phoenician origin. The trireme supported the maritime-based states or thalassocracies of Athens, Carthage, Corinth, Syracuse, Tyre, Caere/Caisra (Cerveteri), Aegina and other Greek, Phoenician and Etruscan city-states. It became the dominant warship in the Mediterranean from the 7th–4th centuries BCE but eventually was superseded by larger warships.

The trireme was about 40 metres long and had 170 oars arranged on three levels, with one man per oar. It was steered using two steering oars at the stern. The ship also had a main-mast and small fore-mast, with square sails taken down for battle. Trireme hulls were constructed of mortise and tenon jointed planks made of softwoods, primarily pine and fir, with larch and plane for the ship's interior parts. Bronze rams or embolon were fitted to the prows of warships and used to rupture an enemy ship's hull.

Classical sources describe the trireme as capable of sustained rowing speeds of 6 knots at a relatively leisurely pace, with short bursts of 8 knots or more. The trireme's two sails were used to help drive the ship when not in battle. In good weather, oarsmen rowing for six to eight hours could propel the trireme 80–100 kilometres, and the Greek historian Thucydides mentions a trireme travelling 300 kilometres in one day.

The trireme was the primary Greek warship up to the Hellenistic period at the beginning of the 4th century BCE. After that, several larger galley types were introduced, such as tetrereis or fours and pentereis or fives. Even larger ships were then developed, so by the mid-4th century BCE, there were sixes and sevens, going up to thirteens, and by the 3rd century BCE, there was a sixteen. These larger ship types probably had two to three banks of oars. They were bigger versions of the bireme and trireme but with more than one rower per oar, from which came their classification as fours, five, sixes, etc.

Ancient Naval Warfare

Plato – (the Royal City's outermost water zone) 'became a harbour, and leaving an opening sufficient to enable the largest vessels to find ingress (via the Canal to the Sea)'…'as they (the Atlanteans) quarried, they at the same time hollowed out double docks, having roofs formed out of the native rock'… 'The docks were full of triremes and naval stores, and all things were quite ready for use.'

As stated by Plato, the Royal City's outermost circular water zone was a military harbour, and the Atlanteans possessed a fleet of at least 1,200 warships with 240,000 sailors or 200 men per ship. Despite no evidence of naval warfare in the Americas, large

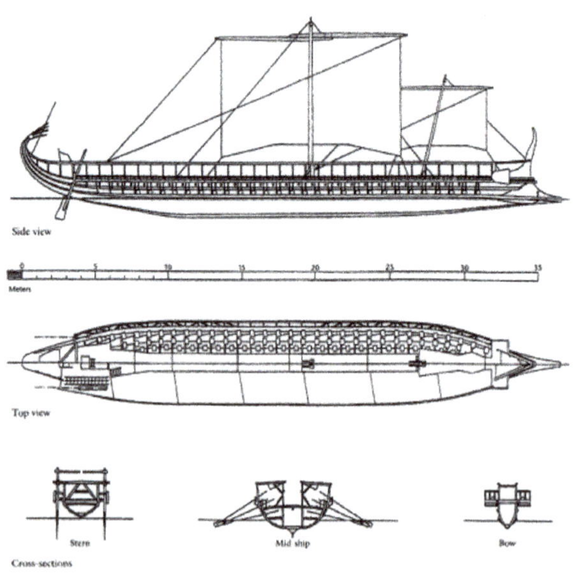

Trireme Plan

The Reconstructed Trireme Olympias
Source: Wikimedia Commons – George E. Koronaios

naval forces and sea battles were common in ancient Old World civilisations.

Egyptian troops were transported by naval vessels as early as the Late Old Kingdom, before 2200 BCE. By the later intermediate period, around 1000 BCE, the Egyptian navy was highly sophisticated and used complicated naval manoeuvres in sea battles. The first dateable recorded sea battle occurred around 1210 BCE when Suppiluliuma II, King of the Hittites, defeated a fleet from Cyprus and burned their ships at sea.

By around 2000 BCE, the Bronze Age Minoan civilisation on the island of Crete had a large navy and evolved into a naval power that controlled the sea of the Eastern Mediterranean. In about 1200 BCE, the Bronze Age Mycenaean Greeks are thought to have sent a naval force hundreds of kilometres from Greece to invade Troy in Asia Minor. In Homer's *Iliad*, the Catalogue of Ships that went to Troy names twenty-nine contingents from various cities around Greece. It gives a total of 1,186 ships, commanded by forty-six captains and possibly carrying 150,000 men.

The Graeco-Persian Wars in the 5th century BCE were the first known to feature large-scale naval operations. Herodotus reports that the Persian fleet invading Greece consisted of 1,207 triremes, with 3,000 lesser fighting and supply ships; the Greeks' opposing force was around 400 triremes. The Greeks defeated the Persian fleet at the decisive naval battle of Salamis near Athens. Following the Graeco-Persian Wars, Athens had a fleet of 400 triremes manned by around 80,000 free citizens, not slaves.

The Punic Wars were a series of three wars fought between Rome and Carthage from 264–146 BCE. The First Punic War (264–241 BCE) was fought partly on land in Sicily and Africa but mainly was a naval war. In 260 BCE, the Carthaginian navy defeated the inexperienced Roman navy at the Battle of the Lipari Islands. In response, the Roman Republic ordered and built a fleet of 150 warships and drilled their crews in two months. In 256 BCE, the greatest naval battle of the First Punic War was part of the Roman invasion of Carthage in North-West Africa. At that time, Carthage gathered its largest fleet of around 350 ships, while the Roman fleet was 330.

The Roman navy consisted of a wide variety of different classes of warships, from heavy polyremes to light raiding and scouting vessels. In 31 BCE, around 750 warships were involved in a decisive civil war between competing Roman factions at the Battle of Actium. It was the last massive sea battle in the Mediterranean. After Actium, Rome dominated the entire Mediterranean, so later Roman fleets comprised relatively small vessels, mainly for policing and escort duties. After the fall of Rome in the 5th century CE, the Byzantine Empire from its capital of Constantinople was a continuation of the Roman Empire. The dromon was the primary warship of the Byzantine navy from the 5th–12th century CE. The largest class of dromon had a crew of 230 rowers and 70 marines. During the 13th and 14th centuries CE, the Mediterranean war galley evolved from the dromon into a design that remained essentially the same until it was phased out in the early 19th century CE.

The naval history of China dates back thousands of years, with archives from the late Spring and Autumn Period (722–481 BCE) describing the various ship types used in war. Though numerous naval battles took place before the 12th century CE, it was during the Song Dynasty (960–1279 CE) that the Chinese established a permanent standing navy. At its height by the late 12th century CE, there were 20 squadrons of some 52,000 marines. In 1363 CE, on Lake Poyang, China's largest freshwater lake, what is claimed as the largest naval battle in history involved up to 850,000 fighters: 200,000 sailors from Ming forces against a Han force of 650,000.

India's maritime history dates back over 5,000 years, with the world's first known tidal dock built during the Indus Valley Civilisation around 2300 BCE. The *Rig Vedas*, written around 1700 BCE, describes the knowledge of ocean routes and naval expeditions. The sea lanes between India and neighbouring lands in the Indian Ocean region were the usual trade routes for centuries.

From the 4th century BCE, powerful Indian navies included those of the Maurya, Satavahana, Chola, Vijayanagara, Kalinga, Maratha, and Mughal Empires. The navy in ancient India transported troops to distant battlefields and participated in actual warfare but primarily protected trade on navigable rivers and maritime trade routes. India's trade with Egypt, West Asia, Greece, and Rome led to the growth of navies along the west coast. On the east coast, naval actions led to colonizing expeditions to Southeast Asia, whereas the navies of the South Indian powers mainly launched invasions of Sri Lanka.

The Atlanteans extended their empire into the Mediterranean

CHAPTER 7

The Atlantean Empire and the Prehistoric Mediterranean

Plato – 'In this Atlantic island a combination of kings was formed, who with mighty and wonderful power subdued the whole (Atlantic) island, together with many other islands and parts of the continent (the Americas); and, besides this, subjected to their dominion all Libya (North Africa), as far as to Egypt; and Europe, as far as to the Tyrrhene sea (north-west Italy).'

Plato states that the early Kings of Atlantis 'with mighty and wonderful power subdued the whole (Atlantic) island'. This statement implies that long before 11,600 BP, the Atlanteans defeated any pre-existing cultures on the Atlantic Island after an armed struggle and used superior military power to do so. Possibly hundreds or thousands of years later, at the peak of their civilisation in 11,600 BP, the Atlanteans possessed a well-equipped and well-organised army and navy of over one million men. As well, they fortified their Royal City with several defensive walls.

A huge Atlantean military force and extensive city defences would not have existed to maintain peace on the Atlantic Island after the original inhabitants were subdued. It is more likely that the Atlanteans built up their military to wage wars of expansion into adjoining lands in the Americas and then across the Atlantic.

The Atlanteans probably faced initial armed resistance from organised cultures in the Americas, but that does not explain why they needed an enormous standing army and navy by 11,600 BP. The Atlanteans likely created and maintained their military to dominate and control any conquered lands in the Americas and to repel any rebellion or attack on the Atlantic Island itself, particularly on the Royal City.

Once the Atlanteans crossed the North Atlantic Ocean, they would have subdued any local cultures they found there. Once they had achieved that, they likely established armed colonies and outposts to control those cultures and to expand the Atlantean Empire further. Any initial Atlantean colonies were possibly located outside the Pillars of Atlas on the Atlantic coasts of Africa and Europe. The Atlanteans would eventually extend their empire into the Mediterranean along the shores of Southern Europe as far as Italy and North Africa as far as Egypt.

An empire is defined as a state with politico-military power over populations culturally and ethnically distinct from the ruling ethnic group and its culture. This definition is in contrast to a federation: an extensive state voluntarily composed of autonomous states and peoples. When applied to the Atlantean civilisation, Atlantis's ten kingdoms formed a federation, which then conquered distant lands and controlled an extensive empire.

Empires appear to be a common form of predatory state expansion into adjoining territories. Once a sufficiently large state forms with a ruling elite controlling a military force, a desire to expand its territory often follows. The Atlanteans were modern humans with the same mental capabilities and drives as us. The Kings of Atlantis and their subjects probably behaved the same way many expansionist human civilisations have done over thousands of years of recorded history.

The Possible Extent of the Atlantean Empire
Source: Wikipedia Map Template

Empires are usually created by military conquest, with the empire incorporating the vanquished states into a political union. A local monarchy or oligarchy continues to dominate the politics of the conquered states. To create an empire is one thing, but it is quite another to control it. The empire's longevity depends on the competence of the following rulers and how they cope with internal and external threats to its stability. Over thousands of years in different regions of the world, many known empires expanded and then collapsed or were conquered, often over only a few hundred years or less.

Repeatedly in the past, an individual leader or a dynasty of leaders harnessed enough military power to conquer new territories in a generation or two. A few Old World examples are Alexander the Great, Julius Caesar, Attila the Hun and Genghis Khan, with the more recent examples of Napoleon Bonaparte and Adolf Hitler. Ever since the distant past, there must have been many similar but forgotten individuals from now-forgotten cultures who controlled enough military power to conquer neighbouring cultures and create an empire.

The Akkadian Empire in Mesopotamia was one of the earliest known Old World empires. Following the conquests by its founder, Sargon of Akkad (2334–2279 BCE), it reached its political peak between the 24th and 22nd centuries BCE.

In the 15th century BCE, the New Kingdom of Ancient Egypt was ruled by Thutmose III, who incorporated Nubia and the ancient city-states of the Levant, thereby creating an Egyptian empire. In the 13th century BCE, Ramesses II led several military expeditions into the Levant to reassert Egyptian control over Canaan, and he also led expeditions south into Nubia.

The Hittites were an ancient Anatolian people who established an empire centred on Hattusa in north-central Anatolia around 1600 BCE. After ca. 1180 BCE, the Hittite Empire ended and splintered into several independent Neo-Hittite city-states, some of which survived until the 8th century BCE. The Neo-Assyrian Empire (916–612 BCE) was the first known empire comparable in organisation to the much later Roman Empire, and Assyria became the most powerful state in Mesopotamia. By the 6th century BCE, the Medes allied with the Babylonians to defeat the Neo-Assyrian Empire and establish the Median Empire, which was the largest of its time and lasted around sixty years. The Achaemenid Empire or First Persian Empire (550–330 BCE) defeated the Medes and absorbed Mesopotamia, Egypt, Thrace, parts of Greece, the Middle East, much of Central Asia and Pakistan. The Persian Empire was then overthrown by Alexander the Great in 331 BCE and replaced by the Macedonian Empire.

Rome had been a relatively unimportant city-state in Italy from the 8th century BCE. Its expansion started with successful warfare in the 5th century BCE against other populations of central Italy, such as the Etruscans, Latins, Volsci, and Aequi. The defeat of the Carthaginians in the Punic Wars (264–146 BCE) gave Rome control of the Western Mediterranean, including Carthaginian territories in Iberia. Further conquests of Gaul and Britain followed in the west, and most of the remnants of Alexander the Great's Macedonian Empire in the east. The Roman Empire lasted 500 years and was one of the largest in history, with territories throughout Europe, North Africa, and the Middle East.

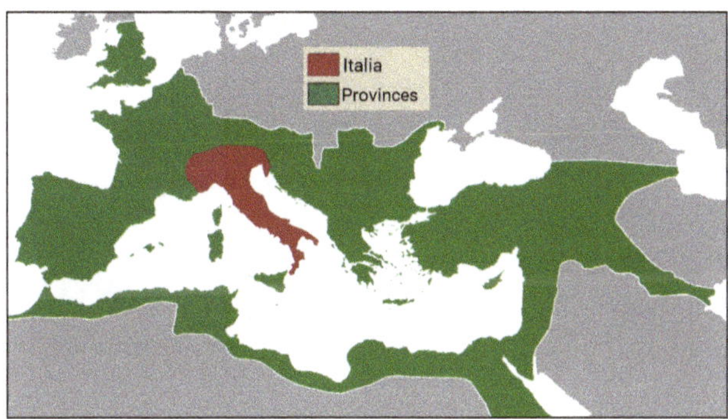

Roman Empire at its Greatest Extent
Source: Wikimedia Commons – Tataryn

In India, the Indus Valley Civilization was an urbanised culture in north-western India and Pakistan from around 3300–1900 BCE. This civilisation collapsed at the start of the 2nd millennium BCE and was followed by the Iron Age Vedic Civilization (ca. 1750–500 BCE), which developed into sixteen kingdoms and oligarchic republics. The Mauryan Empire was founded in 322 BCE by Chandragupta Maurya, who rapidly expanded his power westward across central and western India, with the Maurya Dynasty ruling the empire until 185 BCE. The later Gupta Empire, founded by Maharaja Sri Gupta, existed from approximately 320–550 CE and controlled much of the Indian Subcontinent. The 7th–11th centuries CE saw the Tripartite struggle to control India between the Pala Empire, Rashtrakuta Empire, and the Gurjara Pratihara Empire. In the 11th century CE, the Chola Dynasty conquered Southern India and successfully invaded parts of South-East Asia and Sri Lanka.

Imperial China began with the Qin Dynasty (221–206 BCE) when the First Qin Emperor conquered six other states during the Warring States period from 230–221 BCE. Successive imperial dynasties developed bureaucratic systems that enabled the Emperor of China to control vast territories. China's last dynasty was the Qing (1644–1912 CE).

The Khmer Empire began in the 8th century CE and was a powerful Hindu-Buddhist empire in Southeast Asia. The empire grew out of the former Kingdoms of Funan and Chenla in present-day Cambodia. At times it ruled over most of mainland South-East Asia, including parts of present-day Laos, Thailand and southern Vietnam.

The Mongol Empire unified nomadic tribes of historical Mongolia under Genghis Khan's leadership. He was proclaimed ruler of all Mongols in 1206 CE and the empire grew rapidly under his reign. By the time he died in 1227 CE, the Mongol Empire ruled from the Pacific Ocean to the Caspian Sea and was over twice the size of the Roman Empire. It grew further under Genghis Khan's descendants but by 1294 CE, it had fractured into four separate khanates or empires.

Mongol Empire at its Greatest Extent
Source: Wikimedia Commons – Astrokey44

From the 2nd millennium BCE, several successive empires developed in the Americas. The earliest known empires in Mesoamerica appeared ever since the Olmec, Maya and Zapotecs, and in northern South America since the Norte Chico and Chavin cultures. The final indigenous empires in the Americas were the powerful and extensive Aztec and Inca Empires. In turn, they were cut short by the conquests of the Spanish, who then created their empire in the Americas.

Previously, Chapter 4 described possible cultural connections in the Americas with the remnants of an Atlantean Empire, particularly in Mesoamerica and north-eastern South America. The following sections discuss Plato's 'other islands' the Atlanteans controlled on the way to the Americas and the 'divers islands' in the Atlantic where the Atlanteans may have established colonies.

Plato states the Atlantean Empire extended its control into the Mediterranean, so the region's cultures will also be described from before and after the Mediterranean War in 11,600 BP. All those Mediterranean cultures would have faced the more advanced technology of the invading Atlanteans, and despite resisting, most would have been easily overpowered.

The 'other islands' of the Caribbean

Plato – 'the (Atlantic) island…was the way to other islands, and from these you may pass to the whole of the opposite continent (North and South America)'…'(the Kings of Atlantis) had rule over the whole (Atlantic) island and several others.'

Hispaniola and Puerto Rico should not be considered 'other islands' on the way to the Americas as they were part of the complete Atlantic Island when it was fully emergent. Nevertheless, several 'other islands' did lie between the Atlantic Island and the Americas. To the south were the Leeward Antilles, Trinidad and Tobago; to the east were the Lesser Antilles; to the west were Jamaica and Cuba.

Trinidad and Tobago is a twin-island group off the northern edge of South America, lying just off the coast of north-eastern Venezuela. The Leeward Antilles chain of islands comprises the ABC Islands of Aruba, Bonaire and Curacao, plus most of Venezuela's small off-shore islands. All of these islands lie less than 200 kilometres off the northern coast of South America, so one could pass from the Atlantic Island to these southern islands and then on to 'the opposite continent' of South America.

By at least 7,000 BP, both Trinidad and Tobago seem to have been settled by pre-agricultural Amerindians of South American origin, making them the earliest known settled part of the Caribbean. The earliest known settlements on the Leeward Islands date to 1000 CE, with the first known inhabitants thought to have been Amerindians from the Arawak tribe, who migrated there from Venezuela.

The Lesser Antilles form a long, partly volcanic island arc between the Greater Antilles and South America. Being close to the Atlantic Island, the Atlanteans would likely have occupied them early in their territorial expansion. The earliest known settlements in the Lesser Antilles were after 7,000 BP when the Banwari culture travelled northward by sea from Trinidad and Tobago.

Jamaica and Cuba lay west of the Atlantic Island and were the way to 'the opposite continent' of

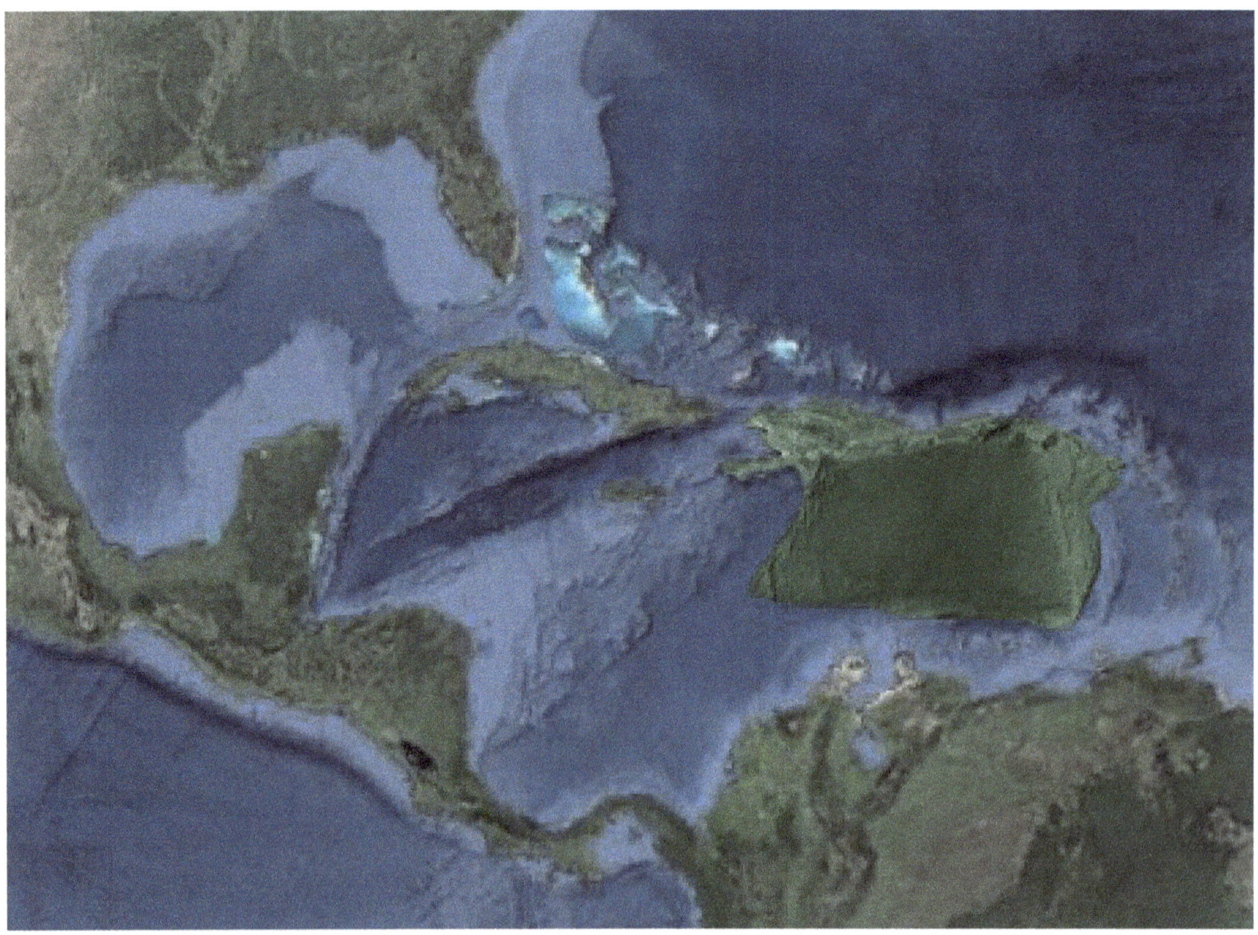

The Atlantic Island and the Americas
Source: Modified from Google Earth

(From L to R) The Leeward Antilles, Trinidad and Tobago
Source: Google Earth

The Lesser Antilles
Source: Google Earth

Jamaica
Source: Google Earth

Cuba
Source: Google Earth

North America. Jamaica is 191 kilometres west of Hispaniola, and at 10,990km^2 it is the third-largest island of the Greater Antilles. The earliest known settlers were the Arawak and Taino indigenous people who originated in South America and settled in Jamaica between 6,000 and 3,000 BP.

Cuba is an archipelago of islands located in the northern Caribbean Sea, with a total land area of 110,000km^2. The main island is 1,199 kilometres long and is the largest island in the Caribbean

Many of Cuba's oldest known occupation sites are in caves and rock shelters on the interior valleys and along the coast. The Levisa rock shelter is the most ancient, dating to around 6,000 BP. The first known group to settle in Cuba was the Casimiroid, who later migrated east to Hispaniola. The Casimiroid settlers probably came from Belize in Central America, as there are similar stone tools found there and in Cuba dating to this time.

The 'divers islands' of the North Atlantic

Plato – 'All these (Kings of Atlantis) and their descendants for many generations were the inhabitants and rulers of divers islands in the open sea (the Atlantic Ocean).'

The Atlanteans were a sea-faring civilisation with ships capable of long-distance, open-ocean voyages. As they expanded their empire outside the Caribbean, they would have encountered 'divers islands' close to North America: the Bahamas and Bermuda. Other island groups in the North Atlantic were closer to Africa and Europe: Cape Verde, the Canaries, Madeira, and the Azores. They would have made natural stopping points when the Atlanteans sailed between the Americas and the Mediterranean.

The Bahamas is located in the Atlantic Ocean north of Cuba and Hispaniola. It comprises 29 islands, 661 cays and 2,387 islets, with a total land area of 13,878km^2. The Bahama Banks are shallow submerged carbonate platforms, generally no deeper than 25 metres, that make up much of the Bahama Archipelago.

The first known human occupation occurred sometime between 500–800 CE when Tainos began crossing from Hispaniola and or Cuba to

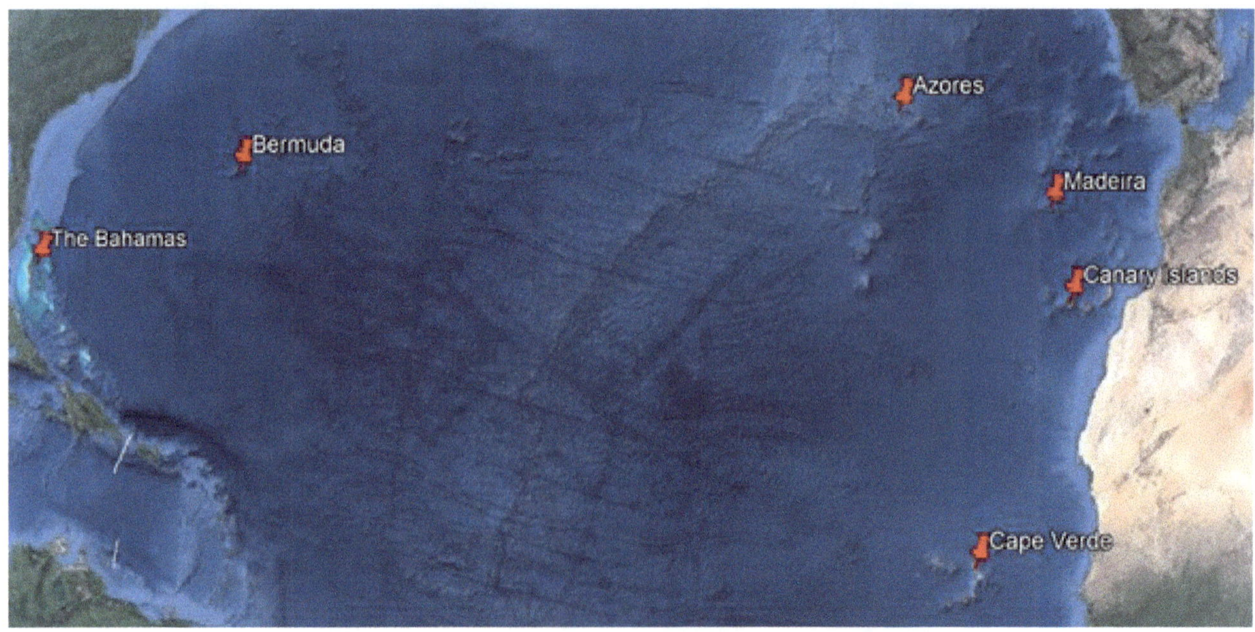

North Atlantic Islands
Source: Modified from Google Earth

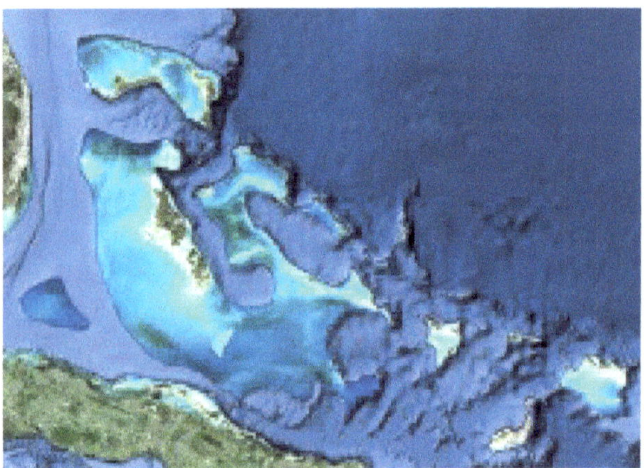

The Bahamas
Source: Google Earth

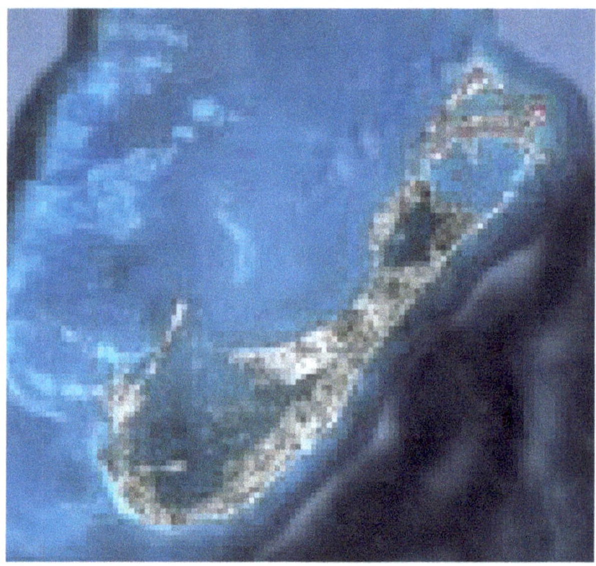

Bermuda
Source: Google Earth

Cape Verde
Source: Google Earth

the Bahamas. These people became known as the Lucayans, who grew root crops, hunted, fished, and gathered wild foods.

The Bahama Banks were dry land during past glacial periods, including 11,600 BP when the sea level was 60 metres lower. The land area of the Bahama Archipelago today is a small fraction of its prehistoric size. Its present area is 14,000km^2, with around 140,000km^2 of shallow bank around it that would once have been dry land. Earlier Amerindian cultures may have inhabited them then.

Bermuda is 1,030 kilometres off the east coast of the United States. The territory comprises 181 small islands, with a total area of 53km^2. Bermuda was discovered in 1505 CE by Spanish navigator Juan de Bermudez, after whom the islands were named. He claimed to find the island inhabited only by pigs, probably left after an earlier European shipwreck.

The Republic of Cape Verde is an archipelago of ten islands in the central Atlantic Ocean, 570 kilometres off the coast of West Africa; they have a combined area of slightly over 4,000km^2. When

Italian and Portuguese navigators discovered the islands around 1456 CE, they were uninhabited. The Canary Islands, also known as the Canaries, is an archipelago of seven main islands with a land area of around 7,500km^2, located 100 kilometres off the north-west coast of Africa. When Europeans explored the islands in the 15th century CE, they encountered several Neolithic indigenous populations, who became known as the Guanches.

Archaeological and ethnographic studies indicate that the Guanche shared common origins with North African Berber tribes from the Atlas Mountains region. They are thought to have arrived in the Canaries by sea around 1000 BCE or earlier. To reach the Canaries from the coast of Africa, those people had to cross 100 kilometres of open water, so they were capable of open-sea travel.

The Canary Islands (Canaries)
Source: Google Earth

They brought domestic animals such as goats, sheep, pigs, and dogs; and cereals such as wheat and barley, and lentils.

King Juba, a Numidian ally of Rome, is credited with discovering the Canary Islands in the early 1st century CE, but the Phoenicians, Greeks and Carthaginians had visited the islands earlier. According to the 1st century CE Roman author and philosopher Pliny the Elder (23–79 CE), the islands were uninhabited when Carthaginians under Hanno the Navigator visited in the 5th century BCE. Still, those Carthaginians claimed they saw the 'ruins of great buildings' despite not seeing any Guanche. The Carthaginians' story suggests that other, more advanced cultures may have inhabited the islands before the Guanche. Otherwise, the Guanche once had a higher technology level before regressing to a Neolithic subsistence level.

Madeira is an archipelago with an area of 740km^2 and lies 400 kilometres north of the Canary Islands. Some knowledge of Madeira existed before the Portuguese's official discovery and settlement in the 15th century CE. In the 1st century CE, Pliny the Elder mentioned the 'Purple Islands', which may have referred to the islands of Madeira. The islands were uninhabited when the Portuguese arrived, but archaeological evidence indicates Vikings visited the islands between 900 and 1030 CE.

Madeira
Source: Google Earth

The Azores archipelago comprises nine volcanic islands in the middle of the North Atlantic Ocean. With an area of 2,300km^2, it is around 1,500 kilometres west of Spain and 3,900 kilometres east of North America. Some chroniclers noted that sailors knew of the islands and visited them during return voyages from the Canary Islands around 1340–1345 CE.

Recent controversial finds of possible rock art and megalithic structures may be evidence of the islands' Neolithic or pre-Bronze age occupation. If that is true, ancient inhabitants of the Azores had to sail there over hundreds of kilometres of open ocean. However, the islands were first officially discovered by the Portuguese in 1431 CE and were uninhabited then.

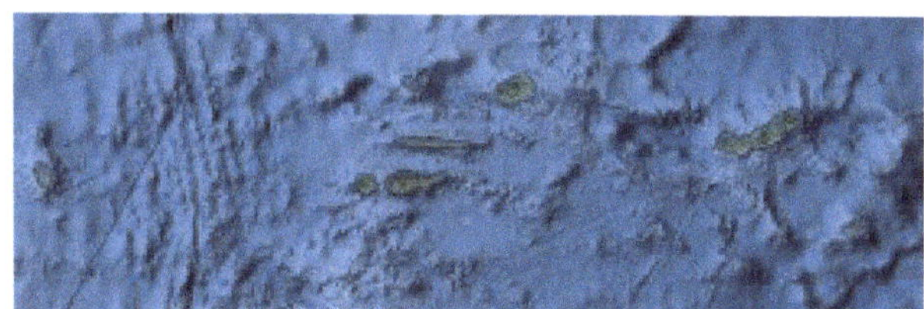

The Azores
Source: Google Earth

If the Atlanteans sailed north along the Atlantic coast of Europe, they possibly had contact with the British Isles. The earliest evidence of human occupation of Great Britain (the island now comprising Scotland, England and Wales) is of *Homo heidelbergensis*, dated to 700,000 BP. *Homo neanderthalensis* settled there sometime around 130,000 BP, and the oldest evidence of *Homo sapiens* is from 33,000 BP. All of these human species crossed to the island of Great Britain over a land bridge that connected it to Europe when the sea level was much lower, which happened several times in the past million years. The first evidence of *Homo sapiens* found on the island of Ireland is from 12,500 BP, and they must have reached there by sea. The Neolithic period only commenced on the British

Source: Google Earth

Isles at about 6,000 BP, so around 11,600 BP, the inhabitants would at most have had a Mesolithic level of culture.

The Prehistoric Cultures of the Mediterranean

Plato – '(the Atlanteans) subjected to their dominion all Libya (North Africa), as far as to Egypt; and Europe, as far as to the Tyrrhene sea.'

At the peak of the Atlantean Empire around 11,600 BP, it conquered and controlled many Mediterranean cultures and lands. Those Atlantean conquests may have taken tens or hundreds of years, depending on how long the Mediterranean cultures could resist the Atlantean military.

The Atlantean Empire extended to the 'Tyrrhene sea' on the northern Mediterranean coast, located between western Italy, Corsica, and Sardinia. Tyrrhenia is a region of central Italy that Greek and Latin texts called Etruria, home of the ancient Etruscan civilisation. The conquered peoples of the northern Mediterranean coast between the Atlantic and Tyrrhenia would have included cultures in

The Mediterranean Lands
Source: Wikimedia Commons

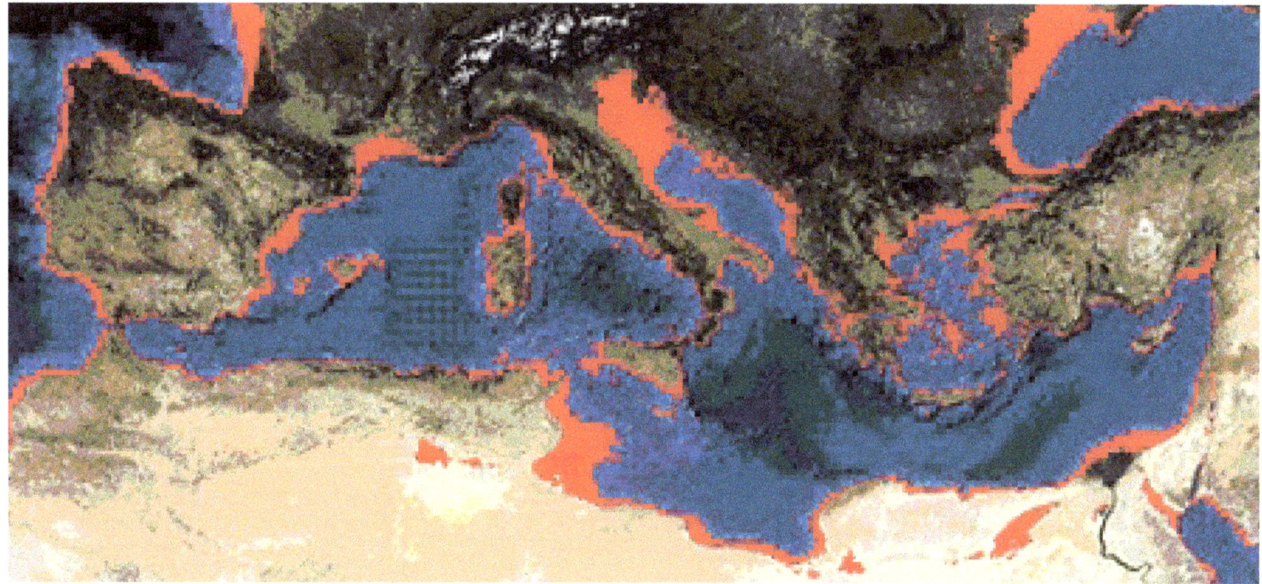

Mediterranean at LGM 20,000 BP (Additional Exposed Land in Red)
Source: From Vincent Gaffney

what are now the southern parts of Portugal, Spain, France, and north-western Italy.

The Atlanteans controlled North Africa up to the boundary between Egypt and Libya on the southern Mediterranean coast. This territory included the northern parts of what are now Morocco, Algeria, Tunisia, and Libya. As well as these mainland regions, the Balearic Islands, Corsica, and Sardinia may have been under Atlantean control.

In the Mediterranean War against the Atlanteans around 11,600 BP, Plato states that Athens was the leader of various non-Athenian Greek cultures and the other free cultures of the Eastern Mediterranean. In the south, the only free culture was Egypt. In the east were the cultures of the Levant, Cyprus, and what is now Turkey. In the north, apart from Greece, were the cultures of the southern Balkans, present-day Italy, including Sicily, and possibly the island of Malta.

Our species *Homo sapiens* inhabited the northern lands of the Mediterranean since at least 50,000 BP. We occupied the southern Mediterranean lands of North Africa for tens of thousands of years before then. While numerous cultures developed in those lands over that time, they declined and disappeared. They left few material traces of their culture, mainly due to the passage of time and the 120-metre rise in sea levels from 20,000 to 6,000 BP.

By the time of the Atlantis story of 11,600 BP, the Atlanteans had conquered the lands of the Western Mediterranean and incorporated them into the Atlantean Empire. The Atlanteans dominated the native people and possibly enslaved them.

Archaeological evidence indicates that the people of the Mediterranean region lived either in hunter-gatherer societies or early farming communities. Nevertheless, coastal lands then extended seaward many more kilometres than now, so more advanced cultures may once have lived there. The 60-metre increase in sea level after 11,600 BP inundated many wide coastal plains and large parts of islands, making them uninhabitable.

Prehistoric Western Europe

The Palaeolithic (Old Stone Age) period of Europe began when those early human species before *Homo sapiens* introduced stone tools, and it ended with the introduction of agriculture after 12,000 BP. The Palaeolithic was an age of purely hunting and gathering, whereas the Neolithic introduced the domestication of plants and animals. Mesolithic refers to cultures falling between the Palaeolithic and the Neolithic. Though some Mesolithic cultures continued with intensive hunting, others began domesticating plants and animals in villages.

Homo erectus originated in Africa and left there around two million years ago to migrate throughout Eurasia. The earliest known evidence of *Homo erectus* in Europe are 1.8 million-year-old remains found in Dmanisi, Georgia. A later species, *Homo heidelbergensis*, evolved in Africa from *Homo erectus* and then left Africa around 500,000 years ago, spreading throughout Europe and West Asia.

Homo heidelbergensis was the likely ancestor of Modern Humans like us (*Homo sapiens*), who first evolved in Africa and the Neanderthals (*Homo neanderthalensis*) who evolved separately in Europe. Our species replaced the Neanderthals when we migrated out of Africa and entered Europe by about 50,000 BP. The Palaeolithic European cultures of *Homo sapiens* were hunter-gatherer societies of a few hundred individuals. While each small tribe was primarily nomadic, some groups may have had permanent territories and dwellings.

Horse Paintings from Chauvet Cave, ca. 25,000 BP

As the Neolithic Package consisting of farming, herding, polished stone axes, timber longhouses, and pottery spread from the East into Europe, the Mesolithic way of life eventually disappeared. The start and end dates of the Mesolithic vary significantly by geographical region. Although it applies to the Levant in the Eastern Mediterranean from 22,000–11,500 BP, it also applies to North-West Europe from 12,000–7,000 BP.

The various European Palaeolithic and Mesolithic cultures are named by the location where archaeologists first discovered the cultures' artefacts and remains. Western Europe's Palaeolithic Magdalenian Culture (ca. 17,000–10,000 BP) developed into a Mesolithic culture by 12,000 BP. After around 12,000 BP, the Mesolithic Azilian Culture in south-west France and Spain co-existed with several similar early Mesolithic cultures of Northern Europe. From 20,000–8,000 BP, the Epigravettian Cultures developed in Italy and various parts of Europe, including the Creswellian Culture in Britain.

In Western Europe around the time of the Mediterranean War of 11,600 BP, the Magdalenian or early Azilian and Epigravettian cultures were evolving into Mesolithic cultures. With their much more advanced Bronze Age military technology, the Atlanteans would have met little resistance from these Mesolithic cultures, which probably consisted of small scattered tribes and settlements.

Even though the time of the Atlantean domination of the Western Mediterranean coincides with Mesolithic cultures in most of Western Europe, Plato describes an advanced Neolithic culture for prehistoric Athens/Attica. The people of Attica farmed domestic crops and animals, with Athens being a sizeable permanent settlement of tens of thousands. In what remains of the *Critias* dialogue, there is no depiction of any other Eastern Mediterranean cultures, though they may have been at a Mesolithic or Neolithic level.

Archaeologists believe Neolithic societies first emerged in the Levant in the Eastern Mediterranean around 14,000 BP. Recent evidence suggests that Neolithic culture was then introduced from Anatolia into Europe, where it developed into several regionally distinctive cultures by the 10th millennium BP. Because of this spread from east to west, all Neolithic sites in Europe contain the plants and animals first domesticated in South-West Asia, such as einkorn, emmer, barley, lentils, pigs, goats, sheep and cattle.

The duration of the Neolithic varies from place to place, with its end marked by the introduction of

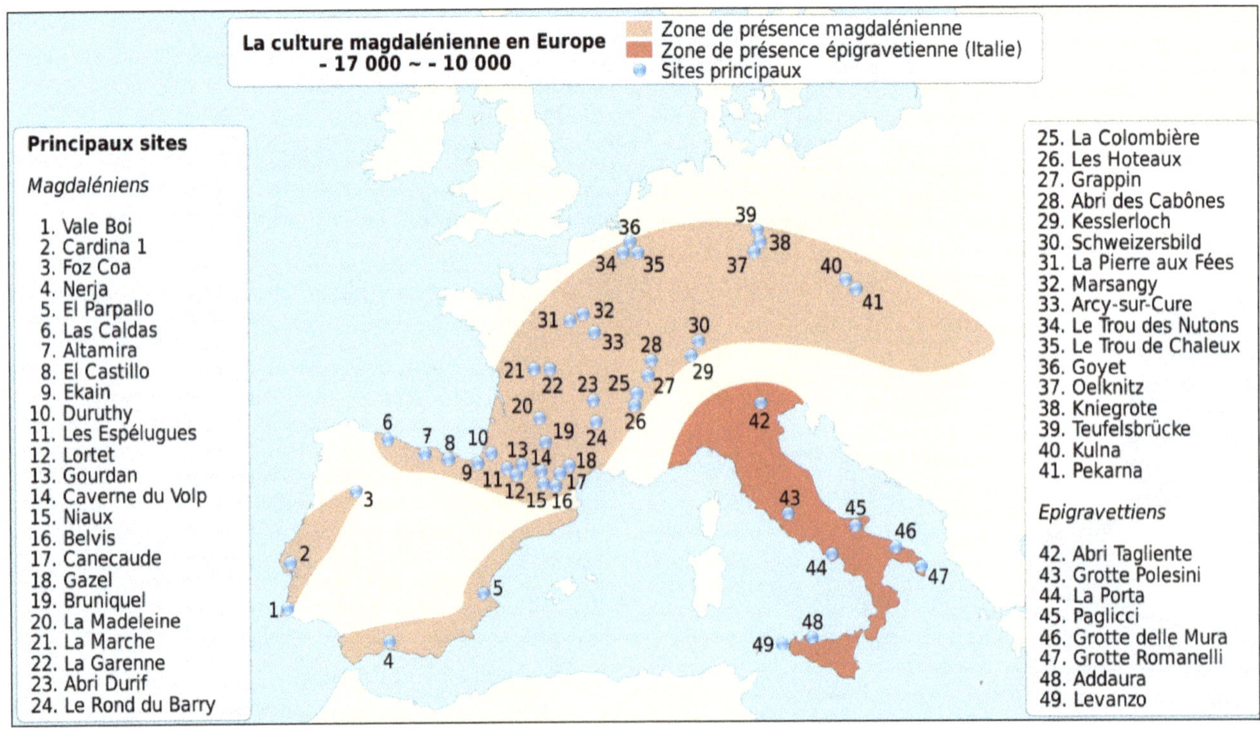

Map of Magdalenian (in pink) and Epigravettian (in red) Cultures, 19,000–12,000 BP
Source: Wikimedia Commons – Semhur

bronze implements, commencing the Bronze Age in those places. The Neolithic in Europe is thought to have begun around 9,000 BP when the first known farming societies appeared in Greece; it continued to around 3,700 BP when farming reached North-Western Europe.

European Neolithic groups shared some essential characteristics of the Neolithic Package. They lived in small-scale, family-based communities and subsisted on domesticated plants and animals supplemented with wild plant foods and hunting. Still, there were also some differences depending on the region. Several Neolithic communities in South-Eastern Europe lived in heavily fortified settlements of 3,000–4,000 people, but in Britain, the groups were small, with possibly 50–100 people who were highly mobile cattle herders.

Cardium Culture (Cardial Culture) is the central culture of the Mediterranean Neolithic period. It extended from the Adriatic Sea to the Atlantic coasts of Portugal and south to Morocco. The earliest known Cardium Culture sites in Europe date

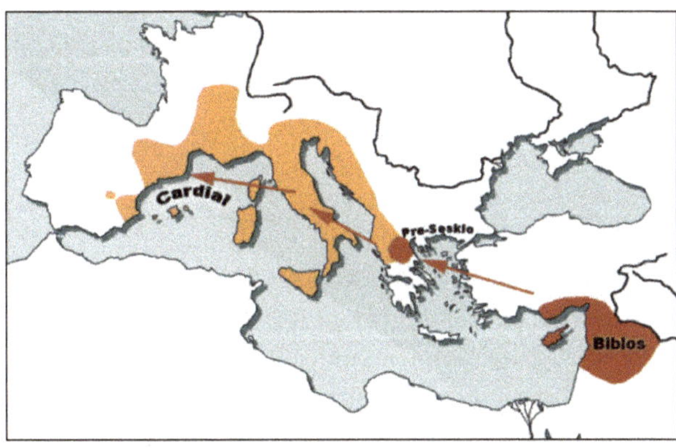

Approximate distribution of Cardium Pottery 8th–7th millennium BP
Source: Wikimedia Commons – Jose-Manuel Benito Alvarez

to 8,400–8,200 BP in Epirus and Corfu in western Greece. Settlements then rapidly spread west, with dates in Iberia from 7,500 BP. This 2,000-kilometre spread of Cardium and related cultures over probably no more than 100–200 years suggests swift expansion by sea, with colonies established along the coast.

Although the first known European locations of the Cardium Culture are on the west coast of Greece from around 8,400–8,200 BP, the Neolithic Package was introduced to Europe from western Anatolia sometime after 14,000 BP. Therefore, the Neolithic Package must have entered Eastern Greece before Cardium Culture appeared in Western Greece, possibly a few thousand years before. If a Neolithic culture did develop much earlier in Eastern Greece before migrating westward, it could match a Neolithic Athens/Attica of 11,600 BP.

Plato – 'she (Athens) defeated and triumphed over the invaders (the Atlanteans), and preserved from slavery those who were not yet subjugated, and generously liberated all the rest of us who dwell within the pillars (the Mediterranean region).'

Plato states that sometime after the Mediterranean War, the Athenians freed the cultures of the Western Mediterranean from Atlantean domination. This action of the Athenians might match the seaborne westward movement of Cardium Culture to Iberia over one or two hundred years. If that feat did happen, the Athenians and possibly their allies had sea-going ships capable of sailing long distances in the Mediterranean. They may have challenged and defeated Atlantean military forces within the Mediterranean.

Prehistoric North-West Africa

Anatomically modern humans were present in North-West Africa during the Middle Palaeolithic (220,000–45,000 BP), forming the Aterian Culture around the Atlas Mountains and the northern Sahara. Personal adornments of pierced and ochred Nassarius shell beads were found in at least one Aterian site dated 82,000 BP. Around 22,000 BP, the Aterian was succeeded by the Iberomaurusian Culture, which possibly shared similarities with Iberian cultures that lived in present-day Spain and Portugal.

The Iberomaurusian Culture existed in the region from around the Last Glacial Maximum at 20,000 BP until 12,900 BP. The Mesolithic Capsian Culture succeeded the Iberomaurusian Culture, lasting from 12,000 to 8,000 BP. It was concentrated mainly in modern Tunisia, Algeria and Libya, with some sites in Europe from southern Spain to Sicily.

In the Atlantis story, as the Atlanteans invaded the Mediterranean, North-West Africa to the west of Egypt became part of the Atlantean Empire. Mesolithic Iberomaurusian and possibly early Capsian Cultures would have occupied that area during the Atlantean conquests.

Around 9,000 BP, the Sahara entered a wet phase, attracting Neolithic peoples from the Near East and Sub-Saharan Africans. A Neolithic culture with

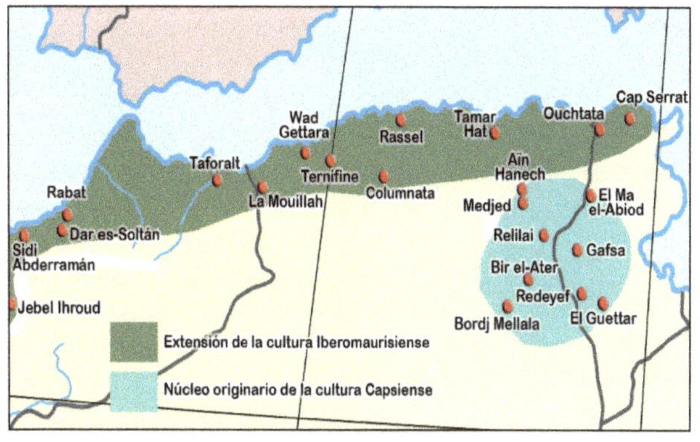

Iberomaurusian (dark green) and Capsian (light green) Cultures
Source: Wikimedia Commons – Jose-Manuel Benito Alvarez

animal domestication and subsistence agriculture developed between 8,000 and 4,000 BP in North Africa. By 7,000 BP, the populations of North Africa were an amalgamation of Iberomaurusian and Capsian stock, blended with the more recent Neolithic culture from the Near East. Berber tribes formed from these mixed populations during the Late Bronze to Early Iron Age. Berbers are the indigenous peoples of North Africa to the west of the Nile Valley; they occupied from the Atlantic coast to the Western Desert of Egypt and from the Mediterranean coast to the Niger River.

The Eastern Mediterranean

In the Mediterranean War, the Atlanteans fought against the free cultures of the Eastern Mediterranean. In the incomplete *Critias* dialogue, Plato states that there were Hellenic cultures besides the Athenians, but none are named. Also, other than the Egyptians, Plato does not name any free non-Hellenic cultures or their territories. Nevertheless, those free cultures could have occupied the lands of what are now the southern Balkans, the Levant, Cyprus, Turkey, Italy and Sicily, and possibly the island of Malta. Though not mentioned in the incomplete *Critias* dialogue, the lost part of that dialogue may have described them.

During the Mediterranean War, Plato states that the Athenians were the military leaders of the free cultures of the Eastern Mediterranean. The Athenians prevailed in battles against the Atlantean aggressors, whereas the other free cultures were contained or defeated. The Atlanteans were eventually beaten back and withdrew from the Mediterranean, but Plato does not state how long that took. The Atlantean retreat may have taken years, decades or centuries.

Greece

Plato describes a thriving Neolithic culture in Attica before 11,600 BP, with varied agriculture and a relatively large population. Although a known Mesolithic culture did exist in Greece then, there is no archaeological evidence of Neolithic culture before 9,000 BP. Even so, *Homo sapiens* has inhabited Greece since at least 30,000 BP, or around 20,000 years before the prehistoric Athens/Attica of the Atlantis story. A Neolithic culture may have developed in the Greek region before 11,600 BP, but any remains are undiscovered.

Palaeolithic Greece

A *Homo erectus* skull in a cave at Petralona in Chalkidiki, Northern Greece, is dated between 160,000–240,000 BP. Other discoveries, such as stone tools from Thessaly prove that *Homo erectus* inhabited Greece since 300,000–400,000 BP.

A *Homo sapiens* skull from Apidima Cave in Mani, southern Greece, was dated to around 210,000 BP. This find indicates a much earlier migration of our species out of Africa into Europe than previously thought, but it is argued that those initial migrants became extinct. They seem to have been followed by a later *Homo sapiens* migration from Africa into Eurasia around 100,000 years ago. Those people supposedly created all of the Earth's present human population outside Africa.

Homo sapiens remains were identified in burials in central Greece at the caves of Apidima from 30,000 BP and in Theopetra from 16,500 BP. The burials at Theopetra provide the first evidence in Greece of pots manufactured from wood and clay. The people there used hard flint for arrowheads, flakes, endscrapers, drills, blades and bladelets.

Neolithic Greece and the Pelasgians

The known Neolithic period in Greece lasted more than three thousand years, from around 9,500 BP until the beginning of the Bronze Age around 6,000 BP. There are approximately 1,000 Neolithic sites recorded or excavated in Greece. The size of the most thoroughly investigated settlements, such as Sesklo, Dimini and Makriyialos, ranges from 500–6,000 square metres. The first farming and stock-rearing communities are estimated to have numbered 100–300 individuals. Initial settlements consisted of huts with wooden walls, whereas later houses were one-roomed or had an open or closed porch and had stone foundations with walls of unfired mud-bricks. The houses were built independently of each other, usually with a single-storey, but there also were two-storey dwellings.

When Plato describes Athens as the 'leader of the Hellenes' in 11,600 BP, the people who inhabited Greece at that time were what later Greeks of Solon and Plato's time called Pelasgians. Some Ancient Greek writers used the name Pelasgian for populations that were either the ancestors of the Greeks or preceded Greek-speaking peoples in Greece. Ancient Greek literary tradition describes the Athenians as the direct descendants of Pelasgians, who were the Neolithic inhabitants of Thessaly to the north.

During the Classical Greek period of Solon and Plato, Pelasgian enclaves survived in several locations of mainland Greece, Crete, and western Anatolia. They spoke a language or languages that Classical Greeks identified as not Greek, even though some ancient writers described the Pelasgians as Greeks. A tradition also survived that large parts of Greece had once been Pelasgian before being Hellenised.

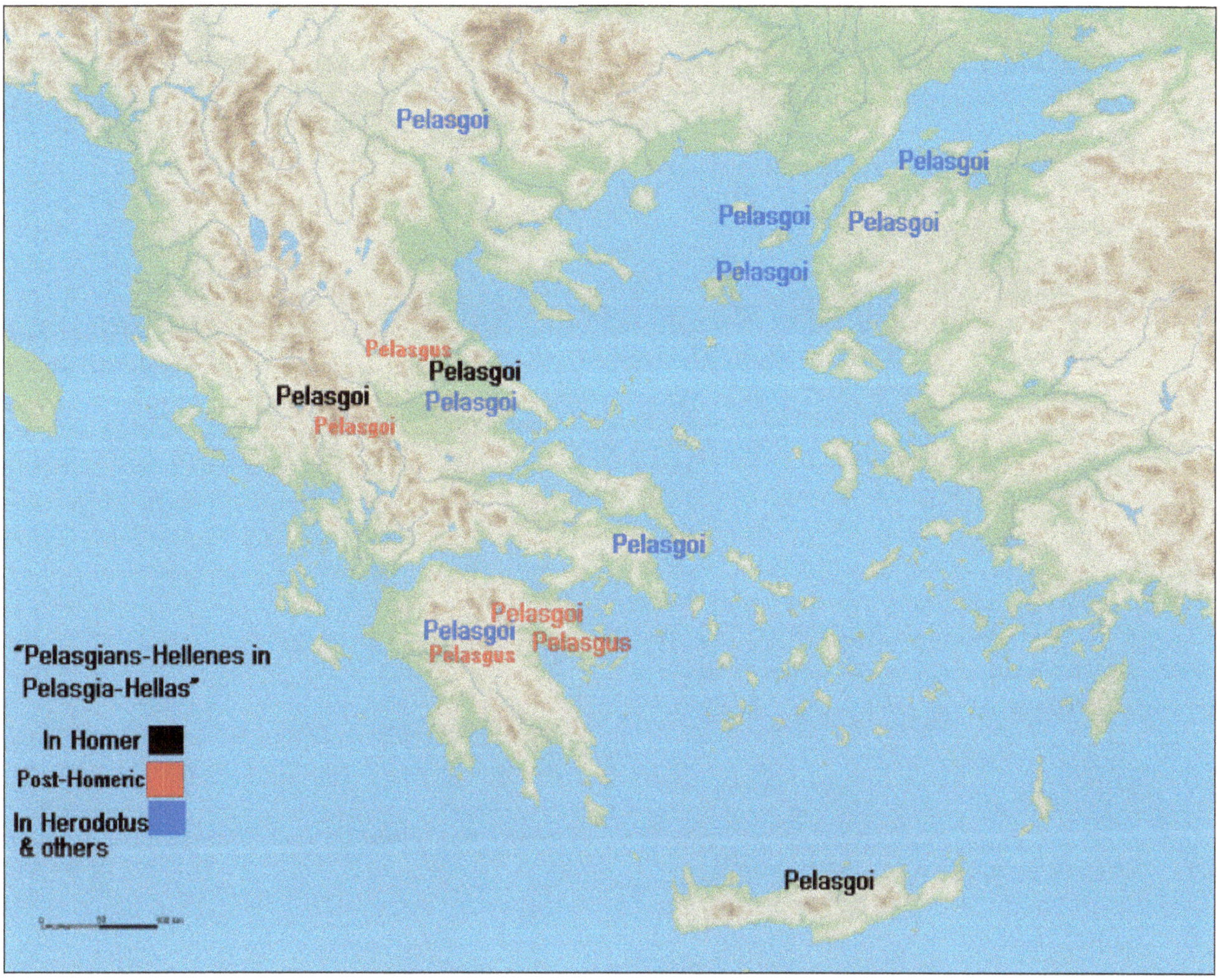

Pelasgian Presence Mentioned by Ancient Writers
Source: Wikimedia Commons – Megistias

Archaeological excavations have unearthed artefacts in areas traditionally inhabited by the Pelasgians, like Thessaly, Attica and Lemnos. Archaeologists have described Pelasgian material culture as being Neolithic.

Franchthi Cave overlooks the Argolic Gulf in the Peloponnese, southern Greece. The cave was occupied by *Homo sapiens* from the Palaeolithic around 20,000 BP and possibly earlier. Occupation continued through the Mesolithic and Neolithic periods, but it was abandoned by 5,000 BP. The people who occupied the cave during that entire time would have been Pelasgians. Obsidian from the island of Melos, 130 kilometres away by sea, appears at Franchthi Cave as early as 13,000 BP, which indicates that the people of that time had seafaring and navigational skills. Furthermore, large fish bones were also found, which is characteristic of deep-sea fishing from boats.

Franchthi Cave also contains some of the earliest evidence of agriculture in Greece. The first inhabitants of the cave were probably hunter-gatherers, but from around 13,000 BP, almonds, pistachios, bitter vetch and lentils appear in the cave. Wild oats and wild barley appear from 12,500 BP, and peas and wild pears appear from 9,300 BP. None of these plants is native to the region, and two are certainly from Anatolia. Around 8,000 BP, there is evidence of the domestication of animals and plants such as emmer and einkorn wheat.

From the archaeological evidence in Franchthi Cave, after around 13,000 BP, the Pelasgian culture in Greece appears to have been in regular contact with the early Neolithic cultures of Anatolia, who probably also were Pelasgians.

The Pelasgians in Greece likely obtained several domesticated plant species and domesticated animals such as pigs, goats, sheep and cattle from Anatolia. Therefore, between 13,000 and 11,600 BP,

Franchthi Cave, Peloponnese

the Greek Pelasgians may have had sufficient time to develop the more advanced Neolithic culture Plato describes for Athens.

Bronze Age Aegean Civilisation

Aegean Civilisation is a general term for the Bronze Age Greek cultures located around the Aegean Sea. It covers three distinct geographical regions: the Greek mainland, Crete, and the Cycladic Islands. These three regions communicated with each other and interacted for over two thousand years, from 3000–1000 BCE.

Many Ancient Greek myths and legends of Solon and Plato's time refer to people and events from the Greek Bronze Age, particularly the latter part. Some modern scholars believe that Plato based his Atlantis story on those myths and legends, but none of those ancient stories mention Atlantis or any events of the Atlantis story. Nothing is vaguely similar to Plato's descriptions of the Atlantic Island in the geography of Bronze Age Greece and the Aegean.

The Cyclades

The Cyclades comprise about 2,200 islands, islets and rocks in the southern part of the Aegean Sea, but only 33 are inhabited. Around 20,000 BP at the time of the low sea level at the LGM, most of the Cyclades islands were joined into one large landmass, sometimes called Cycladia. As the sea level rose, the Aegean Sea flooded Cycladia and formed many small islands.

Evidence from excavations at a chert quarry on the island of Naxos in the middle of the Cyclades suggests that hominins, probably Neanderthals, were present in the region 200,000 years ago. The chert was used to make tools, and these Neanderthals are thought to have reached the chert quarry during low sea levels around the second-last Glacial Maximum, around 200,000 years ago. At that time, exposed land may have connected Anatolia to continental Southeast Europe, so the Neanderthals might have walked there but possibly arrived by sea on watercraft.

Early *Homo sapiens* occupied or traversed the Cyclades region 40,000–30,000 years ago and may have arrived there by boat. The later arrival of Mesolithic hunter-gatherers after 12,000 BP was definitely by sea. Then, a Neolithic culture that combined Anatolian and mainland Greek elements arose in the Cyclades before 8,000 BP and must have reached the islands by sea. They brought with them components of the Neolithic Package, probably

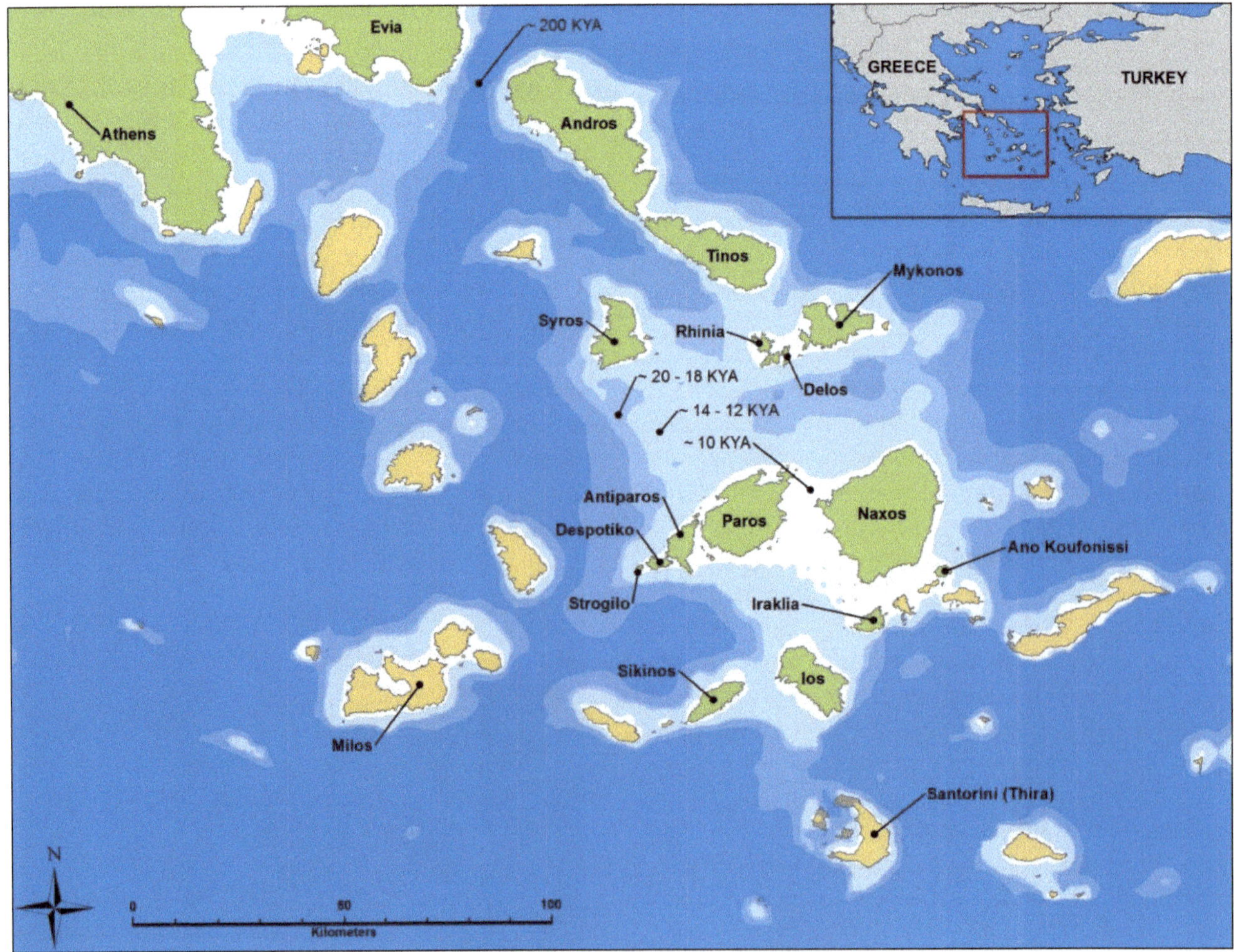

The Fragmentation of Cycladia and the Timing of the Inundations (KYA)
Source: Stephen Roussos – Deciphering the past to ensure viper's future on the Cyclades – Biodiversity Science

from Anatolia. This Neolithic Cycladic culture was based on emmer wheat and wild-type barley, sheep, goats, pigs, and tuna caught from boats.

From the LGM of 20,000 BP to the Mediterranean War of 11,600 BP, there was around 60 metres of sea level rise, with a further 60 metres rise until 6,000 BP. In that case, a substantial part of the large island landmass of Cycladia was still present by 11,600 BP. The inhabitants of Cycladia may have taken part in the war against the Atlanteans, and they probably had at least a Mesolithic level of culture and possibly Neolithic by 11,600 BP.

Following the Neolithic period, the Cycladic Bronze Age civilisation spans from around 3000–2000 BCE. It was a highly developed maritime trading culture, with trade links to Asia Minor, mainland Greece, Crete, North Africa, and Europe. It was probably the most advanced civilisation in the Aegean region for a time, more sophisticated than Crete or the Greek mainland. When the organised palace culture of the Minoans in Crete developed, the Cycladic islands lost significance except for the island of Delos, which continued as a religious sanctuary right through the period of later Classical Greek civilisation. By around 2000 BCE, the Minoan civilisation of Crete had largely absorbed the Cycladic culture.

Thera, also known as Santorini, is a Cycladic island located 200km south-east of the Greek mainland. During Minoan times, it was the site of one of the largest volcanic eruptions in recorded history. There has been much recent speculation that Plato based his Atlantis story on the catastrophic volcanic eruption of Thera.

Thera Island Group
Source: Wikimedia Commons – NASA

The oldest signs of human settlement on Thera are from the 6th millennium BP. Initially, Thera was a centre of Cycladic culture but peaked as a centre of the Minoan civilisation from 2000–1580 BCE. The Minoan eruption, also called the Thera eruption, occurred in the mid-2nd millennium BCE at the height of the Minoan civilisation centred on Crete. Dates for the volcanic eruption range from 1645 to 1500 BCE.

The explosive force of the Thera eruption ejected 60 cubic kilometres of rock material, or up to four times as much as the eruption of Krakatoa in 1883 CE. The Thera eruption generated a megatsunami, once considered to have caused the collapse of the Minoan civilisation on the island of Crete, 110 kilometres to the south. This hypothesis is unlikely because archaeological evidence shows Minoan civilisation did not collapse at the time of the tsunami but many years later.

Thera Caldera
Source: Wikimedia Commons

Excavations in the south of Thera at the site called Akrotiri have uncovered a large Bronze Age town of around twenty hectares in size, entirely buried under the solidified ash of the Thera eruption. Around 2000–1650 BCE, Akrotiri developed into one of the Aegean's major trading ports, with excavated objects coming from Crete, Anatolia, Cyprus, Syria, Egypt, and the Greek mainland. Despite excavations of only the southern tip of the town, it has exposed complexes of multi-storeyed buildings, elaborate drainage systems, streets, and squares.

The town of Akrotiri was an advanced settlement of the Bronze Age Aegean, and there may have been several similar towns on Thera before the volcano erupted. No human remains have been found at

Akrotiri
Source: Wikimedia Commons – F. Eveleens

Akrotiri, which indicates the inhabitants had enough warning of the eruption to leave the island well before it occurred.

Plato is precise about the Atlantic Island's location, shape and size. It is nothing like the 76km^2 island of Thera situated in the middle of the Aegean Sea, not in the Atlantic. If the tiny island of Thera inspired the Atlantis story, all of Plato's details of the Atlantic Island would have been a fabrication of the Egyptian priests, Solon, or Plato himself. Though the Thera eruption did devastate much of the island, it did not destroy its population or the Minoan civilisation. That historical ending is very different from the subsidence below the sea of the enormous Atlantic Island.

Crete

The earliest human inhabitants of Crete were probably the species *Homo erectus*, who may have settled there by 130,000 BP or possibly earlier. They must have somehow travelled to the island of Crete over many kilometres of the open sea, either from Africa, Anatolia or the Greek mainland. Recent finds of cave art are evidence of the possible presence of *Homo sapiens* on Crete from around 20,000 BP, and they also would have arrived there by sea. The first well-documented *Homo sapiens* activity in Crete comes from 9,000–8,500 BP. Neolithic remains are widespread, and the population dwelt in open villages of wattle and daub huts, kept animals, and grew crops.

The Bronze Age began in Crete around 2700 BCE, and Crete's Minoan civilisation represents the first known civilisation in Europe. What the Minoans called themselves is unknown. The archaeologist Arthur Evans, who discovered the city of Knossos in 1900 CE, named the culture Minoan after the mythical Cretan King Minos.

The Minoan civilisation was much more advanced and sophisticated than the cultures of that time on the Greek mainland. The Minoan people were not Indo-European and were probably the same as the pre-Greek Pelasgians of the Greek mainland and western Anatolia. The Minoans had a writing system called Linear A. It has not yet been deciphered and seems to represent a non-Greek Aegean language unrelated to any Indo-European language.

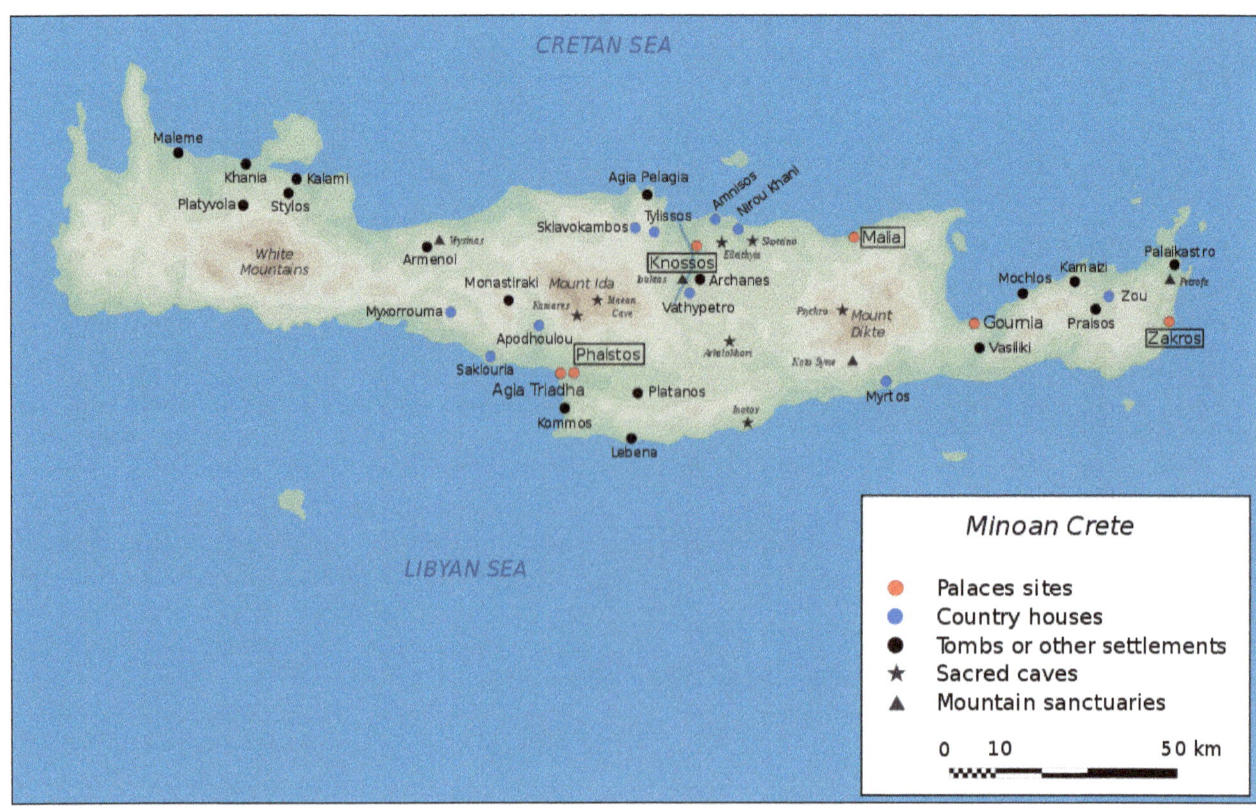

Map of Minoan Crete
Source: Wikimedia Commons – Bibi Saint-Pol

Homer recorded a tradition that Bronze Age Crete had ninety cities, with the four known main palace sites of Knossos, Phaistos, Malia and Zakros. Each site had large, complex, two- or three-storied palace structures covering several thousand square metres. The palaces acted as local administrative, trade, religious and possibly political centres. With an area of 20,000 square metres, the Palace of Knossos was the largest of the Minoan palace centres. It was multi-storied, built of finely cut stone blocks, and decorated with frescoes on its interior walls.

The Ruins at Knossos
The Palace Complex of Knossos
Source: Wikimedia Commons – Mmoyaq

The Palace Complex of Knossos
Source: Wikimedia Commons – Mmoyaq

The Knossos Throne Room
Source: Wikimedia Commons – Rolf Dietrich Brecher

The Minoans were seagoing traders. Their cultural contacts included the Greek mainland and Cyclades, Egypt's Old Kingdom, Cyprus, Anatolia, Canaan and the Levantine coasts. They exported ceramics to Egypt and imported several items from Egypt, especially papyrus, which they would have used for writing. The Egyptians influenced Minoan architecture and art, and after around 1700 BCE, Minoan culture influenced the Greek mainland.

Around 1450 BC, Minoan culture reached a turning point due to a natural catastrophe, possibly an earthquake. Several important palaces, in locations such as Malia, Tylissos, Phaistos and Hagia Triada, and the living quarters of Knossos were destroyed. After a century of partial recovery, most Cretan cities and palaces declined during the 13th century BCE.

The later Greeks of Solon and Plato's time appear to have completely forgotten the existence of Minoan civilisation. There are a few myths but no histories of individuals and events of that period.

Mainland Greece

The Helladic Period is a sequence of Bronze Age cultural periods in mainland Greece. Early Helladic cultures (2800–2100 BCE) were agriculturalists who used basic bronze-working techniques first developed in Anatolia, with which they had cultural contacts. The Middle Helladic period (2100–1500 BCE) began with the emergence of Minyan Ware, a form of monochrome burnished pottery. Ancient Greek historians wrote of the Minyans, apparently indigenous pre-Greek people who may be related to the Pelasgians.

Mycenaean Greece developed out of Early and Middle Helladic cultures. It flourished during the Late Helladic period (1500–1100 BCE) due to new influences from the more advanced cultures of Minoan Crete and the Cyclades. Mycenaean Greece takes its name from the archaeological site of Mycenae, located in the Peloponnese in southern Greece. At its peak in 1350 BCE, Mycenae's citadel and lower town had an area of 32 hectares and a population of around 30,000. Other important Mycenaean cities included Athens, Pylos, Thebes and Tiryns.

In the *Iliad* and *Odyssey*, Homer freely interchanges the terms Achaeans, Argives and Danaans for the Mycenaeans. They are thought to have spoken the earliest known dialect of the Greek language, different to the pre-Greek language of the Pelasgians. In around 1600 BCE, the Mycenaeans modified the pre-Greek Linear A script of the Minoans and developed their own syllabic Linear B script, a form of Greek.

The decline of the Minoan civilization on Crete allowed the Mycenaeans to spread their influence

Mycenae Ruins and Reconstruction

throughout the Aegean. By around 1450 BCE, the Mycenaeans controlled Crete, including Knossos, and colonized several other Aegean islands, reaching as far as Rhodes. Regular Mycenaean sea trade routes extended throughout the Mediterranean as far west as southern Spain. The Mycenaeans imported raw materials such as metals, ivory and glass by sea. They exported manufactured products made from those imported materials and local products such as oil, perfume, wine, wool and pottery. Mycenaean pottery has been found in Sardinia, Southern Italy and Sicily, Anatolia, Cyprus, the Levant, and Egypt.

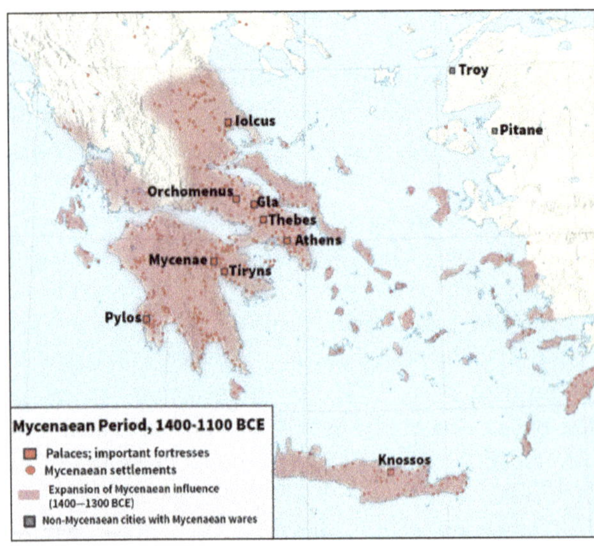

Source: Wikimedia Commons

Mycenaean bronze double-axes and other objects dating from the 13th century BCE have been found in Ireland, and Wessex and Cornwall in England.

From around 1200 BCE, the Mycenaeans' palace centres and outlying settlements began to be abandoned or destroyed. By 1050 BCE, the features of Mycenaean Culture had almost disappeared in Greece. The Mycenaean civilisation's fall was part of the Late Bronze Age Collapse in the Eastern Mediterranean. During a relatively short period between 1206 and 1150 BCE, there was simultaneous violent destruction and cultural collapse of the Mycenaean kingdoms, the Hittite Empire in Anatolia and Syria, and the New Kingdom of Egypt in Syria and Canaan.

Though several possible explanations exist for the Late Bronze Age Collapse, no single answer fits the available archaeological evidence. Some of the reasons may be climatic or environmental catastrophes combined with an invasion by Dorians from northern Greece, raids by a confederation of marauding Sea Peoples, or the widespread availability of iron weapons and changes in warfare.

When the Mycenaean palatial centres collapsed in Greece, there was no more construction of monumental stone buildings; writing in Linear B script ceased; trade links were lost, and towns and villages were abandoned. The population of Greece markedly decreased, and organised state armies, kings, officials, and distribution systems disappeared. This Greek Dark Age lasted until the 8th century BCE. It was followed by the emergence of the Greek city-states and the Classical Greek period of Solon, Socrates and Plato.

Some scholars believe Plato based his Atlantis story on the devastation of the Late Bronze Age Collapse. Despite Mycenaean Greece being the basis of much Ancient Greek literature and myth, including Homer's epic poems the *Iliad* and *Odyssey* concerning the Trojan War, no stories based on the Mycenaean period refer to Atlantis or the role of Athens in a Mediterranean War.

Egypt

The Egyptian priests who told Solon the Atlantis story believed their culture was so ancient that it fought against the Atlanteans in the Mediterranean War of 11,600 BP. This version of prehistoric Egyptian culture has often been criticised because it is assumed that the inhabitants of Egypt lived at a subsistence hunter-gatherer level for thousands of years before and after 11,600 BP. However, there was no sudden shift from hunter-gatherers to the more advanced Egyptian civilisation under the pharaohs. Instead, prehistoric Egyptian cultures developed gradually over thousands of years into Mesolithic and then Neolithic cultures before 11,600

BP. The later Ancient Egyptians recorded dynasties of Egypt's mythical rulers from tens of thousands of years before their own time.

Palaeolithic Period

Egypt and ancient Canaan to the north were probably the migration route for successive waves of human species, from *Homo erectus* to *Homo sapiens*, to travel out of Africa into Mesopotamia and Europe. The earliest evidence of humans in Egypt dates from around 700,000–500,000 BP, and they are *Homo erectus*.

The earliest evidence of our *Homo sapiens* species in Egypt is a child's skeleton with an estimated age between 80,000–50,000 BP. Nomadic *Homo sapiens* hunter-gatherers lived along the Nile by that time and probably well before. A *Homo sapiens* jawbone found in a cave in Israel was dated to 170,000–190,000 BP, meaning that *Homo sapiens* must have been present in Egypt before.

The Nile Valley of the Palaeolithic was much larger than it is today, but annual flooding made a permanent occupation of its floodplain impossible. As the climate became drier and flooding decreased, people were able to settle in the Nile Valley. The Khormusan industry began in Egypt between 40,000–30,000 BP. The hunter-gatherer Khormusans developed tools from stone, animal bones and haematite; they also produced small arrowheads, but no bows have been found.

The Khormusan industry ended around 18,000 BP with the appearance of other regional cultures. The Halfan Culture flourished along the Nile Valley of Egypt and Nubia between 19,000 and 14,000 BP, with its people surviving on a diet of large herd animals and fish. From 15,000–12,000 BP, the Sebilian Culture of southern Egypt (also known as the Esna Culture) gathered wild wheat and barley. From 15,000–11,000 BP in Upper Nubia, a grain-grinding Mesolithic people called the Qadan Culture practised wild grain harvesting along the Nile.

Neolithic Period

The Neolithic period in Egypt coincides with the Mediterranean War around 11,600 BP and the founding of Sais around 10,600 BP.

Along the Nile in the 14th millennium BP, a grain-grinding culture that used sickle blades was replaced by another culture of hunter-gatherers and fishers. Before 10,000 BP, human habitation and cattle herding occurred near the Sudan border in south-western Egypt. Although there was pastoralism and cultivation of cereals in the 9th millennium BP in the Eastern Sahara, there is little evidence of it from 11,600–8,000 BP.

Natural climate changes around 10,000 BP began to dry out the extensive pastoral lands of North Africa, eventually forming the Sahara Desert by around 4,500 BP. This continuing desertification forced the early ancestors of the Egyptians to settle permanently around the Nile. Early tribes in the region tended to gather close to the Nile River, where they developed a settled agricultural economy and more centralised society. So, by around 8,000 BP, Neolithic settlements had appeared throughout Egypt.

Sais and the Neolithic Nile Delta

With the 120-metre increase in sea level from 20,000–6,000 BP, any coastal Neolithic settlements of the Nile Delta dating before 6,000 BP would now be tens of metres underwater and kilometres out to sea in the Mediterranean or under metres of accumulated silt from the Nile's flooding.

There is limited knowledge of prehistoric settlement patterns in the Nile Delta since few sites have been found and excavated. Nearly all the known sites are covered either by the water-table or modern communities. The earliest known Neolithic settlement in the Nile Valley or Delta is Merimda on the western Delta margin of the desert, whose beginnings date from 7,000–6,800 BP.

From what the Egyptian priests told Solon, the city of Sais was founded around 10,600 BP. Archaeological excavations at the site of Sais that Solon visited around 600 BCE indicate it was a fishing camp in the Early Neolithic (6,500–6,200 BP). It was then settled in the Middle to Late Neolithic Period (6,000–5,800 BP), and the community changed from seasonal fishers to settled pig and grain farmers.

Although the earliest occupation of the present archaeological site of Sais is dated to the 7th millennium BP, it may not be the site of the prehistoric city the Egyptian priests described to Solon. The various branches of the Nile in the Delta have often changed course. Until around 3,000 BP, there were seven branches of the Nile in the Delta, but now there are only two. There is geological evidence that the Rosetta branch of the Nile, now two kilometres west of the Sais archaeological site, shifted west in the Middle to Late Neolithic around 6,000 BP. Still, other unknown changes in the Rosetta branch's course may have been earlier than 6,000 BP.

If there were a prehistoric settlement at Sais from 10,600 BP, it might have been abandoned once it became uninhabitable due to a change in the Nile's course or rising sea level. Otherwise, if Plato's prehistoric Sais is the present archaeological site, it is in an unexcavated area, or the excavations are not yet deep enough to find it.

Predynastic Period

By around 8,000 BP, there was organised agriculture and the construction of large buildings in the Nile Valley. Between 7,500 and 5,100 BP, many small settlements flourished along the Nile. Various cultures appeared in Lower Egypt (northern Egypt including the Nile Delta), such as the Merimda, El Omari and Maadi Cultures. During the same time, in Upper Egypt (southern Egypt) cultures such as the Tasian, Badarian and Amratian (Naqada I) appeared. A significant drop in rainfall then occurred, so that farming produced most of the population's food.

The Gerzean (Naqada II) Culture from 5,500–5,200 BP was the foundation of Dynastic Egypt. Gerzean Culture developed out of Amratian (Naqada I) Culture, which started in the Nile Delta and then moved south. With increased food supplies, the larger settlements grew to mud brick cities with about 5,000 residents. Copper was used increasingly instead of stone to make tools and weaponry; ornaments were made from silver, gold, lapis lazuli and faience. Foreign objects and art forms entered Egypt during this period, indicating contacts with Asia and sea-based trade.

The Naqada III period from 5,200–5,000 BP is called Dynasty 0 or the Protodynastic Period, when various small city-states arose along the Nile. By 5,300 BP, just before the first Egyptian dynasty, Egypt was divided into two kingdoms known as Upper Egypt (Ta Shemau) to the south of modern Cairo and Lower Egypt (Ta Mehu) to the north.

Centuries of inter-state warfare had reduced Upper Egypt to three major competing states: Thinis, Naqada and Nekhen. Located between Thinis and Nekhen, Naqada was the first state to fall. Nekhen's relationship with Thinis is uncertain, but these two remaining states may have merged peacefully. The societies of Lower Egypt (the Nile Delta) also underwent a unification process over many centuries. There was frequent warfare between Upper and Lower Egypt, but they were unified around 5,100 BP (3100 BCE), and the royal family of Thinis then ruled all of Egypt.

Early Dynastic Period

Ancient Egypt's historical records begin with Egypt as a unified state. Menes was the first King of united Upper and Lower Egypt in Egyptian tradition. From then on, Egypt's history is divided into several different periods based on the dynasty of the ruling King or Pharaoh. The following list is the conventional Egyptian chronology:

- Predynastic Period – before 3100 BCE
- Protodynastic Period – approximately 3100 – 3000 BCE
- Early Dynastic Period – 1st–2nd Dynasties
- Old Kingdom – 3rd–6th Dynasties
- First Intermediate Period –7th–11th Dynasties
- Middle Kingdom – 12th–13th Dynasties
- Second Intermediate Period – 14th–17th Dynasties
- New Kingdom – 18th–20th Dynasties
- Third Intermediate Period – 21st–25th Dynasties
- Late Period – 26th–31st Dynasties

The Unknown Prehistoric Egyptian Kings

If the timing of the Atlantis story is correct, the Mediterranean War against the Atlanteans occurred around 11,600 BP. Plato states that the Egyptian people fought in that war as allies of the Athenians. Archaeological evidence indicates that Egypt was in a Neolithic state of cultural development then, but there are no surviving records from those prehistoric times. Over thousands of years, later Egyptians must have either copied and preserved extremely ancient records from the time of the Atlantis story's events, or they recorded an earlier oral history and maintained it until Solon's time.

Several surviving Ancient Egyptian references document the Predynastic rulers of Egypt, who date back thousands of years before Egypt's unification around 5,100 BP. If any prehistoric rulers existed around 11,600 BP, they would likely have led the Egyptian people against the invading Atlanteans.

Manetho's King List

The Aegyptiaca was written in Ancient Greek by the Egyptian priest and historian Manetho in

Dynasty	Commenced	Duration
Dynasty of Gods	30,544 BP	13,900 yrs.
Dynasty of Demi-gods	16,644 BP	1,255 yrs.
The First Line of Kings	15,389 BP	1,817 yrs.
Thirty more Kings of Memphis	13,572 BP	1,790 yrs.
Ten Kings of This	11,782 BP	350 yrs.
Spirits of the Dead	11,432 BP	5,813 yrs.
First Dynasty – Menes	5,619 BCE	253 yrs.

Manetho's Chronology: The divine and pre-dynastic dynasties until Menes

the 3rd century BCE. Manetho served as a priest in Egyptian temples at Sebennytos and Heliopolis during the reigns of Ptolemy I Soter and Ptolemy II, who were Hellenistic kings of Egypt.

Manetho had access to temple libraries containing kings' lists and other historical documents. The Aegyptiaca has not survived intact, but fragments are preserved in the works of later ancient historians. Manetho's King List forms the basis of the modern division of Egyptian history into dynasties.

Book I begins from the earliest times, listing gods and demigods as rulers of Egypt. Manetho gives Greek name equivalents for the Egyptian gods in a custom that predates him, such as Hephaistos for Ptah, Demeter for Isis, Hermes for Thoth, Apollo for Horus, and Typhon for Seth. Manetho then proceeds to Dynastic Egypt, from Dynasty I to XI, beginning with the first human King, Menes.

In Manetho's chronology, the rule of the Ten Kings of This would match the period of the Mediterranean War. Interestingly, if ten kings reigned for three hundred and fifty years, that duration would be realistic if the kings were human and not divine.

The Palermo Stone

The Palermo Stone
Source: Wikimedia Commons

The Palermo Stone is in the Salinas Regional Archaeological Museum in Palermo, Italy. It is a large fragment of a stele known as the Royal Annals of the Old Kingdom of Egypt and was engraved toward the end of the 5th Dynasty in the 25th century BCE. The complete black basalt stele is believed to have been approximately 2.2 metres long, 0.61 metres high, and 6.5 cm thick.

The text begins by listing several thousand years of rulers who are presumed to be mythical. The first human ruler listed is Menes, whom the text credits with the unification of Egypt. It then records the kings of Egypt from the 1st Dynasty through to the 5th Dynasty.

The Turin King List

The Turin King List is a papyrus in Egyptian hieratic script, thought to date from the reign of Ramesses II (1279–1213 BCE). The Italian traveller Bernardino Drovetti found the papyrus at Luxor (Thebes) in Egypt in 1820 CE; it is now in the Museo Egizio (Egyptian Museum) in Turin, Italy. The Turin King List is the most extensive known list of kings compiled by the Egyptians, and it is the basis for most chronology before the reign of Ramesses II. It was initially a tax roll, but on its back is written a list of rulers of Egypt, including gods, demi-gods, spirits and human kings.

The papyrus is divided into eleven columns and lists the rulers' names and the lengths of reigns in years, months, and days for individual kings. The King List was written on the back of a recycled older papyrus, indicating that its contents were not unique, and the writer did not consider them of great importance. In that case, the list's contents must have been common knowledge in Egypt in the 13th century BCE.

Hecetaeus and Herodotus in Thebes

Thebes is the Greek name for the Egyptian city of Luxor, known as Waset by the Ancient Egyptians. It has no direct connection with the Ancient Greek city-state of Thebes. Egyptian Thebes is located on the east bank of the Nile, 800 kilometres south of the Mediterranean.

Hecataeus of Miletus (ca. 550–476 BCE) is the first known Greek historian. After travelling extensively, he settled in his native city of Miletus in Anatolia, where he composed geographical and historical works. The later Greek historian Herodotus tells a story in his work, the *Histories*, of a visit by Hecataeus to an Egyptian temple at Thebes around 500 BCE.

Karnak Temple Complex, 1914
Source: Wikimedia Commons – Cornell University Library

Herodotus visited the same temple around fifty years later, around 450 BCE. The Egyptian temple priests showed Herodotus a series of statues, with each statue set up by the high priest of that generation. These statues would probably have been kept in a temple building in the Karnak Temple Complex in Thebes. The complex's construction began just after 2000 BCE and now comprises ruined temples, chapels, pylons and several other buildings

Herodotus says that when Hecataeus saw the same series of statues fifty years before him, Hecetaeus mentioned to the Egyptian priests that he traced his descent from a god through sixteen generations. The Egyptians compared Hecetaeus' claim with the number of statues of their high priests. As there were three hundred and forty-one statues or generations of high priests, all of them mortal men, the Egyptians refused to believe Hecataeus' claim of a human descending from a god in just sixteen generations. The statues Hecetaeus and Herodotus saw were extremely ancient and were likely housed somewhere in a much older temple or structure before being moved to the Karnak temple after 2000 BCE.

Herodotus' account of his visit to Karnak around 450 BCE is from the *Histories*:

'So far in the story, the Egyptians and the priests were they who made the report, declaring that from the first king down to this priest of Hephaistos (Ptah) who reigned last, there had been three hundred and forty-one generations of men, and that in them there had been the same number of chief-priests and of kings: but three hundred generations of men are equal to ten thousand years, for a hundred years is three generations of men; and in the one-and-forty generations which remain, those I mean which were added to the three hundred, there are one thousand three hundred and forty years.'

'Thus in the period of eleven thousand three hundred and forty years, they said that there had arisen no god in human form; nor even before that time or afterwards among the remaining kings who arise in Egypt, did they report that anything of that kind had come to pass.'…'And formerly when Hecataios the historian was in Thebes, and had traced his descent and connected his family with a god in the sixteenth generation before, the priests of Zeus (Amun) did for him much the same as they did for me though I had not traced my descent.'

'They led me into the sanctuary of the temple, which is of great size, and they counted up the number, showing colossal wooden statues in number the same as they said; for each chief-priest there sets up in his lifetime an image of himself: accordingly the priests, counting and showing me these, declared to me that each one of them was a son succeeding his own father, and they went up through the series of images from the image of the one who had died last, until they had declared this of the whole number. And when Hecataios had traced his descent and connected his family with a god in the sixteenth generation, they traced a descent in opposition to his, besides their numbering, not accepting it from him that a man had been born from a god; and they traced their counter-descent thus, saying that each one of the statues had been /piromis/ son of /piromis/, until they had declared this of the whole three hundred and forty-five statues, each one being surnamed /piromis/; and neither with a god nor a hero did they connect their descent.'

'Now /piromis/ means in the tongue of Hellas (Greece) "honourable and good man". From their declaration then it followed, that they of whom the images were had been of form like this, and far removed from being gods: but in the time before these men they said that gods were the rulers in Egypt, not mingling with men, and that of these always one had power at a time.'

Herodotus calculated that up to his time in the 5th century BCE, 11,340 years had passed since the Egyptians erected the first priest's statue. If what Herodotus saw and wrote about was true, the time of Egypt's first recorded human rulers and priests would be around 14,000 BP. This chronology indicates that the Egyptians probably did have an advanced Neolithic culture, at least in Lower Egypt around Karnak, well before 11,600 BP. There would likely have been similar Neolithic cultures in the fertile lands of the Nile Delta and on the Mediterranean coast of Egypt before the sea level rose.

The Egyptian priests who spoke to Herodotus also claimed that gods had ruled Egypt before human rulers, as do the various King Lists so far discovered. These god-rulers may correspond to earlier forgotten Egyptian cultures known to have inhabited Egypt from at least 40,000 BP.

The Balkans

The Balkans is a peninsula in south-eastern Europe, with the current territory of Greece at

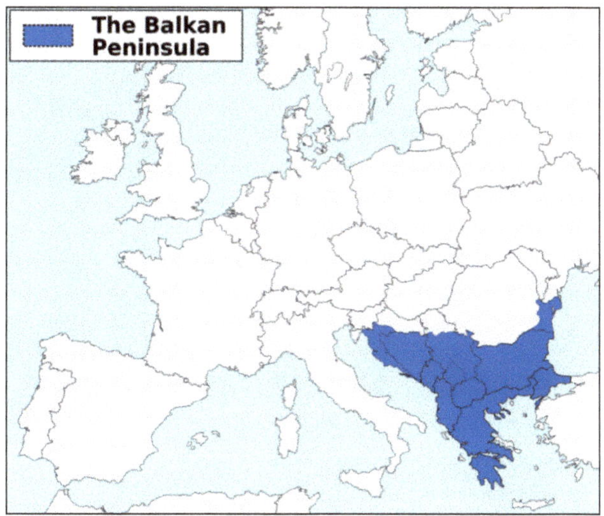

The Balkan Peninsula
Source: Wikimedia Commons – ArnoldPlaton

its southernmost tip. There is evidence of early humans, including *Homo erectus*, *Homo heidelbergensis* and Neanderthals in the Balkans from the Lower Palaeolithic onwards. The oldest confirmed *Homo sapiens* remains outside of Greece are from 44,000 BP. The Palaeolithic lasted until 10,000 BP in the Balkans and was followed by a Mesolithic period.

The Balkan's known Palaeolithic or possibly early Mesolithic period coincides with the Mediterranean War of 11,600 BP. The Balkans may have been home to some of the 'many barbarous nations and Grecian tribes (Pelasgians) which then existed', who fought with the Athenians against the Atlanteans.

Following a Mesolithic period, the Balkans were the site of several important early Neolithic cultures, including the Vinča, Varna, Karanovo and Hamangia. The Vinča Culture of 7,700–6,500 BP was widespread, extending over the course of the Danube in what is now Serbia, Croatia, Romania, Bulgaria, Montenegro, Kosovo, and Albania. However, traces of it can be found all around the Balkans, parts of Central Europe, and Asia Minor. The Vinča Culture practised a mixed subsistence of agriculture, animal husbandry, hunting and foraging economy. The world's earliest example of copper smelting and copper tools was found at the Vinča site of Plocnik and dated to 7,500 BP.

Anatolia

Anatolia, also known as Asia Minor, is the geographical and historical term denoting the westernmost protrusion of Asia. By the time of the Mediterranean War of 11,600 BP, the people of Anatolia had a Mesolithic or early Neolithic culture and possibly participated in the war. It appears that the Pelasgian cultures of Anatolia and Greece made contact before then and shared similar features.

Remains of a Mesolithic culture in Anatolia have been found along the Mediterranean coast, in Thrace, and in the western Black Sea area. As with all other Mediterranean regions, much evidence of early cultures in coastal areas would have been inundated by the rising sea level after 11,600 BP.

Neolithic settlements in Anatolia include Çatalhöyük, Çayönü, Nevalı Çori, Hacilar, Göbekli Tepe, Norşuntepe, Köşk and Mersin. They represent some of the world's oldest known agricultural villages, where humans first domesticated plants and animals. These Neolithic villages in Anatolia were settled around the same time as the Sesklo Culture developed in Greece. They domesticated the same plants and animals, so there would likely have been ongoing communication between the cultures.

Following the Neolithic, the Chalcolithic era in Anatolia lasted from 7,500–5,000 BP; it is when the first copper implements appeared there. The earliest defined civilisation in Anatolia was an indigenous people named the Hattians (ca. 4,500–4,000 BP), who had settlements that traded with each other. Anatolia was one of the first areas to develop bronze-making because the Hattians came into contact with Assyrian traders from Mesopotamia, who provided them with the tin required to make bronze.

From 2000–1700 BCE, the Indo-European Hittite people gradually absorbed the indigenous Hattians of Anatolia. The Hittites are thought to have migrated into Anatolia from the east before 2000 BCE. They established the Hittite Empire centred on Hattusa in north-central Anatolia around 1600 BCE. The empire disintegrated after 1180 BCE, with the territory gradually falling under the control of the Neo-Assyrian Empire.

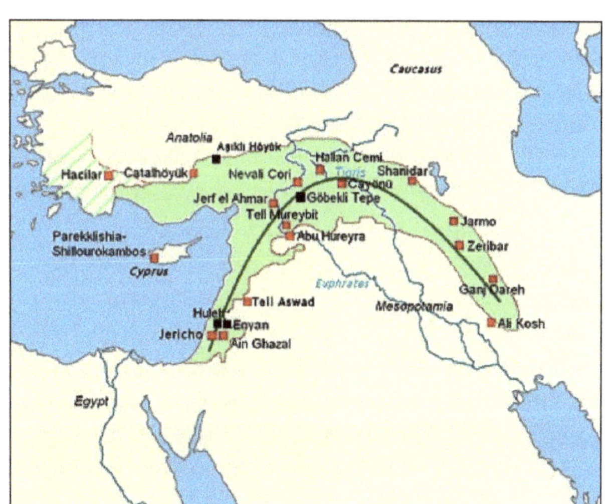

Göbekli Tepe Location – part of the Fertile Crescent ca. 9,500 BP
Source: Wikimedia Commons – from Bjeortvedt

Göbekli Tepe

The archaeological site of Göbekli Tepe in Eastern Anatolia contains the oldest monumental structures in the world and the earliest human-made place of worship yet found. It was once part of the Fertile Crescent, where the earliest known agriculture in the Old World developed.

Göbekli Tepe was only discovered in 1996 CE, with less than five percent of the site excavated. The site is a series of mainly circular and oval-shaped

Göbekli Tepe Excavation
Source: Wikimedia Commons – Teomancimit

structures built over nearly three thousand years. It is believed that hunter-gatherers constructed them thousands of years before the known development of agriculture in the region. Radiocarbon dating places the construction of the first structures at 11,600–10,800 BP. While larger structures are considered temples, some smaller domestic buildings have also been excavated.

The oldest occupation layer (Stratum III), dating from 11,600 BP, contains circular or oval structures with diameters between 10–30 metres. Only four such buildings have been uncovered, but surveys indicate sixteen more structures. The walls are made of unworked dry stone and contain numerous T-shaped limestone pillars, with a larger pair of pillars located in the centre of the circular structures. The structures were probably roofed, with the central pair of pillars supporting the roof. Stratum II, dated to 10,800–10,000 BP, has several adjacent rectangular rather than circular rooms, with smaller T-shaped pillars and terrazzo floors of polished lime.

There are more than two hundred known pillars in the twenty buildings. Each pillar is up to six metres tall, weighs up to twenty tonnes, and is fitted into sockets cut into the bedrock. Abstract pictograms and carved animal reliefs decorate many of the pillars. The quarries for the pillars are located 100–500 metres from the site, and the builders used stone picks for the quarrying. Some unfinished pillars were found at the quarries; the largest was 6.9 metres long and would have had a finished length of nine metres, much larger than any other found.

The Göbekli Tepe site was deliberately backfilled sometime after 10,000 BP, and it is so well-preserved

Göbekli Tepe Pillar Carving
Source: Wikimedia Commons – Teomancimit

until now because it was buried. The buildings were covered with a fill of mostly flinty gravel, with some stone tools and animal and human bones.

The earliest large-building construction at Göbekli Tepe occurred around the same time as the Mediterranean War of 11,600 BP. Such monumental structures indicate that the region's people were technologically and socially advanced thousands of years earlier than previously thought. The local population could organise and support itself in sufficient numbers to build many large communal structures over more than two thousand years. Because domestic structures were also found at the site, there was likely a permanent settlement and possibly some early agriculture to support that population.

Göbekli Tepe is probably not an isolated example of this early culture in Anatolia because some known Neolithic settlements of the region were inhabited from very early times. The culture that built Göbekli Tepe from 11,600 BP may have been Mesolithic and possibly began to develop agriculture, but there is no clear evidence for this. As there is evidence of contact between Anatolian and Greek Pelasgian cultures from 13,000 BP, it is possible that a culture similar to Göbekli Tepe's co-existed in Greece but is so far undiscovered.

Çatalhöyük Model – Museum for Prehistory in Thuringia
Source: Wikimedia Commons – Wolfgang Sauber

Çatalhöyük

Çatalhöyük is one example of a large Neolithic and Chalcolithic proto-city in southern Anatolia that existed from approximately 9,500–7,700 BP and flourished around 9,000 BP. It had an average population of 5,000–8,000 but may have been up to 10,000. Numerous Neolithic villages of Anatolia, similar to Çatalhöyük, were occupied during the same period as the Pelasgian Neolithic villages of Greece.

Çatalhöyük House Reconstruction
Source: Wikimedia Commons – Elelicht

Çatalhöyük comprised only domestic buildings, with no separate public buildings. The inhabitants lived in interconnected mud-brick houses without footpaths or streets between the dwellings. Most houses were accessed by openings in the ceiling reached by ladders and stairs; the rooftops then acted as streets. The ceiling openings were the only source of ventilation, allowing smoke to escape from the houses' open hearths and ovens.

Houses had plaster interiors with vivid murals, and figurines found throughout the settlement were placed on the interior and exterior walls. Heads of animals, especially cattle, were mounted on walls and rooms with concentrations of these items that may have been shrines or public meeting areas.

The Levant

The Levant is the name for the coastal lands and islands of the far-eastern Mediterranean, and it includes present-day Syria, Lebanon, Jordan, Israel, and Palestine.

The Levant (Cyprus upper left)
Source: Google Earth

The earliest traces of *Homo erectus* in the Levant were found in the Jordan Valley of the Southern Levant, dated to 1.4mya. Anatomically modern *Homo sapiens* moved out of Africa into the Levant during the Middle Palaeolithic, before 90,000 BP and possibly by 200,000 BP. Then by 60,000 BP, *Homo sapiens* seem to have disappeared from the region, replaced by Neanderthal groups migrating south from Europe. A second movement of *Homo sapiens* out of Africa into the Levant seems to have occurred around 50,000 BP.

By 40,000 BP, the Ahmarian Culture occupied the region until 25,000 BP. Then, the Mesolithic Kebaran Culture appears in southern Palestine from 20,000–12,500 BP. The Kebarans used the bow and arrow, and grinding stones for harvested wild grains. Kebaran Culture may have been ancestral to the later Neolithic Natufian Culture (12,500–10,500 BP) present throughout the Levant.

Natufian Culture coincides with the time of 11,600 BP for the war with the Atlanteans. The Natufians pioneered some of the first known sedentary settlements and agricultural societies, and they used wild grains later supplemented with domesticated sheep and goats. Although the Natufians may have supported themselves by fishing, there is no evidence of long-distance sea travel.

Cyprus
Source: Google Earth

Cyprus

Cyprus is situated in the north-eastern corner of the Mediterranean Sea and is the third-largest Mediterranean island after Sicily and Sardinia. The earliest confirmed site of human activity on Cyprus indicates that hunter-gatherers were active on the island from around 12,000 BP. To get to the island, they must have travelled at least 100 kilometres by sea from the Asian mainland.

The earliest known village communities in Cyprus date from 10,200 BP. The first settlers were already agriculturalists before they arrived on Cyprus by ship, possibly from Anatolia or the Levant. Though they did not produce pottery, they did introduce dogs, sheep, goats and possibly cattle and pigs, as well as numerous wild animals like foxes and Persian fallow deer. The remains of an 8-month-old cat were found buried with its human owner in a grave estimated to be 9,500 years old, pushing back the earliest known feline-human association by several thousand years. Water wells discovered by archaeologists in western Cyprus are believed to be among the oldest known in the world, dating to 10,500–9,000 BP.

Khirokitia Reconstruction
Source: Wikimedia Commons – Ophelia2

In southern Cyprus, the Neolithic village of Khirokitia dates to approximately 8,800 BP. It is surrounded by a stone wall 2.5 metres thick and 3 metres high at its highest preserved level. Access into the village was probably at several entry points through the wall. The buildings consist of closely grouped round structures with external diameters between 2.3–9.2 metres and internal diameters between 1.4–4.8 metres.

There possibly were Neolithic communities in Cyprus around the time of the Mediterranean War of 11,600 BP, and they may have fought against the Atlanteans. They probably had sea-going vessels, as the earliest settlers could sail at least 100km to get there from the nearest mainland.

Italy, Corsica and Sardinia

Italy, Corsica and Sardinia
Source: Google Earth

The island of Sicily was connected to the Italian mainland when sea levels were lower during past glaciations. Also, the Adriatic Sea was far smaller, with a fertile plain extending north of the Gargano Peninsula, located halfway up the eastern Italian coast. The plain was 75,000km^2 or one-third the size of present-day mainland Italy. During the Last Glacial Maximum at 20,000 BP, Corsica and Sardinia were connected and joined to Tuscany on the Italian mainland until 12,000 BP.

Italy has some of the oldest modern *Homo sapiens* remains discovered anywhere in Europe, dating from between 45,000–43,000 BP. The Epigravettian Culture (20,000–8,000 BP) would have been the dominant Mesolithic culture in Italy, Corsica and Sardinia for several thousand years before and after the war against the Atlanteans around 11,600 BP. Whether or not the Mesolithic cultures present in Italy, Corsica and Sardinia fought in the Mediterranean War, they would not have offered much resistance to the more technically advanced Atlanteans.

The Maltese Islands
Source: Google Earth

Malta

Malta is an archipelago located 100 kilometres south of Sicily, with its three largest islands being Malta, Gozo and Comino. Pottery resembling that found in Italy suggests the Maltese Islands were first settled around 7,200 BP. The settlers were Neolithic hunters or farmers who grew cereals and raised domestic livestock, and they travelled 100 kilometres to Malta from Sicily by ship. If these were the first people to colonise Malta, the islands would have been uninhabited in the Mediterranean War of 11,600 BP.

A culture of temple-builders either replaced or arose from the population of the early Neolithic period. They built some of the oldest existing free-standing structures in the world in the form of megalithic temples. Nearly twenty known temples were in use from 6,000–4,500 BP, including the Ggantija temples on Gozo and those at Hagarr Qim and Mnajdra. The temples have a distinctive architecture with a complicated trefoil design and were probably covered with roofs.

Ggantija Temple Complex
Source: Wikimedia Commons – Michael Gunther

The temple-building culture seems to have disappeared from the Maltese Islands around 4,500 BP. The islands were depopulated for several decades until a new influx of Bronze Age immigrants, probably from Sicily. The Greeks and the Phoenicians colonised the islands sometime after 800 BCE. Malta later came under the control of the Carthaginians in around 400 BCE, then fell to the Romans in 218 BCE.

The inhabitants of Athens and Attica created a thriving Neolithic civilisation by 11,600 BP

CHAPTER 8

Prehistoric Attica and Athens

The existence and contribution of the prehistoric city of Athens is a vital element of the Atlantis story but is rarely discussed. Most scholars completely ignore Athens; instead, they speculate about what past events may have inspired Plato to create the Atlantis story. Some go further and suggest various locations for Atlantis while rejecting the truth of the entire story.

If Plato's depiction of prehistoric Athens is correct, it again indicates that he did not fabricate the Atlantis story. Plato states that the inhabitants of Athens and Attica created a thriving Neolithic civilisation by the time of the Mediterranean War in 11,600 BP. Then, several significant environmental changes and destructions after 11,600 BP caused later Athenian society to break down more than once.

The earliest archaeological evidence of Neolithic cultures found in Greece begins at around 9,000 BP, a relatively small gap of some 2,000 years from the time of the Atlantis story. However, from at least 13,000 BP, the prehistoric Pelasgians of Greece seem to have had contact with Anatolia's early Neolithic Pelasgian cultures. They likely would have shared the same domesticated plants, animals and farming techniques, so the Athenians possibly did have an earlier Neolithic period that began before 11,600 BP. Yet, it may have been buried or ruined by the various later destructions of Athens and Attica that Plato describes.

The Origin of the Athenians

Our species, *Homo sapiens*, has occupied Greece continually since at least 30,000 BP. During Antiquity, the Athenians claimed to be *autochthonic*, meaning they were the area's original inhabitants and had not moved into Attica from another place.

Entirely separate from the Atlantis story, an Athenian founding myth tells that Athena refused a union with the god Hephaestus because of his unsightly appearance and crippled nature. When Hephaestus became angry and forceful with her, she disappeared from the bed. His ejaculation landed on the Earth and impregnated Gaia (the Earth goddess). Gaia then gave birth to Erichthonius (an early mythological ruler of Athens) and gave the child to Athena to foster, guarded by a serpent.

In the Atlantis story, Plato states that the Egyptian priests at Sais described the origin of the Athenians to Solon: 'In days of old the gods had the whole Earth distributed among them by allotment'...'Hephaestus and Athena, who were brother and sister, and sprang from the same father (who was Zeus in the Greek mythology of Solon and Plato's time), having a common nature, and being united also in the love of philosophy and art, both obtained as their common portion this land (Greece/Attica)'...'She (Athena/Neith) founded your city (Athens) a thousand years before ours (Sais), receiving from the Earth and Hephaestus the seed of your race, and afterwards she founded ours, of which the constitution is recorded in our sacred registers to be eight thousand years old'...'Wherefore the goddess (Athena), who was a lover both of war and of wisdom, selected and first of all settled that spot (Athens/Attica) which was the most likely to produce men likest herself'...'there they (Hephaestus and Athena) implanted brave children of the soil.'

The Egyptian priests told Solon that Athena and Hephaestus founded Athens 9,000 years before Solon's time, at around 11,600 BP. As the Mediterranean War was also 9,000 years before Solon's time, the war must have commenced soon after the founding of Athens. These two events were well before the founding of the city of Sais one thousand years later, around 10,600 BP.

The Atlantis story describes how Poseidon arrived on the Atlantic Island many generations before the Mediterranean War of 11,600 BP. In contrast, Athena and Hephaestus went to Attica and 'founded' the city of Athens around the time of the war. Just as Poseidon may have been an actual cultural leader who went to the Atlantic Island and civilised the native population already living there, Athena and Hephaestus may have civilised the original inhabitants of Attica and Athens, who were the 'children of the soil'. Those people probably had a hunter-gatherer, Mesolithic, or early Neolithic level of culture before 11,600 BP.

To the later Ancient Greeks, Athena was the goddess of wisdom, courage, inspiration, civilisation, law and justice, strategic warfare, defender of cities, mathematics, strength, strategy, the arts and literature, agriculture, crafts and skill. Athena's overall attribute is that she taught the Greeks most aspects of civilisation. Hephaestus was the god of blacksmiths, craftsmen, artisans, sculptors, metals and metallurgy. Considering the particular technologies Athena and Hephaestus gave the Greeks, they include most Neolithic and Bronze Age technology.

Present Day Attica

One very ancient myth of Athena claims that she was born in Libya. The Atlantean Empire would have been expanding into the Mediterranean for many years before the Mediterranean War of 11,600 BP, and Plato states it controlled Libya by then. Athena and Hephaestus might have been real people; they possibly were Libyans or even disenchanted Atlantean leaders who escaped the Atlantean occupation of Libya and sailed with others to Attica and colonised it. If this colonising group knew Atlantean technology, they might have taught it to the native Athenians and perhaps the other Hellenes. Particular attributes of Athena are strategic warfare and the technology of warfare, so when the war against the Atlanteans eventually began, the Athenians may have had the military organisation and technology to challenge the Atlanteans and ultimately defeat them.

Attica

Attica is a triangular peninsula of mainland Greece extending into the Aegean Sea. In ancient times, the city of Athens controlled the region of Attica.

Plato – 'The whole country (Attica) is only a long promontory extending far into the sea away from the rest of the continent, while the surrounding basin of the sea is everywhere deep in the neighbourhood of the shore.'

Plato – 'Concerning the country (Attica)...the boundaries were in those days (11,600 BP) fixed by the Isthmus (of Corinth in the south-west), and that in the direction of the continent (north) they extended as far as the heights of (Mounts) Cithaeron and Parnes; the boundary line came down in the direction of the sea, having the district of Oropus on the right (north-east), and with the river Asopus as the limit on the left (north-west).'

Plato – 'Many great deluges have taken place (in Attica) during the nine thousand years (since the Mediterranean War), for that is the number of years which have elapsed since the time of which I am speaking; and during all this time and through so many changes, there has never been any considerable accumulation of the soil coming down from the mountains, as in other places, but the Earth has fallen away all round and sunk out of sight'... 'Even the remnant of Attica which now exists may compare with any region in the world for the variety and excellence of its fruits and the suitableness of its pastures to every sort of animal'...'but in those days (9,000 years before Solon, or 11,600 BP) the country was fair as now and yielded far more abundant produce'...'in comparison of what then was, there are remaining only the bones of the wasted body, as they may be called, as in the case of small islands, all the richer and softer parts of the soil having fallen away, and the mere skeleton of the land being

Map of Attica in Socrates and Plato's time
Source: Bernard Suzanne, 1998

left'...'But in the primitive state of the country, its mountains were high hills covered with soil, and the plains, as they are termed by us, of Phelleus (a mountain near Mt Parnes, north-west of Attica) were full of rich Earth, and there was abundance of wood in the mountains.'

Prehistoric Athens and the Acropolis Hill

When Plato lived in Athens in the 5th century BCE, the city was located on the south-west slope of Mount Lycabettus, between the small rivers of Cephissus to the west, Ilissos to the south, and Eridanos (which flowed through the city) to the north. Athens was 6km from the sea then, but when sea levels were 60 metres lower at around 11,600 BP, the coastline would have been 11km away.

Population estimates for Athens in the 5th century BCE range from 120,000 to 180,000. The walled city was 1.5km in diameter; the Athenian Acropolis was just south of the centre of the walled city. The defensive walls enclosed an area of approximately 3.5km^2, including Piraeus's harbour district. Also, there were suburbs beyond the walls.

The Egyptian priests at Sais declare that the site of the prehistoric Athenian Acropolis in 11,600 BP was much larger than in Solon and Plato's time, which then looked the same as now.

Plato – 'the Acropolis was not as now'...'in primitive times the hill of the Acropolis extended to the (River) Eridanus (north) and (River) Ilissus (south), and included the Pnyx (hill to the west) on one side, and the Lycabettus (hill to the east) as a boundary on the opposite side to the Pnyx, and was all well covered with soil, and level at the top, except in one or two places.'

The approximate distance between the outer edges of the Pnyx and Lycabettus is 4km, while the distance between the rivers Eridanus and Ilissus averages 1.5km. Those dimensions give the base of the prehistoric Acropolis Hill an area of 6km^2 or 600 hectares – two hundred times larger than the three hectares of the present Acropolis.

The summit of the present Athenian Acropolis is 150 metres above sea level; Mount Lycabettus is the highest point in Athens at 277 metres above sea level; the Pnyx is 107 metres above sea level. The ground level around these three rocky outcrops is around 50 metres above sea level.

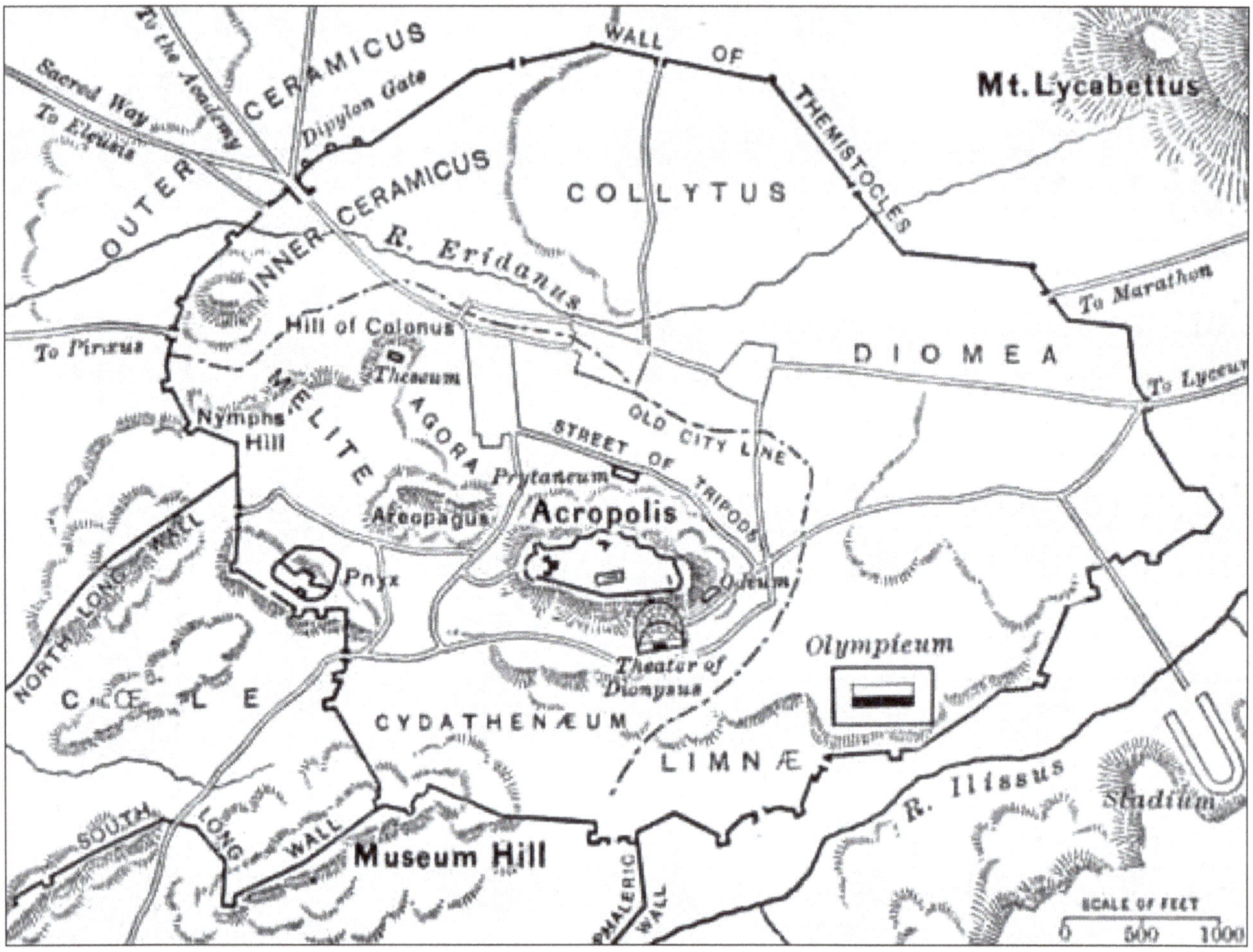

Map of Athens in Socrates and Plato's time

The Pnyx, Present Acropolis and Lycabettus
Source: Modified from Google Earth

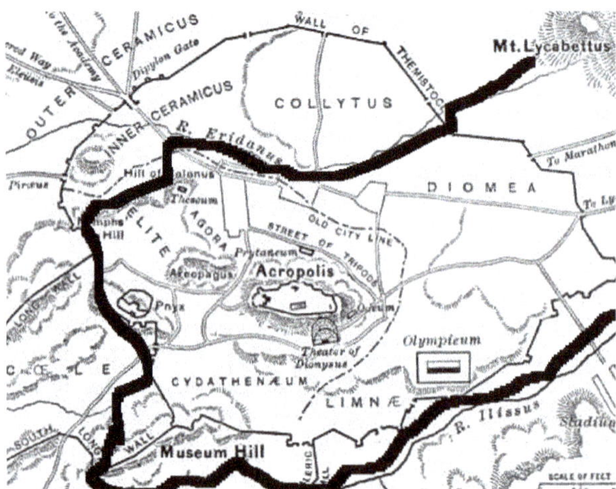

Rough Outline of the Prehistoric Acropolis Hill of 11,600 BP

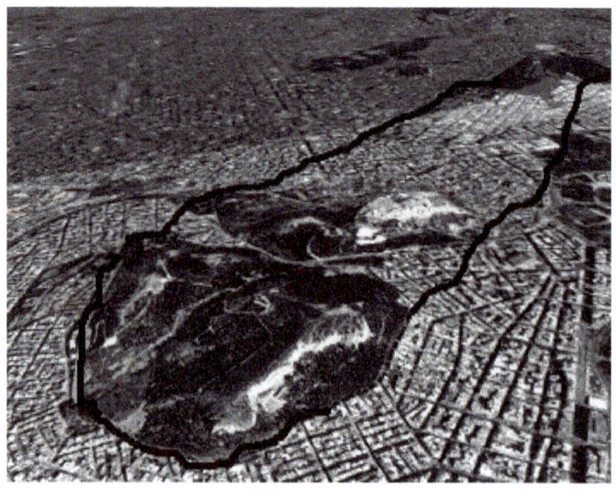

Rough Outline of the Prehistoric Acropolis Hill on Present-day Athens Source: Modified from Google Earth

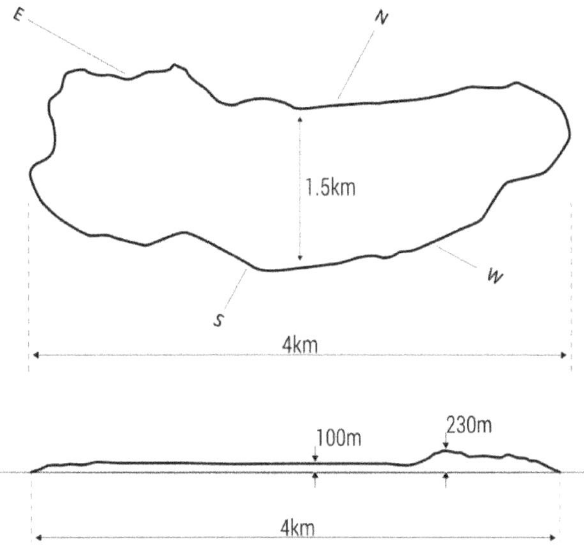

The Dimensions of the Prehistoric Acropolis Hill

Plato describes the summit of the prehistoric Acropolis Hill as being level between the Pnyx and Mount Lycabettus. The summit's average height is assumed to be the same as the present Acropolis at 150 metres above sea level. If the surrounding ground level was 50 metres above sea level as it is now, removing that 50 metres would give the Acropolis Hill an average height of 100 metres, with Lycabettus rising to 230 metres above the surrounding land.

Climate and Vegetation in Prehistoric Greece and the Aegean

Plato describes the climate of prehistoric Attica around 11,600 BP as mild enough to allow diverse plant and forest growth and bountiful agriculture. Attica had distinct summer and winter seasons at that time, with adequate annual rainfall and permanent rivers.

Plato – 'Such was the natural state of the country (Attica of 11,600 BP), which was cultivated...and had a soil the best in the world, and abundance of water, and in the heaven above an excellently attempered climate'...'the land reaped the benefit of the annual rainfall, not as now (Plato's time) losing the water which flows off the bare Earth into the sea, but, having an abundant supply in all places, and receiving it into herself and treasuring it up in the close clay soil, it let off into the hollows the streams which it absorbed from the heights, providing everywhere abundant fountains and rivers'...'although some of the mountains now only afford sustenance to bees, not so very long ago there were still to be seen roofs of timber cut from trees growing there, which were of a size sufficient to cover the largest houses; and there were many other high trees, cultivated by man and bearing abundance of food for cattle'...'Even the remnant of Attica which now exists may compare with any region in the world for the variety and excellence of its fruits and the suitableness of its pastures to every sort of animal, which proves what I am saying; but in those days the country was fair as now and yielded far more abundant produce.'

The present climate of Greece is a Mediterranean Climate type, with hot, dry summers and relatively mild, wet winters. Yet, during the 2.5 million years of the Quaternary Ice Age, numerous glacial/interglacial cycles caused large climate fluctuations at different stages of each cycle. During the Last Glacial Maximum at 20,000 BP, there were widespread glaciations in the northern Mediterranean. Average annual temperatures were 8–9°C lower than now, with average yearly rainfall similar to present values

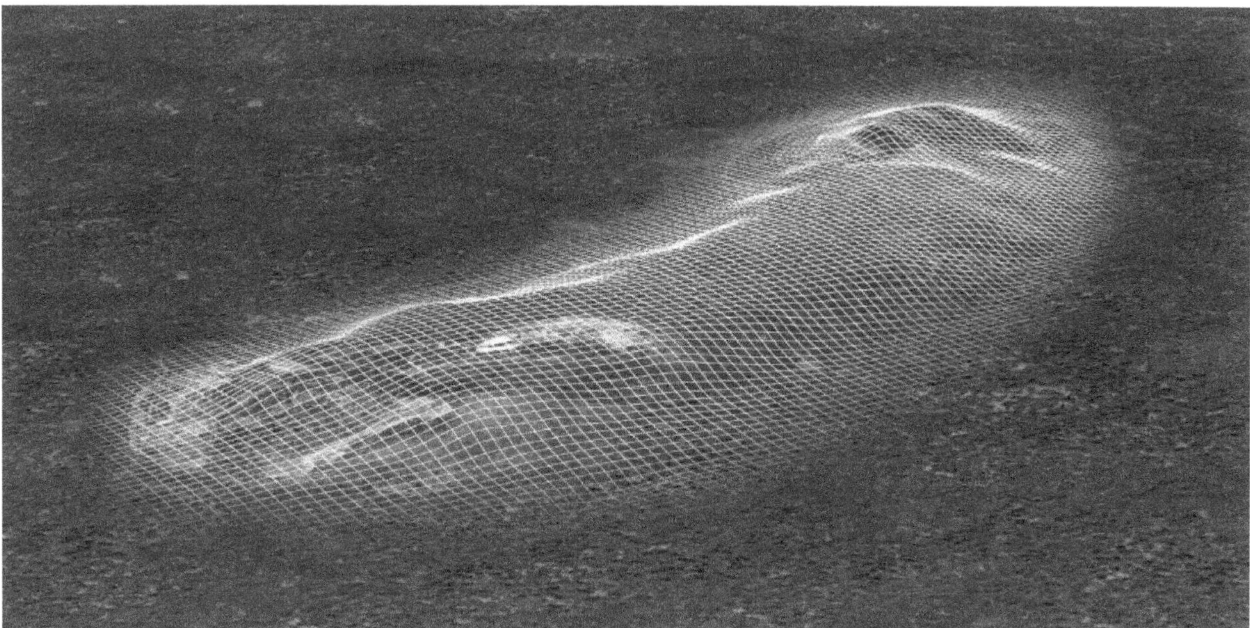

Wireframe Image of the Prehistoric Acropolis Hill

of more than 2,000 mm. As glacial ice melted in Northern Europe from 17,000–13,000 BP, there was a 2–3°C warming and a gradual increase in rainfall.

From 12,900 to 11,600 BP, there was a rapid worldwide return to glacial conditions over just a few decades in what is called the Younger Dryas. In the Eastern Mediterranean, including Greece, it was a dry, cold period that lasted roughly 1,300 years. The Younger Dryas ended abruptly around 11,600 BP; for example, in Greenland, the average temperature rose 10°C in a decade.

In the Atlantis story, the cultural development of prehistoric Attica and Athens occurred around 11,600 BP, when Plato states the climate there was temperate. The climate in Greece improved rapidly at the end of the cold period of the Younger Dryas, possibly for some time before 11,600 BP. The lowlands had higher annual rainfall with no summer drought and frost-free winters. This stable climate period would give prehistoric Athens and Attica an 'excellently attempered climate' and would include the time of the war with the Atlanteans around 11,600 BP.

There was a climate optimum in Greece from around 9,000–7,500 BP. After that, summer rainfall and winter temperature decreased for a few hundred years. The climate became more favourable around 7,000 BP; by 6,000 BP, the present Mediterranean Climate began, with increased summer rainfall and warmer winters.

Although the vegetation in Greece has suffered through human activities for thousands of years, more than 5,000 species of flowering plants grow wild, making Greece one of Europe's most diversified countries for plant life. The Mediterranean Climate in Greece supported a diversified mixed oak forest. Plato states that Attica remained forested until his time in the 4th century BCE despite a significant loss of soil from heavy rains over thousands of years. In Greece, few forests have survived the intense deforestation for shipbuilding, which began in the Bronze Age and continued for centuries after Plato's time. The only remaining forests are in northern Greece, with chestnut, fir, and pine trees.

The Social Organisation of Prehistoric Athens

The Egyptian priests tell Solon that Egypt has social divisions in his time similar to those of prehistoric Athens in 11,600 BP.

Plato – 'In the first place, (in Egypt 600 BCE) there is the caste of priests, which is separated from all the others; next, there are the artificers (artisans), who ply their several crafts by themselves and do not intermix; and also there is the class of shepherds and of hunters, as well as that of husbandmen (farmers); and you will observe, too, that the warriors in Egypt are distinct from all the other classes, and are commanded by the law to devote themselves solely to military pursuits.'

Plato – 'Now the country (Athens/Attica) was inhabited in those days (11,600 BP) by various classes of citizens; there were artisans, and there were husbandmen, and there was also a warrior class originally set apart by divine men. The latter (warriors) dwelt by themselves, and had all things suitable for nurture and education; neither had any of them anything of their own, but they regarded all that they had as common property; nor did they claim to receive of the other citizens anything more than their necessary food'...'Outside the (prehistoric) Acropolis and under the sides of the hill there dwelt artisans, and such of the husbandmen as were tilling the ground near'...'Such was the natural state of the country, which was cultivated, as we may well believe.'

Plato describes Athens/Attica of 11,600 BP as having a culture with some social divisions and work specialisation. There is no mention of 'priests' as in Egypt, but there appear to have been leaders and philosophers, as well as warriors, artisans, and 'husbandmen' or farmers who grew crops or tended domestic animals.

Plato – 'Such were the ancient Athenians, and after this manner they righteously administered their own land (Attica) and the rest of Hellas (Greece); they were renowned all over Europe and Asia for the beauty of their persons and for the many virtues of their souls.'

The prehistoric Athenians appear to have had some administrative control over other tribes or towns and regions in Greece. Also, some form of communication existed between the Athenians and surrounding foreign cultures to the west and east of Greece.

The Leaders and 'wisest of men'

Plato – 'Then as to wisdom, do you observe how our (Egyptian) law from the very first made a study of the whole order of things, extending even to prophecy and medicine which gives health, out of these divine elements deriving what was needful for human life, and adding every sort of knowledge which was akin to them. All this order and arrangement the goddess (Athena/Neith) first imparted to you (Athenians) when establishing your city (Athens); and she chose the spot of Earth in which you were born, because she saw that the happy temperament of the seasons in that land (Athens/Attica) would produce the wisest of men'...'and put into their minds the order of government; their names are preserved, but their actions have disappeared by reason of the destruction of those who received the tradition, and the lapse of ages.'

Reconstruction of the Prehistoric Acropolis Hill

Plato – '(prehistoric) Athens was the best governed of all cities' and 'had the fairest constitution of any of which tradition tells.'

Plato credits the goddess Athena with initially giving the prehistoric Athenians 'every sort of knowledge' to create their civilisation. Then, there appear to be leaders and thinkers who further advance the culture's knowledge, but their individual achievements are forgotten, with only their names remembered.

If prehistoric Athens had a 'constitution', it might have been written in a pre-Greek script like the Linear A script of the Minoans. However, unlike Atlantean or Egyptian written records, Plato does not mention a Greek writing system or the recording of any information. An absence or later loss of written records could explain why the prehistoric Athenians' achievements were unknown to the later Greeks of Solon and Plato's time.

The Athenian Warrior Class

The nature and organisation of the prehistoric Athenian warrior class are entirely different from that of virtually all Greek city-states in Solon and Plato's time. Ancient Greece usually had no permanent armies; only the Spartans had a warrior class made up exclusively of Spartan citizens who trained for war from a young age. In the rest of the Greek world, the free citizens of each city-state supplied their own weapons and formed a militia that waged war when required, usually against the militias of other Greek city-states.

The entire prehistoric Athenian elite 'warrior class' lived communally and separately from the rest of the Athenian population in a garrison on the Acropolis Hill.

Plato – 'the warrior class dwelt by themselves around the temples of Athena and Hephaestus at the summit (of the Acropolis Hill), which moreover they had enclosed with a single fence like the garden of a single house'...'None of them, however, had any private property; for all of them considered all things as common.'...'On the north side (of the Acropolis Hill) they had dwellings in common and had erected halls for dining in winter, and had all the buildings which they needed for their common life, besides temples, but there was no adorning of them with gold and silver, for they made no use of these for any purpose'...'in summer-time they left their gardens and gymnasia and dining halls, and then the southern side of the (Acropolis) hill was made use of by them for the same purpose.'

As well as living communally on the summit of the Acropolis Hill, the Athenian warriors also used other communal buildings on the northern and southern slopes. Plato also describes a single 'fence' on the summit, which probably means a palisade made from wooden poles rather than a stone wall. There is no mention of other defensive structures on the prehistoric Hill. The phrase 'the temples of Athena and Hephaestus at the summit, which moreover they had enclosed with a single fence' could mean either a fence around the entire summit or just around the temples.

Plato describes the Acropolis Hill as level at the summit, with sloping sides where the Athenians could construct large communal buildings. If the base of the Acropolis Hill was 6km^2 or 600 hectares, the level summit might have had an area of 3–4km^2 or

300–400 hectares. That is one hundred times larger than the summit of the present Athenian Acropolis. The sloping sides of the prehistoric Acropolis Hill would have made up another 2–3km^2, or 200–300 hectares.

Plato – 'The land (of Attica) was the best in the world, and was therefore able in those days to support a vast army, raised from the surrounding people'… 'they took care to preserve the same number of men and women through all time, being so many as were required for warlike purposes, then as now (Plato's time) that is to say, about twenty thousand.'

As stated previously, the size of ancient military forces is usually considered to be 1/6 the size of a city during peace and 1/5 the size during times of crisis. If the prehistoric Athenian warrior class numbered 20,000, the population of prehistoric Attica of 11,600 BCE could have been 120,000.

Plato – 'military pursuits (in Athens/Attica) were then (11,600 BP) common to men and women.'

The prehistoric Athenians seem to have had equal duties for men and women in their warrior class, including combat roles. Male and female warriors may have been full-time career soldiers or have performed military service for some years. In contrast to the Athenians, the Atlantean military was a male-only force conscripted from the local population.

The *Timaeus* states there were women in the prehistoric Athenian military, but women were never part of any historic Ancient Egyptian or Greek military. Though the Spartans did have a warrior class for hundreds of years, it never included women. The *Republic* was Plato's earlier work on an ideal society. In that dialogue, Plato does discuss the possibility that exceptional females could become warriors, but he does not consider it a usual or expected role for women. Because Plato emphasises that women had a routine function in the prehistoric Athenian military, it again indicates that he did not fabricate the Atlantis story.

Plato – 'the men of those days in accordance with the custom of the time (11,600 BP) set up a figure and image of the goddess (Athena) in full armour, to be a testimony that all animals which associate together, male as well as female, may, if they please, practise in common the virtue which belongs to them without distinction of sex.'

Plato refers to the 'figure and image of the goddess', which might mean the most venerated object in ancient Athens, even in Plato's own time. That object was an exceptionally ancient olivewood statue of Athena Polias (Athena of the city). In legend, it was not made by human hands but had fallen from the sky.

The wooden statue was probably life-sized and was movable because it was evacuated from the Acropolis during the Persian invasion in 480 BCE. It likely stood upright and wore cloth as well as gold. The statue functioned as a mannequin and was dressed in special clothing in Athenian festival rituals. Every year in Athens, during the Panathenaea festival, it was dressed in a new saffron-coloured woollen robe, or peplos, woven by selected Athenian girls and women. The peplos was decorated with scenes from the mythical battle between the gods and giants – the Gigantomachy.

In Classical Greece, Athena continued to be portrayed with a helmet, spear, shield, and often in body armour. Very ancient warlike images of Athena may reflect the role of women in the military of prehistoric Athens.

Plato – 'the weapons which they (the prehistoric Athenian warriors) carry are shields and spears, a style of equipment which the goddess (Athena/Neith) taught of Asiatics first to us (Egyptians), as in your part of the world first to you (Athenians)'…'the image of the goddess (Athena) in full armour'.

The huge Atlantean military of over one million men had heavy-armed and light-armed troops, specialised 'slingers', 'javelin men' and 'stone shooters'. The Atlanteans also used horse-drawn chariots and may have had cavalry. They also had a large navy of at least 1,200 warships. In contrast, the 20,000 Athenian warriors had no weapons other than shields and spears, though they may have had some body armour. In the lost *Critias*, a full account of the Mediterranean War might have mentioned whether the Athenians or their allies used any other military technology, especially ships to counter an Atlantean navy.

Our very early *Homo* ancestors used wooden hunting spears since at least 400,000 BP. Neanderthals shaped stone spearheads fixed to the spear shaft from as early as 300,000 BP. By the Magdalenian period in Europe, around 17,000–11,500 BP, we *Homo sapiens* used spear-throwers similar to the atlatl. In prehistory and during the earliest civilisations, shields were made of wood, animal hide, woven reeds or wicker, and they later incorporated metal. Body armour was used throughout recorded history and was made from various materials, with initial leather or fabric body protection evolving into metal plate and mail, and eventually full-plated suits-of-armour.

The first Mesopotamian cultures and Ancient Egyptian dynasties used a shield and short, one-handed spears with socketed metal heads. In Greece, most of the weapons and armour types used by Mycenaean armies in the 2nd millennium BCE originated in the earlier Minoan civilisation in Crete, which had regular trade contacts with Mesopotamia and Egypt.

Minoan and Mycenaean offensive arms were made of bronze and consisted of spears and javelins, swords of different sizes, daggers, and the bow and arrow. Several elements of Mycenaean body armour

Athena Promachos Statuette, 5th Century BCE
Source: National Archaeological Museum, Athens

Dendra Panoply, 15th century BCE
Source: Wikimedia Commons – Archaeological Museum of Nafplion

were found at Thebes, Mycenae and Phaistos. The Dendra Panoply is an example of full-body armour or panoply made of bronze plates and dates to the end of the 15th century BCE. The Mycenaean army was composed of men drawn from all levels of society. It was organised and supplied by a highly centralised, palace-based military bureaucracy.

By the time of Solon and Plato, Greek weapons and armour were geared towards combat between militias of armoured citizen-soldiers called hoplites. Hoplites were free citizens of the Greek city-states or polis, such as propertied farmers and artisans, able to afford their own bronze armour and weapons.

There were frequent wars in the Ancient Greek world, usually between individual Greek polis. The hoplite militia was called upon to fight during a conflict but usually received only basic military training. Male citizens aged from eighteen to forty and sometimes up to sixty were required to serve as hoplites, and they made up a third to a half of the polis' able-bodied adult male population.

The hoplite's primary weapon was a two to three-metre-long spear or dory with an iron leaf-shaped blade at one end and a short iron spike at the other. The spear was used one-handed while the other hand supported the soldier's shield or hoplon: a round wooden shield usually one metre in diameter and covered by a thin sheet of bronze. Hoplites carried a short sword made from iron or bronze as a secondary weapon. The hoplite wore a leather-lined bronze helmet, with bronze greaves to protect the lower legs. The most common form of infantry torso armour was a heavy bronze breastplate, but for those who could not afford bronze, it was made out of linen fabric glued together and was called a linothorax. A hoplite's full panoply of body armour could weigh up to 35 kilograms.

Hoplite combat remained virtually unchanged from the 8th–5th centuries BCE. The most common combat formation was the phalanx: a rectangular massed shield-wall of hoplites lined up several rows deep. The hoplites would lock their shields together, and the first few ranks of soldiers would project their spears out over the first rank of shields. The

Greek Hoplites – Detail from the Chigi Vase, 6th century BCE
Source: Wikimedia Commons

opposing armies would approach each other in phalanx formation on a battlefield and engage until one side was defeated.

By the 5th century BCE, archers comprised roughly ten percent of an Ancient Greek city's military force. Another armed fighter was a peltast: light infantry who gradually became more important in the battles between Greek city-states after the 5th century BCE. Peltasts carried a crescent-shaped wicker shield called a pelte as their main protection; their weapons consisted of several javelins. The Greeks did not use much cavalry until the 4th century BCE, well after the time of Plato.

Plato was in military service from 409–404 BCE towards the end of the Peloponnesian War between Athens and Sparta. It was virtually a civil war between Greeks that lasted almost thirty years. Plato would have been very familiar with the weapons and strategies of the Greek militaries of his time. Yet, the prehistoric Athenians do not use metals for spear tips, helmets, breastplates, swords and daggers, and they have no bows and arrows or javelins. Unlike the Atlantean military, the Athenians have no horse-driven chariots, which the Greeks had used for many hundreds of years but were outdated by Plato's time.

The prehistoric Athenians had weapons of spears and shields, which is appropriate for a Neolithic culture. The spears would likely have been stone-tipped; the shields made of wood, wicker or animal hide. Any body armour would be toughened leather or thick fabric. The lack of typical Bronze Age Minoan and Mycenaean weapons or later Iron Age weapons for the prehistoric Athenian warriors again indicates that Plato did not invent the Atlantis story.

Artisans and Husbandmen

Plato – 'Outside the (prehistoric) Acropolis and under the sides of the hill there dwelt artisans, and such of the husbandmen as were tilling the ground near.'

There is no particular mention of the type of work of the Athenian 'artisans'. In a Neolithic society, they likely would have included wood, stone and leather workers, weavers, and potters.

Plato – 'temples of Athena and Hephaestus'... 'gymnasia and dining halls'...'modest houses'.

The prehistoric Athenians constructed permanent buildings, including large monumental and communal structures. Unlike the Atlanteans, who built with cut stone and metals, there is no mention of the building materials the Athenians used, but they likely were mud bricks, wattle and daub, timber, and uncut stone.

Plato – 'there was no adorning of them (the Athenian warrior class' buildings) with gold and silver, for they made no use of these for any purpose.'

Though the Atlanteans commonly used several different metals, there is no mention of any metal used by the Athenians. Plato only states that the Athenian warrior class did not use gold and silver.

Plato – 'the men of those days in accordance with the custom of the time set up a figure and image of the goddess (Athena) in full armour.'

Reconstruction of the Prehistoric Acropolis Hill and Surrounding Countryside

The prehistoric statue of Athena wears 'full armour'. In the time of Solon and Plato, body armour would primarily have been bronze, but in Neolithic Athenian culture, it may have been made from toughened leather or thick fabric.

Plato – 'Such was the natural state of the country (Athens/Attica), which was cultivated, as we may well believe, by true husbandmen, who made husbandry their business'…'suitableness of its pastures to every sort of animal'…'most fertile pastures for cattle'… 'there were many other high trees, cultivated by man and bearing abundance of food for cattle.'

Plato states that the prehistoric Athenians planted crops on tilled land, although he does not specify the types of crops. He also mentions domesticated tree crops but not any particular species. The Athenians also had pastures for 'cattle' and 'every sort of (domesticated) animal'.

There is evidence of crop and animal domestication in Greece from at least the 9th millennium BP. Since Neolithic farming cultures were nearby in Anatolia and the Middle East before 11,000 BP, farming might also have been present in Greece by 11,600 BP. Virtually all the domesticated plants and animals in Neolithic Greece came from Anatolia.

A possible model of Neolithic culture in Greece from around 11,600 BP is the prehistoric settlement of Sesklo in Thessaly, Central Greece. Sesklo gives its name to the first known Neolithic culture of Europe. This Sesklo Culture inhabited Thessaly and parts of Macedonia in Northern Greece, where they built their villages on hillsides near fertile valleys. They practised advanced agriculture and made pottery comparable to the very early pottery of the Near East.

The earliest archaeological evidence from the settlement of Sesklo places the culture's initial development to 9,500 BP. At its peak period around 7,000 BP, Sesklo covered twenty hectares and comprised 500–800 houses, with a population of up to 5,000 people. Initially, the houses had only one or two rooms, but some had two levels by the 8th millennium BP. A stone wall enclosed large parts of the settlement and likely was defensive.

The Sesklo Culture grew wheat, barley, and pulses like broad beans and chickpeas. They supplemented their diet with fruit and nuts such as acorns, pistachios, almonds, prunella, cherries, plums, apples, pears, olives, grapes and mulberries. They mainly kept herds of sheep and goats, though they also had cattle, pigs and dogs.

Domesticated wheat, barley and probably pulses were introduced into Greece from Anatolia. Still, it is uncertain whether the fruits and nuts were gathered from wild tree varieties rather than domesticated ones. Orchards in Ancient Greece included olive, fig, apple, almond and pear trees since at least the Bronze Age, but these species were cultivated much earlier in Anatolia and the Middle East. They may have been introduced to the Sesklo Culture or its predecessors in Greece because of known cultural contact between Anatolia and Greece from 13,000 BP.

Olives were cultivated in the Middle East from at least 6,000 BP, and figs from before the 12th

Clay Vase from Greek Neolithic 7,300–5,300 BP
Source: Wikimedia Commons – Gary Todd, National Archaeological Museum, Athens

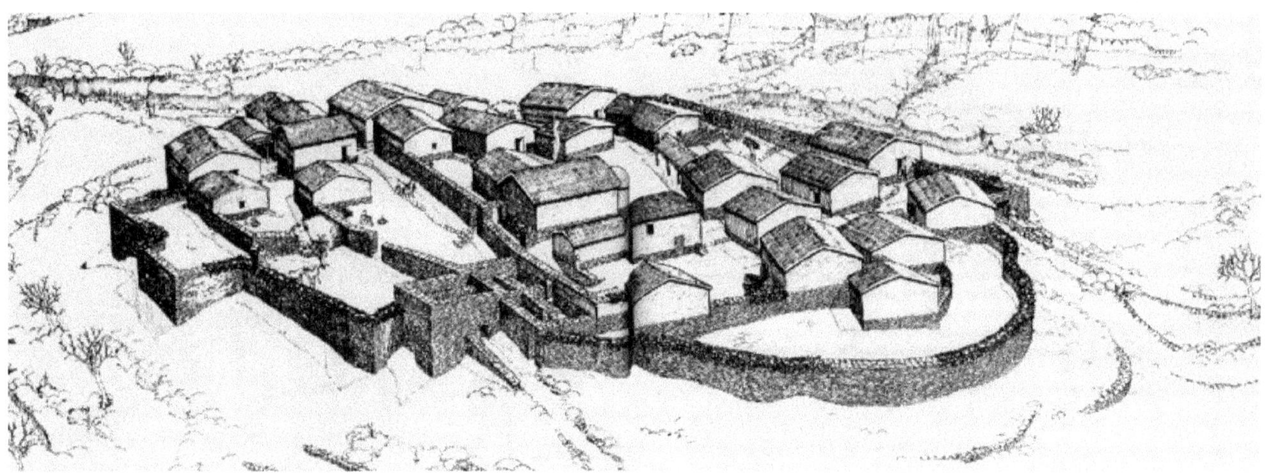

Sesklo Neolithic Settlement Reconstruction
Source: E. R. Theocharis, 1973

millennium BP. The apple tree originated in Central Asia and was perhaps the earliest tree to be cultivated; apple seeds found in Anatolia are carbon-dated to around 8,500 BP. The almond is native to the Middle East and eastward as far as the Indus Valley, with domesticated almonds appearing from at least the Early Bronze Age (3000–2000 BCE). The pear has been a food since prehistoric times; it is native to coastal regions ranging from Western Europe to North Africa and across Asia.

Sheep and goats were probably domesticated first by the Zarzian Culture in Central Asia, sometime between 20,000–10,000 BP. Wild cattle (Bos primigenius) were likely domesticated independently three times between 10,000–8,000 BP in the Indus Valley, the Fertile Crescent, and North Africa. Pigs were domesticated from wild boar as early as 15,000–14,700 BP in the Near East in the Tigris Basin. The origin of the domestic dog (Canis lupus familiaris) began with the domestication of the Grey Wolf (Canis lupus) at 15,000 BP at the latest, possibly as early as 33,000 BP.

The Mediterranean War

Plato – 'All these (Kings of Atlantis) and their descendants for many generations were the inhabitants and rulers of divers islands in the open sea; and also, as has been already said, they held sway in our direction (toward the Eastern Mediterranean) over the country within the Pillars as far as Egypt and Tyrrhenia'...'And when they were collected in a powerful league, they endeavoured to enslave all our regions and yours (Egypt and Greece), and besides this all those places situated within the mouth of the Atlantic sea (the entire Mediterranean region).'

Plato – 'nine thousand was the sum of years which had elapsed since the war which was said to have taken place between those who dwelt outside the Pillars of Heracles (the Atlanteans) and all who dwelt within them'...'these histories tell of a mighty power which unprovoked made an expedition against the whole of Europe and Asia, and to which your city (Athens) put an end'...'Of those, therefore, that dwelt within the pillars of Heracles, this city (Athens) was the leader, and is said to have fought in every battle'...'the combatants on the other side were commanded by the Kings of Atlantis'...'The course of our narration, indeed, will unfold the many barbarous nations and Grecian tribes which then existed, as they may happen to present themselves to our view.

Plato – 'For, as its (Athens/Attica) armies surpassed all others both in magnanimity and military skill, so with respect to its contests, whether it was assisted by the rest of the Greeks, over whom it presided in warlike affairs, or whether it was deserted by them through the incursions of the enemies, and became situated in extreme danger, yet still it remained triumphant'...'the greatest action which the Athenians ever did, and which ought to have been the most famous, but, through the lapse of time and the destruction of the actors, it has not come down to us (Greeks)'...'the (Egyptian) priests in their narrative of that war mentioned most of the names which are recorded prior to the time of Theseus, such as Cecrops, and Erechtheus, and Erichthonius, and Erysichthon, and the names of the women in like manner'...'And when the rest (of Athens' allies) fell off from her, being compelled to stand alone, after having undergone the very extremity of danger, she (Athens) defeated and triumphed over the invaders (the Atlanteans), and preserved from slavery those who were not yet subjugated, and generously liberated all the rest of us who dwell within the pillars (the Mediterranean region).'

What remains of the *Critias* dialogue contains no narrative of the Mediterranean War. This omission is despite Plato explicitly stating 'the (Egyptian) priests in their narrative of that war'. Plato gives no particulars of several subjects he introduces earlier. There are none of 'the many barbarous nations and Grecian tribes'; no individual episodes when the Athenians 'fought in every battle'; no exploits of 'the (Athenian) names which are recorded prior to the time of Theseus', and no events that 'liberated all the rest of us (non-Greeks) who dwell within the pillars (the Mediterranean)'.

The absence of any narrative of the Mediterranean War, which Plato clearly states will come later in his Atlantis story, is most likely because the remainder of the *Critias* dialogue is lost rather than him not writing it. A complete *Critias* might have described a war that possibly lasted years or decades and involved many combatant nations other than the Athenians. The *Critias* may also have described individual battles fought over a large area within the Mediterranean; battles that would have continued until the Atlanteans were defeated and expelled from the lands they had occupied.

Plato – 'Solon said that the (Egyptian) priests in their narrative of that war (in the Mediterranean) mentioned most of the names which are recorded prior to the time of Theseus, such as Cecrops, and Erechtheus, and Erichthonius, and Erysichthon, and the names of the women in like manner'...'For when there were any survivors (of various catastrophes of mankind), as I have already said, they were men who dwelt in the mountains; and they were ignorant of the art of writing, and had heard only the names of the chiefs of the land, but very little about their actions'...'for mythology and the enquiry into antiquity are first introduced into cities when they begin to have leisure, and when they see that the necessaries of life have already been provided, but not before'...'this is the reason why the names of the ancients have been preserved to us and not their actions'...'The names they (later Greeks) were willing enough to give to their children; but the virtues and the laws of their predecessors, they knew only by obscure traditions.'

Plato names several mythical or legendary figures directly associated with Athens but not with other parts of Greece. He states that these names are of prehistoric Athenian leaders, the 'chiefs of the land', who fought in the war against the Atlanteans, but their exploits were forgotten by Solon and Plato's time. The Egyptian priests would have given Solon these leaders' achievements in the 'narrative of that war', which the lost *Critias* dialogue likely described. That lost dialogue also would have included 'the names of the women in like manner', but no Greek women appear in either the *Timaeus* or *Critias*. Their absence further confirms that a complete *Critias* dialogue once did exist and contained much more regarding the Mediterranean War.

Migrants from the East probably introduced the Greek language into Greece in the 3rd millennium BCE. At the time of the Atlantis story of 11,600 BP, the Pelasgians in Greece must have spoken some unknown pre-Greek language or languages. Therefore, the names the Egyptians recorded for the prehistoric Hellenes in the Atlantis story would have been in a pre-Greek language, or they were Egyptian translations of those pre-Greek names.

Plato – 'the names of the chiefs of the land'...'most of the names which are recorded prior to the time of Theseus, such as Cecrops, and Erechtheus, and Erichthonius, and Erysichthon.'

Plato states that the prehistoric Athenian 'chiefs' involved in the Mediterranean War predated Theseus, the legendary Bronze Age founding hero of Athens of the late 2nd millennium BCE. The Athenians considered Theseus to be their great political reformer. He was responsible for the *synoikismos*, or dwelling together, which was the political unification of Attica under Athens. Theseus built and occupied a palace on the fortress of the Athenian Acropolis, which may have been similar to the Bronze Age palace excavated at Mycenae.

Cecrops was a mythical king of Athens. The Greek historian Strabo (ca. 64 BCE–24 CE) claimed that Cecrops' name was not of Greek origin. He was said to be born from the Earth (autochthonous), with his top half shaped like a man and the bottom half in serpent or fish-tail form. In myth, he founded Athens and was its first King, though the autochthonous King Actaeus of Attica preceded him in the region. Cecrops divided the Athenians into four tribes: Cecropis, Autochthon, Actea, and Paralia. He was a culture-hero, teaching the Athenians marriage, ceremonial burial, reading and writing, and navigation.

King Erichthonius was an early mythological ruler of Athens. Early Greek texts do not distinguish between him and his grandson Erectheus, but they are different figures by the 4th century BCE. Some legends claim that he was autochthonous and raised by the goddess Athena. He taught the Athenians to yoke horses and use them to pull chariots, to smelt silver, and to till with a plough.

Erechtheus was the name of an archaic king and the re-founder of the Athenian polis. The Athenians considered themselves Erechtheidai, the sons of Erechtheus. He was associated with Poseidon in Athens as Poseidon Erechtheus.

Erysichthon of Attica was the son of King Cecrops I of Athens and Aglaulus, the daughter of King Actaeus. Erysichthon died in Prasiae on the east coast of Attica while returning from the holy island of Delos with a statue of Eileithyia, the goddess of childbirth.

One particular issue about Greek names is that the mythical or legendary figures known by the Greeks of Plato's time may not be the original prehistoric Athenians of 11,600 BP. They may be much more recent individuals who received the same names passed down by 'obscure traditions' over thousands of years. As Plato declares, they were ancient names that later Greeks were 'willing enough to give to their children' without knowing anything about the names' original owners or their deeds.

Prehistoric Battles – Titanomachy, Gigantomachy, Athena and Poseidon

In Greek mythology, the Titanomachy and Gigantomachy were two separate mythical wars between rival groups of gods in prehistoric Greece (*machy* means war in Greek). On one side were the Titans and the Giants, who modern scholars think may represent the original gods of the prehistoric Pelasgian occupants of Greece. On the opposing side were the Olympian gods, some of whom are thought to have been introduced from the East by later immigrants to Greece, but as Herodotus claims, several were based on very ancient Egyptian gods.

An alternative interpretation is that the Titanomachy and Gigantomachy may be mythical representations of the Mediterranean War between the prehistoric Greeks and Atlanteans. The locations described in the myths could be the sites of actual battles. Atlas is one of the named Titans, so the names of the Titans and Giants may be the names of Atlantean leaders. Some of the Olympian gods' names may be those of prehistoric Athenian or other tribal leaders in Greece who were involved in the war and were victorious over the Atlanteans.

In Greek myth, the Titans were descendants of the primordial deities Gaia (Earth) and Uranus (Sky). The Titans were immortal giants of enormous strength who ruled during the mythical Golden Age. In the first generation of twelve Titans, the males were named Oceanus, Hyperion, Coeus, Cronus, Crius and Iapetus; the females were Mnemosyne, Tethys, Theia, Phoebe, Rhea, and Themis. The second generation of Titans consisted of Hyperion's children named Eos, Helios and Selene; Coeus's daughters Leto and Asteria; Iapetus' children Atlas, Prometheus, Epimetheus and Menoetius; Oceanus' daughter Metis; and Crius' sons Astraeus, Pallas and Perses.

Opposing the Titans were the twelve Olympian gods, who were the principal deities of the later Greek pantheon. They are usually considered to be Zeus, Hera, Poseidon, Demeter, Athena, Apollo, Artemis, Ares, Aphrodite, Hephaestus, Hermes, and either Hestia or Dionysus.

The Titanomachy was a ten-year-long series of battles between the Titans and the Olympians, fought in Thessaly in Central Greece. The Titans were based on Mount Othrys and the Olympians on Mount Olympus. The Olympian gods eventually defeated the Titans and imprisoned them in Tartarus, a deep abyss in the Earth used as a dungeon for the wicked.

The goddess Gaia was angered by her Titan children's imprisonment and pressed the Giants or *Gigantes*, who also were her children, to fight the Olympians and restore the Titans' rule. The Gigantomachy was the resulting war between the Giants and Olympians. Some named Giants were Eurymedon, Alcyoneus, Porphyrion, Agrios, Clytius, Enceladus, Ephialtes of the Aloadae, Eurytus, Gration, Hippolytus, Leon, Mimas, Otus of the Aloadae, Pallas, Pelorus, Polybotes, Thoon, and Damasen.

The Giants and the Gigantomachy were associated with several different places. Ancient writers such as the Greek poet Pindar (ca. 522–443 BCE) regarded Phlegra as the Giants' home ground during the Gigantomachy. Phlegra is an ancient name for Pallene, the westernmost of the three headlands of the Chalkidiki Peninsula in Northern Greece. Also, the name Phlegra and the Gigantomachy were often associated with a large volcanic area in Italy to the west of Naples called the Phlegraean Fields, and at least one tradition placed Phlegra in Thessaly.

The Greek historian Diodorus Siculus (ca. 1st century BCE) describes the Gigantomachy as a war with multiple battles: one at Pallene, one on the Phlegraean Fields, and one on Crete. The Greek historian Strabo mentions an account of Heracles battling Giants at Phanagoria, a Greek colony on the shores of the Black Sea. The Greek geographer Pausanias (ca. 110–180 CE) wrote that the Arcadians of the Peloponnese claimed the battle took place 'not at Pellene in Thrace' but in the plain of Megalopolis where 'rises up fire'. Another tradition placed the battle at Tartessus in south-western Spain.

At the end of the Gigantomachy, the Olympian gods defeated the Giants and continued to reign over the Earth. The Olympians killed some of the Giants in battle, while the surviving Giants were said to be buried under volcanos, which caused volcanic eruptions and earthquakes.

In many Greek myths, Poseidon disputed the possession of particular areas of Greece with the other gods. With Athena it was Athos and Troezene; with Helios it was Corinth; with Hera it was Argolis; with Zeus it was Aegina; and with Dionysus it was Naxos. Since Plato associates Poseidon with Atlantis, these very ancient myths may also be memories of individual battles fought between the Atlanteans and the prehistoric Greeks.

Homer claimed that Poseidon's palace was beneath the sea near Aegae, an ancient town on the west coast of the island of Euboea, north of Attica, and Strabo records a sanctuary of Aegean Poseidon on a nearby mountain. The myth of Poseidon's palace under the sea may represent the location of a decisive naval battle between the Atlanteans and Athenians. Otherwise, it may be the buildings of a colony of the Atlanteans submerged by the subsequent rise in sea levels.

Possible Sites of Prehistoric Battles
Source: Modified from Google Earth

In Greek mythology, Athena became the patron goddess of Athens after she defeated Poseidon in a competition on the Acropolis. After the contest and angered at his loss, Poseidon sent a great flood to the Attic Plain to punish the Athenians for not choosing him. This story may represent a memory of the war between Athens and the Atlanteans, and a deluge Plato describes that destroyed Athens/Attica.

The Panathenaea was an ancient annual festival honouring Athena Polias (Athena of the City) and Erechtheus. It was said to be founded by an Athenian King, either Erechtheus or Erichthonius, 729 years before the first Olympiad of 776 BCE, or around 1500 BCE. Plato states that some of the names later Athenians called themselves were from forgotten leaders and heroes of the war with the Atlanteans of 11,600 BP. As Erechtheus and Erichthonius were Athenians apparently involved in the Mediterranean War, the Bronze Age King Erechtheus or Erichthonius who founded the Panathenaea would have been a much later namesake rather than an original prehistoric figure.

Every year during the Panathenaea festival, there was a grand procession of the whole citizen population of Athens through the city, finishing on the Acropolis. The procession's purpose was to transfer offerings to the goddess Athena, and the principal offering was the sacred peplos used to clothe the ancient olivewood statue of Athena Polias. This statue was usually housed in the Erechtheum, a small temple near the Parthenon on the Acropolis.

The peplos was a rectangular textile showing the Gigantomachy and the goddess Athena's distinguished part in the battles. A new peplos was woven yearly for the Panathenaea by a group of chosen Athenian girls, taking nine months to weave. During the Panathenaea procession, the finished peplos was set like a sail on a ceremonial ship-on-wheels pulled through the city. When it reached the Areopagus Hill, to the north-west of the Acropolis, the peplos was taken down and carried onward by hand to the Erechtheum and placed on the goddess' statue by female attendants.

Athena's role in the Gigantomachy may be a myth about Athens' decisive role in the war against the Atlanteans. Otherwise, an original warrior-queen of Attica called Athena might have led the Athenians in battle against the Atlanteans and was deified by later Athenians. Amongst her other military attributes, the goddess Athena taught the Greeks the art of shipbuilding, so the ceremonial ship-on-wheels carrying her peplos may symbolise naval battles where the Athenians and their allies defeated the Atlanteans.

Erechtheum
Source: Wikimedia Commons – LevineDS

'In a single day and night of misfortune all your warlike men in a body sank into the Earth, and the island of Atlantis in like manner disappeared in the depths of the sea'

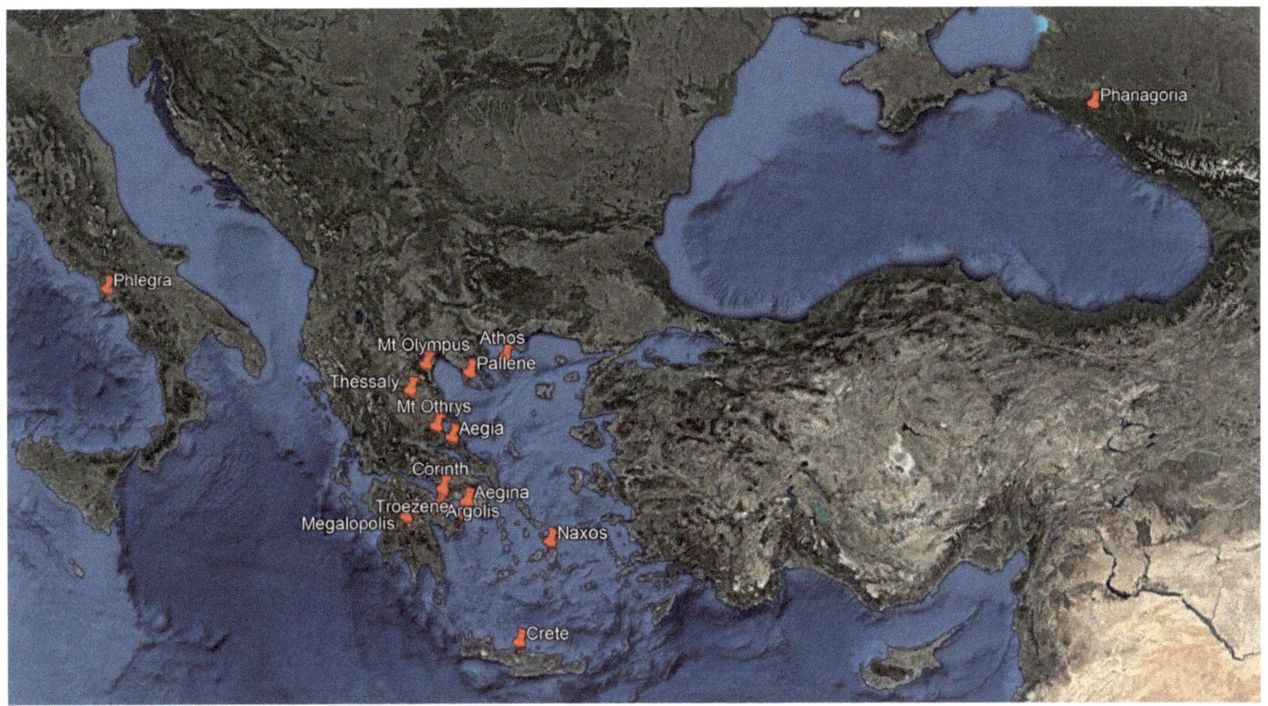

Possible Sites of Prehistoric Battles
Source: Modified from Google Earth

In Greek mythology, Athena became the patron goddess of Athens after she defeated Poseidon in a competition on the Acropolis. After the contest and angered at his loss, Poseidon sent a great flood to the Attic Plain to punish the Athenians for not choosing him. This story may represent a memory of the war between Athens and the Atlanteans, and a deluge Plato describes that destroyed Athens/Attica.

The Panathenaea was an ancient annual festival honouring Athena Polias (Athena of the City) and Erechtheus. It was said to be founded by an Athenian King, either Erechtheus or Erichthonius, 729 years before the first Olympiad of 776 BCE, or around 1500 BCE. Plato states that some of the names later Athenians called themselves were from forgotten leaders and heroes of the war with the Atlanteans of 11,600 BP. As Erechtheus and Erichthonius were Athenians apparently involved in the Mediterranean War, the Bronze Age King Erechtheus or Erichthonius who founded the Panathenaea would have been a much later namesake rather than an original prehistoric figure.

Every year during the Panathenaea festival, there was a grand procession of the whole citizen population of Athens through the city, finishing on the Acropolis. The procession's purpose was to transfer offerings to the goddess Athena, and the principal offering was the sacred peplos used to clothe the ancient olivewood statue of Athena Polias. This statue was usually housed in the Erechtheum, a small temple near the Parthenon on the Acropolis.

The peplos was a rectangular textile showing the Gigantomachy and the goddess Athena's distinguished part in the battles. A new peplos was woven yearly for the Panathenaea by a group of chosen Athenian girls, taking nine months to weave. During the Panathenaea procession, the finished peplos was set like a sail on a ceremonial ship-on-wheels pulled through the city. When it reached the Areopagus Hill, to the north-west of the Acropolis, the peplos was taken down and carried onward by hand to the Erechtheum and placed on the goddess' statue by female attendants.

Athena's role in the Gigantomachy may be a myth about Athens' decisive role in the war against the Atlanteans. Otherwise, an original warrior-queen of Attica called Athena might have led the Athenians in battle against the Atlanteans and was deified by later Athenians. Amongst her other military attributes, the goddess Athena taught the Greeks the art of shipbuilding, so the ceremonial ship-on-wheels carrying her peplos may symbolise naval battles where the Athenians and their allies defeated the Atlanteans.

Erechtheum
Source: Wikimedia Commons – LevineDS

'In a single day and night of misfortune all your warlike men in a body sank into the Earth, and the island of Atlantis in like manner disappeared in the depths of the sea'

CHAPTER 9

The Separate Destructions of the Athenian Acropolis and Atlantic Island

Plato (Jowett) – 'afterwards (after the Mediterranean War) there occurred violent earthquakes and floods; and in a single day and night of misfortune all your warlike men (the Athenian warrior class) in a body sank into the Earth, and the island of Atlantis in like manner disappeared in the depths of the sea. For which reason the sea in those parts is impassable and impenetrable, because there is a shoal of mud in the way; and this was caused by the subsidence of the (Atlantic) island' and '(the Atlantic Island) when afterwards (after the war) sunk by an earthquake, became an impassable barrier of mud to voyagers sailing from hence to any part of the (Atlantic) ocean.'

Plato (Taylor) – 'in succeeding time (after the Mediterranean War) prodigious earthquakes and deluges taking place, and bringing with them desolation in the space of one day and night, all that warlike race of Athenians was at once merged under the Earth; and the Atlantic island itself, being absorbed in the sea, entirely disappeared. And hence that sea (Atlantic Ocean) is at present innavigable, arising from the gradually impeding mud which the subsiding island produced' and '(the Atlantic Island) is now a mass of impervious mud, through concussions of the Earth; so that those who are sailing in the vast sea (Atlantic Ocean) can no longer find a passage from hence thither.'

The above passages from Plato are often assumed to mean the prehistoric Athenian Acropolis and the Atlantic Island were destroyed simultaneously and in the same way. In both translations, they were destroyed at some unspecified time after the Mediterranean War of 11,600 BP. Yet, these two catastrophes were located thousands of kilometres apart, most likely occurring at very different times and from unrelated causes. Either of these separate destructions may have happened tens, hundreds, or thousands of years after 11,600 BP.

Torrential rain and earthquakes destroyed the prehistoric Athenian Acropolis 'in a single day and night of misfortune' when the Athenian warrior class that lived on the Acropolis' summit 'sank' or 'merged' into the Earth. The Atlantic Island 'disappeared in the depths of the sea', but Plato does not specify whether it was before, at the same time, or after the Acropolis' destruction. Still, Plato states that the Atlantic Island was destroyed by 'concussions of the Earth' or earthquakes. In both translations quoted above, the Atlantic Island was 'absorbed', 'subsided', or 'sank' into the sea. These statements mean that a 'deluge', like a rising sea level or a tsunami, did not destroy the Atlantic Island. Instead, it was destroyed in a downward, sinking movement of the land to below sea level.

Unlike the destruction of the Acropolis, which took 'a single day and night', Plato does not describe how long the Atlantic Island took to subside. Taylor's translation states, 'And hence that sea (the Atlantic Ocean) is at present innavigable, arising from the gradually impeding mud which the subsiding (Atlantic) island produced.' So, Taylor describes a subsidence of the Atlantic Island that created a gradual obstruction rather than sudden subsidence due to a single devastating event. Geological events in the Caribbean may have caused a slow or intermittent sinking of the

Atlantic Island that could have continued for tens, hundreds, or thousands of years.

The Decline and Fall of the Atlanteans

Plato – 'For many generations, as long as the divine nature lasted in them, they (the Atlanteans) were obedient to the laws'...'They despised everything but virtue, caring little for their present state of life'...'but when the divine portion began to fade away, and became diluted too often and too much with the mortal admixture, and the human nature got the upper hand, they then, being unable to bear their fortune, behaved unseemly, and to him who had an eye to see grew visibly debased'...'they appeared glorious and blessed at the very time when they were full of avarice and unrighteous power. Zeus, the god of gods, who rules according to law, and is able to see into such things, perceiving that an honourable race was in a woeful plight, and wanting to inflict punishment on them, that they may be chastened and improve, collected all the gods into their most holy habitation, which, being placed in the centre of the world, beholds all created things. And when he had called them together, he spake as follows...' – The rest of the *Critias* dialogue is lost.

While Atlantean civilisation developed on the Atlantic Island over many centuries or millennia and grew into a vast empire, it degenerated as it became ever more powerful. Plato's story stops abruptly when the Gods are preparing to discuss and possibly judge the Atlanteans' behaviour. It is unknown whether the remainder of the lost *Critias* described the Gods' judgement or any punishment of the Atlanteans. However, Plato states that the Atlanteans were defeated in the Mediterranean War and were expelled from the lands they had conquered and enslaved within the Mediterranean. At some undefined time later, catastrophic natural causes destroyed the Atlantic Island.

Edward Gibbon described the decline of Roman civilisation in his *Decline and Fall of the Roman Empire*, written in 1776–88 CE. Gibbon's words can explain the eventual fate of any empire, either before or after Rome, and it echoes Plato's portrayal of the decline of the Atlanteans.

Gibbon – 'The decline of Rome was the natural and inevitable effect of immoderate greatness. Prosperity ripened the principle of decay; the cause of the destruction multiplied with the extent of conquest; and, as soon as time or accident had removed the artificial supports, the stupendous fabric yielded to the pressure of its own weight. The story of the ruin is simple and obvious; and instead of inquiring why the Roman Empire was destroyed, we should rather be surprised that it has subsisted for so long.'

After the Atlanteans were driven from the Mediterranean, a weakening of Atlantean imperial power may have forced them to withdraw from any conquered lands in Africa and Europe outside the Mediterranean. The Atlanteans also may have had less control over their conquered subjects in the Americas, who may have fought wars for their independence.

The Atlantean civilisation's decline after the Mediterranean War of 11,600 BP may have taken centuries or millennia. Its decline may have been like that of the Roman Empire: decay over a long period because of society's degeneration, imperial overreach, an inability to control subject nations, and external military threats. However, the eventual subsidence of the Atlantic Island is an additional destructive factor, unlike Rome's situation. Its effect on the Atlantean Empire would depend on how long after 11,600 BP it occurred and how great the seismic events were that caused the Atlantic Island to subside.

The Atlantean civilisation might have steadily declined if the Atlantic Island experienced a series of many lesser subsidences over hundreds or thousands of years, or a more continuous gradual subsidence. As the Atlantic Island subsided, the sea would have increasingly covered the fertile Plain of Atlantis, disrupting the food source for millions of people. Because the Royal City was close to sea level, it would eventually have subsided and been abandoned. Any remaining Atlantean cities above sea level on the Plain's surrounding mountains may have maintained some political control over what was left of the Atlantic Island until they also subsided or Atlantean civilisation disintegrated.

A different scenario is that one or more sudden catastrophic subsidences of the Atlantic Island, by tens or hundreds of metres, may have caused a swift collapse of the core Atlantean civilisation. An immediate loss of food production and distribution systems would likely have created a complete social breakdown and the failure of law and order. There may have been a post-apocalyptic scenario where millions of urbanised people on the Atlantic Island and possibly any surrounding urbanised lands in the Americas would have suddenly been without the essentials for survival. An enormous initial loss of life from starvation and armed conflict for resources would have been followed by further population decline over years and decades. Any survivors likely regressed to a more subsistence level of hunter-gatherers or Neolithic farmers.

Eventually, the ongoing subsidence of the Atlantic Island submerged the Plain of Atlantis and the Eastern and Western Mountains. That left only the 'remnant islands' Marcellus described, assumed to be Cuba, Jamaica, Hispaniola, Puerto Rico, and the Lesser Antilles.

The Destruction of the Acropolis Hill

Plato states that sometime after the Mediterranean War of 11,600 BP, torrential rain and several earthquakes destroyed the prehistoric Acropolis Hill.

Plato – 'For the fact is that a single night of excessive rain washed away the Earth (on the Acropolis Hill) and laid bare the rock; at the same time there were earthquakes'…'But afterwards (after the Mediterranean War) there occurred violent earthquakes and floods (in Athens/Attica); and in a single day and night of misfortune, all your warlike men (the Athenian warrior class) in a body sank into the Earth.'

The present Aegean region is tectonically active and experiences frequent earthquakes. At the time of prehistoric Athens and Attica, around 11,600 BP, the tectonic forces in the region would have been much the same as today, with a high risk of earthquakes.

Tectonic plates are the rigid segments of the Earth's outer rocky layer called the Lithosphere. They move horizontally relative to one another, with earthquakes, volcanic activity and mountain-

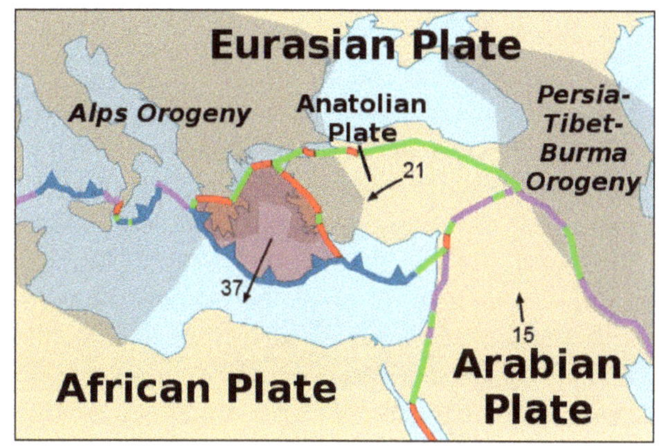

Aegean Plate (red)
Source: Wikimedia Commons – Alataristarion

building occurring along the boundaries between tectonic plates. The Eastern Mediterranean is a boundary region between three major tectonic plates: the Eurasian, African, and Arabian Plates. The relatively small Aegean Plate sits between those three larger plates. Much of southern Greece, including Athens, sits on the Aegean Plate.

The Richter Magnitude Scale describes the energy contained in an earthquake. It is a base-ten logarithmic scale, so an earthquake that measures 6.0 on the Richter scale has an energy output ten

Magnitude	Description	Earthquake Effects	Frequency of Occurrence (estimated)
Less than 2.0	Micro	Microearthquakes, not felt	Continual
2.0–2.9	Minor	Generally not felt, but recorded by instruments.	1,300,000 per year
3.0–3.9		Often felt, but rarely causes damage.	130,000 per year
4.0–4.9	Light	Noticeable shaking of indoor items, rattling noises. Significant damage unlikely.	13,000 per year
5.0–5.9	Moderate	Can cause major damage to poorly constructed buildings over small regions. At most, slight damage to well-designed buildings.	1,319 per year
6.0–6.9	Strong	Can be destructive in areas up to about 160 kilometres across in populated areas.	134 per year
7.0–7.9	Major	Can cause serious damage over larger areas.	15 per year
8.0–8.9	Great	Can cause serious damage in areas several hundred kilometres across.	1 per year
9.0–9.9		Devastation in areas several thousand kilometres across.	1 per 10 years
10.0+	Massive	Never recorded, widespread devastation across very large areas	Extremely rare (Unknown and may not be possible)

Richter Scale Source: Wikimedia Commons – based on USGS documents

times larger than one that measures 5.0; 7.0 is ten times larger than 6.0, and so on.

The Aegean region, including southern Greece and Athens, lies in a highly geologically active area with frequent large earthquakes. In the 20th century CE, the largest earthquakes had magnitudes of around 7.2 on the Richter Scale. However, historical sources and archaeological studies suggest earthquakes centred near Crete in 365 CE and 1303 CE may have been much greater than any 20th-century CE earthquake. The earthquake of 365 CE is considered the largest in historical times, estimated at magnitude 8.0 or higher. It caused widespread destruction in central and southern Greece, northern Libya, Egypt, Cyprus, and Sicily and destroyed nearly all the towns on Crete. The earthquake was followed by a tsunami that devastated the eastern coasts of the Mediterranean, notably Alexandria and the Nile Delta.

Earthquake activity in the Aegean would not have significantly changed over tens of thousands of years. The same tectonic forces that caused the destructive magnitude 8.0 earthquake of 365 CE existed well before the time of the Atlantis story, and they continue now. Aegean earthquakes of magnitude 8.0 or more would likely have occurred numerous times in prehistory, both before and after 11,600 BP.

Athens is built on a plain called the Athens Basin. It is bounded on the north by Mt Parnes, north-east by Mt Penteli, south-east by Mt Hymettos, and west by Mt Aigaleos. The Athens Basin was formed partly by faulting and partly by the erosion of Athens Schist, which mostly consists of Cretaceous (145–66mya) sedimentary rock. It also contains much younger Neogene (past 23 million years) sedimentary rocks.

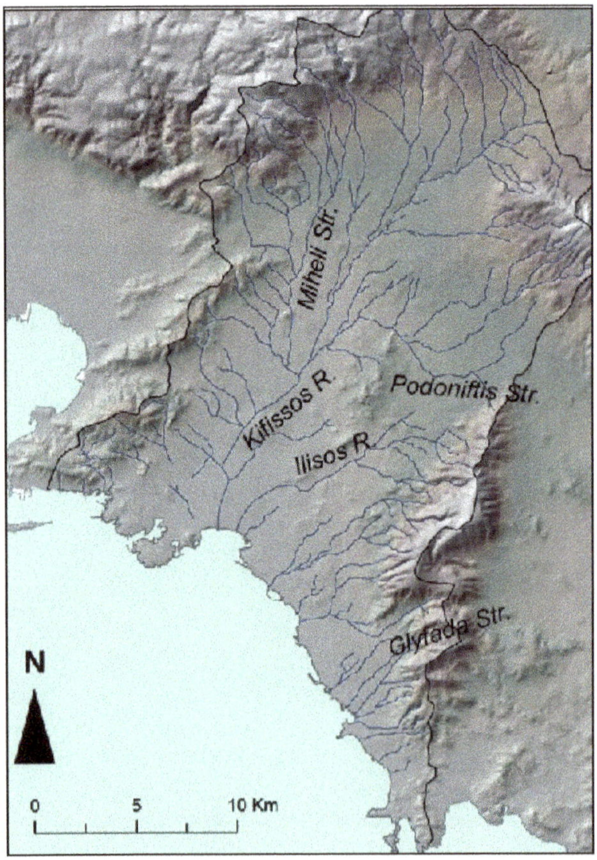

The Athens Basin

In the present Athens Basin, the much older Athens Schist either forms outcrops or underlies the younger Neogene sediments. Many of the hills in the eastern part of the Athens Basin, such as Mount Lycabettus, the Acropolis, the Pnyx, the Areopagus, and the Philopappos hill, are Late Cretaceous (100–66mya) limestone outcrops.

A layer of alluvium up to 20 metres thick covers much of the central and western parts of the Athens Basin. Alluvium is sand, silt, clay, gravel, or other matter deposited by flowing water. Geologists think recent infrequent floods deposited most of the alluvium in the Athens Basin. The 'recent' past in geology often means the Holocene Epoch of the last 12,000 years.

Landslides and Mudslides

Archaeological evidence shows that the present Athenian Acropolis was inhabited as early as the 6th millennium BP, but natural disasters may have obliterated any evidence of earlier occupation.

Plato states that sometime after 11,600 BP, heavy rain combined with earthquakes caused a catastrophe on the prehistoric Acropolis Hill in 'a single day and a night'. That description could literally mean either twenty-four or thirty-six hours. Plato emphasises that thousands of prehistoric Athenians living on the Acropolis Hill 'in a body sank into the Earth'. Some natural event happened before they could escape; a massive landslide is the only geological event that could cause such sudden devastation.

Landslide is a general term for the mass movement of soil or rock downhill. Landslides occur when a slope's condition becomes unstable due to several factors that can act together or alone. Natural causes of landslides include:

- groundwater destabilising the slope
- loss or absence of vegetation

Landslide in Sierra Leone, 2017
Source: Wikimedia Commons – Mark Stedman

- erosion of the toe of a slope by rivers or ocean waves
- weakening of a slope through saturation by snowmelt, glaciers melting, or heavy rains
- earthquakes adding loads to an unstable slope
- earthquake-caused liquefaction where the soil behaves like a liquid
- volcanic eruptions

A mudslide is the most rapid, fluid type of landslide that can travel up to 80km/h. It is caused by the movement of a large mass of mud formed from loose soil and water. Some mudflows are slow, whereas others begin quickly and continue like an avalanche.

Most of the prehistoric Acropolis Hill was probably composed of Neogene (past 23 million years) sediments, which are still present as hills at the northern end of the Athens Basin. Soft sediments are much more like soil than rock. They would have filled what now is mostly empty space between the rocky outcrops of Mt Lycabettus, the present Acropolis, and the Pnyx. These three rocky outcrops consist of much older and harder Late Cretaceous (100–66mya) limestones that have resisted erosion and collapse.

Plato states that the prehistoric Acropolis Hill was saturated by 'a single night of excessive rain' accompanied by several large earthquakes. The combination of saturated soft sediment and the shock of several earthquakes over 'a day and a night' would have destabilised much of the Acropolis Hill. The saturated sediment may have liquefied due to shaking by repeated earthquakes. Then, if a sudden massive mudslide occurred, any buildings and their occupants on and below the Acropolis Hill would have been destroyed and covered by metres-deep mud in a matter of minutes. In this way, thousands of prehistoric Athenian people 'sank into the Earth'.

Some of the up to 20-metre-thick recent alluvium in the central and western parts of the Athens Basin is probably due to the mudslide; it is the remains of the prehistoric Acropolis Hill.

The Estimated Size of the Athenian Mudslide

Mount Lycabettus, the Acropolis, and the Pnyx form a roughly straight line of three separate Cretaceous limestone hills. Plato states that the prehistoric Acropolis Hill between the Pnyx and Lycabettus was 'all well covered with soil, and level at the top, except in one or two places'. It was where 'the warrior class dwelt by themselves around the temples of Athena and Hephaestus at the summit.' The present rocky limestone outcrops of Mt. Lycabettus, the Acropolis or the Pnyx may have been the 'one or two places' on the summit that were not level and covered with soil.

The present Athenian Acropolis rises 100 metres above the surrounding land and appears to have been inhabited from at least the 6th millennium BP. It was also named Cecropia after Cecrops, the first mythical Athenian King. In the 4th millennium BP, the Mycenaeans built a palace on the hill and a massive circuit wall 760 metres long, up to 10 metres high, and from 3.5–6.0 metres thick.

Following the Bronze Age Collapse around 1100 BCE, several later buildings and temples occupied the site during the Greek Dark Ages (1100–800 BCE) and the Archaic Period (800–480 BCE). The top of the Acropolis was levelled with artificial fill up to 14 metres deep behind its more ancient Mycenaean retaining walls. The present Parthenon and Erechtheum Temples were built in the 5th century BCE.

View from the Pnyx past the Acropolis to Mt Lycabettus
Source: Wikimedia Commons – George E. Koronaios

The Present Pnyx, Acropolis and Lycabettus
Source: Modified from Google Earth

Reconstruction of the Athenian Acropolis at the time of Plato
Source: Dr D Josef, 1912

Hillside Village, Morocco
Source: Wikimedia Commons – Luc Viatour

The Pnyx is a small, rocky hill to the west of the present Acropolis, with a large, flat platform of eroded stone set into its side. It was the meeting place of one of the world's earliest known democratic legislatures: the *ekklesia* (assembly), where Athenian citizens gathered to debate and vote.

The flanks of the prehistoric Acropolis Hill were probably sloping because Plato states: 'Outside the Acropolis and under the sides of the hill there dwelt artisans.' Also, for the 20,000 Athenian warriors: 'On the north side (of the Hill) they had dwellings in common and had erected halls for dining in winter, and had all the buildings which they needed for their common life, besides temples'…'in summer-time they left their gardens and gymnasia and dining halls, and then the southern side of the hill was made use of by them for the same purpose.'

In a previous section in Chapter 8, the Acropolis Hill's base was calculated to be 6km^2, with its average height (excluding Mount Lycabettus) assumed to be 100 metres. Using the estimate of the Hill's base of 6km^2 – if the sides were vertical, the volume would be six times 0.1km (100 metres), or 0.6km^3. If the Hill's sides were gently sloping and the top was flat, the actual volume would have been less, so a reasonable estimate of the total volume would be 0.5km^3.

The Earth's most massive historical landslide occurred during the 1980 CE eruption of Mount St. Helens, a volcano in Washington State, USA. The volume of landslide material there was 2.8km^3. The Earth's largest prehistoric mudslide discovered to date is the Saidmarreh Landslide in South-Western Iran. It occurred around 10,000 BP and had a volume of 20km^3, a depth of 300 metres, a travel distance of 14km, and a width of 5km. About 50 billion tonnes of material moved in this single event.

The prehistoric Acropolis Hill's estimated volume of 0.5 km^3 is well within the upper limits of the size of historical landslides and much less than the 2.8 km^3 for Mount St Helens. If the entire Athenian warrior class of 20,000 lived on the Acropolis Hill, a large catastrophic mudslide could explain how 'in a single day and night of misfortune all your warlike men in a body sank into the Earth.'

The initial mudslide would not have entirely destroyed the Acropolis Hill; more erosion would have occurred over the next few thousand years. The alluvium is up to twenty metres thick around the bases of the surviving rocky outcrops of the Pnyx, Acropolis and Lycabettus. That alluvium is what remains of the ancient catastrophic mudslide and any later erosion.

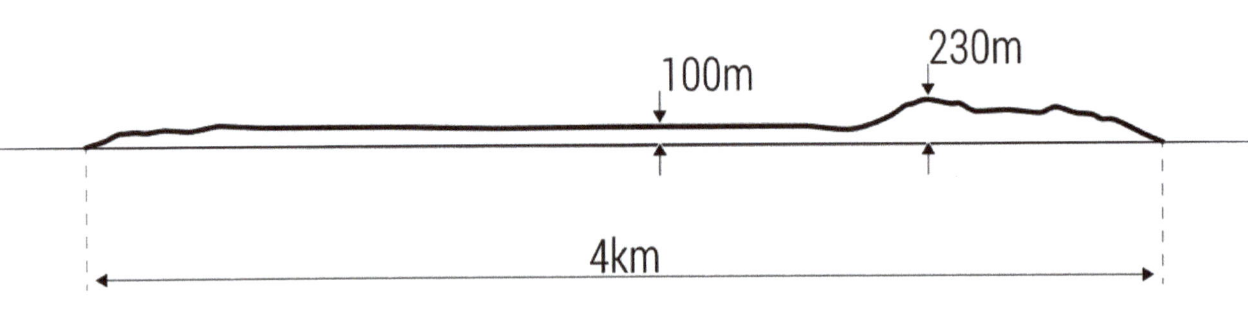

Side View of the Prehistoric Acropolis Hill ca. 11,600 BP

Present Side View from Pnyx (Left) to Lycabettus (Right)

Reconstruction of the Prehistoric Acropolis Hill

As there is evidence of the Neolithic occupation of the present Acropolis from at least the 6th millennium BP, it must have been a prominent rocky outcrop by then, much like it appears today. So, the mudslide that destroyed the prehistoric Acropolis Hill and the Athenian warrior class likely occurred sometime between 11,600 BP and 6,000 BP.

Mount Lycabettus, 1880 CE

Athenian Acropolis with the Parthenon, 1850 CE

'There have been, and will be again, many destructions of mankind arising out of many causes'

CHAPTER 10

Many Catastrophes of 'fire and water' and the Dark Ages of Humanity

When Solon spoke with the Egyptian priests at the Temple of Neith in Sais around 600 BCE, they emphasised that human populations and civilisations rose and fell in the remote past due to many causes. People eventually forgot those past events because the destroyed cultures reverted to a more primitive state.

Plato – 'On one occasion, wishing to draw them (the Egyptian priests) on to speak of antiquity, he (Solon) began to tell about the most ancient things in our part of the world (Greece) – about Phoroneus, who is called 'the first man' and about Niobe; and after the Deluge, of the survival of Deucalion and Pyrrha; and he traced the genealogy of their descendants, and reckoning up the dates, tried to compute how many years ago the events of which he was speaking happened.'

'Thereupon one of the priests, who was of a very great age, said: O Solon, Solon, you Hellenes are never anything but children, and there is not an old man among you. Solon in return asked him what he meant. I mean to say, he replied, that in mind you are all young; there is no old opinion handed down among you by ancient tradition, nor any science which is hoary with age. And I will tell you why'…'There have been, and will be again, many destructions of mankind arising out of many causes; the greatest have been brought about by the agencies of fire and water, and other lesser ones by innumerable other causes'…'wherever the extremity of winter frost or of summer does not prevent, mankind exist, sometimes in greater, sometimes in lesser numbers'…'just when you (Greeks) and other nations are beginning to be provided with letters and the other requisites of civilised life, after the usual interval, the stream from heaven, like a pestilence, comes pouring down, and leaves only those of you who are destitute of letters and education; and so you have to begin all over again like children, and know nothing of what happened in ancient times, either among us (Egyptians) or among yourselves (Greeks).'

'When, on the other hand, the gods purge the Earth with a deluge of water, the survivors in your country (Greece) are herdsmen and shepherds who dwell on the mountains, but those who, like you, live in cities are carried by the rivers into the sea'…'they themselves (the survivors) and their children lacked for many generations the necessaries of life, they directed their attention to the supply of their wants, and of them they conversed, to the neglect of events that had happened in times long past; for mythology and the enquiry into antiquity are first introduced into cities when they begin to have leisure, and when they see that the necessaries of life have already been provided, but not before'…'As for those genealogies of yours which you just now recounted to us, Solon, they are no better than the tales of children.'

The Egyptian priests explain that human cultures rise during periods of climate stability – 'wherever the extremity of winter frost or of summer does not prevent, mankind exist, sometimes in greater, sometimes in lesser numbers.' Cultures then suffer major 'destructions of mankind', mainly due to 'the agencies of fire and water', but lesser destructions are 'by innumerable other causes', which would include war, famine and disease.

This chapter argues that 'the agencies of fire and water' are due to natural climate change. There is firm scientific evidence that over hundreds of thousands of years, there have been many recurring extreme climate cycles on Earth. During each of these cycles, the Earth has had long periods of hot or cold conditions, with enormous changes in sea level at different times in each cycle. These climate cycles occurred well before and throughout the more than two hundred thousand years of our *Homo sapiens* species.

In the remote past, some regular climate cycles have lasted hundreds, thousands, or tens of thousands of years and caused extreme environmental changes. Those profound changes impacted human survival and may have produced the 'many destructions of mankind' that the Egyptian priests described to Solon. The same natural climate cycles continue to the present day and will likely continue into the distant future. These inevitable and possibly devastating climate changes will happen regardless of any current or future human technology and its effect on the global climate.

The Egyptian priests ridiculed Solon's estimates of antiquity that the Greeks of his time commonly believed. Yet, despite the Egyptians' more ancient culture, their belief in the repeated cycles of humanity's destruction would, at most, cover tens of thousands of years. The Egyptians would have had no concept of the much longer time-frames shaping the Earth's climate, which span hundreds of thousands of years.

Plato's English translators in the 18th and 19th centuries wrote at a time when most Christians believed the Bible's Old Testament was an accurate history of the Earth. For devout Christians, God created the entire Universe in six days about six thousand years ago. Plato's accounts of anything that existed thousands of years before then, let alone advanced human civilisations, would have been considered heresy by many Christians in the 18th and 19th centuries.

Science has only recently understood geological time or Deep Time, which began with the writings of James Hutton in the 1780s and Charles Lyell in the 1830s. Lyell was among the first people to believe that the Earth was more than 300 million years old; he based his belief on geological evidence. Lyell's writings influenced Charles Darwin, who in 1859 published his radical book, *On the Origin of Species*, which described the concept of evolution.

One needs to understand extremely long timeframes to explain Plato's 'many destructions of mankind' due to 'the agencies of fire and water'

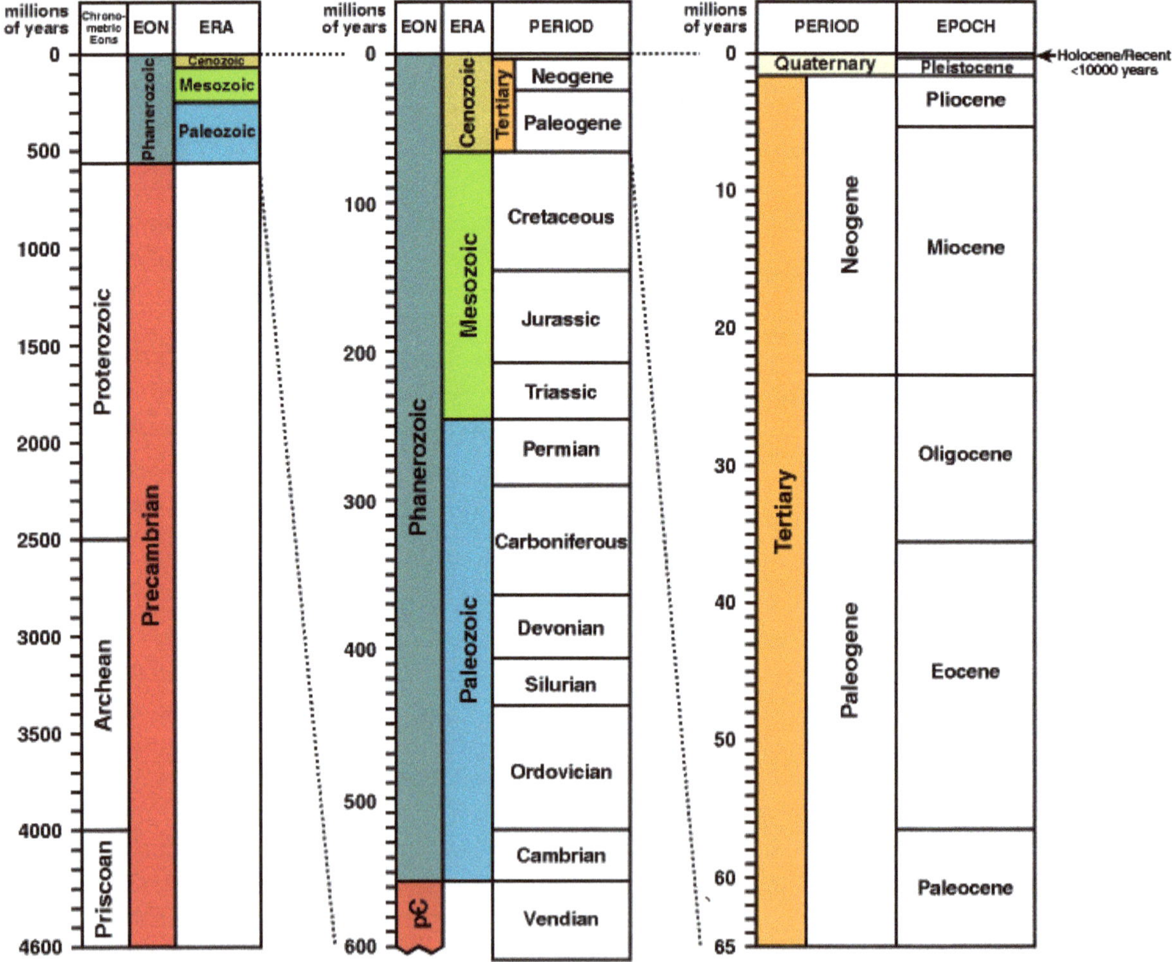

Representation of the Geological Time Scale
Source: Andrew MacRae, 1998

and the creation and destruction of the Atlantic Island. Recent scientific thinking is that the Earth is around 4.6 billion years old. The Geological Time Scale describes the timing and relationships between events on Earth during those 4.6 billion years. The largest defined unit of time is the supereon, which is composed of eons. Eons are then divided into eras, which are divided into periods, epochs and ages.

The Caribbean Hypothesis argues that geological changes created and destroyed the Atlantic Island during the past sixty-five million years. Those sixty-five million years are still a brief time compared to the 4.6 billion years the Earth has existed. They cover the Tertiary and Quaternary Periods of the Earth's existence: the right-hand column on the above Geological Time Scale.

In the Atlantis story, the past environmental changes affecting Atlantean, Egyptian and Greek cultures are a small fraction of the last 65 million years. Those particular changes happened after *Homo sapiens* arrived in the Americas, which at most is only twenty to forty thousand years of the Pleistocene and Holocene Epochs of the Quaternary Period. That is merely the topmost part of the above chart's right-hand column.

Past Major Ice Ages

There were several previous major Ice Ages, but the most important for the Atlantis story is the most recent one, the Pliocene-Quaternary Glaciation, better known as the Quaternary Ice Age. To understand the main geological processes that caused the many past environmental cycles, one must know the effects of glacial ice on the Earth's surface during the Quaternary Ice Age.

There have been at least five major ice ages on Earth in the past 4.6 billion years of our planet's existence. During the ice ages, massive glaciers covered much of the Earth's landmasses. Each ice age lasted between tens of millions and hundreds of millions of years, but between each ice age, the Earth seems to have been ice-free for hundreds of millions of years.

The causes of the major ice ages are not understood entirely, but several factors are significant, and they may interact:

- atmospheric composition, such as the concentrations of carbon dioxide and methane
- changes in the Earth's orbit around the Sun known as Milankovitch cycles
- the movement of tectonic plates with changes in their relative location and the amount of Continental and Oceanic Crust on the Earth's surface that affect wind and ocean currents
- variations in solar energy output
- the orbital dynamics of the Earth-Moon system
- the impact of relatively large meteorites
- volcanism, including eruptions of supervolcanoes

The first major ice age was the Huronian Ice Age, which lasted 300 million years from 2.4 to 2.1 billion years ago. Then came the Cryogenian Ice Age, which lasted 165 million years from 800–635mya and was the most severe. It may have produced a 'Snowball Earth' when the Earth completely iced over. A minor series of glaciations called the Andean-Saharan Ice Age lasted 30 million years from 450–420mya. They were followed by extensive glaciations called the Karoo Ice Age, which lasted 100 million years from 350–250mya.

Name	Period (mya)	Period	Era
Quaternary	2.58–present	Neogene	Cenozoic
Karoo	350–250	Carboniferous and Permian	Palaeozoic
Andean-Saharan	450–420	Ordovician and Silurian	Palaeozoic
Cryogenian	800–635	Cryogenian	Neoproterozoic
Huronian	2,400–2,100	Siderian and Rhyacian	Palaeoproterozoic

Major Ice Ages

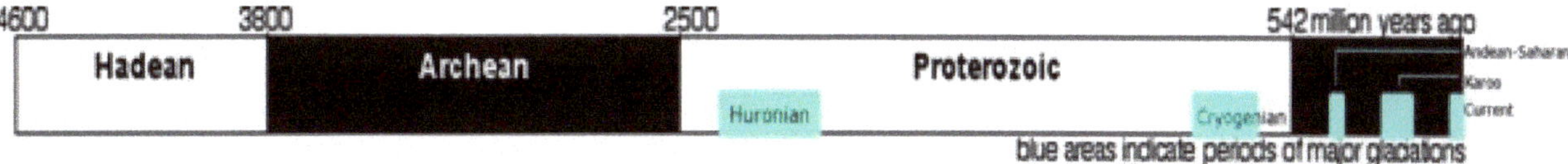

Major Ice Ages (in Blue)
Source: Wikimedia Commons – William M. Connolley

The Present Quaternary Ice Age

After the Karoo Ice Age, there was a long gap of over 245 million years of relatively ice-free conditions. Then came the most recent major ice age, the present Quaternary Ice Age. It began 2.5 million years ago and continues now, and will likely continue for millions more years.

The geological changes that created and destroyed the Atlantic Island can be linked to changes in glacial ice over the Earth's landmasses during the past 36 million years, particularly during the past 2.5 million years of the Quaternary Ice Age.

Well before the Quaternary Ice Age began, an initial increase in glaciation on Earth started 36mya when glacial ice began to build up over the landmass of Antarctica. This glaciation increased as the oceans cooled due to the formation of the Antarctic Circumpolar Current when ocean currents started to circle the Antarctic continent without reaching warmer latitudes. Worldwide temperatures markedly decreased by 15mya, probably due to accelerating ice growth on Antarctica, and then the Antarctic ice cap began to grow into its present form. There was a further acceleration in the rate of ice growth on Antarctica around 5mya. In the Northern Hemisphere, the Greenland ice cap began developing around 3mya.

The Quaternary Ice Age is considered to have started around 2.5mya when ice sheets began to spread over North America and Eurasia. Before then, Arctic areas were comparatively warm, with trees and bushes growing far north of the present tree-line. During the Quaternary Ice Age, there were many cycles of colder periods followed by warmer ones. These regular climate changes are called glacial/interglacial cycles. Massive ice sheets advance during cold glacial periods and retreat during warm interglacial periods. Each prior glacial/interglacial cycle has lasted tens of thousands of years, yet there is no single, simple explanation for them.

Despite a common notion that the 'Ice Age' ended 12,000 years ago, that belief is mistaken. Instead, the Earth is in a relatively warm interglacial period of the Quaternary Ice Age called the Holocene Epoch. By convention, it began at 12,000 BP. Nevertheless, the Quaternary Ice Age continues, and another cold glacial period will eventually return. We are still in a major ice age likely to persist for millions of years, as have all past ice ages.

In the previous 2.5 million years of the Quaternary Ice Age, there have probably been thirty to fifty glacial/interglacial cycles of alternating cold and warm periods that lasted many thousands of years. Before 800,000 BP, each glacial/interglacial cycle continued for around 40,000 years; after that, much longer cycles lasted around 100,000 years. Before 800,000 BP, there was a repeated build-up of relatively small-to-moderate-sized ice sheets at the high northern latitudes of North America and Eurasia. During the more intense glaciations after 800,000 BP, there was repeated growth of kilometres-thick continental-scale ice sheets with much greater volumes of ice on land than in earlier glaciations.

There have been eight to ten more intense Northern Hemisphere glaciations during the past 800,000 years. The two most extensive glaciations are the most recent one, with its maximum at 20,000 BP, and the one before that, with its maximum at 130,000 BP. During each peak of these last two glaciations, massive ice sheets covered vast areas above 40–50° North in Eurasia and North America. There was also a much greater amount of glacial ice covering Antarctica.

Homo sapiens appear to have migrated out of Africa during the last extreme glaciation, sometime after 100,000 years ago. It was a time when the great ice sheets in the Northern Hemisphere were

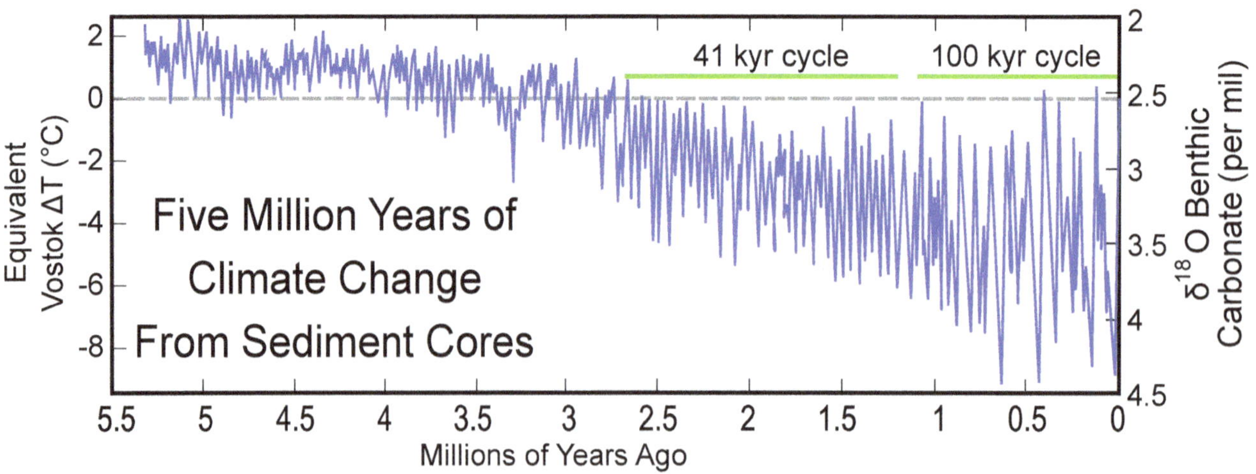

Glacials and Interglacials over the last 5 million years
Source: Wikimedia Commons – Robert A. Rohde

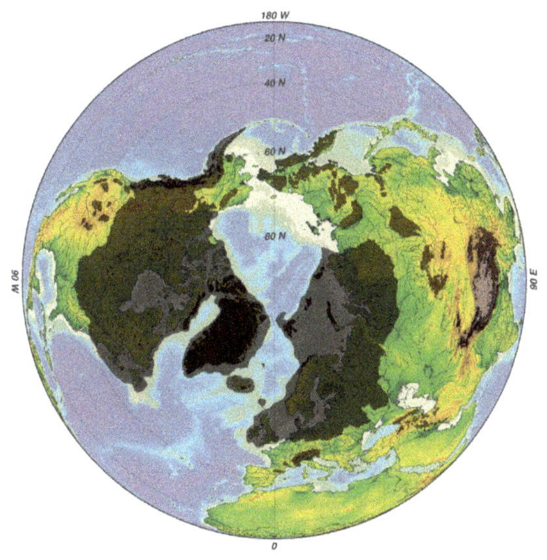

Minimum (interglacial, black) and maximum (glacial, grey) glaciation of the Northern Hemisphere

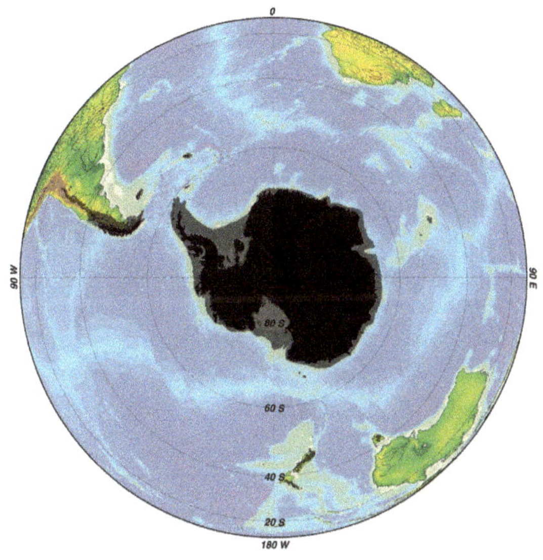

Minimum (interglacial, black) and maximum (glacial, grey) glaciation of the Southern Hemisphere
Source: Wikimedia Commons – Hannes Grobe

advancing. Our species then migrated to Europe between 50,000–40,000 BP and into the Americas at an uncertain time between 40,000–20,000 BP.

The last glacial advance peaked at 20,000 BP, called the Last Glacial Maximum or LGM. Then, the Earth began to warm, and the glaciers melted and retreated. The ice sheets continued to retreat until around 6,000 BP, and all that now remains of the great continental ice sheets are the Greenland and Antarctic ice sheets, with some smaller glaciers.

By convention, the last cold glacial period ended at approximately 12,000 BP. That time marks the beginning of the Holocene Epoch, the name of the warm interglacial period we now live in. The events of the Atlantis story begin on the Atlantic Island several thousand years after the LGM of 20,000 BP, with the Mediterranean War of 11,600 BP at the beginning of the present warmer Holocene Epoch.

The Quaternary Ice Age is unlikely to have ended, so regular glacial/interglacial cycles will probably continue for millions more years. Ice core data shows that over the last 400,000 years, several short interglacials were about as warm as the present Holocene Epoch. Each previous interglacial lasted 10,000–30,000 years and was followed by a longer 70,000–90,000-year cold glacial. In that case, the current warm interglacial that began at the LGM 20,000 years ago will likely end within 10,000 years. Then, massive glaciers will advance from the north to cover much of North America and Eurasia again.

Ross Ice Shelf, Antarctica
Source: Wikimedia Commons – lin padgham

There were many glacial/interglacial cycles during the one million years while our species' predecessors, *Homo erectus* and *Homo heidelbergensis*, had already left Africa and lived in Eurasia. The last two extreme glacial/interglacial cycles occurred since our *Homo sapiens* species evolved in Africa 200,000 years ago and would have directly affected our species. Those relatively recent changes in glaciation caused drastic environmental changes and most likely caused devastations by 'the agencies of fire and water' and probably some of Plato's 'destructions of mankind'.

Destruction by Fire

Plato (Jowett) – 'There is a story, which even you (Greeks) have preserved, that once upon a time Phaethon, the son of Helios (the Greek sun god), having yoked the steeds in his father's chariot (a symbol of the sun going across the sky), because he was not able to drive them in the path of his father, burnt up all that was upon the Earth'…'Now this has the form of a myth, but really a declination of the bodies moving in the heavens around the Earth, and a great conflagration of things upon the Earth, which recurs after long intervals; at such times those who live upon the mountains and in dry and lofty places are more liable to destruction than those who dwell by rivers or on the seashore'…'after the usual interval, the stream from heaven, like a pestilence, comes pouring down.'

Plato (Taylor) – 'For it expresses the mutation of the bodies revolving in the heavens about the Earth, and indicates that, through long periods of time, a destruction of terrestrial natures ensues from the devastations of fire.'

The Egyptian priests at Sais reject the Greeks' myth of the Sun directly burning the Earth on only one occasion in the past. Instead, they describe regular celestial events that recur at 'long intervals' and cause large fires or 'a great conflagration' on mountains and dry, elevated land. An explanation for these great fires may be recurring cycles of long wet periods followed by prolonged severe drought. During long periods of increased rainfall, forests, grasslands and other vegetation would thrive; when prolonged drought follows, the increased vegetation dries out and fuels vast fires.

Milankovitch Cycles

Regular cyclical changes in the Earth's orbit around the Sun are considered the leading cause of the many glacial/interglacial cycles during the Quaternary Ice Age. They are named Milankovitch Cycles after Milutin Milankovitch, the Serbian astronomer and mathematician who calculated them. Three cycles describe variations in the Earth's orbit: eccentricity, axial tilt, and precession. Each of these three cycles lasts tens of thousands of years.

- Eccentricity describes the shape of the Earth's orbit around the Sun. It fluctuates between a greater and a lesser elliptical shape (0 to 5% ellipticity) on a 100,000-year cycle.
- Axial tilt is the inclination of the Earth's axis to its plane of orbit around the Sun. It varies from 21.5 to 24.5 degrees over a 41,000-year cycle.
- Precession is the Earth's wobble as it spins on its axis over a 23,000-year cycle.

When they combine, the regular variations in the three Milankovitch Cycles increase or decrease the amount of the Sun's radiation that reaches the Earth's surface. These times of increased or decreased solar radiation directly influence the Earth's climate system. They drive the advance and

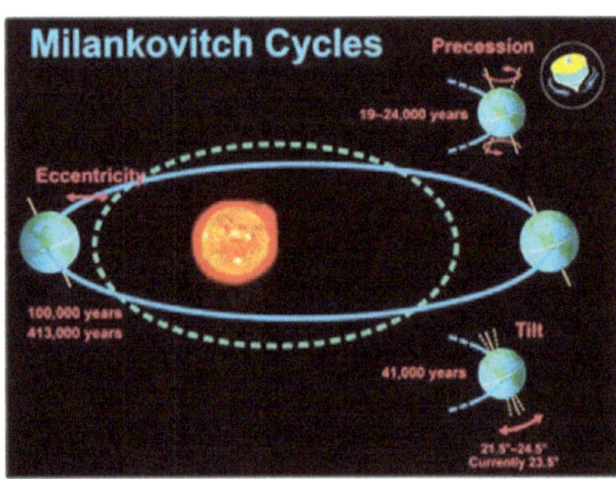

Milankovitch Cycles

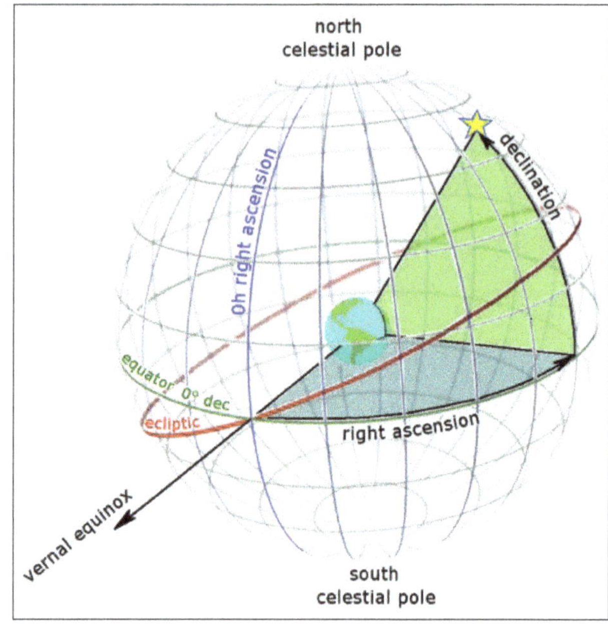

Ascension and Declination on the Celestial Sphere
Source: Wikimedia Commons – Tfr000

retreat of the Earth's ice sheets and cause significant changes in global rainfall patterns.

While speaking with Solon, the Egyptians describe 'a declination of the bodies moving in the heavens around the Earth'...'which recurs after long intervals.' The Egyptian priests associate this 'declination' with devastating fires. In astronomy, declination and ascension are two angles that locate a point on the celestial sphere. It is an imaginary sphere in the sky on which the stars and planets appear placed, with the Earth at its centre. When observers on Earth look up at the night sky, they can imagine the stars and planets projected on the celestial sphere's inside surface. So, each object seen in the sky has a particular declination and ascension.

Egyptian astronomy began in prehistoric times. Long before Solon visited Egypt, the Egyptians studied the movement of the stars and planets for

Nabta Playa Stone Circle – Reconstruction
Source: Wikimedia Commons – Raymbetz

thousands of years. Stone circles at Nabta Playa in the Nubian Desert date from the 7th millennium BP; they are the world's oldest known astronomical alignment of megaliths. The complex positioning of the stones must mean the Egyptians had been observing the movements of the stars and planets long before 7,000 BP.

Cyclical variations in the Earth's orbit and rotation during Milankovitch Cycles could be observed as changes in the stars' and planets' declination and ascension on the celestial sphere. That observation may be what the Egyptians called 'a declination of the bodies moving in the heavens around the Earth'...'which recurs after long intervals.'

Climate Fluctuations During the Last Glacial/Interglacial Cycle

The Egyptian priests at Sais tell Solon that the prehistoric Egyptians recorded important events for at least 9,000 years before Solon visited Egypt. If so, over that time and possibly for thousands of years before then, the prehistoric Egyptians may have recorded significant climate changes and their effects on the environment. They also may have observed and recorded changes in the 'declination' of various celestial bodies due to the Milankovitch Cycles that coincided with those climate changes.

While each glacial and interglacial period lasts tens of thousands of years, there are much shorter but still significant regular climate cycles within each of those periods. An interstadial is a short, warm period within a cold glacial period. A stadial is a short, cold period within a warm interglacial period. During the most recent 120,000-year-long glacial/interglacial cycle, there were many shorter cycles of warmer and colder periods. Similar episodes likely occurred in the previous 30–50 glacial/interglacial cycles during the entire 2.5 million years of the Quaternary Ice Age.

Dansgaard–Oeschger Events (D-O Events) are climate fluctuations that have occurred twenty-five times during the 100,000 years of the last cold glacial

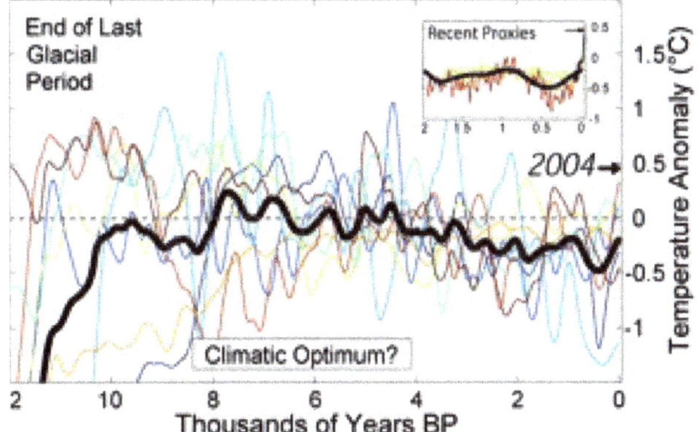

Holocene Temperature Variations
Source: Wikimedia Commons – Robert A. Rohde

period. D-O Events are rapidly warming interstadials that last a few decades, followed by gradual cooling stadials that last a few hundred years. One example was 11,500 years ago when average annual temperatures on the Greenland ice sheet increased by more than 8°C over 40 years in three steps of five years. D-O Events seem to have regular cycles around every 1,500 years and probably were also present during the many previous glacial periods.

Several climate fluctuations called Bond Events have occurred during the current Holocene warm interglacial period. Bond Events are probably the equivalent of D-O Events and have also occurred around every 1,500 years. They are characterised by a cold period followed by significant warming at the end of the cycle. Eight Bond Events have been identified since the Holocene interglacial began at around 12,000 BP.

Prehistoric cultures of *Homo sapiens* lived around the Mediterranean for tens of thousands of years and had to survive many D-O and Bond Events. More recently, several D-O and Bond Events occurred since the Last Glacial Maximum (LGM) of 20,000 BP. Each episode had a short warm and wet period followed by a longer cold and dry period. The warm, wet periods would have accelerated plant growth in grasslands and forests. The following prolonged cold, dry period would kill off much of that vegetation and produce large amounts of fuel that could feed extensive fires. Those fires may have caused 'a great conflagration of things upon the Earth', which the Egyptian priests described to Solon.

Three cold stadial periods interrupted the gradual warming between the LGM of 20,000 BP and the beginning of the Holocene Epoch at 12,000 BP. These three stadials are named after the plant Dryas, whose fossil deposits are found in higher concentrations in colder periods. The Oldest Dryas was followed by the Older Dryas, followed by the Younger Dryas. There was a warm interstadial between each of these cold stadial periods.

The Oldest Dryas lasted 3,000 years, from approximately 18,000–15,000 BP, and had a sharply defined end-point. The following Older Dryas was much shorter, starting around 14,000 BP and lasting around 300 years. Next came the Younger Dryas from 12,900–11,600 BP, the longest and most extreme stadial. It is also called the Big Freeze and was a roughly 1,300-year period of severe cold conditions and drought. A rapid return to glacial conditions in the Northern Hemisphere severely reduced temperatures within a decade. The Younger Dryas ended over just 40–50 years in three discrete steps, each lasting around five years.

If humans inhabited the Atlantic Island sometime after 20,000 BP, they would have been there during the three cold Dryas stadials. The Oldest and

Older Dryas would have been during a Palaeolithic and then Neolithic culture on the Atlantic Island. The severe climate change of the Younger Dryas between 12,900 and 11,600 BP may have coincided with a developing Atlantean Bronze Age civilisation. As the Atlantic Island was in the equatorial region of the Caribbean, it would not have experienced the extremely low temperatures of more northern areas during the three Dryas stadials.

Greece was occupied by *Homo sapiens* long before the three Dryas stadials, and they would have had a Palaeolithic culture during the Oldest and Older Dryas. In Greece, the Younger Dryas was an arid and cold period with dry summers and cold winters, but when it ended around 11,600 BP, the climate in Greece improved rapidly with higher annual rainfall and no summer drought. This improved climate coincides with Athens's supposed founding and Neolithic culture.

Like Greece, Egypt was occupied by *Homo sapiens* long before the three Dryas stadials. They also would have had a Palaeolithic culture during the Oldest and Older Dryas. During the Younger Dryas in Egypt and the rest of North Africa, the climate cooled with substantially less rainfall. If Sais were founded around 10,600 BP, it would have been during the warmer, wetter period in Egypt that followed the Younger Dryas, when early Neolithic cultures began in Egypt.

During the extreme effects of the three cold Dryas stadials after 20,000 BP, the prehistoric Egyptians would likely have experienced a climate change with each of them. However, several Bond Events after 11,600 BP also profoundly affected the climate and cultures of Egypt and Western Asia.

The 8.2 kiloyear event (Bond event 5) was a sudden decrease in global temperatures that started at 8,200 BP and lasted for the next two to four centuries. Drier conditions were notable in North Africa including Egypt, East Africa, and West Asia, especially Mesopotamia.

The 5.9 kiloyear event (Bond Event 4) occurred around 5,900 BP and was one of the most intense aridification events during the Holocene Epoch. Before the 5.9 kiloyear event, there was an extended period of fertile climate in North Africa called the Neolithic Subpluvial, with wet and rainy conditions that lasted from 9,500–6,000 BP. What is now the Sahara Desert supported a vast savannah-type ecosystem with elephants, giraffes and other grassland and woodland animals, along with some now-extinct megafauna. Those fertile conditions led to increased human settlement in the Nile Valley in Egypt and Neolithic societies in Sudan and throughout the present-day Sahara. The 5.9 kiloyear event ended the Neolithic Subpluvial and probably started the most recent desertification of the Sahara. It also triggered migration to river valleys in different regions, such as from central North Africa to the Nile Valley. That migration eventually created the complex and highly organised Egyptian societies of the 6th millennium BP.

The 4.2 kiloyear event (Bond event 3) was a severe aridification event that caused critical cultural upheaval. Drought conditions started at 4,200 BP and probably lasted an entire century. It likely caused the collapse of the Old Kingdom in Egypt and the Akkadian Empire in Mesopotamia.

Around 3,300 BP, several important Old World civilisations, including the Mycenaeans, the

Bond Event	Time (BP)	Climate Manifestation
0	~0.5kya	Little Ice Age
1	~1.4kya	Migration Period; the period of the Barbarian invasions
2	~2.8kya	Early 1st millennium BCE drought in the Eastern Mediterranean, possibly triggering the collapse of Late Bronze Age cultures
3	~4.2kya	4.2 kiloyear event; collapse of the Akkadian Empire and Egyptian Old Kingdom
4	~5.9kya	5.9 kiloyear event
5	~8.2kya	8.2 kiloyear event
6	~9.4kya	Erdalen event of glacier activity in Norway, as well as with a cold event in China
7	~10.3kya	
8	~11.1kya	Transition from the Younger Dryas to the boreal

Bond events Source: Wikipedia

Hittites, and the Egyptian New Kingdom, suddenly disintegrated in the Bronze Age Collapse. One final cause was probably a severe prolonged drought that coincided with the rapid and extended cooling period of the 2.8 kiloyear event (Bond Event 2).

For all those extreme cyclical climate changes going back many thousands of years, the Egyptians may have associated each one with cyclical changes in the observed position in the sky of stars and planets. All of the critical climate events occurred long before Solon visited Egypt. Over thousands of years, the Egyptians may have recorded those disastrous events, and the Egyptian priests in Sais described their effects to Solon. The events would have included prolonged droughts and 'a great conflagration of things upon the Earth' when vast grasslands and forests withered from a lack of rainfall and then burned out of control.

Two more Bond Events have occurred since Plato wrote the Atlantis story and are relevant to present concerns about climate change. They highlight relatively recent climate variability without any connection to industrialisation and CO_2 emissions.

The Bond Event 1 was a period of rapid cooling during what is known as the Migration Period, which lasted from 375 CE to 568 CE. It followed The Roman Warm Period, a period of unusually warm weather in Europe and the North Atlantic from approximately 250 BCE to 400 CE. During the Migration Period, widespread invasions of peoples occurred within or into Europe, notably of Germanic tribes and Huns, during and after the decline of the Western Roman Empire.

The Bond Event 0 coincides with the Little Ice Age of the 16th to 19th centuries CE; however, some experts prefer an alternative period from 1300 CE to 1850 CE. The Little Ice Age followed The Medieval Warm Period, a time of warm climate in the North Atlantic region lasting from 950 CE to 1250 CE. The Little Ice Age brought much colder winters to parts of Europe and North America, but colder conditions were also all around the Earth. Advancing glaciers destroyed farms and villages in the Swiss Alps during the mid-17th century CE. Canals and rivers in Great Britain and the Netherlands froze enough to support ice skating and winter festivals.

If the Little Ice Age or Bond Event 0 ended in the mid-19th century CE, the Earth's present climate might be the warm period before the next Bond Event. Today, what seems to be global warming may be the same as the Roman Warm Period, which lasted 150 years, or the Medieval Warm Period, which lasted 300 years. Following each of these preindustrial warming episodes, a rapid fall in global temperatures (Bond Events) continued for several hundred years until the next warm period.

Destruction by Water

Many cultures worldwide have a myth of a great flood sent by a god or gods to destroy civilisation as an act of divine retribution. Most flood myths also contain a culture hero who ensures humanity's rebirth after the devastation.

The Egyptian priests tell Solon of many prior 'deluges' on Earth. In Greece, they claim that the deluges are due to flooding rivers, whereas in Egypt, they say the water level rises but is not due to rain or flood-swollen rivers.

Plato – 'you (Solon) only mention one deluge of the Earth, when at the same time many have happened'...'when the gods purge the Earth with a deluge of water, the survivors in your country (Greece) are herdsmen and shepherds who dwell on the mountains, but those who, like you, live in cities are carried by the rivers into the sea'...'in our region (of Egypt), neither then, nor at any other time, did the waters descending from on high pour with desolation on the plains; but they are naturally impelled upwards from the bosom of the Earth.'

Unusually heavy rains or glacial ice meltwater may have flooded rivers in the distant past and led to some flood myths; other flood myths may have come from tsunamis flooding coastal areas. These short-term causes of a 'deluge' would last hours, days, weeks or months, and they might explain the flood phenomena the Egyptians describe for Greece but not Egypt. In contrast to short-term flooding, past cyclical global sea-level changes have caused extreme flooding that lasted hundreds or thousands of years. The Egyptians may have described those longer-lasting floods as deluges 'naturally impelled upwards from the bosom of the Earth'.

As already discussed, over the past 2.5 million years of the current Quaternary Ice Age, there were 30–50 glacial/interglacial cycles. Over the last 800,000 years, there were eight to ten more extreme glaciations than before. Each glaciation caused the global sea level to fall by over 100 metres within 100,000 years. Nearly all the water removed from the sea was deposited as glacial ice on land. After tens of thousands of years of glacial conditions and low sea level, a warm interglacial period eventually arrived at the end of each extreme glacial period. Then, the ice melted, and the sea level rose by over 100 metres in little more than 10,000 years.

The global sea level also fluctuated within each glacial/interglacial cycle, as seen in the next chart. During the past 120,000 years of the most recent cycle, the sea level varied by tens of metres in many shorter periods throughout much of our *Homo sapiens* species' existence. Each of these shorter periods lasted thousands of years and would have caused 'deluges', which might be the origin of various prehistoric flood myths.

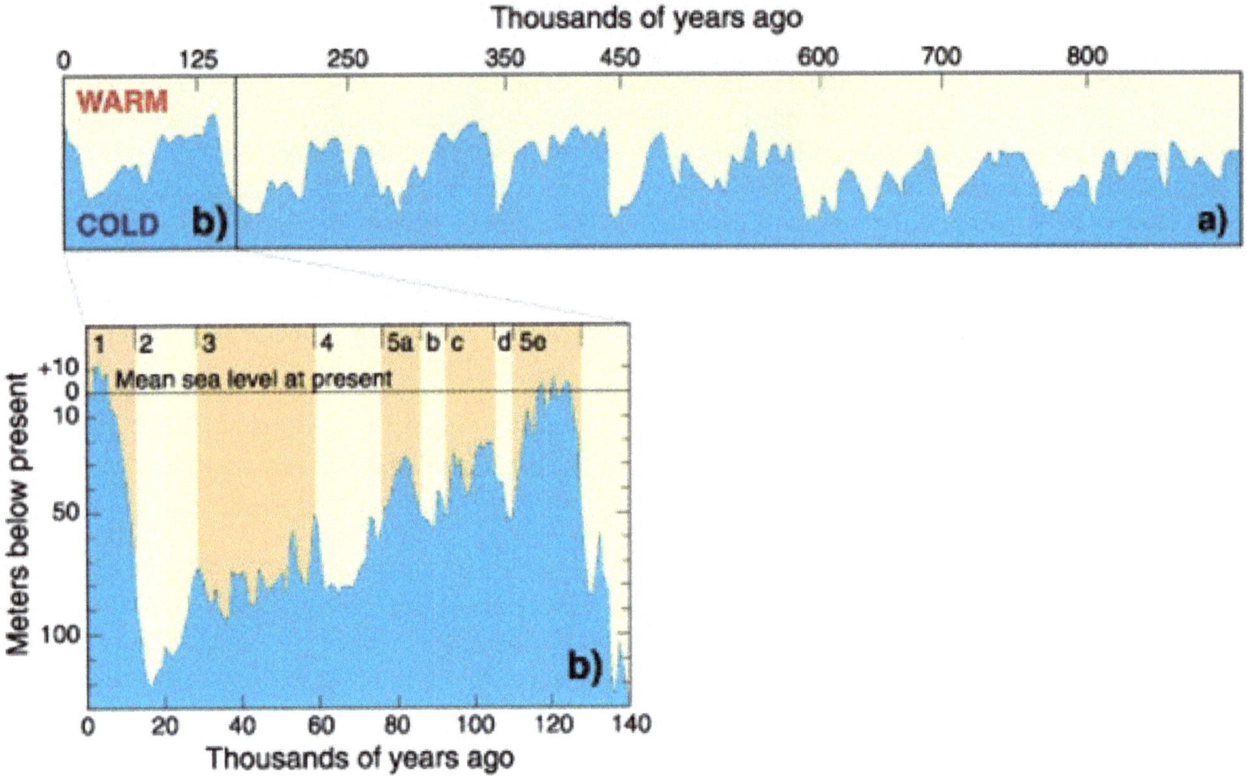

Sea Levels over the Last Million Years
Source: Wikimedia Commons – U.S. National Oceanic and Atmospheric Administration

Every metre rise or fall in sea level would have affected large areas of flat or gently sloping coastal land. When the sea level fell by tens of metres, our species could live on millions of extra square kilometres of exposed coastal land for thousands of years. When the sea level rose, those exposed areas were once again covered by metres of seawater for thousands of years, becoming uninhabitable.

The last glacial period began at around 120,000 BP, with the sea level falling 120 metres until the LGM, around 20,000 BP. After 20,000 BP, glacial ice melted, and the sea level rose at least 120 metres until it eventually stabilised to around its present level between 8,000–6,000 BP. For tens of thousands of years, our species had well-established material cultures in North Africa, Europe, and probably in the Americas. Therefore, many cultural remains in coastal areas worldwide that were once above sea level from 120,000–6,000 BP may now be up to 120 metres underwater.

The global sea level is now nearly the same as in the previous warm interglacial period 120,000 years ago, however, it did continue rising six metres higher than today. The sea level continues to rise naturally during the present warm Holocene interglacial, and it may rise to that level or possibly higher. If so, millions of square kilometres of what is now coastal land may be covered by a future 'deluge' that lasts until the next glacial period begins and the sea level falls again.

Sea Level Change Since the Last Glacial Maximum (LGM)

By the LGM of 20,000 BP, worldwide coastlines lay many kilometres beyond where they are now. Entire islands and vast plains of millions of square kilometres once existed that are now metres underwater.

After 20,000 BP, global warming melted glacial ice, and the sea level rose for the next 14,000 years until it stabilised around 6,000 BP. Still, the rate of glacial melting varied greatly over those 14,000 years, with three phases of extreme deglaciation called Meltwater Pulses. Each of those three phases caused a sudden, large, and exceptionally rapid sea level rise.

The Bolling-Allerod interstadial was a warm, moist period lasting 2,000 years, from 14,700 to 12,700 BP. It began at the end of the Oldest Dryas cold period and ended abruptly with the onset of the Younger Dryas. During the Bolling-Allerod interstadial, a combined melting of the Antarctic, Laurentide and Fennoscandian Ice Sheets produced a massive pulse of meltwater called Meltwater Pulse 1A (MWP-1A). It caused the sea level to rise more than 80 metres over 2,000 years. The highest rate of increase occurred around 13,800 BP when it rose 20 metres in only 200–500 years.

MWP-1A was followed in Antarctica and the Southern Hemisphere by a renewed cooling period called the Antarctic Cold Reversal. It started around

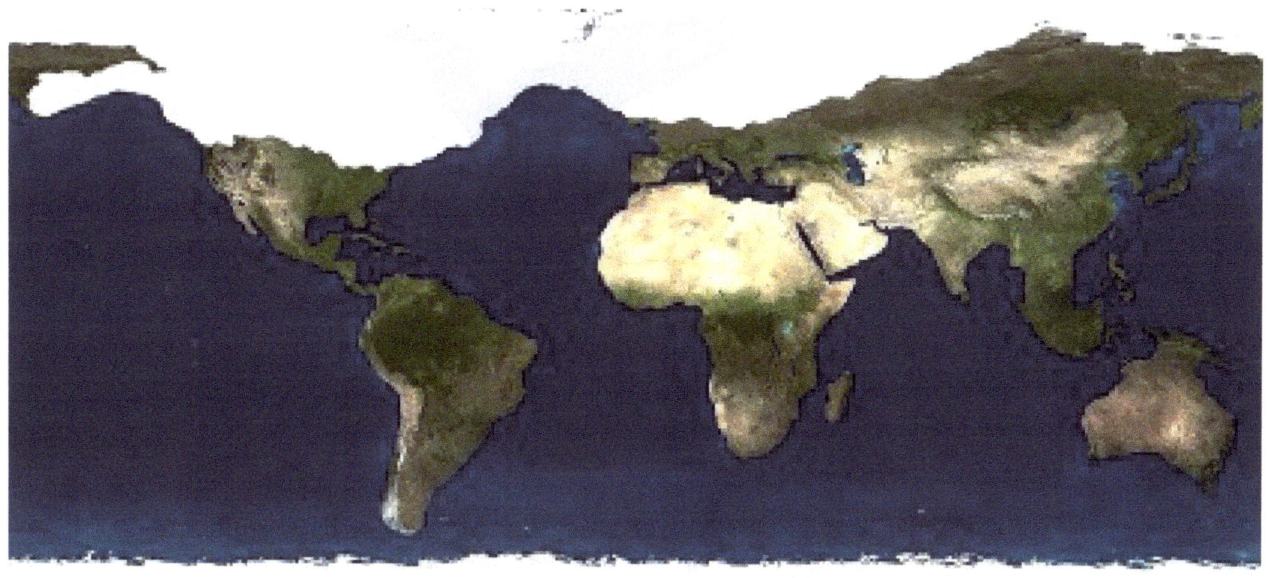

Estimated Glaciation and Coastlines at LGM 20,000 BP

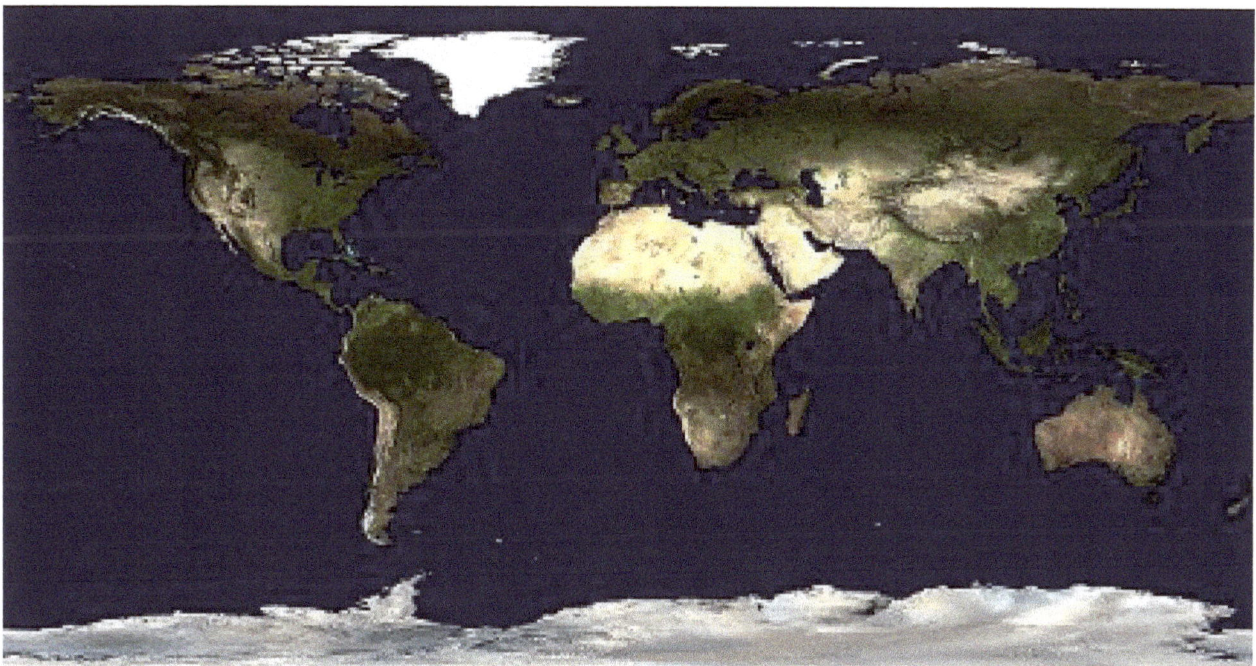

Present Glaciation and Coastlines

14,000 BP and lasted between 1,500–2,000 years. During that colder period, sea levels probably would have been stable or dropped slightly. This period of climate stability and steady sea level between 14,000–12,000 BP would likely have coincided with the early development of Atlantean civilisation.

The onset of the present warmer Holocene Epoch around 12,000 BP has been linked to the rapid global sea level rise due to Meltwater Pulse 1B (MWP-1B), which occurred just after the end of the Younger Dryas cold period. Over almost 3,000 years, from 11,500–8,800 BP, MWP-1B produced a 30-metre sea level increase, with rates of up to 2.5 metres a century. This period coincides with the Mediterranean War's aftermath and Atlantean civilisation's decline. It also coincides with the beginning of known Neolithic cultures in Egypt, around the Aegean, and in the Americas.

Meltwater Pulse 1C (MWP-1C) at around 8,200–7,600 BP was a relatively minor Meltwater Pulse correlating with Bond event 5. It was probably due to the final collapse of the Laurentide Ice Sheet of north-eastern North America and the catastrophic drainage of Agassiz and Ojibway glacial lakes. The initial meltwater pulse caused an estimated 0.5–4.0-metre rise in sea level.

Of the total 120-metre increase in global sea level after the LGM 20,000 years ago, around sixty metres occurred before the Holocene Epoch began around 12,000 BP; the remaining 60-metre increase occurred after 12,000 BP. At the beginning of the Holocene, the Laurentide Ice Sheet of

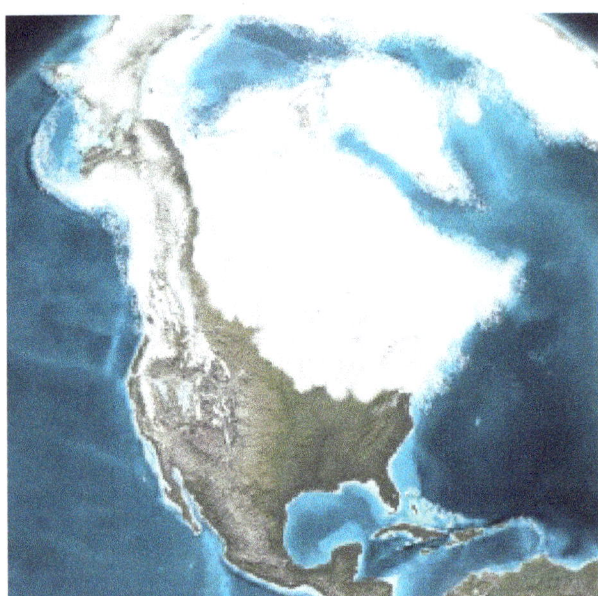

From W–E: the Cordilleran, Laurentide, Greenland and Fennoscandian Ice Sheets *Source: Ron Blakey, NAU*

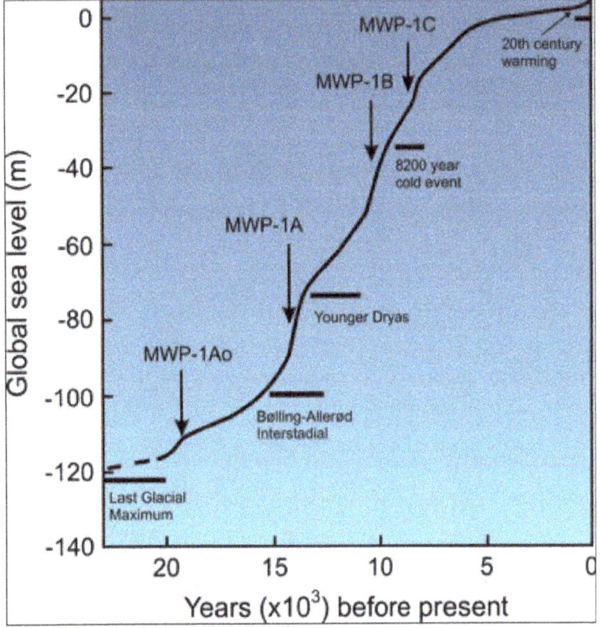

Sea level Rise since the LGM
Source: Wikimedia Commons – Vivien Gomez, NASA

North America was several times the size of the present Greenland Ice Sheet, but it had gone by around 7,000 BP. The Fennoscandian Ice Sheet also disappeared before 9,000 BP, and there would have been additional melting of the Greenland and Antarctic Ice Sheets. Most glacial melting ended by 6,000 BP; since then, the Earth's sea level has gradually approached today's level.

If Atlantean civilisation peaked at around 11,600 BP, it would have had to survive sixty metres of sea level increase over the next 5,000 years. Even without the subsidence of the Atlantic Island, the rapidly rising sea level would have inundated sizeable areas of the island and surrounding coastal lands in the Americas.

The global sea level has been rising at an average rate of 1.8 mm per year since 1961 and 3.1 mm per year since 1993. The main contributors to this rise are melting glaciers and ice caps, and thermal expansion of the ocean. Compared to recent changes, the average sea level rise between 20,000 BP and 6,000 BP was 8.6 mm per year. But this average does not indicate the enormous surges in sea level during the three Meltwater Pulses.

Even though all that remains of the continental ice sheets are the Greenland and Antarctic Ice Sheets, if more glacial ice does melt, the sea level will continue to rise above its present level. Estimates are that if it entirely melted, the Antarctic Ice Sheet would contribute more than 60 metres of sea level rise, while the Greenland Ice Sheet would add another 7 metres. That extreme melting will not happen because the Quaternary Ice Age will continue for probably millions of years. So, apart from a few more metres of sea level rise similar to the previous interglacial, the next glacial episode will advance glacial ice and lower the sea level.

Ice Age Sea levels in the Mediterranean and Aegean

When the sea level around 20,000 BP was at least 120 metres lower, the amount of land available in the Mediterranean for humans to live on was much

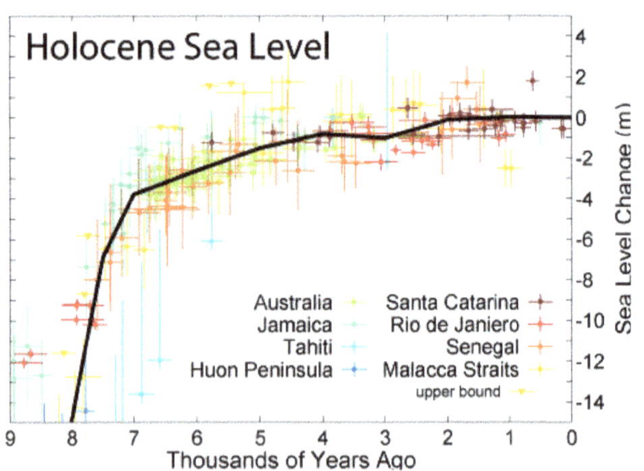

Holocene Sea level
Source: Wikimedia Commons – Robert A. Rohde

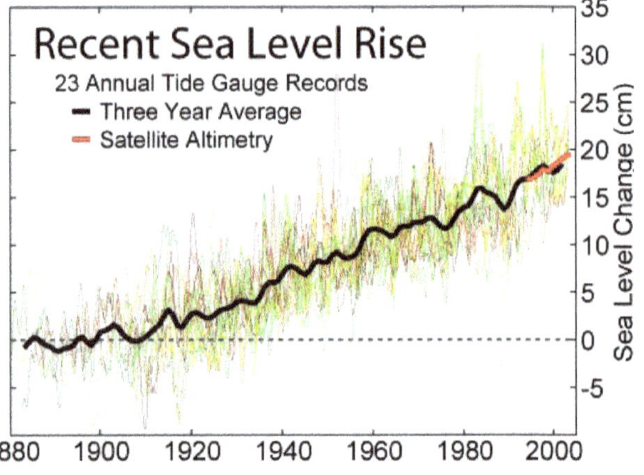

Recent Sea Level Rise
Source: Wikimedia Commons – Robert A. Rohde

different to now. There were many broad, fertile coastal plains, larger islands, and some land bridges between islands and the mainland.

By the time of the Mediterranean War around 11,600 BP, the sea level had risen by 50–60 metres, but it was still 50–60 metres below its present level. Apart from the Athenians, Plato states that other tribes of 'Hellenes' and 'barbarians' fought in the war against the Atlanteans, but what remains of the *Critias* dialogue does not mention their names or territories. Many prehistoric Aegean cultures other than the Athenians may once have existed on the large coastal areas that are now underwater.

There were broad, well-watered coastal plains over much of the northern Aegean. The islands around Attica, such as Aegina, Salamis and Euboea, were part of the Greek mainland. The Peloponnese and the mainland were connected, with no Corinthian Gulf separating them. The present Cycladic Islands joined to form the single large island of Cycladia, three-quarters of which is now submerged. The Bosporus and Hellespont had not yet formed, so the Black Sea was not connected to the Mediterranean.

Around 11,600 BP, the sea level was 50–60 metres lower on Egypt's Mediterranean coast. It would have extended many kilometres out to sea, with extensive fertile plains now submerged. The Nile Delta began to form because of the 60-metre increase in sea level after 20,000 BP. Currently, the Nile Delta has an average elevation of approximately one metre above sea level within 30 kilometres of the Mediterranean coast. So, even a few metres change in sea level would have severely impacted the Nile Delta's habitable land, while each of the Meltwater Pulses would have drowned thousands of square kilometres of land.

Present Coastline of the Aegean
Source: Google Earth

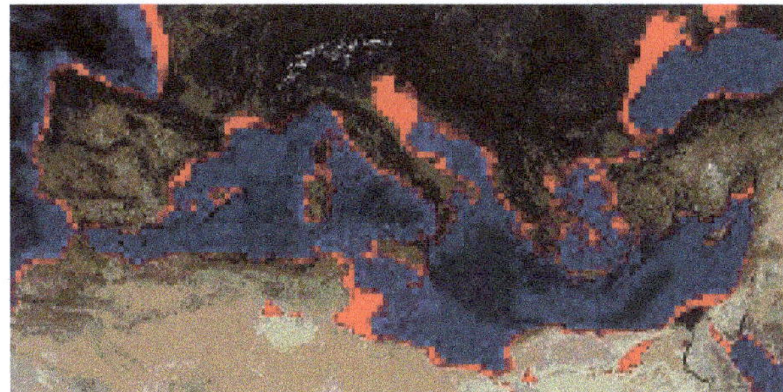

Aegean Coastline (Red) at LGM 20,000 BP
Source: From Simon Fitch and Ben Geary

Plato states that the city of Sais was established around 10,600 BP, 1,000 years after the Mediterranean War of 11,600 BP. Still, Plato also states the prehistoric Egyptians took part in the Mediterranean War as Athens' allies. Those Egyptians must have come from settlements more ancient than Sais and possibly closer to the Mediterranean coast. As the sea level rose, they would have abandoned those older settlements to establish newer ones further inland. They may have had to resettle several times over thousands of years until the sea level stabilised around 6,000 BP. By then, the Egyptians could create more permanent settlements, with no further inundations 'impelled upwards from the bosom of the Earth' due to the rising sea level.

The present archaeological site of Sais that Solon visited in the 6th century BCE is sixty kilometres inland from the Mediterranean coast of Egypt. If prehistoric Sais were located at this same site and founded in 10,600 BP when the sea level was many metres lower, it would have been much further inland than sixty kilometres. Another possibility is that the present site of Sais is a more recent resettlement after the rising sea level inundated a much older original city called Sais.

Deluges in the Mediterranean

Plato – 'In the first place you (Solon) remember a single deluge (of Deucalion) only, but there were many previous ones'…'prior, O Solon, to that mighty deluge (of Deucalion) which we have just mentioned, a city of Athenians existed'…'a single night of excessive rain washed away the earth and laid bare the rock; at the same time there were earthquakes, and then occurred the extraordinary inundation, which was the third before the great destruction of Deucalion'…'many and mighty deluges happened in that period of nine thousand years (from the war with Atlantis up to Solon's time).'

The Egyptian priests state there were many deluges in the remote past, but they were unknown to

Present Coastline of the Aegean
Source: Google Earth

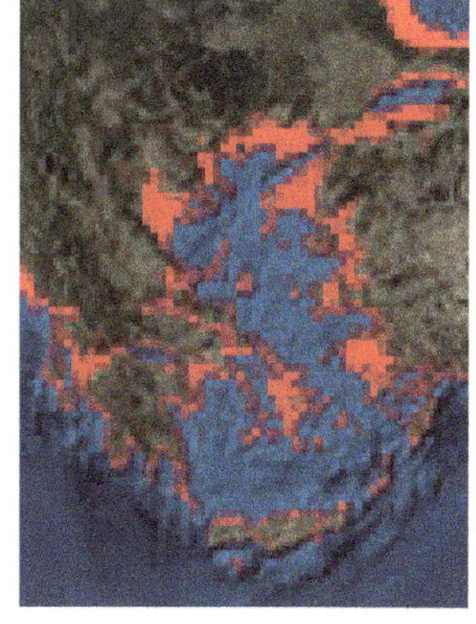

Aegean Coastline (Red) at LGM 20,000 BP
Source: From Simon Fitch and Ben Geary

the Greeks of Solon's time in the 6th century BCE. Heavy rain and earthquakes destroyed the prehistoric Athenian Acropolis Hill at some unspecified time after the Mediterranean War of 11,600 BP. Then, that destruction was followed by an 'extraordinary inundation', which may have caused further devastation in what remained of Athens and the coastal areas of Greece and Egypt. In addition to that 'extraordinary inundation', numerous other 'mighty deluges' were said to have occurred later.

The Ages of Man

In Greek mythology, the Ages of Man are the stages of human existence on Earth. Virtually all the Greeks of Solon's time in the 6th century BCE would have believed these stages were fact; so would most Greeks of Plato's time in the 4th century BCE. As Plato does not include any of the Greeks' Ages of Man in his Atlantis story, it further proves that the story is original and started with the Egyptians since they did not believe in that feature of Greek mythology.

The first surviving account of the Ages of Man comes from the *Works and Days*, written by the Greek poet Hesiod in the 7th century BCE. Though none of the Ages of Man directly relate to any events of the Atlantis story, they may represent four possible destructions of prehistoric civilisations in Greece and its surroundings long before the time of Solon and Plato.

- The Golden Age – The Golden Age is the only age within the rule of the primordial god Cronus, before the ascendancy of the Olympian gods. These humans were moulded from the Earth by the Titan Prometheus and lived 'among the gods, and freely mingled with them'. Peace and harmony prevailed during this age, and humans did not have to work to feed themselves as the Earth provided abundant food. They lived to a very old age but with a youthful appearance and eventually died peacefully. Their spirits lived on as the 'guardians' of mortals.
- The Silver Age – The Silver Age and every age that follows fall within the rule of the Olympian god Zeus (Cronus' son and successor). Men in the Silver Age lived under the dominion of their mothers for one hundred years. They lived only a short time as grown adults and spent that time in strife with one another. During this Age, 'men refused to worship the gods', so Zeus destroyed them for their impiety. After death, humans of this age became 'blessed spirits' of the underworld.
- The Bronze Age – Men of the Bronze Age were hardened and tough, as war was their purpose and passion. Zeus created these humans out of the ash tree. Their armour was forged of bronze, as were their homes and tools. The men of this Age were undone by their violent ways and left no named spirits; instead, they dwell in the 'dank house of Hades'. This Age ended with the Flood of Deucalion.
- The Heroic Age – The Heroic Age is the only age that does not correspond with any metal and is the only age that is better than the one before. Humans were created through the actions of Deucalion and Pyrrha, the only survivors following the Flood of Deucalion. In this period, 'men lived with noble demigods and heroes.' This race of humans died and went to Elysium, a paradise on the western edge of the Earth, by the stream of Okeanos, the single encircling ocean. The heroes of this Age were the subjects of Homer's *Odyssey* and *Iliad*.
- The Iron Age – The Greeks of Solon and Plato's time believed they lived in the Iron Age. During this age, humans live an existence of toil and misery. Children dishonour their parents; brother fights with brother, and the social contract between guest and host (*xenia*) is forgotten. During this age, might makes right, and bad men use lies to be thought good. At the height of this age, humans no longer feel shame or indignation at wrongdoing; 'the gods will have completely forsaken humanity', and 'there will be no help against evil.'

Ancient Greek Flood Myths and the 'extraordinary inundation'

Greek mythology describes a series of three great floods. They were the Flood of Ogyges, the Flood of Deucalion, and the Flood of Dardanus. Two of these floods ended two of the mythical Ages of Man: the Flood of Ogyges ended the Silver Age; the Flood of Deucalion ended the Bronze Age.

The Egyptian priests mention the 'extraordinary inundation' that occurred sometime after the war of 11,600 BP and the destruction of the prehistoric Acropolis Hill in Athens. They state it was 'the third before the great destruction of (the Flood of) Deucalion' or two inundations before the Flood of Ogyges. As the Flood of Ogyges was the first mythical inundation known to the Greeks of Plato's time, they knew nothing of those two prior inundations. Again, it is doubtful Plato fabricated this part of the Atlantis story.

Meltwater Pulse-1A (MWP 1A) occurred from 14,300–12,800 BP, so it is far too early to be the 'extraordinary inundation' after 11,600 BP. MWP 1A was followed by Meltwater Pulse-1B (MWP-1B), which lasted almost 3,000 years from 11,500–8,800 BP. So MWP-1B was at the right time for the Egyptian priests' 'extraordinary inundation'.

Although MWP-1B caused a total 30-metre sea level increase over 3,000 years, there were peak rates of rise of up to 2.5 metres in a century. In a short time of decades or centuries, those peak increases during MWP-1B would have inundated vast areas of coastal land in Egypt, so the prehistoric Egyptians would likely have considered them 'deluges'. If there were two unusually large short-term peaks in MWP 1B between 11,500–8,800 BP, it might explain the two deluges before the Flood of Ogyges that were unknown to the Greeks. Specifically, those two deluges may have been the Egyptians' 'extraordinary inundation' and the unnamed deluge that followed it.

The Flood of Ogyges

The Flood of Ogyges is the first flood in Greek mythology. It occurred in the time of Ogyges, a mythical primaeval ruler in Ancient Greece. Some ancient sources considered it a local flood associated with Boeotia or Attica in Greece, whereas others claimed it covered the entire world. It possibly coincides with the flooding and loss of vast areas of coastal land on mainland Greece and the large island of Cycladia on the Cycladic Plateau in the Aegean, the high points of which now form the much smaller Cyclades Islands.

The source of the Ogyges Flood myth could be another large short-term peak in MWP 1B. If that was the source, it must have occurred before MWP 1B ended around 8,800 BP. Otherwise, Meltwater Pulse-1C (MWP-1C) may have been the source of the myth. Even though MWP-1C was relatively small, with an estimated sea level rise of only 0.5–4.0 metres between 8,200–7,600 BP, that would still have been enough to cover hundreds or thousands of square kilometres of low-lying coastal land around the Mediterranean. It would also have been considered a 'deluge' by the prehistoric Greeks and Egyptians.

The Flood of Deucalion

The next flood in Greek myth is that of Deucalion. In the myth, Zeus was angered by the Pelasgians' hubris (extreme pride), so he decided to end the mythical Bronze Age. He created a deluge so the rivers ran in torrents, the sea flooded the coastal plain and washed everything clean. With the aid of his Titan father Prometheus, Deucalion built a chest and used it to save himself and his wife, Pyrrah. After floating in the chest for nine days and nights, they reached land and created a new race of humans.

The historical Greek Bronze Age starts at the beginning of the 3rd millennium BCE and covers the duration of the Minoan and Mycenaean civilisations in the Aegean. It ends during the 12th century BCE with the Bronze Age Collapse of several important civilisations in the Eastern Mediterranean. When combined, the Greeks' mythical Bronze and Heroic Ages were part of the historical Bronze Age.

The eruption of the Aegean island of Thera in the mid-2nd millennium BCE generated a megatsunami that was 35–150 metres high. It devastated the north coast of Crete 110 kilometres away and may have severely affected the Bronze Age Minoan civilisation on Crete. Also, the megatsunami would have devastated any Bronze Age coastal cities and towns around the Western Mediterranean. These extreme catastrophic events may have given rise to the Greeks' myth of Deucalion and the end of the mythical Bronze Age, which could also mark the end of the Minoan civilisation. The mythical Heroic Age probably ended with the rapid decline of the Mycenaean civilisation during the Bronze Age Collapse in the 12th century BCE.

The Flood of Dardanus

The third mythical Greek flood is that of Dardanus, a son of Zeus and Electra. After killing his brother Iasius, Dardanus fled from Arcadia in the central Peloponnesus and colonised a land in the north-east Aegean Sea. The Flood of Dardanus covered that land, and the mountain on which Dardanus and his family survived formed the island of Samothrace.

Dardanus later left Samothrace and went to Anatolia. He settled on Mount Ida in north-west Anatolia, where he founded the city of Dardania. Dardanus' grandson Tros eventually moved from the mountains down to a large plain and built a city named Troy after him. The region surrounding Troy became known as the Troad.

Hisarlik is the modern name for the site of ancient Troy, which was also called Ilion in ancient

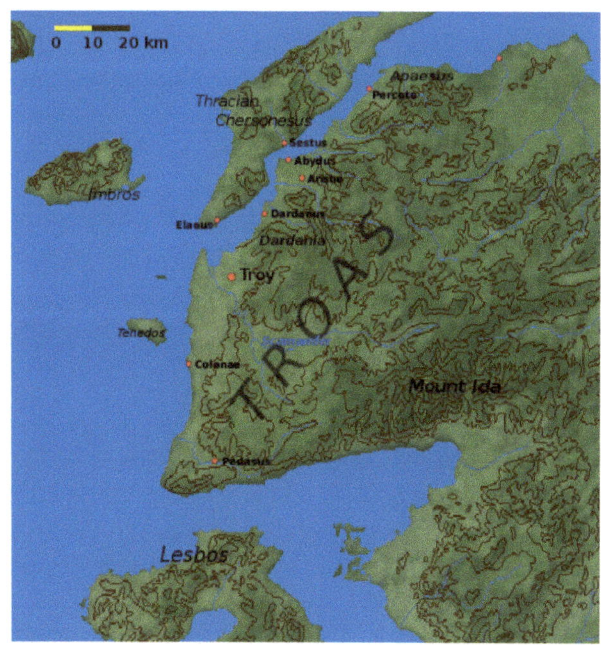

The Troad, N-W Anatolia
Source: Wikimedia Commons – D. Bachmann

Dardanelles Strait (Yellow), Bosphorus (Red)
Source: Wikimedia Commons – Interiot

times. The archaeological site of Troy has nine distinct layers, with the earliest remains from the 5th millennium BP. As there was a thriving Neolithic culture throughout Anatolia at least as early as the 9th millennium BP, earlier settlements at or near the site of Troy may have left no remains.

If the Dardanus myth is based on fact and Dardanus' grandson Tros founded the city of Troy, it must have been before the 5th millennium BP at the latest, placing it before the beginning of the Bronze Age. If so, the Flood of Dardanus may be another myth based on MWP-1C between 8,200–7,600 BP, possibly the same event as the Flood of Ogyges.

Apart from MWP-1C, there was a more local cause of flooding in the north-east Aegean between 9,500–7,000 BP. During deglaciation after 20,000 BP, the Aegean sea level rose over the strait of the Hellespont or Dardanelles (named after Dardanus) from 11,600–9,500 BP. The rising sea level caused seawater to flow from the Aegean, through the Dardanelles, and into the Sea of Marmara.

Then, at about 9,500 BP, glacial meltwater that had accumulated in the Black Sea broke through the Bosphorus into the Sea of Marmara. It developed into a high southward flow through the Dardanelles into the Aegean Sea. This high outflow persisted for around 1,500 years until around 7,000 BP; it may have caused local flooding in the north-east Aegean, which led to the myth of the Flood of Dardanus.

'Many Great Deluges'

Plato – 'Many great deluges have taken place during the nine thousand years (since the war with Atlantis)'.

For a few thousand years after 11,600 BP, MWP 1B and MWP 1C may have had several short periods of rapid sea level increase. These brief episodes could have occurred within tens or hundreds rather than thousands of years. Any individual episode would have flooded many square kilometres of coastal lands and settlements, so its inhabitants considered it a 'great deluge'.

As well as the Meltwater Pulses, the prehistoric Egyptians may have recorded deluges caused by tsunamis, which can devastate coastal lands in hours instead of hundreds or thousands of years. These shorter tsunami episodes may account for some of the 'many great deluges' the priests describe to Solon.

Other than the megatsunami caused by the Thera eruption, many great tsunamis probably occurred in the Mediterranean and Aegean in prehistoric times. Still, the rise in sea level before 6,000 BP would have covered any evidence of them. One prominent known example is a volcanic avalanche in Sicily in about 8,000 BP. It triggered an underwater mudslide and a megatsunami with wave heights of up to 40 metres and maximum speeds of up to 700 kilometres per hour. Those huge waves would have crossed the entire Eastern Mediterranean in three and a half hours, striking the coastal areas of Greece and Egypt before finally reaching the coasts of the Levant.

The Aegean region is tectonically active and prone to earthquakes and tsunamis. As an indication of how frequently they occur, numerous tsunamis were reported in the Aegean in historical times. Two tsunamis were from 1628–550 BCE, 14 from 550 BCE–300 CE, 29 from 300–1550 CE, 37 from 1550–1845 CE, and 77 from 1845 CE to the present.

Tsunami after a magnitude 9.0 earthquake, Japan 2011
Source: AAP Photo/Kyodo News

CHAPTER 11

The Hydraulic Hypothesis – The Earth's Internal Hydraulic System

As already described in Chapter 10, during the past 2.5 million years of the current Quaternary Ice Age, many great cyclical changes occurred in the worldwide sea level. When the sea level fell, almost all of the water that left the Earth's oceans became kilometres-thick glacial ice sheets that covered the landmasses of North America, Eurasia, and Antarctica. A novel geological hypothesis – the Hydraulic Hypothesis – describes how those massive changes in glacial ice thickness could have caused extreme geological changes on parts of the Earth's surface, including the Atlantic Island.

Plato – '(the Atlantic Island) when afterwards (after 11,600 BP) sunk by an earthquake' and 'disappeared in the depths of the sea.'

If Plato's geographical descriptions are accurate, the Caribbean region is the only possible site for his 'Atlantic island'. But the most challenging problem with a Caribbean location is explaining the Atlantic Island's initial existence and later destruction. The Hydraulic Hypothesis radically departs from accepted geological theories, but it could explain the creation and sinking of the Atlantic Island.

Plato describes a diverse collection of plants and animals on the Atlantic Island. His account must mean the Atlantic Island was above sea level long enough for many complex life forms to colonise it and thrive there. At the least, such a process would have taken tens of thousands of years. Plato also states that the Atlantic Island 'sank' under the sea sometime after 11,600 BP, so a 'deluge' or flood alone did not destroy it. In that case, the Atlantic Island submerged relatively quickly, within a few thousand years after 11,600 BP.

In order to understand the Hydraulic Hypothesis, it is essential to know a few basic facts about the Earth's geological structure. The Earth has several

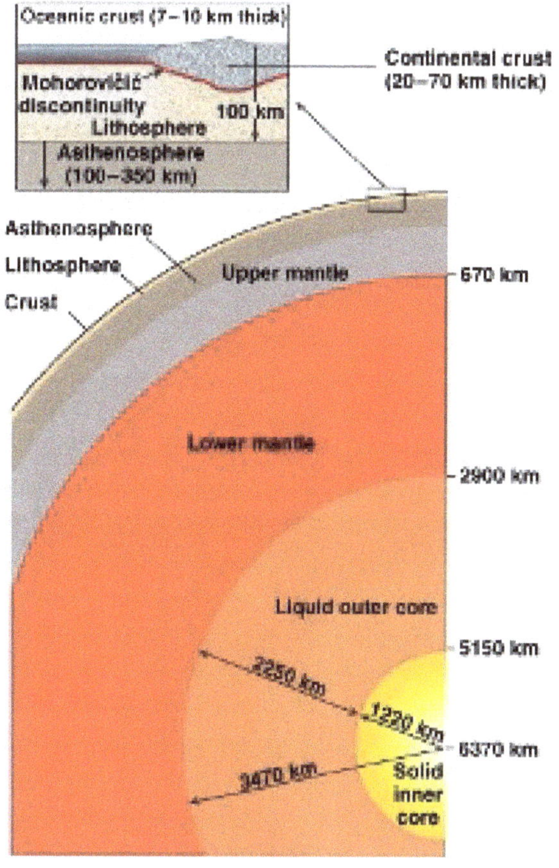

The Earth's Internal Structure
Source: Harold L. Levin

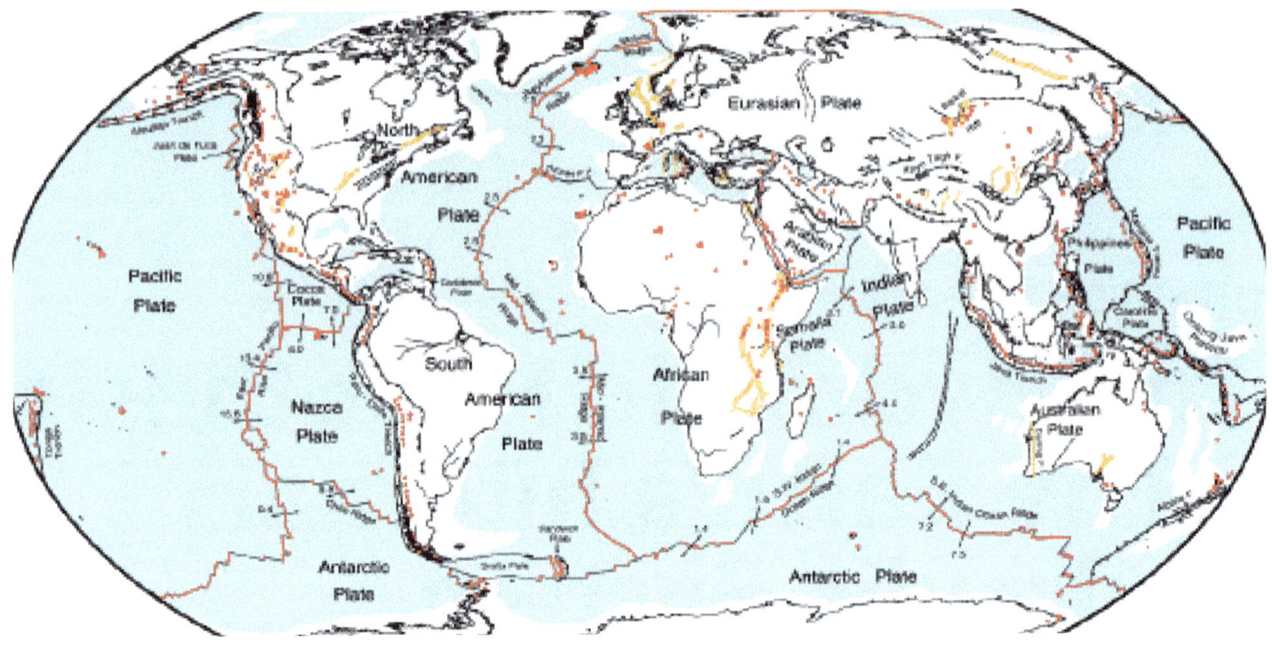

Major Tectonic Plates
Source: NASA

outer layers surrounding a solid inner Core. The solid outermost shell of the Earth is called the Lithosphere, which is the rigid Crust and the hard upper portion of the Mantle. The layer located directly below the Lithosphere is the Asthenosphere, which contains the more fluid parts of the Mantle.

The solid outer layer of the Lithosphere is divided into many large rigid pieces called tectonic plates. There are seven primary and eight secondary tectonic plates, plus dozens of smaller tertiary microplates. All the tectonic plates float on the fluid Asthenosphere beneath them, much like a solid iceberg floats on water. Depending on their location on the Earth, the tectonic plates consist of two main Lithosphere types: a thin Oceanic Crust under the oceans or a thicker Continental Crust of the Earth's continents.

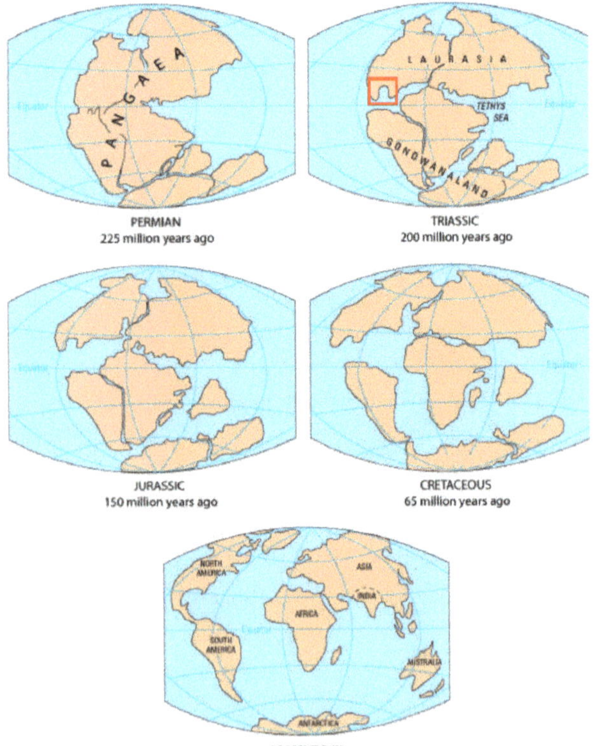

Continental Drift - The Breakup of Pangaea
Red square is the early Gulf of Mexico
Source: USGS

The accepted geological theory of plate tectonics describes how the Earth's tectonic plates move horizontally in a process called continental drift. Some plates move toward each other, some move away from each other, whereas others slide sideways along each other. The plates move slowly at speeds of between zero to ten centimetres per year.

In geological processes that take many millions of years, the slow horizontal motion of the plates creates stresses at the boundaries between the plates. The conventional view is that this slow sideways plate movement has caused almost all vertical plate movements over millions of years. These vertical movements can be either up or down and are assumed to cause all mountain-building and oceanic trench formation along plate boundaries.

Another known cause of vertical plate movement is cyclical changes in the thickness of the glacial ice sheets on ice-covered plates. During the past 2.5 million years, kilometres-thick ice sheets repeatedly covered tens of millions of square kilometres of land on North America, Eurasia and Antarctica. Geologists know that the weight of the overlying glacial ice at the Earth's northern and southern poles can push down the landmasses by hundreds of metres.

What has not been considered up to now is a possible connection between the vertical movement of those plates covered by ice and the vertical movement of distant plates not covered by ice. The Hydraulic Hypothesis describes such a link, but it

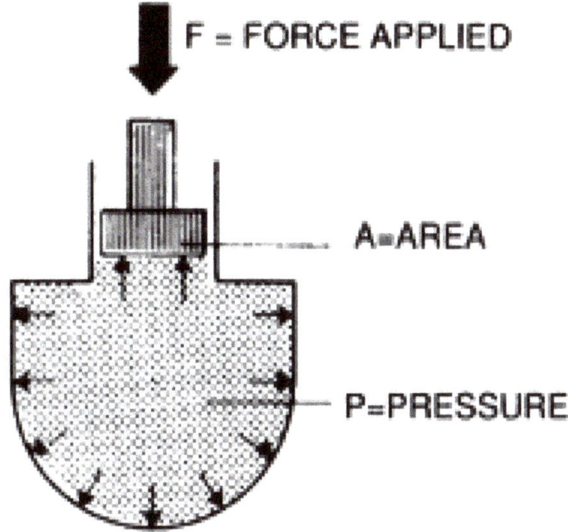

Pascal's Law

is an alternative and so far unproven concept of how the Earth's surface structure behaves. It does not replace continental drift; instead, the Hydraulic Hypothesis is an additional geological mechanism entirely separate from continental drift. It is a mechanical cause for large and relatively rapid vertical tectonic plate movements very different from continental drift's extremely slow horizontal movements.

The Hydraulic Hypothesis describes a natural hydraulic system below Earth's surface. This hydraulic system transfers forces from ice-covered plates to distant plates not covered by ice. The physical basis for the Hydraulic Hypothesis is Pascal's Law, which is the basis of all engineered hydraulic systems where pressurised hydraulic fluid powers machinery. Pascal's Law is also known as the *Principle of Transmission of Fluid Pressure*; it states: 'Pressure exerted anywhere in a confined incompressible fluid is transmitted equally in all directions throughout the fluid such that the pressure ratio remains the same.'

Pascal's Law applies to any mechanical hydraulic system where an 'incompressible' hydraulic fluid transmits energy from one point to another. In a hydraulic system, the pressure is the same throughout the closed or 'confined' system. Because the hydraulic fluid is 'incompressible', it can instantly transmit power from one part of the system to another. Commonly used hydraulic fluids are usually based on mineral oil or water.

In the accompanying hydraulic system diagram, when either the small or large piston is pushed down, it displaces an incompressible fluid such as oil. For a given distance of movement, the small piston displaces a smaller amount of fluid than the large piston. So, the small piston must move down a greater distance for the large piston to move up significantly. In contrast, the large piston needs to move down a lesser distance for the small piston to move up significantly.

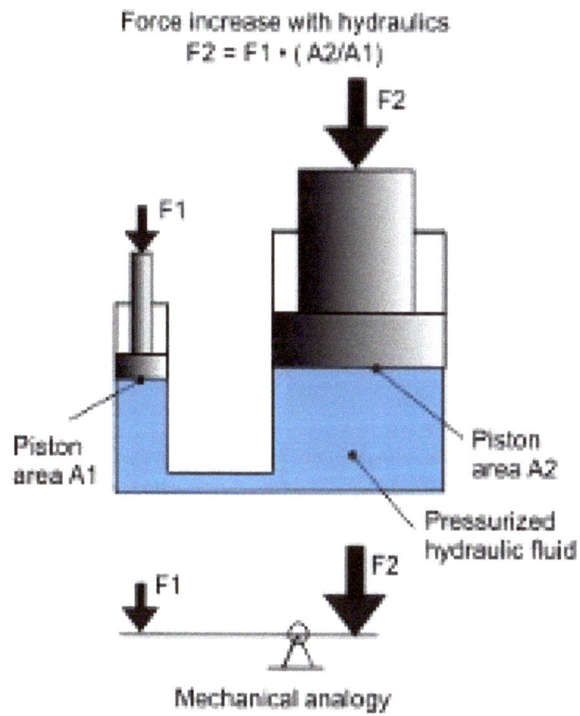

A Hydraulic System

A simple mechanical analogy for the Hydraulic Hypothesis is an automobile's hydraulic brake system, where rigid pipes transmit the pressure in a master cylinder to remote wheel cylinders. Incompressible brake fluid completely fills the closed system and immediately transmits hydraulic pressure evenly between all of the cylinders.

A foot pushing on the brake pedal causes a force on the piston in the master cylinder and pressure on the brake fluid. In line with Pascal's Law, hydraulic pressure is transmitted evenly throughout the sealed, continuous brake system. All of the cylinders experience the same pressure, regardless of whether the pipes that link them are of different lengths. The transmitted pressure forces the piston in each wheel cylinder to act on the brake shoe, which slows the

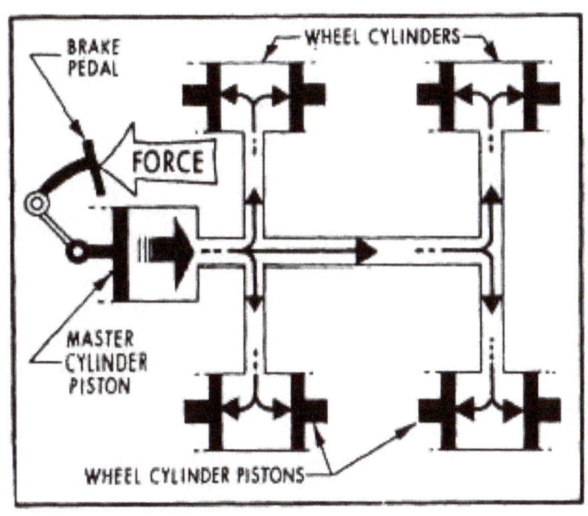

Hydraulic Brake System

vehicle. Releasing the push on the master cylinder releases the force on the wheel cylinders and releases the brakes.

It is essential to understand that hydraulic systems do not need an actual movement of fluid between the large cylinder and the smaller cylinders. Because pressure is 'transmitted equally in all directions' throughout the closed system, the fluid itself does not need to move from any one cylinder to another; only pressure is transmitted.

During each of the many past cold glacial periods of the current Quaternary Ice Age, the enormous weight of glacial ice on land caused parts of the Earth's solid Lithosphere to bend downward. That downward movement forced the underlying fluid Mantle material in the Asthenosphere to flow away from the ice-loaded region. The glaciers retreated when the climate eventually warmed at the end of the glacial period. The weight was removed from the ice-loaded Lithosphere, allowing the land's uplift, or rebound. The fluid Mantle material then flowed back under the deglaciated area. The amount of rebound depends on the local ice load so that the land may rebound several hundred metres near the centre of the ice load.

The Hydraulic Hypothesis proposes that the most fluid part of the Asthenosphere behaves like the 'confined incompressible fluid' in a hydraulic system. By using the hydraulic brake analogy, the master cylinder is the combined glaciated tectonic plates of Antarctica, North America, and Eurasia; the wheel cylinders are distant unglaciated tectonic plates, and the brake fluid is in the fluid Asthenosphere. According to Pascal's Law, changes in the downward pressure of glacial ice on the master cylinder tectonic plates should transmit that

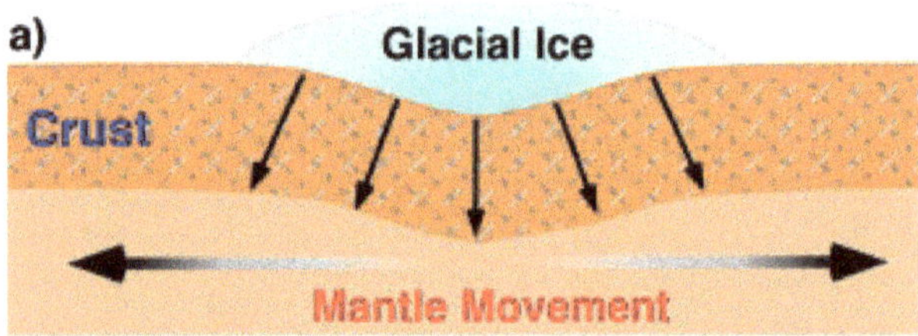

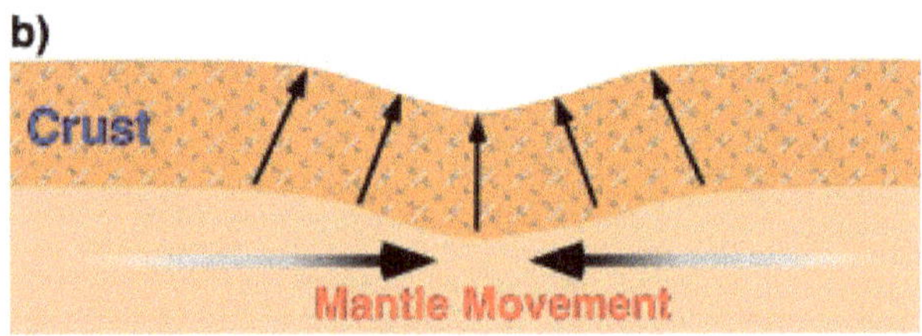

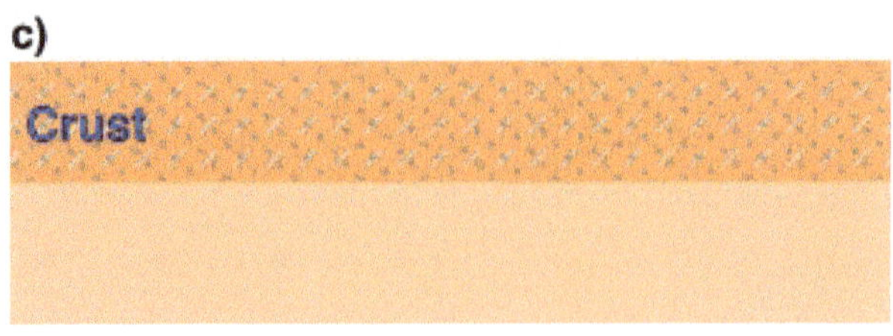

Mantle Flow and Ice Load

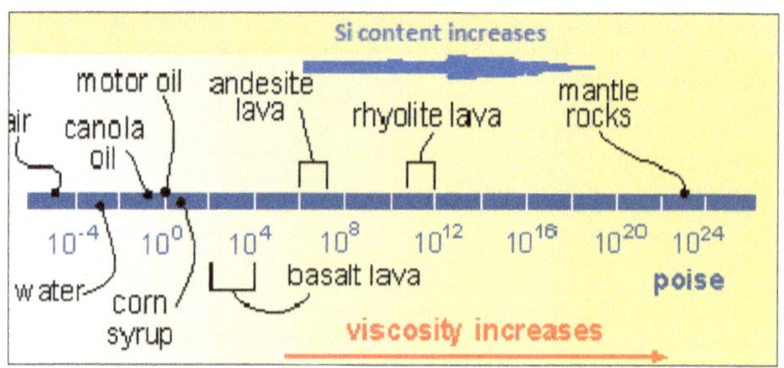

Viscosity of Fluids
Source: University of British Columbia

Visualisation of a 3D network
Source: Wikimedia Commons – From the Opte Project

pressure change instantaneously through the brake fluid in the Asthenosphere to the remote wheel cylinder tectonic plates.

Magma is a mixture of molten or semi-molten rock in the Asthenosphere and is located directly beneath the Earth's solid Lithosphere. When magma reaches the Earth's surface from volcanic eruptions, it is called lava. Viscosity describes a fluid's thickness and is measured in Poise (Pa s) units. For example, honey is thicker than water, so it has a higher viscosity than water. Some naturally occurring magmas can be hundreds of thousands of times more fluid than others, with the most fluid magmas having a consistency about the same as motor oil.

The mechanism of the Hydraulic Hypothesis can only function effectively if particular parts of the Asthenosphere form a confined, interconnected network of highly fluid magma. In the following explanation of the Hydraulic Hypothesis, that network will be called the Ultra-Low-Viscosity Zone or ULVZ. The ULVZ contains all the 'brake fluid' that transmits hydraulic forces between the 'master cylinder' and the 'wheel cylinders'.

There is increasing geological evidence that layers and channels of highly fluid magma do exist within the Asthenosphere. These ultra-low-viscosity structures seem to occur mainly at the Lithosphere-Asthenosphere Boundary, or LAB, located immediately below the solid Lithosphere. When magma is less dense than the surrounding rock, it rises from the Asthenosphere towards the Earth's surface and accumulates at the LAB. As a result, very low-viscosity magma could form

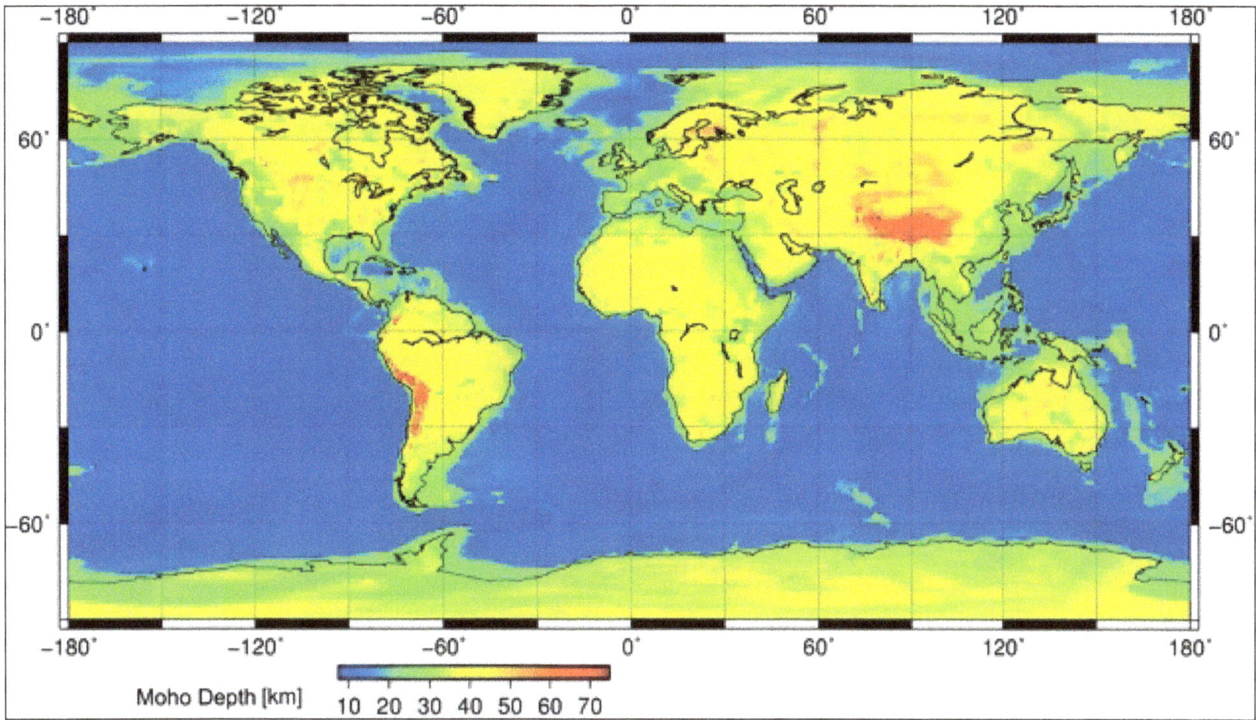

The Position and Depth of the Moho Discontinuity
Source: Wikimedia Commons – AllenMcC

interconnected layers and channels at the LAB. All of these interlinked structures would be confined by any solid rock or thicker magma around them, and the structures would then form a continuous, three-dimensional (3D) enclosed fluid network.

In the Hydraulic Hypothesis, this worldwide 3D network of very fluid magma forms the ULVZ of 'confined incompressible fluid'. The ULVZ would behave according to Pascal's Law and allow the Earth's hydraulic system to transmit any change in force beneath one tectonic plate to another. Again, using the hydraulic brake analogy, the master cylinder is the ice-covered polar tectonic plates, and the wheel cylinders are the remote unglaciated plates. The very fluid magma of the ULVZ would act like the hydraulic brake fluid. The brake lines would be the 3D network of the ULVZ, which connects all of the Earth's tectonic plate cylinders into one closed hydraulic system.

When glacial ice sheets thicken over the master cylinder of glaciated polar plates, those plates are pushed down and displace the underlying magma. The ULVZ should transmit that downward force and cause an upward force on the wheel cylinders of remote unglaciated plates, pushing them up. When the ice sheets melt, magma returns below the master cylinder of glaciated plates. That backflow causes an upward force on the master cylinder and a downward force on the wheel cylinders of unglaciated plates, pulling them down.

Following Pascal's Law, any changes in hydraulic force would be transmitted evenly around the entire Earth through the confined, continuous fluid network of the ULVZ. As in the hydraulic brake analogy, the magma beneath the glaciated plates does not need to flow directly to and from the unglaciated plates. Any vertical movement of the tectonic plates is purely from the transmission of hydraulic force beneath each plate.

The Mohorovicic discontinuity or Moho is a boundary surface that marks the lower limit of the Earth's outer Crust. The Moho is five to ten kilometres below the ocean floor and 20–90 kilometres beneath the continents. The solid part of the Mantle lies below the Moho, and the Lithosphere-Asthenosphere Boundary (LAB) lies directly below that. The Earth's LAB is where the most fluid magma rises and accumulates.

If the Moho's depth is an estimate of the LAB's depth, greater volumes of very fluid magma should rise and accumulate at the shallowest Moho. The accompanying map of the Moho shows its shallow levels coloured blue and green. The Earth's hypothetical hydraulic system should work most effectively where the ULVZ is thickest and closest to the Earth's surface. Therefore, the most likely areas to accumulate very fluid magma are beneath the Oceanic Lithosphere and along the continental shelves of the Continental Lithosphere: the blue and green zones on the map.

As the blue zones of Oceanic Lithosphere lay beneath thousands of metres of seawater, the immense weight of that water would likely cancel out any hydraulic effects under the deep oceans. Consequently, the impact of the Hydraulic Hypothesis should be highest at the green zones, which appear to be in either shallower water or above water.

Much more technical detail about a ULVZ can be found in Appendix 2 – The Hydraulic Hypothesis.

The Closure of the Panama Isthmus and Onset of the Quaternary Ice Age

One geological effect of the Hydraulic Hypothesis may have begun the Quaternary Ice Age about 2.5 million years ago. That key geological event blocked the flow of ocean currents between the Pacific and Atlantic Oceans.

The Panama Isthmus between Costa Rica and Colombia is the narrow strip of land that connects the North and South American continents. However, the Panama Isthmus was submerged for many millions of years, so the gap between the American continents allowed water to circulate between the Pacific and Atlantic Oceans. The Panama Isthmus partially emerged and subsided a few times from 4.5–3.0mya before finally emerging between 3.0 and 2.5mya. Since then, it has completely closed the connection between the Pacific and Atlantic Oceans.

There is shallow Moho beneath the Panama Isthmus, which sits on the southernmost part of the Caribbean Plate at its boundary with the Nazca Plate. According to the Hydraulic Hypothesis, the increasing amounts of glacial ice accumulating on the Antarctic Plate after 5mya caused an increase in hydraulic force below the Panama Isthmus. That increased pressure could have caused partial uplifts and subsidences there. As hydraulic pressure increased further, possibly from some early Northern Hemisphere glaciation around 3mya, the Panama Isthmus finally closed by 2.5mya. This closure completely blocked the flow of ocean currents between the Pacific and Atlantic Oceans.

The end of free flow between the Pacific and Atlantic Oceans caused a reorganization of the Earth's ocean-climate system. Those critical changes in ocean circulation are thought to have created the ongoing Quaternary Ice Age with its frequent, recurring Northern Hemisphere glaciations over the past 2.5 million years. Those much greater amounts of glacial ice on the Earth's polar tectonic plates produced even greater worldwide effects of the Hydraulic Hypothesis.

Late Cenozoic Uplift

Geologists have described what appears to have been a large, rapid uplift of many separate mountain ranges and plateaus all around the Earth. This virtually simultaneous uplift began around five million years ago and continued through the Pliocene and Quaternary Epochs – also known as the Late Cenozoic or Late Neogene.

The global geological phenomenon, called the Late Cenozoic Uplift, appears in many widely separated mountain ranges with very different ages. Until now, no single simple cause exists to explain these global geological changes. However, the Hydraulic Hypothesis could explain all of the following major uplift events:

- Appalachians in the USA
- Central Andes in South America
- Atlas Mountains in North Africa
- Pyrenees in South-West Europe
- Hugger Range in the Sahara
- Palaeozoic mountains of Central Europe

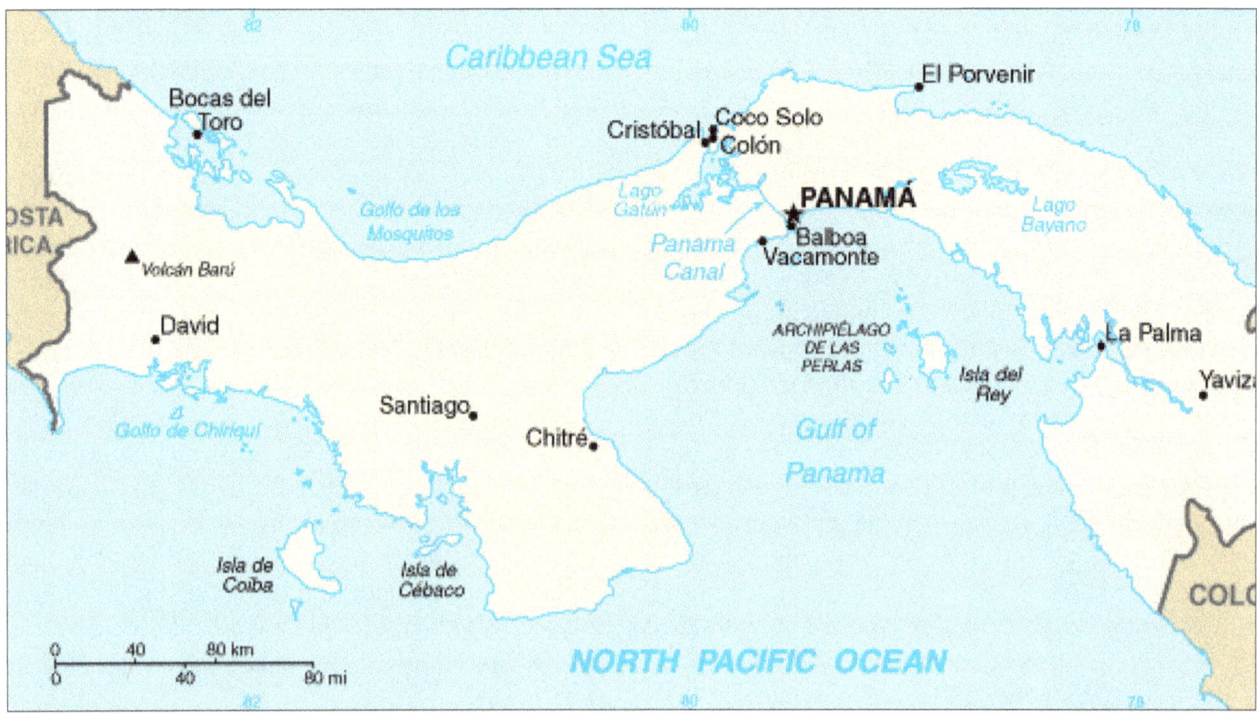

Panama Isthmus
Source: Wikimedia Commons – CIA World Factbook

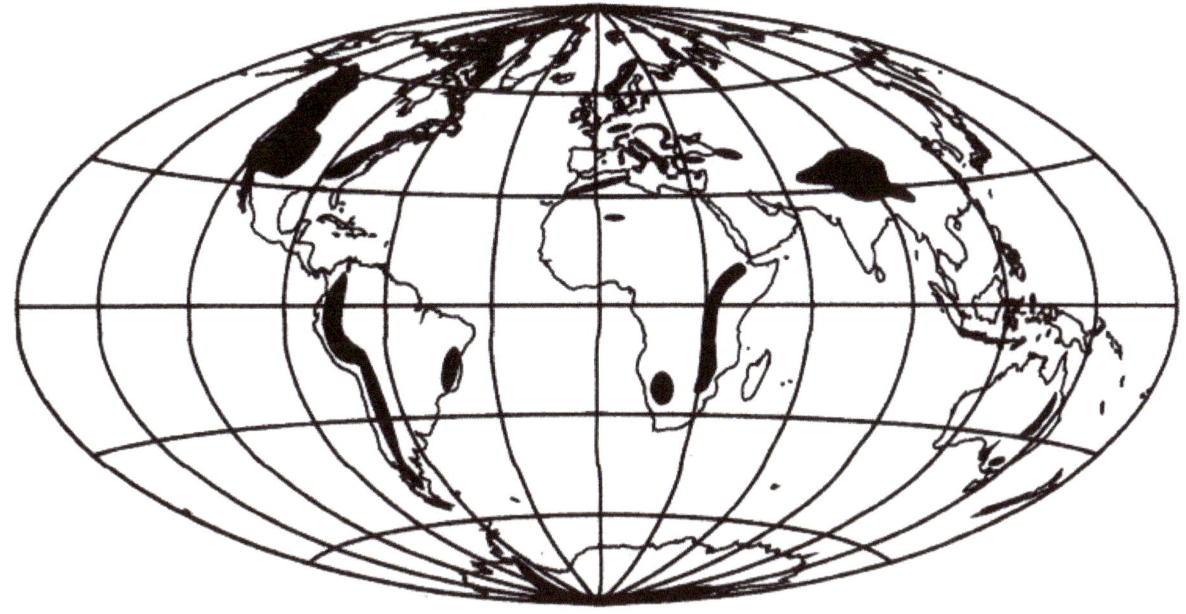

Areas of Possible Uplift in the Late Cenozoic
Source: W. W. Hay, E. Soeding, R. M. DeConto, C. N. Wold – The Late Cenozoic uplift – climate change paradox – Int J Earth Sci (Geol Rundsch) (2002) 91:746–774 DOI 10.1007/s00531-002-0263-1

- European Alps
- Sierra Nevada of California
- Southern Alps of New Zealand
- Himalayas in Asia
- East African Rift
- Southern California Borderland
- Polar Urals in western Russia
- Indonesia
- Mountains of Scandinavia
- Tibet
- Rocky Mountains and High Plains in the USA
- Transantarctic Mountains in Antarctica
- Altai and Tien Shan mountain ranges in Central Asia
- Much of South-Eastern Asia
- Japan
- Apennines in Italy
- Palaeozoic fold belts forming the Australian Alps and the Great Dividing Range
- Kalahari Plateau in Africa

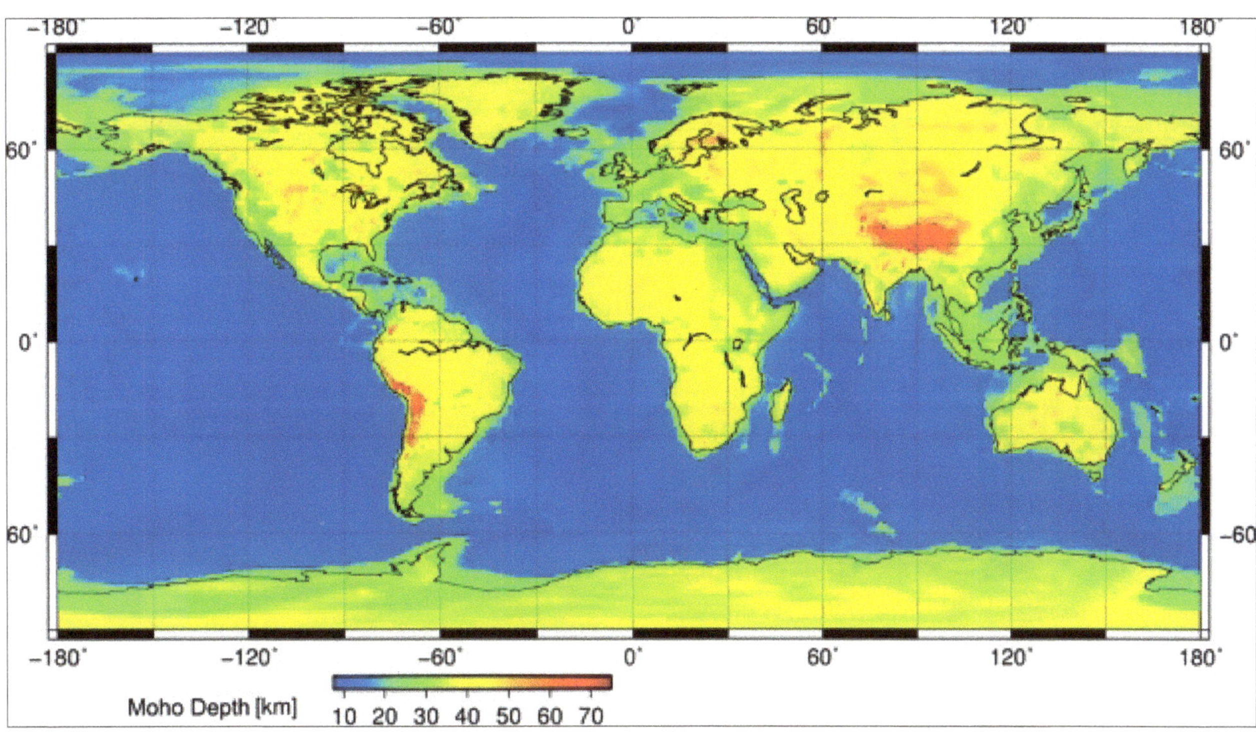

The Position and Depth of the Moho Discontinuity
Source: Wikimedia Commons – AllenMcC

Each uplifted mountain range and plateau appears to have risen by thousands of metres in the geologically short time of merely the last few million years (see the accompanying map). In the conventional theory of the Earth's plate tectonics, all mountain-building and uplift are supposed to be due to the plates' slow, regular horizontal movements. These geological processes take tens of millions of years, but in contrast, Late Cenozoic Uplift seems to have occurred in less than five million years. Significantly, the uplift occurred in regions that had not been tectonically active for many millions of years, so a relatively recent force must have caused the uplift.

So far, no single geological mechanism has explained the rapid, synchronous uplift of such geographically diverse mountain regions after 5mya. However, the transmission of hydraulic force in the ULVZ could have caused it. Uplift may have started when the Antarctic ice sheet began to grow around 15mya and then accelerated around 5mya. Once the Quaternary Ice Age began 2.5mya with the closure of the Panama Isthmus, uplift would have accelerated further because of the much larger glacial ice loads on Antarctica, North America, and Eurasia.

Most, if not all, of the worldwide uplift occurred in regions with a shallow Moho: the green areas on the accompanying map. These are the locations where the Hydraulic Hypothesis predicts the greatest focus of hydraulic force and the greatest vertical movement of the overlying Lithosphere.

Late Cenozoic Volcanism

Another effect of the Hydraulic Hypothesis could be two significant increases in past volcanic activity on Earth. There is geological evidence of increased worldwide tectonic activity in the Late Cenozoic, from 5mya to the present. Over that time, there was a substantial increase in volcanic deposits in the deep sea, a sign of increased volcanic eruptions. There was also an earlier, less pronounced peak in tectonic activity in the Middle Miocene, sometime between 16 and 11mya.

The increased global volcanism in the Late Cenozoic after 5mya may be due to additional hydraulic pressure in the Asthenosphere from increasing glaciation over the polar tectonic plates, initially over Antarctica. Volcanism would have further intensified in the past 2.5 million years of the Quaternary Ice Age when far larger amounts of glacial ice accumulated at the poles. There was also a marked increase in glaciation over Antarctica around 15mya, which may have produced the earlier peak in global volcanism from 16–11mya.

CHAPTER 12

The Caribbean Hypothesis – The Atlantic Island's Creation and Destruction

Plato states that the Atlantic Island subsided and disappeared below the sea sometime after 11,600 BP. He describes the cause as 'concussions of the Earth' or 'an earthquake', which means tectonic forces.

Plato (Jowett) – 'For which reason, the sea in those parts is impassable and impenetrable, because there is a shoal of mud in the way; and this was caused by the subsidence of the (Atlantic) island'…'(the Atlantic Island) is now a mass of impervious mud, through concussions of the Earth; so that those who are sailing in the vast sea (Atlantic Ocean) can no longer find a passage from hence thither.'

Plato (Taylor) – 'And hence that sea (Atlantic Ocean) is at present innavigable, arising from the gradually impeding mud which the subsiding (Atlantic) island produced'…'(the Atlantic Island)

The Present Caribbean Region
Source: Google Earth

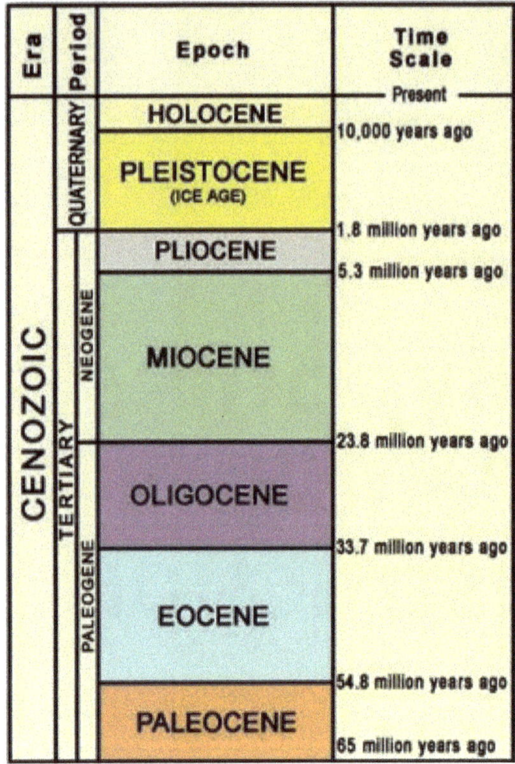

Time-scale of the most recent 65 million years
Source: USGS

when afterwards (after 11,600 BP) sunk by an earthquake, became an impassable barrier of mud to voyagers sailing from hence to any part of the (Atlantic) ocean.'

The Hydraulic Hypothesis might explain large vertical tectonic plate movements in the past and could explain the creation and destruction of Plato's Atlantic Island. The Caribbean Hypothesis argues that a large part of the eastern Caribbean Sea's floor rose above sea level in the extremely distant past, forming the Atlantic Island. Initially, as the North American, Eurasian, and Antarctic Plates were pushed down because of glacial ice accumulating there, some parts of the Caribbean Plate were pushed up to form the entire Atlantic Island. The reverse happened when glacial ice melted on the large polar plates; they moved up while much of the Caribbean Plate 'sank' below sea level.

As the Venezuelan Basin and the adjoining Aves and Beata Ridges emerged and formed land, they attached to the already emergent islands of Hispaniola and Puerto Rico. They remained connected for hundreds of thousands, possibly one million years or more. This combination of landmasses in the eastern Caribbean formed Plato's 'Atlantic island' of one million square kilometres. Then, sometime after 11,600 BP, most of the Atlantic Island subsided hundreds to thousands of metres below sea level, where it once again formed part of the Caribbean Sea's floor. All that remained of the Atlantic Island were some Caribbean islands that Marcellus described in his lost work, *Aethiopica*.

The earliest geological events that could have created the Atlantic Island began 65mya, in the Palaeocene Epoch. But the most important geological events started 23mya in the Miocene Epoch and continued into the present Holocene Epoch, which began 12,000 years ago.

It is worth repeating some facts about the past changes in glacial ice load on Earth as they caused the geological effects of the Hydraulic Hypothesis. Hundreds of millions of years ago, during each of several previous major Ice Ages, there were extremely long periods of glaciation on Earth lasting tens and hundreds of millions of years. These Ice Ages were followed by long ice-free periods lasting tens and hundreds of millions of years.

After the previous major Ice Age ended about 250mya, an ice-free period lasted over two hundred million years. The most recent increase in glaciation started 36mya when glacial ice began to accumulate over Antarctica. Later, at 15mya, worldwide temperatures dropped markedly, and the Antarctic ice cap began to grow into its present form. There was a further acceleration in Antarctic ice cap growth from 5mya, and the Greenland ice cap began to develop 3mya. The current Quaternary Ice Age started 2.5mya when glacial ice sheets began to spread over North America and Eurasia and increased on Antarctica.

During the past 2.5 million years of the Quaternary Ice Age, there were an estimated 30–50 glacial/interglacial cycles, each lasting tens of thousands of years. Ice on land repeatedly reached depths of thousands of metres during each long, cold glacial period. Then, it partially melted during the relatively short, warm interglacial period that followed.

The most recent cold glacial period began around 110,000 BP and lasted about 90,000 years before it peaked at the Last Glacial Maximum (LGM) at 20,000 BP. The global sea level at the LGM was at least 120 metres lower than today. Virtually all the water missing from the oceans was stored on land in ice sheets up to four thousand metres thick. The ice sheets were thickest over most of North America and Eurasia and were much thicker than now on Antarctica.

After 20,000 BP, the ice sheets melted as the Earth began to warm again. The global sea level rose by 120 metres over a relatively short period of about 14,000 years before reaching present levels around 6,000 BP. Only over the last 12,000 years has the Earth been in the stable, warm interglacial period called the Holocene Epoch.

The sea level rise after 20,000 BP inundated millions of square kilometres of coastal land all over the Earth. That relatively rapid and enormous sea level rise may have caused the many 'deluges' described in myths worldwide. Yet, it does not explain how most of the enormous Atlantic Island

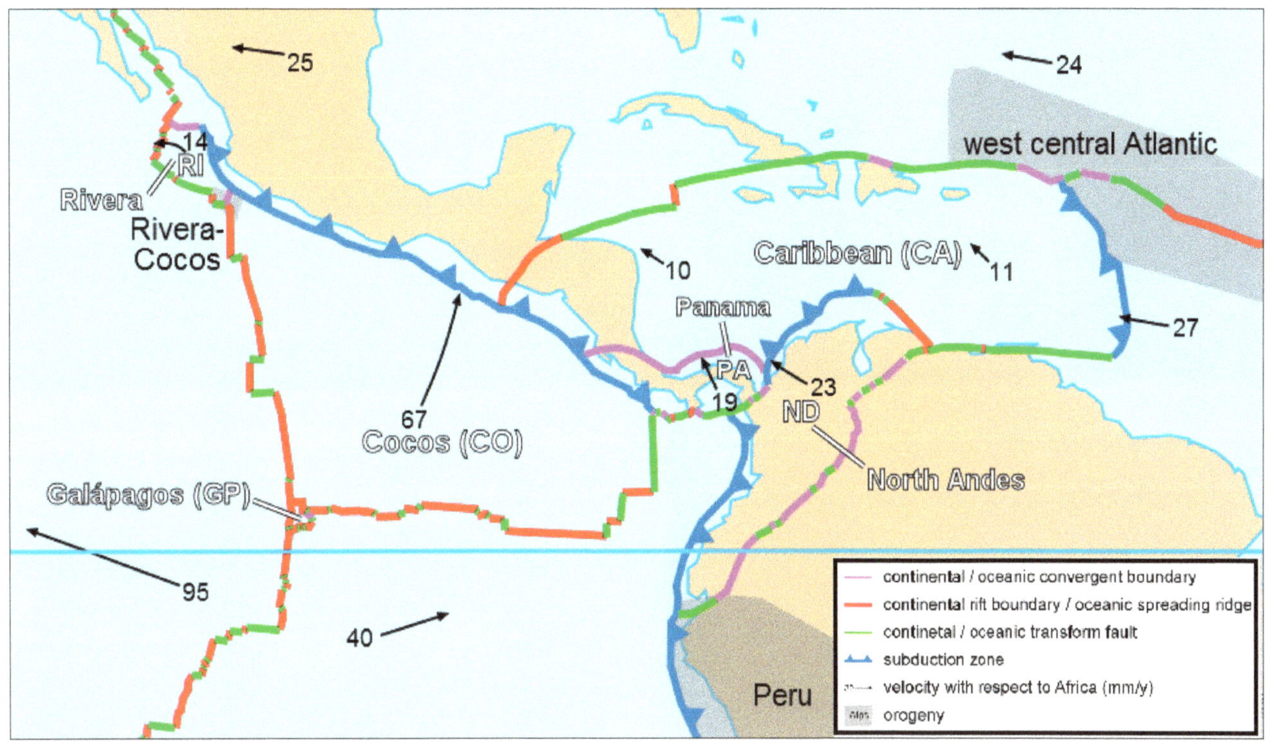

Map of Plate Tectonics in the Caribbean region
Source: Wikimedia Commons – Sting and Woudloper

'sank' by thousands of metres sometime after 11,600 BP.

Modern geology rejects the sinking or subsidence of lost continents because the Earth's rigid outer layer, or Crust, consists of lighter sial rocks (rich in aluminium silicates) that float on a heavier layer of sima rocks (rich in magnesium silicates) below the Crust. The lighter sial rock of the Crust is absent or only a few kilometres thick at the bottom of the oceans, whereas the continents are blocks of sial Crust tens of kilometres thick. Therefore, the lighter sial continents float on the heavier sima layer below them, just as icebergs float on water. Consequently, geologists rightly claim that a continent cannot sink into the ocean.

Nevertheless, the Crust of the Caribbean Plate has an unusual geological structure, so the conventional argument that continents cannot sink may not apply to it. The Caribbean Plate is not a continent because its Crust is much thinner than Continental Crust. Most of the Caribbean Plate's Crust is only 5–15 kilometres thick compared to Continental Crust, which is usually 40–70 kilometres thick.

Most of the Caribbean Sea sits on the Caribbean Plate, which borders the North American, South American, Nazca and Cocos Plates. The Caribbean Plate is a separate, relatively small, isolated structure compared to the larger tectonic plates around it. Therefore, it may have been more affected by changes in hydraulic pressure below than its large surrounding plates. Also, because most of the Caribbean Plate has a relatively thin Crust, it could have responded more to changes in underlying hydraulic pressure than the much thicker Continental Crust.

The Caribbean Plate has numerous fault lines and microplates, dividing it into smaller parts. These separate components could move up or down independently because of differences in hydraulic pressure beneath each component. There is an unusually thin Crust in those parts of the eastern Caribbean that would have comprised most of the Atlantic Island. With any changes in hydraulic pressure below them, those thinner components might have had more vertical movement than the plate's thicker parts.

Hydraulic Effects on the Caribbean Plate

The Hydraulic Hypothesis assumes a worldwide layer of highly fluid magma (the Ultra-Low-Viscosity Zone or ULVZ) lies at the Lithosphere-Asthenosphere Boundary (LAB). That highly liquid layer is roughly at the Moho's depth. In that case, the accompanying map of Moho depth indicates a shallow ULVZ of less than 30km – the blue and green areas – beneath the Caribbean Plate. Also, there appears to be a continuous connection of shallow ULVZ that runs south along both edges of North America to the Caribbean Plate. The ULVZ at the eastern and western ends of the Eurasian Plate connects to the ULVZ on both sides of the North American Plate, so the Eurasian Plate also connects to the Caribbean Plate. Another possible ULVZ connection, from the Antarctic Plate to the Caribbean Plate, runs north along both edges of South America.

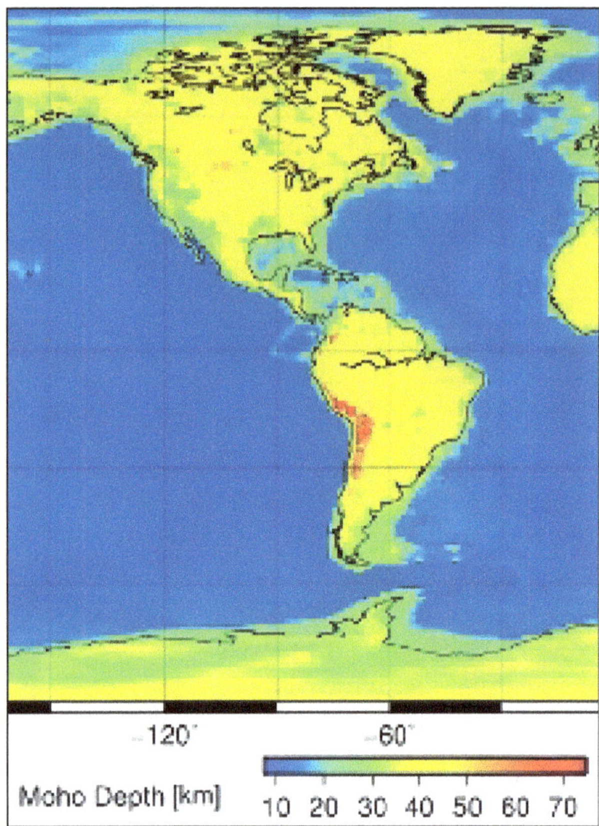

Moho Depth
Source: Wikimedia Commons – From AllenMcC

Using the hydraulic brake system analogy, hydraulic pressure from the large glaciated plates at the poles (the master cylinder of the combined North American, Eurasian, and Antarctic Plates) would travel to the Caribbean Plate (one of the wheel cylinders) through shallow ULVZ connections (the brake lines) along the edges of the North and South American continents.

If the Hydraulic Hypothesis is correct, hydraulic pressure transmitted to the Caribbean Plate caused the past vertical movements of some of the plate's components. Those vertical movements ought to be closely linked to the various phases of glaciation on Earth over the past thirty-five million years. Still, the main plate movements would have occurred over the past 2.5 million years of the Quaternary Ice Age.

The significant phases of glaciation were:

- A gradual build-up of ice over Antarctica, beginning 35mya.
- Accelerating ice cover over Antarctica 15mya, with a further acceleration 5mya.
- Ice sheets formed over the Northern Hemisphere from 2.5mya and increased over Antarctica – marking the start of the Quaternary Ice Age.
- Glacial/interglacial cycles become more extreme ~1mya, with the final two glacial periods since 240,000 years ago being the most extreme. This period includes the rapid deglaciation after the LGM 20,000 years ago.

Appendix 3 – The Caribbean Hypothesis, contains more information about the vertical movements of the Caribbean Plate's components over the past sixty-five million years. The many vertical movements over that time do seem connected to distinct changes in glacial ice thickness over the polar tectonic plates. In particular, the variations in the Caribbean Plate's elevation in the last one million years to the present are the most crucial evidence for the emergence and subsidence of the Atlantic Island.

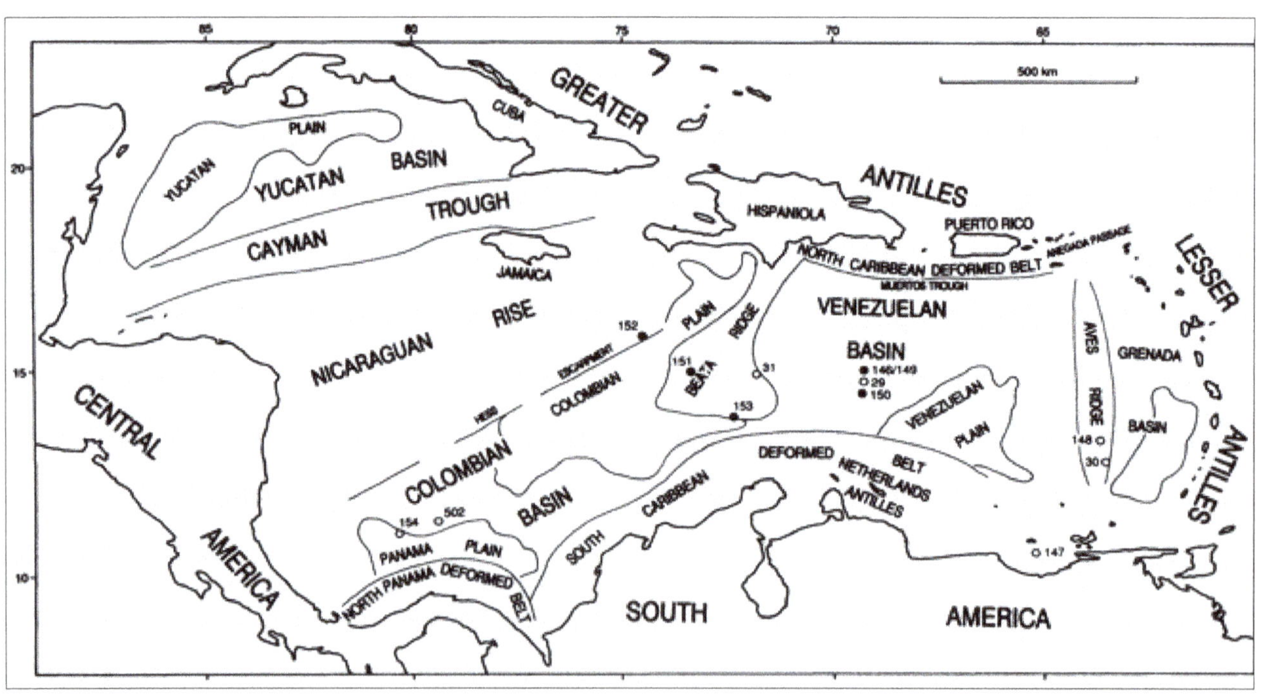

Map of the Caribbean showing the major named features
Source: Case, J.E., MacDonald, W.D. & Fox, P.J. 1990. Caribbean crustal provinces; seismic and gravity evidence: in Dengo, G. & Case, I.E. (eds), The Geology of North America, Volume II, The Caribbean Region, 15-36. Geological Society of America

The Emergence of the Atlantic Island

The Caribbean Hypothesis describes how hydraulic forces pushed up several of the Caribbean Plate's submerged components, which then emerged to form the complete Atlantic Island. To satisfy all of Plato's geographical descriptions, his 'Atlantic island' had to be a landmass that combined Hispaniola, Puerto Rico, the Beata Ridge, the Venezuelan Basin, and the Aves Ridge.

The entire Caribbean Plate did not have to move upward; only some parts of the eastern Caribbean Plate had to rise above sea level to create the Atlantic Island. Because of the unusual geological structure of the eastern Caribbean Plate's Crust, those emerging components may have moved together as a single unit rather than separately.

Any vertical movement of the eastern Caribbean Plate would have occurred at its major fault zones. Several of those faults form a continuous boundary around the eastern Caribbean Plate's components, creating the wheel cylinder of the Caribbean Plate.

- To the west are the Hess Escarpment, the faulted coastlines of Costa Rica and Panama, and the Panama Deformed Belt.
- To the north is the Enriquillo-Plantain Garden Fault on Hispaniola, with faults between the Beata Ridge and Hispaniola that continue along the Muertos Trough into the Anegada Gap.
- To the east are the Kallinago Depression and the steep outer slopes of the Lesser Antilles Islands. The La Desirade Escarpment is at the transition from the steep outer slopes of the northern Lesser Antilles to the steep inner slopes of the southern Lesser Antilles along the Grenada Basin.
- To the south is the South Caribbean Deformed Belt.

The accompanying map shows those parts of the eastern Caribbean Plate that might have tilted upward as a single unit to form the complete Atlantic Island. These components could act as a single movable flap with one fixed hinge and three free edges.

The flap's fixed hinge is in the north where the Venezuelan Basin joins with Hispaniola and the Puerto Rico-Virgin Islands Platform; the flap's mobile free edges are the west, south, and east fault zones. Those free edges would allow the flap to tilt upward along its southern border at the Panama and South Caribbean Deformed Belt.

Over several million years, the Atlantic Island's flap may have risen gradually and lifted the island's submerged components above sea level. Uplift may have started from the beginning of the Quaternary Ice Age 2.5mya, or it may have begun even earlier from 15mya when thicker ice sheets began to form over Antarctica. Around one million years ago, there was a marked increase in the amount of glacial ice that accumulated at the Earth's poles during each glacial period. That increasing glacial ice load might have caused faster and higher uplift of the eastern Caribbean Plate.

In the accompanying graph, the red line estimates the average intensity of past glacial/interglacial cycles. It can be used as a proxy for the increasing amount of glacial ice covering the polar tectonic plates. Increasing average volumes of glacial ice

The Flap portion of the Caribbean Plate
Source: Modified from Google Earth

The Fully Emergent Atlantic Island
Source: Modified from Google Earth

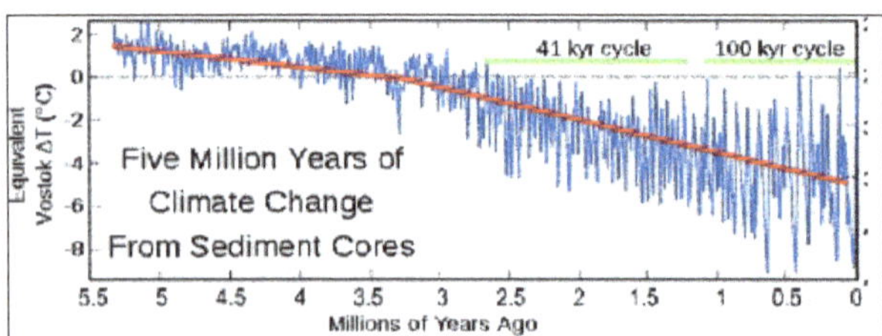

Glacials and Interglacials over the last 5 million years
Source: Wikimedia Commons – From Robert A. Rohde

over the past one to two million years might have accelerated the uplift of the Caribbean Plate's flap. Still, the flap's elevation may not have been steady. Over the last one million years of more intense cycles of glaciation/deglaciation, the flap's elevation may have fluctuated, rising and falling due to cyclical changes in glacial ice loads and hydraulic pressure in the ULVZ below it.

If the Caribbean Hypothesis is correct, when sufficient hydraulic pressure increased below the flap, it began tilting upward from the south, with the Beata and Aves Ridges emerging first. Those two ridges eventually rose some thousands of metres above sea level to form the Western and Eastern Mountains of the Atlantic Island. As the flap rose further, the Venezuelan Basin emerged to become the Plain of Atlantis. In the north, the Plain of Atlantis joined with the already emergent islands of Hispaniola and Puerto Rico, which became the Northern Mountains of the Atlantic Island.

Once the entire Atlantic Island formed, it had to remain above sea level long enough for many animal and plant species to colonise it. Larger animals, such as bison, horses, camelids, and elephants, possibly crossed over now-submerged land bridges from the Americas to reach the Atlantic Island. Otherwise, they and other species may have already been present on Hispaniola and Puerto Rico and then moved onto the newly emergent parts of the Atlantic Island. Eventually, humans arrived and settled on the Atlantic Island, creating the equivalent of a Bronze Age civilisation before 11,600 BP.

The Subsidence of the Atlantic Island

As previously described in the Hydraulic Hypothesis, when ice accumulates on polar tectonic plates during a long, cold glacial period, it pushes down those plates. The underlying fluid Mantle flows away from the plates, and hydraulic pressure increases in the ULVZ worldwide. When the ice melts during the shorter, warm interglacial period, the displaced Mantle moves back under the glaciated plates, and hydraulic pressure decreases in the ULVZ.

During deglaciation, the return flow of the Mantle causes the polar plates to uplift (rebound) in two distinct phases. First, there is an immediate elastic phase of rebound when Mantle material flows back while the ice melts, and this rapid return flow is likely to be the most fluid magma in the Mantle. Then, the elastic phase is followed by a slow viscous phase, with a much slower return of less fluid magma, which continues for thousands of years after the ice stops melting.

Based on the Hydraulic Hypothesis, the immediate elastic rebound phase would rapidly transmit any drop in hydraulic pressure throughout the most fluid parts of the Earth's entire ULVZ. That immediate return flow of magma below glaciated plates would create a rapid drop in hydraulic pressure below unglaciated plates, and they would tend to be pulled

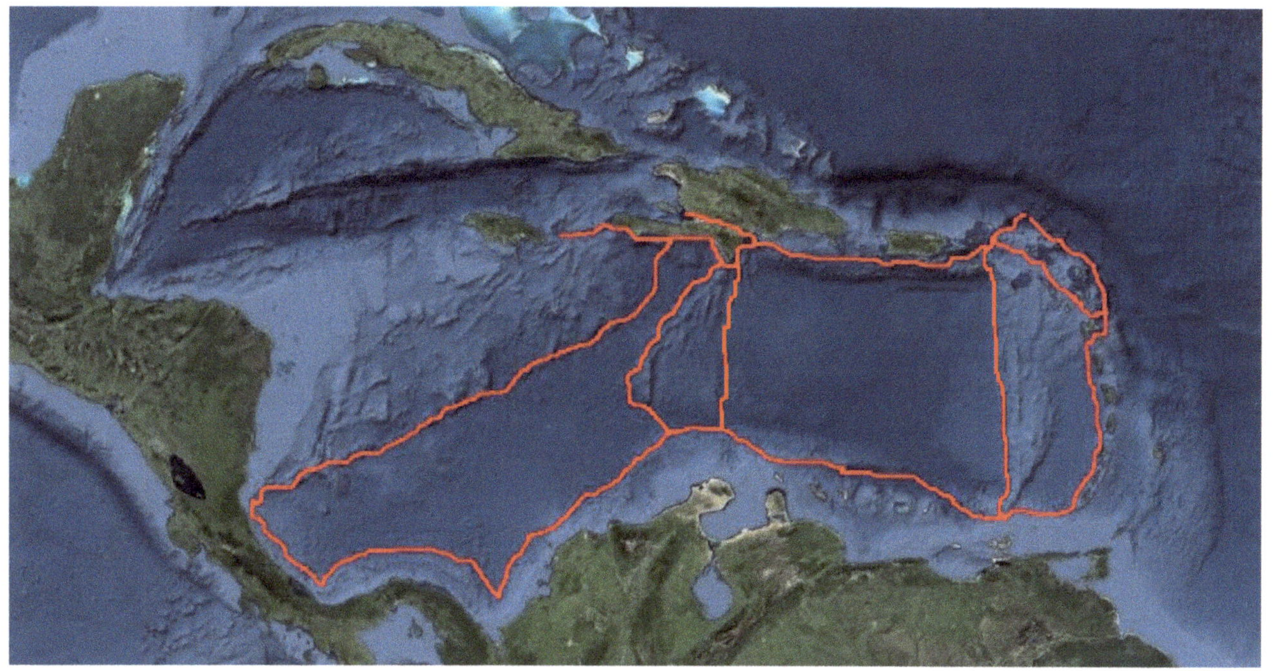

Major Fault Zones of the Caribbean Plate's Flap
Source: Modified from Google Eart

downward. The initial rapid pressure drop would be followed by a more gradual fall in hydraulic pressure over thousands of years during the slower viscous phase of magma flow.

Over the past 250,000 years, the last two glacial periods were the most extreme and produced the greatest amount of glacial ice on Antarctica, North America, and Eurasia. The most recent glacial period began at 110,000 BP; glaciation peaked at the LGM at 20,000 BP, and then the ice started melting rapidly. By convention, the last glacial period ended 12,000 years ago, marking the onset of the present warm Holocene Epoch. However, glacial ice continued to melt rapidly until 6,000 BP. Out of the total amount of glacial ice that melted after the LGM, half was from 20,000 to 12,000 BP, while the other half was from 12,000 to 6,000 BP.

As the glacial ice sheets covering North America, Eurasia, and Antarctica melted, each of those large landmasses rebounded upward by hundreds of metres, which would have greatly reduced hydraulic pressure in the Earth's entire ULVZ. In

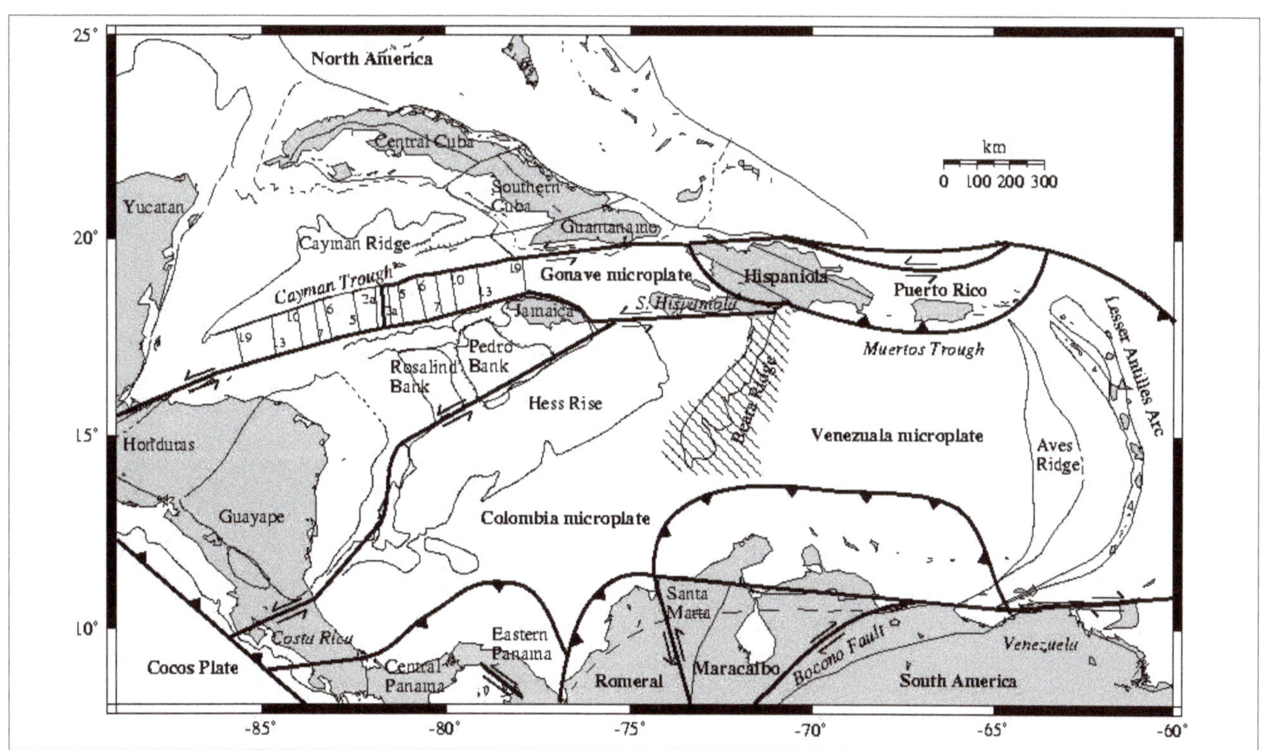

Tectonic map of the Caribbean
Source: R. Dietmar Müller, Jean-Yves Royer, Steven C. Cande, Walter R. Roest, and Sergei Maschenkov – New Constraints on Caribbean Plate Tectonic Evolution

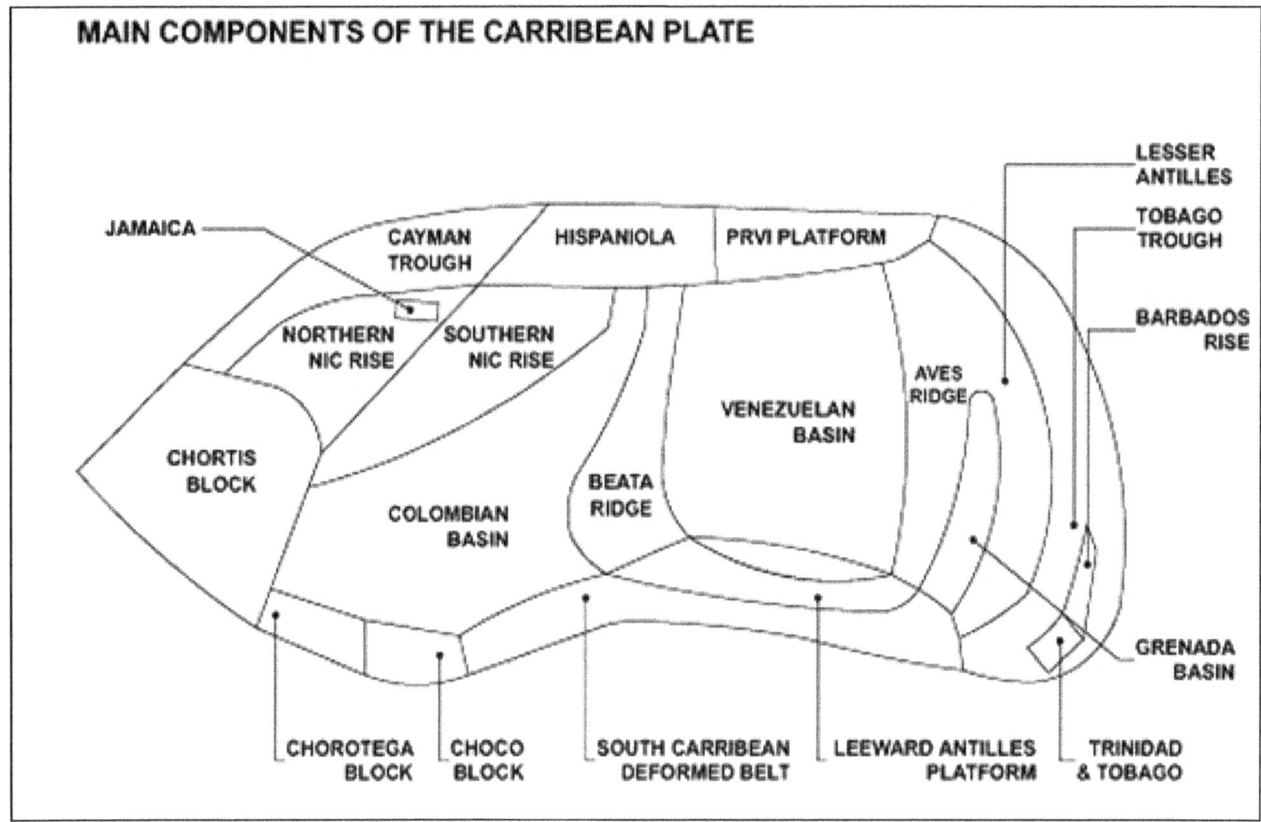

the Caribbean Hypothesis, the large and rapid fall in hydraulic pressure was transmitted to the Caribbean Plate and caused increasing suction underneath it.

The Atlantic Island must have begun to subside sometime after 11,600 BP, or more than 8,400 years after the LGM of 20,000 BP. Over a few thousand years, the downward pull increased to the point where it overcame resistance at the Caribbean Plate's weak boundaries or internal fault lines. Then, certain parts of the Atlantic Island were pulled downwards and subsided below sea level.*h*

Although the Caribbean flap may have risen above sea level in one piece over hundreds of thousands of years or more, it probably did not subside in one piece after 11,600 BP. Because major fault zones exist between each of the Caribbean Plate's components, there could have been different amounts of subsidence and tilting of each component. Some parts may have been relatively stable because of resistance to vertical movement at their boundaries, or they may have had less accumulated fluid magma beneath them. These combined effects would have focussed extra hydraulic force below the most mobile parts of the Caribbean Plate, causing greater downward movement there.

Major subsidences of individual components of the Caribbean Plate may have continued for thousands of years after 11,600 BP. Eventually, those components would have had to subside far enough to form the eastern Caribbean as it appears today. In particular, the Beata and Aves Ridges and the Venezuelan Basin all had to subside by thousands of metres after 11,600 BP. Each subsidence may have been by tens, hundreds, or thousands of metres and would have caused a wide-ranging seismic event. Those great subsidences would explain Plato's statement that the Atlantic Island was 'sunk by an earthquake'.

Some parts of the Atlantic Island may have subsided by many metres in a brief time, and the sea would have quickly covered low-lying areas of the island, such as the Plain of Atlantis – the now-submerged Venezuelan Basin. Over hundreds or thousands of years, large parts of the Atlantic Island may have continued to sink more gradually or in several major subsidences to form most of the present eastern Caribbean Sea.

The following components of the Caribbean Plate had to tilt and subside for the Atlantic Island to become most of the eastern Caribbean Sea's floor.

- The northern part of the Colombian Basin tilted to the east, and the Beata Ridge tilted to the south at their northern margins with Hispaniola.
- The northern Venezuelan Basin subsided as a separate unit at its margin with the PRVI Platform at the Muertos Trough.
- The Venezuelan Basin may also have subsided relative to the Beata and Aves Ridges.
- As well as subsiding, the Venezuelan Basin tilted to the south-east and slid southward toward the Leeward Antilles Platform and the South Caribbean Deformed Belt.
- The Aves Ridge tilted to the south at the Anegada Passage and along its associated fault extensions in the north.

- The Grenada Basin tilted south and subsided along its steep boundary with the southern Lesser Antilles.
- The northern Lesser Antilles Islands tilted south at their steep eastern boundary and possibly west along the Kallinago Depression.

There is much more information about the above geological changes in Appendix 3 – The Caribbean Hypothesis: The Caribbean Plate 250kya–Recent.

Prehistoric Seismic and Volcanic Events in the Caribbean

Over the past 120,000 years, changes in the hydraulic pressure of magma in the ULVZ might have caused several known prehistoric seismic and volcanic events in the Caribbean.

If the Hydraulic Hypothesis is correct, from 120,000–20,000 BP, the gradual increase of glaciation on the polar tectonic plates would have increased hydraulic pressure beneath the Caribbean Plate. Over tens of thousands of years, a gradual pressure increase would have increased volcanic activity in the Caribbean region, but seismic activity should have been relatively stable.

The reverse should have occurred during the rapid deglaciation period from 20,000–6,000 BP. Seismic activity would have increased, but volcanic activity should have decreased because of the rapid drop in hydraulic pressure beneath the Caribbean Plate. That rapid pressure drop from 20,000–6,000 BP would have coincided with the subsidence of the Atlantic Island sometime after 11,600 BP.

Known examples of increased Caribbean volcanic eruptions from 120,000–20,000 BP are at least two eruption deposits less than 40,000 years old in the Lesser Antilles islands of St Lucia and Dominica. With volumes of several tens of cubic kilometres, they are in the same range as the largest historical eruptions on Earth, like the 1883 CE eruption of Krakatoa, which was twenty cubic kilometres. Another example of increased volcanism is bioclastic flow deposits offshore from the Soufriere Hills volcano on Montserrat, deposited in the last 26,000 years.

If large parts of the Caribbean Plate began to subside from 20,000–6,000 BP, thousands of kilometres of plate boundaries and fault lines would have ruptured around and within the Plate. Those ruptures would likely have produced massive earthquakes, much larger than any in historical times. Giant earthquakes can cause submarine landslides, creating thick, widespread sediment beds or turbidites on the ocean floor. Few large submarine landslides are well-dated worldwide, but those that are dated are known to be associated with periods of rapid sea level change. Since rapid sea level increase is due to deglaciation, that indicates a possible connection of earthquakes with reduced pressure in the ULVZ.

The Caribbean region has numerous thick turbidite beds in the Grenada Basin and Puerto Rico Trench. Some but not all Grenada Basin turbidites may be from volcano collapse landslides. However, the turbidites in the Puerto Rico Trench indicate past great earthquakes along the Caribbean-North American Plate boundary, dating from 25kya to 18kya. There may be later but so far unrecognised earthquakes along the other boundaries of the Caribbean Plate, which could indicate subsidence of the more southern parts of the plate.

Three Holocene (after 12,000 BP) tsunami events around 3,500 BP, 1,500 BP and 450–500 BP struck the islands of Aruba, Curacao and Bonaire, which lie in the south-east Caribbean Sea, off the coast of Venezuela. Even though the tsunami waves approached the islands from a north-easterly direction, the source does not appear to be from the Lesser Antilles islands. The Aves Ridge is to the north-east of the islands, so if it did subside in several stages after 11,600 BP, it might be the source of these three tsunamis. There may have been earlier unknown tsunamis on the islands, but the global sea level rise of 60 metres from 11,000–6,000 BP would have submerged any tsunami deposits from before 6,000 BP.

Seismicity and Volcanism in the Caribbean

According to the Hydraulic Hypothesis, from 20,000 to 6,000 BP, the enormous amount of glacial melting over the polar tectonic plates should have caused a large, immediate elastic drop in hydraulic pressure below the Caribbean Plate. This great drop in hydraulic pressure would have created significant subsidences of the Atlantic Island after 11,600 BP.

There was very little deglaciation from 6,000 BP to the present, so there should have been no further large or rapid fall in hydraulic pressure below the Caribbean Plate. However, an ongoing smaller decrease in hydraulic pressure likely continued after 6,000 BP due to the slower viscous phase of magma flow away from the Caribbean Plate. This long, gradual pressure drop would continue for thousands of years after deglaciation stops.

There should be ongoing earthquake activity in the Caribbean region as hydraulic pressure continues to drop below the Caribbean Plate. There should also be a decrease in volcanic activity because of the pressure drop in the underlying magma after 20,000 BP. But, the present eastern Caribbean, particularly the Lesser Antilles, continues to be a region of high tectonic activity, including earthquakes, tsunamis, and volcanic eruptions.

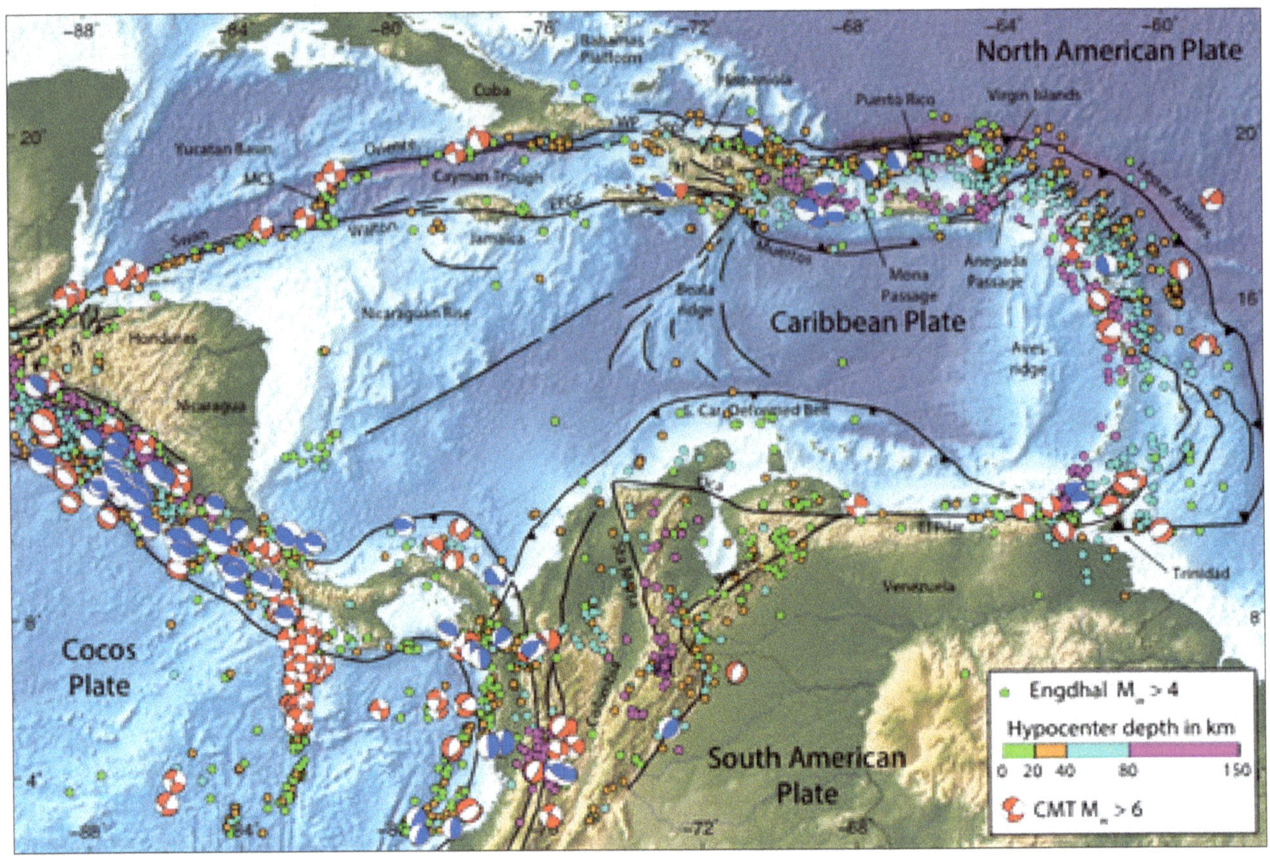

Recent Seismic Events on the Caribbean Plate
Source: Eric Calais – Ecole Normale Supérieure, Department of Geosciences and UMR CNRS 8538

Active faults along the northern and southern boundaries of the Caribbean Plate cause the main geological hazards there. In the north, there is potential for rare but very large earthquakes, particularly along the Puerto Rico Trench. Also, the possibility exists for extremely large plate boundary earthquakes of magnitude 8.5–9.0, which could rupture the 1,000-km-long plate boundary between easternmost Hispaniola and Guadeloupe. A dozen major earthquakes of magnitude 7.0 or greater have occurred in the northern Caribbean near Puerto Rico, the U.S. Virgin Islands and the island of Hispaniola in the past 500 years; several have generated tsunamis. Low to intermediate magnitude earthquakes occur at the Caribbean Plate's southern boundary, which runs east-west across Trinidad and western Venezuela, then south-west into Central Columbia.

Along the arc of the Lesser Antilles, the volcanic front extends northward from Grenada to Saba. While twenty-one volcanoes show evidence of activity during the last 12,000 years of the Holocene Epoch, only seven volcanoes are presently active. That means fourteen have become inactive in the past 12,000 years, possibly due to a reduction in magma pressure below the eastern Caribbean Plate.

Caribbean Tsunamis

For thousands of years after 11,600 BP, any massive earthquakes from subsidences of the Atlantic Island could have caused megatsunamis tens of metres high. Those huge tsunami waves would have travelled rapidly in all directions across the Atlantic Ocean. They likely obliterated much evidence of an Atlantean Empire in the Caribbean, on coastal lands in the Americas near the Caribbean, on islands in the Atlantic, on the Atlantic coasts of Africa and Europe, and possibly coastal areas within the Mediterranean.

Most tsunamis occur in the Pacific Ocean because of the intense continental and oceanic plate activity and volcanism there. The Atlantic Ocean has much less seismic and volcanic activity than the Pacific, so it has fewer tsunamis. Still, the great majority of the North Atlantic Ocean's present seismic and volcanic activity is concentrated in the Caribbean region

The present areas with the potential for Caribbean tsunamis on the accompanying map match the main fault zones of the Caribbean Plate's mobile flap. The flap is where the major downward movements of the Caribbean Plate's components would have caused the subsidence of the Atlantic Island. They will likely continue to subside and cause earthquakes and tsunamis because of the ongoing decrease in hydraulic pressure below them during the slow viscous flow of magma away from the Caribbean Plate.

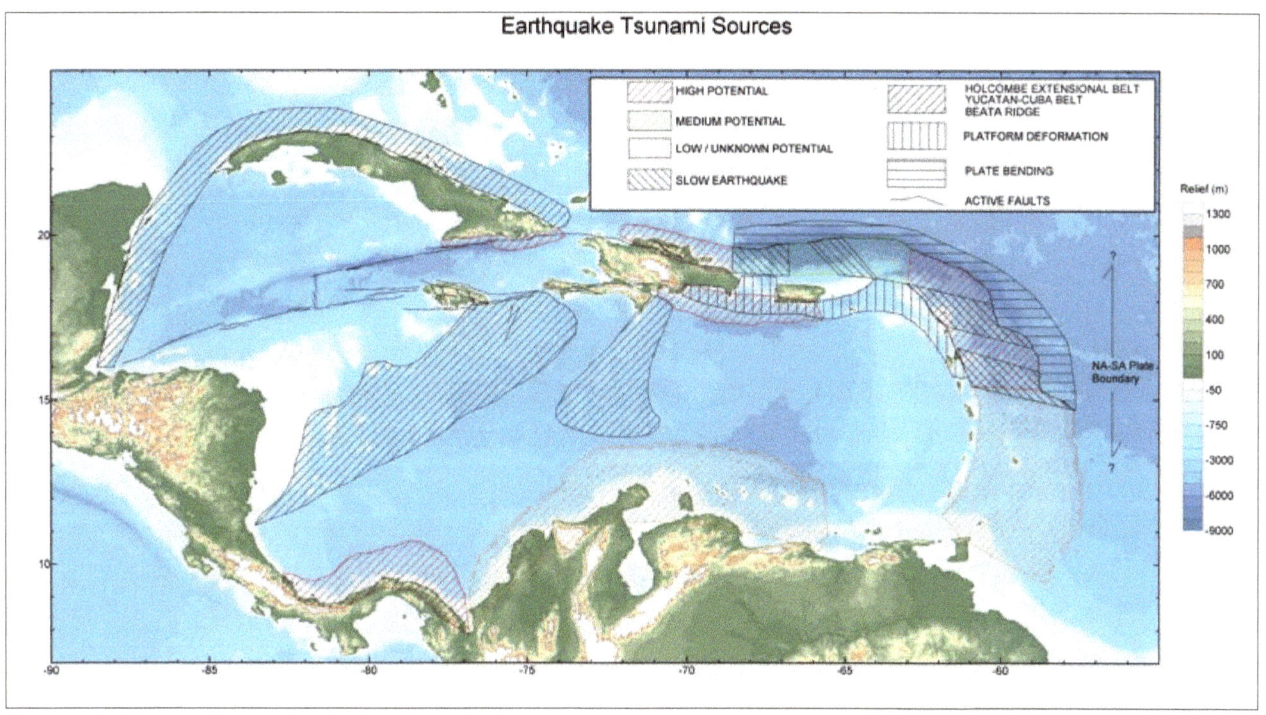

Earthquake Tsunami Sources for the Caribbean Basin
Source: William R. McCann – Estimating the threat of tsunaminogenic earthquakes and earthquake -induced landslide tsunami in the Caribbean

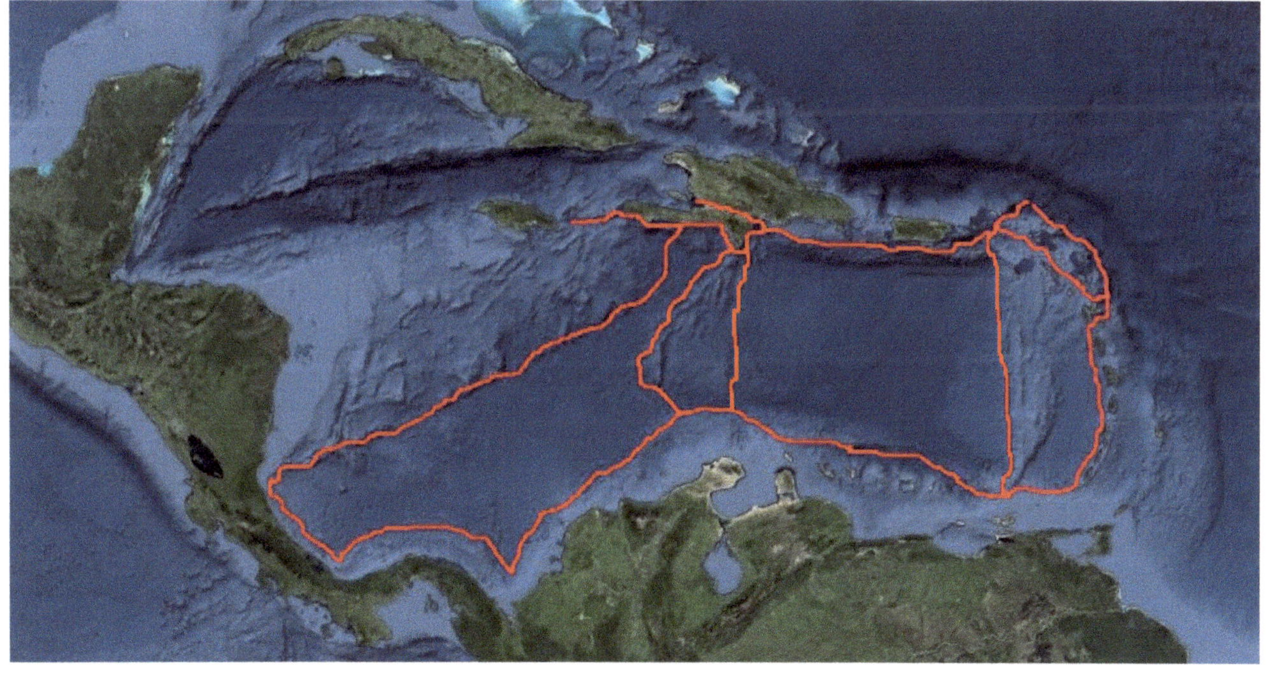

Major Fault Zones of the Caribbean Flap
Source: Modified from Google Earth

Eighty-eight moderate tsunamis have been reported in the Caribbean area since 1489 CE. Volcanic eruptions, volcanic flank failures, debris avalanches, and landslides caused most of them. However, in the past five hundred years in the Caribbean, there have been ten confirmed earthquake-generated tsunamis. A magnitude 7.3 earthquake off the north-west coast of Puerto Rico in 1918 CE generated a tsunami with a run-up height of six metres. A travel-time map for this tsunami is in the accompanying diagram; it shows the speed and reach of Caribbean tsunami waves.

Prehistoric megatsunamis generated by catastrophic subsidences of the Caribbean Plate may have had run-up heights of tens of metres. A tsunami originating in the Caribbean would take one to four hours to strike nearby areas in the Americas and six to seven hours to reach the Atlantic coasts of Europe and North-West Africa. It would then pass through the Strait of Gibraltar and continue into the Mediterranean.

Because the approach to the Strait narrows from a diameter of 500km to less than 20km at Gibraltar, an additional funnelling effect would push a far larger

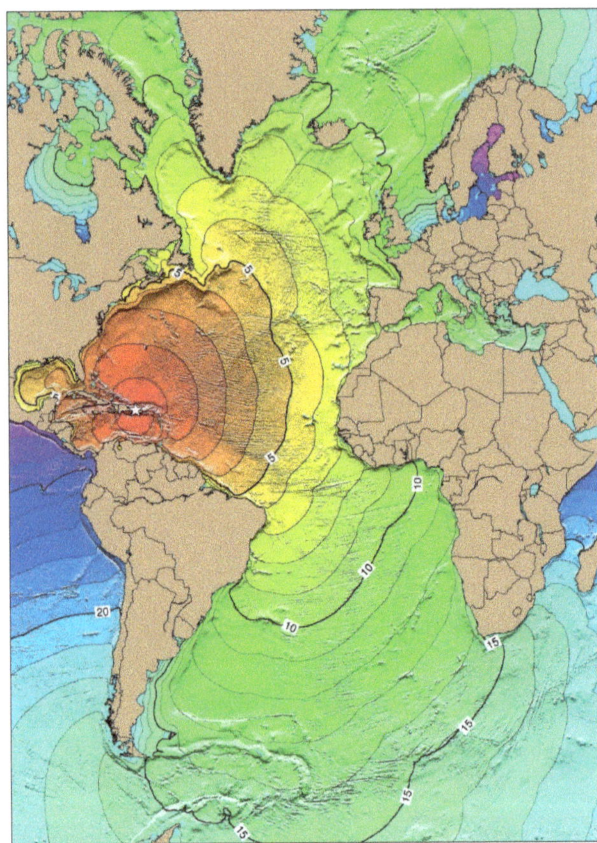

Caribbean Tsunami Travel-Time Map
The contours are in 1-hour time intervals. Red contours are for 1–4 hour arrival times, yellow (5–6 hour arrival times), green (7–14 hour arrival times), and blue (15–21 hour arrival times).
Source: National Oceanic and Atmospheric Organisation

volume of water into the Mediterranean. As the Mediterranean Sea is an enclosed body of water, the tsunami would continue to the farthest point of the sea. A few hours after entering the Mediterranean, it would reach Greece, Egypt, and the Levant.

Around 11,600 BP, the global sea level was 60 metres lower than now. That is roughly halfway between its level at 20,000 BP and its present level, where it stabilised by 6,000 BP. So, between 11,600 and 6,000 BP, Neolithic or Mesolithic cultures within the Mediterranean would have inhabited much larger fertile coastal plains that would have been exposed to devastating tsunamis.

The Caribbean Plate may have subsided in several stages over thousands of years after 11,600 BP, with each abrupt movement generating a separate megatsunami. Any megatsunamis from the Caribbean may have remained metres-high within the Mediterranean and inundated many coastal areas and cultures. By the time a prehistoric megatsunami reached the Eastern Mediterranean, it would have swamped coastal parts of Egypt and the Aegean, possibly giving rise to some ancient Egyptian and Greek flood myths.

Strait of Gibraltar and the Mediterranean
Source: Wikimedia Commons – NASA

Possible Mediterranean Coastline 20,000 BP (red)
Source: From Simon Fitch and Ben Geary

Present Coastline of the Mediterranean
Source: Google Earth

Tartessos and Donana National Park

For several hundred years, the Atlantic coast of southern Spain has been promoted as the location of Atlantis, with the ancient city of Tartessos claimed to be a model for the Atlantis story.

Tartessos, or Tarshish, was a harbour city and surrounding culture at the mouth of the Guadalquivir River in present-day south-eastern Spain. The first known political system in the area emerged and collapsed from the 4th–2nd millennium BCE. Later, the people of Tartessos became important trading partners of the Phoenicians, who were present in Iberia from the 8th century BCE. The Phoenicians then built their own harbour city nearby called Gadir – present-day Cadiz. The culture of Tartessos flourished in this area under Phoenician influence, but it had vanished by the 6th century BCE. It was presumably struck by a natural disaster, possibly a tsunami, sometime between 800 and 500 BCE.

Donana National Park is located north of Cadiz. Satellite photos of Donana's wetlands show buried rectangular buildings and concentric circles, with a canal system connected to the Guadalquivir River. The rectangular forms vary in length between 20–230 metres; the diameters of the circular forms are around 100 metres. Excavations have found Palaeolithic artefacts as well as pottery sherds from the Neolithic, Copper, and early Bronze Ages.

Geological drillings to depths of eighteen metres found a sand layer in the clay subsoil, which probably is evidence of a tsunami during the 3rd millennium BCE. The large buildings buried by a tsunami in the Donana area, possibly dating to the 3rd millennium BCE, indicate an advanced Copper or Bronze Age civilisation was present in the region. Although Donana does not remotely resemble the Atlantic Island, the 3rd millennium BCE tsunami that struck the area may have come from ongoing subsidences of the Atlantic Island.

The 'shoal of mud' and Spartel Island

Plato states that a ship sailing from the Mediterranean Sea could not reach the Atlantic Island's location because of an obstruction of 'mud' caused by the Atlantic Island when it subsided.

Plato (Jowett) – 'For which reason the sea in those parts is impassable and impenetrable, because there is a shoal of in the way; and this was caused by the subsidence of the (Atlantic) island'...'(the Atlantic Island) is now a mass of impervious mud, through concussions of the Earth; so that those who are sailing in the vast sea can no longer find a passage from hence thither.'

Plato (Taylor) – 'And hence that sea is at present innavigable, arising from the gradually impeding mud which the subsiding island produced'...'(the Atlantic Island) when afterwards (after 11,600 BP) sunk by an earthquake, became an impassable barrier of mud to voyagers sailing from hence to any part of the ocean.'

There are two ways to interpret Plato's statements. One is that the Atlantic Island sank gradually and produced a mud barrier, preventing a ship already sailing in the Atlantic Ocean from going to the Americas. The other is that when the Atlantic Island sank, it caused a mud barrier at the Mediterranean's entrance, making it difficult to sail out of the Mediterranean into the Atlantic Ocean.

It is unlikely that the Ancient Egyptians, Solon, or Plato believed it was impossible to sail out of the Mediterranean because of an obstruction at the Strait of Gibraltar. Well before Solon and Plato's time, Aegean people had been sailing out of the Mediterranean since at least the Minoan civilisation of the 3rd millennium BCE. From around 750 BCE, the Ancient Greeks regularly traded with the city of Tartessos outside the Mediterranean in southern Spain.

As people could sail out of the Mediterranean from at least 5,000 BP, it seems likely that Plato's 'impassable barrier of mud' may once have been the distant, partially submerged parts of the Atlantic Island on the eastern Caribbean Plate. Any obstruction would have lasted until those parts of the Atlantic Island subsided far enough to allow ships to pass, which may have been thousands of years after 11,600 BP.

Otherwise, there is another possible explanation for Plato's 'shoal of mud'. Thousands of years ago, there may have been a partial, temporary obstruction at the entrance to the Mediterranean. The Spartel Bank is a submerged former island in the Strait of Gibraltar; its highest point is 56 metres below the surface. The Spartel Bank is one of several seamounts in the bed of Gibraltar Strait, with similar but deeper seamounts at Camarilal Sill and further east.

When the Spartel Bank was emergent, it formed Spartel Island, thought to have been submerged by the rising sea level by 12,000 BP. Nevertheless, the now-submerged area between the Strait of Gibraltar is located in a subduction zone and may once have been up to 40 metres higher than today. If that higher elevation is correct, Spartel Island and other nearby seamounts may have remained above sea level until well after 12,000 BP. They may have caused some obstruction to anyone trying to sail out of the Mediterranean.

A seafloor survey on the Spartel Bank found a 50–120cm-thick sedimentary deposit left after a tsunami struck around 12,000 BP. In prehistoric times, a combination of rising sea level and a Caribbean tsunami, or several tsunamis, that struck Spartel Island and other seamounts in a narrower and shallower Gibraltar Strait may have produced Plato's 'gradually impeding mud' or a 'shoal of mud' at the entrance to the Mediterranean. Those mud shoals may have made sailing in or out of the Mediterranean difficult until the seamounts subsided and sea levels rose further over the next few thousand years. Some investigators have claimed an emergent Spartel Island might have been Atlantis. Still, even when above sea level, Spartel Island did not resemble the enormous Atlantic Island.

Believing that the Atlantic Island and Atlantean Empire were real might inspire investigation and discovery

CHAPTER 13

Searching for Atlantis

The usual academic opinion is that none of Plato's Atlantis story is true. There is an unquestioned belief that Plato's *Timaeus* and *Critias* are complete fiction, merely something Plato fabricated to support a philosophical argument. Any alternative opinion or explanation is considered an impossibility or pseudoscience. This book has argued the exact opposite position. It aims to provide enough connected facts to confirm that Plato believed the Atlantis story and wrote an accurate account of very ancient places and events.

Once there is a belief that the Atlantic Island and Atlantean Empire were real and not fiction, it might inspire someone to investigate and discover physical evidence of them. The following sources and locations could provide further proof that Plato based his Atlantis story on fact:

- Ancient records confirming or adding to Plato's descriptions in his *Timaeus* and *Critias*.
- Geological evidence confirming Plato's 'Atlantic island' once did exist in the Caribbean.
- Physical remains of Atlantean civilisation in the Caribbean and the Americas, on various islands in the Atlantic, on the Atlantic coasts of Africa and Europe, or within the Mediterranean.
- Geological evidence of a mudslide around the present Athenian Acropolis confirming the existence of the Prehistoric Hill of the Acropolis and its destruction after 11,600 BP.
- Prehistoric remains of a Neolithic culture from around 11,600 BP in Attica or other parts of Greece that support Plato's description of Greek society at that time.

Lost Ancient Writings on Atlantis

In the Old World, the ancient libraries of Antiquity or the Mediaeval period likely kept any now-lost works about Atlantis. Some documents may have survived the destruction of those libraries and were transported to safer places but were eventually lost or forgotten. If any of those texts were discovered, they would confirm and add more substance to the Atlantis story.

If any ancient writings about Atlantis were found that dated to before Plato wrote, it would prove that he did not concoct the story. Perhaps some lost original texts other than Plato's lie buried or hidden in an undiscovered ancient site. Alternatively, they may now be unnoticed and unstudied somewhere in a museum or library. There may be a copy or copies of the original works of unknown Egyptian, Greek or Phoenician authors who discussed knowledge of Atlantis. There may also be lost translations of those ancient texts in Latin, Arabic, Irish, English, or other languages.

Another possibility is finding some original New World written references to Atlantis in the Americas. Ancient Mesoamerican civilisations had a known script since at least the 1st millennium BCE, and they may have recorded oral histories of the Atlantic Island and the Atlantean Empire. There are myths in several ancient American cultures where a more ancient civilising culture came from an island to the east.

The Egyptians' 'sacred registers'

Solon was supposed to have seen the Egyptians' 'sacred registers' around 570 BCE. Any original Egyptian documents from that time or before were probably written on papyrus or animal skin, so they are unlikely to have survived to the present day. Although later Egyptian priests may have copied the Atlantis story, those copies would still have had to survive for about two thousand years until the present.

Solon's original Greek translation would have disintegrated long ago, as would any copies written up to Plato's time in the 4th century BCE. There may have been later copies of Solon's translation, but that is unlikely.

Both Crantor and Proclus state that the Egyptians wrote the Atlantis story in hieroglyphs carved on columns at the Temple of Neith in Sais. Finding them would confirm that the Ancient Egyptians did record the Atlantis story. Given the amount of past destruction at the site, it is improbable that anyone will ever discover those columns with intact, legible hieroglyphics. There possibly were hieroglyphs about the Atlantis story on other temple buildings in Egypt; if so, they remain undiscovered.

Plato's Lost *Critias* and Other Ancient Texts on Atlantis

It is argued here that Plato did complete the *Critias* dialogue, but its remainder was lost over the following hundreds of years. In the first part of the *Critias*, Plato implies that it contained a narrative of the Mediterranean War against the Atlanteans. If the remainder were ever found, it would likely describe the military role of the Athenians and their allies. It might include the various battles against the Atlanteans that eventually drove them from the Mediterranean.

Crantor was a follower of Plato who studied at the Academy in Athens shortly after Plato's death in the 4th century BCE. Although he wrote commentaries on Plato's dialogues, only fragments survive. Because Crantor thought Plato's Atlantis story was a historical fact, he probably studied a complete *Critias* dialogue. As Crantor wrote a now-lost commentary on the *Timaeus*, he also may have written one on the *Critias* that included the remainder of the Atlantis story. If he did write one, it is now lost.

A passage from Proclus' 4th century CE commentary on Plato's *Timaeus* describes the islands that remained after the Atlantic Island sank. It is the only surviving work apart from Plato's that suggests a possible location for the Atlantic Island. Proclus states that knowledge of these islands was in a text called the *Aethiopica*, written by an unidentified author named Marcellus. Marcellus' *Aethiopica* is a lost work that might have contained more discussion about the Atlantic Island. Also, suppose a complete *Critias* had survived until Proclus' time in the 4th century CE. In that case, Proclus may have written a now-lost commentary on the *Critias* discussing the remainder of the Atlantis story.

Proclus claimed that in his time in the 4th century CE, the Atlantis story was still visible in Egypt on the columns of the Temple of Neith at Sais. If his claim is valid, for almost one thousand years after Solon visited Egypt, other ancient travellers may have seen those hieroglyphs, translated them, and written their versions of the Atlantis story.

The Temple of Neith was destroyed sometime between the 4th and 14th centuries CE, after which the columns and Atlantis hieroglyphs were probably no longer visible. Although a form of Ancient Egyptian was spoken until the 17th century CE, few Egyptians could read hieroglyphs by the 4th century CE. The meaning of Egyptian hieroglyphs was forgotten until the Rosetta Stone was discovered in 1799 CE and deciphered in the 1820s CE. Therefore, if someone had seen the hieroglyphs at the Temple of Neith between the 4th and 14th century CE, they probably had little or no understanding of them.

Physical Evidence of the Atlantis Story

If anyone finds physical evidence of an Atlantean Empire, it would be a revolutionary archaeological discovery that would change our understanding of when and where human civilisation began. The most obvious question to ask is why no one has found any material evidence of Atlantean civilisation. The most obvious answer is that no one has been looking in the right places for that evidence.

As archaeology became more sophisticated over the past one or two hundred years, archaeologists discovered numerous unknown ancient towns, cities and even previously unknown cultures and entire civilisations. Sometimes, a local legend, myth or ancient written source might stir someone's curiosity to look for evidence of a culture in a particular location. Others may discover an ancient site when they look at a landscape and notice certain features that could mean human occupation. An unusual mound might mean cultural artefacts are buried below it; a fresh-water source such as a river that once flowed in ancient times might indicate the location of a settlement there.

Archaeologists have excavated many once-buried sites of ancient civilisations from around the Earth. Entire cities that once thrived with tens of thousands of people were destroyed or abandoned and then forgotten in a few thousand years and sometimes much sooner. Natural processes eroded or buried them under metres of soil, so they became invisible and unknown to later generations.

The Atlantean civilisation began before 11,600 BP, so even if it lasted two or three thousand years or more, any physical remains on the land's surface would likely be deeply buried or eroded beyond recognition. To find an ancient buried site on land, remote sensing techniques such as aerial photography, Lidar, or satellite imaging can reveal structures covered by dense vegetation or invisible at ground level. Once a potential archaeological site is found, a geophysical survey on the ground can map the site's subsurface. The most common tools used for site-mapping are magnetometers, electrical resistance meters, ground-penetrating radar and electromagnetic conductivity meters. The final step in the discovery process may be the excavation of the site.

The Atlanteans were seafaring people, so the main settlements of the Atlantean Empire beyond the Atlantic Island would probably have been coastal towns and cities. As stated several times, the global sea level is now sixty metres higher than in 11,600 BP. That entire sixty metres increase occurred before 6,000 BP, so evidence of any civilisations located in coastal regions, from well before 11,600 until 6,000 BP, is now likely to be underwater.

The coastal settlements of the Atlanteans or other very ancient cultures would likely have developed where rivers and natural harbours existed long before 6,000 years ago. To find any Atlantean coastal towns or cities, investigators would need to imagine what a coastline in a particular area looked like when the sea level was much lower than now, possibly lower by 60 metres or more.

Underwater archaeology has developed only recently because of the difficulty accessing and working underwater sites. In the initial exploration phase, remote sensing techniques can locate objects and structures on the seafloor and deeper structures covered by many metres of sediment. Bathymetric (hydrographic) maps show seafloor terrain and are created from an echo-sounder (sonar) mounted beneath or over the side of a boat. Sub-bottom profilers towed behind a boat are more powerful echo-sounders that reveal the upper layers of the ocean bottom; commercially available devices can penetrate 300 metres of sediment in 12,000 metres of water. Side-scan sonar towed behind a boat can find objects like shipwrecks on the seafloor's surface.

The maximum depth for a professional scuba diver is less than one hundred metres. However, a remotely operated vehicle (ROV) or an autonomous underwater vehicle (AUV) can be used for waters deeper than divers can safely survey or excavate.

An ROV is a tethered underwater vehicle linked to a ship by a group of cables that carry electrical power, video and data signals between the ROV and the operator on the ship. Most ROVs are equipped with a video camera and lights, while additional equipment may include sonar, magnetometers, a still camera, and a manipulator or cutting arm. Whereas the operating depth for most commercially available ROVs is from 1,000 to 3,000 metres, some can operate at depths of over 7,000 metres.

As an alternative to an ROV, an AUV is a self-propelled, untethered underwater vehicle programmed for use with little or no human supervision. Sizes range from vehicles weighing tens of kilograms to thousands of kilograms, and some can operate to depths of over 6,000 metres.

Material Evidence of an Atlantic Island

If the present eastern Caribbean Sea floor is the location of a large part of the Atlantic Island, it was submerged sometime after 11,600 BP. Unfortunately, existing interpretations of underwater drill cores taken from the Venezuelan Basin and the Beata and Aves Ridges are not precise enough to prove any definite change in their elevation within the past 250,000 years.

Those existing drill cores are stored for future study. If they were reviewed to look for significant emergence or subsidence, the upper levels might show some evidence of recent vertical movements. Otherwise, new drilling investigations could create more specific and accurate drill cores for recent vertical changes. A recordable change in elevation in old or new drill cores could confirm the past emergence and recent subsidence of the Atlantic Island.

Ultimately, the most convincing evidence for Plato's 'Atlantic island' would be the discovery of the Atlantean Royal City with its Circular Zones of sea and land, or the grid of irrigation and transport canals on the Plain of Atlantis, or any submerged provincial Atlantean towns or cities. As this potential evidence might be from tens of metres to 3,000 metres below sea level, remote underwater sensing devices such as a sub-bottom profiler, an ROV or AUV would be required to find any human-built structures there.

The Circum-Caribbean Region

Apart from the submerged Venezuelan Basin or Beata and Aves Ridges, the most likely places to look for any physical evidence of Atlantean culture would be in regions around the present Caribbean. Those locations were probably part of the Atlantean Empire before and after 11,600 BP.

It is unknown how long the Atlantean Empire and its outlying colonies survived before or after the island sank. As sea levels rose sixty metres from 11,600 BP to 6,000 BP, much of the physical evidence of Atlantean civilisation outside the Atlantic Island would now be underwater. Any abandoned cities

Approximate position of the shoreline (dark outline) when sea level was 100 metres lower
Source: Wikimedia Commons – adapted from Derekk2

and towns that remained above sea level would now be buried or destroyed by natural processes.

Marcellus' 'remnant islands' of Atlantis could be the Caribbean Islands of Cuba, Jamaica, Hispaniola, Puerto Rico and some of the Lesser Antilles. The Atlanteans likely inhabited these islands and probably the Leeward Antilles, Trinidad and Tobago.

Thousands of years ago, various sophisticated early civilisations arose in the Americas that are at least as old as the first known civilisations of the Old World. Still, the traces of even earlier civilisations in the Americas may be lost and undiscovered.

The most likely places to search for evidence of Atlantean civilisation, or its early successors, would be in the regions where known complex cultures first arose in the Americas. Examples of very early American cultures are the Old Copper Complex near the Great Lakes; the Mound Builders of south-eastern North America; the Olmec Heartland and the Maya of the Yucatan Peninsula in Mesoamerica; the Muisca and Tairona of Colombia; the Las Vegas culture of Ecuador; and the Norte Chico civilisation of Peru.

The Islands of the Atlantic

The Atlanteans' sailing route between the Caribbean and the Mediterranean possibly included the islands lying off the north-west coast of Africa. To provision their ships as they crossed the Atlantic, the Atlanteans might have developed ports and settlements on the islands of Cape Verde, the Canaries, Madeira and possibly the Azores.

In particular, the Canary Islands may be the most promising for some evidence of an Atlantean settlement that still survives above sea level. When the Carthaginians under Hanno the Navigator visited the Canaries in the 5th century BCE, they claimed to have seen the ruins of great buildings. These buildings were unlikely to have been built by the Guanche, the Neolithic-level inhabitants of the islands thought to have arrived from north-west Africa about 1,000 BCE or possibly earlier. So, the Atlanteans perhaps built on the Canaries thousands of years before the Guanche arrived there.

The Coasts of Northern Africa and Southern Europe

Before extending into the Mediterranean, the Atlanteans may have colonised the Atlantic coasts of Iberia and north-west Africa. In particular, the site of ancient Tartessos in Spain could be the location of a much earlier Atlantean colony.

Within the Mediterranean, Plato states that the Atlantean Empire extended as far as Italy in the north and Egypt in the south. If the Atlanteans occupied those lands for decades, centuries, or longer, they probably built ports and settlements along the coastlines. They also may have colonised the Mediterranean islands of the Balearics, Corsica, Sardinia, and Malta.

The Nile Delta and Sais

Compared to the present, the Nile Delta and the coastline of Egypt of 11,600 BP extended much further into the Mediterranean. Therefore, there may be underwater evidence of a Neolithic Egyptian culture that existed before the founding of Sais around 10,600 BP. Plato stated that an earlier Egyptian culture participated in the Mediterranean War against the Atlanteans. If a site were discovered for a prehistoric settlement of Sais dated to around 10,600 BP, it would confirm Plato's statement that Sais was founded then.

Athens and the Aegean

Plato describes how the people of Athens and Attica had a relatively advanced Neolithic culture around 11,600 BP, despite that being a couple of thousand years before any sign of Neolithic culture so far found in Greece. Nevertheless, some undiscovered evidence of earlier Neolithic settlements in Attica or other parts of mainland Greece may exist. Neolithic culture in Greece is assumed to have come from the Near East, where increasing evidence shows it developed much earlier than previously thought. So, it also may have arrived in Greece before 11,600 BP.

In Athens, finding and dating evidence of a massive prehistoric mudslide between the Pnyx and Mount Lycabettus would confirm the catastrophic destruction of the Hill of the Acropolis. Core drilling may show a sudden and distinct change in sediment type consistent with a mudslide. Analysis of any organic matter found below the mudslide layer could precisely date the catastrophe. If a prehistoric mudslide is confirmed, an excavation may find buried dwellings or the human remains of those Athenians who 'in a body sank into the Earth'.

Outside mainland Greece, the Cycladic Islands and Crete are likely locations for very early Neolithic civilisations because that is where Greece's first sophisticated Bronze Age civilisations developed in the 5th millennium BP. In particular, the culture of the Cycladic islands was once the most advanced in the Aegean, preceding the Minoan civilisation of Crete by hundreds of years. If the sea level on the Cycladic Plateau in the Aegean were sixty metres lower in 11,600 BP than now, individual Cycladic islands would have been much larger. Some would have been joined together, such as the large island of Cycladia, and would have supported larger populations compared to later times.

The Americas should be considered the first 'Cradle of Civilisation' rather than cultures in Mesopotamia, Egypt, India or China

Conclusion

Ultimately, the critical issue is whether Plato based his Atlantis story on fact. Contemporary scholars insist Plato fabricated all of it to prove a philosophical point. Contrary to that dismissive view, the evidence presented here indicates Plato believed the Atlantis story was an accurate historical account, and more of the story existed but is now lost. Supporting evidence from many unconnected scientific fields can explain the details of Plato's Atlantis story. When viewed as a whole, it points to the existence of a powerful prehistoric Bronze Age civilisation centred on an enormous Atlantic Island in the Caribbean.

Plato states that Atlantean civilisation flourished thousands of years before any known ancient civilisation on Earth. If the Atlanteans created their civilisation on the Atlantic Island, the Americas should be considered the first 'Cradle of Civilisation' rather than any Old World cultures in Mesopotamia, Egypt, India or China. Significantly, the Americas were one of the few regions on Earth where complex civilisations developed several thousand years ago without any proven outside influence. Therefore, the Americas may have been where earlier, unknown civilisations developed, including Atlantean culture.

If the Atlanteans ventured east across the Atlantic Ocean to colonise the Mediterranean more than eleven thousand years ago, they might have transferred some features of their advanced civilisation to the Mediterranean's more primitive cultures. It might then have been the Atlanteans who initiated the development of what we know as civilisation in the Mediterranean and the rest of the Old World beyond.

Three crucial questions must be answered when explaining and defending Plato's story of an Atlantic Island and the Atlantean Empire. Firstly, did Plato believe his Atlantis story was true and was it the same as the early Egyptians recorded thousands of years before him? Secondly, if the Atlantis story accurately describes the Atlantic Island, where was it located and were Plato's accounts of its geology, biology, and Atlantean culture possible? Thirdly, what geological mechanism might explain the creation and destruction of the Atlantic Island?

Plato: 'Then listen, Socrates, to a tale which, though strange, is certainly true, having been attested by Solon, who was the wisest of the seven sages.' This statement and several others in the *Timaeus* and *Critias* mean that Plato believed his Atlantis story was an accurate account of very ancient events.

The prominent Athenian historical figure Solon is known to have visited Egypt, where he spoke with senior Egyptian temple priests at Sais. Plato states the Egyptian priests showed Solon their 'sacred registers' about Atlantis, which were recorded and copied continuously until Solon's time in the 6th century BCE. Solon wrote a document in Greek based on the Egyptians' records; Plato accessed and used Solon's document to write his *Timaeus* and *Critias*. If Solon saw and translated all of the particulars in the Egyptians' records, there is no reason for the Egyptian priests, Solon, or Plato to fabricate any of those details, let alone the entire Atlantis story.

Plato states that the 'Atlantic island' was located in the Atlantic Ocean, which he calls 'the true ocean' outside the Mediterranean Sea. The Atlantic Island was opposite the Strait of Heracles (Gibraltar) and was the way to 'the opposite continent which surrounded the true ocean'. That 'continent' can only be the Americas, seemingly unknown to the Greeks of Solon and Plato's time. Plato describes the Atlantic Island as 'larger than Libya and Asia put together', estimated to be over one million square kilometres. If so, the Caribbean region is the only Atlantic site large enough to comfortably fit the Atlantic Island. Besides Plato, the ancient author Marcellus gives a separate, independent account of individual islands that remained above sea level after the Atlantic Island sank. Marcellus' description closely matches some of the present Caribbean islands and further confirms a Caribbean location for the Atlantic Island.

If a large part of the eastern Caribbean Plate were once above sea level, it would accurately match Plato's geographical description of the enormous Atlantic Island: a vast rectangular plain surrounded by extensive mountain ranges, except to the south. The size and shape of the Plain of Atlantis are virtually identical to the now-submerged Venezuelan Basin. The plants and animals on the Atlantic Island match the flora and fauna of the prehistoric Americas. In particular, some of the now-extinct animals in the Americas, such as elephants and horses, would not have co-existed more than 11,000 years ago in any other location proposed for the Atlantic Island.

Modern humans most likely travelled by sea to the Americas at least 20,000 years ago. By then, they were also capable of colonising an emergent Atlantic Island in the Caribbean. Therefore, a human population could have been on the Atlantic Island for thousands of years before the time of the Atlantis story. That would have been enough time for the people on the Atlantic Island to develop from hunter-gatherers to a Neolithic and then a Bronze Age Atlantean civilisation, with all of the technological features Plato describes. The Atlanteans then expanded as an empire into surrounding lands in the Americas and later sailed across the Atlantic to colonise the Mediterranean.

Following the destruction of the Atlantic Island and Atlantean civilisation sometime after 11,600 BP, there may have been a Dark Age in the Americas lasting a few thousand years, with any cultures there regressing to a more primitive level. Later, a sequence of New World civilisations developed their social and technological achievements over thousands of years. Those various cultures in the Americas developed virtually all of the elements of the Atlantean civilisation Plato describes. They used the same natural resources as the Atlanteans but lacked domesticated working animals other than llamas and alpacas.

The Hydraulic Hypothesis describes a geological mechanism below the Earth's surface connected to changes in glacial ice thickness at the Earth's poles. It possibly caused Late Cenozoic Uplift, where many massive mountain ranges around the Earth formed almost simultaneously in the geologically short time of the last few million years.

The Hydraulic Hypothesis' effects on the Caribbean Plate can explain the creation and destruction of the Atlantic Island. The Caribbean Hypothesis describes large vertical movements of components of the Caribbean Plate over the last thirty-five million years. Those vertical movements appear to match the different stages of glacial ice accumulation over the polar tectonic plates. The Atlantis story states the Atlantic Island submerged sometime after 11,600 BP. Unfortunately, there is no definite geological evidence to confirm the precise timing of that catastrophic subsidence.

Once a real Atlantean civilisation is thought possible or probable, a search may begin to find archaeological evidence. Many important past archaeological discoveries were based on someone imagining a historical possibility and then looking for some material proof in the right location. For example, the discoveries of ancient Old World cities, such as Mycenae in the Peloponnese, Troy in Anatolia, and Knossos in Crete, only happened because committed individuals believed that Homer based the *Iliad* and *Odyssey* on actual events. Those individuals then looked for and discovered physical evidence that confirmed the truth of ancient stories, previously thought only to be myths.

The Atlantis story can be interpreted as a warning to humanity about our future as a species. Plato states that many previous 'destructions of mankind' were mainly due to 'the agencies of fire and water' and 'innumerable other causes'. Like the eventual fate of the ambitious Atlanteans, regardless of how powerful and technologically advanced an individual civilisation may be, external and internal factors can destroy it. Irrespective of whether or not they were more moral than the Atlanteans, the prehistoric Athenians were not immune to natural disasters such as the destruction of the Acropolis Hill or many 'deluges' and 'great conflagrations'.

What Plato calls 'the agencies of fire and water' are the effects of natural climate cycles, which the Egyptians had recorded for thousands of years. So far, any measurable climate change due to human activity is minor compared to the huge natural climate fluctuations of the past. Although the stable climate of the past twelve thousand years of the Holocene Epoch is temporary, there were several significant climate fluctuations even within that relatively short time. Those prolonged warmer and colder periods seem to alternate every few hundred years. The more recent climate episodes disrupted regional weather patterns and destroyed the food sources of entire civilisations, contributing to their decline or collapse. Any similar short-term natural climate changes over the next thousand years or so will be mostly unaffected by human-generated climate change.

The Earth may now be in a short natural warming period that may last a few hundred years, followed by a cooling period for a few hundred years. However, those relatively short fluctuations are not the same as the much longer glacial/interglacial cycles of the Quaternary Ice Age. The next cold glacial period will eventually start in the next few thousand years and possibly much earlier. It will be similar to the preceding two glacial/interglacial cycles, so massive ice sheets will again grow over North America and Eurasia.

During a period of one hundred thousand years, kilometres-thick ice sheets will eventually cover millions of square kilometres of land humans now occupy. Any towns or cities in the path of the ice sheets will be scraped off the Earth's surface. On the other hand, the sea level will fall by tens of metres, increasing the Earth's habitable coastal land by millions of square kilometres. This extreme natural climate change may happen soon or thousands of years from now, but it will happen, and humans cannot alter its course.

For the Atlanteans, it seems that geological upheaval and the Atlantic Island's sinking was the primary cause of their final destruction. Yet, there also was a degeneration of Atlantean society. Plato states the Atlanteans 'appeared glorious and blessed at the very time when they were full of avarice and unrighteous power'. Their advanced Bronze Age technology compared to surrounding cultures allowed them to dominate, but imperial expansion may have played a large part in their decline and ultimate downfall. For thousands of years, empires all over the Earth have risen and fallen. Even though one culture's desire and ability to create an empire and control those around it might succeed for hundreds of years, the empire will eventually collapse.

A sustainable political system is vital for any society's development and survival. Plato partly uses the Atlantis story to illustrate the political and social differences between Atlantean and Athenian societies, highlighting some contrasting features of the two cultures. The autocratic Ten Kings of Atlantis ruled the predatory Atlantean Empire, unlike the prehistoric Athenians who led free lives as leaders, warriors, artisans and farmers. The Atlanteans had a huge conscripted military they used to expand the Atlantean Empire by controlling and enslaving conquered people; the Athenians had a voluntary communal warrior class maintained for the state's defence. Plato claims that prehistoric Athens was the 'best governed of all cities' by the 'wisest of men' and 'had the fairest constitution of any of which tradition tells'. He prefers the simple, ordered, law-abiding community of prehistoric Athens to the Atlantean elite's material wealth, military aggression and expansion.

Admittedly, it is a stretch of the imagination to think that the extraordinary Atlantean civilisation once existed in the Americas. Yet, for many thousands of years all over the Earth, modern humans have possessed the intellectual potential and physical ability to organise themselves into societies and develop great civilisations. Those essential human capabilities have existed unchanged for tens of thousands of years and would have existed in the Atlantean people more than eleven thousand years ago.

Human evolution is a very slow process. We *Homo sapiens* are little changed physically, intellectually and emotionally from when we evolved in Africa more than 200,000 years ago. The Atlanteans, prehistoric Egyptians and Athenians of the Atlantis story were humans like us. Any future humans will be fundamentally the same as us, whether one hundred, one thousand, or ten thousand years from now. Those future humans will have the same positive and negative emotions, behavioural strengths and flaws we have now. They will need stable, effective social and political systems to prosper and continue on Earth as a species.

Our human species and global civilisation needs sufficient time for our technologies to become more efficient and resilient, for our global population to stabilise or decline, and for our political systems to nurture productive societies. One can only hope that the next fifty to one hundred years is enough time for those profound changes. In the meantime, let us hope Plato's 'destructions of mankind...by innumerable other causes' do not cut short our modern globalised civilisation and lead to a new Dark Age. That includes human-made factors such as economic collapse, political instability, major wars, and epidemic diseases.

Plato claims the Atlanteans' civilisation existed over ten thousand years ago. Can anyone imagine what civilisations on Earth will be like ten thousand years from now or merely one hundred years from now? Given we *Homo sapiens* have survived on Earth for well over two hundred thousand years, it is ironic and frightening that our fate as an entire species might depend on how we manage our global societies over just the next few decades.

The Timaeus and Critias are the only existing written records describing Atlantis

APPENDIX 1

Plato's Atlantis Dialogues

Two of Plato's dialogues, the *Timaeus* and *Critias*, are the only existing written records describing Atlantis. The dialogues are in the form of conversations between the characters of Socrates, Hermocrates, Timaeus, and Critias. In the *Timaeus* dialogue, the Critias character begins to tell Socrates about something that is 'not a fiction but a true story'; he then continues the story in the following dialogue, called the *Critias*. Unfortunately, the *Critias* dialogue is incomplete; the remainder is probably lost.

The Critias character describes the historical Athenian statesman Solon's travels to Egypt around 570 BCE. While Solon is in Egypt, some senior Egyptian temple priests tell him about the empire of Atlantis and its war against the nations of the Eastern Mediterranean. They tell Solon that the war occurred 9,000 years before his time, which is around 9600 BCE or 11,600 years before the present (11,600 BP). Solon records what the priests tell him in a document he takes back to Athens. Apart from recounting the Atlantis story to Socrates, the Critias character states he possesses a copy of Solon's document about Atlantis. Plato appears to have based the *Timaeus* and *Critias* on Solon's writings.

***Timaeus* – Translated by Benjamin Jowett (1871)**
Written by Plato in about 360 BCE

Plato's *Timaeus* dialogue begins with a summary by Socrates of a prior discussion about ideal societies, followed by a brief introduction to Atlantis and prehistoric Athens. The following passage is the part of the *Timaeus* dialogue that refers to and describes Atlantis and Athens. The remainder of the *Timaeus* dialogue discusses the creation of the universe and natural phenomena; it is omitted as it makes no further reference to Atlantis. However, there is much more about Atlantis in Plato's following dialogue – the *Critias*.

Persons of the *Timaeus* Dialogue
CRITIAS
HERMOCRATES
TIMAEUS
SOCRATES

Crit. Then listen, Socrates, to a tale which, though strange, is certainly true, having been attested by Solon, who was the wisest of the seven sages (of Ancient Greece). He was a relative and a dear friend of my great-grandfather, Dropides, as he himself says in many passages of his poems; and he told the story to Critias, my grandfather, who remembered and repeated it to us. There were of old, he said, great and marvellous actions of the Athenian city, which have passed into oblivion through lapse of time and the destruction of mankind, and one in particular, greater than all the rest. This we will now rehearse. It will be a fitting monument of our gratitude to you, and a hymn of praise true and worthy of the goddess (Athena) on this, her day of festival.

Soc. Very good. And what is this ancient famous action of the Athenians?

Crit. I will tell an old-world story which I heard from an aged man; for Critias (the grandfather), at the time of telling it, was as he said, nearly ninety years of age, and I (the grandson in the dialogue) was about ten. Now the day was that day of the Apaturia (festival) which is called the Registration of Youth, at which, according to custom, our parents gave prizes for recitations, and the poems of several poets were recited by us boys, and many of us sang the poems of Solon, which at that time had not gone out of fashion.

One of our tribe, either because he thought so or to please Critias, said that in his judgment Solon was not only the wisest of men, but also the noblest of poets. The old man, as I very well remember, brightened up at hearing this and said, smiling: Yes, Amynander, and had he not been compelled, by reason of the factions and troubles which he found stirring in his own country (Athens) when he came home, to attend to other matters, in my opinion he would have been as famous as Homer or Hesiod, or any poet.

And what was the tale about, Critias? Said Amynander.

About the greatest action which the Athenians ever did, and which ought to have been the most famous, but, through the lapse of time and the destruction of the actors, it has not come down to us.

Tell us, said the other, the whole story, and how and from whom Solon heard this veritable tradition. He replied:

In the Egyptian Delta, at the head of which the river Nile divides, there is a certain district which is called the district of Sais, and the great city of the district is also called Sais, and is the city from which King (Pharaoh) Amasis came. The citizens have a deity for their foundress; she is called in the Egyptian tongue Neith, and is asserted by them to be the same whom the Hellenes (Greeks) call Athene; they are great lovers of the Athenians and say that they are in some way related to them.

On one occasion, wishing to draw them (the Egyptian priests) on to speak of antiquity, he (Solon) began to tell about the most ancient things in our part of the world – about Phoroneus, who is called the first man, and about Niobe; and after the Deluge, of the survival of Deucalion and Pyrrha; and he traced the genealogy of their descendants, and reckoning up the dates, tried to compute how many years ago the events of which he was speaking happened.

Thereupon one of the priests, who was of a very great age, said: O Solon, Solon, you Hellenes are never anything but children, and there is not an old man among you. Solon in return asked him what he meant. I mean to say, he replied, that in mind you are all young; there is no old opinion handed down among you by ancient tradition, nor any science which is hoary with age. And I will tell you why. There have been, and will be again, many destructions of mankind arising out of many causes; the greatest have been brought about by the agencies of fire and water, and other lesser ones by innumerable other causes.

There is a story, which even you (Greeks) have preserved, that once upon a time Phaethon, the son of Helios (the god of the Sun), having yoked the steeds in his father's chariot (the Sun), because he was not able to drive them in the path of his father, burnt up all that was upon the earth, and was himself destroyed by a thunderbolt. Now this has the form of a myth, but really signifies a declination of the bodies moving in the heavens around the earth, and a great conflagration of things upon the earth, which recurs after long intervals. At such times, those who live upon the mountains and in dry and lofty places are more liable to destruction than those who dwell by rivers or on the seashore. And from this calamity the Nile, who is our never-failing saviour, delivers and preserves us (Egyptians).

When, on the other hand, the gods purge the earth with a deluge of water, the survivors in your country (Greece) are herdsmen and shepherds who dwell on the mountains, but those who, like you, live in cities are carried by the rivers into the sea. While in this land (Egypt), neither then nor at any other time, does the water come down from above on the fields, having always a tendency to come up from below; for which reason the traditions preserved here are the most ancient. The fact is, that wherever the extremity of winter frost or of summer does not prevent, mankind exist, sometimes in greater, sometimes in lesser numbers. And whatever happened either in your country or in ours, or in any other region of which we are informed – if there were any actions noble or great or in any other way remarkable, they have all been written down by us of old, and are preserved in our temples.

While, just when you (Greeks) and other nations are beginning to be provided with letters and the other requisites of civilised life, after the usual interval, the stream from heaven, like a pestilence, comes pouring down and leaves only those of you who are destitute of letters and education; and so you have to begin all over again like children and know nothing of what happened in ancient times, either among us or among yourselves. As for those genealogies of yours which you just now recounted to us, Solon, they are no better than the tales of children.

In the first place you remember a single deluge only, but there were many previous ones; in the next place, you do not know that there formerly dwelt in your land the fairest and noblest race of men which ever lived, and that you and your whole city are descended from a small seed or remnant of them which survived. This was unknown to you because for many generations the survivors of that destruction died, leaving no written word. For there was a time, Solon, before the great deluge of all, when the city which now is Athens was first in war and in every way the best governed of all cities; it is said to have performed the noblest deeds and to have had the fairest constitution of any of which tradition tells, under the face of heaven.

Solon marvelled at his words and earnestly requested the priests to inform him exactly and in order about these former citizens. You are welcome to hear about them, Solon, said the priest, both for your own sake and for that of your city, and above all, for the sake of the goddess (Athena/Neith) who is the common patron and parent and educator of both our cities. She founded your city (Athens) a thousand years before ours (Sais), receiving from the Earth and (the god) Hephaestus the seed of your race, and afterwards she founded ours, of which the constitution is recorded in our sacred registers to be eight thousand years old.

As touching your citizens of nine thousand years ago, I will briefly inform you of their laws and of their most famous action; the exact particulars of the whole we will hereafter go through at our leisure in the sacred registers themselves. If you compare these very laws with ours, you will find that many of ours are the counterpart of yours as they were in the olden time.

In the first place, there is the caste of priests, which is separated from all the others; next, there are the artificers (artisans) who ply their several crafts by themselves and do not intermix; and also there is the class of shepherds and of hunters, as well as that of husbandmen (farmers); and you will observe, too, that the warriors in Egypt are distinct from all the other classes, and are commanded by the law to devote themselves solely to military pursuits; moreover, the weapons which they carry are shields and spears, a style of equipment which the goddess (Athena/Neith) taught of Asiatics first to us, as in your part of the world first to you.

Then as to wisdom, do you observe how our (Egyptian) law from the very first made a study of the whole order of things, extending even to prophecy and medicine which gives health; out of these divine elements deriving what was needful for human life and adding every sort of knowledge which was akin to them. All this order and arrangement the goddess first imparted to you when establishing your city (Athens); and she chose the spot of Earth in which you were born, because she saw that the happy temperament of the seasons in that land would produce the wisest of men. Wherefore the goddess, who was a lover both of war and of wisdom, selected and first of all settled that spot which was the most likely to produce men likest herself. And there you dwelt, having such laws as these and still better ones, and excelled all mankind in all virtue, as became the children and disciples of the gods.

Many great and wonderful deeds are recorded of your state in our histories. But one of them exceeds all the rest in greatness and valour. For these histories tell of a mighty power which unprovoked made an expedition against the whole of Europe and Asia, and to which your city put an end. This power came forth out of the Atlantic Ocean, for in those days the Atlantic was navigable; and there was an island situated in front of the straits which are by you called the Pillars of Heracles; the island was larger than Libya and Asia put together, and was the way to other islands, and from these you may pass to the whole of the opposite continent which surrounded the true ocean; for this sea (the Mediterranean) which is within the Straits of Heracles is only a harbour, having a narrow entrance, but that other is a real sea, and the surrounding land may be most truly called a boundless continent.

Now in this island of Atlantis there was a great and wonderful empire which had rule over the whole island and several others, and over parts of the continent, and, furthermore, the men of Atlantis had subjected the parts of Libya within the columns of Heracles as far as Egypt, and of Europe as far as Tyrrhenia. This vast power, gathered into one, endeavoured to subdue at a blow our country and yours and the whole of the region within the straits; and then, Solon, your country shone forth, in the excellence of her virtue and strength, among all mankind. She was pre-eminent in courage and military skill, and was the leader of the Hellenes. And when the rest fell off from her, being compelled to stand alone, after having undergone the very extremity of danger, she defeated and triumphed over the invaders, and preserved from slavery those who were not yet subjugated, and generously liberated all the rest of us who dwell within the pillars.

But afterwards there occurred violent earthquakes and floods; and in a single day and night of misfortune all your (Athenian) warlike men in a body sank into the earth, and the island of Atlantis in like manner disappeared in the depths of the sea. For which reason the sea in those parts is impassable and impenetrable, because there is a shoal of mud in the way; and this was caused by the subsidence of the island.

I have told you briefly, Socrates, what the aged Critias heard from Solon and related to us. And when you were speaking yesterday about your city and citizens, the tale which I have just been repeating to you came into my mind, and I remarked with astonishment how, by some mysterious coincidence, you agreed in almost every particular with the narrative of Solon; but I did not like to speak at the moment. For a long time had elapsed, and I had forgotten too much; I thought that I must first of all run over the narrative in my own mind, and then I would speak.

And so I readily assented to your request yesterday, considering that in all such cases the chief difficulty is to find a tale suitable to our purpose, and that with such a tale we should be fairly well provided. And therefore, as Hermocrates has told you, on my way home yesterday I at once communicated the tale to my companions as I remembered it; and after I left them, during the night by thinking I recovered nearly the whole of it. Truly, as is often said, the lessons of our childhood make wonderful impression on our memories; for I am not sure that I could remember all the discourse of yesterday, but I should be much surprised if I forgot any of these things which I have heard very long ago. I listened at the time with childlike interest to the old man's narrative; he was very ready to teach me, and I asked him again and again to repeat his words, so that like an indelible picture they were branded into my mind. As soon as the day broke, I rehearsed them as he spoke them to my companions, that they, as well as myself, may have something to say. And now, Socrates, to make an end to my preface, I am ready to tell you the whole tale. I will give you not only the general heads, but the particulars, as they were told to me.

The city and citizens, which you yesterday described to us in fiction, we will now transfer to the world of reality. It shall be the ancient city of Athens, and we will suppose that the citizens whom you imagined, were our veritable ancestors, of whom the priest spoke; they will perfectly harmonise, and there will be no inconsistency in saying that the citizens of your republic are these ancient Athenians. Let us divide the subject among us, and all endeavour according to our ability gracefully to execute the task which you have imposed upon us. Consider then, Socrates, if this narrative is suited to the purpose, or whether we should seek for some other instead.

Soc. And what other, Critias, can we find that will be better than this, which is natural and suitable to the festival of the goddess (Athena), and has the very great advantage of being a fact and not a fiction? How or where shall we find another if we abandon this? We cannot, and therefore you must tell the tale, and good luck to you; and I in return for my yesterday's discourse will now rest and be a listener.

Crit. Let me proceed to explain to you, Socrates, the order in which we have arranged our entertainment. Our intention is, that Timaeus, who is the most of an astronomer amongst us, and has made the nature of the universe his special study, should speak first, beginning with the generation of the world and going down to the creation of man; next, I am to receive the men whom he has created of whom some will have profited by the excellent education which you have given them; and then, in accordance with the tale of Solon, and equally with his law, we will bring them into court and make them citizens, as if they were those very Athenians whom the sacred Egyptian record has recovered from oblivion, and thenceforward we will speak of them as Athenians and fellow-citizens.

Soc. I see that I shall receive in my turn a perfect and splendid feast of reason. And now, Timaeus, you, I suppose, should speak next, after duly calling upon the Gods.

That is the end of any discussion about Atlantis or prehistoric Athens in the *Timaeus*; much more will follow in the *Critias*.

Critias – Translated by Benjamin Jowett (1871) Written by Plato in about 360 BCE

As can be seen from his introduction to the *Critias*, the translator Benjamin Jowett thought Plato's Atlantis story was a complete fiction. Academics have echoed Jowett's negative opinion of the Atlantis story for generations.

Jowett's Introduction:
No one knew better than Plato how to invent 'a noble lie'. Observe (1) the innocent declaration of Socrates, that the truth of the story is a great advantage: (2) the manner in which traditional names and indications of geography are intermingled ('Why, here be truths!'): (3) the extreme minuteness with which the numbers are given, as in the Old Epic poetry: (4) the ingenious reason assigned for the Greek names occurring in the Egyptian tale: (5) the remark that the armed statue of Athena indicated the common warrior life of men and women: (6) the particularity with which the third deluge before that of Deucalion is affirmed to have been the great destruction: (7) the happy guess that great geological changes have been affected by water: (8) the indulgence of the prejudice against sailing beyond the Columns, and the popular belief of the shallowness of the ocean in that part: (9) the confession that the depth of the ditch in the Island of Atlantis was not to be believed, and 'yet he could only repeat what he had heard', compared with the statement made in an earlier passage that Poseidon, being a God, found no difficulty in contriving the water-supply of the centre island: (10) the mention of the old rivalry of Poseidon and Athene, and the creation of the first inhabitants out of the soil. Plato here, as elsewhere, ingeniously gives the impression that he is telling the truth which mythology had corrupted.

The world, like a child, has readily, and for the most part unhesitatingly, accepted the tale of the Island of Atlantis. In modern times we hardly seek for traces of the submerged continent; but even Mr. Grote is inclined to believe in the Egyptian poem of Solon of which there is no evidence in antiquity; while others, like Martin, discuss the Egyptian origin of the legend, or like M. de Humboldt, whom he quotes, are disposed to find in it a vestige of a widely-spread tradition. Others, adopting a different vein of reflection, regard the Island of Atlantis as the anticipation of a still greater island – the Continent of America. 'The tale,' says M. Martin, 'rests upon the authority of the Egyptian priests; and the Egyptian priests took a pleasure in deceiving the Greeks.' He never appears to suspect that there is a greater deceiver or magician than the Egyptian priests, that is to say, Plato himself, from the dominion of whose genius the critic and natural philosopher of modern times are not wholly emancipated. Although worthless in respect of any result which can be attained by them, discussions like those of M. Martin have an interest of their own, and may be compared to the similar discussions regarding the Lost Tribes, as showing how the chance word of some poet or philosopher has given birth to endless religious or historical enquiries.

In contrasting the small Greek city numbering about twenty thousand inhabitants with the barbaric greatness of the island of Atlantis, Plato probably intended to show that a state, such as the ideal Athens, was invincible, though matched against any number of opponents. Even in a great empire there may be a degree of virtue and justice, such as the Greeks believed to have existed under the sway of the first Persian kings. But all such empires were liable to degenerate, and soon incurred the anger of the gods. Their Oriental wealth, and splendour of gold and silver, and variety of colours, seemed also to be at variance with the simplicity of Greek notions. In the island of Atlantis, Plato is describing a sort of Babylonian or Egyptian city, to which he opposes the frugal life of the true Hellenic citizen. It is remarkable that in his brief sketch of them, he idealizes the husbandmen 'who are lovers of honour and true husbandmen,' as well as the warriors who are his sole concern in the *Republic*; and that though he speaks of the common pursuits of men and women, he says nothing of the community of wives and children.

It is singular that Plato should have prefixed the most detested of Athenian names (Critias, a tyrant) to this dialogue, and even more singular that he should have put into the mouth of Socrates a panegyric (tribute) on him. Yet we know that his character was accounted infamous by Xenophon, and that the mere acquaintance with him was made a subject of accusation against Socrates. We can only infer that in this, and perhaps in some other cases, Plato's characters have no reference to the actual facts. The desire to do honour to his own family, and the connection with Solon, may have suggested the introduction of his name. Why the *Critias* was never completed, whether from accident, or from advancing age, or from a sense of the artistic difficulty of the design, cannot be determined.

At the beginning of the *Critias* dialogue, the characters agree on the requirement to accurately describe any facts they have already discussed or any they will discuss. This first part of the dialogue is omitted as it does not directly describe Atlantis or Athens.

Persons of the Critias Dialogue
CRITIAS
HERMOCRATES
TIMAEUS
SOCRATES

Crit. Let me begin by observing first of all, that nine thousand was the sum of years which had elapsed since the war which was said to have taken place between those who dwelt outside the Pillars of Heracles and all who dwelt within them; this war I am going to describe. Of the combatants on the one side, the city of Athens was reported to have been the leader and to have fought out the war; the combatants on the other side were commanded by the Kings of Atlantis, which, as was saying, was an island greater in extent than Libya and Asia, and when afterwards sunk by an earthquake, became an impassable barrier of mud to voyagers sailing from hence to any part of the ocean.

The progress of the history will unfold the various nations of barbarians and families of Hellenes which then existed, as they successively appear on the scene; but I must describe first of all the Athenians of that day, and their enemies who fought with them, and then the respective powers and governments of the two kingdoms. Let us give the precedence to Athens.

In the days of old, the gods had the whole earth distributed among them by allotment. There was no quarrelling; for you cannot rightly suppose that the gods did not know what was proper for each of them to have, or, knowing this, that they would seek to procure for themselves by contention that which more properly belonged to others. They all of them by just apportionment obtained what they wanted, and peopled their own districts; and when they had peopled them they tended us, their nurselings and possessions, as shepherds tend their flocks, excepting only that they did not use blows or bodily force, as shepherds do, but governed us like pilots from the stern of the vessel, which is an easy way of guiding animals, holding our souls by the rudder of persuasion according to their own pleasure; thus did they guide all mortal creatures.

Now different gods had their allotments in different places which they set in order. Hephaestus and Athene, who were brother and sister, and sprang from the same father, having a common nature, and being united also in the love of philosophy and art, both obtained as their common portion this land (Attica/Athens), which was naturally adapted for wisdom and virtue; and there they implanted brave children of the soil, and put into their minds the order of government; their names are preserved, but their actions have disappeared by reason of the destruction of those who received the tradition, and the lapse of ages. For when there were any survivors, as I have already said, they were men who dwelt in the mountains; and they were ignorant of the art of writing and had heard only the names of the chiefs of the land but very little about their actions. The names they were willing enough to give to their children but the virtues and the laws of their predecessors they knew only by obscure traditions; and as they themselves and their children lacked for many generations the necessaries of life, they directed their attention to the supply of their wants, and of them they conversed, to the neglect of events that had happened in times long past; for mythology and the enquiry into antiquity are first introduced into cities when they begin to have leisure, and when they see that the necessaries of life have already been provided, but not before. And this is reason why the names of the ancients have been preserved to us and not their actions. This I infer because Solon said that the (Egyptian) priests in their narrative of that war mentioned most of the names which are recorded prior to the time of Theseus, such as Cecrops, and Erechtheus, and Erichthonius, and Erysichthon, and the names of the women in like manner. Moreover, since military pursuits were then common to men and women, the men of those days in accordance with the custom of the time set up a figure and image of the goddess (Athena) in full armour, to be a testimony that all animals which associate together, male as well as female, may, if they please, practise in common the virtue which belongs to them without distinction of sex.

Now the country (of Attica) was inhabited in those days by various classes of citizens; there were artisans, and there were husbandmen, and there was also a warrior class originally set apart by divine men. The latter dwelt by themselves, and had all things suitable for nurture and education; neither had any of them anything of their own, but they regarded all that they had as common property; nor did they claim to receive of the other citizens anything more than their necessary food. And they practised all the pursuits which we yesterday described as those of our imaginary guardians.

Concerning the country (Attica) the Egyptian priests said what is not only probable but manifestly true, that the boundaries were in those days fixed by the Isthmus (of Corinth), and that in the direction of the continent (of Europe) they extended as far as the heights of Cithaeron and Parnes; the boundary line came down in the direction of the sea, having the district of Oropus on the right, and with the river Asopus as the limit on the left. The land was the best in the world, and was therefore able in those days to support a vast army, raised from the surrounding people.

Even the remnant of Attica which now exists may compare with any region in the world for the variety and excellence of its fruits and the suitableness of its pastures to every sort of animal, which proves what I am saying; but in those days the country was fair as now and yielded far more abundant produce. How shall I establish my words and what part of it can be truly called a remnant of the land that then was? The whole country (of Attica) is only a long promontory extending far into the sea away from the rest of the continent, while the surrounding basin of the sea is everywhere deep in the neighbourhood of the shore.

Many great deluges have taken place during the nine thousand years, for that is the number of years which have elapsed since the time (of the war) of which I am speaking; and during all this time and through so many changes, there has never been any considerable accumulation of the soil coming down from the mountains, as in other places, but the earth has fallen away all round and sunk out of sight. The consequence is, that in comparison of what then was, there are remaining only the bones of the wasted body, as they may be called, as in the case of small islands, all the richer and softer parts of the soil having fallen away, and the mere skeleton of the land being left. But in the primitive state of the country, its mountains were high hills covered with soil, and the plains, as they are termed by us, of Phelleus were full of rich earth, and there was abundance of wood in the mountains. Of this last the traces still remain, for although some of the mountains now only afford sustenance to bees, not so very long ago there were still to be seen roofs of timber cut from trees growing there, which were of a size sufficient to cover the largest houses; and there were many other high trees, cultivated by man and bearing abundance of food for cattle. Moreover, the land reaped the benefit of the annual rainfall, not as now losing the water which flows off the bare earth into the sea, but, having an abundant supply in all places, and receiving it into herself and treasuring it up in the close clay soil, it let off into the hollows the streams which it absorbed from the heights, providing everywhere abundant fountains and rivers, of which there may still be observed sacred memorials in places where fountains once existed; and this proves the truth of what I am saying. Such was the natural state of the country, which was cultivated, as we may well believe, by true husbandmen, who made husbandry their business, and were lovers of honour, and of a noble nature, and had a soil the best in the world, and abundance of water, and in the heaven above an excellently attempered climate.

Now the city (Athens) in those days was arranged on this wise. In the first place the Acropolis was not as now. For the fact is that a single night of excessive rain washed away the earth and laid bare the rock; at the same time there were earthquakes, and then occurred the extraordinary inundation, which was the third before the great destruction of (the Flood of) Deucalion. But in primitive times the hill of the Acropolis extended to the Eridanus and Ilissus (Rivers), and included the Pnyx (Hill) on one side, and the (Mount) Lycabettus as a boundary on the opposite side to the Pnyx, and was all well covered with soil, and level at the top, except in one or two places.

Outside the Acropolis and under the sides of the hill there dwelt artisans and such of the husbandmen as were tilling the ground near; the warrior class dwelt by themselves around the temples of Athene and Hephaestus at the summit, which moreover they had enclosed with a single fence like the garden of a single house. On the north side they had dwellings in common and had erected halls for dining in winter, and had all the buildings which they needed for their common life, besides temples, but there was no adorning of them with gold and silver, for they made no use of these for any purpose; they took a middle course between meanness and ostentation, and built modest houses in which they and their children's children grew old, and they handed them down to others who were like themselves, always the same. But in summer-time they left their gardens and gymnasia and dining halls, and then the southern side of the hill was made use of by them for the same purpose. Where the Acropolis now is there was a fountain, which was choked by the earthquake, and has left only the few small streams which still exist in the vicinity, but in those days the fountain gave an abundant supply of water for all and of suitable temperature in summer and in winter. This is how they dwelt, being the guardians of their own citizens and the leaders of the Hellenes, who were their willing followers. And they took care to preserve the same number of men and women through all time, being so many as were required for warlike purposes, then as now – that is to say, about twenty thousand.

Such were the ancient Athenians, and after this manner they righteously administered their own land and the rest of Hellas (Greece); they were renowned all over Europe and Asia for the beauty of their persons and for the many virtues of their souls, and of all men who lived in those days they were the most illustrious. And next, if I have not forgotten what I heard when I was a child, I will impart to you the character and origin of their adversaries. For friends should not keep their stories to themselves, but have them in common.

Yet, before proceeding further in the narrative, I ought to warn you, that you must not be surprised if you should perhaps hear Hellenic names given to foreigners. I will tell you the reason of this: Solon, who was intending to use the tale for his poem, enquired into the meaning of the names, and found that the early Egyptians in writing them down had translated them into their own language, and he recovered the meaning of the several names and when copying them out again translated them into our (Greek) language. My great-grandfather, Dropides, had the original writing, which is still in my possession, and was carefully studied by me when I was a child. Therefore if you hear names such as are used in this country, you must not be surprised, for I have told how they came to be introduced. The tale, which was of great length, began as follows:

I have before remarked in speaking of the allotments of the gods, that they distributed the whole earth into portions differing in extent, and made for themselves temples and instituted sacrifices. And Poseidon, receiving for his lot the island of Atlantis, begat children by a mortal woman, and settled them in a part of the island, which I will describe. Looking towards the sea, but in the centre of the whole island, there was a plain which is said to have been the fairest of all plains and very fertile. Near the plain again, and also in the centre of the island at a distance of about fifty stadia (the singular stadium is about 200 metres), there was a mountain not very high on any side. In this mountain there dwelt one of the earth-born primaeval men of that country, whose name was Evenor, and he had a wife named Leucippe, and they had an only daughter who was called Cleito. The maiden had already reached womanhood, when her father and mother died; Poseidon fell in love with her and had intercourse with her, and breaking the ground, inclosed the hill in which she dwelt all round, making alternate zones of sea and land larger and smaller, encircling one another; there were two of land and three of water, which he turned as with a lathe, each having its circumference equidistant every way from the centre, so that no man could get to the island, for ships and voyages were not as yet. He himself, being a god, found no difficulty in making special arrangements for the centre island, bringing up two springs of water from beneath the earth, one of warm water and the other of cold, and making every variety of food to spring up abundantly from the soil.

He (Poseidon) also begat and brought up five pairs of twin male children; and dividing the island of Atlantis into ten portions, he gave to the first-born of the eldest pair his mother's dwelling and the surrounding allotment, which was the largest and best, and made him king over the rest; the others he made princes, and gave them rule over many men, and a large territory. And he named them all; the eldest, who was the first king, he named Atlas, and after him the whole island and the ocean were called Atlantic. To his twin brother, who was born after him, and obtained as his lot the extremity of the island towards the Pillars of Heracles, facing the country which is now called the region of Gades (Cadiz) in that part of the world, he gave the name which in the Hellenic language is Eumelus, in the language of the country which is named after him, Gadeirus. Of the second pair of twins he called one Ampheres, and the other Evaemon. To the elder of the third pair of twins he gave the name Mneseus, and Autochthon to the one who followed him. Of the fourth pair of twins he called the elder Elasippus, and the younger Mestor. And of the fifth pair he gave to the elder the name of Azaes, and to the younger that of Diaprepes. All these and their descendants for many generations were the inhabitants and rulers of divers islands in the open sea; and also, as has been already said, they held sway in our direction over the country within the Pillars (the Mediterranean) as far as Egypt and Tyrrhenia.

Now Atlas had a numerous and honourable family, and they retained the kingdom, the eldest son handing it on to his eldest for many generations; and they had such an amount of wealth as was never before possessed by kings and potentates, and is not likely ever to be again, and they were furnished with everything which they needed, both in the city and country. For because of the greatness of their empire, many things were brought to them from foreign countries, and the island itself provided most of what was required by them for the uses of life. In the first place, they dug out of the earth whatever was to be found there, solid as well as fusile, and that which is now only a name and was then something more than a name, orichalcum, was dug out of the earth in many parts of the island, being more precious in those days than anything except gold.

There was an abundance of wood for carpenter's work, and sufficient maintenance for tame and wild animals. Moreover, there were a great number of elephants in the island; for as there was provision for all other sorts of animals, both for those which live in lakes and marshes and rivers, and also for those which live in mountains and on plains, so there was for the animal which is the largest and most voracious of all. Also whatever fragrant things there now are in the earth, whether roots, or herbage, or woods, or essences which distil from fruit and flower, grew and thrived in that land; also the fruit which admits of cultivation, both the dry sort, which is given us for nourishment and any other which we use for food – we call them all by the common name pulse, and the fruits having a hard rind, affording drinks and meats and ointments, and good store of chestnuts and the like, which furnish pleasure and amusement, and are fruits which spoil with keeping, and the pleasant kinds of dessert, with which we console ourselves after dinner, when we are tired of eating – all these that sacred island which then beheld the light of the sun, brought forth fair and wondrous and in infinite abundance.

With such blessings the earth freely furnished them; meanwhile they went on constructing their temples and palaces and harbours and docks. And they arranged the whole country in the following manner:

First of all they bridged over the zones of sea which surrounded the ancient metropolis, making a road to and from the royal palace. And at the very beginning they built the palace in the habitation of the god (Poseidon) and of their ancestors, which they continued to ornament in successive generations, every king surpassing the one who went before him to the utmost of his power, until they made the building a marvel to behold for size and for beauty. And beginning from the sea they bored a canal of three hundred feet in width and one hundred feet in depth and fifty stadia in length, which they carried through to the outermost zone, making a passage from the sea up to this, which became a harbour, and leaving an opening sufficient to enable the largest vessels to find ingress. Moreover, they divided at the bridges the zones of land which parted the zones of sea, leaving room for a single trireme to pass out of one zone into another, and they covered over the channels so as to leave a way underneath for the ships; for the banks were raised considerably above the water.

Now the largest of the zones into which a passage was cut from the sea was three stadia in breadth, and the zone of land which came next of equal breadth; but the next two zones, the one of water, the other of land, were two stadia, and the one which surrounded the central island was a stadium only in width. The (central) island in which the palace was situated had a diameter of five stadia. All this including the zones and the bridge, which was the sixth part of a stadium in width, they surrounded by a stone wall on every side, placing towers and gates on the bridges where the sea passed in. The stone which was used in the work they quarried from underneath the centre island, and from underneath the zones, on the outer as well as the inner side. One kind was white, another black, and a third red, and as they quarried, they at the same time hollowed out double docks, having roofs formed out of the native rock. Some of their buildings were simple, but in others they put together different stones, varying the colour to please the eye, and to be a natural source of delight. The entire circuit of the wall, which went round the outermost zone, they covered with a coating of brass, and the circuit of the next wall they coated with tin, and the third, which encompassed the citadel, flashed with the red light of orichalcum.

The palaces in the interior of the citadel (on the central island) were constructed on this wise: in the centre was a holy temple dedicated to Cleito and Poseidon, which remained inaccessible, and was surrounded by an enclosure of gold. This was the spot where the family of the ten princes first saw the light, and thither the people annually brought the fruits of the earth in their season from all the ten portions, to be an offering to each of the ten. Here was Poseidon's own temple which was a stadium in length, and half a stadium in width, and of a proportionate height, having a strange barbaric appearance. All the outside of the temple, with the exception of the pinnacles, they covered with silver, and the pinnacles with gold. In the interior of the temple the roof was of ivory, curiously wrought everywhere with gold and silver and orichalcum; and all the other parts, the walls and pillars and floor, they coated with orichalcum. In the temple they placed statues of gold: there was the god himself (Poseidon) standing in a chariot – the charioteer of six winged horses – and of such a size that he touched the roof of the building with his head; around him there were a hundred Nereids riding on dolphins, for such was thought to be the number of them by the men of those days. There were also in the interior of the temple other images which had been dedicated by private persons. And around the temple on the outside were placed statues of gold of all the descendants of the ten kings and of their wives, and there were many other great offerings of kings and of private persons, coming both from the city itself and from the foreign cities over which they held sway. There was an altar too, which in size and workmanship corresponded to this magnificence, and the palaces, in like manner, answered to the greatness of the kingdom and the glory of the temple.

In the next place (circular zone of land), they had fountains, one of cold and another of hot water, in gracious plenty flowing; and they were wonderfully adapted for use by reason of the pleasantness and excellence of their waters. They constructed buildings about them and planted suitable trees, also they made cisterns, some open to the heavens, others roofed over, to be used in winter as warm baths; there were the kings' baths, and the baths of private persons, which were kept apart; and there were separate baths for women, and for horses and cattle, and to each of them they gave as much adornment as was suitable. Of the water which ran off they carried some to the grove of Poseidon, where were growing all manner of trees of wonderful height and beauty, owing to the excellence of the soil, while the remainder was conveyed by aqueducts along the bridges to the outer circles; and there were many temples built and dedicated to many gods; also gardens and places of exercise, some for men, and others for horses in both of the two islands formed by the zones; and in the centre of the larger of the two there was set apart a race-course of a stadium in width, and in length allowed to extend all round the island, for horses to race in. Also there were guardhouses at intervals for the guards, the more trusted of whom were appointed-to keep watch in the lesser zone, which was nearer the Acropolis while the most trusted of all had houses given them within the citadel, near the persons of the kings. The docks were full of triremes and naval stores, and all things were quite ready for use.

Enough of the plan of the royal palace. Leaving the palace and passing out across the three (circular zones of water) you came to a wall which began at the sea and went all round: this was everywhere distant fifty stadia from the largest zone or harbour, and enclosed the whole (of the city), the ends meeting at the mouth of the channel which led to the sea. The entire area was densely crowded with habitations; and the canal and the largest of the harbours were full of vessels and merchants coming from all parts, who, from their numbers, kept up a multitudinous sound of human voices, and din and clatter of all sorts night and day.

I have described the city and the environs of the ancient palace nearly in the words of Solon, and now I must endeavour to represent the nature and arrangement of the rest of the land. The whole country was said by him to be very lofty and precipitous on the side of the sea, but the country immediately about and surrounding the city was a level plain, itself surrounded by mountains which descended towards the sea; it was smooth and even, and of an oblong shape, extending in one direction three thousand stadia, but across the centre inland it was two thousand stadia. This part of the island looked towards the south, and was sheltered from the north. The surrounding mountains were celebrated for their number and size and beauty, far beyond any which still exist, having in them also many wealthy villages of country folk, and rivers, and lakes, and meadows supplying food enough for every animal, wild or tame, and much wood of various sorts, abundant for each and every kind of work.

I will now describe the plain, as it was fashioned by nature and by the labours of many generations of kings through long ages. It was for the most part rectangular and oblong, and where falling out of the straight line followed the circular ditch. The depth, and width, and length of this ditch were incredible, and gave the impression that a work of such extent, in addition to so many others, could never have been artificial. Nevertheless I must say what I was told. It was excavated to the depth of a hundred feet, and its breadth was a stadium everywhere; it was carried round the whole of the plain, and was ten thousand stadia in length. It received the streams which came down from the mountains, and winding round the plain and meeting at the city, was there let off into the sea. Further inland, likewise, straight canals of a hundred feet in width were cut from it through the plain, and again let off into the ditch leading to the sea. These canals were at intervals of a hundred stadia, and by them they brought down the wood from the mountains to the city, and conveyed the fruits of the earth in ships, cutting transverse passages from one canal into another, and to the city. Twice in the year they gathered the fruits of the earth – in winter having the benefit of the rains of heaven, and in summer the water which the land supplied by introducing streams from the canals.

As to the population, each of the lots in the plain had to find a leader for the men who were fit for military service, and the size of a lot was a square of ten stadia each way, and the total number of all the lots was sixty thousand. And of the inhabitants of the mountains and of the rest of the country there was also a vast multitude, which was distributed among the lots and had leaders assigned to them according to their districts and villages. The leader was required to furnish for the war the sixth portion of a war-chariot, so as to make up a total of ten thousand chariots; also two horses and riders for them, and a pair of chariot-horses without a seat, accompanied by a horseman who could fight on foot carrying a small shield, and having a charioteer who stood behind the man-at-arms to guide the two horses; also, he was bound to furnish two heavy-armed soldiers, two slingers, three stone-shooters and three javelin-men, who were light-armed, and four sailors to make up the complement of twelve hundred ships. Such was the military order of the royal city – the order of the other nine governments varied, and it would be wearisome to recount their several differences.

As to offices and honours, the following was the arrangement from the first. Each of the ten kings in his own division and in his own city had the absolute control of the citizens, and, in most cases, of the laws, punishing and slaying whomsoever he would. Now the order of precedence among them and their mutual relations were regulated by the commands of Poseidon which the law had handed down. These were inscribed by the first kings on a pillar of orichalcum, which was situated in the middle of the (central) island, at the temple of Poseidon, whither the kings were gathered together every fifth and every sixth year alternately, thus giving equal honour to the odd and to the even number. And when they were gathered together they consulted about their common interests, and enquired if any one had transgressed in anything and passed judgment and before they passed judgment they gave their pledges to one another on this wise:

There were bulls who had the range of the temple of Poseidon; and the ten kings, being left alone in the temple, after they had offered prayers to the god that they may capture the victim which was acceptable to him, hunted the bulls, without weapons but with staves and nooses; and the bull which they caught they led up to the pillar and cut its throat over the top of it so that the blood fell upon the sacred inscription. Now on the pillar, besides the laws, there was inscribed an oath invoking mighty curses on the disobedient. When therefore, after slaying the bull in the accustomed manner, they had burnt its limbs, they filled a bowl of wine and cast in a clot of blood for each of them; the rest of the victim they put in the fire, after having purified the column all round. Then they drew from the bowl in golden cups and pouring a libation on the fire, they swore that they would judge according to the laws on the pillar, and would punish him who in any point had already transgressed them, and that for the future they would not, if they could help, offend against the writing on the pillar, and would neither command others, nor obey any ruler who commanded them, to act otherwise than according to the laws of their father Poseidon. This was the prayer which each of them offered up for himself and for his descendants, at the same time drinking and dedicating the cup out of which he drank in the temple of the god; and after they had supped and satisfied their needs, when darkness came on, and the fire about the sacrifice was cool, all of them put on most beautiful azure robes, and, sitting on the ground, at night, over the embers of the sacrifices by which they had sworn, and extinguishing all the fire about the temple, they received and gave judgment, if any of them had an accusation to bring against any one; and when they had given judgment, at daybreak they wrote down their sentences on a golden tablet, and dedicated it together with their robes to be a memorial.

There were many special laws affecting the several kings inscribed about the temples, but the most important was the following: They were not to take up arms against one another, and they were all to come to the rescue if anyone in any of their cities attempted to overthrow the royal house; like their ancestors, they were to deliberate in common about war and other matters, giving the supremacy to the descendants of Atlas. And the king was not to have the power of life and death over any of his kinsmen unless he had the assent of the majority of the ten.

Such was the vast power which the god settled in the lost island of Atlantis; and this he afterwards directed against our land (Greece) for the following reasons, as tradition tells: For many generations, as long as the divine nature lasted in them (the Atlanteans), they were obedient to the laws, and well-affectioned towards the god, whose seed they were; for they possessed true and in every way great spirits, uniting gentleness with wisdom in the various chances of life, and in their intercourse with one another. They despised everything but virtue, caring little for their present state of life, and thinking lightly of the possession of gold and other property, which seemed only a burden to them; neither were they intoxicated by luxury; nor did wealth deprive them of their self-control; but they were sober, and saw clearly that all these goods are increased by virtue and friendship with one another, while by too great regard and respect for them, they are lost and friendship with them. By such reflections and by the continuance in them of a divine nature, the qualities which we have described grew and increased among them; but when the divine portion began to fade away, and became diluted too often and too much with the mortal admixture, and the human nature got the upper hand, they then, being unable to bear their fortune, behaved unseemly, and to him who had an eye to see, grew visibly debased, for they were losing the fairest of their precious gifts; but to those who had no eye to see the true happiness, they appeared glorious and blessed at the very time when they were full of avarice and unrighteous power.

Zeus, the god of gods, who rules according to law, and is able to see into such things, perceiving that an honourable race was in a woeful plight, and wanting to inflict punishment on them, that they may be chastened and improve, collected all the gods into their most holy habitation, which, being placed in the centre of the world, beholds all created things. And when he had called them together, he spake as follows... – **The rest of Plato's Critias dialogue has been lost.**

A natural hydraulic system transfers forces from ice-covered plates to distant plates not covered by ice

APPENDIX 2

The Hydraulic Hypothesis

A simple analogy for the Hydraulic Hypothesis is an automobile's hydraulic braking system. The pressure in a master cylinder is transmitted via rigid pipes to remote wheel cylinders. Incompressible brake fluid completely fills the closed system and immediately transmits hydraulic pressure evenly between all of the cylinders.

The Hydraulic Hypothesis argues that a natural hydraulic system under the Earth's surface transmits a change in hydraulic pressure below ice-covered tectonic plates (the master cylinders) to remote tectonic plates not covered by glacial ice (the wheel cylinders). Any changes in hydraulic pressure that cause vertical movements of ice-covered plates will cause an opposite vertical movement of uncovered plates.

The Earth's geological structure consists of several layers surrounding a solid inner Core. The Lithosphere is the rigid outer shell of the Earth, comprising the Crust and the brittle upper portion of the Mantle. The Asthenosphere is the layer located directly below the Lithosphere and contains the more fluid parts of the Mantle.

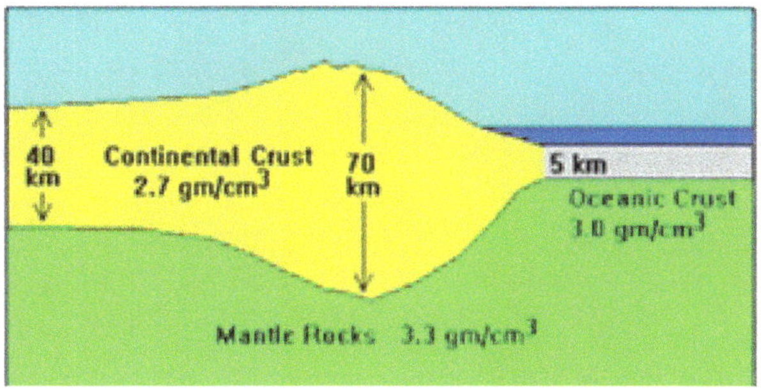

The solid Lithosphere is divided into many tectonic plates. There are seven primary and eight secondary tectonic plates, plus dozens of smaller tertiary microplates. Depending on where they are located on the Earth, the tectonic plates consist of the two main Lithosphere types: thin Oceanic Crust that lies under the oceans or the thicker Continental Crust of the Earth's continents.

The Earth's rigid Lithosphere is less dense than the more fluid underlying Asthenosphere, so the tectonic plates float on the Asthenosphere. Isostasy is the state of gravitational balance between the Lithosphere and the Asthenosphere. This concept of buoyancy explains how different heights can exist at the Earth's surface – thicker Lithosphere sinks deeper but rises higher than thinner Lithosphere.

40 km | Continental Crust 2.7 gm/cm³ | 70 km | 5 km | Oceanic Crust 3.0 gm/cm³ | Mantle Rocks 3.3 gm/cm³

Isostatic Effect on the Crust

Past Global Sea Level Changes and Glaciation

The term eustatic change of global sea level means the changes in the total volume of water in the World Ocean. It is different to the local changes in sea level that occur when an area of land rises or falls because of tectonic forces such as earthquakes.

The main influence on eustatic sea level is a change in the amount of water stored in the Earth's polar ice caps, glaciers, sea ice, rivers, lakes and aquifers. Glacioeustasy refers to the changes in the eustatic sea level due to changes in the volume of glacial ice. Differences in global sea level are almost entirely due to the amount of glacial ice on land because ice does not accumulate on water, where it forms sea-ice only one to three metres thick.

There was no glaciation for hundreds of millions of years after the previous great Ice Age ended. Gradual glaciation over Antarctica began by 36mya, but more extreme falls in global temperature and increased glaciation occurred at 15mya and again at 5mya. Over more than 30 million years, the global sea level fell around 70 metres, with most of that water deposited as glacial ice on Antarctica.

Around 2.5mya, the present Quaternary Ice Age began when ice sheets formed and spread over North America and Eurasia, with additional ice forming on Antarctica. One key feature of the Quaternary Ice Age is recurring glacial/interglacial cycles. They consist of cold periods called glacials, which peak at a Glacial Maximum, followed by warm periods called interglacials. The Quaternary Ice Age has had thirty to fifty glacial/interglacial cycles up until now.

Up to 120metres of World Ocean became glacial ice at each past Glacial Maximum, when the ice was at its greatest extent. Each glacial/interglacial cycle lasted tens of thousands of years. Ice repeatedly reached thicknesses of thousands of metres on land during each long glacial period, partially melting during the relatively short interglacial period that followed.

Glacial/interglacial cycles intensified markedly over the past one million years. During each cold glacial period that lasted 80,000–100,000 years, there was a relatively slow fall in sea level and increased ice accumulation. The warm interglacial periods were much shorter, with rapid deglaciation that caused the sea level to rise in only 10,000–20,000 years..

The most recent cold glacial period began at about 120,000 BP and lasted about 90,000 years before it peaked at the Last Glacial Maximum (LGM) around 20,000 BP. At the LGM, the global sea level was at least 120 metres lower than today, and virtually all that water was stored as ice on land. Hundreds of millions of cubic kilometres of additional ice accumulated in ice sheets up to three kilometres thick on the continents of North America, Eurasia and Antarctica.

When the Earth began to warm again after 20,000 BP, the ice sheets melted over a relatively short period of around 14,000 years. The global sea level rose again by 120 metres until it stabilised to its present level about 6,000 years ago.

If the Antarctic Ice Sheet entirely melted, it would increase the sea level by more than 60 metres, while a melted Greenland Ice Sheet would add another 7 metres. Therefore, the entire range of eustatic sea level between full glacial and non-glacial conditions is 180–200 metres.

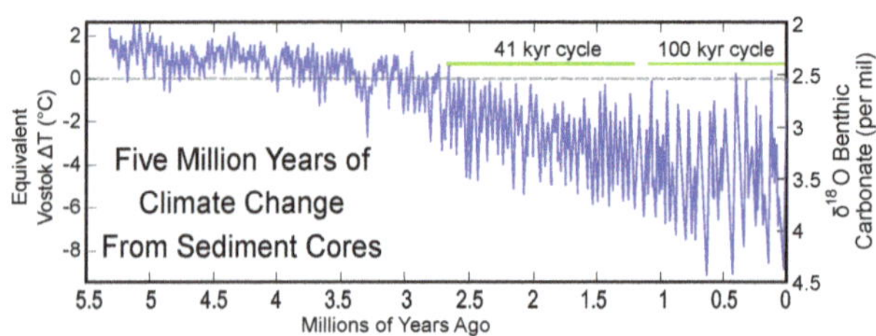

Glacials and Interglacials over the last 5 million years
Source: Wikimedia Commons – Robert A. Rohde

The Hydraulic Effect of Glacial Ice

Glacial isostasy is the Lithosphere's response to any changes in the thickness of the planet's ice sheets. During the LGM around 20,000 BP, the weight of ice over Northern Europe, Asia, North America, Greenland, and Antarctica depressed large areas of land below sea level. It pushed away the underlying liquid part of the Asthenosphere.

When glacial ice melts, the liquid Asthenosphere returns below the tectonic plate, and the Lithosphere rebounds (uplifts) in two distinct stages. The initial uplift is called elastic and occurs immediately while the ice unloads. After this immediate elastic phase, uplift proceeds more slowly and decreases over time, called the slow viscous flow. This two-stage phenomenon occurs because different types of Asthenosphere material have different viscosities. Viscosity describes a fluid's resistance to flow and corresponds to thickness. An example is honey and water, where honey has a much higher viscosity than water and is thicker than water.

During the latest deglaciation, the rapid elastic rebound phase lasted from the LGM of 20,000 BP until deglaciation virtually stopped by 6,000 BP. Now, rebound continues in the slow viscous flow phase, with present uplift rates of 1cm/year or less. Because of the high viscosity of much of the Asthenosphere, the land will continue rising for thousands of years before it reaches its isostatic equilibrium level, possibly for another 10,000 years or more.

The area of the World Ocean is 360 million square kilometres. So, an estimate of the volume of glacial ice that accumulated over Antarctica from 36mya to 2.5mya is 70 metres multiplied by the area of the World Ocean, i.e. 0.07km x 360 million km^2, or 25 million cubic kilometres. The additional volume of water lost from the oceans and converted to glacial ice at the LGM 20,000 years ago is 120 metres multiplied by the area of the World Ocean, i.e. 0.12km x 360 million km^2, or 43 million cubic kilometres. When that extra 43 million km^3 is added to glacial ice accumulated from 36mya to 2.5mya, it gives a total ice volume on land of 70 million cubic kilometres at the LGM.

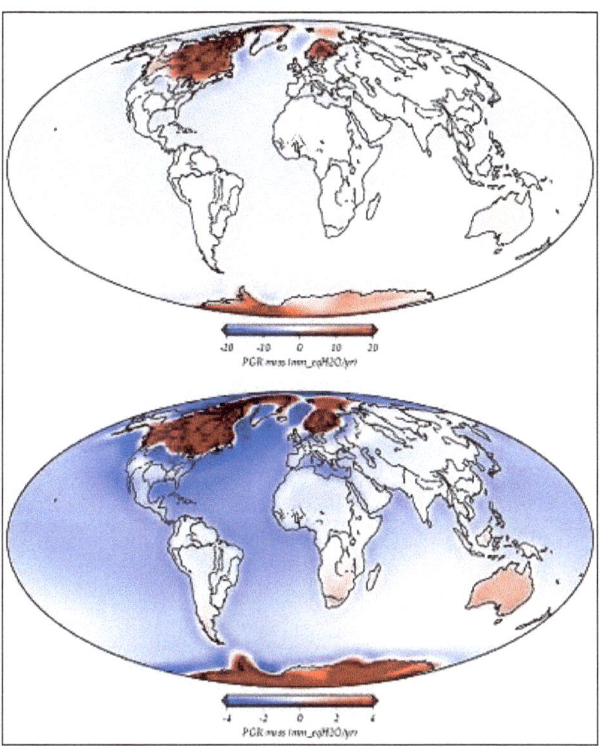

Present-day surface elevation change due to post-glacial rebound and the reloading of the ocean basins with seawater. Red areas are rising due to the removal of the ice sheets. Blue areas are falling due to the re-filling of the ocean basins when the ice sheets melted and because of the collapse of the forebulges around the ice sheets.
Source: Wikimedia Commons – A. Paulson

To estimate the weight of glacial ice on land, one cubic metre of ice weighs roughly one thousand kilograms or one metric tonne. One cubic kilometre of ice is one billion cubic metres, weighing one billion tonnes. So, from 36mya to 2.5mya, the 25 million km^3 of glacial ice accumulated over Antarctica had a total weight of 25 million billion (trillion) tonnes. During the Quaternary Ice Age, at the LGM 20,000 years ago, the additional 43 million km^3 of glacial ice weighed 43 trillion tonnes. So, at the LGM, the combined weight of glacial ice over ice-covered tectonic plates would have been around 70 trillion tonnes.

The potential depression of the Lithosphere beneath an ice sheet 1,000 metres thick is as much as 275 metres or about 30% of ice thickness. The depressed Lithosphere displaces fluid Mantle material away from the ice-loaded region. So, the volume of Mantle displaced should be roughly 30% of the volume of ice over the Lithosphere.

If the volume of glacial ice accumulated before 2.5mya was 25 million km^3, the volume of displaced Mantle would be 30% of that or 8 million km^3. If the maximum volume of additional glacial ice during the Quaternary Ice Age were 43 million km^3, the volume of additional displaced Mantle would be 13 million km^3. This calculation gives a total Mantle displacement at a Glacial Maximum (including at the LGM of 20,000 BP) of 20 million km^3.

Magma Viscosity and Density

Magma is a mixture of molten or semi-molten rock, volatiles and solids found beneath the surface of the Earth. Magma develops within the Mantle or Crust when the temperature and pressure conditions favour a molten state. Three main parameters control the rock-melting process that forms magma: temperature, pressure and composition. Viscosity (fluidity) is measured in pascal-seconds (Pa·s) or Poise. The viscosity of naturally occurring silicate magmas can span more than 15 orders of magnitude (10^{-1}–10^{14} Pa s), with the lowest viscosity magmas being as fluid as motor oil.

Magma viscosity depends on variations in temperature, melt composition and the proportions of dissolved volatiles. In particular, a lower temperature results in a dramatic increase in magma viscosity. Water and carbon dioxide are the two most common volatile components in natural magmas, followed by sulphur, chlorine and fluorine. Magmas that form by the melting of Mantle rocks have low volatile contents, but those formed by partial melting of Crustal rocks are often volatile-rich. Small variations in the concentration of dissolved volatiles can generate large ($>10^5$ or 100,000 times) changes in melt viscosity, which drastically affects magma transport, ascent and eruption dynamics.

Most melts develop in the Lower Crust or the Asthenosphere and have a basaltic composition. Melts developing in the Upper Crust have a higher initial silica content. In general, the viscosity of magma increases as the silica content increases, from basalt to rhyolite. Felsic refers to igneous rocks that are relatively rich in elements that form feldspar and quartz, in contrast to Mafic rocks, which are relatively richer in magnesium and iron. Mafic melts, such as basalts, have a higher density than Felsic melts, such as rhyolite.

Magma differentiates by a complex process based on its viscosity and density so that a single melt can produce a wide variety of different igneous rocks. Less dense magma separates from and migrates above denser magma; paradoxically, the denser the magma, the lower the viscosity. This relationship causes a less viscous magma to rise until it is blocked above by less dense but more viscous material.

The Location of the Ultra-Low Viscosity Zone (ULVZ)

For the mechanism of the Hydraulic Hypothesis to function effectively, particular parts of the Asthenosphere must form an interconnected and contained network of extremely fluid magma. In the Hydraulic Hypothesis, that region is named the Ultra-Low-Viscosity Zone (ULVZ). In the proposed hydraulic system of the Earth, the ULVZ is the confined incompressible fluid that transmits hydraulic forces from one tectonic plate to another.

The Mohorovicic discontinuity (Moho) is the boundary between the Earth's Crust and the Mantle. In geology, the word discontinuity describes a surface where seismic waves change velocity, and that change indicates a variation in the density of matter. The Moho marks the lower limit of the Earth's Crust. It is 5–10 kilometres below the ocean floor and 20–90 kilometres beneath the continents. Below the Moho is the solid part of the Mantle, and below that is the Lithosphere-Asthenosphere Boundary (LAB). The LAB is the boundary between the Earth's solid and more fluid layers.

Fluid magma migrates upward out of the Asthenosphere and accumulates at the LAB. In the Hydraulic Hypothesis, the LAB is where the most fluid magma would create the network of layers and connecting channels of the ULVZ. If the Moho is used as a proxy for the depth of the LAB, then fluid magma will rise and accumulate in larger volumes below the shallowest Moho. The accompanying map of the Moho displays its shallow levels in blue and green. The hypothetical hydraulic system of the Earth should function most effectively in those regions where a ULVZ is shallower and thicker.

The most likely areas for fluid magma to accumulate are beneath Oceanic Lithosphere and along the continental shelves of Continental Lithosphere: the blue and green zones on the accompanying map.

Because the blue zones of Oceanic Lithosphere are mainly submerged below thousands of metres of water, the weight of the overlying deep water may cancel out hydraulic effects there. The green zones appear to be in shallower or emergent regions, where the greatest hydraulic effects should be felt. Magma may also accumulate along plate-boundary subduction zones, intracontinental fault lines and the boundaries of microplates. There may also be connected layers and channels of melt within Continental Lithosphere.

The Volume and Nature of a ULVZ

The following estimates for the ULVZ are based on existing geological research results. Depending on its location, the values of a ULVZ range from a depth of 25–110km and a thickness of 5–30km

The Earth has a mean radius of 6,371km. From the above estimates of a ULVZ, if an arbitrary average value of 30km depth and 20km thickness is assumed for a ULVZ, then:

Earth's radius to 30 km depth (upper limit of ULVZ) = 6,371-30 = 6,341 km

Earth's radius to 50 km depth (lower limit of ULVZ) = 6,371-50 = 6,321 km

The Volume of a sphere $V = \frac{4}{3}\pi r^3$

So if V1 is the Earth's volume at 30 km depth and V2 is the volume at 50 km depth:

$V1 = \frac{4}{3} \times 3.14 \times 6{,}341^3 = 2.55 \times 10^{12}\ km^3$

and

$V2 = \frac{4}{3} \times 3.14 \times 6{,}321^3 = 2.53 \times 10^{12}\ km^3$

The Volume of the ULVZ = V1-V2 = $0.02 \times 10^{12}\ km^3 = 2 \times 10^{10}\ km^3$, or 20 billion km^3

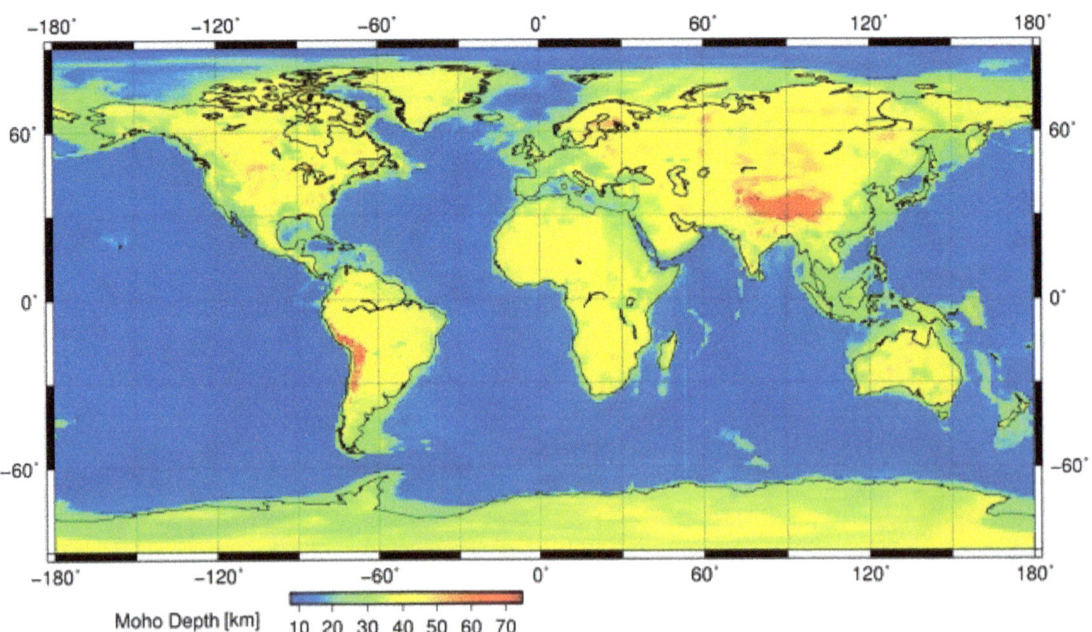

The Position and Depth of the Moho Discontinuity
Source: Wikimedia Commons – AllenMcC

This figure of 20 billion km^3 for the ULVZ would only apply if a uniform layer of partial melt with constant thickness and viscosity extended around the entire Earth. Such a structure would be improbable. A more likely ULVZ structure would be an interconnected combination of shallow layers

Location of ULVZ	Depth km	Thickness km
Oceanic LAB	40–45	3–40
Continental LAB	90–110	<10
Subduction Zone Wedge	Ave. ~70	<20
Intra–Lithosphere	20–60	10–30
Fault Zones	12	~12
Cratons	50–110	50–100

Summary of ULVZ Research

and channels, which form a three-dimensional network around the Earth and vary in thickness from 5–30km. Therefore, a more realistic volume of the ULVZ may be less than one-fifth of the above estimate, possibly less than 4 billion km^3.

If a three-dimensional ULVZ network did connect the Earth's ultra-low-viscosity layers and channels, it might further differentiate due to gradual differences in magma viscosity. Magma viscosities within the ULVZ may vary from 10^{15} Pa s down to 10^{-1} Pa s, and these viscosity variations would be continuous rather than having sharp boundaries. The most fluid magma regions may behave as separate connected structures, which exist within larger fluid structures of gradually increasing viscosity. So, several independent connected structures may form with different viscosities of 10^{-1} Pa s, 10 Pa s, 10^{1} Pa s, and so on, up to 10^{15} Pa s.

ULVZ structures with a viscosity of 10^{15} Pa s or less may form relatively thin layers in the Asthenosphere, possibly only a few kilometres or less in thickness. They may also occur as narrow channels connecting those layers. Therefore, the volume of the lowest viscosity networks of the ULVZ may be only a fraction of the entire ULVZ, much less than one billion km^3 and perhaps only in the hundreds or tens of millions of km^3.

The three-dimensional magma structures within the ULVZ would be dynamic over time. The structures would vary as magma viscosity altered due to changes in volatiles, temperature and pressure. Depending on changes in magma viscosity, any connections between different magma regions could increase or decrease, open or close. Those changes in magma flow would then cause variations in the amount of hydraulic pressure transmitted from one plate to another and to regions within plates.

The Global Effects of Glacial Ice Sheets

The gradual build-up of glacial ice over Antarctica after 35mya does not appear to have had recurring glacial/interglacial cycles. However, glaciation did accelerate markedly around 15mya and again around 5mya. That extensive period of increasing glaciation pushed down the Antarctic Plate and may have caused some remote unglaciated plates to uplift. Still, the many large cyclical changes in glacial ice volumes over the past 2.5 million years of the Quaternary Ice Age would have had a much greater hydraulic effect.

Over the 2.5 million years of the Quaternary Ice Age, there were massive accumulations of glacial ice on the North American, Eurasian and Antarctic Plates. According to the Hydraulic Hypothesis, downward pressure at the Earth's poles would transmit upward pressure to the plates closer to the Equator.

Large equatorial plates such as the Pacific, North and South American, African and Australian Plates are probably too large to experience much vertical displacement. Nevertheless, they could tilt at some of their plate boundaries or internal fault lines. Suppose the vertical movement of larger tectonic plates was limited. In that case, the hydraulic force could then concentrate on the smaller plates closer to the Equator, such as the Cocos, Nazca, Caribbean, Scotia, Arabian, Indian and Philippines Plates.

Some of the smaller plates consist mainly of Oceanic Crust, much thinner than Continental Crust, and they are much more likely to respond to vertical forces from below. As well as the smaller tectonic plates, numerous microplates around the Earth may also respond more readily to changes in underlying hydraulic force.

Any change in hydraulic force beneath smaller plates and microplates could potentially cause greater vertical movement there. The potential vertical movement of the smaller plates depends on the types of boundaries they have with the plates surrounding them. Each boundary may have a degree of lock that either restricts or allows vertical movement at that boundary. Vertical movement may also occur inside a plate at any of its microplate boundaries and internal fault zones. Rather than the entire plate rising or subsiding evenly, plates and microplates may merely tilt at individual boundaries or faults. Over distances of hundreds or thousands of kilometres on a plate, a tilt of only a few degrees could produce vertical displacements of hundreds or thousands of metres at one of the plate's boundaries or faults.

Several factors would affect the degree of vertical movement of an unglaciated remote plate. Those factors would include the depth, quantity and viscosity of magma melt beneath the plate, the thinness of the plate's Lithosphere, and the degree of lock at its boundaries and internal fault zones. Also, the three-dimensional magma structures within the ULVZ would likely change over time as magma viscosity altered due to changes in volatiles, temperature and pressure. Over time, the amount of hydraulic force transmitted from plate to plate, or regions within plates, would vary because of the changing structures and connections within the ULVZ.

The increasing glaciation on Antarctica after 35mya may have caused some uplift on smaller remote tectonic plates. However, the 30–50 slow glaciation phases over the past 2.5 million years of the Quaternary Ice Age could have caused a much greater uplift of the plates. Uplift may have increased over many long glaciation periods as there may not have been much subsidence on some remote plates during the short deglaciation phases. A degree of lock at those plates' boundaries may have prevented or reduced any subsidence there. There could have been a ratchet effect, where the degree of lock at a boundary allowed mainly upward motion with little or no subsidence. Over hundreds of thousands or millions of years, a small plate's accumulated uplift may have been much greater than any subsidence.

While glacial ice melted rapidly during the most recent deglaciation phase from 20,000–6,000 BP, there was an immediate elastic rebound (uplift) of the ice-covered plates at the poles. Magma flowed back quickly beneath those large plates, and the hydraulic pressure fell rapidly below the wheel cylinders of small, remote unglaciated plates. If the Hydraulic Hypothesis is correct, the hydraulic effect would have been greatest under the unglaciated plates during the immediate elastic phase of deglaciation. The rapid reduction in hydraulic pressure from 20,000–6,000 BP would have produced suction under some unglaciated plates. It may have caused those plates to subside rapidly at any of their weak boundaries.

Post-glacial rebound is now in the slow viscous flow phase, which will continue for thousands more years, so there will be a continuing decrease in hydraulic force under the unglaciated plates. Therefore, there is potential for further subsidence of those unglaciated plates and more seismic activity, though probably nowhere near as great as during the immediate elastic phase of the rebound.

When the next glacial period begins, likely within the next ten thousand years, ice will again accumulate for around 100,000 years, and hydraulic pressure will increase in the ULVZ, leading to an uplift on some unglaciated tectonic plates.

Diffusion vs Containment of Hydraulic Pressure in the ULVZ

One essential argument against the Hydraulic Hypothesis is that any change in hydraulic pressure due to glaciation would be diffused within the Asthenosphere and cease before it reached remote tectonic plates. Therefore, if no hydraulic force were transmitted in a ULVZ, there would be no vertical movement of remote unglaciated plates.

Three factors would diffuse hydraulic force in a ULVZ. One factor is whether the hydraulic fluid in the hydraulic system can be compressed by the forces placed on it. If the fluid can be compressed, the hydraulic system loses energy, and hydraulic force will be reduced or absent. Still, as even the lowest viscosity magmas are incompressible fluids, there should be no diffusion of hydraulic force due to fluid compression.

The second factor is whether the hydraulic fluid is contained in the closed system or there is fluid leakage from the system. The ULVZ is contained either by rock or incompressible higher viscosity magma above, below or around it. Because the ULVZ is contained, it would allow the transmission of hydraulic force throughout the entire ULVZ network without diminution of that force.

The third and most important factor is whether the total volume of the contained hydraulic fluid of the ULVZ is much larger than the volume of the displaced fluid, such as if the total volume of the ULVZ was thousands of times more than the displaced fluid. Even if that were so, if all the hydraulic fluid is incompressible and contained, the total volume of the ULVZ should make little difference. Based on Pascal's Law, the hydraulic forces would still be transmitted evenly throughout the contained hydraulic system.

The volume for the entire ULVZ was previously estimated to be one billion cubic kilometres. However, within the ULVZ, some structures with the lowest viscosity of 10^{15} Pa s or less may form relatively thin layers and narrow channels. Within these larger magma structures, there may be even smaller structures with viscosities as low as 10^{-1} Pa s. Therefore, the volume of the most fluid ULVZ structures and networks may be only a fraction of the one billion cubic kilometres of the entire ULVZ. The most fluid structures may have volumes in the hundreds of millions or as low as tens of millions of cubic kilometres.

A previous calculation estimated that during the most recent 100,000-year-long glaciation, accumulated glacial ice displaced 13 million cubic kilometres of magma volume by the time of the LGM of 20,000 BP. As the ice accumulated, it may be assumed that the most fluid (lowest-viscosity) magma of the ULVZ was displaced first. That lowest-viscosity magma, possibly as low as 10^{-1} Pa s, may have a volume of only a hundred million cubic kilometres or less. Therefore, there may not be a significant difference between the volume of the lowest-viscosity networks of a ULVZ and the 13 million km^3 volume of displaced magma due to glaciation.

It must be emphasised that hydraulic force is transmitted immediately throughout a closed hydraulic system; the fluid itself does not need to flow from one part of the system to another. The magma does not need to flow directly from a glaciated to an unglaciated plate – only the hydraulic force is transmitted.

Large vertical movements of the Caribbean Plate created its many fault zones, basins and ridges

APPENDIX 3

The Caribbean Hypothesis

Geologists have studied the Caribbean region for decades, mainly because it is the location of very large commercial quantities of gas and oil. The following information about past structural changes on the Caribbean Plate is based on existing data from field geology and drill cores. That geological data describes changes in the structure of the Caribbean Plate, from 65mya up to the recent past.

Most of the field geology information is from the publication *Caribbean Geology: An Introduction* – a compilation edited by Stephen K. Donovan and Trevor A. Jackson. Also, several other geological research publications provided additional information on the Caribbean Plate. The drill core information is from the Deep Sea Drilling Project (DSDP) expeditions in the Caribbean Sea. The DSDP operated from 1968 to 1983 and was the first of three international scientific ocean drilling programmes.

Hydraulic Pressure Effects on the Caribbean Plate

The Caribbean Plate was in its present location between the North and South American Plates by 65mya, at the beginning of the Cenozoic era. Since then, it has been encircled by active subduction zones to the east and west and complex fault zones to the north and south.

By 35mya, the main components of the Caribbean Plate had already formed and were in their current positions. From east to west, the Plate's components are the Lesser Antilles, Grenada Basin, Aves Ridge, Venezuelan Basin, Beata Ridge, Greater Antilles (other than Cuba), Colombian Basin and Southern Nicaraguan Rise, the Chorotega and Choco Blocks, the Chortis Block and the attached Northern Nicaraguan Rise.

Much of the floor of the Caribbean Sea is normal Oceanic Crust, which is usually six kilometres thick. Despite this underlying structure, some parts of the Caribbean Plate are much thicker than normal Oceanic Crust. They are unusually thick because a Large Igneous Province, or LIP, spread over that Oceanic Crust millions of years ago. An LIP is an extremely large build-up of volcanic rock that forms when hot magma flows out from inside the Earth and solidifies into a thick layer.

The Caribbean's LIP is called the Caribbean Large Igneous Province or CLIP. Volcanic activity created the CLIP between 139–69mya, most forming between 95–88mya. The CLIP layer lies beneath the Colombian Basin, the Beata Ridge, the southern part of the Venezuelan Basin, the Aves Ridge, and the southern part of the Grenada Basin. The CLIP makes the Oceanic Crust at those structures unusually thick: two to three times thicker than normal Oceanic Crust.

The accompanying figures show the present geological understanding of the thickness of the Caribbean Plate's Crust. According to the Hydraulic Hypothesis, the most fluid magma of the ULVZ should build up under the thinnest areas of the Crust because this is where the fluid Asthenosphere is closest to the surface. The Caribbean Plate's thinnest Crust is in the eastern part of the Colombian

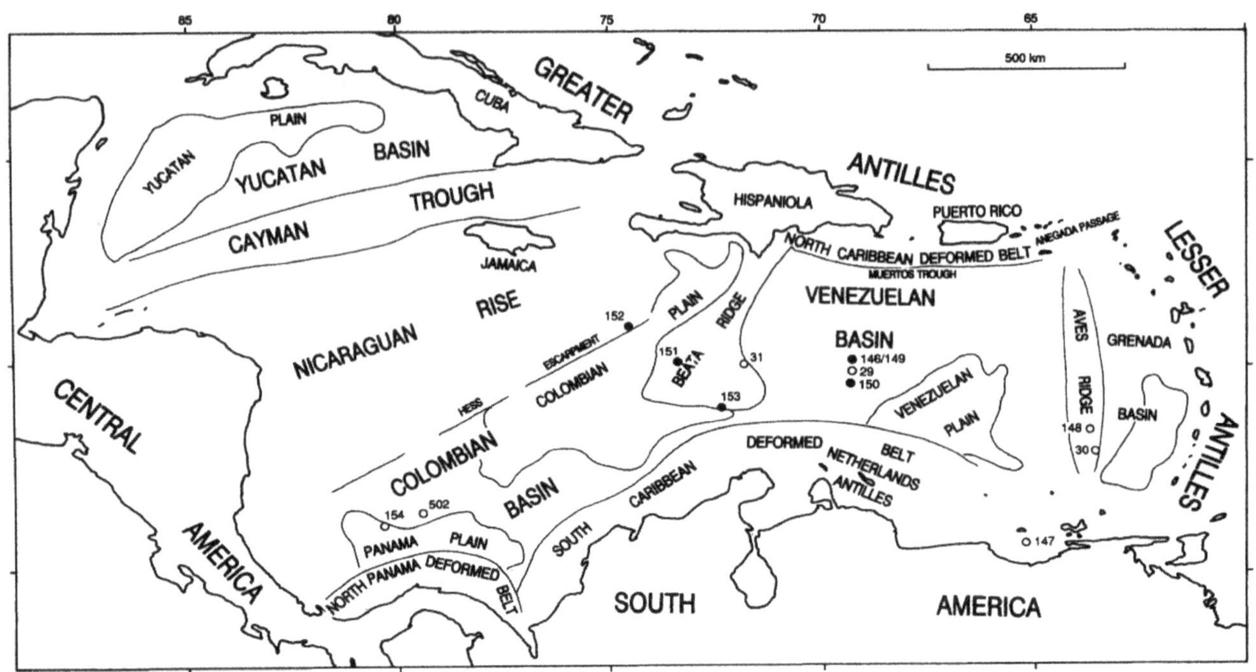

Map of the Caribbean showing the major named features
Source: Case, J.E., MacDonald, W.D. & Fox, P.J. 1990. Caribbean crustal provinces; seismic and gravity evidence: in Dengo, G. & Case, I.E. (eds), The Geology of North America, Volume H, The Caribbean Region, 15-36. Geological Society of America

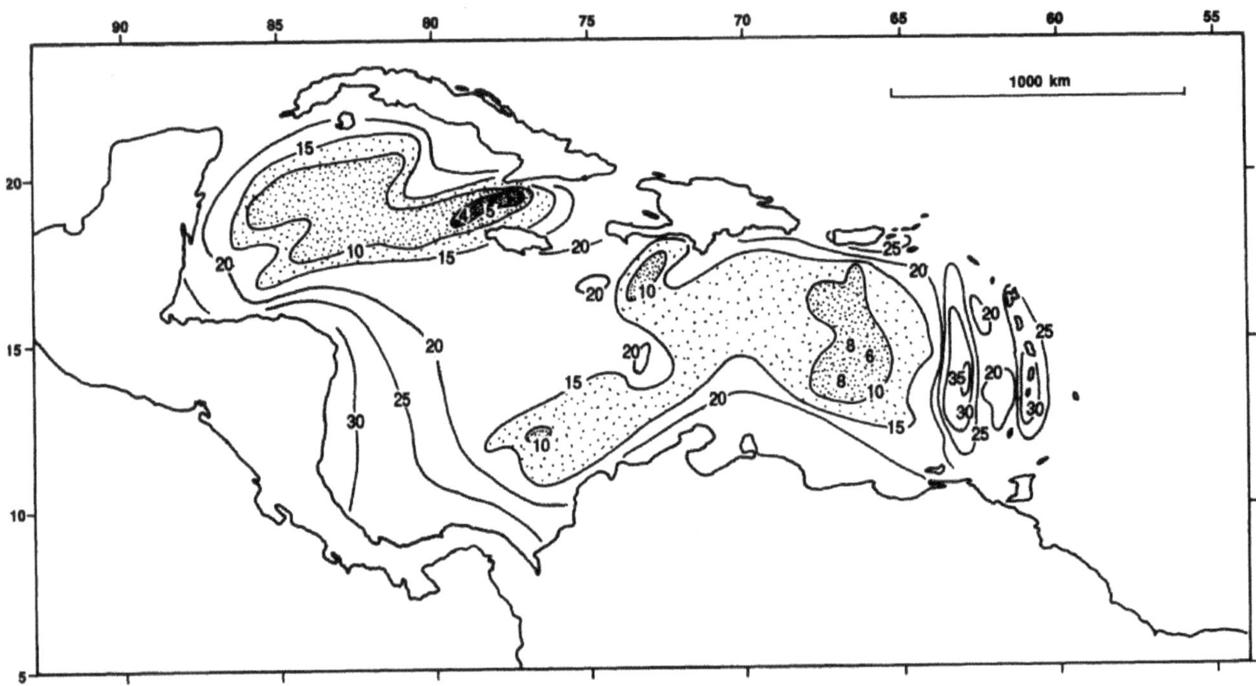

Map of the Caribbean Crust showing its thickness in kilometres

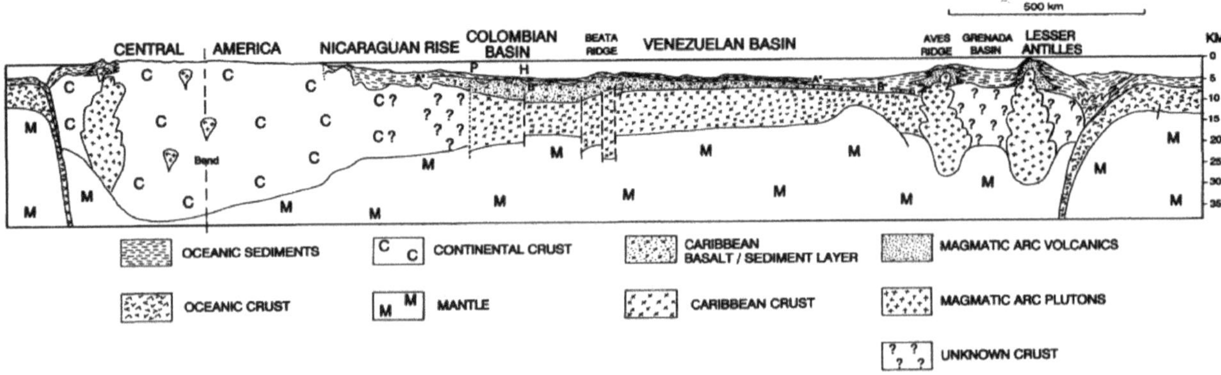

Caribbean East-West cross-section of the Crust
Source: Case, J.E., MacDonald, W.D. & Fox, P.J. 1990. Caribbean crustal provinces; seismic and gravity evidence: in Dengo, G. & Case, I.E. (eds), The Geology of North America, Volume H, The Caribbean Region, 15-36. Geological Society of America

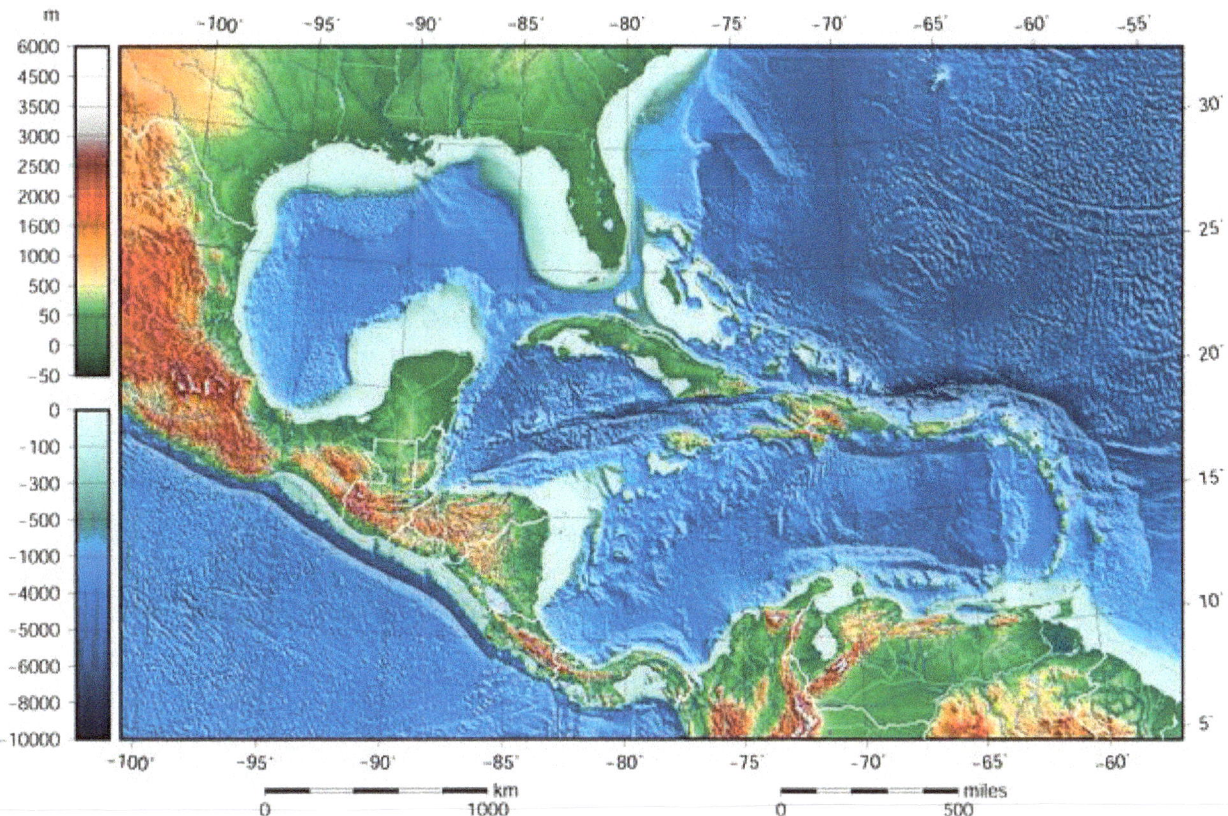

Caribbean Bathymetric Map
Source: Wikimedia Commons – Darekk2

Basin, the Beata Ridge, and the Venezuelan Basin, particularly the eastern part of the Venezuelan Basin. Also, most of the CLIP's structure in the eastern Caribbean appears to be under the thinnest parts of the Crust there.

As the Crust is thin under some components of the eastern Caribbean Plate, more fluid magma would accumulate in the ULVZ beneath them, making them more likely to act like a wheel cylinder in the hydraulic braking system analogy. With any change in underlying hydraulic pressure, the thinner Crust of the eastern Caribbean Plate would probably move vertically much more than the thicker Crust of its western parts. As well as having thin Crust, those components of the eastern Caribbean Plate all share the CLIP's underlying structure, making them more likely to move vertically as one.

At around 35mya, most components of the Caribbean Plate were at the same or a much more equal level relative to each other. Unlike today, there were no deep basins or intervening high ridges, faults or escarpments on the Caribbean Plate. The entire Caribbean region was either a very shallow sea or partly above sea level. The only exception is the Grenada Basin in the east, which appears to have been submerged from when it formed.

Glacial ice started accumulating on Antarctica 35mya, marking the beginning of any hydraulic pressure effects on the Caribbean Plate. After 35mya, large vertical movements of various parts of the Caribbean Plate created the numerous fault zones, basins and ridges that now subdivide the Plate:

- From east to west, there is the Grenada Basin (2,000–3,000m deep), Aves Ridge (0–2,000m deep), Venezuelan Basin (average 4,800m deep), Beata Ridge (0–3,000m deep), and Colombian Basin (average 3,000m deep).
- From east to west, the major faults with large vertical displacement are the eastern and western margins of the Lesser Antilles Islands, the eastern and western margins of the Aves Ridge, the Central Venezuelan Fracture Zone, the eastern and western margins of the Beata Ridge; the Hess Escarpment; and the Pecos Fault Zone.
- In the north are the Puerto Rico Trench and the Muertos Trough; the fault zones around the Gonave, Hispaniola and Puerto Rico-Virgin Islands microplates; and the Cayman Trough.
- In the south, there is the El Pilar Fault Zone, the South Caribbean Deformation Belt, and the Panama Fracture Zone.

It is assumed a ULVZ of very-low-viscosity magma exists at the LAB, which is related to the depth of the Moho. The map below shows shallow Moho beneath the Caribbean Plate at 30km depth or less (the green areas). A structural connection of shallow Moho runs northward along both edges of South America, from the Antarctic Plate to the Caribbean Plate. Another similar shallow Moho connection runs along both edges of North America

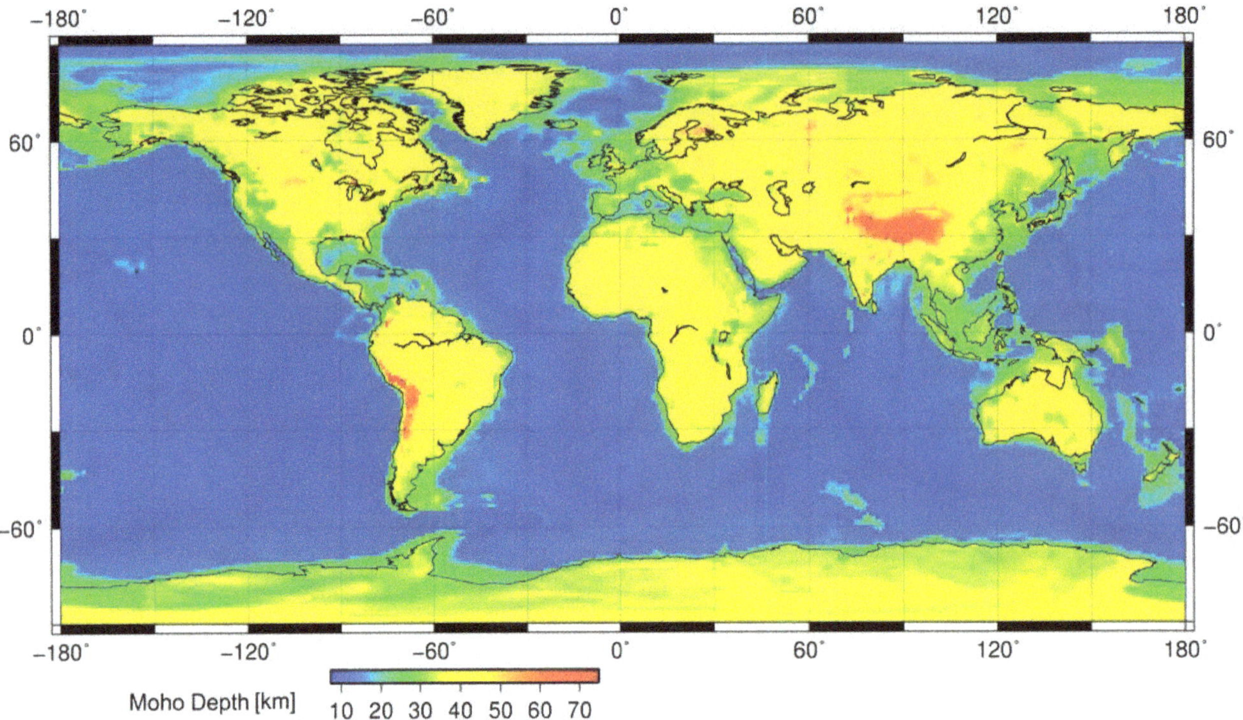

The Position of the Moho Discontinuity
Source: Wikimedia Commons – AllenMcC

to the Caribbean Plate. The Eurasian Plate also has shallow connections to the North American Plate at its eastern and western margins.

The Hydraulic Hypothesis argues that hydraulic pressure from the glaciated plates at the poles would be transmitted to the Caribbean Plate through ULVZ connections along shallow Moho. This hydraulic pressure would mainly transmit along subduction zone wedges and under continental shelves at the edges of the North and South American continents. The transmitted pressure would then cause vertical movements of parts of the Caribbean Plate but not necessarily the entire Plate.

A previous estimate in Appendix 2 was that each major glaciation displaced a magma volume of 13 million km^3 from beneath glaciated polar plates. That displacement would then cause an increase in hydraulic pressure in the ULVZ below remote unglaciated plates. How much uplift could that displacement cause on a remote tectonic plate? As a purely hypothetical example, if all of the upward hydraulic force was transmitted to the Caribbean Plate, would it be enough to raise much of the submerged Plate above sea level from its present depth of 1,000–3,000 metres below sea level?

For this hypothetical example, it is assumed that the 13 million km^3 volume of displaced magma is transmitted evenly beneath the whole Caribbean Plate and that the entire Plate moves as a single unit, like a simple piston in a hydraulic drive. The area of the Caribbean Plate is 3.2 million km^2, which includes all of the Caribbean Plate's components, whether presently below or above sea level. The uplift in kilometres would then be the total volume of displaced magma (13 million km^3) divided by the total area of the Caribbean Plate (3.2 million km^2). The resulting uplift of the entire Caribbean Plate would be 4 kilometres or 4,000 metres, more than enough to lift the Caribbean Plate's submerged components above sea level.

This extreme and very unlikely example illustrates how much uplift displaced magma could cause if focused on a single area the size of the entire Caribbean Plate. A more realistic scenario would be the uplifting or tilting of particular Caribbean Plate components, not the entire 3.2 million km^2.

If a hydraulic effect caused past vertical movements of components of the Caribbean Plate, those movements would need to be linked to the major phases of glaciation on Earth over the past 35 million years. The distinct phases of glaciation were:

- A gradual build-up of ice over Antarctica, beginning 35mya.
- Accelerating ice cover over Antarctica 15mya, with a further acceleration 5mya.
- Ice sheets begin forming over the Northern Hemisphere from 3mya and increase over Antarctica, marking the start of the Quaternary Ice Age.
- Glacial/interglacial cycles become more extreme 1mya, with the final two glacial periods since 240,000 years ago being the most extreme.
- Rapid ice melting and sea level rising after the Last Glacial Maximum 20,000 years ago and continuing until 6,000 years ago.

The Caribbean Plate's Geological Regions

The cartoon maps of the Caribbean Plate illustrate the plate's vertical movements over time. They are based on the present understanding of Caribbean neotectonics. Neotectonics is the sub-discipline of tectonics that studies the current or recent motions and deformations of the Earth's Crust.

Although there is no clear geological definition of 'recent' in neotectonics, it is usually considered to be the past 25 million years, but it can be as long as 60 million years. To further confuse geological definitions, Recent with a capital R can mean just the last 12,000 years of the Holocene Epoch. Therefore, some of the following descriptions use Recent for events confirmed for the last 12,000 years. In contrast, other descriptions use recent for events within the past 250,000 years or less, a very short time compared to 25 or 60 million years for the formal definition of 'neotectonics'.

The cartoon maps show the major vertical movements of the Caribbean Plate's components during each glaciation stage over the past 35 million years. The conclusions come from an analysis of geological field observations and core drilling data.

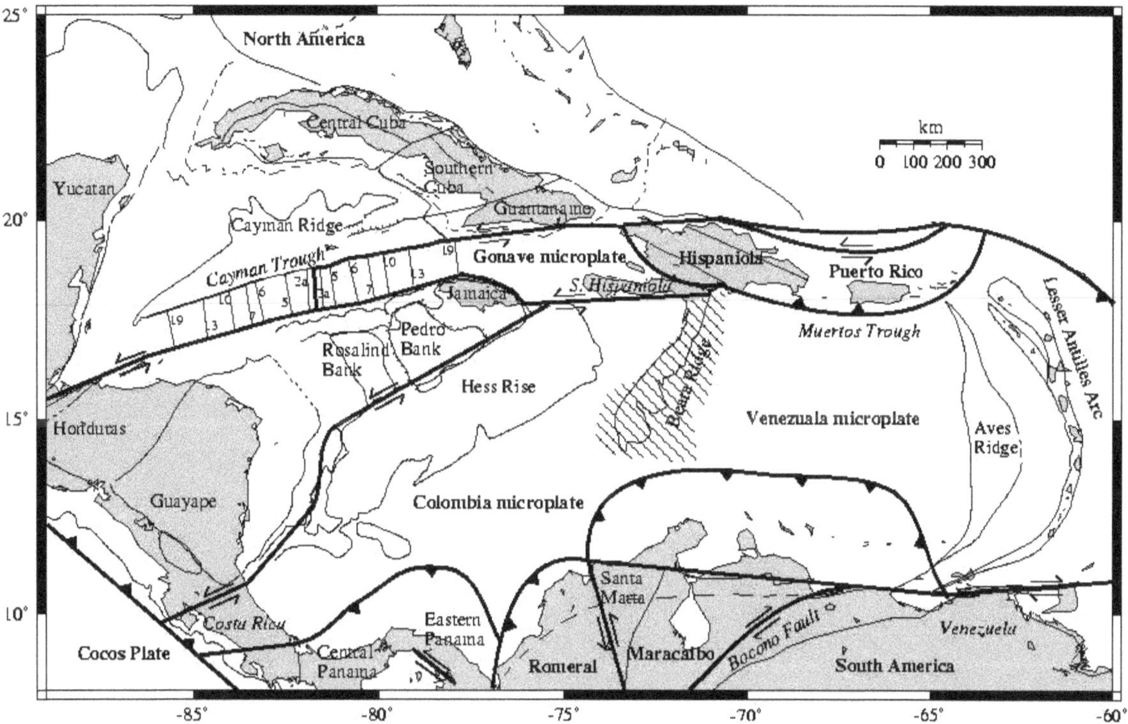

Tectonic map of the Caribbean
Source: R. Dietmar Müller, Jean-Yves Royer, Steven C. Cande, Walter R. Roest, and Sergei Maschenkov – New Constraints on Caribbean Plate Tectonic Evolution

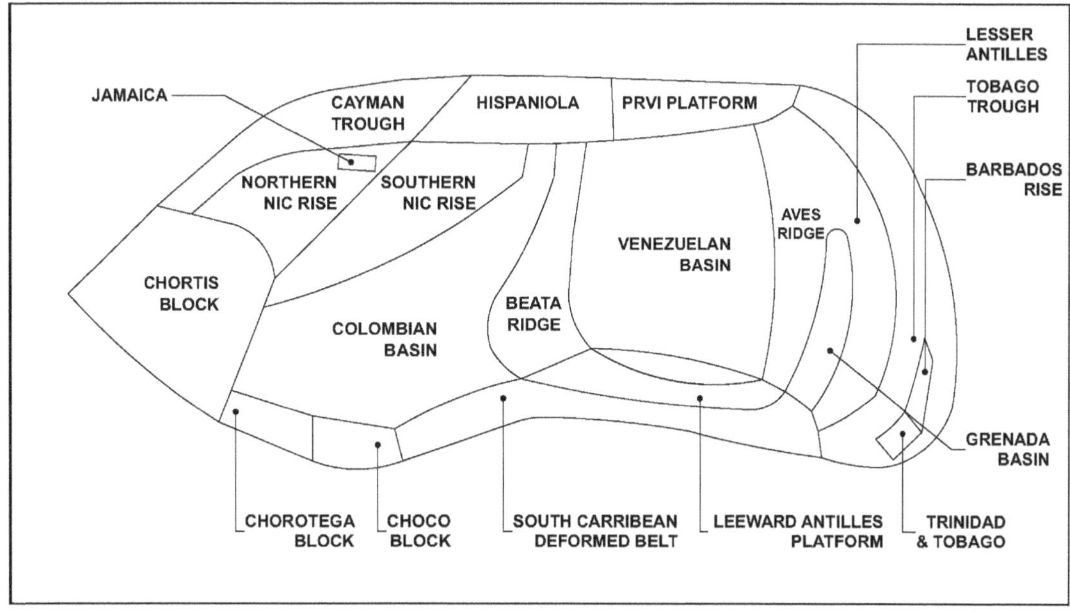

Cartoon Map of the Major Components of the Caribbean Plate

The Caribbean Plate before 35mya

There was no glacial ice on Antarctica or the Northern Hemisphere before 35mya, so no glacial hydraulic forces existed in the ULVZ then. This period can be considered the baseline for any later vertical movements of the Caribbean Plate's components.

West

- The Chortis Block is emergent and remains emergent up to the present.
- The Cayman Trough already exists and will remain a deep region up to the present.

North

- A shallow sea covers Jamaica, the Northern Nicaraguan Rise (NNR), Hispaniola, and the Puerto Rico-Virgin Islands Platform (PRVI).

South

- The Chorotega and Choco Blocks are deeply submerged.
- A shallow sea covers the South Caribbean Deformed Belt (SCDB).

Centre

- The Caribbean Large Igneous Province (CLIP) has already formed the structures of the Southern Nicaraguan Rise (SNR), Beata Ridge, Leeward Antilles Platform, Venezuelan Basin, and Aves Ridge.
- All the above components are at around the same elevation – either emergent or covered by a shallow sea.

East

- A shallow sea covers the Grenada Basin and the Lesser Antilles Islands.

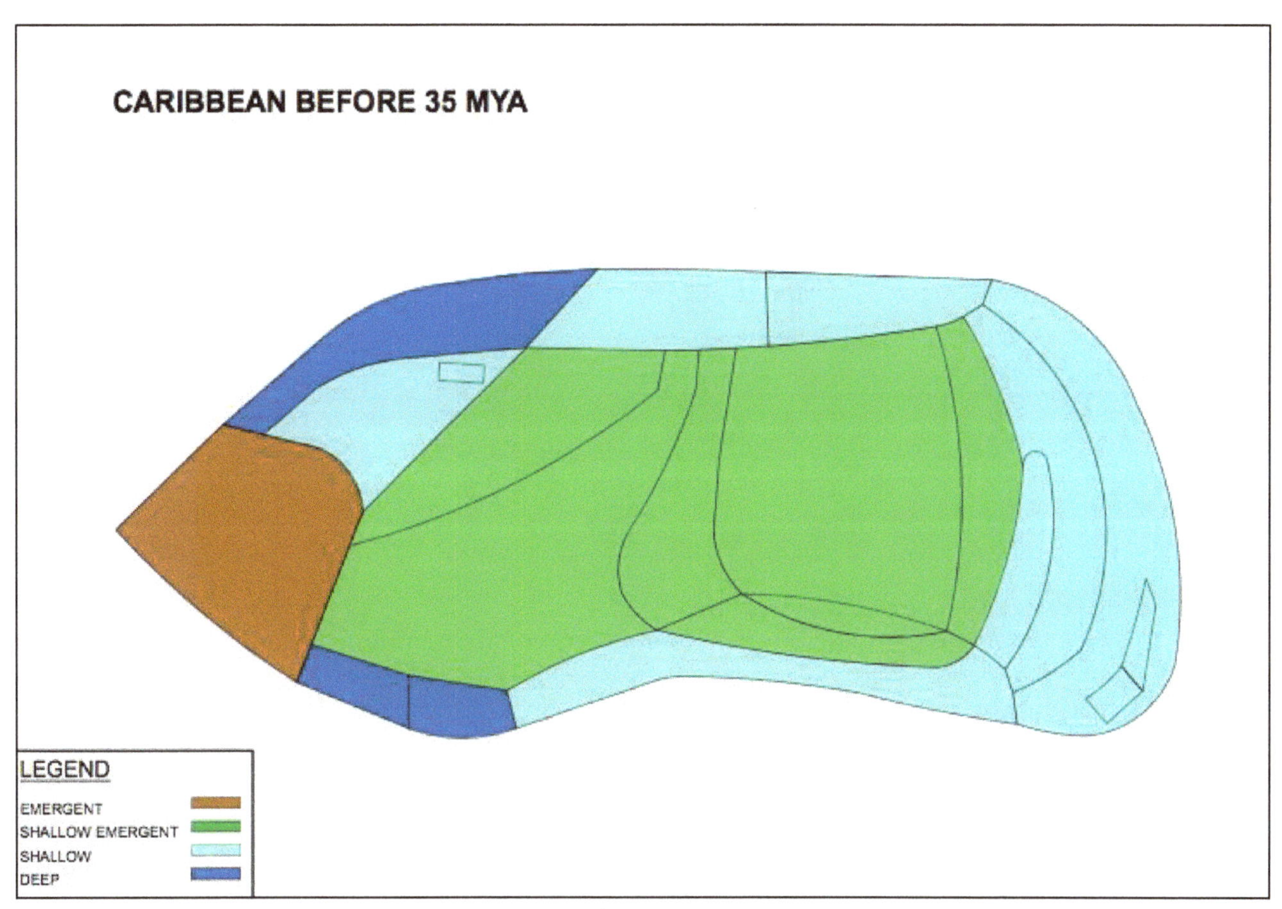

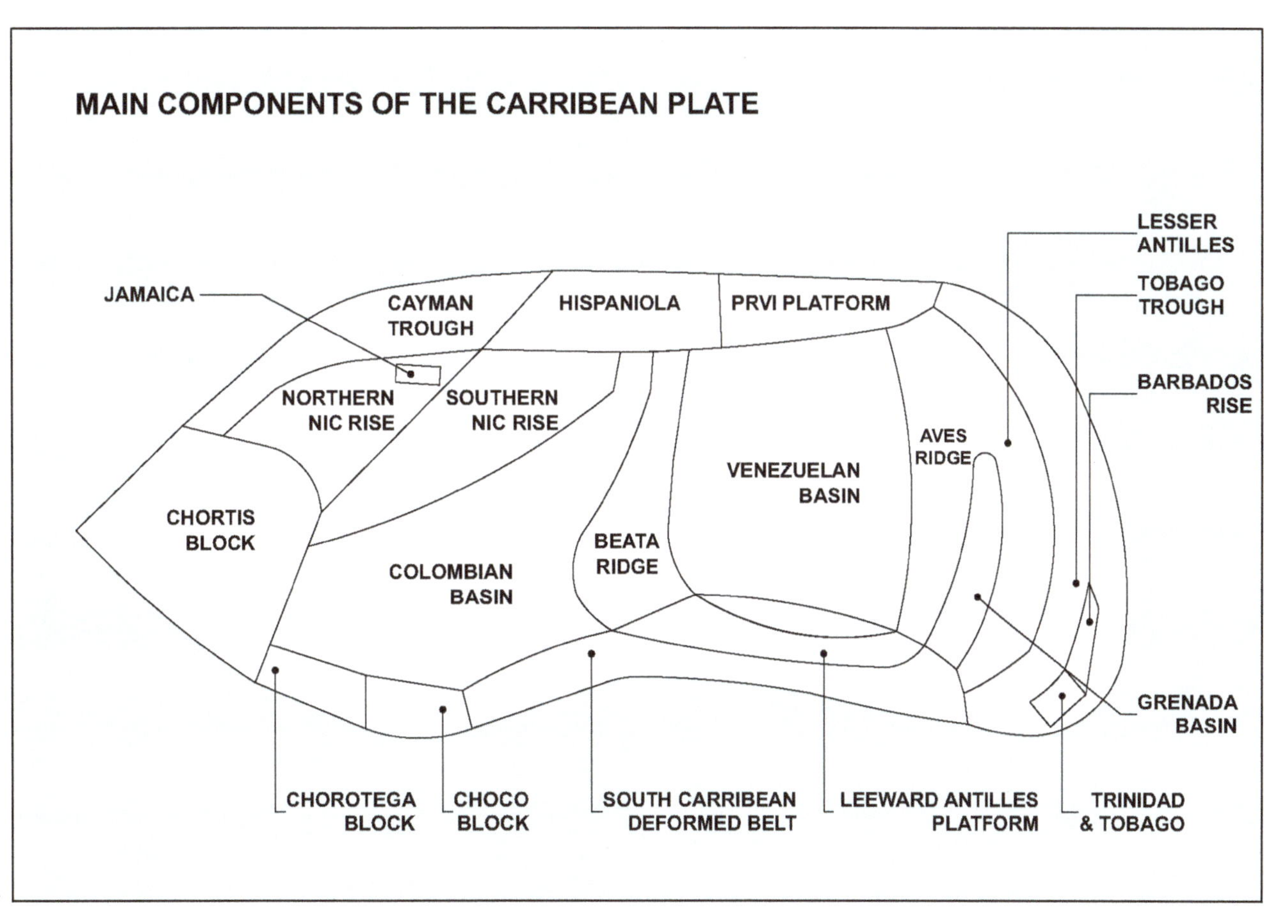

Cartoon Map of the Major Components of the Caribbean Plate

The Caribbean Plate 35–15mya

The period from 35–15mya coincides with the steady build-up of glacial ice on Antarctica. Any effects of hydraulic uplift on the Caribbean Plate would likely have been gradual over those 20 million years.

West

- Increased volcanism occurs on the Chortis Block.
- Rifting intensifies in the Cayman Trough.

North

- Uplift and emergence of Hispaniola, which remains emergent up to the present.
- Uplift of the PRVI Platform.

South

- Uplift of SCDB and Leeward Antilles Platform.

Centre

- Uplift at the northern end of the Colombian Basin and subsidence at its southern end.
- Uplift and emergence of the Beata Ridge.
- Uplift and emergence of the Aves Ridge.
- Venezuelan Basin compresses structures to the south and west in a separate movement to the Beata and Aves Ridges.

East

- Uplift of the Lesser Antilles and increased volcanism there.

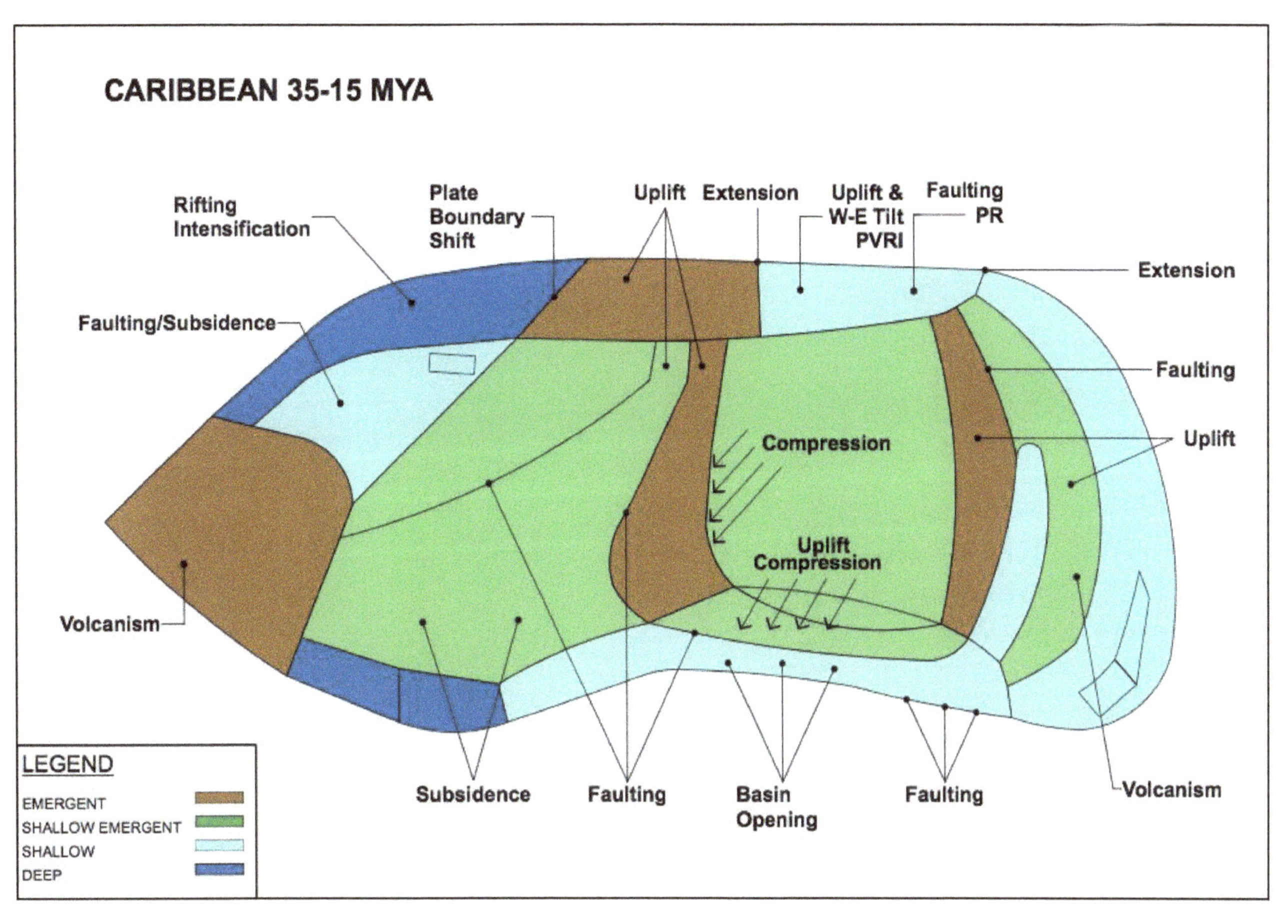

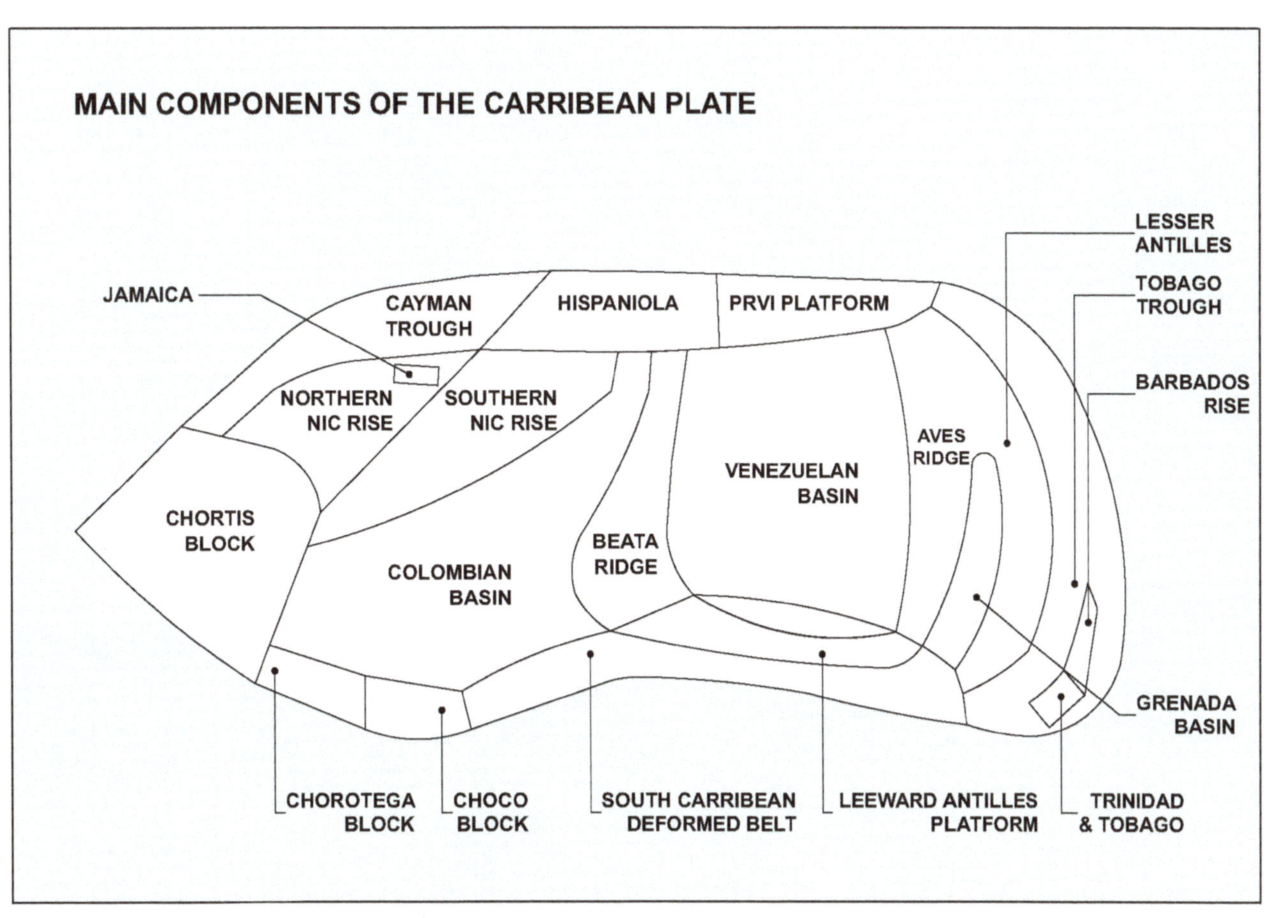

Cartoon Map of the Major Components of the Caribbean Plate

The Caribbean Plate 15–3mya

Compared to the previous 20 million years, the period from 15–3mya had a much more rapid increase in ice sheets over Antarctica. Increasing hydraulic pressure below the Caribbean Plate should cause a more extreme uplift, with increased tilting and faulting of the Plate's components.

North

- Uplift of the NNR and the emergence of Jamaica, which remains emergent up to the present.
- Subsidence of the SNR.
- Uplift and emergence of the PRVI Platform and continued uplift of Hispaniola.
- Emergence of Puerto Rico around 5mya, which remains emergent up to the present.

South

- Uplift of the Chorotega and Choco Blocks.

Centre

- Subsidence of the southern and northern parts of the Colombian Basin.
- The Beata Ridge remains emergent and tilts southward, with increased faulting at its western, eastern and southern margins.
- Venezuelan Basin subsides and tilts to the northwest; along with compression to the west and faulting to the south at the Leeward Antilles Platform.

East

- Uplift and emergence of the Lesser Antilles Islands, which remain emergent up to the present.
- Uplift and emergence of Trinidad and Tobago, which remain emergent up to the present
- Uplift of the eastern boundary of the Caribbean Plate.

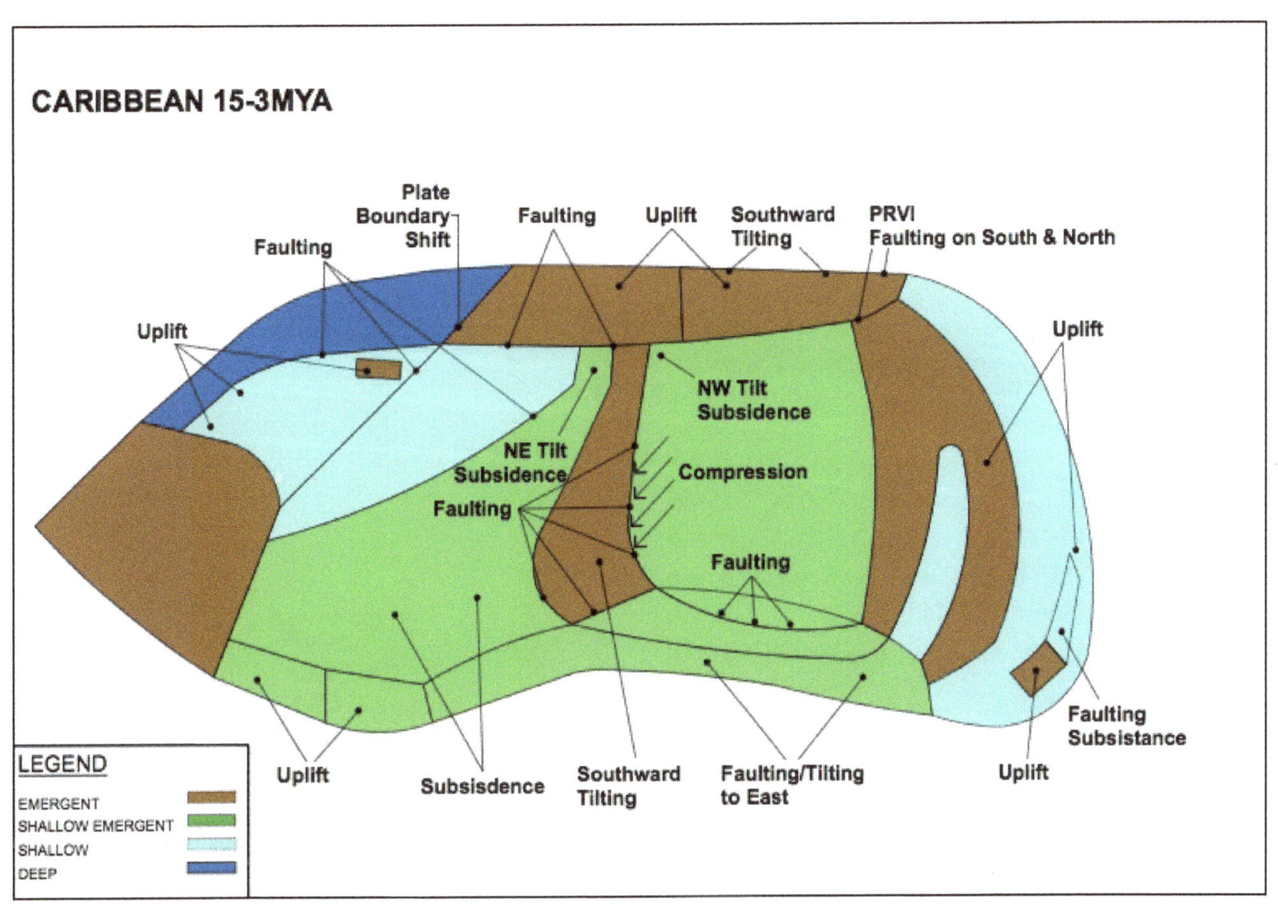

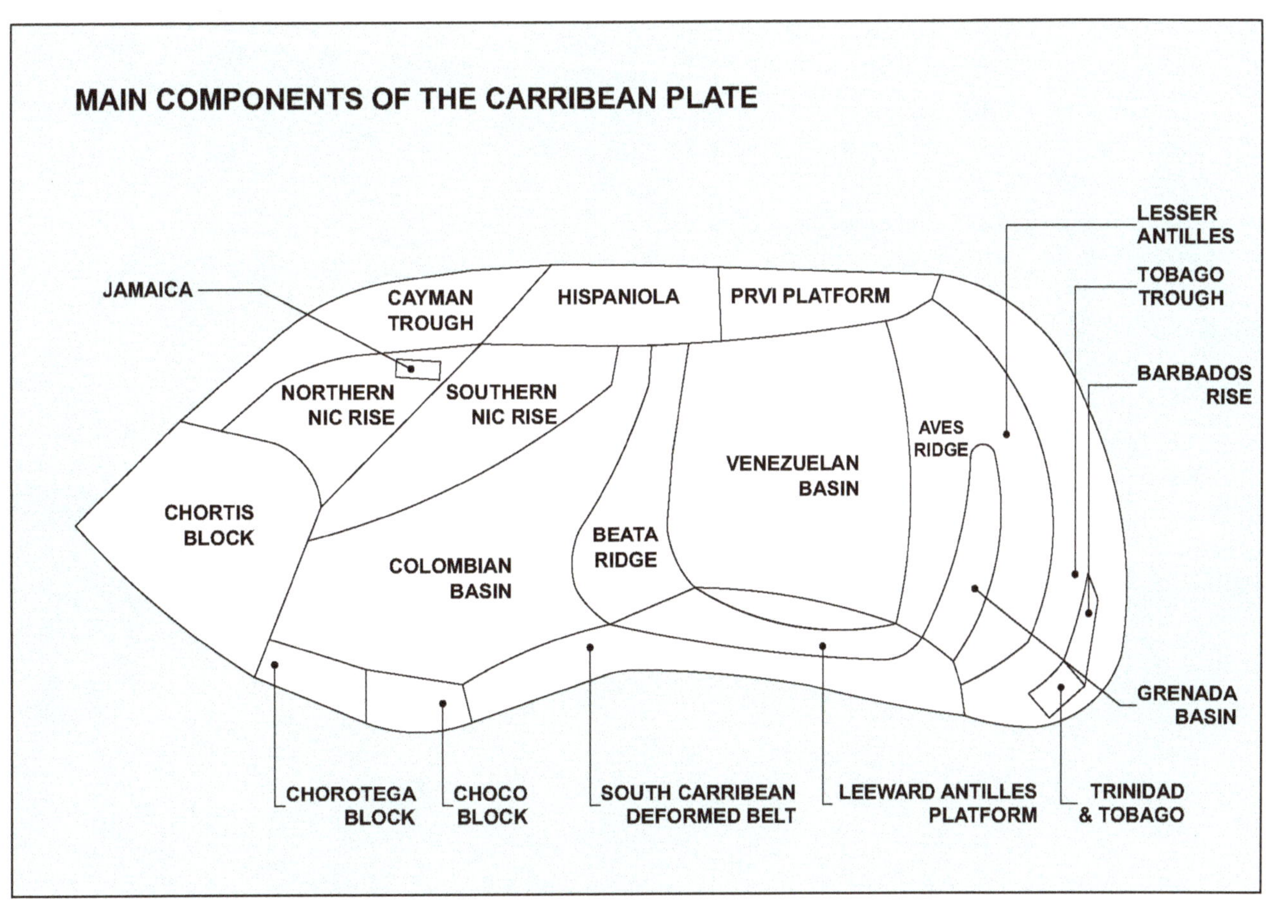

Cartoon Map of the Major Components of the Caribbean Plate

The Caribbean Plate 3–1mya

Around 3mya, glacial ice began to build up over the Northern Hemisphere and Antarctica. Those much quicker and larger accumulations of glacial ice would have greatly increased the underlying hydraulic force and accelerated the uplift, tilting and faulting of the Caribbean Plate's components. However, the large cyclical pressure fluctuations likely caused repeated uplift followed by subsidence of some parts of the Plate.

North

- Continued uplift of Jamaica, Hispaniola, and the PRVI Platform, including Puerto Rico.
- Hispaniola and Puerto Rico become separate structures on the PRVI Platform.
- Rapid subsidence of the Puerto Rico Trench.

South

- Uplift and emergence of the Chorotega and Choco Blocks, which then form the Isthmus of Panama, which remains emergent.
- Faulting and slab break-off of the southern boundary of the Caribbean Plate with Venezuela.

Centre

- Subsidence of the Colombian Basin.
- Southward tilting of the Beata Ridge and faulting at its margin with the Colombian Basin.
- Venezuelan Basin subduction at its Muertos Trough margin with Hispaniola and the PRVI.
- Venezuelan Basin compression and subsidence at its margins with the Beata Ridge and Leeward Antilles Platform.
- Venezuelan Basin faulting and subsidence at its margin with the Aves Ridge.

East

- Compression and uplift of the northern end of the Grenada Basin.
- Faulting at the margin of the Grenada Basin with the southern Lesser Antilles Islands.
- Volcanism in the southern Lesser Antilles Islands.
- Uplift of the northern Lesser Antilles Islands.

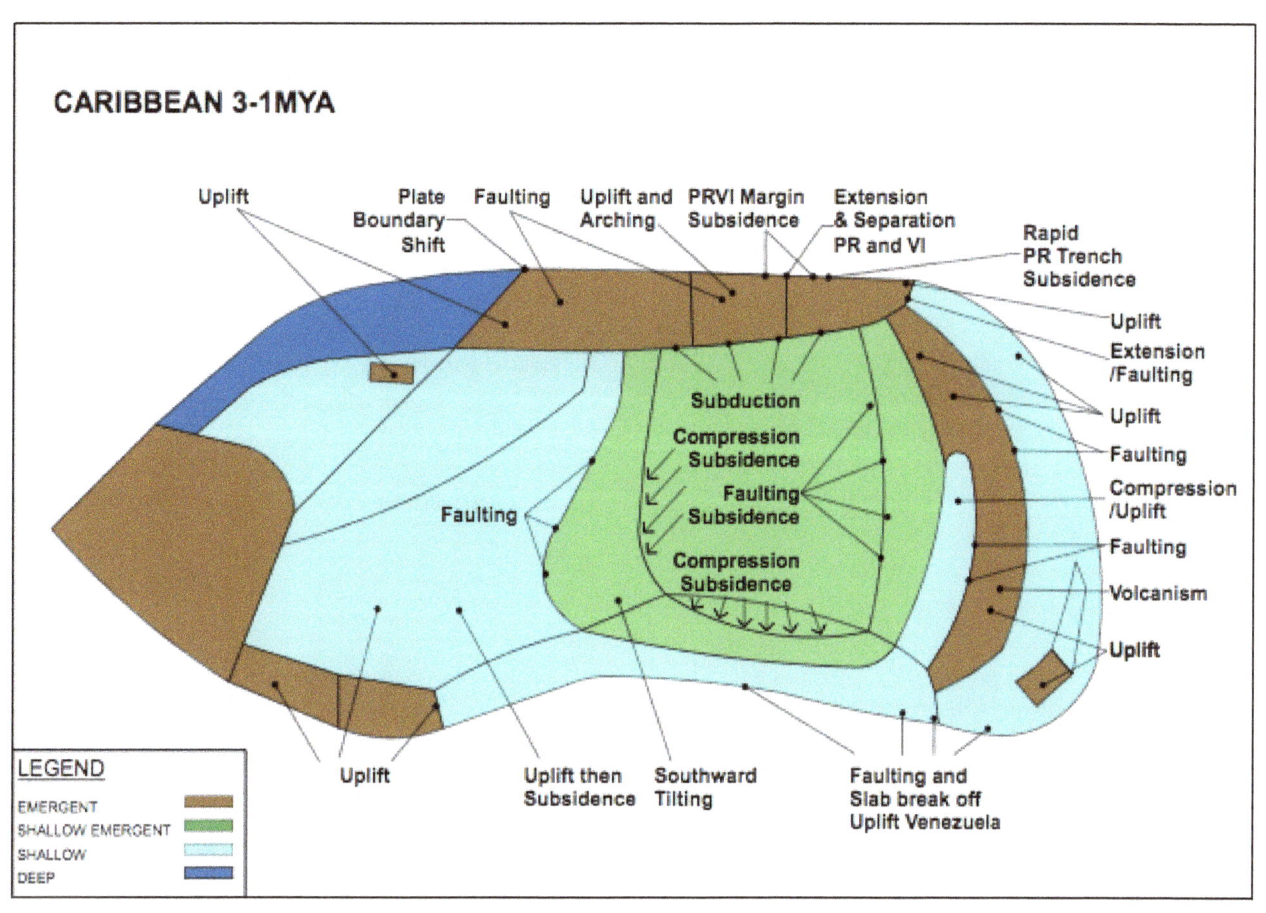

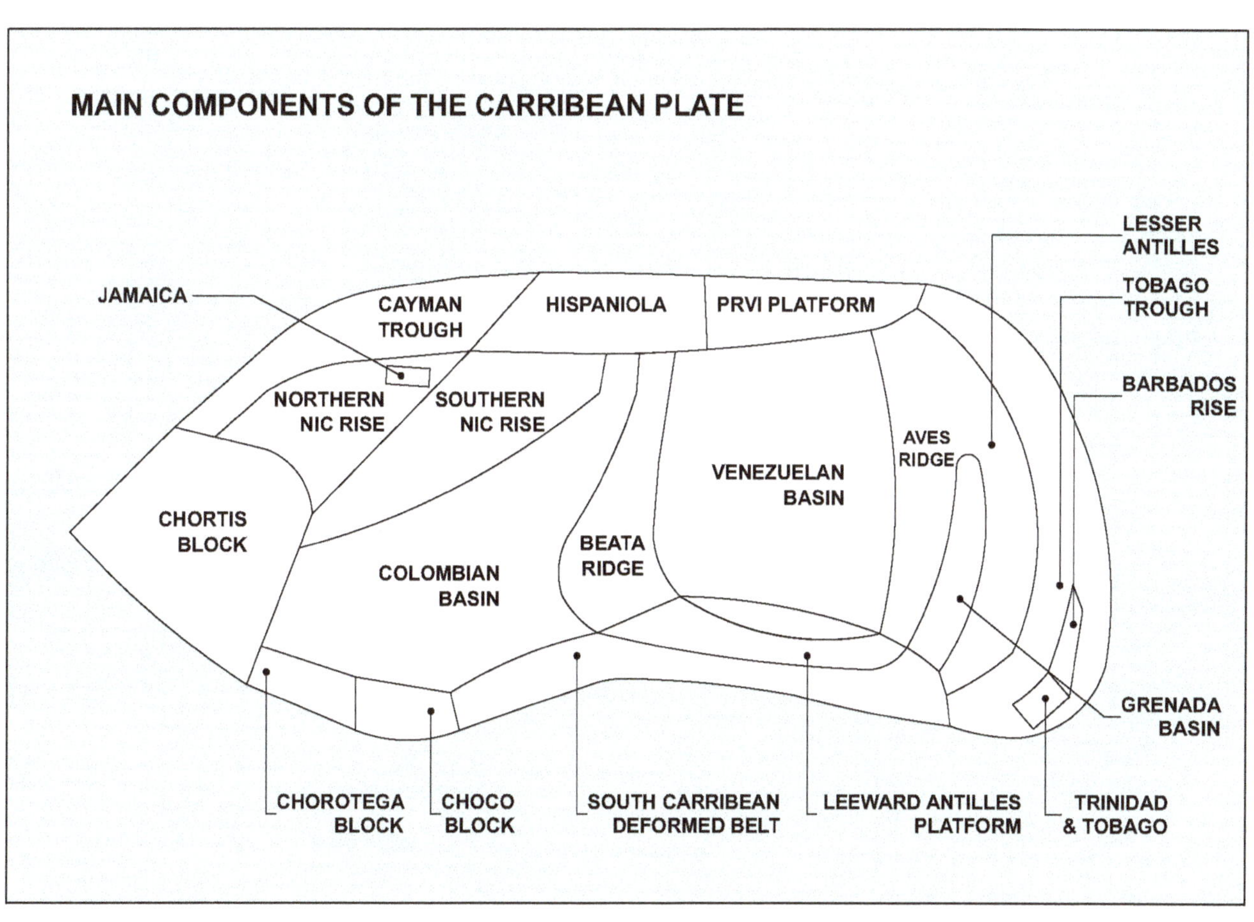

Cartoon Map of the Major Components of the Caribbean Plate

The Caribbean Plate 1mya–Recent

The increasing hydraulic force under the eastern Caribbean Plate pushed up the Atlantic Island's mobile flap, which is bounded by fault zones. The flap is fixed at its northern edge and has three free edges to the east, west, and south – leaving it free to move vertically at its southern edge.

The most likely period for the emergence of the complete Atlantic Island is during the past one million years of more extreme glaciations. Nevertheless, the flap may have emerged gradually over several million years. Uplift may have started from the beginning of the Quaternary Ice Age 2.5mya, or it may have begun even earlier from 15mya when thicker ice sheets began to form over Antarctica.

Around one million years ago, there was a marked acceleration in the amount of glacial ice accumulated during each glacial period. In the accompanying graph, the red line estimates the average intensity of past glacial/interglacial cycles. It can be used as a proxy for the increasing amount of glacial ice covering the polar tectonic plates.

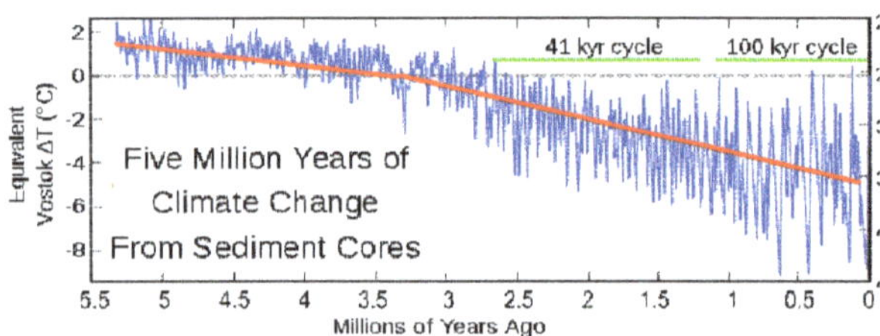

Glacials and Interglacials over the last 5 million years
Source: Wikimedia Commons – From Robert A. RohdeSource: Modified from Google Earth

Increasing average volumes of glacial ice over the past one to two million years would have accelerated the uplift of the Caribbean Plate's flap, even though the flap's elevation may not have been steady. The flap may have repeatedly risen and fallen due to changes in hydraulic pressure below it, particularly over the past one million years of more intense cycles of glaciation/deglaciation. Those pressure fluctuations could have caused different parts of the Plate to rise and fall over time, giving a mixed picture of vertical movements, with some components repeatedly rising and then falling.

The islands of Hispaniola and Puerto Rico have been above sea level for more than 3 million years, and with further uplift, they would have formed a long mountain range on the north of an emergent Atlantic Island. The Aves and Beata Ridges had been uplifted and emergent in the past, and with further uplift, they would have formed long mountain ranges on the east and west of an emergent Atlantic Island.

The final missing portion of the Atlantic Island appeared with the uplift of the Venezuelan Basin from below sea level, forming the Plain of Atlantis. The Venezuelan Basin seems to have been submerged at a shallow depth for millions of years, although it possibly had once been emergent.

Even though the Venezuelan Basin now forms a separate unattached structure within the Caribbean Plate, before 35mya, it was at the same level as the Aves and Beata Ridges. After 35mya, the Venezuelan Basin increasingly detached along fault zones at the Aves and Beata Ridges, subsiding relative to them. It also detached at fault zones to the north at the Muertos Trough and the south at the South Caribbean Deformed Belt.

West

- Increased faulting at the eastern margins of the Chortis Block and along the Cayman Trough.
- Uplift of the NNR and Jamaica.

North

- Volcanism, faulting and tilting of the SNR to the south-east.
- Faulting and uplift on Hispaniola.
- Uplift of the PRVI on the south, with subsidence on the north.

South

- Faulting and uplift of the Chorotega and Choco Blocks (Panama Isthmus) and the southern part of the Colombian Basin.
- Faulting along the southern boundary of the Caribbean Plate.

Centre

- Subsidence of the northern part of the Colombian Basin.
- Southward tilt of the Beata Ridge.
- Increased subsidence of the Venezuelan Basin:
- Subduction at the Muertos Trough in the north.
- Compression and subsidence at the western margin with the Beata Ridge.
- Compression, faulting and subduction at the southern margin with the Leeward Antilles Platform and SCDB.
- Increased faulting at the eastern margin with the Aves Ridge.
- Southward tilt of the Aves Ridge and Grenada Basin.

East

- Increased volcanism on the northern Lesser Antilles Islands.
- Faulting along the eastern margin of the Lesser Antilles Islands.
- Uplift of Trinidad and Tobago and the Barbados Rise.
- Uplift on the eastern boundary of the Caribbean Plate.

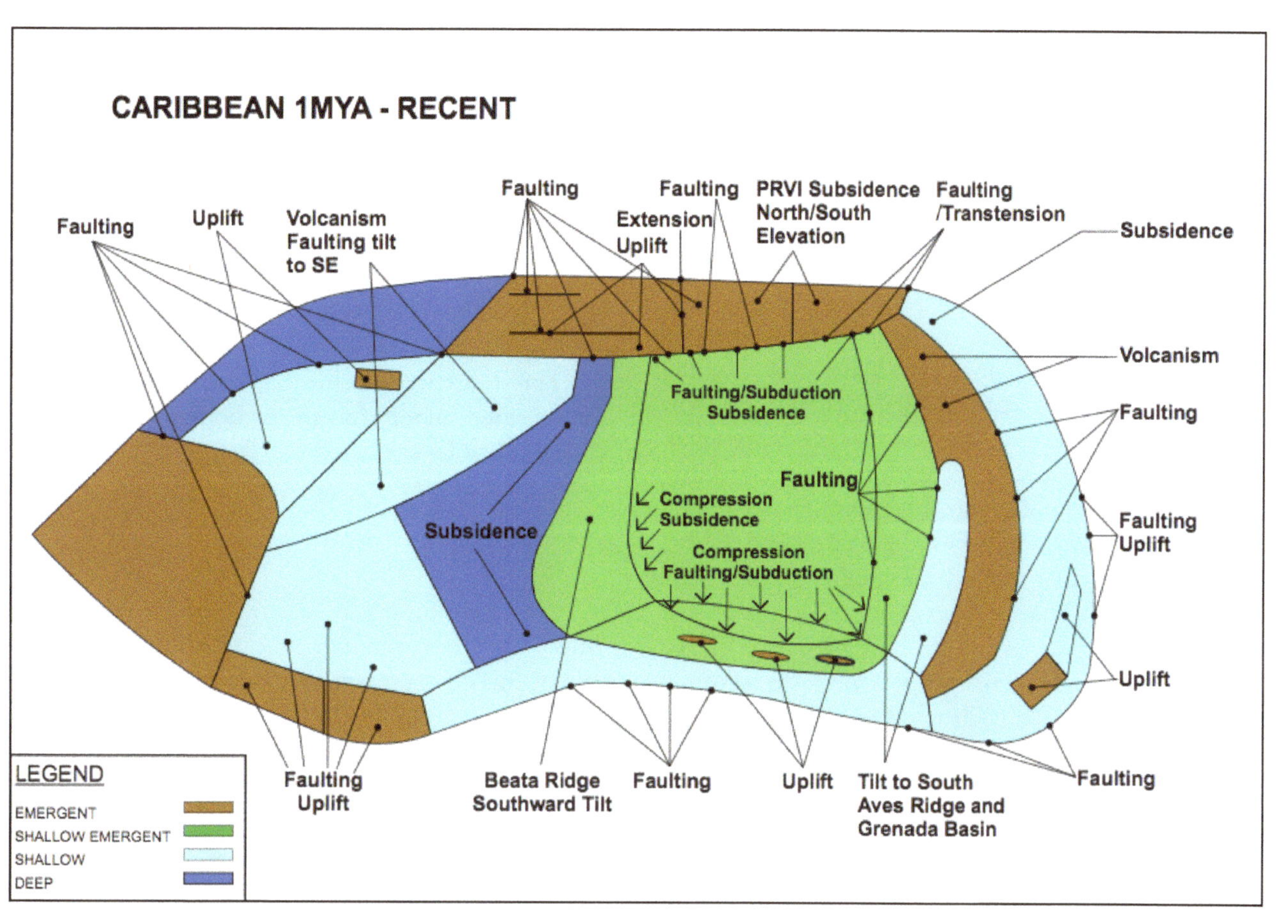

The Flap portion of the Caribbean Plate
Source: Modified from Google Earth

The Caribbean Plate 250kya–Recent

It has already been argued that the complete Atlantic Island most likely formed sometime during the last one million years. The Atlantic Island then remained emergent for possibly hundreds of thousands of years until large parts submerged sometime after 11,600 BP.

This section attempts to describe any vertical movements of the Caribbean Plate that can be limited to the past 250,000 years. It is a period that includes the two last and greatest glacial/interglacial cycles. During these two extreme cycles, there would have been both large increases and decreases in hydraulic pressure below the Caribbean Plate, which would have caused substantial uplifts and subsidences of different parts of the Plate.

During the most recent glacial/interglacial cycle, ice sheets gradually increased over the polar tectonic plates for roughly 100,000 years until they stopped 20,000 years ago at the Last Glacial Maximum. Over those 100,000 years of increasing glaciation, hydraulic pressure would have increased under the mobile flap of the eastern Caribbean Plate and caused an uplift there. All of the Atlantic Island or some parts of it may have already been emergent long before then, and they may have undergone additional uplift.

From 20,000 to 6,000 years ago, the most recent rapid glacial melting would have created a relatively sudden and large hydraulic pressure release below the Caribbean Plate. Such a pressure drop over a relatively short time could have caused recent subsidence and downward tilting of several components of the Caribbean Plate's flap. As Plato describes, those recent downward movements may have caused the sinking of the Atlantic Island sometime after 11,600 BP.

Because of differences in resistance at the various fault zone boundaries of the Caribbean Plate's components, the whole Plate probably did not subside as one piece. There would likely have been more subsidence of those components along fault zones with less resistance to downward movement. There may also have been a larger drop in hydraulic pressure below particular components, which would tend to subside more than others.

The following major subsidences of the eastern Caribbean Plate had to occur for the Atlantic Island to sink and create the present eastern Caribbean Sea bottom:

- The northern part of the Columbian Basin tilted to the east, and the Beata Ridge tilted to the south at their margins with Hispaniola.
- The Venezuelan Basin subsided as a separate unit at its northern margin with the PRVI Platform at the Muertos Trough.
- The Venezuelan Basin may also have subsided relative to the Beata and Aves Ridges.
- As well as subsiding, the Venezuelan Basin tilted to the south-east and slid southward toward the Leeward Antilles Platform and the South Caribbean Deformed Belt.
- The Aves Ridge tilted to the south at the Anegada Passage and along its associated fault extensions in the north.
- The Grenada Basin tilted to the south and subsided along its steep boundary with the southern Lesser Antilles.
- The northern Lesser Antilles Islands tilted to the south at their steep eastern boundary and possibly west along the Kallinago Depression.

Any discontinuity in a drill core would be an important finding, confirming whether an Atlantic Island was once emergent but submerged sometime later. A discontinuity indicates an interruption or change in the local environment at the drill site. There would be a visible discontinuity if the land was once above sea level and later subsided underwater or vice versa.

A recent discontinuity in a drill core from the now-submerged Beata or Aves Ridges or the Venezuelan Basin would indicate a change in the elevation of that structure. Some drill cores suggest changes in the elevation of components of the Caribbean Plate over the past million years or more and may indicate emergence followed by submergence. Unfortunately, current drill core data is not accurate enough for the most recent 250,000 years and gives no obvious picture of very recent change. Specifically, there is no clear evidence of changes in the past 11,600 years when the Atlantic Island was supposed to have submerged.

Even though there is no known distinct discontinuity in available drill cores, existing field geology provides some evidence for the existence and destruction of the Atlantic Island. It does seem to describe relatively recent faulting, elevation and subsidence of several components of the Caribbean Plate.

The following section presents the geological changes that can be confined to the past 250,000 years. There may be a combined picture of uplift and subsidence since there were two glacial/interglacial cycles over those 250,000 years. A previous section discussed older geological changes from one million years ago to Recent. As many older changes remain active, they can be added to those for 250kya to Recent. The cartoon map of 1mya to Recent is included to compare it with the changes for 250kya to Recent.

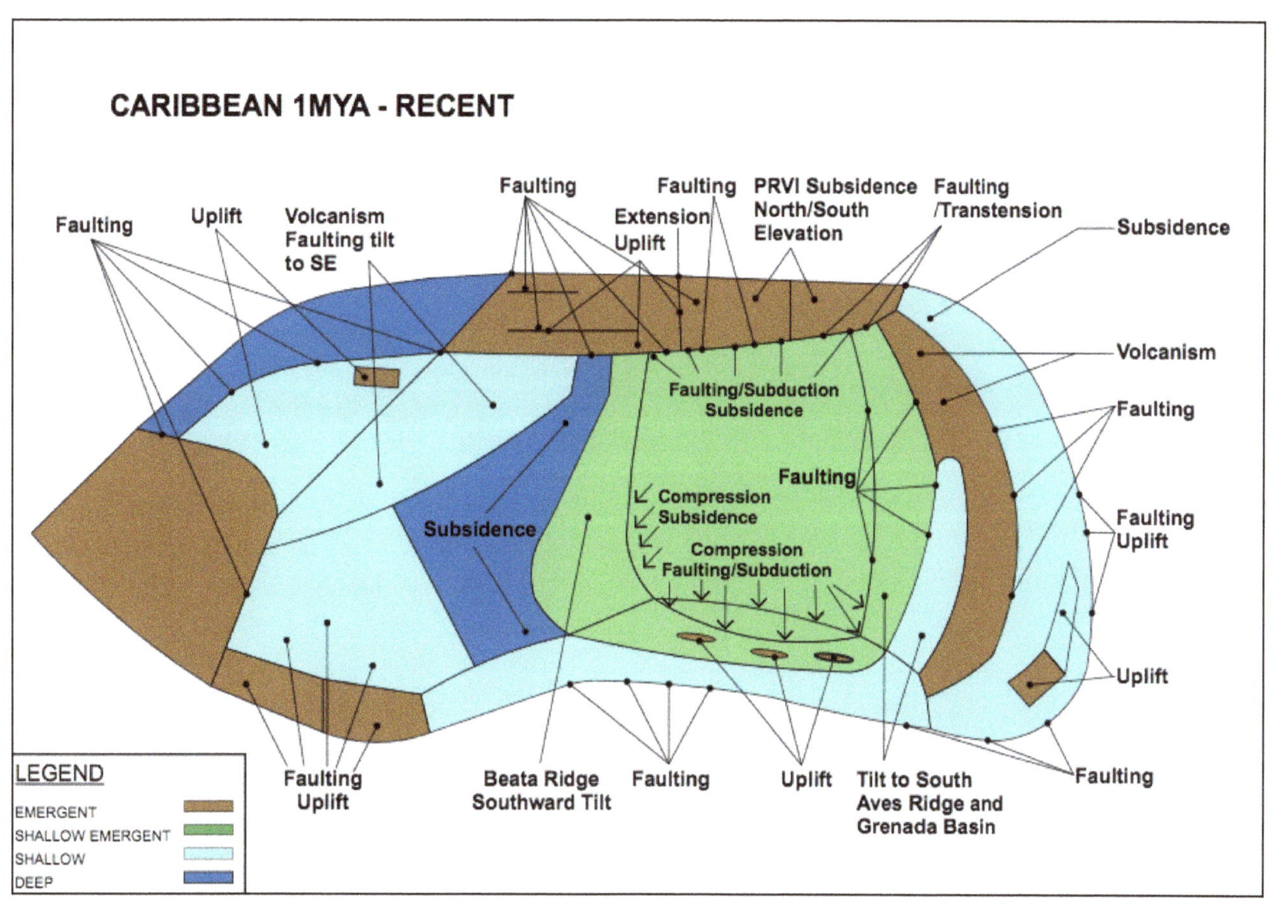
CARIBBEAN 1MYA - RECENT
Faulting
Uplift
Volcanism
Faulting tilt
to SE
Faulting
Faulting
Extension
Uplift
PRVI Subsidence
North/South
Elevation
Faulting
/Transtension
Subsidence
Volcanism
Faulting
Faulting/Subduction
Subsidence
Faulting
Compression
Subsidence
Compression
Faulting/Subduction
Subsidence
Faulting
Uplift
Uplift
LEGEND
EMERGENT
SHALLOW EMERGENT
SHALLOW
DEEP
Faulting
Uplift
Beata Ridge
Southward Tilt
Faulting
Uplift
Tilt to South
Aves Ridge and
Grenada Basin
Faulting

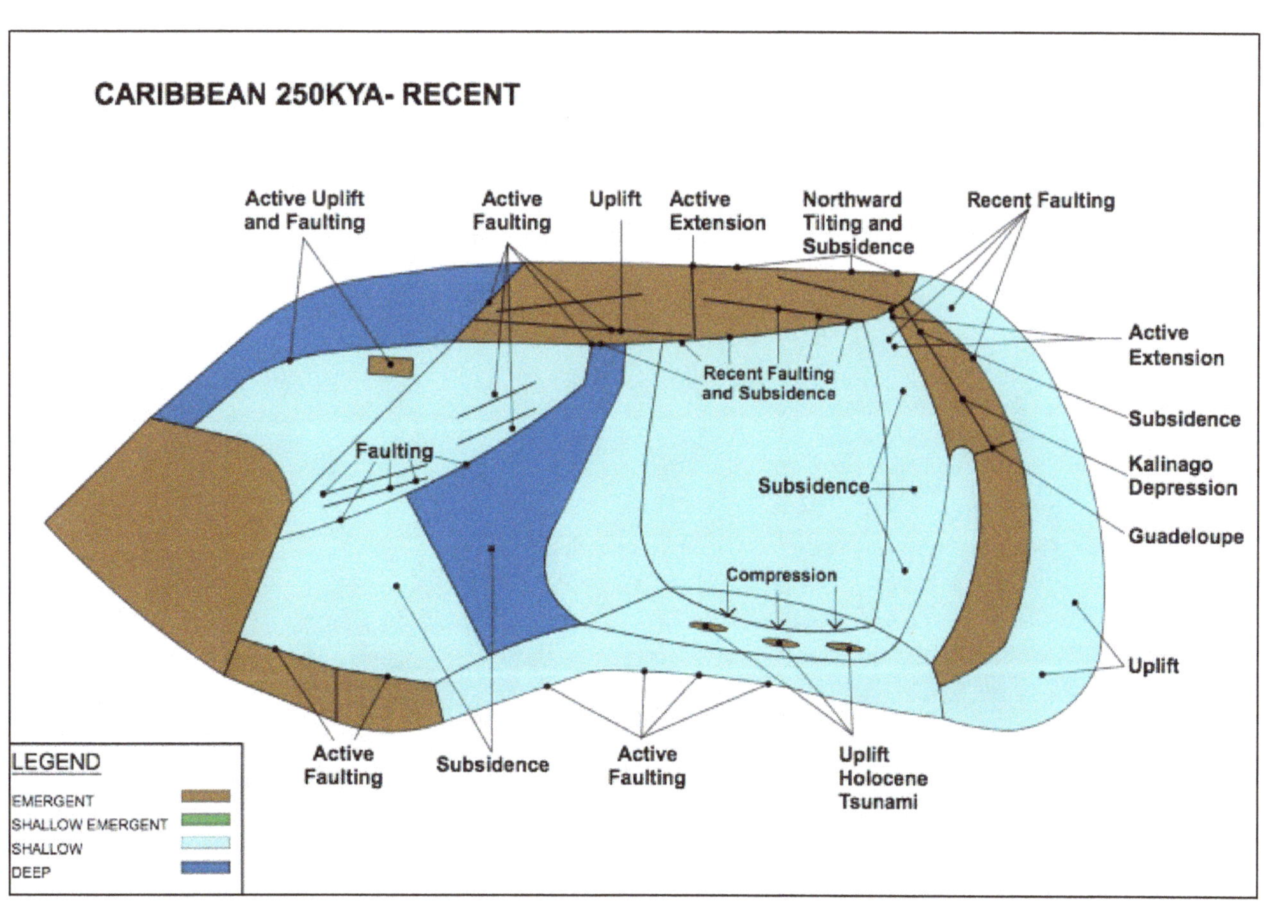
CARIBBEAN 250KYA- RECENT
Active Uplift
and Faulting
Active
Faulting
Uplift
Active
Extension
Northward
Tilting and
Subsidence
Recent Faulting
Active
Extension
Recent Faulting
and Subsidence
Subsidence
Faulting
Subsidence
Kalinago
Depression
Guadeloupe
Compression
Uplift
LEGEND
EMERGENT
SHALLOW EMERGENT
SHALLOW
DEEP
Active
Faulting
Subsidence
Active
Faulting
Uplift
Holocene
Tsunami

West

- The Costa Rica and Panama coastlines of the Chorotega forearc have active faulting.
- Active strike-slip faults are continuous across the N-W Caribbean Plate from Hispaniola to the western end of the Chortis Block.
- The Pedro Fracture Zone divides the Nicaraguan Rise into the Northern Nicaraguan Rise (NNR) and Southern Nicaraguan Rise (SNR).
- There was generalised uplift across the Northern NNR in the Late Pleistocene (~120–12kya).
- There was Late Pleistocene (~120–12kya) uplift at the Swan Islands Platform and Jamaica; both are located on the NNR.
- No major subsidence occurred on the NNR during the Late Pleistocene (~120–12kya), and the NNR appears uncoupled from any recent vertical movement of the Southern Nicaraguan Rise (SNR).
- The SNR lies at a water depth of 2,000–4,000m, with depth increasing to the south-east. This change in depth indicates tilting of the SNR to the south-east.

North

The Windward Passage is an 80-km-wide active fault zone between the islands of Cuba and Hispaniola.

- There is a continuous line of active faults from western Hispaniola through the Muertos Trough and into the Anegada Passage. There is active faulting with recent uplift and subsidence along all those northern fault zones.
- The connected northern faults could allow the combined vertical movement and tilting of southern Hispaniola and the northern part of the Beata Ridge attached to it, the northern margin of the Venezuelan Basin, the Aves Ridge, and the northern islands of the Lesser Antilles.
- On Hispaniola, active fault systems roughly define the northern and southern coasts of the island.
- A fault-bounded depression separates the Southern Peninsula of Hispaniola from the rest of the island.
- There is recent uplift and faulting of the Southern Peninsula of Hispaniola and compression of south-western Hispaniola at its Muertos Trough margin.
- At the Enriquillo-Plantain Garden Fault Zone (EPGFZ), the most recent phase of tectonism involves strong uplifts and open folding along N-W-striking axes.

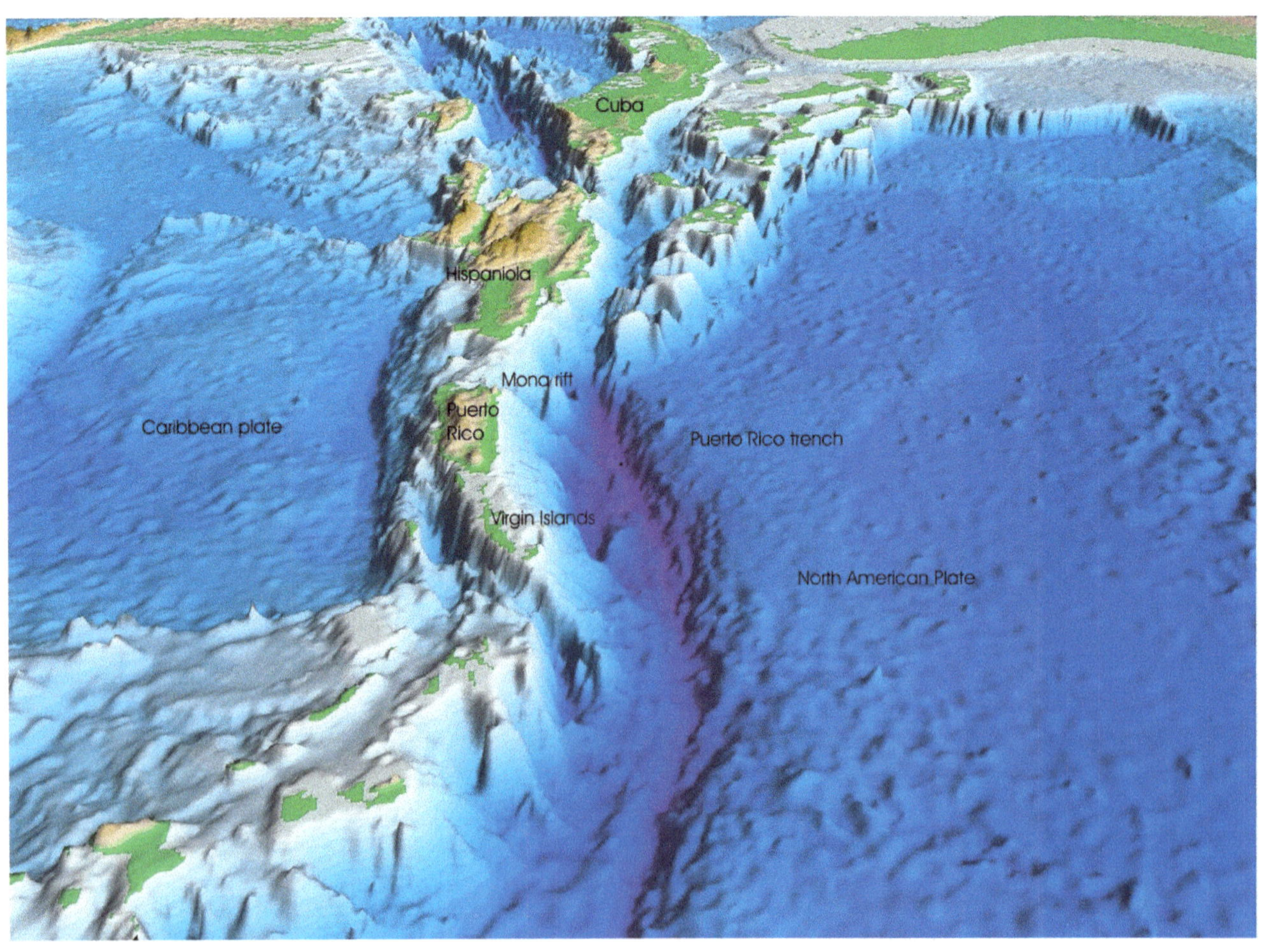

3D Bathymetry of North-East Caribbean
Source: Wikimedia Commons – USGS

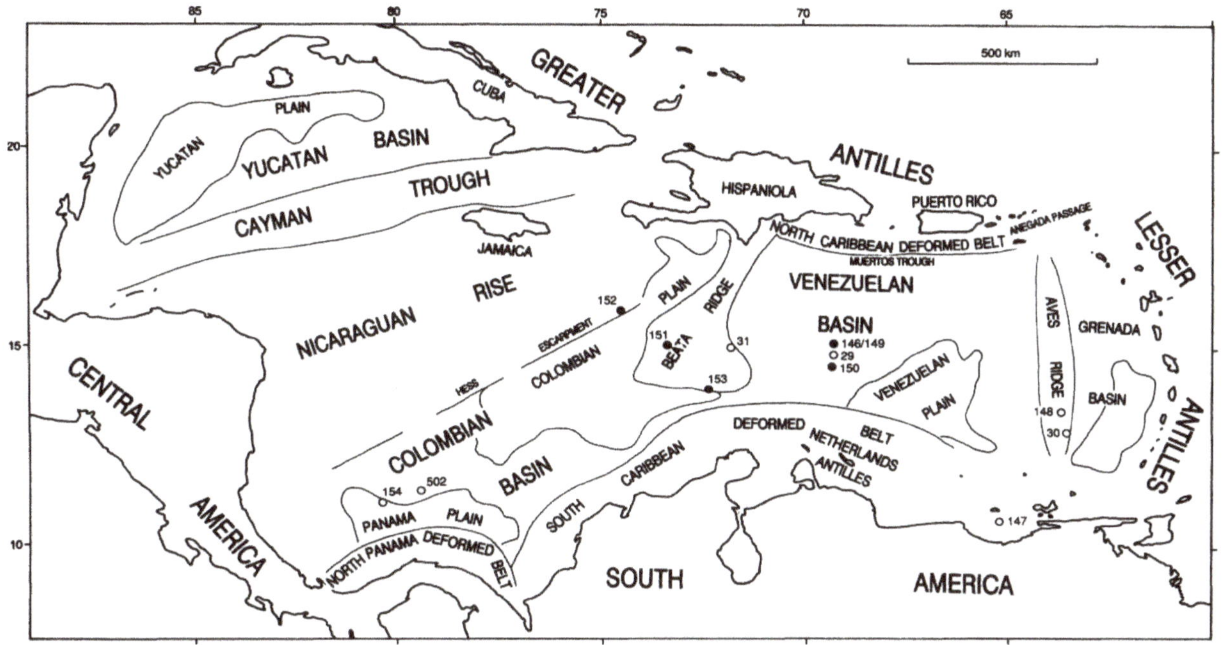

Map of the Caribbean showing the major named features
Source: Case, J.E., MacDonald, W.D. & Fox, P.J. 1990. Caribbean crustal provinces; seismic and gravity evidence: in Dengo, G. & Case, I.E. (eds), The Geology of North America, Volume H, The Caribbean Region, 15–36. Geological Society of America.

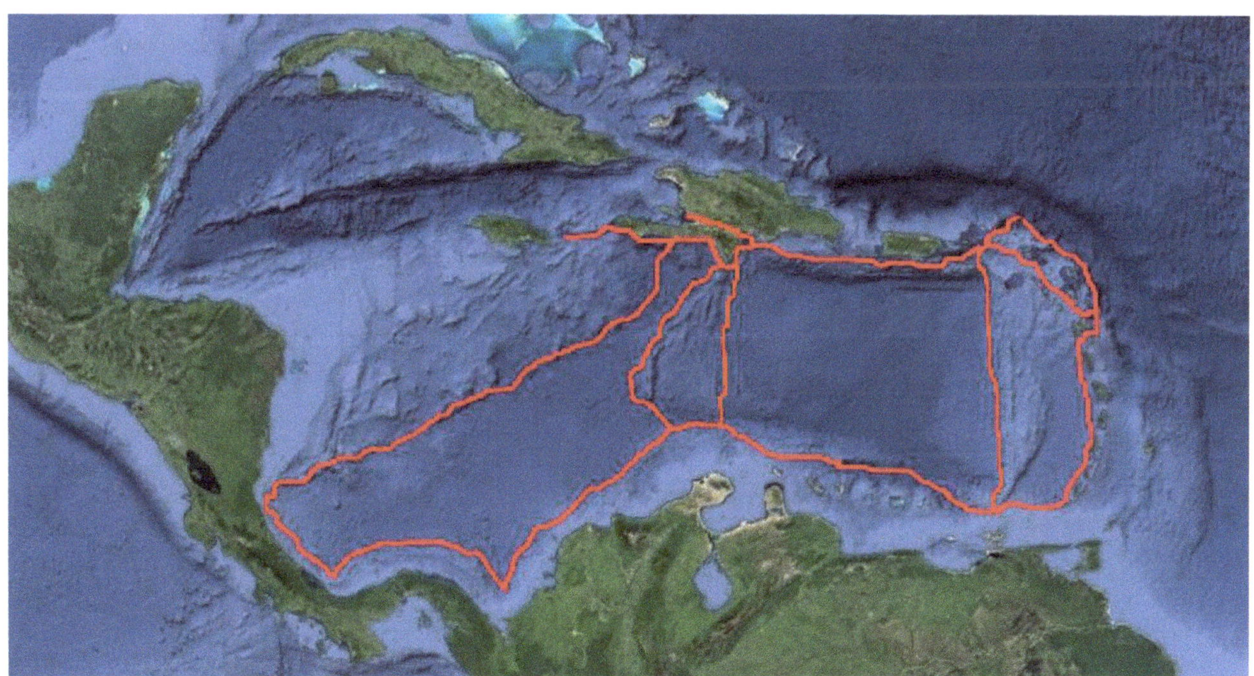

Major Fault Zones of the Caribbean Flap
Source: Modified from Google Earth

- At the Isla de Mona, there has been no tectonic movement of the Mona platform for over 100,000 years, but there is active extension across the Mona Passage between Hispaniola and Puerto Rico.
- Pliocene to Holocene (after 5mya–Recent) northward tilting of the Puerto Rico-Virgin Islands (PRVI) Platform submerged the northern edge of the platform to a depth of 4km, and it elevated the southern edge of the platform to several hundred meters above sea level on Puerto Rico.
- The Southern Carbonate Zone of Puerto Rico contains steeply dipping faults that indicate Recent major faulting and southward tilting.
- Late Quaternary (after ~500kya) faulting occurred in western Puerto Rico with an estimated 4km of vertical throw. It may coincide with the uplift along the south coast of Puerto Rico.
- Late Holocene (after ~10kya ago) seafloor-rupturing, north-east-striking normal faults accommodate south-east extension of the southern margin of Puerto Rico.

- Late Holocene (after ~10kya ago) seafloor-rupturing and left-lateral strike-slip faults occur along the offshore extension of the Great Southern Puerto Rico Fault Zone.
- There are active faults and tilting on the Virgin Islands Platform and the northern margin of the Virgin Islands Basin.
- The Virgin Islands Basin appears to continue to the north-east through the Anegada Passage and intersects with the Lesser Antilles compressional zone.
- The northern margin of the Virgin Islands Basin has active faults.
- The Anegada Passage is 65km wide and divides the Greater Antilles from the Lesser Antilles. It has the greatest depth (more than 2,300m) of any channel in the eastern Caribbean.
- The Anegada Passage links the Muertos Trough's eastern end to the plate boundary's major strand along the Puerto Rico Trench.
- A transtensional event from Pliocene to Recent (after ~5mya) gave the present-day pattern to this area.
- Late Cenozoic (~2.5mya–Recent) extension occurred in the Anegada Gap and a broader region of the eastern Greater Antilles and northern Aves Ridge.
- There is recent faulting in the Anegada Passage.
- A major active fault divides the Saba Bank into a western and eastern platform area.
- At least the latest movement on the fault has been wrenching, and significant lateral movement may have occurred there.
- The platform surface rises from depths of 50m on its western edge to 7–15m on its eastern and south-eastern edges. This difference in depth indicates recent faulting and subsidence, with tilting of the platform to the west.
- During the Pliocene and Pleistocene (~5mya–Recent) the islands of Anguilla, Saint Bartholomew and Saint Martin were probably connected to form one large island. The area is now submerged to form the Anguilla Bank, with the mountainous portions being the present islands. This change indicates recent subsidence in the N-E corner of the Caribbean Plate.

South

- In northern Venezuela, a 1,000-km-long and 100-km-wide active fault system accommodates a 2cm/year relative motion between the Caribbean and South American Plates.
- The South Caribbean Deformed Belt (SCDB) is a 50–100-km-wide submarine prism formed at the interface between the subducting Colombian and Venezuelan Basins and the northern edge of the South American continent.
- The SCDB and subducted Caribbean slab extend 1,500km from Panama in the west to the Aves Ridge in the east.
- The crust under the SCDB has a thickness of 15km and is part of the Caribbean Large Igneous Province (CLIP).
- The Aruba, Bonaire and Curacao islands are aligned along the crest of a 200-km-long east-west trending Leeward Antilles Ridge segment.
- The entire Leeward Antilles Ridge consists of a basement of CLIP and could move vertically as a single structure.
- Because the CLIP also underlies part of the Colombian Basin, Beata Ridge, Venezuelan Basin, Aves Ridge and SCDB, these structures may also have moved vertically with the Leeward Antilles Ridge.
- Pliocene-Quaternary (~5mya–Recent) NNE-trending compression, presumably caused by the southern Venezuelan Basin, produced NW–SE-trending anticlines on Aruba, Curacao, and Bonaire Islands.
- On Curacao, a Late Pleistocene (125–12kya) coral reef terrace is uplifted up to 45m above sea level. As Curacao is part of the Leeward Antilles Ridge, the entire Ridge probably was uplifted to a similar level during the Late Pleistocene. The uplift could indicate a southward tilt of the Venezuelan Basin with compression after 12,000 BP.
- On Trinidad, there was rapid uplift via a reverse fault from the Late Miocene to recent (after ~15mya).
- The uplift on Trinidad may indicate a generalised uplift of the south-eastern Caribbean Plate, but it does not appear to be followed by subsidence. This uplift indicates separate movement from the rest of the Caribbean Plate.
- During the Pleistocene (after 2.5mya), there was normal followed by reverse movement along the Southern Tobago Fault System. This movement accounted for coral limestone deposition and subsequent uplift and tilting.

Centre

- The major fault zone at the Hess Escarpment allows differential vertical movement between the Southern Nicaraguan Rise (SNR) and the Colombian Basin to the south-east.
- Recent faulting and rifts in the SNR indicate tilting and bending of the entire structure to the south-east.
- There are features of both uplift and subsidence in the Colombian Basin up to Recent times.
- The Beata Ridge is joined to the Southern Peninsula of Hispaniola along an active fault zone connected to major faults to the west and the Muertos Trough to the east.
- This combined fault zone could have allowed recent tilting to the south of the entire Beata Ridge.
- An active collision exists between the Beata Ridge's north-eastern tip and the Muertos Trough's western termination. This collision suggests the recent tilting of the northern Beata Ridge to the east.
- The Venezuelan Basin has major active fault zones on each of its four boundaries, which could allow vertical movement of the Basin independently of surrounding structures.
- There has been recent subduction of the Venezuelan Basin at its northern boundary with the Muertos Trough and southern boundary with the South Caribbean Deformed Belt.
- The Venezuelan Basin shallows to the west, indicating greater subsidence or tilting in the east.
- Some DSDP drill sites of the Venezuelan Basin show evidence of a recent change from a shallow or possibly emergent environment, with later subsidence to a much deeper environment.
- There is no recent deformation of the interior of the Venezuelan Basin. If any vertical movement occurred there in the past, it would have been of the entire Venezuelan Basin.
- The Muertos Trough is a key structure as it could allow both the emergence and subsidence of the northern Venezuelan Basin. In the past, the Muertos Trough must have been much shallower to allow the Venezuelan Basin to uplift and emerge to form the Plain of the Atlantic Island.
- The Muertos Trough is tectonically active and separates the Venezuelan Basin from Hispaniola and the Puerto Rico-Virgin Islands Platform (PRVI).
- The Muertos margin structure continues westwards into the Southern Peninsula of Hispaniola.
- The Anegada Passage links the Muertos Trough's eastern end to the plate boundary's major strand along the Puerto Rico Trench.
- Evidence shows that the southern margins of Hispaniola and the PRVI were uplifted, possibly at the same time as the northern Venezuelan Basin along the Muertos Trough.
- There is evidence of recent faulting and vertical movement at the Muertos Trough.
- Recent subsidence of the Venezuelan Basin along the whole length of its northern margin may have produced the present depth of 5,000m of the Muertos Trough.
- The western boundary of the Aves Ridge with the Venezuelan Basin is the 600-km-long Aves Escarpment and its associated parallel faults.
- Any recent subsidence of the Venezuelan Basin relative to the Aves Ridge would have occurred along the Aves Escarpment.
- The Aves Ridge itself subsided 400–1,400m in recent times.
- There is no existing seismic activity on the Aves Ridge.
- The Grenada Basin and Aves Ridge may have tilted southward together at their northern margins around the Anegada Gap.
- An active aseismic extension on the Aves Ridge's eastern margin with the Grenada Basin may extend northward to the Anegada Gap. This continuous extension indicates probable recent and ongoing southward tilting of the combined Aves Ridge and Grenada Basin.
- The water depth of the Grenada Basin decreases to the north, and a very flat sea bottom (average depth of 2,990m) occupies its southern two-thirds. This feature suggests southward tilting of the Grenada Basin with no deformation in the south of the Basin.

East

- The Lesser Antilles' active island arc marks the Caribbean Plate's eastern boundary.
- In the northern Lesser Antilles, the potential exists for great earthquakes of magnitude 8.5–9.0 to rupture the 1,000-km-long plate boundary between easternmost Hispaniola and Guadeloupe, indicating active faulting there.
- It is proposed that much of the eastern edge of the Caribbean Plate subsided after 11,600 BP at fault zones along the Lesser Antilles.
- The northern Lesser Antilles may have tilted southward at the complex of fault zones around the Anegada Gap.

- Subsidence of the Lesser Antilles appears to have involved the islands north of Guadeloupe but not the islands to the south.
- An east-west transition zone that divides the northern from the southern Lesser Antilles Islands may have been located at the La Desirade Escarpment east of Guadeloupe. The La Desirade Escarpment is one of the world's steepest submarine slopes, with a continuous drop of 4,700m and a more than 27° slope. It shows evidence of recent significant tectonic movement.
- Some additional extension and westward tilting may have also occurred in the Kallinago Depression – a 250-km-long trough between the two northern Lesser Antilles' arcs.
- East of the Caribbean, the plate boundary zone between the North American and Caribbean Plates shows recent basement uplift, folding and faulting.
- On Barbados, coral reef terraces of the Middle Pleistocene (~780–126kya) and Late Pleistocene (~125–12kya) were uplifted simultaneously as those on Curacao, suggesting combined uplift of the eastern Caribbean Plate and the Leeward Antilles Platform.

INDEX